Quddús
The First in Rank

BORIS HANDAL

Published: First edition September 2024

Quddús: The First in Rank

ISBN: 978-0-6458963-2-9 (print)
Quddús: The First in Rank

ISBN: 978-0-6458963-3-6 (e-book)
Quddús: The First in Rank

“The importance of exploring the early history of religions cannot be overstated. This is especially important with the 19th century Bábí religion which rapidly evolved from a messianic movement to a globally esteemed Bahá’í Faith. Through his two recent publications, *The Dispensation of the Báb* and *Quddús the First in Rank,* Professor Boris Handal has offered a substantial body of valuable information that enables us to discern the intrinsic connection between the Bábí and the Bahá’í religions despite the stark differences in their worldviews.”

Fereydun Vahman, Professor Emeritus, University of Copenhagen

“Quddús’ exemplary sacrifice and unwavering devotion to the teachings of the Báb, aimed at bringing about a new reality in all spheres of human endeavour, have served as an inspiration to many. Boris Handal’s detailed book on the life of Quddús will surely inspire many more and provide them with complete information about his life.”

Dr Amin Egea, author of the two volumes of “The Apostle of Peace”.

“How can one obtain a better impression of one who was described by the Guardian of the Bahá’í Faith as ‘the essence of sanctity and purity’. most certainly throughout the Bahá’í Dispensation. Bahá’ís will laudably try to get a better impression of this ‘stainless mirror’ of the Báb’s Manifestation. This book is the first time an author has dedicated his whole endeavour to get us closer to Quddús, to enable us to look more closely at the rays of sanctity and holiness reflected upon us. It is a great accompaniment to the immortal pages and passages of the Guardian’s abiding *Dawn-breakers.*”

Dr Khazeh Fananapazir, Bahá'í translator and author

“This gripping book brings to life the extraordinary account of Quddús, one of the most revered figures in Bahá’í history. The author transports readers to the tumultuous dawn of the Bábí religion, which shook the foundations of nineteenth-century Persia. The story of Quddús’s life and sacrifice, unwavering faith, and spiritual conviction—rendered in poignant detail—blaze forth from the chapters of *Quddús: The First in Rank* and resonate in readers long after the final page is turned.”

Dr Omid Ghaemmaghami, Associate Professor of Arabic and Islamic Studies at the State University of New York

To Mercedes Sanchez,
who nurtured me into the Bahá'í Faith.

Thou hast ascended through the realm of existence unto a horizon wherein none hath preceded thee, and been seated upon the Throne of Might in the loftiest mansions of Paradise, a station that none, in the compass of God's knowledge, hath surpassed.

The Báb

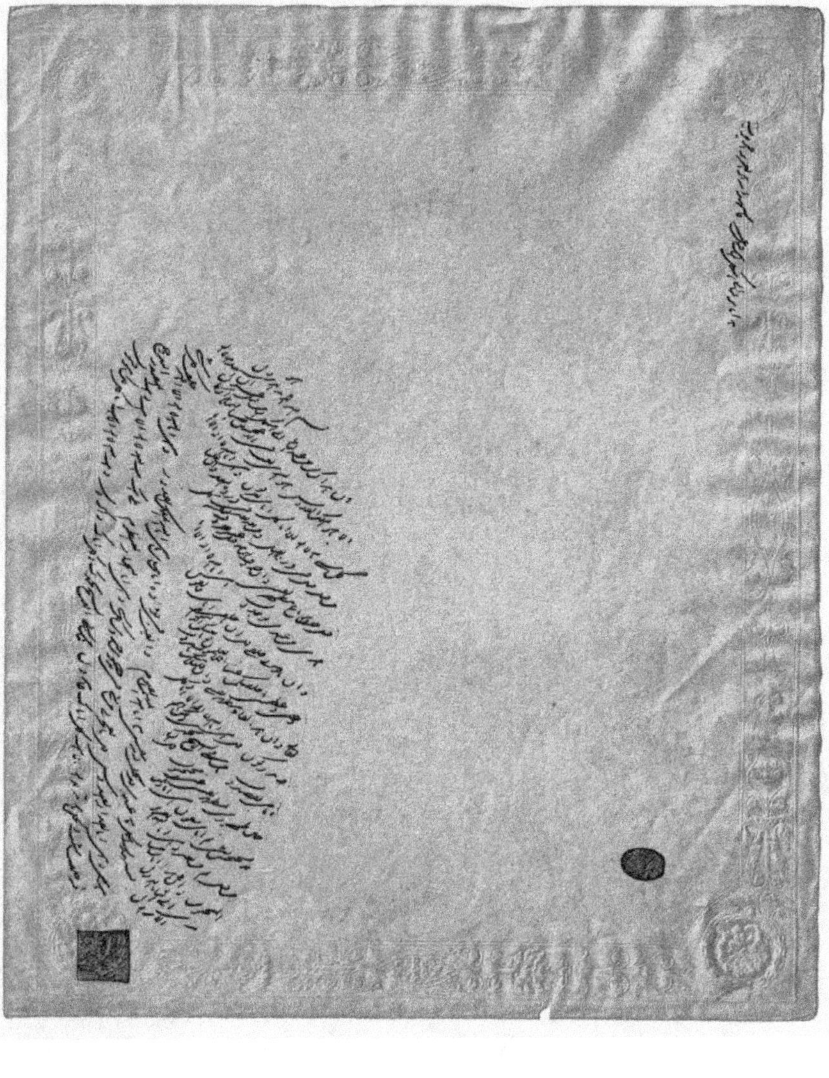

Tablet of the Báb to the 18th Letter of the Living, Quddús

Contents

Acknowledgments.. viii
Illustrations.. xi
Foreword.. xv
Preface.. xvii
Preamble.. xx

Part I
The seeker

1. The early years.. 1
   - Mázindarán Province, Iran.. 1
   - Bárfurúsh, the birthplace of Quddús.. 2
   - Growing up in Bárfurúsh.. 6
   - A farming family.. 7
   - Early education.. 9
   - The rural soul.. 10
2. Years of study.. 12
   - Sárí.. 12
   - Study in a madrasa.. 14
   - The holy city of Mashhad.. 15
   - The seminary of Mírzá Ja'far.. 17
   - Shí'a and Sunní sects of Islam.. 19
   - Who is the "Lord of the Age"?.. 20
   - Shaykh Aḥmad and Siyyid Káẓim.. 22
   - Karbilá, Iraq.. 23
   - Quddús in Karbilá.. 24
   - Karbilá, a centre of Shaykhism.. 24
   - Did Quddús meet the Báb in Karbilá?.. 26
   - The passing of Siyyid Káẓim.. 28
3. Finding the Promised One.. 36
   - Quddús returns to Bárfurúsh.. 36
   - Mullá Ḥusayn is the first.. 38
   - Behold the Promised One.. 40
   - What is the *Qayyúmu'l-Asmá*?.. 40
   - The Letters of the Living.. 41
   - Quddús is the last.. 42
   - The Day of Resurrection.. 45
4. The chosen companion.. 48
   - Mecca, the pilgrimage centre.. 48
   - Búshihr, Iran.. 50
   - Kangán, Iran.. 51
   - Muscat, Oman.. 52
   - Mocha, Yemen.. 53
   - Jeddah, Ottoman Empire.. 55

Theft of Writings.. 55
Public declaration of the Báb in Mecca.. 56
Return to Mocha, Yemen.. 58
Return to Muscat, Oman.. 58
Return to Shíráz, Persia.. 59
Associating with a Manifestation of God.. 60

5. "First to suffer persecution in Persia".. 63
The Báb farewells Quddús.. 63
Quddús and Mullá Ṣádiq in Shíráz.. 65
Their beards are burnt.. 67
Qayyúmu'l-Asmá' message to Muḥammad Sháh.. 69
Worldwide publicity.. 69

Part II
The promoter

6. A special mission from the Báb.. 81
Kirmán, Persia.. 81
Quddús departs Shíráz.. 82
The mission in Kirmán.. 84
Karím Khán Kirmání.. 85
Quddús in Kirmán.. 86
Karím Khán confronts Quddús.. 88
Ḥájí Siyyid Javád confronts Karím Khán.. 89
Quddús visits Bahá'u'lláh in Ṭihrán.. 90

7. Quddús in Mázindarán.. 93
Bárfurúsh description.. 93
Settling into Bárfurúsh.. 94
Living in Bárfurúsh. 95
Regent to the "Lord of the Age".. 96
The opposition of Mullá Qásim.. 98
Quddús and the Sa'ídu'l-'Ulamá'.. 99
Exchanges between Quddús and the Sa'ídu'l-'Ulamá'.. 101
Quddús predicts his martyrdom.. 102

8. Two extraordinary friends reunited.. 104
Two prominent friends.. 104
Two Bábí leaders.. 105
Brilliant service records.. 106
The Hidden Treasure of God.. 108
Mullá Ḥusayn and Quddús reunited.. 109
Ascendency of Quddús.. 110
Leadership upon shoulders of Quddús.. 111
Mullá Ḥusayn and the Sa'ídu'l-'Ulamá'.. 112
Hands of the Cause of God.. 113

9. The House of Bábíyyih.. 115
About dates.. 121
Friends working together.. 122

Reactions of local authorities.. 124
Mullá Ḥusayn's retreat.. 125
Departure of Quddús.. 127
Mázindarán visit.. 127
Rendezvous with Bahá'u'lláh at Badas<u>sh</u>t.. 128

Part III:
The leader

10. The Bada<u>sh</u>t conference.. 133
Renewal of religion.. 133
Bada<u>sh</u>t village.. 136
Conference purpose.. 137
Old World Order abrogated.. 139
Laws of the Bayán.. 141
Conference organisation.. 143
A pre-arrranged plan.. 144
"Him Whom God shall make manifest".. 145
Ṭáhirih and *"Him Whom God shall make manifest"*.. 147
Quddús and Bahá'u'lláh.. 148
Ṭáhirih removes her veil.. 149
The role of the Báb in the conference 152
New Day celebrated.. 153
New Order proclaimed.. 153
11. August 1848 – Five stories.. 155
Ṭáhirih's journey to Núr 156
Quddús in Sárí.. 158
The Báb in the <u>Ch</u>ihríq Castle.. 161
Bahá'u'lláh in Bandar-i-Gaz.. 164
The long march to Bárfurú<u>sh</u>.. 165
12. The long march of Mullá Ḥusayn.. 168
Departure from Ma<u>sh</u>had.. 173
Ní<u>sh</u>ápúr.. 176
Sabzivár.. 176
Message received when in Mazínán.. 176
<u>Kh</u>án-i-<u>Kh</u>údí and Bíyár Jumand.. 177
Mayámay.. 178
Dih-Mullá.. 179
Basṭám.. 179
Mihmán-Dúst.. 179
<u>Ch</u>a<u>sh</u>mah-'Alí.. 180
Fúlád Maḥallih.. 181
Message received in <u>Kh</u>úríyih.. 182
<u>Ch</u>á<u>sh</u>m.. 182
Message from the new governor.. 183
Fírúzkúh.. 185
Úrím.. 185

Shír-Gáh.... 186
Bárfurúsh (Babol).... 187
The sardár arrives.... 189
13. Settling into Shaykh Ṭabarsí.... 191
Leaving Bárfurúsh.... 195
The treason of Khusraw.... 196
Finding a refuge.... 197
Building the initial fort.... 198
Words of the Báb about the victory of His Faith 200

Part IV
The hero

14. The eight Shaykh Ṭabarsí battles.... 205
First battle—the horsemen from Qáḍí-Kalá (October 1848).... 209
Visit by Bahá'u'lláh and arrival of Quddús.... 212
A regional army is formed.... 216
An imperial army is formed.... 234
Third battle—Quddús is injured (January 1849).... 239
Fourth battle—death of Mullá Ḥusayn (February 1849).... 244
Fifth battle—treason and triumph (March 1849).... 252
Celebrating Naw-Rúz in the camp 255
Sixth battle— the enemy tower is captured (March 1849).... 257
Seventh battle—new warfare technologies (April 1849) 261
Eighth battle—the last engagements (May 1849).... 267
15. Living conditions in Shaykh Ṭabarsí fort.... 269
Shaykh Ṭabarsí as an early Bábí settlement.... 276
Arrivals at Shaykh Ṭabarsí.... 277
Teaching the Faith.... 283
Devotional environment.... 284
Community celebrations.... 286
Bábí heroism.... 287
Attacks on the fortifications.... 289
Hunger and starvation.... 291
16. The massacre of 10 May 1849.... 296
Deceiving the Bábís: the final strategy.... 296
The Thursday massacre.... 302
Killing the survivors.... 305
Three poignant stories.... 305
Departure to Bárfurúsh.... 307

Part V
The martyr

17. Martyrdom of Quddús.... 311
Entry into Bárfurúsh.... 311
The mob rejoices.... 312
Quddús' confinement.... 313
Demands for the right to kill Quddús.... 315

The trial.. 316
The role of the prince.. 323
The execution.. 326
After the martyrdom.. 331
Remains are recovered.. 334
Nuptials of fire.. 337
Other martyrdoms that same week.. 338
Martyrdom as a rendezvous.. 340
Further thoughts.. 341
Chronology of the life of Quddús.. 342

18. The family of Quddús.. 344
Áqá Ṣáliḥ.. 350
The stepmother.. 351
Siblings.. 351

Part VI
The saint

19. The station of Quddús.. 357
Testimonies from the Báb.. 357
Testimonies from Bahá'u'lláh.. 363
Testimonies from 'Abdu'l-Bahá.. 371
Testimonies from Shoghi Effendi.. 373
The Last Name of God.. 373

20. Reverence for Quddús.. 376
Love for Quddús.. 377
A source of guidance.. 378
Obeisance.. 379
Spiritual authority.. 380
Turning to Quddús.. 380
Circumabulating his chamber.. 382
Spoke from behind a curtain.. 382
Future predictions.. 383

21. The pen of Quddús.. 385
A prolific writer.. 385
Commentary on the letter Ṣad.. 388
The Sermon on the Eternal Witness.. 390

Part VII
His legacy

22. In retrospect.. 395
Ministry of Quddús.. 395
Sorrow of the Báb.. 397
The fate of the enemies.. 399
The Persian religious leaders.. 404
Sharí'atmadár and the Bábís.. 405
The lasting impact of the siege.. 406

23. What happened next.. 409

Growth of the Bábí-Bahá'í Faith.. 409
Abrogation of some Islamic practices.. 410
Triumph of good over evil.. 412
Ignorance versus truth.. 413
Fruits of determination.. 414

24. Quddús as the mirror of the Báb.. 417
The Báb and Quddús.. 417
Religious hatred.. 422
A monument to infamy.. 425
Saints and heroes.. 427
Shaykh Ṭabarsí and Bahá'í Identity.. 429
Message for the youth.. 431
Postscript.. 432

Part VIII
Miscellanea

25. Shrine of Quddús.. 437
History of the shrine.. 438
Confiscation and demolition.. 440
International pressure.. 441
Relics of Quddús.. 444
Recent persecutions in Babol.. 445
The fate of the fort.. 446
The shrines of the Letters of the Living.. 450

26. Conceptions of the early Bábís.. 452
Transience of the Bábí Revelation.. 456
Internal confusion.. 458
Myths, legends and folklore about Quddús.. 459
Misconceptions about Quddús.. 460
First chronicles.. 461
The Shaykh Ṭabarsí fort defenders.. 465
Progressive claims and delegation of functions.. 466
The Qá'im.. 469
Quddús and Jesus Christ.. 471
Practising the new laws.. 473
Devotion over knowledge.. 475

27. The role of women and families in Shaykh Ṭabarsí.. 477
Teachings of the Báb regarding women.. 477
Cultural restrictions and hardships.. 478
Women members of the family of Mullá Ḥusayn.. 480
Brides and grooms.. 482
Mothers and sons.. 482
Fathers and sons.. 487
The elderly.. 488

28. Prayers and letters by Quddús.. 490
Prayers revealed by Quddús.. 490

Letters to Sa'ídu'l-'Ulamá'.. 493
Other extracts from the writings of Quddús.. 496
29. Quddús in the arts.. 498
Film The Gate.. 499
Fictional images.. 499
Is there a photograph of Quddús?.. 500
Horrific death inflicted by a crazed mob.. 501
Poetry.. 503
30. Social impact.. 508
The beginning of communal life.. 508
Allegations of communal sharing.. 509
Insurrectionist allegations.. 511
Holy war allegations.. 514
What happened at Shaykh Ṭabarsí?.. 518
Socialist allegations.. 518
A progressive social agenda.. 520
Echoes from the past.. 523
The rural factor.. 524
Popularity of the Bábís.. 525
The village of Ívil 527
Afterword - My writing journey 528
Before the journey.. 528
During the journey.. 529
After the journey.. 530

Appendix

1. Tablet of Visitation for Mullá Ḥusayn and Quddús.. 532
2. Tablet of Visitation for Quddús.. 537
3. A tribute to Mullá Ḥusayn 539
Glossary and pronunciation guide.. 546
Glossary.. 546
Arabic and Persian pronunciation guide.. 548
Index of names. 549
Bibliography. 554

Acknowledgments

I would like to thank the following persons for their assistance with translation: Farzad Naziri, Mohiman Shafa, Dr Khazeh Fananapazir, Mehran and Samiheh Oboodi, Prof Bijan Samali, Dr Vargha Bolodo-Taefi, Mansoor Adami, Hoda Seioshansian, Mary Victoria, Hélène Safajou, and Muneer Rushdy. The "Tablet of Visitation for Mullá Ḥusayn and Quddús" by Bahá'u'lláh and the "Tablet of Visitation for Quddús" by the Báb were translated by Adib Masumian and Babak Mohajerin. Babak also translated the writings of Quddús presented in 28. After review and modifications from the Research Department of the Bahá'í World Centre, these renderings from the Holy Writings were kindly approved for publication.

My thanks also go to the friends who provided historical advice throughout the research, namely, Dr Felicity Rawlings-Sanaei, Dr Melanie Lotfali, Simin and Qudrat Motallebi, Janet Ruhe-Schoen, Ann Hinton, Michael W. Thomas and Dr Yvonne I. Woźniak, Dr Soroush Sedaghat, Hooshmand Dehghan, Dr Necati Alkan, Dr Chris Buck, Dr Farin Sanaei, Mohinam Shafa, Hamid Kazemi, Dr Omar Brdarevic, Manuel Rosas, Fardin Heydari, Farhad Shahidi, Camelia Handal, Parvin Handal, Ghobad Momtazian, Dr Moojan Momen, Dr Steven Phelps, Dr Nader Saiedi, Bahman Mousavi, Adel Shafipour, Dr Javid Atai, Nafha Maani Ebrahimi, Dr Farshad Esmailian, Dr Grover Gonzales, Ḥusayn Villar, Adel Adl, Dr Siyamak Zabihi-Moghaddam, Dr Amin Egea, Sepehr Manuchehri, Professor Seena Fazel, Dr Muin Afnani, Dr Iraj Ayman, Mr and Mrs Farhad Toghyani and Michael V. Day. Likewise, I would like to acknowledge Cambridge University Library for providing copies of Quddús' writings from their Oriental and India Office Collection.

I also would like to acknowledge Ernie and Diana Jones for her proofreading and editorial assistance, Gregg Suhm, Michael W. Thomas for his expert cartographic work, Pedro Donaires for the maps portraying de travel of Quddús, Mullá Ḥusayn, and the conference of Bada<u>sh</u>t. Dr Amir Badei for his permission to use his story about Mírzá Ḥaydar-'Alí from the book *Dreams of Destiny in the Bábí and Bahá'í Faiths.* Several friends in the Cradle of the Faith assisted me by providing historical information about the early periods of the Faith.

Similarly, I would like to express my gratitude to Sue Podger and Ivan Lloyd for sharing their beautiful illustration of <u>Sh</u>ay<u>kh</u> Ṭabarsí and Fariba Rosas Heydari for the cover design illustrating the physical fire that burnt Quddús' body but also the fire of the love of God that consumed his searching soul.

Dr Yvonne Ingrid Woźniak and Michael W. Thomas did a marvellous job with the proofreading and editing of the final manuscript getting it to ready for publication. They went the extra mile proving very valuable critical feedback to strengthen the quality of the final product.

My thanks to poets Carl Fraver and John Etheridge for sharing their poems about Quddús, and to artists Ivan Lloyd and Kamal Ma'ani for giving me permission to use their beautiful and inspiring illustrations. Steve Sarowitz gave permission to use an image from his film "The Gate" and Armin Awan assisted with formatting it. Likewise, Fara Narwariya assisted with photographic work. Thanks also to Anthony Lee of Kalimát Press for providing a map from book *Mullá Ḥusayn*. I also would like to acknowledge the National Spiritual Assembly of the Bahá'ís of the United States for allowing to reproduce extracts from the article "Visit to Fort Ṭabarsí" by Guy Murchie.

The Bahá'í World Centre kindly provided the images of the ring of Quddús, a cannon ball from the fort of Shaykh Ṭabarsí, and the sword of Mullá Ḥusayn. The Review Committee of the National Spiritual Assembly of the Bahá'ís of Australia was very resourceful with their suggestions and valuable recommendations. Likewise, without the help of my wife Parvin and daughter Camelia this book might never have seen the light of day.

List of Illustrations

1. Views of the house of Quddús' father in Bárfurúsh (Source: Bahá'í Media)
2. Views of the house of Quddús' father in Bárfurúsh (Source: Bahá'í Media)
3. A view of Bárfurúsh around 1865 (Public domain)
4. Babolsar, port city north of Babol in the 1930s (Public domain)
5. Two Iranian stamps showing Mázandaráni i people's traditional attire
6. Sharí'atmadár's school in Bárfurúsh (old view) (Source: *Ganj-i-Pinhán*)
7. A madrasa, late 19th or early 20th century (© The Nelson Collection of Qajar Photography)
8. Mírzá Ja'far seminary where Quddús studied, Mashhad (Public domain)
9. Siyyid Káẓim
10. Shrine of the Imám Ḥusayn in Karbilá by Robert Clive (1827 - 1902) (Public domain).
11. General view of Shíráz in the early 1930s (Source: Bahá'í Media)
12. Persia (Courtesy Pedro Donaires and M. W. Thomas)
13. Qur'án Gate, Shíráz, 1888 (Source: Bahá'í Media)
14. Old picture of the House of the Báb in Shíráz
15. View of the interior of the House of the Báb in Shíráz (Source: Bahá'í Media)
16. Coat worn by the Báb during His pilgrimage to Mecca (Source: Bahá'í Media)
17. Shíráz to Mecca pilgrim caravan, 1912 (Source: National Geographic Magazine, 1921)
18. Sketch of old Mecca (Source: Bahá'í Media)
19. Masjid-i-Naw, Shíráz
20. Early coverage of Bábís in Shíráz (The Times London, 1 Nov 1845)
21. Transcript of the writings of Quddús - Cambridge University Library.
22. The travels of Quddús (Courtesy of Pedro Donaires and M. W. Thomas)
23. Mírzá Karím Khán of Kirmán (Source: Bahá'í Media)
24. Áqáy-i Kalím, brother of Bahá'u'lláh (Source: Bahá'í Media)
25. House of Bahá'u'lláh in Ṭihrán (Source: Bahá'í Media)
26. Castle of Máh-Kú (Source: Bahá'í Media)
27. The ring of Quddús © Bahá'í World Centre
28. Quddús' shirt and shawl (courtesy of Hooshmand Dehghan)
29. House of Sa'ídu'l-'Ulamá' in Bárfurúsh
30. José Rey and Adam Mondschein as Quddús and Mullá Ḥusayn in the film "The Gate" (with permission)
31. The travels of Mullá Ḥusayn (Courtesy of Pedro Donaires)
32. Muḥammad Sháh (r. 1834-1848)
33. Northern Iran (Courtesy M. W. Thomas)
34. Bábíyyih house, Mashhad (Source: Bahá'í Media)

35. Bábíyyih house, Mashhad (Source: Bahá'í Media)
36. Route between Ṭihrán and Badasht (courtesy of Pedro Donaires)
37. Route between Badasht and Níyalá (courtesy of Pedro Donaires)
38. Old view of Badasht
39. Quddús wrongly attributed photograph – unknown source
40. Chihríq castle ridge (Source: Bahá'í Media)
41. The long march (courtesy of M. W. Thomas)
42. The long march – eastern end (courtesy of M. W. Thomas)
43. Village of Níshápúr (Source: Bahá'í Media)
44. Village of Míyámay (Source: Bahá'í Media)
45. Village of Shír-Gáh (Source: Bahá'í Media)
46. Old view of the Caravanserai, Sabzih-Maydán, Bárfurúsh (Source: Bahá'í Media)
47. The sword of Mullá Ḥusayn © Bahá'í World Centre
48. Portrait of Násirí'd-Dín Sháh (r. 1848-1896)
49. Násirí'd-Dín Sháh's edict of December 1848 to crush the Bábís
50. Doorway to Shaykh Ṭabarsí shrine
51. Old view of entrance to Shaykh Ṭabarsí shrine (Source: Bahá'í Media)
52. Old interior of Shaykh Ṭabarsí shrine
53. Old photo of Shaykh Ṭabarsí shrine (Source: Bahá'í Media)
54. Old photo of Shaykh Ṭabarsí shrine (Source: Bahá'í Media)
55. Old photo of Shaykh Ṭabarsí shrine (Public domain)
56. Well dug by the Bábís near Shaykh Ṭabarsí (Source: *Bahá'í News*, no. 411, 1965)
57. Modern interior of Shaykh Ṭabarsí shrine
58. Modern exterior of Shaykh Ṭabarsí shrine (Public domain)
59. View of Shaykh Ṭabarsí from a distance, 1964
60. Shaykh Ṭabarsí plan (courtesy of Sue Podger)
61. Layout of the Shrine of Shaykh Ṭabarsí by E.G. Browne
62. Sulaymán Khán-i-Afshár, military commander at Shaykh Ṭabarsí (Source: George Ronald Publisher)
63. Village of Afrá next to the Fort Shaykh Ṭabarsí
64. Route from the Vás-Kas military camp to Shaykh Ṭabarsí (Courtesy Kalimát Press)
65. Fictional image of Quddús (courtesy of Ivan Lloyd)
66. A cannon ball from the fort of Shaykh Ṭabarsí © Bahá'í World Centre
67. The defenders of Shaykh Ṭabarsí (courtesy of Ivan Lloyd)
68. The defenders of Shaykh Ṭabarsí (courtesy of Ivan Lloyd)
69. Old Bárfurúsh sketch (Adapted from Ganj-i-Pinhán, p. 215) (Courtesy of M. W. Thomas)
70. Portrait of Sa'ídu'l-'Ulamá'
71. Old view of the Jum'ih mosque of Bárfurúsh where Quddús was trialled
72. The Governor House where Quddús was arrested during his trial (public domain)
73. The bridge to the Governor House located in an island in the Bágh-i-Sháh

74. Park (Sabzih Maydán) where Quddús was martyred (Source: Bahá'í Media)
75. Aerial view of the Sabzih Maydán (Source: Google Earth)
76. View of the old caravanserai gate where Quddús was beaten to bleed profusely
77. The lower border of the photo shows the possible span where Quddús was killed facing the caravanserai
78. Duzdekchál in the eastern side of Bahru'l-Arim lake where Quddús remains were scattered (photo around 1866)
79. The martyrdom of Quddús at the Sabzih Maydán (Courtesy of Kamal Ma'ani)
80. Old view of the Panj-Shambih bazar of Bárfurúsh scene of various martyrdoms (public domain)
81. Ḥaẓír-Fúrúshan (mat-weaver) alley near Quddús' grave
82. Mírzá Zakí Madrasih where Quddús was buried (Source: Bahá'í Media)
83. Mírzá Zakí Madrasih where Quddús was buried (Source: Bahá'í Media)
84. Shrine of Quddús in Bárfurúsh being demolished, 2004 (Source: Bahá'í Media)
85. Shrine of Quddús in Bárfurúsh being demolished, 2004 (Source: Bahá'í Media)
86. Shrine of Quddús in Bárfurúsh being demolished, 2004 (Source: *Ganj-i-Pinhán*)
87. Place where the shrine of Quddús was located (four-storey building)

Foreword

The Universal House of Justice writes that "the forces of disintegration have rent the fabric of society".[1] This rending, says the infallible body, takes the form of selfishness, suspicion, fear, fraud, the feverish pursuit of earthly vanities, riches and pleasures, the weakening of family solidarity, the perversion of human nature, the degradation of human conduct, as well as the corruption and dissolution of human institutions.

The reason for this disintegration is largely due to the decline of religion as a social force. In the words of Bahá'u'lláh: *"Should the lamp of religion be obscured, chaos and confusion will ensue, and the lights of fairness, of justice, of tranquillity and peace cease to shine."*[2]

In this socio-historical context then, the short life of the youthful Quddús, referred to by the beloved Guardian as a hero and a trail-breaker of the New Day, served as a channel for the integrative forces, and continues to serve as a reminder of the potency of those forces that "will continue to gain in strength, no matter how bleak the immediate horizons",[3] and ultimately lead to the total reorganisation of human affairs and the inauguration of an era of universal peace.

Quddús' life constitutes a role-model to everyone who would seek to live a life worthy of the name Bahá'í; for he is one of

> ... the Báb's chosen disciples, the Letters of the Living, and their companions, the trail-breakers of the New Day, who to so much intrigue, ignorance, depravity, cruelty, superstition and cowardice opposed a spirit exalted, unquenchable and awe-inspiring, a knowledge surprisingly profound, an eloquence sweeping in its force, a piety unexcelled in fervor, a courage leonine in its fierceness, a self-abnegation saintly in its purity, a resolve granite-like in its firmness, a vision stupendous in its range, a veneration for the Prophet and His Imáms disconcerting to... adversaries, a power of persuasion alarming to ... antagonists, a standard of faith and a code of conduct that challenged and revolutionized the lives of their countrymen.[4]

Professor Handal's biography of Quddús has the potential to draw us closer—spiritually, emotionally and intellectually—to the faith and the sacrifices of the early believers, those God-intoxicated lovers, from whose legacy we benefit, on whose shoulders we stand, and in whose footsteps we strive to tread. A deeper knowledge of the intimate details of his life can bring Quddús alive for us, such that though separated by expanses of time and of place, his example serves to

---

1 The Universal House of Justice, Riḍván Message 2006, para. 4.

2 Bahá'u'lláh, *Tablets of Bahá'u'lláh*, p. 125.

3 The Universal House of Justice, dated 2 March 2013 to the Bahá'ís of Iran.

4 Shoghi Effendi, *God Passes By*, p. 5.

strengthen our faith, perseverance, commitment, readiness to learn, ability to foster unity of thought and to learn about effective action in our current time and place, as we arise to play our part in the unfoldment of the very same Divine Plan.

The Universal House of Justice states that advancement is associated with action and that those who advance most rapidly are those who do not hesitate to act. Action is at the heart of the Faith for which Quddús sacrificed his life and it was through action that Quddús demonstrated his dedication. From the moment he first set eyes on the Báb, to the moment of his own public execution following the betrayal at Shaykh Ṭabarsí, Quddús' faith was manifest in selfless, tireless action wholly directed by the Manifestation of God. Let us then, immerse ourselves in this biography by Professor Handal, and then, inspired by Quddús' life, arise to play our part in the divine drama within the framework for action provided to us by the Centre of the Covenant.

Dr Melanie Lotfali
Queensland, Australia

Preface

The story of Quddús rings as fresh as the first time I heard of it forty-five years ago at a youth deepening seminar, at which a presenter talked about that young man's heroism and sanctity.

The "immortal Quddús"[1] represents a stellar example of sacrifice and detachment for the Bahá'í youth as exemplified by the outstanding nature of his services. His exploits are profound narratives to transform the individual and society because these represent the triumph of the human spirit over adversity, opposition and prejudice. The following accounts are the celebration of the triumph of the human spirit over barbarism and bigotry. In no other personage of the Bábí Faith could we find a better reflection of the Báb's refulgent lights. The best veneration of Quddús' sacred memory therefore can be translated today through continuing the spiritual edifice he began to build and for which he died so gloriously.

The stellar career of service and devotion, lasting only five years, was enough to demonstrate his position as the most outstanding disciple in the religion of the Báb. In a letter written on his behalf, Shoghi Effendi affirmed:

> Regarding the station of Quddús, he should by no means be considered having had the station of a Prophet .... Quddús reflected more than any of the disciples of the Báb the light of His teaching.[2]

Quddús, meaning *Holy*, became the *First in Rank* not only because of the extraordinary designations given to him by the Báb and Bahá'u'lláh but also for what he made of himself by being worthy of these very exalted titles. This book is therefore a testament of his inspiring life and service to the Cause of God which is indeed a story of personal transformation.

The central protagonist of this book is the youthful, saintly and courageous Quddús. Along with him stands the brave and staunch Mullá Ḥusayn as his sworn companion coming in and out of the narrative in the most fascinating circumstances appearing like a mythological duo. These two extraordinary characters gravitate like celestial satellites around the majestic figures of the Twin Manifestations of God, Bahá'u'lláh and the Báb.

Stories such as these about Quddús are to be treasured by the believers. As per 'Abdu'l-Bahá's exhortation that Bahá'ís *"should recount the high deeds and sacrifices of the lovers of God in Persia, and tell of the martyrs' detachment from the world, and their ecstasy, and of how the believers there stood by one another and gave up everything they had."*[3]

---

1 Shoghi Effendi, *Citadel of Faith*, p. 66.

2 Letter written on behalf of Shoghi Effendi to an individual believer dated 11 November 1936. In The Universal House of Justice, "Letters of Living ...."

3 'Abdu'l-Bahá in *Compilation of Compilations*, vol. 1, p. 428.

The book has been divided into five parts portraying Quddús as a *seeker, promoter, leader, hero, saint* as well as an *erudite man*, in brief, a man of many colours The initial three parts relates to the life of Quddús, signalising distinctive stages of his journey as a *seeker*. The first refers to the preparatory years of his trajectory, culminating with his conversion to the Cause of the Báb and participation in the initial persecutions. If the first part concerns learning, the next refers to teaching the Bábí Faith throughout Iran with zeal and passion while networking the dispersed community as much as possible. Here we see Quddús arising distinctively as the *promoter* of the Faith. The third part brings out a Quddús as a *leader* guiding the believers in various events. In turn, the fourth depicts him as a *hero* defending the integrity of the Bábí community and shining forth uniquely in the tragic episode of Shaykh Ṭabarsí. The fifth and sixth components of the book focus on his station as a *martyr* and as a *saint*, as well as on his writings and his shrine in Bábul . This shrine can be considered the most sacred sepulchre in Iran for the Bahá'ís. Chapters 21 and 28 establish Quddús' position as a celebrated *erudite man*, focusing on his writings. The book closes with reflections on Quddús' legacy.

This biographical study on Quddús has been enriched from various sources in Persian, Arabic, French and German, many of which are not yet translated into English. This biography about Quddús includes new translations from the Writings of the Báb and Bahá'u'lláh paying homage to his exalted rank, which are located in the Appendix. There is also new and exclusive information about the history of Quddús' shrine. A short tribute about Mullá Ḥusayn has been added in Appendix III.

How to read this book

This book has thirty-one self-contained chapters each involving a central concept like modules. As such, readers may go through the book content linearly or in any order. Therefore, each chapter can be read individually and used for story-telling purposes. If there are repetitions, they are intended to ensure each chapter stands alone and to keep the reader aware of crucial details.

Secondly, although history books are to be read chronologically, this biography permits any reading entry point. Readers might like focus on any of these nine dimensions extracted from Quddús' life in any order:

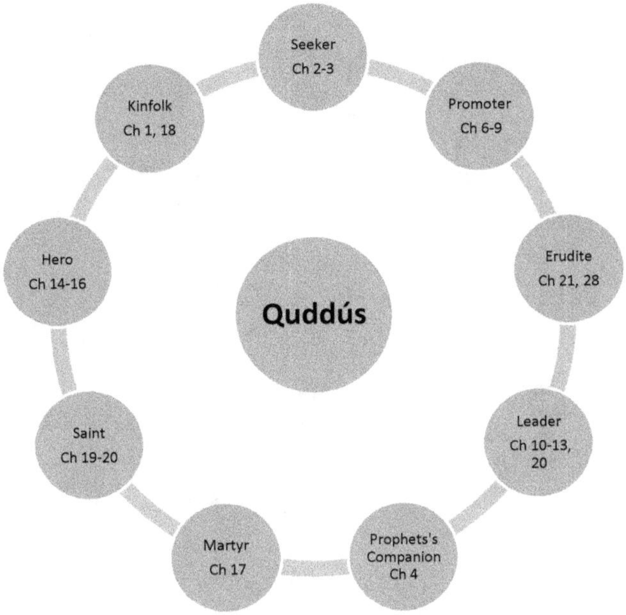

The nine dimensions of Quddús' life

Preamble

Quddús (pronounced as Kod-doos) awoke his compatriots from their spiritual slumber. His memory will always remain, and his name will echo through the ages. Quddús' legacy is forever bright, guiding each generation with his example of service, obedience and sacrifice.

During his relatively short lifetime, Quddús experienced the realities of being raised in a farming family, the airiness of the academic rooms, the sublimity of the divine presence, the wonders of the distant travels, the affronts of the ecclesiastics, the harshness of the battlefield and the ultimate altar of sacrifice.

He was a radiant star from the dawn of the Faith of the Báb. He journeyed far away with His Beloved, and later he shared His message, undeterred, to cultivate once-barren souls with the waters of his faith and knowledge. Educated personally by the Prophet Himself during a year, Quddús best embodied His attributes, and, therefore can be considered the finest mirrors reflecting His Revelation.

Quddús embraced the path of sacrifice with love and became a strong pillar never to fall. With unyielding courage, he stood tall and steadfast. On becoming the most eminent disciple of the Báb and His mirror, he guided the faithful with leadership, wisdom, authority and love.

Touching many hearts, his life has enthralled both the simple believer and the educated follower, the adversary and the admirer, the ill-informed and the scholar. His soul, a detached spirit, glowed with sublime values and love and compassion for his fellowman.

During the battles and the violent conflicts that followed, his spirit remained unwavering and rejuvenated. In deadly clashes, Quddús displayed matchless bravery leaving a testament of his unwavering certainty, leadership and uncompromising defence of his belief.

Amidst a prevailing atmosphere of deceit, opposition and hostility, Quddús always remained worthy of being the bearer of such a sacred name. His light burns brightly in the garden of the martyrs for giving his life so heroically to vivify humanity.

Part I
The seeker

1
The early years

Mázindarán Province, Iran

Chapter content
Mázindarán Province, Iran
Bárfurú<u>sh</u>, the birthplace of Quddús
Growing up in Bárfurú<u>sh</u>
A farming family
Early education
The rural soul

From the sandy Caspian Sea beaches into the country, the green province of Mázindarán, unfolds through dense forests to the imposing Alborz Mountain range. This luxuriant and bountiful region is the birthplace of Quddús, the protagonist of this book.

Situated between Asia and Europe, the magnificent Caspian Sea bestows generous showers of rain upon the coastlines of the old Russian and Persian empires on each side of it.

Beyond Mázindarán, on the other side of the majestic Alborz Mountain range, several important cities emerge, including the capital city of Ṭihrán. And like an immense carpet of sand, the Kabir desert—the Great Desert—with its scattered salt flats and occasional lakes, shapes the middle of the vast Iranian plateau.

Mázindarán is abundantly crossed by streams and colonised by extensive woodlands, creating an exotic and lush environment, which Iranians refer to as a "jungle". On these merits, the Báb called it His "Green Island"[1] a term that derived from ancient Islamic prophecies regarding the Last Days.[2] Full of flowers and trees, and a unique fauna, Mázindarán Province provides travellers with an exuberantly beautiful and colourful landscape with which to refresh their spirits. Mázindarán in old Persian means "the gate or the valley of the giants".[3]

Throughout Mázindarán's diverse and rich topography, a number of cities, towns and villages were the scenarios of the glorious first years of the Heroic Age of the Bahá'í Faith. Within its borders is located the village Núr ("Light"), the ancestral home of Bahá'u'lláh. The Arabic word "Bahá'u'lláh" means the "Glory of God", but it can also be translated as the "Light of God". The *Qur'án* prophesises:

---

1 Nabíl-i-A'ẓam, *The Dawn-Breakers*, p. 325.

2 Abbas Amanat, *Resurrection and Renewal*, p. 187.

3 Ehsan Yarshater, *Iranian National History*, p. 445.

"It is light upon Light ..."[1] Bahá'u'lláh once said, *"My name is Bahá'u'lláh (Light of God), and My country is Núr (Light). Be ye apprized of it".*[2]

The Count of Gobineau wrote about the simple-mindedness nature of the locals:

> They are thought little inclined to religious speculation. Good marksmen, they do not like war, and if the circumstances in any way permit they dedicate themselves exclusively to agricultural tasks, which they love above all. The main concerns of their life are their enormous rice fields, their fruit trees, which bring them considerable profits from exportation to Russia, and wood- cutting. There is nothing chivalrous about them, and they are so little concerned with the notion of honour that when the Turkmen tribes see fit to invade from the Northeast of their country to carry off prisoners, they generally offer no resistance, flee, hide or give themselves up, but do not defend themselves.[3]

Many mystics and sages found in this region an appropriate place to pray, meditate and think. Several legends emerged about this province. For instance, it has been said that there would grow a sacred tree whose branches were to reach heaven and that the fruit of that tree would benefit all humanity.[4] Perhaps the legend was referring to the appearance of Bahá'u'lláh, who frequently visited the home of His ancestors. There are still people who go to Mázindarán looking for this tree.

Bárfurú<u>sh</u>, the birthplace of Quddús

Quddús, the protagonist of our story, was born on the family property in a small village to the north of Bárfurú<u>sh</u> (now the city of Babol) during the reign of Fatḥ-'Alí <u>Sh</u>áh Qájár (1772–1834).[5] Bárfurú<u>sh</u> literally means "the place where loads are sold", "place for selling" or "market town". Quddús' birthplace has now been encompassed by the old suburb, <u>Ch</u>ahár <u>Sh</u>anbih Pí<u>sh</u> of Babol on the banks of the Áqá-rúd river.[6] The name <u>Ch</u>ahár <u>Sh</u>anbih Pí<u>sh</u> ("Last Wednesday") was originally used to represent a farmers' market that was held every Wednesday. Malgonov, a Russian traveller there, mentioned the existence of this market of 1860 in his chronicles.[7]

---

1 *Qur'án* 24:35.

2 Bahá'u'lláh in Shoghi Effendi, *God Passes By*, p. 190. See Qur'án 24:35.

3 Gobineau in Nash and O'Donoghue, *Comte de Gobineau and Orientalism,* pp. 151-152.

4 Fazel Mazandarani, *The Life of Bahá'u'lláh*, p. 291.

5 Fatḥ-'Alí <u>Sh</u>áh Qájár (1772–1834), the second Qájár monarch, whose notable achievement is having a harem of 160 wives. His reign saw the irrevocable ceding of Persia's northern territories in the Caucasus (present day Georgia, Dagestan, Azerbaijan and Armenia) to the Russian Empire following the Russo-Persian Wars of 1804–1813 and 1826–1828.

6 There is a shrine of the same name (36.553683, 52.685930) in the village of Áq-Rúd.

7 Morteza Nouraei and Elena Andreeva, *Russian Migrants and Their Settlements in Iran*

Babol is the second largest city of the province of Mázandarán. It is known as the "Orange Blossom City" due to its famous orange orchards. It is 20 km south of the southern Caspian Sea coast. The word Babol means "city with abundant water supply" because it is located on a very wet and flat section of the Babol River basin. A place of abundant rain,[1] Bárfurúsh was an important commercial centre connected to one of the major harbours at the time (now Babolsar) on the southern shores of the Caspian Sea, with goods being traded between Iran and Russian ports on the Caspian Sea.[2] Its population was predominantly Muslim, as was the rest of the country. There were some Armenian Christians and Jews living in Bárfurúsh, the latter having two synagogues. The Muslims were hostile towards the Jewish population.[3]

The main agricultural products of the plains were rice and cotton. It is notable that the peasants of Mázandarán usually owned the land they cultivated, and therefore they were better off than their counterparts in the rest of the country.[4] Russian ships were the main carriers of goods to Iran that they used to purchase precious metals, bolstering local businesses, and propelling Bárfurúsh ahead of the rest of the region, at least economically. According to the eminent Iranian historian Abbas Amanat, there were about four hundred shops and four caravanserais (inns) in Bárfurúsh.[5] Apart from farming, the second main occupation was fishing as the town was close to the sea. The preferred catch was sturgeon, whose eggs are the famous caviar—the black oil—which was sold as a delicacy inside and outside of Iran. Apart from farmers and fishermen, there were traders and merchants. In general, the economy was based on basic subsistence farming.

By the early 1840's, Russia was the most potent of Persia's military foes controlling most of the Caspian Sea coastline with its strong navy. They introduced steam ship navigation and effectively displaced Persian sailing vessels. "Hardly 20 ships sail on the Caspian Sea under the Persian flag", Gödel wrote in 1849, "and these are commanded by foreign [mostly Russian] captains".[6] Russia was the only Christian country adjacent to Iran, against whom they had recently finished a bloody war with significant territorial losses incurred by Iran.

There were many clergymen based at the mosques (masjids) living in Bárfurúsh. Their fame for corrupting and commercializing religious practices

---

in the Early 20th Century: A New Stage of Colonization, p. 24.

1 Average rainfall is less than 700 mm, but this is high compared with the arid climate of Iran south of the Alburz mountains. The coastal plain of Mazandaran Province is hot and humid, very flat, low lying (elevations are less than 2 m), and the ground is often water logged.

2 Abbas Amanat, *Resurrection and Renewal*, p. 181.

3 Daniel Tsadik, *Between Foreigners and Shi'is*, pp. 61–62.

4 Mohammad Ali Kazembeyki, *Society, Politics and Economics in Mazandaran*, p. 131.

5 Abbas Amanat, *Resurrection and Renewal*, p. 183.

6 Rudolf Gödel, *Ueber den pontischen Handelsweg*, p. 68.

was notorious. Madrasahs (religious schools or seminaries), which mostly taught Quranic related subjects, were located in most neighbourhoods. By 1843, there were 6,000 families, 25 mosques and 500 shops.[1]

The daily life of a Bárfurú<u>sh</u> boy can be reconstructed from these elements. Depending on varying socio-economic backgrounds, the children from poor families would be helping their parents in their trades or farms throughout the day. Those from more affluent households would have private tutors at home where mostly literacy, numeracy and Islamic instruction were provided. Boys from the lower socio-economic spectrum would probably obtain some basic reading instruction at the local masjids, mainly focused on reading the *Qur'án*. Only the brightest boys would break out of the prevailing cycle of poverty and illiteracy. Any boy who was able to complete his theological studies at the local level would be consecrated as a mullá[2] serving as a preacher, and a marriage or funeral celebrant, among other parochial duties. From that ordained group, some would manage to undertake more advanced studies at more prestigious centres such as in the cities of Ma<u>sh</u>had in Persia or Karbilá in Iraq. These places were associated with Islamic pilgrimage to the family of the Prophet Muḥammad. Quddús was one of the lucky youths who followed this path.

Youths who did not follow the clerical path remained in towns as apprentices of various mainstream trades such as butchers, candy makers, book repairers, carpenters, cooks, bakers, builders, quacks, blacksmiths, carpet weavers, potters, tailors, etc. Those from more affluent families became merchants who were an influential social class in Iranian politics and governance. In general, the social status a person was born into—a peasant or an aristocrat, for example—determined that person's life and his future.

Rural youngsters were more likely to work on farms with few connections to city life and to be at the bottom of a serfdom-style economy. It is not surprising therefore that the illiteracy rate was about 90%,[3] and even higher for girls for whom education was forbidden. Such a depressing pattern was almost the same across 19th century Persia—the product of centuries of obscurantism perpetuating intergenerational prejudice, corruption and ignorance. It is against this backdrop of religious divisions and immorality, burgeoning trade, and Russian dominance in Bárfurú<u>sh</u>, situated between sea and forest, that Quddús grew up. This is the explanation given by 'Abdu'l-Bahá regarding the status of the country:

> *In Persia previous to the middle of the nineteenth century, among the various tribes and peoples, sects and denominations there existed the greatest animosity, strife and hatred. At that time too all the other nations of the East were in the same condition. Religionists were hostile and bigoted, sects were*

---

1 Mohammad Ali Kazembeyki, *Society, Politics and Economics in Mazandaran*, p. 120.

2 Mullá means a religious tutor, someone who knows, normally a low-level Muslim local priest.

3 Willem Floor, *The Economic Role of the Ulama in Qajar Persia*, p. 54.

at enmity, races hated each other, tribes were constantly at war; everywhere antagonism and conflict prevailed. Men shunned and were suspicious of each other. The man who could kill a number of his fellow-creatures was glorified for his heroism and strength. Among religionists it was esteemed a praiseworthy deed to take the life of one who held an opposite belief.[1]

Although there was a civil authority in Bárfurú<u>sh</u>, the clerical influence was dominant in government affairs and local decisions. There were also religious "secret wars" waged between the two leading divines[2] that split the city into two main Muslim religious factions. On one side, there was the "hysterical, the cruel and overbearing Sa'ídu'l-'Ulamá'",[3] and on the other, a cleric named <u>Sh</u>arí'atmadár[4] who had been Quddús' mentor. Each of these two divines belonged to a different sect. The Sa'ídu'l-'Ulamá' represented a more traditional orientation of Islamic teaching, while <u>Sh</u>arí'atmadár belonged to the <u>Sh</u>ay<u>kh</u>í school advocating a symbolic interpretation of the Qu'rán.[5] Furthermore, the Sa'ídu'l-'Ulamá' represented the Ḥaydari tradition while the latter advocated the Ni'matí school. According to Hamid Dabashi, "The popularity of the [Ni'matí] Sufi order rightly jeopardized the monopoly that the clerical establishment wanted to exercise over religious symbols, rituals, and doctrines, in a cozy and mutually beneficial arrangement with the Qájár dynasty."[6] At times, the contention between the two factions turned violent in Iran.

<u>Sh</u>arí'atmadár was the preacher at the Káẓim Bayk Mosque;[7] while Sa'ídu'l-'Ulamá' had the oversight of the Masjid <u>Sh</u>ahádát ("Martyrs Mosque"), which is less than 1 km to the SSW, and a short distance north of the central city mosque. <u>Sh</u>arí'atmadár was the owner of "a caravanserai, ten shops, four houses, all in Bárfurú<u>sh</u>, two pastures as well as farms in the villages of Hamza Kulá, Rad'ia Kula, Bundár Kulá etc."[8] This gives an indication of his prominence as a businessman. Moojan Momen wrote that "He was a popular religious leader, who preached in the local Mazandarani dialect. Rather than concentrating on the sorrows of the martyrdoms of the Imáms as most <u>Sh</u>í'i preachers do, he made his audiences laugh and happy. It is said that at times the crowds attending his mosque were so large that they overflowed onto the street outside."[9]

---

1 'Abdu'l-Bahá, *Foundations of World Unity*, p. 25.

2 Abbas Amanat, *Resurrection and Renewal*, p. 182.

3 Shoghi Effendi, *God Passes By*, p. 39. Sa'ídu'l-'Ulamá ("Chief of the Scholars") is a title indicating a prestigious clergyman. His name was Muḥammad Sa'íd Dív-Kullá'í (Bárfurú<u>sh</u>í).

4 The title of <u>Sh</u>arí'atmadár or "scholar of religious law" of God was held by Ḥájí Mullá Muḥammad-i-Ḥamza.

5 Mohammad Ali Kazembeyki, *Society, Politics and Economics in Mazandaran*, p. 117.

6 Hamid Dabashi, *Shi'ism: A Religion of Protest*, p. 173

7 Grid reference: 36.547248, 52.682688.

8 Mohammad Ali Kazembeyki, *Society, Politics and Economics in Mazandaran*, p. 264.

9 Moojan Momen, *The Bahá'í Communities of Iran*, vol. I, p. 305.

The city areas around both mosques basically marked the jurisdictional territories held by the two clerics.[1] Quddús' family and the Sharí'atmadár were followers of the Shaykhí school of religious thought, therefore they were strongly opposed by the Sa'ídu'l-'Ulamá', a cleric who ultimately dominated decision-making in the town. At one point, before the Declaration of the Báb, "he succeeded in having Sharí'atmadár arrested and taken in chains to Sárí, where the governor resided."[2]

Growing up in Bárfurúsh

The year of Quddús' birth is disputed although most texts refer to 1822.[3] [4] He was named Muḥammad-'Alí, however, he became known by the title Quddús that he received from Bahá'u'lláh and this was confirmed by the Báb.[5] A non-Bahá'í source from that time indicates that he was also called *Mamdalí*,[6] which is an abbreviation for Muḥammad-'Alí. Muḥammad-'Alí is a popular Islamic name: Muḥammad representing the Prophet and Alí being the most revered personage in Shí'ih Islam.

---

1 Abbas Amanat, *Resurrection and Renewal*, p. 182.

2 Moojan Momen, *The Bahá'í Communities of Iran*, vol. I, p. 305.

3 1238 AH. See Nosratollah Mohammad-Hosseini, "Qoddus, Moḥammad-'Ali Bārforuši". Nabíl states that Quddús was twenty-years old when he accepted the Báb in 1844, i.e. he would have been born in 1822 (*The Dawn-Breakers*, p. 351). Abbas Amanat in *Resurrection and Renewal*, p. 181, suggests 1819–1820 (1235 AH) as the time of birth. Fazel Mazandarani wrote that when Quddús returned from pilgrimage (about May 1845) he was 21 years of age (*Ẓuhúr al-Ḥaqq*, vol. 2, p. 71). In turn, Sharí'atmadár, Quddús' mentor, wrote in his book *Ásrár al-Sháhadá* that his mentee was a little older than the Báb (*Ẓuhúr al-Ḥaqq*, vol. 3, p. 438). Another source indicates that Quddús was thirty years old at the time of his martyrdom (Browne, *Kitáb-i-Nuqtatu'l-Káf*, p. 208; Amanat, *Resurrection and Renewal*, p. 181). More importantly, in *Ẓuhúr al-Ḥaqq* (vol. 3, p. 413), Fazel Mazandarani notes Quddús himself mentioning that he left his town when he was twelve years old and came back after thirteen years. The Islamic lunar year is shorter consisting of 354–355 days and there is a difference of one year with the Gregorian calendar for every 33 lunar years. If Quddús came back to Bárfurúsh after 24 Gregorian years, hence, he would have been born around 1819–1820. The Báb was born in 1819.

4 In old Persia, a person's age at birth was calculated, as being one year old on the day after having born. In other words, the year of everyone's life is calculated from the day of conception rather that year of birth (Nader Saiedi, The Ethiopian King, p. 182). Hence, a person on his 24th birthday would be considered as twenty-five years old. For instance, the chronological age of the Báb when He declared His mission has been calculated in twenty-four years in both Islamic (1 Muḥarram 1235 A.H. – 5 Jamádíyu'l-Avval 1260 A.H.) and Gregorian calendar (20 October 1819 – 23 May 1844) in the case of the latter. He would have turned twenty-five about another quarter into the year. The Báb wrote in the *Persian Bayán* (2:1) that He was twenty-four years old when He declared His mission. However, Shoghi Effendi gives as twenty-five the age for that occasion (*God Passes By*, p. 5) — two different systems to represent the same event.

5 Nosratollah Mohammad-Hosseini, *Qoddus, Moḥammad-'Ali Bārforuši, n.p.*

6 Habib Borjian, *A Mazandarani Account of the Babi Incident at Shaikh Tabarsi*, p. 386.

Quddús' father, Áqá Muḥammad-Ṣáliḥ, who was an illiterate man of modest background, was engaged in farming and cultivating rice along the Áq-Rúd river to the north of Bárfurúsh. The family lived in a predominantly Ni'matí ṣúfí religious area.

Quddús' mother was a Sayyida, a descendant of the Prophet Muḥammad.[1] For this reason she was entitled to special consideration and respect in the social and religious milieu of nineteenth-century Persia.[2] Quddús' mother passed away when Quddús was still very young, and eventually, his father married another woman who found in Quddús a true son, showing the child exceptional affection and love.

Quddús had a sister whom he called Maryam (Mary), and who was very dear to him. He also had two half-brothers, Mírzá Ḥaydar and Áqá Muḥammad-Ṣádiq. Historian Hushmand Dehghan described Mírzá Ḥaydar as "the son of the wife of the father of Quddús, who believed in Quddús and was extremely attached to him and used to serve Quddús, and Quddús used to call him brother" and Áqá Muḥammad-Ṣádiq as "the son of the second wife of Quddús' family".[3] Quddús never married.

A farming family

As Quddús had been born into a farming family, it is logical to assume that he helped his father with agricultural tasks, work that was alleviated by occasional visits to the nearby seaside. British Consul E. G. Abbott described in 1844 the rudimentary rice agriculture of Mázindarán Province during spring and summer:

> Rice is sown at the Vernal Equinox [around 21 March]. It is first raised in a heap and 20 or 30 days afterwards when the plants are of a sufficient size they are separated and planted by women in the fields which have already undergone the necessary ploughing and saturation. The plants are placed at a few inches apart from each other and each one yields several stalks—in about 100 days the crop is ready for harvest.[4]

Given the extremes of temperatures throughout the year, many peasants would migrate with their cattle to land they owned or purchase other land to establish a small settlement. During the summer, many peasants moved with their animals to cooler areas due to soaring temperatures. Conversely, in winter, they would move their cows and sheep to warmer areas as temperature fell to nearly zero degrees. The men generally turned to herding which was supported by their children —mainly boys— while the women and girls remained behind

---

1 Nosratollah Mohammad-Hosseini, *Qoddus, Moḥammad-'Ali Bārforuši, n.p.* Also Nabil, *Dawn Breakers*, pp. 292–3.

2 Sayyid (feminine Sayyida) is a title of Muḥammad's direct descendants through His daughter, Fáṭimah.

3 Hooshmand Dehghan, *Ganj-i-Pinhán*, pp. 113–122.

4 K. E. Abbott, *Narrative of a Journey from Tabriz*, pp. 193–4.

tending to home chores. Such was the life cycle of most of the Mázindaráni families.

Quddús was raised in a rural setting. Coming from a poor family of rice growers meant that he was accustomed to hardship. Peasants, in general, endure the hardship of living in isolated areas and working under difficult conditions on their farms, a living very often associated with destitute people. Interestingly, the Faith of the Báb elevated the rank of this occupation in society. In the *Kitábu'l-Asmá'* ("Book of Divine Names"), the Báb portrays God and Himself as divine farmers sowing the seeds of Their words in people's hearts: "*God verily cultivateth on earth as He pleaseth, at His bidding. Will ye not behold? Think ye that ye are the sowers? Say! Glorified be God! We are, verily, the Cultivators*".[1]

Planting rice was the most popular harvest in the region one which was very labour intensive because of the deployment of artisanal techniques, although women were not normally involved in rice cultivation.[2] One can imagine Quddús being expected to help his father over the years with the many stages involved in rice production, from sowing to harvesting, collecting firewood for cooking and heating, protecting the crops from wildlife, and so on. As profoundly sad as it would have been for a young child to lose his mother, a heavenly compensation no doubt for Quddús was having gained an affectionate step-mother who loved him dearly as well as two new half-brothers to play with at home.

Exploring the natural surrounding around his home, the river and the forest jungle must have also provided an excellent playground to discover nature. Quddús' home, some 100 metres from the river, offered ample space to be with his friends and siblings, probably swimming in summer, playing in the forest, fishing, hunting wild ducks or playing ball games or marbles, like any other peasant child.

Beyond that, he might have enjoyed going to the Panj Shanbih bazaar, which opened on Thursdays, about a twenty-minute walk from his home. Perhaps he accompanied his father, selling the family agricultural produce. The market was a central hub; a noisy conglomerate of alleys where locals chatted and shared news and where the whole gamut of merchandise was displayed, not to mention the presence of foreign citizens. The traditional street Persian puppetry known as Khaymih-shab-bází was likely enacted to the children's delight in public.

Another source of home entertainment was the evening family reading of the epic Shahnameh legends[3] by a literate family member. These books also had fascinating illustrations of the epic stories contained therein, thus captivating the

---

1 The Báb in Nader Saiedi, *Gate of the Heart*, pp. 80–81. In *Kitábu'l-Asmá'* (29:383-86), provisional translation. The original term is *zári'* (a farmer, grower, planter, producer) who is involved with *zirá'at* (agriculture, farming).

2 Mohammad Ali Kazembeyki, *Society, Politics and Economics in Mazandaran, Iran 1848-1914*, p. 153.

3 The Shahnameh is an epic Persian poem by Ferdowsi (born 940 CE) describing Persia's mythical history, heroes, kings and battles.

children's imaginations. Occasional short trips to the Caspian Sea, perhaps on some family business, involving a five-hour trip by mule to see the powerful Russian steamers, either warships or commercial ships, arriving with goods or encounters with other traders such as Armenian Christians would, no doubt, have been a source of excitement.

Mosques dotted the landscape, calling the faithful in ringing tones from the minarets five times a day from dawn till evening to perform the congregational obligatory Islamic prayer. Two major religious events were on the Islamic calendar. One was the fasting month of Ramaḍán, which concluded with community celebrations with a feast at the local mosque, accompanied by gift giving, charity and fellowship. The second was Muḥarram, the month of mourning, where Muslim religious ceremonies were performed to grieve the martyrdom of Imám Ḥusayn[1] as well as public dramatic performances to represent his martyrdom in 680 CE called Ta'zíyih ("Consolation"). On those occasions, people would take to the streets and publicly flagellate themselves to express their sorrow for the tragic death of the Imám.

Such was, more likely than not, the life experienced by peasant boys like Quddús living on the outskirts of Bárfurú<u>sh</u>. it would have likely been a simple lifestyle, provincial and markedly religious.

Early education

There is not much information about Quddús' childhood. It appears that, unlike many other underprivileged children, he began his education within the establishment of <u>Sh</u>arí'atmadár,[2] [3] a local cleric who would become one of his life-long mentors. According to Hushmand Dehghan:

> Muḥammad-'Alí [Quddús] was a handsome and lovable child, and at the same time, at an early age, his intelligence and piety were visible. As it was the custom of that time, Áqá Muḥammad Salih, the father of His Holiness [Quddús], introduced him to the study of the basics of religious sciences ... According to a tradition, he studied under Hájí Mullá Muḥammad-'Alí [<u>Sh</u>arí'atmadár] at a young age.[4]

At that time there were rudimentary one-room schools called *maktab.* The Arabic term maktab means a place of study. In those spaces the basics of reading and writing were taught, some mathematics as well as some religious education which included scriptural Arabic and reading the *Qur'án* in its original language. There was not a set curriculum, and methods of teaching were idiosyncratic and more aligned with rote learning and memorisation. Sometimes women served as maktab instructors. Maktabs for children from poor backgrounds lasted until noon so that they could help with house chores or assist parents in their trades.

---

1 Prophet Muḥammad's beloved grandson who was killed in Karbilá, Iraq in 860 CE.

2 Abbas Amanat, *Resurrection and Renewal*, p. 182.

3 Mírzá Muḥammad-Taqí Lisan al-Mulk Sipihr, *Nasi<u>kh</u> al-tawari<u>kh</u>* Qájáríyyah, p.238.

4 Hooshmand Dehghan, *Ganj-i-Pinhán, p. 33*

Education was not compulsory and not always supported by parents. Only up until the age of nine, did boys and girls study together, since the age of nine was considered to be the age of puberty and the minimum age for girls to marry. Subsequently, gender segregation took place.

After reaching ten years of age, a few select number of boys chosen by ability progressed to schools called madrasahs which were like secondary schools, which typically included boarding. Children from rural backgrounds would attend maktabs only in winter so as to help their parents with farming work during other seasons.

Normally, maktabs were attached to a mosque. Quddús' school was attached to the Káẓim Bayk Mosque.[1] Accessing this form of informal instruction opened a window for him to a world beyond his farm-life rearing. From there, he would be progressively attending a chain of more prestigious educational institutions for twelve years in Iran and later, overseas in Iraq.

> In general, Bárfurúsh had two famous central schools in those days. One is the central school in the neighborhood of Panj Shanbih (Thursday) bazaar and the other is the Káẓim Bayk school in the public bath neighbourhood in the direction of the Sadr school built in 1806 at the expense of Mirzá Muḥammad Shafí, the chancellor.[2]

Only the children from wealthy families were fortunate enough to receive more advanced instruction in numeracy, literature and the humanities as well as the rudiments of commerce from home tutors and mentors.

The rural soul

Growing up on the edge of the Mázindarán forest, Quddús had an affinity with the natural world. His connection with nature and the opportunity to attend school were all powerful sources of influences which helped shape the great person he became for the benefit of his country and in reality, humankind. Quddús' home and school were 1,400 metres away from it, a short walk, by going through the main bazaar.

Mázandarán was the happy province of Persia. The Báb called it the "Green Isle"[3] for her greenery. Women and men wore colourful dresses and their cheerful dances and love for music reflected the joyfulness of the people. Daily life in Mázandarán was deeply influenced by the natural environment. For instance, the villages were normally named after plants, animals or flowers. Those names were taken from the trees or plants growing predominantly in a particular locality. Picturesque names would include the Oak Flower Village (آزاد گله) or Flowers Village(گِله محله) or names of plants such as Buxus (شمشاد) and Under the Fern (چمازین). Toponymies based on trees are frequent: Under the Walnut

---

1 Hooshmand Dehghan, *Ganj-i-Pinhán,* pp. 113–122; & p. 34.

2 Hooshmand Dehghan, *Ganj-i-Pinhán,* p. 33

3 Nabíl-i-A'ẓam, *The Dawn-Breakers,* p. 325.

Tree (آغوزبن), Under the Maple Tree (افرا داربن), Under the Plain Tree (چناربن), Under the Elm (درخت اوجابن), Syrup Tree (شیردار), Oak (درخت آزاد), The Willow Village (بیدآباد محله). The names of some villages indicated location such as The Oak Trees Row (موزی رج), The Jungle Edge (بیشه سر) or Grove Village (بیشه محل).

It is reasonable to assume that Quddús' early rural environment had an indelible mark on his life, as is reflected in his writings which draw on natural elements to give expression to spiritual concepts such as the nightingale, sweet scented heavenly leaves, fish, air, warbling, waters, fire, trees, seas, sun, fruits, mountains, valleys, birds, stars, animals, stars and clouds,[1] [2] [3] [4] among other motifs. Fifteen years later, Quddús still recalled an incident where he got lost in the forest when his father sent him out to look for firewood.[5]

1 Hooshmand Dehghan. *Ganj-i-Pinhán: Sargozasht va Asare Hazrate Ghodoos*, p. 209.
2 Fazel Mazandarani, *Ẓuhúr al-Ḥaqq*, vol. 3, pp. 337-339.
3 Fazel Mazandarani, *Ẓuhúr al-Ḥaqq*, vol. 3, pp. 322-323.
4 Translated from E. G. Browne. *Catalogue and Description of 27 Bábí Manuscripts*, pp. 485–7.
5 E. G. Browne, *Kitáb-i-Nuqtatu'l-Káf*, pp. 199–200.

2
Years of study

Chapter content
Sárí
Study in a madrasa
The holy city of Mashhad
The seminary of Mírzá Ja'far
Shí'a and Sunní sects of Islam
Who is the "Lord of the Age"?
Shaykh Aḥmad and Siyyid Káẓim
Karbilá, Iraq
Quddús in Karbilá
Karbilá, a centre of Shaykhism
Did Quddús meet the Báb in Karbilá?
The passing of Siyyid Káẓim

Sárí

According to Nosrat Mohammad-Hosseini, Quddús completed "his basic schooling in Bárfurúsh and Sárí at the age of twelve".[1] "From the early childhood Quddús was a prodigy", the same author wrote, "and his intellectual and spiritual gifts were apparent".[2] Abbas Amanat called him a "bright youngster".[3]

Fazel Mazandarani argues that Quddús was chosen to go the Sárí to complete his next level of education after the maktab stage[4] "presumably with the encouragement of Sharí'atmadár.[5] Muḥammad-'Alí Kazembeyki said that it was because of Quddús connections to Mírzá Muḥammad-Taqí,[6] who was his relative. In any case, having such a continuing education in a more advanced city constituted an extra life benefit for the son of a modest farmer who normally lived in social and economic disadvantage. Quddús studied in madrasahs in Sárí, Mashhad and Karbilá for the next ten years becoming a religious erudite, and who became the successful story of a farm boy who spiritually conquered Iran.

---

1 Nosratollah Mohammad-Hosseini, *Qoddus, Moḥammad-'Ali Bārforuši, n.p.*

2 Nosratollah Mohammad-Hosseini, *Qoddus, Moḥammad-'Ali Bārforuši, n.p.*

3 Abbas Amanat, *Resurrection and Renewal,* p. 182.

4 Fazel Mazandarani, *Ẓuhúr al-Ḥaqq*, vol. 3, p. 413.

5 Abbas Amanat, *Resurrection and Renewal,* p. 182.

6 Mohammad Ali Kazembeyki. *Society, Politics and Economics in Mazandaran, Iran 1848-1914,* p. 117.

Our hero, Quddús, went to study in Sárí, the capital city of Mázindarán Province. He attended a madrasa (a school)[1] from the age of twelve,[2] circa 1834. Sárí is about 30 km east of Bárfurúsh on the banks of the Táján River and, with its 6,000-year history, it was considered more culturally advanced than Bárfurúsh. Since both cities were geographically close, it meant Quddús, as a teenager, stayed connected to his home. It has been said that the chief cleric of Sárí, Mírzá Muḥammad-Taqí, was related to him.[3]

By 1834, the Great Plague that had affected Persia began to fade in the region. Mázindarán was one of the provinces that was hardest hit. It was a terrible epidemic in which 80,000 people had died in Bárfurúsh alone. Once a flourishing and prosperous trading city, it became a desolate place. A European source wrote in 1834 that "'... the grass was growing in the shops ... where the merchant used to sit ...."[4] The epidemic was proliferated because of a lack of sanitation and medical facilities. Doctors could only be afforded by the rich, and sewage was allowed to flow along open drains in the middle of the streets. The situation was greatly exacerbated by the absurd religious beliefs of the people. For instance, Ahmad Seyf reported there was a "fanatical belief that the flow of water can never be polluted and is always safe".[5] He cited a report that cooking utensils and house linen were washed in one household water supply tank, and that the polluted water then flowed into the water tank of the next house. Hence, "water generally used for drinking purposes is polluted and contaminated. The water of the hammams (*ḥamámát*) or public baths is only changed once or twice a year."[6] The latter practice was reviled by the Báb, Who, in the *Bayán*, forbade the use of such communal baths.[7]

Sanitary practices in agrarian Persia, and in general, were poor and there was no knowledge of antiseptics, germs, and hygiene with proliferating quack-medicine vendors abounding, or religious invokers taking the role of healers. Public health systems did not exist, and, more often than not, couples would assume that at least one of their children was to die since the mortality rate was alarming; as high as eighty-five per cent in 1915.[8]

---

1 Madrasa or Madrasah (Arabic), "literally, 'a place where learning and studying occur' or a 'place of study'; a religious boarding school associated with a mosque; school. Pers. also madrasih, madrisih." (Michael Thomas, *Glossary and transcription for Arabic & Persian terms,* Madrasa entry).

2 Abbas Amanat, *Resurrection and Renewal,* p. 182.

3 Nabíl-i-A'ẓam, *The Dawn-Breakers*, p. 351.

4 Fraser, *A Winter's Journey*, vol. 2, p. 486.

5 Ahmad Seyf, Iran and the Great Plague, 1830–1831, p. 152.

6 Ahmad Seyf, Iran and the Great Plague, 1830–1831, p. 152.

7 The Báb, *Persian Bayán* 6:2.

8 Shireen Mahdavi, *Childhood in Qajar Iran,* p. 308.

Study in a madrasa

Quddús wrote, in 1843 CE (1259 AH),[1] that he returned from Karbilá after thirteen years of study,[2] meaning he left Bárfurúsh around 1830. He must have left home by the age of twelve or so —1842 being his year of birth—[3] as Abbas Amanat has suggested.[4] Interestingly, according to Islamic belief, boys would be circumcised at the age of thirteen with a public and family celebration constituting a major ritual of passage into adulthood symbolising new roles and responsibilities.

As mentioned earlier, in the first half of the nineteenth century, there was no formal educational system for children or youth. The only facility provided was the madrasa, which has been described by C. R. Markham as:

> The Madrasahs, or Persian colleges, are entirely in the hands of the clergy, and there are several in every large town. They generally consist of a court, surrounded by buildings containing chambers for students and masters, with a gate on one side, and frequently a garden and a well in the centre of the court ... Many of the madrasahs have been founded and endowed by kings or pious persons.[5]

Only promising children and youth were selected to attend a madrasah in preparation for an ecclesiastic career. The madrasas were seminaries focusing on Muslim theology and philosophy, Quranic studies, and history and Islamic law in order to prepare young people for careers in the clergy. Other areas included calligraphy, which was appreciated as an artform in those times. In general, their academic activity revolved around metaphysical discussions and orthodox studies. Any effort to learn from the Western world was perceived as an act of religious uncleanliness.

Most of these Islamic sciences were referred by Bahá'u'lláh as sciences that "*begin with words and end with words*"[6] rather than those that "*can profit the peoples of the earth*".[7] In the words of Ruhollah Mehrabkhani:

> The subjects of their [Islamic theologians] study were mostly superstitious and pointless arguments. They held endless discussions on the proper way to wash the different parts of the body before prayer; on the various acts and objects that might nullify one's prayers, and so on. Heated debates

---

1 AH stands for *Anno Hegirae* in Latin, literally "In the year of the Hijrah", representing the Islamic calendar.

2 Fazel Mazandarani, *Ẓuhúr al-Ḥaqq*, vol. 3, p. 413.

3 We assume that Quddús died when he was 27 years old in 1849 (1265 AH), as Nabíl-i-A'ẓam inferred (*The Dawn-Breakers*, p. 415) and therefore born in 1842 (1257 AH).

4 Abbas Amanat, *Resurrection and Renewal*, p. 182.

5 C. R. Markham, *A General Sketch of the History of Persia*, p. 365.

6 Bahá'u'lláh, *Tablets of Bahá'u'lláh*, p. 52.

7 Bahá'u'lláh, *Tablets of Bahá'u'lláh Revealed*, p. 52.

> might arise over such questions as whether the urine of the holy Imám was ritually clean, or whether the Prophet Muḥammad had a shadow. Could He be in 40 places at the same time? Could the Imám travel long distances in the twinkling of an eye? Such subjects kept them occupied for months, or even years.[1]

It is not clear why Quddús went to Sárí to study, since he could have attended any one of the local madrasas or remained in the Sharí'atmadár madrasa, where food and accommodation were freely provided. Fazel Mazandarani argues that the "bright youngster",[2] Quddús, went to Sárí with the encouragement of Sharí'atmadár. On the other hand, Kazembeyki stated that it was because of Quddús' connections to Mírzá Muḥammad-Taqí, the leading divine.[3] In either case, continuing his education in a more advanced city constituted an extra life benefit for the son of a modest farmer who normally lived a life of social and economic disadvantage.

The holy city of Mashhad

After finishing his studies in Sárí, the young Quddús was sent to continue his studies in Mashhad, 800 km east of his home, where he joined the prestigious seminary of Mírzá Ja'far.

Mashhad is the capital of Khurásán Province (it was divided into three provinces in 2004) and literally means the "Place of martyrdom". This name relates to the murder of Imám Riḍá (Reza)—the eighth Imám, an illustrious direct descendant of the Prophet Muḥammad—whose life was taken in the year 818 CE[4] by orders of the Caliph 'Abdu'lláh al-Ma'mún (r. 813–33 CE), an adversary and detractor of the Imám. It is reported that the Prophet Muḥammad once said, alluding to the eventual resting-place of Imám Riḍá, "A part of my body is to be buried in Khurásán,"[5] adding sacredness to the place.

Quddús stayed in Mashhad for four years. At this time, as well as in modern times, the city is known for the number of pilgrims visiting the shrine of Imám Riḍá and also for the monetary practices associated with it. The percentage of the city population belonging to the clerical class was about 25–30%.[6]

"It is natural to imagine," wrote Hushmand Dehghan, "that Quddús was a daily pilgrim to that holy place, and that he rose from his comfortable bed at dawn and sought refuge in that blessed place, praying and supplicating, preparing for the

1 Ruhollah Mehrabkhani, *Mullá Ḥusayn*, pp. 5–6.

2 Abbas Amanat, *Resurrection and Renewal*, p. 182.

3 Mohammad Ali Kazembeyki, *Society, Politics and Economics in Mazandaran, Iran 1848-1914*, p. 266.

4 CE stands for *Christian Era*.

5 'Abdu'l-Bahá, *Memorials of the Faithful*, p. 184.

6 Willem Floor, "The Economic Role of the Ulama in Qajar Persia", p. 55.

time of the appearance of the Promised One".[1] About the quality of his devotion, the Báb wrote:

> *[There is no one] who doth not dwell beneath thy shadow, or praise God as thou didst praise Him; who hath not sanctified God in the manner thou didst sanctify Him; who is not a true believer in the Unity of God, just as thou hast believed; and who doth not magnify God even as thou didst magnify Him.*[2]

A. L. M. Nicolas (1864–1939), a renowned French historian, wrote about the two walled faces of this city:

> Mas͟hhad is the greatest place of pilgrimage in all Persia, Karbilá being, as everyone knows in Ottoman territory. It is in Mas͟hhad that the holy shrine of the Imám Riḍá is located. I shall not enlarge upon the hundreds of miracles that have taken place and still take place at this shrine; it is enough to know that every year thousands of pilgrims visit the tomb and return home only after the shrewd exploiters of that productive business have separated them from their last penny. The stream of gold flows on and on for the benefit of the greedy officials; but these officials need the co-operation of many partners to catch their innumerable dupes in their nets. This is, without doubt, the best organized industry in Persia. If one half of the city derives its living from the Mosque, the other half is likewise keenly interested in the great concourse of pilgrims.[3]

Finally, it is noteworthy that the memory of the Imáms is highly celebrated, as are the places associated with their followers. Mas͟hhad, consequently, became a highly revered place, the most sacred in Persia, since Imám Riḍá was buried there. The other Imáms were killed beyond the limits of Persian territory.

The shrine of Imám Riḍá became the main Persian pilgrimage centre of S͟hí'ih Islam. Around this building, fanaticism has fabricated the most absurd legends, which have been perpetuated in popular thought. The shrine is credited with the power to heal the sick, perform miracles and many other things, as well as being an inviolable asylum precinct for criminals and the persecuted.

It is said that on the day the Promised One of Islam appears, he will leave the sanctuary to show himself to the world. Imám Riḍá's sister is buried in the city of Qum, where the Imám is alleged to make regular "visits". It had been also affirmed that the Promised One lived hidden on the Spanish coasts.[4] Despite this religiosity, intolerance was rampant to such extent that a Christian who was found within the sanctuary could have been charged with profanation and killed.[5]

---

1 Hushmand Dehghan, *Ganj-i-Pinhán*, p. 38.

2 The Báb, *Tablet of Visitation for Quddús*. See Appendix part 2.

3 A. L. M. Nicolas, *Seyyèd Ali-Mohammed dit le Bâb*, pp. 258–259.

4 Omid Ghaemmaghami, *To the Abode of the Hidden One*, p. 154.

5 James Baillie Fraser, *A Narrative of a Journey into Khorasan in the Years 1821 and 1822, including some Account of the Countries to the North-East of Persia*, p. 473.

The seminary of Mírzá Ja'far

As mentioned in the previous section, Quddús joined the prestigious seminary of Mírzá Ja'far in Mas_h_had. Mullá Ḥusayn, another student and future Bábí hero, also studied there probably starting before Quddús did.[1] According to historian Hasan Fuadi Bushru'I, "Mullá Ḥusayn and Quddús did not overlap in time in the school of Mírzá Ja'far."[2] These events took place around mid 1830s.

In Mas_h_had, Quddús befriended Áqá 'Alí-Riḍá Tájir-i-S_h_írází. It seems that he and Quddús were part of a group that once included Mullá Ḥusayn.[3] Hasan Fuadi Bushru'i wrote:

> Áqá 'Alí-Rizá, a businessman from Shíráz, was a famous merchant in Khurásán, and through Mullá Ḥusayn Bus_h_rúí had the honor of attaining the Faith. Before the Declaration of the Báb, he was studying at Mírzá Ja'far's school, next to the Holy Shrine [the Imám Reza sanctuary], and used to meet with Quddús. Such a strong friendship blossomed between them, that they each considered the other a true brother.
>
> At that time the Báb had not yet revealed Himself. Quddús had returned from Mas_h_had and was bidding farewell to Áqá 'Alí-Rizá. Quddús said to him, "I grant you the birthright of fraternity[4] and I hope you will be able to undertake it".
>
> When Mullá Ḥusayn Bushrúí arrived in Mas_h_had, Áqá 'Alí-Rizá rendered valuable services to him and his companions, and when they departed, Áqá 'Alí-Rizá tarried for a while in Mas_h_had, in order to settle accounts with local merchants, overcome his attachments, and later join the companions.
>
> However, sometime after the death of Muḥammad S_h_áh, Sam K_h_án Bíghlarbíghí [a senior provincial administrator] was informed of Áqá 'Alí-Rizá's intentions, and with the pretext of his religious beliefs, pounded him extracting a lot of money for himself. Therefore, Áqá 'Alí-Rizá was not able to leave for Mázindarán [with Mullá Ḥusayn].[5]

Under the oath of fraternity Quddús had said to Áqá 'Alí-Rizá: "I grant you the right of fraternity, because it will be possible for you to take care of Mullá Ḥusayn when he arrives to Mas_h_had". This happened before the Declaration of the Báb in 1844.

Every Muslim has thirty rights over his fellow Muslim brother, and he will not be relieved of them except if he fulfills them or if the one with the right forgives him. The rights of the oath of fraternity can be summarised as follows:

---

1 Hushmand Dehghan, *Ganj-i-Pinhán*, p. 38.

2 In Ahang Rabbani, *The Genesis of the Bahá'í Faith in K_h_urásán*, Chapter 2, p. 2.

3 Abbas Amanat, *The Shaping of the Babi Community*, p. 127.

4 Moojan Momen, *The Bahá'í Communities of Iran*, vol. 1, pp. 219-23.

5 Hasan Fuadi Bushru'i, *The History of the Bahá'í Faith in Khorasan*, p. 100.

> (1) to overlook his mistakes; (2) to have mercy on his tears; (3) to keep his secrets and be a trustworthy confidant; (4) to compensate for his slips (mistakes);(5) to accept his apologies;(6) to refute his defamation; (7) to be always well-wishing towards him; (8) to persevere his friendship; (9) if he has made a commitment to him, he should fulfill it and act upon it; (10) to visit him when he is sick; (11) to participate in his funeral procession; (12) to accept his invitation; (13) to accept his gifts; (14) to repay his kindness with kindness; (15) to thank and praise him for the blessings that he has bestowed upon him; (16) to assist him to the utmost of his ability; (17) to guard his family and honour; (18) to fulfill his request; (19) he should hasten to fulfill his request; (20) if he sneezes, he should say "May God have mercy on you", and show concern for him; (21) to find his lost things; (22) to respond to his greeting; (23) to speak with him with gentleness and kindness; (24) to repay his favours with kindness; (25) if he swears, he should confirm his oath; (26) he should be friends with his friend, and not be his enemy; (27) to help him, whether he is oppressive or in the time of oppression, but his help in the time of oppression means to prevent him from oppression, (28) helping him in the time of his oppression means to help him to obtain his rights; (29) in the time of distress, he should not humiliate him, and leave him alone; and (30) to love for him what he loves for himself, and to hate for him what he hates for himself. [1]

The seminary of Mírzá Ja'far was built in 1649 as an educational centre for religious scholars of Ma<u>sh</u>had. The school is still located inside the grandiose complex of the Imám Riḍá [Reza] Shrine. The seminary is currently part of the Razavi University of Islamic Sciences. James Baillie Fraser (1783 – 1856) a Scottish traveller who visited the madrasah around 1822 and 1823, found about fifty to sixty students (mullás) studying there. [2] At that time, the city theological circles were heavily influenced by <u>Sh</u>ay<u>kh</u>í ideas, so it is possible that Quddús had been studying under teachers from that religious tradition.

Ruhollah Mehrabkhani[3] narrates the story of Mullá Ḥusayn in Ma<u>sh</u>had, years later, and comments about the perceived value of these institutions:

> One of Mullá Ḥusayn's fellow countrymen, Ḥájí Mummin-i-<u>Kh</u>urásání, has left a fascinating story. He had attended school with Mullá Ḥusayn and in later years came to believe in the Báb through his former classmate. He relates: "Once I was walking with Mullá Ḥusayn in the street and we passed a religious school for mullás. Mullá Ḥusayn looked at it and recited this poetry:
>
> > "Never from this school has come learning,
> > This house of ignorance is fit for burning."

1 Imám'Alí, Cited in *Muslim Traditions of Human Rights*, p. 2

2 James Baillie Fraser, *A Narrative of a Journey into Khorasan in the Years 1821 and 1822, including some Account of the Countries to the North-East of Persia*, p. 458.

3 Ruhollah Mehrabkhani, *Mullá Ḥusayn*, p. 71.

I asked him: "Why should we complain about these schools, when they have produced a man like you?" "No, my friend", interrupted, "if it were not for the education I received in these schools, I would not have argued with my Lord."[1]

Shí'a and Sunní sects of Islam

To understand the social and religious contradictions of this city where Quddús lived as a student, it is important to know a little of the history of Islam and its two main branches.

The Muslim religion was divided into two large sects, Sunní and Shí'ih, each claiming absolute possession of the truth of this Faith. This deep split among the majority of the followers of the Prophet of Arabia dates back to Muḥammad's death when Abú-Bakr, one of the early believers and foremost "Companions" of the Prophet, assumed leadership of the community with their approval. But, in fact, Muḥammad is believed to have placed the mantle of leadership on 'Alí ibn Abú-Ṭálib (c. 600–661 CE)—the cousin and, at the same time, the son-in-law of the Prophet of God. 'Alí was a young man known for his wisdom, holiness and courage. At a very young age, he embraced the Revelation of Muḥammad and arose in its defence.

'Alí had lived in close association with Muḥammad, later marrying his daughter, Fáṭimih, a woman known as the most prominent female in the history of the Faith of Islam. Shí'ih Muslim followers believe 'Alí is the legitimate successor of Muḥammad, that is, the recognised interpreter of his doctrines, not only because of his brilliant qualities; but also because of the explicit references made about him by the Messenger of God himself, who granted high prerogatives to his family. In His last pilgrimage Muḥammad said, "Verily, I leave amongst you My twin weighty testimonies: The Book of God and My Family".[2] [3]

'Alí and eleven of his direct descendants in the direct line of successors are called Imáms and they constitute the exponents of the truths of the Islamic religion. The last Imám disappeared in 874 CE. It is prophesised that the twelfth Imám will reappear in the "last days". The Báb identifies Himself with the return of the twelfth Imám, the Imám Mahdí,[4] or the Qá'im, which means the One who will arise—thus fulfilling this prophecy.

---

1 Mullá Ḥusayn did not instantly accept the Báb at their first encounter as is seen at the beginning of the next chapter.

2 Bahá'u'lláh, *The Kitáb-i-Íqán*, p. 201.

3 Prophet Muḥammad stayed at the pond (Ghadír) of the Khumm oasis during his last trip to Mecca from Medina in 632 CE, three months before His passing. At the pond, in public, He proclaimed 'Alí's spiritual authority through a sermon. While Shí'ihs consider that Muḥammad had pronounced 'Alí as His successor, Sunnís believe that the Prophet was only extolling 'Ali's special attributes. Such a fundamental difference of opinions later created the major schism in the Islamic world once Muḥammad passed away.

4 The term *Mahdí* means the "Rightly Guided One". *Mahdí* and *Qá'im* are used

The Shí'ih world

Today Shí'ih Muslims are still the followers of Imám 'Alí. The vast majority of them live within the borders of Iran, Iraq, Azerbaijan, and Bahrain, with about 30% of the population in Lebanon. The Báb and Bahá'u'lláh grew up in the Shí'a Islam environment of Persia, and the Báb was a descendant of the Prophet Muḥammad from both the maternal and paternal sides of His family, entitling Him to be called a Siyyid.

In contrast, the Sunní Islam sect consists of all the believers who accepted Abú-Bakr's leadership, civil and religious. Sunní Muslims are in the majority in over 40 countries from Morocco to Indonesia, except Iran. Those who succeeded Abú-Bakr were given the title of Caliph (Khalífa, "successor").

To date, antagonism and hatred incited by fanaticism and prejudice have moved Muslims to commit innumerable inhumane acts of bloodshed against each other, and against non-Muslims, thus tarnishing the lustre of Islam. Sunnís have a stubborn aversion to Imáms and Siyyids. The Shí'ihs respond to this enmity with contempt for everything representing the doctrines and clerical orders of the Sunní Muslims.

The work of the twelve Imáms of Shí'a Islam represents a valuable contribution and a unique legacy to Islam's history, literature and theology, adding significantly to the elucidation of profound issues contained in the *Qur'án*. Bahá'u'lláh in the *Kitáb-i-Íqán* (Book of Certitude) has referred to them as the *"unquenchable lights of divine guidance"*.[1]

Quddús' family, like the majority of the Persian nation, belonged to the Shí'ih branch of Islam. He explained in one of his letters how God provides continuous guidance to humanity, particularly through the Imáms or descendants of the Prophet Muḥammad:

> It is imperative that a deputy from God of the universe, may his name be exalted, should always be apparent among people. Otherwise, the ministry [of the prophets] and revelations of their scriptures would be futile.[2]

Who is the "Lord of the Age"?

The Promised One of Islam is referred to as the Qá'im ("He Who Will Arise") and is a title assumed by the Báb. According to the Shí'ih Muslim belief, the 12th Imám, a linear descendant of Muḥammad, disappeared in 874 CE and was expected to return on the Day of Judgement. The Báb fulfilled this prophecy as the Promised One of Islám.

A central topic of learning in the Persian religious seminaries was the study of the prophecies regarding the Qá'im, also known as "the Lord of the Age". In this

---

interchangeably.

1 Bahá'u'lláh, *The Kitáb-i-Íqán*, pp. 143–144.

2 Abbas Amanat, *Resurrection and Renewal*, p. 184.

regard, Bahá'u'lláh in the *Kitáb-i-Íqán* ("Book of Certitude") mentions a famous Islamic tradition or oral saying: *"Knowledge is twenty and seven letters. All that the Prophets have revealed are two letters thereof. No man thus far hath known more than these two letters. But when the Qá'im shall arise, He will cause the remaining twenty and five letters to be made manifest."*[1] Bahá'u'lláh goes on to state that this oral saying from the sixth Imám reflects how elevated was the position of the Báb: *"Behold from this utterance how great and lofty is His* [*Qá'im's*] *station! His rank excelleth that of all the Prophets, and His Revelation transcendeth the comprehension and understanding of all their chosen ones"*.[2]

The appearance of this prophetic figure was eagerly expected in nineteenth century Iran. Years later, after the Cause of the Báb was born and subsequently proclaimed, Quddús became known as the regent to the Lord of the Age.[3]

Just as the coming of Jesus was announced by John the Baptist, and anticipated by the Wise Men (*Matthew* 2:1–2) along with many other prophecies from the *Bible*,[4] so also the advent of the Báb was foretold by many Biblical and Quranic prophecies, as well as by various oriental sages. In the case of the Báb, both Shaykh Aḥmad al-Aḥsá'í (1753–1826), founder of Shaykhism, and his successor Siyyid Káẓim (1793–1843), predicted His arrival. These two sages were praised by the Báb and referred by Bahá'u'lláh as *"twin shining lights"*.[5]

The Occultation

The notion of the "Lord of the Age" in Islam is related to the theological concept of Occultation. The period after the disappearance of the 12th Imám in 874 CE, according to the Shí'ih belief, is called the Occultation. This Occultation would end when the Lord of the Age returns to earth. Quddús had described this as a period of "heaviest burden" when humanity is left only with "the Book, the Traditions, and those who would understand them, those who embody the word of the Imám, peace be upon him, and what has been related from him. They are appointed by him as his proof as he himself [Quddús] stated, 'They are my proofs to you and I am the proof of God'; their command is his command and denial of them is denial of him and denial of him is denial of God."[6]

In Islam Shí'ih, the end of the period of Occultation will mark the advent of the Day of Judgement. According to historian Dr Vahid Rafati:

> Islamic eschatology holds that the Day of Judgment will definitely come, but only God knows when it will occur. Its advent will be announced by the appearance of certain signs: "mountains will be like carded wool";

---

1 Bahá'u'lláh, *The Kitáb-i-Íqán*, pp. 243–244.

2 Bahá'u'lláh, *The Kitáb-i-Íqán*, pp. 243–244.

3 A reference to the Báb.

4 *Malachi* 4:5; *Isaiah* 66:15–16, 66:14–16; *Micah* 5:2; *Daniel* 9:26; *Zechariah* 9:9, 12:10.

5 Bahá'u'lláh, *The Kitáb-i-Íqán*, p. 65.

6 Abbas Amanat, *Resurrection and Renewal*, p. 184–185

> "heaven shall be rent asunder"; "the stars shall be dispersed"; "the seas shall be commingled"; and "the earth and the mountains will be borne away, and both of them crushed (to dust at a single crushing)." The Antichrist, al-Dajjál, who leads people away from the right path, will appear. The sun will rise from the west, the Beast will appear, and Gog and Magog will come. Dense smoke, which will cover the earth for days, and several eclipses will proclaim the approach of the Day of Judgment. On that Day, the trumpet will blast twice. At the first blast, all living things will die; at the second, the dead will be resurrected. Then they will assemble in the gathering place, in the presence of God, for His judgment. God will ask them questions, weigh their deeds and then, in accordance with their conduct, send them to Hell or to Paradise. One of the major events of that Day will be the advent of the Mahdí (Guided One), who will be followed by the return of Christ.[1]

Similarly, in the West, William Miller (1782–1849) had identified 1844 as the year of Jesus Christ's Second Coming.[2] The year 1844 was considered a pivotal year for Christianity in the nineteenth century. For the "Adventist" churches, particularly for the Millerites, 1844 signified the "cleaning of the sanctuary" in relation to the "abomination of desolation" that Daniel foretold would appear at the conclusion of 2,300 years (*Daniel* 8:13–14; *Matthew* 24:30).[3] It was considered that the time of the Gentiles was fulfilled in 1844, the year when Jews were permitted to return to their native land (Luke 21:24–27).[4]

Shaykh Aḥmad and Siyyid Káẓim

Shaykh Aḥmad al-Aḥsá'í (1753–1826) regarding the advent of the Qá'im stated that, "Ere long shall ye behold the countenance of your Lord resplendent as the moon in its full glory ...", and "One of the most mighty signs that shall signalise the advent of the promised Hour is this: 'A woman shall give birth to One who shall be her Lord.'"[5]

Siyyid Káẓim Rashtí (1793–1843), Shaykh Aḥmad's successor, went even further declaring that the Promised One was already present in the world, living among the population and would soon manifest Himself. The Shaykhis also taught that the interpretation of the prophecies of the Holy Books was more symbolic than literal, a suggestion that was severely rejected by the more

---

1 See Vahid Rafati, *The Development of Shaykhí Thought in Shí'í Islam*, p. 106.

2 Carolyn Sparey Fox, *Seeking a State of Heaven*, p. 12.

3 The Millerites were the followers of the teachings of William Miller, who in 1831 publicly declared his belief that the Second Advent of Jesus Christ would occur about the year 1843–1844. The calculation starts from the time of the third edict to rebuild Jerusalem, issued by Artaxerxes in 457 BCE. See Sears, *Thief in the Night*, pp. 75, 6, & 27.

4 'Abdu'l-Bahá, *Some Answered Questions*, pp. 40–41.

5 Nabíl-i-A'ẓam, *The Dawn-Breakers*, p. 12.

conservative of the Muslim clerics. The French historian A. L. M. Nicolas commented on the effects of Siyyid Káẓim's preaching:

> Indeed, the sermons of Siyyid Káẓim had deeply stirred Muslim consciences. His undisputed science, his eloquence, the clarity of explanations had propagated in an unexpected way the opinions of Shaykh Aḥmad. The official clergy was terrified to see teachings about the non-resurrection of bodies and the material non-existence of the body of Muḥammad in his miraculous ascension to heaven. The legal and ritual purity of the Christians,[1] possessors of the Gospels, proclaimed by Shaykh Aḥmad, heightened their fury. They felt threatened in their doctrines, which are few, but also in their influence and in their interests, which was otherwise serious. Therefore, they wanted to resort to the only means at their disposal and which, until then, had proved effective: to declare Siyyid Káẓim and all the Shaykhís[2] convicted of impiety and apostasy and condemn them to death.[3]

Of these two personages, Bahá'u'lláh stated, "*Likewise, there appeared on earth Aḥmad and Káẓim, those twin resplendent lights—may God sanctify their resting-place!*"[4]

Karbilá, Iraq

The city of Karbilá is located in the neighbouring country of Iraq, 1,200 km west of Bárfurúsh. Iraq was then part of the Ottoman Empire. Karbilá is famous for its religious history. The tragic 680 CE battle of Karbilá is commemorated as one of the greatest passionate dramas in Shí'a Islam. The battle ended when Imám Ḥusayn, the revered grandson of the Prophet Muḥammad, was brutally beheaded. Over twenty of his family members, including women and children, along with about fifty early Muslim believers, were inhumanely killed in the battle.

Karbilá is renowned as a centre of Islamic Shí'ih theology and religious pilgrimage to visit and venerate the site where the remains of Imám Ḥusayn (626–680 CE), the martyred grandson of the Prophet Muḥammad, are entombed.

The number of Shí'ih and Sunní pilgrims going on the "greater" 5-day pilgrimage to Mecca varied between 2 and 3 million people between the years of 2000 and 2019. At times the number has been limited by the physical restraints of the location. The number of pilgrims going on the "lesser" pilgrimage (the off-season of the main pilgrimage season) can exceed 24 million per year. In contrast, Mashhad and Karbilá may receive 20 and 30 million respectively, solely regarding the Shí'ih pilgrims. A pilgrim to Mecca, Mashhad and Karbilá is referred to as Ḥájí, Mashdí and Karbilá'í (abbreviated as Kal) respectively. People used these titles

---

1 The Muslim clergy taught that Christians were ritually impure and spiritually unclean.

2 Plural form is Shaykhiyún.

3 A. L. M. Nicolas, *Seyyèd Ali-Mohammed dit le Bâb,* pp. 251–252.

4 Bahá'u'lláh, *The Kitáb-i-Íqán,* p. 65.

in daily life to add to their names as a sign of moral reputation. Quddús was therefore a Ḥájí, a Mashdí and a Kal.

Quddús in Karbilá

At the age of eighteen years, Quddús moved further away from home to Karbilá. He stayed there for four years[1] and became the "most esteemed disciple of Siyyid Kaẓím."[2]

It seems that he did not pass through Bárfurúsh but travelled probably through the southeast route Yazd - Bandar 'Abbás – Baṣrih - Búshihr - Baghdád.[3] The journey involved thousands of kilometres but was worthwhile as Karbilá was one of the prime centres of Islamic learning.

It was likely that Quddús' devotion to the Lord of the Age—The Promised One of Islam—led him to study at the Shaykhí school founded by Shaykh Aḥmad al-Aḥsá'í and run by Siyyid Káẓim, since its focus was on the advent of that Divine Personage. The school, with ideas differing from those prevalent, was attracting considerable attention at that time from the Islamic religious circles. Many of the early Bábís attended this famous school. It was during this Mashhad-Karbilá period, when he was between twelve and twenty-two years of age, that Quddús' "veneration of the Imám, the Lord of the Time, and a longing for his speedy Advent" evolved to perfection.[4]

What moved a promising eighteen-year-old boy such as Quddús to move to a distant and foreign land, to study at a school of antithetical religious orientation? We can only hypothesise that Quddús was being encouraged and supported by his family mentor, Sharí'atmadár, to study at the Shaykhí school run by Siyyid Káẓim. Himself a Shaykhí, Sharí'atmadár probably had in mind to further train Quddús in that tradition so that, once back in Bárfurúsh, he might strengthen his congregation. According to Sharí'atmadár, "in my attendance at the classes of Shaykh Aḥmad-i-Aḥsá'í at Iṣfahán (1238 AH /1822 CE), I gained much benefit during a short period."[5] Quddús was certainly a gifted youth, one who was destined to succeed Sharí'atmadár as the main cleric of his mosque and the leader of the local Shaykhí community.

Karbilá, a centre of Shaykhism

It appears that Siyyid Káẓim's followers would identify potentially gifted Persian students and invite them to study at the Shaykhí school in Karbilá.[6] He was careful as to which students to take. According to Hushmand Dehghan:

---

1 Abbas Amanat, *Resurrection and Renewal*, p. 182.

2 Shoghi Effendi, *God Passes By*, p. 7.

3 This route was once taken by Badí (See Hasan Balyuzi, *Bahá'u'lláh, King of Glory*, p. 296).

4 Abbas Amanat, *Resurrection and Renewal*, p. 184.

5 Mohammad Ali Kazembeyki, *Society, Politics and Economics in Mazandaran*, p. 264.

6 Hushmand Dehghan, *Ganj-i-Pinhán*, p. 38.

> Sharí'atmadár was one of the students and followers of Shaykh Aḥmad-i-Aḥsá'í .... Shaykh Aḥmad-i-Aḥsá'í instructed him to return to his hometown in Bárfurúsh after completing his studies in Karbilá to spread the teachings of Shaykh Aḥmad-i-Aḥsá'í. When Sharí'atmadár returned to Bárfurúsh, he began teaching the works of Shaykh Aḥmad-i-Aḥsá'í at [his] Káẓim Bayk school[1] .... Quddús was probably one of his pupils and became acquainted with the teachings of Shaykh Aḥmad—planting thus the seeds of love for Shaykh Aḥmad's philosophy in his heart .... It is in this Káẓim Bayk school that Ṭáhirih[2] once gave a talk .... Káẓim Bayk was a branch of the Shaykhí in Bárfurúsh.[3]

It is noteworthy that at the time of Quddús' sojourn in Mashhad, there was significant support for the Shaykhí movement. According to Moojan Momen: "... several of the leading clerics of Mashhad were favourable to the movement, including Mírzá 'Askarí (d. 1862), who was probably the most influential cleric in the city".[4]

In Karbilá, Quddús became a disciple of Siyyid Káẓim, who, as previously stated, led the Shaykhí movement that was followed by Sharí'atmadár of Bárfurúsh. His four-year sojourn in that city was very special to Quddús, as he remarked, "I was brought up in the holy land and grew up on that pure soil and reached what was bestowed upon me by my Lord on that sublime threshold".[5] We do not have historical evidence that Quddús met the Báb in Karbilá, although it is very likely that both lived together in the same city at the same time, upon visiting Siyyid Káẓim's religious seminary.

Quddús remained in Karbilá, learning advanced Islamic theology from Siyyid Káẓim, particularly concerning the prophecies of the Qá'im, the Promised One of Islam. Quddús was distinguished by his humility and the mastery of theological and mystical subjects acquired during his training. Siyyid Káẓim praised Quddús and said, "Amongst you, there is one who enters after everyone and leaves before everyone; he does not mix with anyone".[6] Siyyid Káẓim was worried that jealousy might be endangered with such exemplary behaviour. According to Nabíl:

> It has been reported by those who attended the lectures of Siyyid Káẓim that in the last years of the latter's life, Quddús enrolled himself as one of Siyyid's disciples. He was the last to arrive and invariably occupied the lowliest seat in the assembly. He was the first to depart upon the

1 Hushmand Dehghan, *Ganj-i-Pinhán,* p. 24.

2 Fáṭimih Baraqání Qazvíní (c. 1817/1818–1852) was given the title Ṭáhirih by the Báb. She was an illustrious poet, theologian and vehement defender of women's rights. She was the 17th person to become a Letter of the Living. She was executed for her beliefs in 1852. Ṭáhirih is considered the most prominent woman in the Bábí Faith.

3 Hushmand Dehghan, *Ganj-i-Pinhán,* p. 30.

4 Moojan Momen, *The Bahá'í Communities of Iran*, vol. 1, p. 120.

5 Abbas Amanat, *Resurrection and Renewal*, p. 182

6 Ruhollah Mehrabkhani, *La Aurora del Día Prometido*, p. 63.

> conclusion of every meeting. The silence he observed and the modesty of his behaviour distinguished him from the rest of his companions. Siyyid Káẓim was often heard to remark that certain ones among his disciples, though they occupied the lowliest of seats, and observed the strictest silence, were none the less so exalted in the sight of God that he himself felt unworthy to rank among their servants. His disciples, although they observed the humility of Quddús and acknowledged the exemplary character of his behaviour, remained unaware of the purpose of Siyyid Káẓim.[1]

"Quddús stayed with that master for four years," wrote Ruhollah Mehrabkhani, "reaching excellent theological knowledge and acquiring an incomparable spirit achieved after fruitful meditations, prayers and retreats."[2]

Did Quddús meet the Báb in Karbilá?

Historian Fazel Mazandarani, a Bárfurú<u>sh</u>í like Quddús, stated in his book Taríkh-i-Ẓuhúr al-Ḥaqq ("History of the Manifestation of Truth"), that "Mírzá Muhammad-'Alí (His Honour Quddús) met the Báb during the days of Karbilá" before their later encounter in Shíráz, "as he had [previously] met the Báb in Karbilá". [3]

Hushmand Dehghan in his book Ganj-i-Pinhán ("The Hidden Treasure"), takes this interesting question one step further.

> ... the tomb of Siyyidu'<u>sh</u>-<u>Sh</u>uhadá ("prince of Martyrs", a reference to Imám Ḥusayn) held a special sanctity and reverence for the students of Siyyid Káẓim's school. Siyyid Káẓim used to visit the shrine every day before attending school. We can consider the same routine to be true for Quddús.[4]

Hushmand Dehghan produces no historical evidence to substantiate this claim. However, from the standpoint of a teacher-student relationship, especially engendered within a pious Shaykhi kernel of devotion—where visiting shrines of holy Imáms is a legitimate act of worship— provide ample grounds for entertaining his hypothesis. Ibn Shu'ba al-Harrani narrates a hadíth from the tenth Imám of the Twelver Shí'as: "There are definite places in which God likes the servants to supplicate to Him. One of these places is the tomb of Al-Ḥusayn."[5]

Dehghan continues to demonstrate this devotion and intense love which Quddús had always expressed towards the holy Shrine of the Third Imám. Therefore, it is not surprising to see the same level of utmost respect and

---

1 Nabíl-i-A'ẓam, *The Dawn-Breakers,* pp. 71–72.

2 Ruhollah Mehrabkhani, *La Aurora del Día Prometido*, p. 63.

3 Fazel Mazandarani, *Taríkh Ẓuhúr al-Ḥaqq*, vol. 2, p. 38.

4 Fazel Mazandarani, *Ẓuhúr al-Ḥaqq*, vol. 3, p. 413.

5 Ibn Shu'ba al-Harrani, Tuhaf al-'Uqul ("The Masterpiece of the Mind"), p. 366.

reverence in the Sacred Writings of the Báb and Bahá'u'lláh towards the shrine of Imám Ḥusayn. For instance, in the *Kitáb-i-Iqán* we read,

> For instance, consider the pervading power of those drops of the blood of Ḥusayn which besprinkled the earth. What ascendancy and influence hath the dust itself, through the sacredness and potency of that blood [Imám Ḥusayn's], exercised over the bodies and souls of men! So much so, that he who sought deliverance from his ills, was healed by touching the dust of that holy ground, and whosoever, wishing to protect his property, treasured with absolute faith and understanding, a little of that holy earth within his house, safeguarded all his possessions.[1]

Perhaps in trying to find a logical historical venue for Fazel Mazandarani's statement above, Dehghan, places this encounter at the holy Shrine, without any historical evidence when the latter wrote "It was in this holy tomb that probably His Holiness met a young man who, at the end of his prayers, visited the shrine of Siyyidu'sh-Shuhadá (Imám Ḥusayn) with attentiveness and humility."[2] However, Dehghan continues with absolute confidence and conviction the following statement which is well-founded in the historical data and testimonies of eyewitnesses:

> During the pilgrimage [to Imám Ḥusayn's shrine], He [the Báb] attracted everyone's attention.[3] This young man was none other than Siyyid 'Alí-Muḥammad Shírází, a young man who claimed to be the Báb a few months later, and now millions of Bahá'ís around the world call Him His Holiness the Báb. Historical documents show that during his seven-month stay in Karbilá, His Holiness the Báb visited the school of Siyyid Káẓim many times.[4] Thus there is no doubt that he met with His Holiness the Báb many times in Karbilá.[5]

There is abundant historical evidence to corroborate Dehghan's statement in the previous paragraph. For instance, al-Qatíl ibn al-Karbalá'í confirms that,

> ... no one from the committed people of that region [the 'Atabat[6]] remained who had not heard or did not understand . . . and all those who had seen

---

1 Bahá'u'lláh, *The Kitáb-i-Íqán*, p.p. 127-128.

2 Hushmand Dehghan, *Ganj-i-Pinhán*, p. 42.

3 In 1841 the Báb went to Karbilá and stayed for seven-eight months attending the Shaykhí school several times (Fereydun Vahman, *The Báb: A Sun in a Night not Followed by Dawn*, pp.18-21), He stayed in Karbilá from spring to the fall of 1841 (Denis MacEoin, *Early Shaykhí reactions to the Báb and his claims*, p. 15).

4 "According to a treatise by Ibn Karbilá'í, the Báb attended the Shaykhí school once every three days (*Ẓuhúr al-Ḥaqq*, vol. 3, p. 529), and according to Mírzá Ḥádíy-Nahrí, the Báb often attended that school (*Memories and Letters*, p. 10)"; in Hushmand Dehghan, *Ganj-i-Pinhán*, p. 42n.

5 Hushmand Dehghan, *Ganj-i-Pinhán*, p. 42.

6 "'Atabát" stands for "the Shi'ite holy shrines in Iraq and the cities where they are located: the tombs of the first six Imáms; and the cities of Karbalá', Najaf, Káẓimayn,

the Báb previously said that if the claimant is the one we know of, then we will be among his followers.[1]

E.G. Browne has relayed the following account:

> One day I was seated with a holy and just person [Muqqadas-i-salib] at the head of the tomb of that Holy One (i.e. Ḥusayn), when we saw that same Siyyid (i.e. the Báb) enter. And he stood at the entrance of the holy place, and performed his visit (ziyárat), and turned back from that same place. I asked of that holy person [Muqqadas] "Who is this person?" That holy one replied, "This man is Mír 'Alí-Muḥammad Shírázi, and he is one of the pupils of Ḥájí Siyyid Káẓim."[2]

Fazel Mazandarani adds,

> To this Ḥájí Rasúl, a Shaykhí merchant from Qazvín, adds that he never saw any other person "whether from divines, mystics, spiritual guides, nobles, and merchants" who could match "the humility, devotion, or magnificence" in his visits. [3]

As we have seen, and which Hushmand Dehghan has so successfully proven, the humility, devotion, magnificence and the nobility with which the Báb conducted in His daily affairs and religious observances in Karbilá did not go unnoticed by a number of eyewitnesses and perhaps future devoted believers. Whether these qualities attracted the attention of Quddús, and whether the arena for it was at the sanctuary of the holy Shrine of the Imám Ḥusayn, or not, the matter requires further study from new primary and secondary historical sources.

The passing of Siyyid Káẓim

Siyyid Káẓim had spent his life promoting the advent of the Promised Messenger prophesied by all the religions of the world. To varying degrees, he succeeded in instilling this idea in the hearts of his pupils. They were all instructed carefully in the prophecies revealed about the glorious Day of God and were urged to arise after his death, in a spirit of detachment and consecration, and to gain the invaluable blessing of attaining the presence of the Promised One. For this reason, Siyyid Káẓim did not appoint any successor. Rather, he encouraged his students to cross the vastness of the world until they finally discovered the Qá'im. Siyyid Káẓim passed away on the last day of 1843.

Mullá Ḥusayn and a group of Siyyid Káẓim's disciples decided to travel back to Persia to find the Promised One. Before departing, Mullá Ḥusayn "established a

---

and Sámarrá", Michael W Thomas, in "*Glossary and transcription for Arabic & Persian terms*", p. 31.

1 Cited in Abbas Amanat, *Resurrection and Renewal*, p. 214.

2 Browne, E. G., *The Bábís of Persia. Vol. II: Their Literature and Doctrines*, pp. 894-895.

3 Fazel Mazandarani, *Ẓuhúr al-Ḥaqq*, vol. 3, p. 379.

pact with his companions that if any one of them should hear the Call of the Truth, he would inform the others at once".[1]

The search for the Promised One had begun.

[1] Afnán, Mírzá Ḥabíbu'lláh, *The Genesis of the Bábí-Bahá'í Faiths,* pp. 22–23.

Figure1: Views of the house of Quddús' father in Bárfurúsh
(Source: Bahá'í Media)

Figure 2: Views of the house of Quddús' father in Bárfurúsh
(Source: Bahá'í Media)

Figure 3: A view of Bárfurú<u>sh</u> around 1865 (Public domain)

Figure 4: Babolsar, port city north of Babol in the 1930s
(Public domain)

Figure 5: Two Iranian stamps showing Mázandaráni i people's traditional attire

Figure 6: Sharí'atmadár's school in Bárfurúsh (old view) (Source: Ganj-i-Pinhán)

Figure 7: A madrasa, late 19th or early 20th century
(© The Nelson Collection of Qajar Photography)

Figure 8: Mírzá Ja'far seminary where Quddús studied, Mashhad
(Public domain)

Figure 9: Siyyid Káẓim

Figure 10: Shrine of the Imám Ḥusayn in Karbilá by Robert Clive (1827 - 1902) (Public domain)

Figure 11: General view of Shíráz in the early 1930s (Source: Bahá'í Media)

3
Finding the Promised One

Chapter content
Quddús returns to Bárfurús͟h
Mullá Ḥusayn is the first
Behold the Promised One
What is the *Qayyúmu'l-Asmá*?
The Letters of the Living
Quddús is the last
The Day of Resurrection

Quddús returns to Bárfurús͟h

After having lived in Karbilá for four years, Quddús returned to Bárfurús͟h in about March 1844[1] at the insistence of his family. Another source states that he left Karbilá a few months before the passing of Siyyid Káẓim (at the end of 1843).[2] Quddús had by this time become a recognized religious scholar, having completed about ten years of continuous theological studies in Sárí, Mas͟hhad and Karbilá.

After leaving Karbilá, Quddús began his search for the Promised One. He returned triumphantly to Bárfurús͟h and stayed with his sister Maryam and stepmother.[3] He received a warm welcome at home:

> The moment of his arrival at Bárfurús͟h was recounted by the wife of Mullá Áminá, a loyal servant of Muḥammad-'Alí [Quddús] as follows: "I was washing dishes by the river when a voice of an announcer was heard and people were saying that Mullá Muḥammad-'Alí had come from Karbilá. I also put my dishes aside and I happily went to welcome him. At this time, I saw that his father's wife had put a mullá's clothes on a tray; they brought them to Mullá Muḥammad-'Alí and he put the clothes on. The kind woman said: "How fitting these clothes are for you!"[4]

During the short time that Quddús remained in Bárfurús͟h, he only maintained contact with S͟harí'atmadár, a clergyman who had been his mentor for many years.

---

[1] Hushmand Dehghan, *Ganj-i-Pinhán*, p. 291.
[2] Fazel Mazandarani, *Tarík͟h Ẓuhúr al-Ḥaqq*, vol. 3, pp. 405–407.
[3] Sources do not specify the stepmother's name.
[4] Hushmand Dehghan, *Ganj-i-Pinhán*, p. 45.

"People, especially from the Ni'matí neighborhood,"[1] wrote Hushmand Dehghan, "used to love him and were amazed at his good behaviour and the breadth of his knowledge".[2]

However, Quddús was constantly ostracised by the Sa'ídu'l-'Ulamá', the chief cleric of the city, because he was a close companion of the Sharí'atmadár and a consummate Shaykhí theologian, and a follower of Shaykh Aḥmad al-Aḥsá'í and Siyyid Káẓim. Sharí'atmadár used to praise Quddús in meetings and public circles, which added to his popularity, and would have further antagonised Sa'ídu'l-'Ulamá'. We should bear in mind that Sa'ídu'l-'Ulamá' was 50 years older than Quddús —a significant age difference that might partly explain the jealousy and envy of the former. Moreover, Sa'ídu'l-'Ulamá' had had theological disputes with Siyyid Káẓim when he was in Karbilá.[3]

After the passing of Siyyid Kázim, who had foretold the imminent appearance of the Promised One, a group of about forty of his students, which included Mullá Ḥusayn and Quddús, undertook a 40-day period of intense meditation and fasting in the Masjid Kufih and Masjid Sahlih. According to a relative of the Báb, Mírzá Ḥabíbu'lláh Afnán, at the end of this period of ascetic observance, Mullá Ḥusayn had "established a pact with his companions that if any one of them should hear the Call of the Truth, he would inform the others at once."[4]

Around Naw-Rúz (21 March) of 1844, Quddús dreamed about his meeting with the Promised One. Historian Ahang Rabbani, wrote that:

> In his writings, Quddús describes his vision of the Báb some time prior to the Latter's declaration that enabled him to recognize the promised Manifestation. He further states that on the first day of Jamádíyu'l-Avval [18 May 1844], he left his native town for Shíráz.[5]

Quddús recognized his dream as the spiritual "Call of Truth". Mírzá Ḥabíbu'lláh Afnán, a relative of the Báb, wrote that, "no sooner had he [Quddús] heard this Call than he set out for Shíráz to investigate the matter ...."[6]

Quddús headed to Shíráz with the intention of going to Mecca.[7] His decision to go to Mecca seems strange, since the liturgic pilgrimage season would not begin until December 1844, a long way off. Going to Mecca was perhaps an excuse to leave town and begin the search for the Promised One.

According to historian Abbas Amanat:

---

1 The predominantly Ni'matí ṣúfí religious part of Bárfurúsh was where Quddús lived as well as the jurisdiction of Sharí'atmadár.

2 Hushmand Dehghan, *Ganj-i-Pinhán*, p. 46.

3 Mohammad Ali Kazembeyki, *Society, Politics and Economics in Mazandaran*, p. 117.

4 Ḥabíbu'lláh Afnán, *The Genesis of the Bábí-Bahá'í Faiths in Shíráz and Fárs*, pp. 22–23

5 Ahang Rabbani in Ḥabíbu'lláh Afnán, *The Genesis of the Bábí-Bahá'í Faiths*, p. 30.

6 Ḥabíbu'lláh Afnán, *The Genesis of the Bábí-Bahá'í Faiths in Shíráz and Fárs*, p. 30.

7 Muhammad Mu'ín al-Saltanih, *Tarikh-i Amr*, pp. 63-64

> Neither is it unlikely that in his search for the true representative of the Imám, Mullá Muḥammad-'Alí [Quddús] should have acquired some vague knowledge of the sayyid [siyyid] of Shíráz [the Báb] even before his instant recognition of the Báb upon His arrival in that city.[1]

In any case, to go to Mecca from Mázindarán, Quddús had to embark from the port of Búshihr necessarily passing through the city of Shíráz. It is in this city where he would find his companions from his Karbilá seminary who were searching for the Promised One.

Mullá Ḥusayn is the first

Shíráz is a beautiful city in the south of Persia, famous for its innumerable nightingales, candle-like cypresses, roses, and fruits, and especially the lemon trees, which perfume the neighbourhoods with their unique fragrance. A gentle climate favours both its natural environment and its human inhabitants. It is also the cradle of great Persian poets such as Ḥáfiẓ and Sa'dí.[2] Furthermore, the city is known for the domes of its mosques, and for the unique atmosphere created by the exquisitely designed tiles, with their vibrant colours and patterns, that adorn its shrines and residences. The Báb called it *"the mother of all cities"*.[3]

In his vigorous search for the Promised One, Mullá Ḥusayn—that staunch disciple of Siyyid Káẓim—arrived in Shíráz in May of 1844. While he was walking alone an hour before sunset around the old city gate[4] on the Kázirún to Shíráz road, a younger man suddenly approached him, welcomed him with unusual affability. At first, Mullá Ḥusayn thought that perhaps the person was another one of his classmates from the Shaykhí religious seminary in Karbilá. However, he would later realise that this Young Man was none other than the Promised Messenger, the Báb.

The Báb was wearing a green turban, signifying that He was a descendant of the Prophet Muḥammad. In contrast, Mullá Ḥusayn, a poor traveller, had no shoes, and no buttons on his shirt.[5] Mullá Ḥusayn was described by locals previously as a "ragged student".[6]

---

1 Abbas Amanat, *Resurrection and Renewal,* p. 184.

2 Khwája Shams ad-Dín Muḥammad Ḥáfiẓ-i-Shírází (1320–1390) and Sa'dí Shírází (1210–c. 1291/1292).

3 Abbas Amanat, *The Persian Bayan and the Shaping of the Bábí Renewal,* p. 347.

4 The gate was on the northwest side of the old city through which the Kázirún passed. All the old city gates have since been destroyed. The *Qur'án* gate on the north side is a recreation of one of the gates.

5 Bahá'í Blogcast with Rainn Wilson—Ep. 48: *A Declaration of the Bab: Conversation with Nader Saiedi.* 17 September 2020. (With Dr Saiedi's permission). Transcript available at www.scribd.com/document/476399968/Transcripts-Baha-i-Blogcast-With-Rainn-Wilson-Ep-48-a-Declaration-of-the-Bab-Conversation-With-Nader-Saiedi

6 The Báb in *Dalá'il-i-Sab'ih.* In Emily McBride Périgord, *Translation of French Footnotes of the Dawn-Breakers,* p. 4.

To Mullá Ḥusayn's surprise, he received an extremely courteous invitation to visit the Báb's home, which was a twelve-minute walk from the gate. The allure of the Young Man's voice, the dignity of that first meeting and, moreover, His respectful demeanour, as well as the delicacy and warmth of His expressions, moved Mullá Ḥusayn so much that he could not resist the invitation and he was impelled to show great reverence to the Báb.

Mullá Ḥusayn was led into a modest house, the door of which was opened by a servant. "'*Enter therein in peace, secure*'," were the Báb's words as he crossed the threshold "and motioned for me to follow Him."[1]

Khadíjih Bagum,[2] the wife of the Báb, recounted that He was expecting the coming of Mullá Ḥusayn on the night of 22 May 1844:

> What an extraordinary night that was! The Báb said to me: *"Tonight we will entertain a dear guest"*. His whole being was ablaze. I was most eager to hear what He had to say, but He turned to me and told me: *"It is better if you go and sleep."*[3]

Once inside, Mullá Ḥusayn found himself surrounded with such tokens of kindness and loving courtesy that his heart pulsated with the premonition that God had prepared this strange experience for him.

> Might not my visit to this house, I thought to myself, enable me to draw nearer to the Object of my quest? Might it not hasten the termination of a period of intense longing, of strenuous search, of increasing anxiety, which such a quest involves? As I entered the house and followed my Host to His chamber, a feeling of unutterable joy invaded my being. Immediately we were seated, He ordered an ewer of water to be brought, and bade me wash away from my hands and feet the stains of travel. I pleaded permission to retire from His presence and perform my ablutions in an adjoining room. He refused to grant my request, and proceeded to pour the water over my hands. He then gave me to drink of a refreshing beverage, after which He asked for the samovar and Himself prepared the tea which He offered me.[4]

Mullá Ḥusayn performed his customary ablutions, and then, stood upright to pray beside the Báb. He eagerly avowed in his prayer, "I have striven with all my soul, O my God, and until now have failed to find Thy promised Messenger. I testify that Thy word faileth not, and that Thy promise is sure".[5]

Afterwards, the Báb asked Mullá Ḥusayn about what signs the Messenger of God should show according to what Siyyid Káẓim had taught him. "He is of a pure

---

1 Nabíl-i-A'ẓam, *The Dawn-Breakers*, p. 53.

2 Khadíjih Bagum (1822–1882) was referred to by the Báb as *"O thou who art the chosen one among women!"* (The Báb, *Selections*, p. 63).

3 Munírih Khanum, *Memoirs and Letters*, p. 34.

4 Nabíl-i-A'ẓam, *The Dawn-Breakers*, pp. 54–55.

5 Nabíl-i-A'ẓam, *The Dawn-Breakers*, p. 55.

lineage, is of illustrious descent, and of the seed of Fáṭimih.[1] As to His age, He is more than twenty and less than thirty. He is endowed with innate knowledge. He is of medium height, abstains from smoking, and is free from bodily deficiency".[2]

Behold the Promised One

After a pause, Mullá Ḥusayn then received the great Declaration of the Báb *"Behold, all these signs are manifest in Me!"*[3] At that moment, Mullá Ḥusayn was tested by a powerful summons. His mind was suddenly confused and his heart was seized with anguish to the point that he felt inclined to reject the Báb's statement and consider it more prudently later.

Without the Báb being asked, and much to Mullá Ḥusayn's astonishment, a lengthy and comprehensive theological treatise about the life of Joseph[4] began to flow from the Báb, the very earnest and secret longing for that Mullá Ḥusayn had not disclosed. Mesmerised, Mullá Ḥusayn said that he "sat enraptured by the magic of His [the Báb's] voice and the sweeping force of His revelation.[5]

Khadíjih Bagum, the wife of the Báb, said that she "... I remained awake all night and could hear His blessed voice until the morning, conversing with the Bábu'l-Báb, chanting verses, and presenting proofs and arguments".[6]

Then, during the meeting, these prophetic and historical words were addressed to Mullá Ḥusayn:

> *O thou who art the first to believe in Me! Verily I say, I am the Báb, the Gate of God, and thou art the Bábu'l-Báb, the gate of that Gate.*

About Mullá Ḥusayn's singular station of being the first to accept the Báb's revelation, Bahá'u'lláh wrote:

> *... and glory be upon him who was the first* [*Mullá Ḥusayn*] *to believe in Him and in His verses, whom Thou didst make a throne for the ascendancy of Thy most sublime Word, a focal-point for the manifestation of Thy most excellent names, a dayspring of the radiance of the Sun of Thy providence, a dawning-place for the appearance of Thy names and attributes, and a treasury of the pearls of Thy wisdom and Thy commandments.*[7]

What is the Qayyúmu'l-Asmá?

The verses revealed to Mullá Ḥusayn that night constitute the first of the 111 chapters of the Báb's book entitled the *Qayyúmu'l-Asmá*. The term has been

---

1 Fáṭimih was Prophet Muḥammad's daughter.

2 Nabíl-i-A'ẓam, *The Dawn-Breakers*, p. 57.

3 Nabíl-i-A'ẓam, *The Dawn-Breakers*, p. 57.

4 *Genesis* 37-50, *Qur'án* Sura 12,

5 Nabíl-i-A'ẓam, *The Dawn-Breakers*, p. 61.

6 Munírih Khanum, *Memoirs and Letters*, p. 34.

7 Bahá'í World Centre, *The Importance of Obligatory Prayers and a Fasting.*

translated as "The Self-Subsisting Lord of All Names"[1] or "the one who sustains the divine names".[2]

The *Qayyúmu'l-Asmá* is also called the Commentary on the Surah of Joseph, which has been characterized by Bahá'u'lláh as *"the first, the greatest, and mightiest of all books"*.[3] The *Qayyúmu'l-Asmá* is considered to be the *Qur'án* of the Bábís.[4] About the *Qayyúmu'l-Asmá*, the Báb wrote, *"This book is the Remembrance of God that, in truth, is revealed unto the Most Great Word for the entire world"*[5] and *"This is our Book proclaiming the truth unto you"*.[6] The book was also a re-interpretation by the Báb of the story of Joseph told in the book of *Genesis* (chapters 37–50) and in the *Qur'án* (Súra 12 Yúsuf, 111 verses).

During that night, the following verses were revealed to Mullá Ḥusayn from that Holy Book:

> *All praise be to God Who hath, through the power of Truth, sent down this Book unto His servant, that it may serve as a shining light for all mankind.... Verily this is none other than the sovereign Truth; it is the Path which God hath laid out for all that are in heaven and on earth. Let him then who will, take for himself the right path unto his Lord. Verily this is the true Faith of God, and sufficient witness are God and such as are endowed with the knowledge of the Book. This is indeed the eternal Truth which God, the Ancient of Days, hath revealed unto His omnipotent Word—He Who hath been raised up from the midst of the Burning Bush. This is the Mystery which hath been hidden from all that are in heaven and on earth, and in this wondrous Revelation it hath, in very truth, been set forth in the Mother Book by the hand of God, the Exalted ....*[7]

The Letters of the Living

Immediately following His declaration, the Báb informed Mullá Ḥusayn about the enrolment of the first eighteen believers over the next forty days. These first eighteen believers who accepted the new Message constitute the Letters of the Living.[8] Their paths leading them to believe in the Báb differed significantly. As

---

1 Nader Saiedi, *Gate of the Heart*, p. 130.

2 Afnán, Muḥammad, *A General Introduction to the Qayyúmu'l-Asmá*, p. 1.

3 Bahá'u'lláh in Shoghi Effendi, *God Passes By*, p. 23.

4 Shoghi Effendi, *God Passes By*, p. 23.

5 The Báb in Nader Saiedi, *Gate of the Heart*, p. 141.

6 Muḥammad Afnán, *A General Introduction to the Qayyúmu'l-Asmá*, p. 1.

7 The Báb, *Selections*, p. 41.

8 "The title 'Letters of the Living' (Ḥurúf-i-Ḥayy) is used specifically to refer to the first eighteen followers of the Báb, who independently searched for and found the Báb and became believers in His Revelation .... 'Ḥayy', meaning 'living', is numerically equal to eighteen." Letter dated 11 November 1936, written on behalf of Shoghi Effendi to an individual believer, the Universal House of Justice, "Letters of Living, Dawn-Breakers, Quddús, Terraces".

we know, Mullá Ḥusayn was the first of the letters of the Living to believe in the Báb through theological studies and his meeting with the Báb. The others attained this high position through prolonged retreats, while in an attitude of prayer, meditation and contemplation. Among those eighteen souls, was a woman, Ṭáhirih, who read some writings of the Báb and hastened to declare her belief to Him in writing.

"Every day, from then on," Khadíjih Bagum stated, regarding the way the remaining Letters converted, "the Báb entertained an unknown guest and they would converse in the same way."[1]

The Báb revealed the remaining verses of the *Qayyúmu'l-Asmá* over the next 40 days.[2]

Without a doubt, it must have been a wonderful, but challenging, experience being in the presence of the Manifestation of God as He was revealing the Word of the Supreme. It has been said that when the Báb revealed divine verses, people were enchanted by the "gentle intonation" and "the soft and gentle murmur of His voice".[3]

It is important to note that the Letters of the Living were accomplished theologians, most of whom had pursued advanced Islamic studies in the renowned city of Karbilá. As such, they could be considered as the equivalent of modern-day graduate students in their fields. In this regard Bahá'u'lláh wrote in the *Kitáb-i-Íqán*:

> *In this most resplendent Dispensation, however, this most mighty Sovereignty, a number of illumined divines, of men of consummate learning, of doctors of mature wisdom, have attained unto His Court, drunk the cup of His divine Presence, and been invested with the honor of His most excellent favor. They have renounced, for the sake of the Beloved, the world and all that is therein.*[4]

Quddús is the last

Quddús, a graceful young man of profound knowledge and sanctity, was able to recognize the Báb by His gait while He was walking along one of the streets of Shíráz. Quddús had left his native Bárfurúsh to begin the long journey to Mecca to arrive during the annual pilgrimage season.[5] On his travels, he eventually reached Shíráz in the south of Persia. It appears that the presence of his Karbilá classmates in Shíráz gave him a clue as to the whereabouts of the Promised One.[6]

---

1 Munírih Khánum, *Memoirs and Letters*, p. 34.

2 Afnán, Muḥammad, *A General Introduction to the Qayyúmu'l-Asmá*, p. 2.

3 Nabíl-i-A'ẓam, *The Dawn-Breakers*, p. 61, 175, & 202.

4 Bahá'u'lláh, *Kitáb-i-Íqán*, pp. 223-224.

5 Abbas Amanat, *Resurrection and Renewal*, pp. 181–182

6 Abbas Amanat, *Resurrection and Renewal*, p. 178.

The way Quddús accepted the Báb and became the last Letter of the Living was described by Nabíl, the outstanding historian of the Faith:

> One night, in the course of His conversation with Mullá Ḥusayn; the Báb spoke these words: "Seventeen Letters have thus far enlisted under the standard of the Faith of God. There remains one more to complete the number. These Letters of the Living shall arise to proclaim My Cause and to establish My Faith. Tomorrow night the remaining Letter will arrive and will complete the number of My chosen disciples."
>
> The next day, in the evening hour, as the Báb, followed by Mullá Ḥusayn, was returning to His home, a youth dishevelled and travel-stained appeared. He approached Mullá Ḥusayn, embraced him, and asked whether he had attained his goal. Mullá Ḥusayn tried to calm his agitation and advised him to rest for the moment, promising that he would subsequently enlighten him. That youth, however, refused to heed his advice.
>
> Fixing his gaze upon the Báb, he said to Mullá Ḥusayn: "Why seek you to hide Him from me? I can recognize Him by His gait .... None other can manifest the power and majesty that radiate from His holy person".[1]

It is interesting to note that in the above account Nabíl indicates that Mullá Ḥusayn, in a sign of reverence, walked behind the Báb. This means that Quddús could not see the face of the Báb and, therefore, recognised the Báb by His gait.

A similar version of Quddús' acceptance of the Báb is rendered below:

> Mullá Ḥusayn ... refused in the first weeks after his conversion, to disclose the personal details of the Báb to his S͟hayk͟hí compatriots in S͟híráz. This caused resentment amongst some of them who took their grievance to the newly arrive[d] Quddús: "Jináb-i-Ák͟húnd [Mullá Ḥusayn] has attained the presence of the Lord, recognised His station and remains unwilling to disclose His details." Mullá Ḥusayn was forced to explain instructions from the Báb requiring the concealment of His name. At this time the Báb was seen to be passing by. Quddús immediately looked up and said: "I do not see this Cause as distinct from this young Siyyid." Mullá Ḥusayn then responded by a verse from Rúmí "I desire a sharp vision who recognises the King in disguise."[2]

Nabíl added:

> Mullá Ḥusayn marvelled at his words. He pleaded to be excused, however, and induced him to restrain his feelings until he could acquaint him with the truth. Leaving him, he hastened to join the Báb, and informed Him of his conversation with that youth. *"Marvel not,"* observed the Báb, *"at his strange behaviour. We have in the world of the spirit been communing with*

1 Nabíl-i-A'ẓam, *The Dawn-Breakers,* p. 69.

2 Sepehr Manuchehri, *Taqiyyah,* p. 223.

> *that youth. We know him already. We indeed awaited his coming. Go to him and summon him forthwith to Our presence".*[1]

Quddús immediately accepted the Báb, never asking of Him for any proof of the validity of His mission—He simply accepted it immediately. That indicates the purity of his heart. Mystical associations between these holy souls cannot be characterised by human logic. Situated in a dimension where oral or written language do not have space, communication between them certainly "rise[s] above words and letters and transcend the murmur of syllables and sounds".[2] Talking about the magical link between the Báb and Quddús, Nabíl remarked, "Though distant in body, these heroic souls are engaged in daily communion with their Beloved, partake of the bounty of His utterance, and share the supreme privilege of His companionship."[3]

As one historian wrote, "because of the purity of his heart, he [Quddús] at once believed without seeking further sign or proof."[4] The way Quddús converted brought to Mullá Ḥusayn's mind the words of an old Islamic tradition:

> On the last Day, the Men of the Unseen shall, on the wings of the spirit, traverse the immensity of the earth, shall attain the presence of the promised Qá'im, and shall seek from Him the secret that will resolve their problems and remove their perplexities.[5]

From that day onwards, Quddús consecrated his life to the service of the Báb with the utmost devotion and fervour as recorded in a prayer he wrote:

> O my God, my Lord, my Beloved, and my heart's desire.
> Thy Glory beareth witness, there is no desire for me but Thee,
> no station but in Thy presence,
> no companion except Thee,
> and no place of dwelling but Thine.[6]

If, as the Báb predicted, the last Letter was to convert before the end of the 40th day following His declaration to Mullá Ḥusayn on 23 May 1844, then Quddús must have accepted the Báb's Message near the end of June 1844. In coming years, both Bahá'u'lláh and the Báb used the designation "the Last to Attain" to refer to Quddús".[7]

---

1 Nabíl-i-A'ẓam, *The Dawn-Breakers,* p. 70.

2 'Abdu'l-Bahá, *Bahá'í Prayers,* pp. 69–70

3 Nabíl-i-A'ẓam, *The Dawn-Breakers,* p. 70.

4 "The New History", p. 39, cited in Thomas Kelly Cheyne, *The Reconciliation of Races and Religions,* p. 84.

5 Nabíl-i-A'ẓam, *The Dawn-Breakers,* p. 70.

6 Hooshmand Dehghan, *Ganj-i-Pinhán,* p. 175.

7 Bahá'u'lláh, *Tablet of Visitation for Mullá Ḥusayn and Quddús.* See Appendix part I.

The Day of Resurrection

During April-May 1844, with the acceptance of the Báb's Message by Quddús, the number of the Letters of the Living plus the Báb reached 19, the number specified by the Báb. This was a wonderful day for Quddús because he was witnessing the dawn of the Day of Resurrection[1] spoken of in the Holy Books of the past, also referred as the "Day of God":

> *O My servants! This is God's appointed Day which the merciful Lord hath promised you in His Book; wherefore, in very truth, glorify ye abundantly the name of God while treading the Path of the Most Great Remembrance* [the Báb] ....[2]

According to the Báb, *resurrection* did not mean the literal rising of the dead from their graves, but the spiritual resurrection of the previous Manifestation of God with the emergence of the next Manifestation of God. For the Báb, it was the resurrection of the spiritual Being, the "Word" "made flesh", similar to the way that the Spirit of Jesus was resurrected when Muḥammad declared His Mission.

The Day of Resurrection therefore occurs each time a Manifestation of God appears in the world with a new revelation, and the Day ends when the Manifestation passes away. As stated by the Báb:

> *... what is meant by the Day of Resurrection is this, that from the time of the appearance of Him Who is the Tree of divine Reality, at whatever period and under whatever name, until the moment of His disappearance, is the Day of Resurrection.*[3]
>
> *For example, from the inception of the mission of Jesus ... till the day of His ascension was the Resurrection of Moses .... And from the inception of the Revelation of the Apostle of God—may the blessings of God be upon Him—till the day of His ascension was the Resurrection of Jesus—peace be upon Him—wherein the Tree of Divine Reality appeared in the person of Muḥammad .... And from the moment when the Tree of the Bayán appeared until it disappeareth is the Resurrection of the Apostle of God, as is divinely foretold in the Qur'án.*[4]

As per the *Persian Bayán* (2:9), upon the arrival of a new Manifestation of God, the spiritual existence of all Earth's inhabitants comes to an end. Those who embrace Him will experience a revival of their spiritual beings. Those who turn away from Him remain in their spiritual graves. The *Persian Bayán* (2:10) conveys the notion that the bodies of people once allegorically dead become their own graves. When the Manifestation of God emerges, a spiritual resurrection will unfold, during which every soul will be questioned regarding their faith (2:10).

---

1 *Daniel* 12:2; 1 *Corinthians* 15:52; & *Qur'án* 4:87.

2 The Báb, *Selections*, p. 72.

3 The Báb, *Selections*, pp. 107–107.

4 The Báb in Nader Saiedi, *Gate of the Heart*, p. 107.

Should one be a believer, their sepulchre will transform into a heavenly garden; conversely, lack of belief leads to damnation. In the words of the Báb:

> *... the soul of no believer shall be taken but his grave shall become as a garden of the Gardens of Paradise, wherein God hath created that which he loves ready for him. So also there is none who shall disbelieve in the Bayán but shall suffer what the pen dares not write. Happy that person whose soul shall be taken after that he hath believed in Him whom God shall manifest and his words, for he is a believer in the Bayán and all that is in the Bayán.*[1]

Contrary to a literal interpretation of the prophecies, the Day of Resurrection was going to be a typical day. *"The Day of Resurrection is a day on which the sun riseth and setteth like unto any other day".* The Báb stated, *"How oft hath the Day of Resurrection dawned, and the people of the land where it occurred did not learn of the event."*[2] Further, the Báb affirmed, "*... the Day of Resurrection is said to be the greatest of all days, yet it is like unto any other day ....*"[3]

Quddús understood the spiritual meaning of the Day of Resurrection and that is why he was so happy to be living in that Day, a day he had hoped to arrive ever since he left Bárfurúsh, twelve years before. His dream had come true when he met the Promised One, the object of his constant search, study and reflection. He could then say: "I confidently testify that none besides Him, whether in the East or in the West, can claim to be the Truth."[4] Of the potentialities of that new Day, the Báb stated:

> *The newly born Babe of that Day excels the wisest and most venerable men of this time, and the lowliest and most unlearned of that period shall surpass in understanding the most erudite and accomplished divines of this age ....*[5]

> *Know thou, verily, that God revealed the Qur'án even as He hath created all things. Therefore, in this day, should a tiny ant desire to unravel all its verses, and its abstruse meanings, and its stations, through the black of its own eye, it shall be capable of achieving that, inasmuch as the mystery of Lordship and the effulgence of the Eternal vibrate within the very atoms of all created things.*[6]

'Abdu'l-Bahá further explained the greatness of that new Day with the dawning of the light of the Promised One:

> *Now, concerning the recorded tradition that in former times only two letters were revealed but in the days of the Qá'im all the remaining ones shall be made manifest, the following is meant. All the works and sciences, laws and*

---

1 The Báb in Momen, *Selections from the Writings of E. G. Browne*, p. 326.

2 The Báb, *Selections*, p. 78.

3 The Báb, *Selections*, p. 79.

4 Nabíl-i-A'ẓam, *The Dawn-Breakers*, p. 69.

5 The Báb in Nabíl-i-A'ẓam, *The Dawn-Breakers*, p. 94.

6 The Báb in Nader Saiedi, *Gate of the Heart*, p. 59.

ordinances, inventions and wonders, and the perfections of the human world that had been manifested in bygone times, were even as two letters. But in this wondrous Dispensation, and with the appearance of the glorious Treasure, the perfections and attainments of the world of humanity and its limitless sciences and arts shall advance to such a degree that they may be likened unto all the remaining letters.[1]

[1] 'Abdu'l-Bahá, *Light of the World,* section 75, para. 2.

4
The chosen companion

Chapter content
Mecca, the pilgrimage centre
Búshihr, Iran
Kangán, Iran
Muscat, Oman
Mocha, Yemen
Jeddah, Ottoman Empire
Theft of Writings
Public declaration of the Báb in Mecca
Return to Mocha, Yemen
Return to Muscat, Oman
Return to Shíráz, Persia
Associating with a Manifestation of God

One day, the Báb called the Letters of the Living to His presence for their farewell and He inspired them to propagate the new Faith with zeal and devotion. These believers were assigned to visit certain provinces, especially their native ones, and to summon the people and proclaim the Good News of the appearance of the Manifestation of Providence. However, Quddús was selected by the Báb to accompany Him on His pilgrimage to Mecca and Medina, the twin holy cities of Islam.

To the Letters of the Living, the Báb said that they were *"the bearers of the name of God in this Day"* and had *"been chosen as the repositories of His mystery"*,[1] and He asked them to emulate the actions of the disciples of Jesus by dispersing throughout the land, and to dedicate themselves, even the last ounce of their energies, to the teaching of the nascent Faith. With the call *"Arise in His name, put your trust wholly in Him, and be assured of ultimate victory"*[2] these future heroes set out to lay the first foundations of the Cause of the Báb in the world.

Mecca, the pilgrimage centre

The Báb travelled with Quddús to Mecca in the Ottoman Empire (now Saudi Arabia) for the sole purpose of proclaiming His divine mission in the heart of the Islamic world.

According to Stephen Lambden, as shown in His Khuṭbiy-i-Jiddah ("Sermon of Jiddah"), the Báb "strongly believed that He was acting in accordance with a

1 Nabíl-i-A'ẓam, *The Dawn-Breakers*, p. 92.
2 Nabíl-i-A'ẓam, *The Dawn-Breakers*, p. 94.

predestined plan".[1] Such was also the prophecy of Muslim traditions concerning the appearance of the Promised One at that holy place:[2]

> He [the Qá'im, the Promised One] will stand between the *Rukn* [Pillar] and the *Maqám* [place (of Ibráhim)] and call loudly: 'O! My noble men and my companions and those whom God spared for the purpose of my assistance prior to the day of my appearance on the face of the earth, now come to me.'"[3]

Muḥammad was born in Mecca, whose ancient city centre is dominated by the Ka'ba (literally, "the cube"), an ancient cubic structure that has been a place of worship for millennia. *"Fulfill the pilgrimage to Mecca"*, the *Qur'án* exhorts, *"at least once in life and visit the Temple (the Ka'ba) in honor of God .... The pilgrimage is made in the prescribed months .... Take provisions for the journey and know that the best provision is piety"* (*Qur'án* 2:196–197).

The five central precepts of Islam are: observing the profession of faith, praying, fasting, almsgiving and pilgrimage to Mecca. The profession of faith consists in averring the Oneness of God and explicitly declaring that Muḥammad is a Messenger of God. As such, He came after Jesus in the chain of successive stages in God's progressive revelation to humanity. Muḥammad appeared around the year 622 CE, fulfilling numerous prophecies from the Old and New Testaments regarding the appearance of a divine Messenger, the *Saint of Mount Paran* (Habbakuk 3:3) and the *Periklitos* referred to several times in the Gospel of John (4:16, 25; 15:26; 16:7).

The pilgrimage journey of the Báb was in the company of Quddús, as His secretary, and His Ethiopian servant, Mubárak, who was much loved by the Báb. Abu'l-Qásim Afnán has written the following about Mubárak:

> In 1842, upon His return to His home in Shiraz from a six-year sojourn in Bushihr and Karbala, the Báb—as was the custom—acquired a young Ethiopian slave. The man was nineteen years old and was named Mubárak (meaning, "Blessed"). The bill of purchase, which still exists among the Báb's business accounts, is dated 1842 and indicates that the price paid was fourteen túmáns (about twenty-eight dollars).
>
> Ḥájí Mírzá Abu'l-Qásim, the brother-in-law of the Báb, had purchased Mubárak from slave traders when he was a child of only five years and had adopted him into his own family. The education and upbringing that Mubárak received was exemplary. The Báb, approving of his instruction and his abilities, purchased him and brought him to the holy household. His quarters were arranged in the southern courtyard of the Báb's house.[4]

---

1 Stephen Lambden, *From a Primal Point to an Archetypical Book,* p. 194.

2 Omid Ghaemmaghami, *A Youth of Medium Height,* pp. 175–195.

3 Abbas Amanat, *Resurrection and Renewal,* p. 195.

4 Abu'l-Qasim Afnan, *Black Pearls,* pp. 4–5.

It was an extraordinarily good combination: Quddús attended to the spiritual matters related to the Báb and Mubárak was in charge of the logistics, like closing a full circle. Interestingly, the three of them were of about the same age, in their early twenties.

The journey of these three men began three months after the enrolment of the eighteen Letters of the Living. The time of their departure was dictated by the predetermined dates in the Islamic calendar on which to perform the five-day greater pilgrimage (12 December 1844 to 19 January 1845).[1]

Today, a direct flight from Shíráz to Mecca takes about two-and-half hours. However, in the first half of the nineteenth century, the trip would involve an arduous and agonizing 5,000 km trip, mostly by sea, of about two or three months.

Búshihr, Iran

The Báb departed from Shíráz for pilgrimage on 10 September 1844. The 200 km overland trip from Shíráz to the port of Búshihr took about ten days as travelling was only safe during the daytime and nights had to be spent in caravanserais set along on the route for travellers.

From Búshihr the Báb wrote to His beloved wife, Khadíjih Khánum:[2]

O the best of Protectors! In the Name of God, the Exalted.
My sweet life! May thou be guarded by God!
It was not because of sadness that I did not write sooner,
Nor was it due to My heart being sorrowed
Nay, My hand wrote thee,
But My tears washed away the words.

God is My witness that I have been overcome with so much sorrow since our separation that it cannot be described. However, since we are all seized in the grasp of destiny, such has been decreed for us. May the Lord of the world, by the righteousness of the Five Near-Ones, ordain My return.

It is now two days since we arrived in Búshihr. The temperature is extremely hot, but the Lord of creation will protect [us]. Apparently, our ship will sail this very month. May God watch over Us, out of His mercy. At the time of departure, it was not possible to meet My esteemed mother. Therefore, kindly convey My greetings to her and ask for her prayers. Regarding the silk cloth, I will write to Bombay. I am also intent on securing a maidservant for

---

1 In the *Persian Bayán* (4:16), revealed between 1847–1848, the Báb designated His House in Shíráz as the new place of pilgrimage replacing Mecca. (See: Armin Eschraghi, *Undermining the Foundations of Orthodoxy,* p. 231)

2 The marriage of the Báb to Khadíjih Bagum occurred in Shíráz in August 1842. She was born in 1822 and passed away in the same city on 15 September 1882. Their only son died stillborn or possibly in very early infancy.

you. God willing, that which is ordained will come to pass. Upon thee rest the peace, favors, and grace of God.[1]

They had to wait until the 2 October to board, with many other pilgrims, a sailing ship that was leaving for Mecca. The ship's departure date was organised to allow its passengers to arrive in Mecca before the start of the thirty-day Islamic fasting month, known as Ramaḍán, from 14 September to 13 October 1844.

According to Mírzá Ḥabíbu'lláh Afnán, there were some notable passengers on the ship:

> That year a large contingent of the city's [Búshihr's] inhabitants, including many of the 'ulamá and merchants, were also travelling to Mecca. Shaykh Háshim (a brother of the Imám-Jum'ih of Shíráz, Shaykh Abú-Turáb) who was much hated and very quarrelsome, was also among this group of pilgrims.[2]

Mírzá Ḥabíbu'lláh Afnán quotes the words of a companion travelling with the Báb, Hájí Abú'l-Ḥasan, who described another obnoxious pilgrim on board the vessel as "... Shaykh Abú-Háshim who molested [The Báb] both verbally and physically, and would cause great discomfort for His Holiness".[3]

Shoghi Effendi has stated that during the nine month journey, the Báb "was assiduously preparing [Quddús] for the assumption of his future office."[4] The Báb and Quddús were together for about a year, from Quddús' conversion in Shíráz in June 1844, the pilgrimage to Mecca and back to Shíráz, and his departure from Shíráz in May 1845. We can only imagine the effects that such a close association produced in the young Quddús, galvanizing his inner being to achieve formidable spiritual victories in the ensuing years. In the Tablet of Visitation that the Báb revealed for Quddús, He wrote:

> *I take God and creation to witness that God hath sanctified thee from all likeness, and bestowed upon thee what hath never been conferred on any of His creatures: not the sovereignty of the earth and whatsoever is on it, but that of Paradise and those who dwell therein.*[5]

Kangán, Iran

The ship, which the Báb called an "*oppressive ship*",[6] took 18 days travelling south along the Persian Gulf to reach the vital port of Masqat (also now written as Mascat or Muscat) in Oman. After two days sailing from Búshihr a stop was

---

1 The Báb, quoted in a footnote in Mírzá Ḥabíbu'lláh Afnán, *The Genesis of the Bábí-Bahá'í Faiths,* p. 31.

2 Mírzá Ḥabíbu'lláh Afnán, *The Genesis of the Bábí-Bahá'í Faiths,* pp. 30–31.

3 Hájí Abú'l-Hasan quoted in Mírzá Ḥabíbu'lláh Afnán, *The Genesis of the Bábí-Bahá'í Faiths,* p. 31

4 Shoghi Effendi, *God Passes By,* p. 9.

5 The Báb, *Tablet of Visitation for Quddús.* See Appendix part 2.

6 Stephen Lambden, *The Khutba al-Jidda,* p. 152.

made at the Bandar ("port of") Kangán. It was an uncomfortable trip. The weather was stormy with wind gusts blowing in the opposite direction accompanied by high temperatures. In addition, there was a lack of cleanliness among the passengers and the condition of the vessel was very unhygienic. Conditions were made worse when the ship ran out of fresh water. According to the Báb:

> *It is thus that I myself saw, on the voyage to Mecca, a notable who was spending considerable sums of money but who hesitated to spend the price of a glass of water for his fellow-traveler. This happened on the boat where the water was scarce, so scarce in fact, during the voyage from Búshihr to Mascat, which lasted twelve days with no opportunity to get water, that I had to content myself with sweet lemons.*[1]

The Báb disliked the trip also owing to the innumerable disputes among the pilgrims:

> *However, nothing is more important in the path of pilgrimage than adornment with virtuous conduct, so that should he be in the company of another, neither he himself nor his companion should have cause for sadness. I have observed (on the way to Mecca) acts which, in the sight of God, are of the vilest kind, sufficient to undo the good that results from the act of pilgrimage. These were the quarrels among the pilgrims! For quarrels are forbidden at all times and under any condition, and the ways of the faithful have never been, nor will ever be, aught but forbearance, patience, shame, and tranquility. Verily, the House of God hath no need of such people!*[2]

"In spite of these unfavorable circumstances," according to Fereydun Vahman, "the Báb's time on the ship was spent revealing sermons, prayers, and commentaries on Surahs of the *Qur'án*, all of which Quddús would write down as the Báb spoke".[3] It is therefore exciting to realize that some of the early pieces of the Báb's divine revelation are extant in the pen of Quddús, His secretary. During the trip, the Báb called Quddús Ḥabíb ("Beloved").[4]

Muscat, Oman

The southern end of the Persian Gulf ends when the gulf passes the Strait of Hormuz and enters the Gulf of Oman. The port of Muscat (Masqaṭ) is about 350 km southeast along the Gulf of Oman. Here the pilgrims rested for a few days after a long and tiring 1,000 km sea voyage from the port of Bú<u>sh</u>ihr. They arrived on 14 October 1844. According to Nabíl, in Muscat:

---

1 The Báb in A. L. M. Nicolas, *Le Bayán Persan*, vol. 2, p. 154. Cited in *Dawn-Breakers*, p. 130.

2 The Báb in Nader Saiedi, *Gate of the Heart*, p. 324.

3 Fereydun Vahman, "The Báb: A Sun in a Night not Followed by Dawn", pp. 39–40.

4 Abbas Amanat, *Resurrection and Renewal*, p. 184

> ... He [the Báb] sought to convert the people of that country but without success. He spoke to one among them, a religious man probably, one of high rank, whose conversion might also have been followed by that of his fellow citizens, at least so I believe, though he gives us no details upon this subject. Evidently, he did not attempt to convert the first comer who would have had no influence on the other inhabitants of the city. That he attempted a conversion and did not succeed is an indisputable fact because He Himself affirms it:
>
> *The mention of God, in truth, descended upon the earth of Muscat and made the way of God come to one of the inhabitants of the country. It may be possible that he understood our verses and became one of those who are guided. Say: This man obeyed his passions after having read our verses and in truth this man is by the rules of the Book, among the transgressors. Say: We have not seen in Muscat men of the Book willing to help him, because they are lost in ignorance. And the same was true of all these voyagers on the boat with the exception of one who believed in our verses and became one of those who fear God.*[1]

The above theologian might have been Shaykh Sulaymán, "a famous and powerful Sunni mujtahid"[2] because when the Báb returns five-and-a half-months later on His way back to Persia, He addresses Shaykh Sulaymán with these words:

> *From this land* [Muscat] *We then proceeded to the sacred House, and on Our return journey We landed once again at this spot, when We perceived that thou hadst heeded not that which We sent thee, nor art thou of them that truly believe. Although We had created thee to behold Our countenance, and We did actually alight in thy locality, yet thou didst fail to attain the object of thy creation, and this despite thy worshipping God all thy life. Wherefore vain shall be the deeds thou hast wrought, by reason of thy being shut out as by a veil from Our presence and from Our Writings.*[3]

Mocha, Yemen

The ship left Muscat and travelled 2,500 km through the Arabian Sea and the Gulf of Oman to reach the port of Mocha (al-Mukhá) in southwest Yemen. Probably the most fascinating aspect of the voyage for the Báb, Quddús and the servant Mubárak was to contemplate the clear waters of the Arabian Sea and its tonalites between blue and green reflecting the majesty of the skies and the glory of creation. The author gained some insight into the magnitude of that historical journey, when he flew over the Arabian Sea at an altitude of 10,000 m and observed the beauty of this captivating mantle of water. As an endless maritime gateway originating in Persia, the Arabian Sea embraces countless vessels

---

1 The Báb in A. L. M. Nicolas, *Seyyèd Ali-Mohammed dit le Bâb,* pp. 207–208. Cited in Nabíl-i-A'ẓam, *The Dawn-Breakers,* pp. 129–130.

2 Abu'l-Qasim Afnan (p. 80) cited in Peter Terry, *A Prophet of Modern Times* (p. 111).

3 The Báb, *Selections,* p. 35.

traversing its trade routes between Europe, Asia and Australasia, while having blended many nationalities and races for millennia.

It is unknown how long the Báb stayed in Mocha. These stops were part of the itinerary, becoming stopovers for the crew and passengers to purchase food provisions, pick new passengers and temporarily recover from the arduous sea journey, perhaps in some local caravanserai. An independent research report states that, "The Báb passed through the port city of Mokha, on Yemen's Red Sea Coast, during a trip from Iran to Mecca to spread the message of the faith. During his stopover, the Báb spread his teachings to local Yemenis".[1] According to the Bahá'ís of Yemen, the Báb "set foot there [in Mocha] on his journey in which He announced to the world the dawning of the light of a new day of God, to fulfil what millions had been waiting for and eagerly anticipating".[2]

From the port of Mocha there were still more than 1,000 km to travel before reaching the port of Jiddah, the start of a major land access route to the city of Mecca. It was a turbulent voyage in which the Báb and Quddús continued writing and praying as though in a state of perfect tranquility. During the long voyage, the Báb dictated His verses to Quddús, as recalled by a witness in the following story:

> During the entire period of approximately two months, from the day we embarked at Búshihr to the day when we landed at Jiddah, the port of Ḥijáz, whenever by day or night I chanced to meet either the Báb or Quddús, I invariably found them together, both absorbed in their work. The Báb seemed to be dictating, and Quddús was busily engaged in taking down whatever fell from His lips. Even at a time when panic seemed to have seized the passengers of that storm-tossed vessel, they would be seen pursuing their labours with unperturbed confidence and calm. Neither the violence of the elements nor the tumult of the people around them could either ruffle the serenity of their countenance or turn them from their purpose.[3]

As stated earlier, the main reason for the Báb's pilgrimage to Mecca was to proclaim His mission in that centre of Islamic worship. The Báb spent time on the ship teaching His Cause to the passengers, although not all went well as the following story reveals:

> One incident illustrates the source of the Báb's grievance. His constant composition of khuṭbas (sermons) and letters prompted a troublesome fellow citizen, Shaykh Abú-Háshim Shírází to ridicule and insult the young sayyid with "extraordinary and strange behavior." But as his attacks became increasingly intolerable, the captain, probably fearing a full-scale

1 Maysaa Shuja Al-Deen, Casey Coombs and Abdullah Olofi, *The Bahá'ís in Yemen: From Obscurity to persecution and exile,* p. 14.

2 Bahá'ís of Yemen. (2015). Available online at: https://bahaiye.org/

3 Nabíl-i-A'ẓam, *The Dawn-Breakers,* p. 130.

fight aboard his overcrowded vessel, apparently ordered Abú Háshim to be seized and thrown into the sea. However, the Báb stepped forward to intercede for him. Mírzá Abu'l-Ḥasan, a merchant on board and a later convert, recounts that "the captain, who was impressed by the Báb's innocence and his attempt at mediation, finally yielded". Yet Abú-Háshim lost no time in creating more trouble for the Báb by reporting his activity to the 'Ulamá even before he returned to Shíráz.[1]

Jeddah, Ottoman Empire

The ship sailed the final 1,000 km to arrive at the port of Jeddah (Jidda), which was then a part of the Ottoman Empire (present day Saudi Arabia). The whole trip from Búshihr had taken seventy-one days. Mecca is located 80 km inland from Jeddah. The pilgrims arrived in Mecca on 12 December 1844. Nabíl tells us about the journey from Jeddah to Mecca:

> Upon His arrival in Jaddih the Báb donned the pilgrim's garb, mounted a camel, and set out on His journey to Mecca. Quddús, however, notwithstanding the repeatedly expressed desire of his Master, preferred to accompany Him on foot all the way from Jaddih to that holy city. Holding in his hand the bridle of the camel upon which the Báb was riding, he walked along joyously and prayerfully, ministering to his master's needs, wholly indifferent to the fatigues of his arduous march. Every night, from eventide until the break of day, Quddús, sacrificing comfort and sleep, would continue with unrelaxing vigilance to watch beside his Beloved, ready to provide for His wants and to ensure the means of His protection and safety.[2]

Theft of Writings

A startling episode happened when a Bedouin stole the Báb's saddlebag containing His Sacred Writings. In the words of the historian Nabíl-i-A'ẓam:

> One day, when the Báb had dismounted close to a well in order to offer His morning prayer, a roving Bedouin suddenly appeared on the horizon, drew near to Him, and, snatching the saddle bag that had been lying on the ground beside Him, and which contained His writings and papers, vanished into the unknown desert. His Ethiopian servant set out to pursue him, but was prevented by his Master, who, as He was praying, motioned to him with His hand to give up his pursuit.
>
> *"Had I allowed you"*, the Báb later on affectionately assured him, *"you would surely have overtaken and punished him. But this was not to be. The papers and writings which that bag contained are destined to reach, through the instrumentality of this Arab, such places as we could never have succeeded*

---

1 Abbas Amanat, *Resurrection and Renewal,* p. 242.

2 Nabíl-i-A'ẓam, *The Dawn-Breakers,* p. 132.

in attaining. Grieve not, therefore, at his action, for this was decreed by God, the Ordainer, the Almighty".[1]

Of this incident the Báb wrote:

> *Wherefore, O thou concourse! The stealing of* [revealed] *materials from God took place within the domain of justice* [mulk al-'adl], *the land of the sanctuary of God* [Ḥaram Alláh, Mecca]. *There was nothing about it in line with justice for it consisted of the treasures of the inhabitants of the heavens and of the earth. And God is witness to* [the truth of] *that which I relate, for God, in this respect, is sufficient* [witness] *along with whomsoever recites the decrees of the Qur'án in an informed manner. And if God thy Lord should will it he would assuredly, in very truth, bring his verses to light for he, verily, no God is there except him.*[2]

Public declaration of the Báb in Mecca

In Mecca, the Báb proclaimed His Station as the Promised Qá'im to Mírzá Muḥíṭ al-Kirmání, a well-known Islamic theologian, and also to the Sharíf (Sherif), the chief priest of Mecca and magistrate of the country. The Sharíf received a letter hand delivered by Quddús. Lowell Johnson described the episode as follows:

> It was the Báb's purpose in writing this letter to inform the head Chief of the Muslim Faith that the Promised One had arrived, the Promised One that all the faithful Muslims were waiting for. The Báb gave this very important letter to Quddús to deliver to the Sharif. Quddús followed his Master's instructions and delivered it, sealed, into the Sharíf's own hands.
>
> The Sharíf was a good man. However, he was very busy and had no time to read. A few days later Quddús went back to the Sharíf and asked him if he had any answer for the Báb. The Sharíf told him that he was too busy at the moment. He would read the message and answer it at a later time. Little did the Sharíf know that he was too busy to read a Message from God.[3]

On this incident, Shoghi Effendi commented that the Sharíf of Mecca accorded to Quddús "a reception that betrayed by its icy indifference the contemptuous disregard in which the Cause of a Youth of Shíráz was held by the ruler of Ḥijáz and custodian of the Ka'bih".[4]

---

1 Nabíl-i-A'ẓam, *The Dawn-Breakers,* p. 132.

2 Stephen Lambden, *The Khutba al-Jidda,* p. 158. (provisional translation)

3 Lowell Johnson, *Quddús,* p. 8.

4 Nabíl-i-A'ẓam, *The Dawn-Breakers,* p. 652.

Mírzá Muḥíṭ met personally with the Báb. Mírzá Muḥíṭ was summoned to write his questions about the Báb's mission to Him directly. In the following weeks, Mírzá Muḥíṭ received a response from the Báb, but he fled away.[1]

Abbas Amanat in his book, *Resurrection and Renewal,* summarises the experiences of an observer:

> Mírzá Abu'l-Ḥasan Shirází alone clearly states that at the end of Hajj rites, when the floor and the roof of Masjid al-Ḥaram [Ka'bih, precincts] were entirely filled with pilgrims, the Báb stood against the wall, holding the ring knob of the Ka'bih, door, and three times in "the most eloquent and exquisite voice" announced, "I am the Qá'im whom you were expecting." Abul-Ḥasan continues: "It was extraordinary, that in spite of the noise, immediately the crowd became so silent that even the flapping of the wings of a passing sparrow was audible." All the pilgrims heard the Báb's call, he maintains, and interpreted it for one another. They discussed it, and reported the new proclamation in letters to the people in their homelands.[2]

In the *Persian Bayán,* the Báb made the following pronouncement regarding how His message was received in the heart of the Islamic world:

> Twelve hundred and seventy years have elapsed since the declaration of Muḥammad, and each year unnumbered people have circumambulated the House of God [Mecca]. In the concluding year of this period He Who is Himself the Founder of the House [The Báb] went on pilgrimage. Great God! There was a vast concourse of pilgrims from every sect. Yet not one recognized Him, though He recognized every one of them—souls tightly held in the grasp of His former commandment.[3]

Seventy thousand pilgrims were in Mecca at that time. The Báb stayed on the pilgrimage in Mecca for three weeks after which all the pilgrims left on 7 January 1845 to travel to Medina, where the sepulchre of the Prophet Muḥammad is located. They arrived on 16 January, the birthday of the Báb according to the Islamic calendar (the 1st of Muḥarram), and the pilgrims stayed for twenty-seven days until 12 February 1845.[4]

Nabíl reported that during the pilgrimage, according to the customary practice:

> He [the Báb] purchased nineteen lambs of the choicest breed, of which He sacrificed nine in His own name, seven in the name of Quddús, and three in the name of His Ethiopian servant. He refused to partake of the meat of

---

1 Nabíl-i-A'ẓam, *The Dawn-Breakers,* p. 137.

2 Abbas Amanat, *Resurrections and Renewal,* pp. 243–344.

3 The Báb, *Selections,* pp. 89–90.

4 The Báb gives the exact chronology of His travels in a Khuṭbih [Sermon] (Ishráq-Khávarí, *Kitáb Muhádirát,* pp. 729–31).

> this consecrated sacrifice, preferring instead to distribute it freely among the poor and needy of that neighbourhood.[1]

In general, the Báb's expectations about this pilgrimage were much higher. As Shoghi Effendi stated, "The plan He had, at the very outset of His career, conceived of inaugurating His mission with a public proclamation in the holy cities of Mecca and Medina failed to materialise as He had hoped".[2]

The Báb, Quddús and Mubárak returned to the port of Jeddah on 27 February to embark on the same vessel that had carried them thither, which then set sail on 4 March.

Return to Mocha, Yemen

"On the return trip to Persia", historian Omid Ghaemmaghami wrote, "from the port of Makhá (Mocha in present-day Yemen) He addressed a letter to His uncle and a tablet to His followers, in which He exhorted them to proclaim His Cause".[3]

Return to Muscat, Oman

At Muscat the Báb visited and stayed with the Sulṭán of Muscat:

> The Báb had earlier, on his journey to Mecca, become acquainted with the Sultan of Muscat and had received an invitation to stay at his home on the return journey. There are documents to indicate that the Báb remained in Muscat for a month and a half, for all of the month of Rabí'u'th-Thání and the first half of the month of Jamádíyu'l-Avval. During His sojourn, voluminous writings emanated from His pen and the new-born Faith was proclaimed to the chief clergymen of Najaf, Karbilá, Búshihr, and Muscat. The recipient of one of His epistles was the erudite Shaykh Sulaymán, the mujtahid of Muscat.[4]

In addition to having proclaimed His Mission to the Sunní leader Shaykh Sulaymán in His first visit to Muscat, in His second visit to the same city, the Báb wrote an epistle[5] to 'Abdu'l-Majíd (r. 1839-1861), Sulṭán of the Ottoman Empire proclaiming His Revelation:

> *Read the Book of your Lord, O Majíd, through the command of your Lord in the preserved Book. Know that God has knowledge of all things in the heavens and on earth, and that you are, on account of the verdict passed on*

---

1 Nabíl-i-A'ẓam, *The Dawn-Breakers*, p. 133.

2 Nabíl-i-A'ẓam, *The Dawn-Breakers*, p. 652.

3 Omid Ghaemmaghami, *The Life of the Báb*, p. 20,

4 Abu'l-Qasim Afnan, *Black Pearls*, p. 13.

5 Stephen Lambden, *From a Primal Point to an Archetypal Book*, p. 170.

the messenger,[1] *the lord of great oppression. Fear God, O man, for today no place is there for anyone to flee to except that he believes in the signs of your Lord and is accounted among those who prostrate* [before Him].[2]

O man, Thou hast followed Satan regarding the verdict to imprison the messenger of the Remembrance. Fear God after you have read a single wondrous letter from Our Book. Do not repudiate the command of God and send the messenger in accordance with the command We have send down in the Book addressed to you .... You are not aware of the decree of the caliphate. The messenger is a weak servant in those lands. Yet know full well that it is We that sent him .... Know God's decree and send him after [you have read] this Book. ... Follow God's command, O Majid, and not your idle imaginings that lead you astray from the path of God.[3]

Return to S͟híráz, Persia

After nine months, or about 250 days, since they had left S͟híráz, the entourage returned to the Persian port of Búshihr. According to the K͟huṭba al-Jiddah (the Báb's "Sermon at Jeddah"), the Báb, Quddús and Mubárak safely arrived back in Búshihr on 15 May 1845.[4] This was the month of the first anniversary of the Declaration of the Báb. The Báb stayed about a month in the port of Búshihr and they arrived back in S͟híráz in early July of 1845.

Continuing with the proclamation of His mission to important dignitaries such as the Sherif from Mecca and the Sulṭán 'Abdu'l-Majíd from Muscat, the Báb from Búshihr revealed His first of several epistles to Muḥammad S͟háh, the Persian monarch. The sovereign had been previously addressed to in a "Book" [Epistle] which was carried by Mullá Ḥusayn but was not delivered to him because of interferences from the royal court.[5] [6] Excerpts from this Tablet include:

We indeed sent down a Book ... unto thee [Muhammad Shah] to the end that thou command that there be written the like of what We sent down therein in golden ink (al-midád al-dhahab) in a noble, naskh script (khattt, naskh karím). Then shall thou dispatch this Book [Epistle] of thy Lord unto the Ottoman Sovereign (malik al-rúm) [i.e. Sultan 'Ard al-Majíd] then unto all

---

1 A reference to Mullá 'Alí-i-Bastámí who was sent by the Báb to teach the Faith to a high Muslim cleric in Iraq. Upon his arrival he was trialled on the charges of heresy and sent to forced labour in Istanbul where he died in 1846. Mullá 'Alí-i-Bastámí was the second Letter of the Living and is considered the first Bábí martyr.

2 The Báb in Alkan Necati, *Dissent and Heterodoxy*, p. 53.

3 The Báb in Alkan Necati, *Dissent and Heterodoxy*, p. 54.

4 D. M. MacEoin, "Bāb, 'Ali Moḥammad Širāzi, pp. 278–284. According to Abu'l-Qasim Afnan, on 4 June 1845 "the Báb arrived in Bushihr on the last leg of His journey home. He remained only a few days, and on the afternoon of Wednesday, the nineteenth of the same month, He departed for Shiraz, accompanied by Mubárak" (*Black Pearls*, p. 13)

5 The Báb, *Selections*, p. 13.

6 Ruhu'llah Mehrabkhani, *Mullá Ḥusayn*, p. 102.

the [other] kings (mulúk). This to the end that We might know which faction (tá'ifa) among them hath been just with respect to the command of God and which faction (tá'ifa) among them hath been untruthful. Wherefore shall We judge between them with justice.

So recite, O thou king (malik), the Book [Epistle] of thy Lord to the end that thou be numbered among such as have attained.

Render victorious the Religion of God (dín Alláh) that the Day of Resurrection (yawm al-qiyáma) be realized through such as are inclined towards victory.

"The [personified] Word of God (kalimát Alláh) does not desire worldly dominion (mulk al-dunyá) nor [that of] the world to come [Hereafter] (al-akhira); neither the decree of religious judgement (fatwá) after the fashion of the clerics of the True God (haqq). [1]

In general, the Báb did not enjoy the sea trip and in His Writings, He discouraged others from undertaking the journey:

Know that the sea voyages are hard. We do not favor them for the faithful; travel by land.[2]

One cannot imagine on the sea anything but discomfort. One cannot have all the necessities as in land travel. The mariners are obliged to live thus but by their services they come nearer to God, and God rewards actions performed on the land and on the sea but He grants a two-fold recompense for those services accomplished by one of the servants on the sea, because their work is more arduous.[3]

Associating with a Manifestation of God

The intimate and sacred association between Quddús and the Báb during the eight months they were together during their pilgrimage to the most Holy Place at that time leaves us wondering as to what transpired during the countless hours they spent together. Enshrouded in the veils of history are the untold tales of their companionship, leaving us to ponder the myriad conversations and exchanges that must have transpired during those many days.

We learn of the Báb's personal magnetism as perceived by people who met Him, whether believers or non-believers. One wonders what impact such proximity to the sacred and Holy Being of the Báb had on Quddús?

Throughout history, personal association with a Manifestation of God has had a remarkable effect on people's personalities. Bahá'u'lláh explains that the bodies

---

1 Sholeh Quinn, *Muhammad Shah Qajar in Four Early Writings of the Báb*, pp. 162-169. (Provisional translation by Stephen Lambden and Sholeh Quinn)

2 The Báb in A. L. M. Nicolas, *Seyyèd Ali-Mohammed dit le Bâb,* pp. 207–208. Cited in Nabíl-i-A'ẓam, *The Dawn-Breakers*, p. 129.

3 The Báb in A. L. M. Nicolas, *Seyyèd Ali-Mohammed dit le Bâb,* pp. 155–156. Cited in Nabíl-i-A'ẓam, *The Dawn-Breakers*, p. 131.

of each Divine Manifestations of God "*become the Throne of the Merciful God, and the realities of all things that are created in heaven revolve around them.*"[1] In addition, the Báb explains that attaining the presence of a Manifestation of God during His earthly life is equivalent of reaching the presence of God (*Qur'án* 83:4–6; *Qur'án* 33:44; *Psalm* 140:13; & 2 *Thessalonians* 1:9):

> *There is no paradise more wondrous for any soul than to be exposed to God's Manifestation in His Day, to hear His verses and believe in them, to attain His presence, which is naught but the presence of God, to sail upon the sea of the heavenly kingdom of His good-pleasure, and to partake of the choice fruits of the paradise of His divine Oneness.*[2]

Individuals who met the Báb in Búshihr before the declaration of His mission in 1844, referred emphatically to His "good nature, his equanimity, his dignified bearing, his piety, his virtue, his work ethic, his generosity, his contentment, and his insight".[3] They also spoke about "His downcast eyes, his extreme courtesy, and the serene expression of his face ..."[4] and described Him as a "... a handsome man with a thin beard, dressed in clean clothes, wearing a green shawl and a black turban."[5] The French consular diplomat A. L. M. Nicolas has recorded the following words of an early Bábí, Mullá Ṣadíq-i-Khurásání who met the Báb in Karbilá:

> On a certain day, I entered the Shrine of the Imám Ḥusayn, intending to make pilgrimage there, when I beheld a youth in a kind of spiritual trance. He was immersed in a silent state of sanctification, and tears were streaming down his face ....[6]

Later Mullá Ṣadíq-i-Khurásání. was able to speak to the Báb and stated about Him, "So courteous was His demeanour, so cheerful His face as He spoke these words that I could not help but be totally captivated by Him."[7]

Another account depicts the Báb in the following terms:

> People thought of him as possessing a mystical consciousness. When it came to his peculiarity and his incomprehensible utterances, they attributed them to his profound wisdom. It was especially through the

---

1 Bahá'u'lláh in Horace H. Holley, *Bahá'í Scriptures*, p. 207.

2 The Báb, *Selections*, p. 77.

3 Fereydun Vahman, *The Báb: A Sun in a Night not Followed by Dawn*, p. 11.

4 Haji Sayyid Javad Karbala'i in Fereydun Vahman, *The Báb: A Sun in a Night not Followed by Dawn*, p. 17.

5 Abbas Amanat, *Resurrection and Renewal*, p. 133.

6 Nicolas quoted in Fereydun Vahman, *The Báb: A Sun in a Night not Followed by Dawn*, p. 19.

7 Nicolas quoted in Fereydun Vahman, *The Báb: A Sun in a Night not Followed by Dawn*, p. 19.

Shírází pilgrims, the ordinary people who returned from Karbilá, that his fame spread in his homeland.[1]

In addition, Mullá Ḥusayn once commented on his initial meeting with the Báb in Shíráz. He described himself as being "overwhelmed" by the Young Man's "expressions of affection and loving-kindness", being "profoundly impressed by the gentle yet compelling manner in which that strange Youth spoke", and becoming fascinated by "His gait, the charm of His voice, the dignity of His bearing."[2]

Dr William Cormick, an Irish doctor who attended the Báb in the prison of Tabríz in 1848 stated:

> He was a very mild and delicate-looking man, rather small in stature and very fair for a Persian, with a melodious soft voice, which struck me much .... To all enquiries he merely regarded us with a mild look, chanting in a low melodious voice some hymns, I suppose .... Being a Sayyid, he was dressed in the habits of that sect, as were also his two companions.[3]

"The power and majesty with which He spoke confounded me", commented a religious dignitary who met the Báb in Iṣfahán, "I am convinced He is the promised Qá'im ...."[4] The recipient of the famous *Tablet of Aḥmad* narrated: "His beautiful face and His powerful Words and presence sufficed all things".[5]

While the chronicles have not recorded the nature of their time together, one may wonder about the many different topics spoken about and how the Báb prepared Quddús for the heroic and illustrious services he was destined to perform. One cannot help but wonder about the effect the Báb had on Quddús' very essence. Could it be that the Báb unveiled the magnificent destiny that awaited the Faith they held so dear, sharing secrets that illuminated the path ahead?

Might the Báb have disclosed the wondrous destiny of the Faith? How did their words weave a tapestry of understanding, and how did the Báb shape Quddús' spirit for the bold and illustrious acts he was fated to undertake?

---

1 Abbas Amanat, *Resurrection and Renewal*, p. 148.

2 Nabíl-i-A'ẓam, *The Dawn-Breakers*, pp. 69–70.

3 E. G. Browne, *Materials for the Study of the Bábí Religion*, pp. 260–262.

4 Cited in Houri Faláhi-Skuce, *A Radiant Gem*, p. 172.

5 Naysan and Zohre Faizi, *Penned by A. Q. Faizi*, p. 52.

5
"First to suffer persecution in Persia"

Chapter content
The Báb farewells Quddús
Quddús and Mullá Ṣádiq in S͟híráz
Their beards are burnt
Qayyúmu'l-Asmá' message to Muḥammad S͟háh
Worldwide publicity

During His pilgrimage, the Báb began writing the treatise *K͟haṣá'il-i Sab'ih* ("The Seven Proofs") in which He *"set forth the essential requirements from those who had attained to the knowledge of the new Revelation and had recognized its claims."*[1] This was the first occasion where the Báb promulgated new laws to the believers. Years later, the Báb would reveal the *Bayán* ("Exposition"), which abrogated many Islamic laws and replaced them with new ordinances.

In the *K͟haṣá'il-i Sab'ih*, the Báb prohibited the smoking of tobacco, prescribed that believers should wear an object around their necks containing the names of God, and also should wear a ring engraved with the Greatest Name. In addition, the believers were exhorted to drink tea with the utmost refinement and cleanliness, and recite a specific Grand Visitation Tablet on Friday and on other holy occasions.

In particular, the Báb exhorted the believers to modify the *ad͟hán* the official religious call to congregational prayer, by adding an innovative verse: *"I bear witness that He whose name is 'Alí-Qabl-i-Muḥammad* [i.e. *'Alí before Muḥammad*] *is the servant of the Baqíyyatu'lláh".*[2] The name of the Báb was 'Alí-Muḥammad and the original *ad͟hán* consisted only of the words, "I bear witness that Muḥammad is the Messenger of God". The expression *Baqíyyatu'lláh* alludes to the Báb and Bahá'u'lláh, respectively.[3] Muslim clerics were greatly offended by the new call, which they considered to represent a heretical statement. Anyone using the creed had to be punished and the call was to be strongly repressed.

The Báb's farewell to Quddús

The Báb, while still in Bús͟hihr, requested Quddús to return to S͟híráz, 300 km distant, to carry a copy of the *K͟haṣá'il-i-Sab'ih* and to deliver it to his beloved maternal uncle. His uncle, Ḥájí Mírzá Siyyid 'Alí, was the first person to support his Nephew's Faith after the Letters of the Living. The Báb also foretold his

---

[1] Nabíl-i-A'ẓam, *The Dawn-Breakers*, p. 143.
[2] The Báb in Nabíl-i-A'ẓam, *The Dawn-Breakers*, p. 144. The term *Baqíyyatu'lláh* ("the Remnant of God") is mentioned in the Qur'an (11:86) and refers to the Promised One of Islam.
[3] Nabíl-i-A'ẓam, *The Dawn-Breakers*, p. 674.

uncle's eventual martyrdom. In February 1850, this uncle gave his life as one of Ṭihrán's Seven Martyrs.

At his last farewell, the Báb told Quddús about his future path of service and the fact that, eventually, he would pay the ultimate sacrifice. The Báb also asked Quddús to convey His love to all the believers in Shíráz, and promised Quddús that one day he would meet Bahá'u'lláh. According to Nabíl, the Báb said to Quddús:

> *The days of your companionship with Me are drawing to a close. The hour of separation has struck, a separation which no reunion will follow except in the Kingdom of God, in the presence of the King of Glory. In this world of dust, no more than nine fleeting months of association with Me have been allotted to you. On the shores of the Great Beyond, however, in the realm of immortality, joy of eternal reunion awaits us. The hand of destiny will ere long plunge you into an ocean of tribulation for His sake. I, too, will follow you; I, too, will be immersed beneath its depths. Rejoice with exceeding gladness, for you have been chosen as the standard-bearer of the host of affliction, and are standing in the vanguard of the noble army that will suffer martyrdom in His name. In the streets of Shíráz, indignities will be heaped upon you, and the severest injuries will afflict your body. You will survive the ignominious behaviour of your foes, and will attain the presence of Him*[1] *who is the one object of our adoration and love. In His presence you will forget all the harm and disgrace that shall have befallen you. The hosts of the Unseen will hasten forth to assist you, and will proclaim to all the world your heroism and glory. Yours will be the ineffable joy of quaffing the cup of martyrdom for His sake. I, too, shall tread the path of sacrifice, and will join you in the realm of eternity.*[2]

Thus, in Búshihr, we find Quddús beginning a tireless journey on foot towards Shíráz, spreading the Faith, and enduring tribulations, with a high sense of devotion, courage and strength. Walking with persistence and courage, and on the path of thorns, as the Báb had affirmed, were among Quddús' best and indisputable qualities.

Upon reaching the house of the Báb's uncle, Ḥájí Mírzá Siyyid 'Alí, Quddús was received with great affection and asked to report about the health and provide news of his dear nephew. The uncle had already heard about the Bábí Faith, but at that time, he had little knowledge of the Báb's Message. Quddús nurtured in him a greater understanding of the Faith of his beloved Nephew to the point that he was finally added to the ranks of the first Bábí adherents. The uncle had raised the Báb from His tender youth, and he would prove to be one of the Bábs most loyal followers and strongest supporters within the Báb's Household along with the wife of the Báb, Khadíjih Khánum. In the ensuing years, Ḥájí Mírzá Siyyid 'Alí

---

1 A reference to Bahá'u'lláh

2 The Báb in Nabíl-i-A'ẓam, *The Dawn-Breakers*, pp. 142–3.

would become a true and faithful believer. He devotedly served the interests of the new religion until 1850 when he offered his life as a Bábí martyr.

A historian referred to Quddús as the "náíb" (deputy, representative) of the Báb while in Shíráz:

> But the náíb was unfortunate enough to have to deal with a hardened unbeliever in Hussein Khan, who after his return from England had been appointed governor-general of the province of Fars. By his orders the náíb was seized and bastinadoed, and, in order, to prevent him from going from house to house, the governor ordered that the tendons of his legs should be severed.[1] [2]

Quddús and Mullá Ṣádiq in Shíráz

Quddús later found in Shíráz a believer previously converted by Mullá Ḥusayn. His name was Mullá Ṣádiq (1799–1889)[3] and he was about 23 years older than Quddús. A resident of Iṣfahán, he had attended the same classes of Siyyid Káẓim in Karbilá, prior to the Báb's declaration of His Mission. He had also known the Báb in Karbilá. Upon arriving in Shíráz while searching for the Promised One, Mullá Ṣádiq recognized the Báb through a vision. Afterwards, he spoke publicly about the prophecies concerning the appearance of the Báb. Nobody could refute him with authority because, in that field, he was virtually a teacher of teachers. Of him, 'Abdu'l-Bahá said:

> *... he was a great scholar and among the most renowned of matchless and unique divines. As a teacher of the Faith, he spoke with such eloquence, such extraordinary power, that his hearers were won over with great ease.*[4]

Quddús shared with him a copy of the *Khaṣá'il-i-Sab'ih* ("Seven Proofs") in which, as previously mentioned at the beginning of this chapter, the Báb had ordered a change to the *adhán*—the formula to the call for congregational prayers. Mullá Ṣádiq did not vacillate in implementing the new ordinance, which caused great havoc in the city.

The Masjid-i-Naw ("New Mosque") was less than 300 m from the House of the Báb. The Masjid is a beautiful and impressive building across the main road from the alley leading to the House of the Báb. The Báb used to visit it frequently and His famous granduncle received his basic education at its school. It was built in 590 CE and represented the largest mosque in the country and the second oldest in the city of Shíráz. Today there are about 70,000 mosques in Iran.

---

1 Robert Grant Watson, *A history of Persia from the Beginning of the Nineteenth Century to the Year 1858*, p. 349.

2 It is not clear what the invasive procedure was.

3 Boris Handal, *A Trilogy of Consecration*, pp. 97–123.

4 'Abdu'l-Bahá, *Memorials of the Faithful*, pp. 5–6.

The following is the story of Mullá Ṣádiq[1] who, along with Quddús and another believer, Mullá 'Alí-Akbar, were among the first to suffer persecution for the Cause of God on Persian soil. As Nabíl has related:

> Mullá Ṣádiq, who in those days had been extolling from the pulpit-top to large audiences the virtues of the Imáms of the Faith, was so enraptured by the theme and language of that treatise that he unhesitatingly resolved to carry out all the observances it ordained. Driven by the impelling force inherent in that Tablet, he, one day as he was leading his congregation in prayer in the Masjid-i-Naw, suddenly proclaimed, as he was sounding the a<u>dh</u>án, the additional words prescribed by the Báb.
>
> The multitude that heard him was astounded by his cry. Dismay and consternation seized the entire congregation. The distinguished divines, who occupied the front seats and who were greatly revered for their pious orthodoxy, raised a clamour, loudly protesting: "Woe betide us, the guardians and protectors of the Faith of God! Behold, this man has hoisted the standard of heresy. Down with this infamous traitor! He has spoken blasphemy. Arrest him, for he is a disgrace to our Faith." "Who," they angrily exclaimed, "dared authorise such grave departure from the established precepts of Islám? Who has presumed to arrogate to himself this supreme prerogative?"[2]

In Islamic terms, such a liturgical alteration constituted *Bid'at* ("innovation"), the equivalent to blasphemy, in particular a "reprehensible innovation in matters of faith". Professor Fereydun Vahman adds:

> Prior to the Báb's own subsequent arrival at <u>Sh</u>íráz, Mullá 'Alí-Akbar-i-Ardistání ascended the minaret of the Masjid-i-Naw and began to sound the call to prayer, to which he added a sentence testifying to the Báb's station. Quddús likewise went to that same mosque, ascended the minaret, and began to recite from the *Qayyúmu'l-Asmá'* there he unreservedly proclaimed the name of Sayyid 'Alí-Muḥammad, which until that time had been kept secret. Mullá Ṣádiqi-<u>Kh</u>urásání (Muqaddas)[3] then took to the mosques, streets, and bazaars of <u>Sh</u>íráz, where he declared, without the slightest inhibition, that "the Gate to the Hidden Imám" had appeared.[4]

The above actions continued for five days.[5] The news that riots threatened to break out and seriously disrupt public order also reached the provincial governor. He was told that the Báb, a <u>Sh</u>íráz citizen, had claimed to speak in the

---

1 Mullá Ṣádiq was posthumously appointed a Hand of the Cause of God by 'Abdu'l-Bahá.

2 Nabíl-i-A'ẓam, *The Dawn-Breakers,* p. 145.

3 *Muqaddas* means "saint" and that is how the believers addressed Mullá Muḥammad-Ṣádiq-i-<u>Kh</u>urásání, also called Mullá Ṣádiq.

4 Fereydun Vahman, *The Báb: A Sun in a Night not Followed by Dawn,* p. 43.

5 Hasan Fuadi Bushru'i, *The History of the Bahá'í Faith in Khorasan*, p. 112.

name of God, that He still resided in Búshihr, and that His disciples were engaged in disturbing activities. The governor was informed that the Báb was urging all Muslims to accept His faith since that was the responsibility of a real Muslim believer.

Their beards are burnt

Quddús, Mullá Ṣádiq, and most likely Mullá 'Alí-Akbar, were all taken into custody by the governor at the request of the local clergy. The captives were led to the governor in chains. The truth of the Báb's words at the farewell in Búshihr was now apparent: *"In the streets of Shíráz ... the severest injuries will afflict your body"*.[1]

This governor had read the first passages of the Báb's book entitled *Qayyúmu'l-Asmá'*, which the police had snatched from Mullá Ṣádiq as he was fervently and loudly reading to the congregation. In the initial passages of the *Qayyúmu'l-Asmá'* the Báb urged the earth's kings and rulers to abdicate their positions of authority.

The governor read it and was baffled by such forceful language. Given that he was the governor of Fars Province, he vehemently questioned Mullá Ṣádiq[2] to see if he and the Sháh of Persia should abdicate their positions. The dialogue that occurred is reported by A. L. M. Nicolas:

> Governor: "I heard that you have changed the Qibla?"[3]
>
> Mullá Ṣádiq: "Yes."
>
> Governor: "You have also modified the formula for the adhán?"
>
> Mullá Ṣádiq: "Yes."
>
> Governor: "Did you recite and comment on these new verses?"
>
> Mullá Ṣádiq: "Yes."
>
> Governor: "What do you mean by these words: *"O kings, O son of kings."*[4] [Quoting from the *Qayyúmu'l-Asmá'*] "Here it says:
>
> > *'Divest yourselves of the robe of sovereignty, for He who is the King in truth, hath been made manifest! The Kingdom is God's, the Most Exalted. Thus hath the Pen of the Most High decreed!'*[5]
>
> That young Shirází [the Báb]?"
>
> Mullá Ṣádiq: "Yes."

1 The Báb in Nabíl-i-A'ẓam, *The Dawn-Breakers*, pp. 142–143.
2 Boris Handal, *A Trilogy of Consecration*, pp. 106–107.
3 Qibla, that is, the direction towards which one turns in prayer.
4 Nabíl-i-A'ẓam, *The Dawn-Breakers*, p. 146.
5 Nabíl-i-A'ẓam, *The Dawn-Breakers*, p. 146.

Governor: "So Muḥammad Sháh should not reign without asking His permission? And when that happens, would the globe fall into ashes? So I am no longer governor of this city, unless I request permission from Him to govern?"

Mullá Ṣádiq: "You said it."

Ḥusayn Khán flew into a rage, and the ulamá (divines) took advantage of this to issue a *fatvá* (religious decree) condemning the two blasphemers to death. However, the governor would not consent to this. He ordered Muqaddas to be stripped of his clothes, then taken to the garden where, in his presence, Muqaddas was given five hundred lashes. This being done, his beard was burned and he was imprisoned with Quddús, who had received twelve slaps.[1]

According to Nabíl:

> He [the Governor] then commanded that the beards of both Quddús and Mullá Ṣádiq should be burned, [and shaved][2] their noses be pierced, that through this incision a cord should be passed, and with this halter they should be led through the streets of the city. "It will be an object lesson to the people of Shíráz," Ḥusayn Khán declared, "who will know what the penalty of heresy will be." Mullá Ṣádiq, calm and self-possessed and with eyes upraised to heaven, was heard reciting this prayer: "O Lord, our God! We have indeed heard the voice of One that called. He called us to the Faith—'Believe ye on the Lord your God!'—and we have believed. O God, our God! Forgive us, then, our sins, and hide away from us our evil deeds, and cause us to die with the righteous." With magnificent fortitude both resigned themselves to their fate. Those who had been instructed to inflict this savage punishment performed their task with alacrity and vigour. None intervened on behalf of these sufferers, none was inclined to plead their cause. Soon after this, they were both expelled from Shíráz. Before their expulsion, they were warned that if they ever attempted to return to this city, they would both be crucified.[3]

Another account recalled:

> A merchant, by whose place of business they were passing, stopped them in their tracks and told them: 'That being so, let me have a share of this righteous deed and inflict more pain on these men.' Having said this, he brought a long and stout piece of timber and put one end on the shoulder of Quddús and the other on the shoulder of Mullá Ṣádiq. Next he attached a measuring device to the pole and had eighty bales of sugar weighed and

---

1 A. L. M. Nicolas, *Seyyèd Ali-Mohammed dit le Bâb*, pp. 225–226.

2 Hasan Fuadi Bushru'i, *The History of the Bahá'í Faith in Khorasan*, p. 113. Shaving a beard was a sign of dishonour.

3 Nabíl-i-A'ẓam, *The Dawn-Breakers,* pp. 146–147.

placed on it. It was a hot day. Whenever Quddús and Mullá Ṣádiq, overcome by the heaviness of the load and the heat of the day, tried to shift their feet [because of the heat of the street floor as they were without shoes],[1] their tormentors lashed them mercilessly.[2]

Qayyúmu'l-Asmá' message to Muḥammad Sháh

> *O King of Islám! Aid thou, with the truth, after having aided the Book, Him Who is Our Most Great Remembrance, for God hath, in very truth, destined for thee, and for such as circle round thee, on the Day of Judgment, a responsible position in His Path. I swear by God, O Sháh! If thou showest enmity unto Him Who is His Remembrance, God will, on the Day of Resurrection, condemn thee, before the kings, unto hellfire, and thou shalt not, in very truth, find on that Day any helper except God, the Exalted. Purge thou, O Sháh, the Sacred Land* [Ṭihrán] *from such as have repudiated the Book, ere the day whereon the Remembrance of God cometh, terribly and of a sudden, with His potent Cause, by the leave of God, the Most High. God, verily, hath prescribed to thee to submit unto Him Who is His Remembrance, and unto His Cause, and to subdue, with the truth and by His leave, the countries, for in this world thou hast been mercifully invested with sovereignty, and wilt, in the next, dwell, nigh unto the Seat of Holiness, with the inmates of the Paradise of His good-pleasure. ... By God! If ye do well, to your own behoof will ye do well; and if ye deny God and His signs, We, in very truth, having God, can well dispense with all creatures and all earthly dominion.*[3]

Worldwide publicity

It is important to note that the suffering of Quddús and Mullá Ṣádiq was not in vain because a few months later, a version of these events appeared in an article titled "Persia" in the 1 November 1845 issue of *The Times* of London, the most widely read Western newspaper. The article also covered the Báb's claim of Prophethood, His voyage to Mecca, His return to Persia, and subsequent arrest and trial in Shíráz.

Eventually *The Times* article was reproduced in newspapers in the United States, United Kingdom, Australia and New Zealand. The episode was also chronicled in *The Bombay Courier* on 19 September 1845 as well as in several journals in France and Germany.[4]

---

1 Hasan Fuadi Bushru'i, *The History of the Bahá'í Faith in Khorasan*, p.113.

2 Hasan Balyuzi, *Eminent Bahá'ís in the Time of Bahá'u'lláh*, p. 14.

3 The Báb, *Selections*, p. 41.

4 Amín Egea, *The Apostle of Peace*, vol. 1, p. xvi. "A Modern Mahomet". *Boon's Lick Times.* Fayette, Arkansas. 4 April 1846. p. 1. "Mahometan Schism": *Troy Daily Whig.* Troy, New York. 26 January 1846. pp. 2; *Vermont Watchman and State Journal.* Montpelier, Vermont. 19 February 1845. p. 4; *Ann Arbor,* Michigan. 23 February 1846. p. 3; *The Eclectic Magazine of Foreign Literature, Science, and Art.* Jan.–Feb. 1846. p.

The article in *The Times* describes the extreme cruelty of the punishment in the following terms (see Figure 20):

> We have been favoured with the following letter, dated Bú<u>sh</u>ihr, August 10:
>
> A Persian merchant, who has lately returned from a pilgrimage to Mecca, had been for sometime endeavouring here to prove that he was one of the successors of Muḥammad, and therefore had a right to demand of all true Mussulmans to mention him as such in their profession of faith; he had already collected a good number of followers, who secretly aided him in forwarding his views. On the evening of the 23rd June last, I have been informed from a creditable source, four persons being heard at Shíráz repeating their profession of faith according to the form prescribed by the new impostor were apprehended, tried, and found guilty of unpardonable blasphemy. They were sentenced to lose their beards by fire being set to them. The sentence was put into execution with all the zeal and fanaticism becoming a true believer in Muḥammad. Not deeming the loss of beards a sufficient punishment for the believers in the impostor, they were further sentenced on the next day to have their faces blacked and exposed throughout the city. Each of them was led by a Mirgazah (executioner), who had made a hole in his nose and passed through it a string, which he sometimes pulled with such violence that the unfortunate felloes cried out alternately for mercy from the executioner and for vengeance from Heaven. It is the custom in Persia on such occasions for the executioners to collect money from the spectators, and particularly from the shopkeepers in the bazaar. In the evening, when the pockets of the executioners were well filled with money, they led the unfortunate fellows to the city gate, and there told them
>
> > 'The world was all before them where to choose
> > 'Their place of rest, and Providence their guide.'
>
> After which the Mullás[1] at <u>Sh</u>íráz sent the men to Bú<u>sh</u>ihr with power to seize the impostor, and take him to <u>Sh</u>íráz, where, on being tried, he very wisely denied the charge of apostacy laid against him and thus escaped from punishment.[2]

As we can see, this article presents incorrect information about the Báb and His teachings, and what happened during the incident in <u>Sh</u>íráz. Yet, it was the

---

142; *Morning Chronicle*. Sydney, New South Wales. 4 April 1846. p. 4; *South Australian*. Adelaide, South Australia. 7 April 1846. p. 3; *New Zealand Spectator Cook's Strait Guardian*. Wellington. 15 July 1846. p. 3. "Persia": *The Times*. London. 1 November 1845. p. 5; *South Australian Register*. Adelaide, South Australia. 11 April 1846. p. 3.

1 Muslim clergy or 'ulamá.

2 Moojan Momen, *The Bábí and Bahá'í Religions, 1844–1944*, p. 69. The article was published first in India. It was also published in Spain and Puerto Rico.

means by which an early global awareness occurred about fourteen months after the Báb's Declaration. "For as the lightning comes from the east and shines as far as the west", as Matthew (24:27) stated, the announcement of the Manifestation of the Báb lighted the continents of Europe, America and Asia, as well as other parts of the earth.

Figure 12: Persia (Courtesy Pedro Donaires and M. W. Thomas)

Figure 13: Qur'án Gate, Shíráz , 1888 (Source: Bahá'í Media)

Figure 14: Old picture of the House of the Báb in Shíráz

Figure 15: View of the interior of the House of the Báb in Shíráz (Source: Bahá'í Media)

Figure 16: Coat worn by the Báb during His pilgrimage to Mecca (Source: Bahá'í Media)

Figure 17: Shíráz to Mecca pilgrim caravan, 1912 (Source: National Geographic Magazine, 1921)

Figure 18: Sketch of old Mecca (Source: Bahá'í Media)

Figure 19: Masjid-i-Naw, Shíráz

PERSIA.

We have been favoured with the following letter, dated Bushire, August 1st:—

A Persian merchant, who has lately returned from a pilgrimage to Mecca, had been for some time endeavouring here to prove that he was one of the successors of Mahomet, and therefore had a right to demand of all true Mussulmans to mention him as such in their profession of faith; he had already collected a good number of followers, who secretly aided him in forwarding his views. On the evening of the 23d of June last, I have been informed from a creditable source, four persons being heard at Shiraz repeating their profession of faith according to the form prescribed by the new impostor were apprehended, tried, and found guilty of unpardonable blasphemy. They were sentenced to lose their beards by fire being set to them. The sentence was put into execution with all the zeal and fanaticism becoming a true believer in Mahomet. Not deeming the loss of beards a sufficient punishment for the believers in the impostor, they were further sentenced on the next day to have their faces blacked and exposed throughout the city. Each of them was led by a Mirgazab (executioner), who had made a hole in his nose and passed through it a string, which he sometimes pulled with such violence that the unfortunate fellows cried out alternately for mercy from the executioner and for vengeance from Heaven. It is the custom in Persia on such occasions for the executioners to collect money from the spectators, and particularly from the shopkeepers in the bazaar. In the evening, when the pockets of the executioners were well filled with money, they led the unfortunate fellows to the city gate, and there told them

" The world was all before them where to choose
" Their place of rest, and Providence their guide."

" After which the Mollahs at Shiraz sent men to Bushire with power to seize the impostor, and take him to Shiraz, where, on being tried, he very wisely denied the charge of apostacy laid against him, and thus escaped from punishment.

Figure 20: Early coverage of Bábís in <u>Sh</u>íráz (The Times London, 1 Nov 1845)

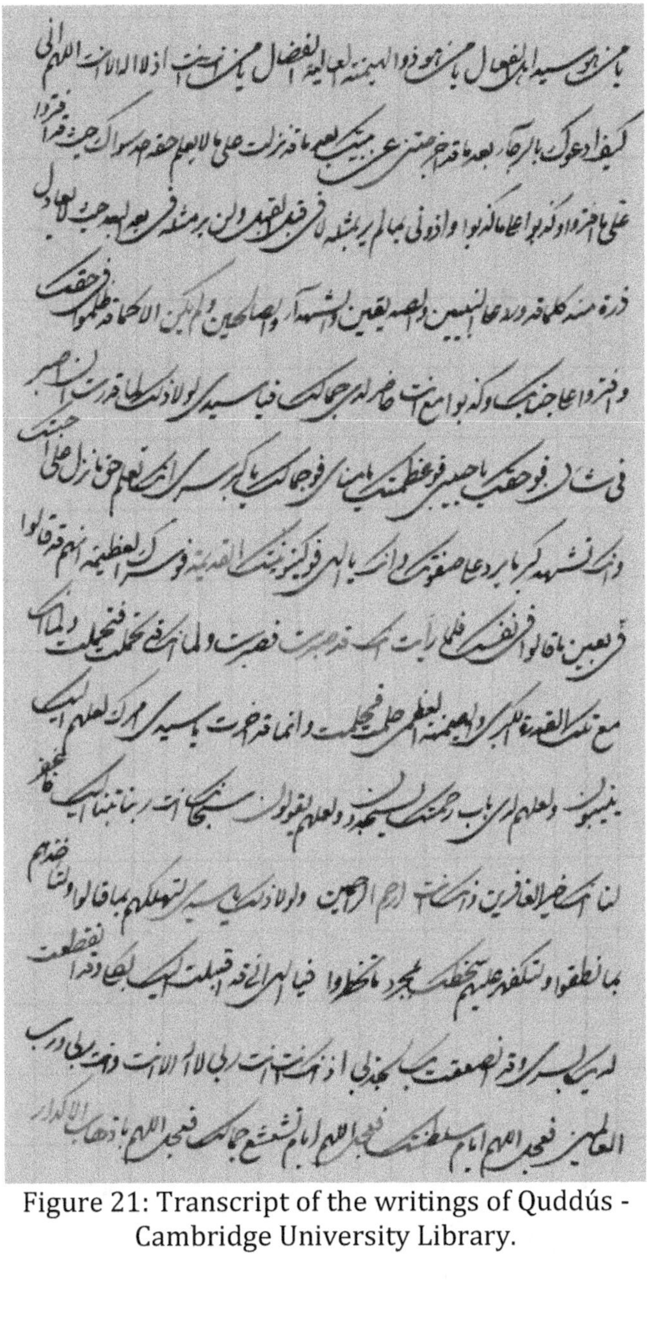

Figure 21: Transcript of the writings of Quddús - Cambridge University Library.

Part II
The promoter

6
A special mission from the Báb

Chapter content
Kirmán, Persia
Quddús departs Shíráz
The mission in Kirmán
Karím Khán Kirmání
Quddús in Kirmán
Karím Khán confronts Quddús
Ḥájí Siyyid Javád confronts Karím Khán
Quddús visits Bahá'u'lláh in Ṭihrán

Kirmán, Persia

Caravans, consisting of groups of traders, pilgrims or other travellers, engaged in long-distance travel, often travelled 15–20 km per day, and they occasionally rested for a day, especially after a particularly taxing journey. Hence, allowing for time spent in each settlement, Quddús' travels might have lasted about one year.

After their expulsion from Shíráz in June 1845, Quddús and Mullá Ṣádiq travelled together for a short time. Mullá Ṣádiq (1799–1889) was about 20 years older than Quddús, making them an interesting travelling duo. Mullá Ṣádiq was considered a muhtajid, that is, the highest rank in Islamic theology and jurisprudence. Of him, 'Abdu'l-Bahá said: *"He was a surging sea, a falcon that soared high. His visage shone, his tongue was eloquent, his strength and steadfastness astounding."*[1] They separated when Quddús went to Kirmán and Mullá Ṣádiq to Yazd.[2] Another source reports that Mullá Ṣádiq arrived in Kirmán shortly after Quddús arrived there.[3]

Kirmán is an old mud-brick city sitting like an oasis in the Iranian desert and famous for its production of palm dates, pistachios and carpets. Several historical mosques and some ancient Zoroastrian fire temples are located in Kirmán. The modern province of Kirmán is the largest of the 31 provinces in Iran today, the population density is the 27th lowest, and the Kirmán along with the Sístán and Balúchistán Provinces are the most isolated due to their geographical location. The vast salt desert of Lut (Dasht-i-Lút, the "Emptiness Plain"; 51,800 km^2) is spread across both provinces. Shahdád Kalút is the name given to 20% of the desert that is dominated by *kaluts*, meaning large wind sculptured sand ridges or outcrops, like enormous towers in a barren wilderness. This desert is one of the hottest and driest regions of the planet.

---

1 'Abdu'l-Bahá, *Memorials of the Faithful*, p. 8.

2 Nabíl-i-A'ẓam, *The Dawn-Breakers*, p. 180.

3 Denis McEoin, *Sources for early Bábí Doctrine and History*, p. 22.

In summer, temperatures can reach 42 °C (surface temperatures are significantly higher) and drop to -10 °C in winter. As a result of the extremely arid climate, the people of Kirmán build *qanats*, which are sloping underground channels, with a series of vertical access shafts, to transport water from an aquifer under a hill. They are used to distribute water to farms and the beautiful gardens in the area.

The people of Kirmán are also famous for using wind towers in their homes, which resemble modern air conditioners, called *badgirs* (wind-catchers). The *badgirs* are built on top of houses with openings facing the prevailing winds. The wind forces fresh air into the buildings to cool the interior. Openings on the downwind side drag out stale hot air.

Kirmán lies on a southern branch of the famous Silk Road. The city was visited by Marco Polo in 1272 CE, who remarked about its environment:

> On quitting the city you ride on for seven days, always finding towns, villages, and handsome dwelling-houses, so that it is very pleasant travelling; and there is excellent sport also to be had by the way in hunting and hawking. When you have ridden those seven days over a plain country, you come to a great mountain; and when you have got to the top of the pass you find a great descent which occupies some two days to go down. All along you find a variety and abundance of fruits; and in former days there were plenty of inhabited places on the road, but now there are none; and you meet with only a few people looking after their cattle at pasture. From the city of Kirmán to this descent the cold in winter is so great that you can scarcely abide it, even with a great quantity of clothing.[1]

Quddús departs Shíráz

For three days, Muqaddas and Quddús remained concealed in the Báb's home where they were given instructions for the next stage of their travels.[2] Another source indicated that Mullá Ṣádiq (Muqaddas) and Quddús moved to the former village of Saadi (Sa'dí), about 3 km north of the Shíráz city centre, to allow time for their wounds to heal and to await further orders from the Báb. Shortly after, the Báb, who had just returned from Búshihr, arrived at the residence. According to Hasan Fuadi Bushru'i:

> When the Báb was returning from Búshihr to Shíráz, [after the three Bábís had been paraded on the streets], these three people [including Quddús] came to His presence, in Sa'díh, and the Báb took them to His holy house. When they reached His house, the Báb put His hand on His holy neck, wept loudly and said, "*With which eyes can I look at your faces?*[3] *This Ḥusayn*

---

1 Marco Polo in Henry Yule, *The Travels of Marco Polo*, pp. 91–92.

2 Peter Terry, *A Prophet in Modern Times*, p. 172.

3 A Persian expression, meaning to be ashamed.

> *Khán* [the Governor] *is the same Shimr*[1] *that in this Revelation has appeared with the name Ḥusayn."*[2] Then, Muqaddas presented several pages containing abstruse questions, and the Báb, without delay and without stopping His pen, wrote the answers. In short, for two days Muqaddas had the honor of being in the presence of the Báb, and from the holy mouth, heard the promise of a new meeting.[3]

Once Muqaddas and Quddús received instructions from the Báb, they journeyed together for a few days and then parted. In particular, Quddús had been given an important mission to undertake in the city of Kirmán. Muqaddas instead had to go to Yazd and to his province of Khurásán for teaching the Faith.[4]

Mullá 'Alí-Akbar remained in Shíráz sheltering in the ruins outside the town. According to Julio Savi:

> In those circumstances he addressed a letter to the Báb. In that letter he [Mullá 'Alí-Akbar] wrote that he had taught the Cause in three towns, Yazd, Kirmán and Shíráz, asked permission to meet the Báb and a guidance on his behavior. From Shíráz Mullá 'Alí-Akbar returned to Ardistán where he continued serving the Faith of the Báb, while keeping afar from any dangerous situation.[5]

Moojan Momen adds that "After this [the Shíráz episode], he [Mullá 'Alí-Akbar-i-Ardistání] came to his home town [Ardistán] with Quddús and Mullá Ṣádiq (Muqqadas) and they succeeded in converting many."[6] Hasan Balyuzi adds that

> Mírzá Fatḥ 'Alí, surnamed Fatḥ-i-A'ẓam ["the Most Great Victory"] by Bahá'u'lláh, was one of the leading Bahá'ís of Ardistán, near Iṣfahán. He had accepted the Báb, with others in Ardistán when Mullá 'Alí-Akbar Ardistání[7] and Mullá Ṣádiq-i-Muqaddas passed through the town after their persecution in 1845, with Quddús, in Shíráz.[8]

A few months later Quddús returned to Ardistán. Hushmand Dehghan confirmed that Quddús "stayed in Ardistán for some time and stopped in a village of Márbín, the property of Zaynab Begum of Ardistán, who was the maternal

---

1 Abú as-Sábigha Shimr killed Imám Ḥusayn, Muḥammad's beloved grandson, in 680 CE.

2 Peter Terry, *A Prophet in Modern Times*, p. 172.

3 Hasan Fuadi Bushru'i, *The History of the Bahá'í Faith in Khorasan*, p. 113 (author's translation).

4 Peter Terry, *A Prophet in Modern Times*, p. 173.

5 Julio Savi and Faezeh Mardani, *Prayers and rituals in the Bahá'í Faith*, p. 322.

6 Moojan Momen, *The Bahá'í Communities of Iran*, vol. II, p. 147.

7 Former member of the Universal House of Justice Hushmand Fatheazam (1924-2013) was the great grandson of Mullá 'Alí-Akbar Ardistání. Mr Fatheazam married Shafiqih Farzar who was Muqqadas' great granddaughter (Shahbaz Fatheazam, *In Memoriam: Hushmand Fatheazam, Lights of Irfán*, no. 15, p. 408).

8 Bahá'u'lláh, *King of Glory*, p. 471.

grandmother of Nuṣratu'lláh Muḥammad-Ḥusayn (the author of the book *Ḥaẓrat-i-Báb*) succeeding in guiding a few noble people."[1]

Nabíl affirms that "For a few days they [Quddús and Muqqadas] continued to journey together, after which they separated, Quddús departing for Kirmán in order to interview Ḥájí Mírzá Karím Khán, and Mullá Ṣádiq (Muqqadas) directing his steps towards Yazd..."[2]

From the above, it seems that Quddús' route from Shíráz to Kirmán was north to Ardistán and then southeast towards Kirmán. It is likely that he passed through Ná'ín, Ardikán and Yazd on his way.

Quddús went first to Kirmán followed later by Mullá Ṣádiq who journeyed to Yazd.[3] Mullá Ṣádiq stayed in Yazd for two months teaching the Cause of the Báb before proceeding towards Kirmán.[4] Four years after going their separate ways, both would be reunited together in the heroic events of Fort Ṭabarsí. Mullá Ṣádiq continued to direct his efforts and use his knowledge for the progress of the Faith until his death in Hamadán at about 90 years of age.

The mission in Kirmán

After being released from his arrest in Shíráz, Quddús had dreamed that the Báb placed His blessed robe upon Quddús' shoulders.[5] It seems that this dream, was a portent of the mission assigned to him by the Báb to instruct a reprehensible Muslim cleric of Kirmán, Mírzá Karím Khán. Quddús carried a number of Divine Tablets and Sacred Texts in the handwriting of the Báb and in the handwriting of other amanuenses.[6]

Among these documents was a letter from the Báb to the impostor, Mírzá Karím Khán,[7] as previously mentioned, a cleric that pretended to be the successor of Siyyid Káẓim. According to Abbas Amanat, "Quddús conveyed a 'red sheet' from the Báb in which the new prophet invited [Mírzá Karím Khán] Kirmání to

---

1 In *Ḥaẓrat Báb,* p. 462. Cited in Hushmand Dehghan, *Ganj-i-Pinhán*, pp. 60–61.

2 Nabíl-i-A'ẓam, *The Dawn-Breakers,* p. 180.

3 According to historian A.L.M. Nicolas, "They [Quddús and Muqaddas] went then to Yazd where they remained for the duration of forty days, restricting themselves to discussions with prominent persons, civic as well as religious and military" (In Peter Terry, *A Prophet in Modern Times,* p. 173). Nabíl does not mention the presence of Quddús in Muqqadas activities in Yazd (*The Dawn-Breakers,* p. 186). Further, Nabíl affirms that they had separated before (*The Dawn-Breakers,* p. 180).

4 Hasan Balyuzi, *Eminent Bahá'ís in the Time of Bahá'u'lláh*, p. 14.

5 In Ibrahim Ruhi, *Kitáb-i-Quddúsiyyíh*, p. 57. Cited in Hushmand Dehghan, *Ganj-i-Pinhán*, pp. 60–61.

6 Ibrahim Ruhi, *Kitáb-i-Quddúsiyyih*, p. 57. Cited in Hushmand Dehghan, *Ganj-i-Pinhán*, pp. 60–61.

7 Denis McEoin, *Sources for early Bábí Doctrine and History*, p. 22.

'obey the order of his Lord' and 'renew covenant with the Remnant of God' by paying allegiance to the *Zikr* [the Báb]."[1]

It was the summer of 1845. Quddús had decided to try to stop the attacks and slanders of Mírzá Karím Khán Kirmání against the Báb. He was a man of considerable influence in royal circles and had written 278 books on a variety of philosophical and scientific matters. [2]

Karím Khán Kirmání

After the death of Siyyid Káẓim in 1843, Ḥájí Mírzá Karím Khán (or Karím Khán) had assumed the leadership of his disciples, even though Siyyid Káẓim himself had made it clear that there would be no successor. Rather, Siyyid Káẓim had left very precise instructions that, after his death, all his disciples should disperse in search of the Promised Messenger.

There is also evidence that Karím Khán had not followed the Shaykhí School principles during the last years of Siyyid Káẓim's life. Karím Khán went even further by ignoring the instructions to search for the Promised One and by pretending to be Siyyid Káẓim's successor. Karím Khán then introduced an even more blatant deviation by rejecting the Báb and doing everything possible to stop His Cause from spreading. In his arrogance, he wrote a treatise that attacked the Báb while allying himself with those people seeking to undermine the progress of the Cause of God. In one of his treatises, he wrote that the Báb "was the perpetrator of ... innovations that contradicted the exigencies of Islam, Shi'ism, and their essential nature."[3] Bahá'u'lláh said of him that he "*imagined himself a learned man and regarded the rest of the people ignorant*".[4] As an author stated, Quddús "was probably the best acquainted of all the Báb's followers with His teachings at this stage"[5] to confront the impostor.

Karím Khán usually signed his name as the servant who is *Athím* (Sinful) pretending to be humble. However, Bahá'u'lláh wrote of him in the *Kitáb-i-Íqán*:

> *And as to this man's attainments, his ignorance, understanding and belief, behold what the Book which embraceth all things hath revealed; 'Verily, the tree of Zaqqúm (Infernal tree) shall be the food of the Athím.'* (Sinner or sinful—*Qur'án* 44:43–44) *And then follow certain verses, until He saith: 'Taste this, for thou forsooth art the mighty Karím!'"* (Honourable—*Qur'án* 44:49). *Consider how clearly and explicitly he hath been described in God's incorruptible Book! This man, moreover, feigning humility, hath in his own*

---

1 Abbas Amanat, *Resurrection and Renewal,* p. 297.

2 Stephen Lambden, *Antichrist-Dajjal: Some Notes on the Christian and Islamic Antichrist Traditions and their Bahá'í Interpretation,* part II, p. 19.

3 Mohamad Tavakoli-Targhi, *Anti-Baha'ism and Islamism in Iran*, p. 212.

4 Bahá'u'lláh, *Kitáb-i-Íqán,* p. 185.

5 Denis MacEoin, *Early Shaykhī Reactions to the Báb and His Claims*, p. 29.

book referred to himself as the '*a<u>th</u>ím servant*': '*A<u>th</u>ím*' in the Book of God, mighty among the common herd, '*Karím*' in name!¹

Quddús in Kirmán

Some details of Quddús' arrival in Kirmán have been recorded in the book *Ganj-i-Pinhán*:

> ... He travelled the distance from <u>Sh</u>íráz to Kirmán on foot and alleviated his hunger by eating the plants and vegetations of the desert .... He entered Kirmán with a worn-out hat, torn out shoes, and ragged clothes.
>
> The people started wondering about an individual who has arrived to Kirmán from <u>Sh</u>íráz, that as he passes by the people in the marketplaces and ally-ways, they stop their daily work, gaze their attention towards him and say to themselves, "Who is this dignified and noble person, who has come to our city? Everyone was wondering, even though in appearance he was not wearing expensive clothes and was dressed like a poor man.²

Ganj-i-Pinhán relates Quddús' activities when he arrived in Kirmán:

> ... Quddús was coming to the house located around the late 'Abbás <u>Kh</u>án and Mírzá <u>Gh</u>ulám-Ḥusayn which is in front of the arcade;³ when you pass the house of Ḥájí Riḍá-Qulí <u>Kh</u>án and enter the neighbourhood near the street, which in the past was the house of Mullá Ibráhím.
>
> In order to be honoured by his presence, I (Mullá Ja'far) and two or three other people who were awaiting for his arrival, went to that house of that blessed soul and we sat in the room facing the hallway .... Some of the women from that house were sitting at the end of the same room. We were watching the hallway when he entered ....⁴
>
> In many gatherings, we were blessed with the honour of seeing Quddús .... One of these occasions was when he came to the Á<u>kh</u>únd's⁵ house in the upper room above the hallway at the house of Á<u>kh</u>únd's father ....
>
> At these gatherings, apart from giving sermons and counsels, and alluding to the false nature of this world, he was urging all to observe what would benefit them in the next world, and never discussed anything about any other worldly matters ....⁶ To teach the Cause of God, he used to visit the

---

1 Bahá'u'lláh, *Kitáb-i-Íqán*, p. 190.
2 Ibrahim Ruhi, *Kitáb-i-Quddúsiyyíh*, p. 57. Cited in Hushmand Dehghan, *Ganj-i-Pinhán*, pp. 60–61.
3 A covered yard.
4 Ibrahim Ruhi, *Kitáb-i-Quddúsiyyíh*, p. 59. Cited in Hushmand Dehghan, *Ganj-i-Pinhán*, pp. 60–61.
5 Á<u>kh</u>únd means a Muslim priest.
6 Ibrahim Ruhi, *Kitáb-i-Quddúsiyyíh*, p. 61. Cited in Hushmand Dehghan, *Ganj-i-Pinhán*, pp. 60–61.

grand mosque of Kirmán. Quddús himself would stand on the street near the courtyard of the mosque and grand stone,[1] which it is said that it was so shiny that the reflection of the mosque could be seen in it. He used to recite the Divine Verses with a melodious and loud voice. In those days, each time the spiritual leader of the Friday Prayer, the late Ḥájí Siyyid Javád Shírází, visited the mosque, he [Ḥájí Siyyid Javád Shírází] would stand upright while leaning on his walking stick listening attentively to the Divine Verses but not uttering a word of approval or disapproval ....[2]

Quddús arrived in Kirmán and was the guest of a distinguished citizen named Ḥájí Siyyid Javád. Highly respected by the population of Kirmán because of his learning and pious knowledge, Ḥájí Siyyid Javád[3] had also been a disciple of Siyyid Káẓim for over 10 years. He was not on good terms with Karím Khán. Ḥájí Siyyid Javád knew the Báb when He was still a child[4] and he was a distant paternal cousin of the Báb.[5] Through Quddús, Ḥájí Siyyid Javád accepted the Faith of the Báb. For a period of time, Ḥájí Siyyid Javád preferred to hide his faith, believing that thus he could better help the growth of the Cause. He was also the Imám Jum'ih of the city, that is, the chief divine and the preacher for the Friday congregational prayers. "At all the gatherings held in his home," Nabíl related, "He [Ḥájí Siyyid Javád] invariably assigned to his youthful guest the seat of honour and treated him with extreme deference and courtesy."[6] Nabíl added:

> In the privacy of his home, Ḥájí Siyyid Javád heard Quddús recounting all the details of his activities from the day of his departure from Karbilá until his arrival at Kirmán. The circumstances of his conversion and his subsequent pilgrimage with the Báb stirred the imagination and kindled the flame of faith in the heart of his host, who preferred, however, to conceal his belief, in the hope of being able to guard more effectively the interests of the newly established community. "Your noble resolve", Quddús lovingly assured him, "will in itself be regarded as a notable service rendered to the Cause of God. The Almighty will reinforce your efforts and will establish for all time your ascendancy over your opponents".[7]

Nabíl reported that Karím Khán experienced intense feelings of jealousy as a result of the preferential treatment given to Quddús:

> So marked a preference for so young and seemingly mediocre a person kindled the envy of the disciples of Ḥájí Mírzá Karím Khán, who, describing

1 "The author [Hushmand Dehghan] observed this stone closely during his trip to Kirmán in AH 1375. The locals call it the mirror stone but due to the passage of time, it has become unclear." In Hushmand Dehghan, *Ganj-i-Pinhán*, pp. 60–61.

2 Hushmand Dehghan, *Ganj-i-Pinhán*, pp. 60–61.

3 In 1881, he died in Kirmán aged nearly 100.

4 Soli Shahvar et al, *The Bahá'ís of Iran,* vol. 1, p. 108.

5 Abbas Amanat, *Resurrection and Renewal,* p. 288.

6 Nabíl-i-A'ẓam, *The Dawn-Breakers,* pp. 180–181.

7 Nabíl-i-A'ẓam, *The Dawn-Breakers,* pp. 180–181.

in vivid and exaggerated language the honours which were being lavished upon Quddús, sought to excite the dormant hostility of their chief. "Behold," they whispered in his ears, "he who is the best beloved, the trusted and most intimate companion of the Siyyid-i-Báb, is now the honoured guest of one who is admittedly the most powerful inhabitant of Kirmán. If he be allowed to live in close companionship with Ḥájí Siyyid Javád, he will no doubt instill his poison into his soul, and will fashion him as the instrument whereby he will succeed in disrupting your authority and in extinguishing your fame."[1]

Such was Karím Khán's arrogance that he once wrote:

> Whoever seeks guidance in matters of faith, this is with us. Let him come to us and receive [answers] because these matters are to be found with us, not with shopkeepers (baqqál) and bakers.[2]

Karím Khán confronts Quddús

Quddús went to Kirmán to present the holy verses from the Báb to Karím Khán. According to Hushmand Dehghan:

> Quddús requested the Athím [Karím Khán] that he should organise and appear at assembly for a debate accompanied with whoever he wants from among his subjects (followers). A large number showed up, particularly his disciples, but Quddús was alone. After presenting his arguments and denying all the proofs and statements by the Athím, Quddús presented the verses of the Báb which are the statements of Siyyid 'Alí-Muḥammad-i-Shírází [the Báb], and he said to Karím Khán, "Either yourself or any of your followers bring verses similar to these or admit your helplessness and inability". No one from the audience had the strength to reply. All were amazed and bewildered except the Athím who said: "I do not understand anything from these words that you just read, except the words "they know" and "they reason". Then Karím Khán, after asking a few questions and hearing the answers, threatened Quddús that either [he] leave voluntarily, otherwise that cleric would order his expulsion ....[3]
>
> So far the quoted phrases were from Mullá Muḥammad-Ja'far. However, Karím Khán Kirmání himself mentioned about this meeting in a treatise and wrote: "And the surah that (the Báb) had sent down to me through

---

1 Nabíl-i-A'ẓam, *The Dawn-Breakers,* pp. 180–181.

2 Eschraghi, Armin, *Undermining the Foundations of Orthodoxy,* p. 236.

3 In the same place, pp. 70–1, Modarris Chahar-Dehi writes: "But Ḥájí Muḥammad Karím Khán invited the distinguished people of the city and invited two representatives and delegates of the Báb, who were among the most prominent followers and pillars of the Bábí movement, and from this very meeting, he obstinately started opposing the Báb, as he ordered them to be expelled from Kirmán." Bábigeri Sheikhigeri, p. 241, cited in Hushmand Dehghan, *Ganj-i-Pinhán,* pp. 60–61.

Mullá Muḥammad-'Alí [Quddús], named Mazándaráni, He had written in His own handwriting, and there he had ordered me to gather troops and come to Fárs ... and I dismissed that mentioned Muḥammad-'Alí with indignation and humiliation. And in another place, he writes about this: "He wrote me a Letter in his own handwriting, that is, Siyyid 'Alí-Muḥammad Báb, and gave it to one of his apostate students. He brought the Letter to me, and still it exists. In it, He asked me to assist Him and ordered me that I should tell the muezzins to mention His name in the call to daily prayers. When that infidel came (Quddús), I answered to that letter, comprehensively, and sent him away disappointed and wretched".[1]

Historian Mangol Bayat described Karím Khán's hostile attitude towards the Báb:

> He directed his most openly vicious, polemical attacks against the Báb. He wrote several essays to refute the latter's claim to divine knowledge and to ridicule the *Bayán,* the Báb's "revealed book," for its blasphemous pretensions. "Our Prophet is the last prophet," he emphatically proclaimed, "and there will be no other after him, ever. Our Koran is God's and the Prophet's miracle. Anyone who pretends to be a new prophet bringing a new message is a heretic" .... He called the Báb "the gate to hell", and "the devil's disciple", charging he had abused and corrupted [Shaykh Aḥmad] Aḥsá'í knowledge, and used it to achieve his own worldly ends. Karím Khán insisted that "the real Báb exists, a person who carries the Imám's light; God has commanded his existence," as the gate to the Imám's knowledge, obviously meaning himself.[2]

Ḥájí Siyyid Javád confronts Karím Khán

Nabíl also reported that Karím Khán was envious of the high position of Quddús in the community of Kirmán as a result of the preferential treatment given to him:

> ... the cowardly Ḥájí Mírzá Karím Khán appealed to the governor and induced him to call in person upon Ḥájí Siyyid Javád and demand that he terminates that dangerous association [with Quddús]. The representations of the governor inflamed the wrath of the intemperate Ḥájí Siyyid Javád.
>
> "How often," he violently protested, "have I advised you to ignore the whisperings of this evil plotter! My forbearance has emboldened him. Let him beware lest he overstep his bounds. Does he desire to usurp my position? Is he not the man who receives into his home thousands of abject and ignoble people and overwhelms them with servile flattery? Has he not, again and again, striven to exalt the ungodly and to silence the innocent?

1 *Yadgar Magazine* No. 6 and 7, Bahman and Esfand 1327, p. 70. Cited in Hushmand Dehghan, *Ganj-i-Pinhán*, pp. 60–61.

2 Mangol Bayat, *Mysticism and Dissent*, p. 80.

Has he not, year after year, by reinforcing the hand of the evil-doer, sought to ally himself with him and gratify his carnal desires? Does he not until this day persist in uttering his blasphemies against all that is pure and holy in Islám? My silence seems to have added to his temerity and insolence. He gives himself the liberty of committing the foulest deeds, and refuses to allow me to receive and honour in my own home a man of such integrity, such learning and nobleness. Should he refuse to desist from his practice, let him be warned that the worst elements of the city will, at my instigation, expel him from Kirmán."

Disconcerted by such vehement denunciations, the governor apologised for his action. Ere he retired, he assured Ḥájí Siyyid Javád that he needs entertain no fear, that he himself would endeavour to awaken Ḥájí Mírzá Karím Khán to the folly of his behaviour, and would induce him to repent.

The siyyid's message stung Ḥájí Mírzá Karím Khán. Convulsed by a feeling of intense resentment which he could neither suppress nor gratify, he relinquished all hopes of acquiring the undisputed leadership of the people of Kirmán. That open challenge sounded the death-knell of his cherished ambitions.[1]

Thus, Quddús could move more freely within the city and proclaim the teachings of the Faith to the people. From Kirmán, he visited several other cities till he finally reached Ṭihrán, the capital of Persia. In visiting the villages and towns along his route, Quddús widely proclaimed the good news of the Manifestation of the Báb.

After Kirmán

From Kirmán, Quddús came back to Ardistán via Yazd, Ardikán and Ná'ín.[2] After Ardistán, Quddús went to the capital Tihran passing through Iṣfahán, Qum and Káshán. In Káshán, in the company of 'Aẓím, Quddús stayed "in the house of two Bábí brothers named Áqá Abu'l-Qásim and Áqá Mihdí, who were respectable merchants of Káshán,[3] then he left for Qum and finally arrived in Ṭihrán."[4]

Quddús visits Bahá'u'lláh in Ṭihrán

A few months earlier, the Báb had received a letter from Mullá Ḥusayn reporting that he had successfully delivered a scroll of the Báb's Writings to

---

1 Nabíl-i-A'ẓam, *The Dawn-Breakers,* pp. 180–181.

2 Nabíl-i-A'ẓam, *The Dawn-Breakers,* p. 180.

3 *Taríkh Ẓuhúr al-Ḥaqq*, vol. 3, p. 394. "Fazel Mazandarani writes that the two mentioned brothers believed in the presence of Mírzá Jání with the agreement of Ḥájí Mírzá Jání (p. 394). Considering the fact that Ḥaẓrat Báb entered that region months after Quddús' visit to Káshán in Rabí'u'th-Thání AH 1283 (Nabíl Zarandí, p. 188), the said report is questionable and also considering the subsequent events in the short life of Quddús makes it unlikely that he went to Káshán in the following years." Cited in Hushmand Dehghan, *Ganj-i-Pinhán*, pp. 60–61.

4 Hushmand Dehghan, *Ganj-i-Pinhán*, pp. 60–61.

Bahá'u'lláh through a messenger in Ṭihrán. Upon reading the text, Bahá'u'lláh remarked:

> *Verily I say, whose believes in the Qur'án and recognises its Divine origin, and yet hesitates, though it be for a moment, to admit that these soul-stirring words are endowed with the same regenerating power, has most assuredly erred in his judgement and has strayed far from the path of justice.*[1]

When the Báb read Mullá Ḥusayn's report, He shared His great joy and delight with Quddús. According to a witness of that moment, "This was sufficient, however, to convince me that in the city of Ṭihrán there lay hidden a Mystery which, when revealed to the world, would bring unspeakable joy to the hearts of both the Báb and Quddús."[2]

In Ṭihrán, Quddús met Bahá'u'lláh in late 1845 or early 1846[3] During his few days in Ṭihrán, he stayed in the home of Riḍá [Reza] Khán the son of a noble Persian who converted to the Cause of the Báb. His story is told with more detail in the section "Arrivals at Shaykh Ṭabarsí" of chapter 15.

As previously stated, on the eve of his ultimate separation from the Báb in the port of Búshihr, Quddús was given the assurance that after his ordeals on the streets of Shíráz, he would one day be in the presence of Bahá'u'lláh, "Him who is the one object of our adoration and love .... In His presence you will forget all the harm and disgrace that shall have befallen you".[4] During the Báb's time, only a few believers were assured that they would meet the next Manifestation of God. These included Mullá Báqir, Sayyáḥ, Mullá Ḥusayn, Shaykh Ḥasan-i-Zunúzí, Dayyán, and 'Aẓím.[5]

On Quddús' visit to Bahá'u'lláh in Ṭihrán, Áqáy-i-Kalím, His brother, said:

> Whoever was intimately associated with him was seized with an insatiable admiration for the charm of that youth. We watched him one day perform his ablutions, and were struck by the gracefulness which distinguished him from the rest of the worshippers in the performance of so ordinary a rite. He seemed, in our eyes, to be the very incarnation of purity and grace.[6]

It is important to note that Quddús was a model of piousness and religiousness while observing meticulously the Islamic ritual of the daily obligatory prayer. This and other dimensions of his personality were highlighted by the Báb:

> *Thou hast drawn nigh, and none is there besides thee whose nearness is like unto thine. Each and every being doth lift up its voice in praise by means of thy praise. Each and every subtle reality hath voiced its thanksgiving out of*

---

1 Nabíl-i-A'ẓam, *The Dawn-Breakers*, p. 107.
2 Adib Taherzadeh, *The Covenant of Bahá'u'lláh*, p. 37.
3 Nabíl-i-A'ẓam, *The Dawn-Breakers*, p. 183.
4 Nabíl-i-A'ẓam, *The Dawn-Breakers*, pp. 142–143.
5 Shoghi Effendi, *God Passes By*, p. 28.
6 Nabíl-i-A'ẓam, *The Dawn-Breakers*, p. 183.

the quintessence of thy thanksgiving. Each and every soul hath been united by the power of thy unity. Each and every living thing hath worshipped through the transcendence of thy worship"[1]

Quddús and Bahá'u'lláh would meet again in June-July 1848 at the conference of Badasht, when Quddús bowed down in the presence of Bahá'u'lláh and treated Him with absolute respect and reverence. The third meeting occurred when Bahá'u'lláh visited Quddús during his confinement in Sárí in the third quarter of 1848.[2]

When Quddús arrived in Shaykh Ṭabarsí in October 1848, he referred to Bahá'u'lláh as the "Baqíyyatu'lláh" ("the Remnant of God").[3] With these words he associated Bahá'u'lláh[4] with a messianic Islamic figure and indirectly relating Bahá'u'lláh with *"Him Whom God shall make manifest"*[5] promised by the Báb. Quddús dedicated his lengthy interpretation of the Sád of Ṣamad, written mostly in Shaykh Ṭabarsí, to Bahá'u'lláh. The Báb also referred to Bahá'u'lláh when He told Mullá Ḥusayn back in 1844 that Ṭihrán *"enshrines a Mystery of such transcendent holiness as neither Hijáz nor Shíráz can hope to rival"*.[6]

After Ṭihrán

After his meeting with Bahá'u'lláh in Ṭihrán, Quddús travelled to Bárfurúsh. He visited small villages between these cities. It is probably during this trip that he visited Qazvín and taught the Faith at the home of the Farhadi family.[7]

According to Nabíl "in the home of his father, he [Quddús] lived for about two years, during which time he was surrounded by the loving devotion of his family and kindred."[8] At the end of that time it was 1847.[9]

Quddús' travels represent an extensive movement from the south to the east and then to the north of the country. (See *The Travels of Quddús* map in Figure 22).

---

1 The Báb, *Tablet of Visitation for Quddús.* See Appendix part 2.

2 Adib Taherzadeh, *The Covenant of Bahá'u'lláh,* p. 56; and Moojan Momen, *Two Episodes from the Life of Bahá'u'lláh in Iran,* p. 143.

3 *Qur'án* 11:86.

4 Shoghi Effendi, *God Passes By,* p. 69.

5 Man Yuẓhiruhu'lláh.

6 Nabíl-i-A'ẓam, *The Dawn-Breakers,* p. 96.

7 John Walbridge, *Essays and Notes on Babi and Baha'i History,* p. 38.

8 Nabíl-i-A'ẓam, *The Dawn-Breakers,* p. 183.

9 Nosratollah Mohammad-Hosseini, *Qoddus, Moḥammad-'Ali Bārforuši, n.p.*

7
Quddús in Mázindarán

Chapter content
Bárfurús͟h description
Settling into Bárfurús͟h
Living in Bárfurús͟h
Regent to the "Lord of the Age"
The opposition of Mullá Qásim
Quddús and the Sa'ídu'l-'Ulamá'
Exchanges between Quddús and the Sa'ídu'l-'Ulamá'
Quddús predicts his martyrdom

Bárfurús͟h description

In the early 1800s Bárfurús͟h consisted of nearly 18 neighbourhoods that were separated from each other by dense woodlands. Even neighbouring houses were sometimes hidden from each other by gardens and trees. Several small villages flourished around the town's periphery, each having its own civil autonomy, mostly following traditional tribal practices. "The old centre of Bárfurús͟h," according to Amanat, "appears to have been originally surrounded by a cluster of agricultural districts, which were gradually integrated into a city."[1]

The people in Bárfurús͟h speak Mazání, a northwestern Iranian language, that is today spoken by approximately two million people in the north of Iran. The predominant religion is S͟hí'ih Islám, and the city has a number of mosques and Muslim religious institutions. Bárfurús͟h was known for its large number of clerics.[2]

The city has been described as "a small dam or floodgate located in the intersection of roads, connecting cities and villages; to this, like many other residential places around the northern part of the country, a weekly bazaar was formed in that place, and the neighbours gathered there in special days with the purpose of a transaction. Since this bazaar was active on Thursdays, gradually, it has been called Panj S͟hambih [Thursday] bazaar."[3] The western side of Bárfurús͟h was once mainly an area of rice fields irrigated by the Babol River prior to the last century's rapid urbanisation of the city.

To the south of the 19th century city, there was a vast natural space known as Sabzih-Maydán or Green Square. This spacious grazing land formed the southern entrance to the city. The Palangh ("Panther") Caravanserai, or local inn, was built there to accommodate travellers, their trade goods, and riding and pack animals.

---

[1] Abbas Amanat, *Resurrection and Renewal*, p. 182.
[2] Mohammad Ali Kazembeyki, *Society, Politics and Economics in Mazandaran*, p. 117.
[3] Poursoleiman et al, *An Investigation on Elements Creating Sense of Place*, pp. 14–15.

On the western side of the Sabzih-Maydán there lies the garden of the Baḥru'l-Arim ("Sea of Paradise"). This was an inland lake, the size of a racetrack, with an island in the middle on which there was a handsome palace with beautiful flower gardens and cypress trees. The home of the governor was on the island and it was here that visiting royalty stayed when visiting Bárfurú<u>sh</u>. Hence, the island was also known as Bá<u>gh</u>-i-<u>Sh</u>áh ("Garden of the King"). Access to the island was via a 150 m wooden bridge or by boat. There were lotus plants in the lake and it was a habitat for ducks. The swamps were also a popular place for duck hunting. Unfortunately, over time the quality of the water declined and most of the lake became a swamp due to a lack of maintenance. In the first half of the 19th century, the lake was filled with soil to create land for two new residential developments: East Baḥru'l-Árám and West Baḥru'l-Árám. The Sabzih-Maydán is now a sizeable local park surrounded by local institutions such as a medical university and the municipality.

Settling into Bárfurú<u>sh</u>

The young Quddús, known for his kind and benevolent character, eagerly rejoined his family when he returned to his native Bárfurú<u>sh</u>, residing in the house that belonged to his father. Two-and-a-half years had passed since the Báb declared His mission in <u>Sh</u>íráz.[1] He came back as a Ḥájí, that is, a person who had made his pilgrimage to Mecca. Ḥájís were well-respected people in the Muslim community, since undertaking such a long, difficult and expensive trip, travelling in precarious embarkations through five major seas, was a sign of piousness and sacrifice. A non-Bábí source remarked that:

> After some years, he came back [to Bárfurú<u>sh</u>] and stayed in his father's residence. People frequently visited him. He was so-good natured that people approved of his habits. The people would always pay him visits.[2]
>
> According to Nabíl, Quddús "freely associated with all classes of people, and by the gentleness of his character and the wide range of his learning had won the affection and unqualified admiration of the inhabitants of that town".[3]

Opposition from fanatical Muslims began on the second day after his arrival[4] either for being a Bábí or for being known as a follower of the <u>Sh</u>aykhí teachings of Siyyid Kázim. Sadly, "No prophet is accepted in his hometown" (*Luke* 4:24), as the *Bible* warns. And so, Quddús' challenges with the local ecclesiastical hierarchy began to grow into resentment and hate.

---

1 According to Abbas Amanat, Quddús returned to Bárfurú<u>sh</u> from pilgrimage to Mecca in 1261 AH / 1845 CE. See Abbas Amanat, *Resurrection and Renewal*, p. 184.

2 Habib Borjian, *A Mázandarání Account of the Babi Incident at Shaikh Ṭabarsí*, p. 391.

3 Nabíl-i-A'ẓam, *The Dawn-Breakers*, p. 261.

4 Fazel Mazandarani, *Ẓuhúr al-Ḥaqq*, vol. 3, p. 431.

For his teaching activities, Quddús has been called the "Apostle of Mázandarán".[1] Each of the Letters of the Living had been assigned their native province as their primary area of focus. During two years, his activities and energies were devoted to building a community of believers by making the Faith of the Báb known within the local and neighbouring population.[2] It is claimed that in less than a week he had brought 300 souls into the ranks of the Faith.[3]

These teaching activities angered the Muslim clerics who complained to the government. However, Khánlár Mírzá, the prince-governor, rejected their accusations and rebuked them for their behaviour. The clergymen continued to hassle Quddús to the point that he was left isolated at his father's house.[4] It was 1847, the third year after the Declaration of the Báb.

The French historian A. L. M. Nicolas[5] remarked that one of Quddús' roles in Bárfurúsh was to receive news from the provinces and give instructions to the followers regarding their pilgrimages to the Báb's presence.[6] "He was appointed deputy by the Báb in his own country, Mázindarán," the Count of Gobineau commented, "and there he obtained very great successes, which were to occupy a considerable place in the history of Bábísm."[7] During that period, Gobineau adds, "Knowing that Mullá Ḥusayn Bushrú'í was in Ṭihrán, He [the Báb] had established contact with him and kept him [Quddús] informed of all His actions, for the future steps depended on the success or failure of the Báb's first vicar." [8]

Living in Bárfurúsh

Quddús' family background was simple. His father, Áqá Ṣáliḥ, was a "poor rice cultivator in the outskirts of Bárfurúsh."[9] Áqá Muḥammad-Ṣádiq, his brother, had the job of "weaving quilts".[10] The family lived by a river in the farming area known as Chihár Shanbih Písh [literally, "After Wednesday"].[11] There are two photographs of their rural house, now demolished, showing how modest their plight was. Quddús once wrote to the Sa'ídu'l-'Ulamá', "I am staying at my own

1 Gobineau in Nash and O'Donoghue, *Comte de Gobineau and Orientalism,* p. 146.

2 Nosratollah Mohammad-Hosseini, *Qoddus, Moḥammad-'Ali Bārforuši, n.p.*

3 A. L. M. Nicolas, *Seyyèd Ali-Mohammed dit le Bâb,* pp. 296–297. Cited in Nabíl-i-A'ẓam, *The Dawn-Breakers,* p. 262.

4 Hushmand Dehghan, *Ganj-i-Pinhán,* p. 66.

5 Louis Alphonse Daniel Nicolas (1864–1937) was a Persian-born, French diplomat who wrote several books about the religion of the Báb. His historical research was based on nineteenth-century publications in Persian and French as well as from local oral sources.

6 A. L. M. Nicolas, *Seyyèd Ali-Mohammed dit le Bâb,* p. 300.

7 Joseph Arthur Gobineau, *Les Religions et les Philosophies dans l'Asie Centrale,* p. 166.

8 Gobineau in Nash and O'Donoghue, *Comte de Gobineau and Orientalism,* p. 145.

9 Abbas Amanat, *Resurrection and Renewal,* p. 158.

10 Hooshmand Dehghan, *Ganj-i-Pinhán,* p. 120.

11 Hushmand Dehghan, *Ganj-i-Pinhán,* p. 45.

dwelling, busy with perusing the Holy Book, and holding fast to the Cord of God's holy family." [1]

This then begs the question, *What was then Quddús occupation in Bárfurúsh?*

The straight answer is that we do not know exactly. We can only surmise that he was assisting his father with the family farm since agriculture tends to be a family-centred endeavour where everyone helps. On the other hand, or simultaneously, Quddús could have worked as a scribe. Well-educated citizens or people involved in theology were able to make a living by copying religious treatises in the absence of printing presses, resulting in books only being produced by hand. Being a scribe (kátib), a "man of letters", also required knowledge of Arabic typically the written language of Islamic texts and of the ecclesiastical elite. Having it was a plus in a country where the literacy rate was less than 10%.[2] Scribes held a reputable status among the population. They could work independently, for a patron, for the government or for a religious institution.

Well-known Bábí believers such as Shaykh Ḥasan,[3] Mírzá Muḥammad-Taqíy-i-Juvayní,[4] Mullá Ḥusayn-Dákhil-i-Marághi'í and Mullá Ḥusayn-i-Bushrú'í[5] worked as scribes to earn a livelihood.[6] Nabíl recalled that his mentor, Mírzá Aḥmad,[7] used to make copies of the Writings of the Báb and send them as gifts.[8] We can also imagine Quddús engaged in such a generous endeavour for the believers in the absence of Bábí literature. Scribes were also good calligraphers, an art extolled by the Báb particularly for transcribing the verses of God.[9] [10] Quddús could have also worked as a teacher at the school attached to the mosque of Sharí'atmadár, his local mentor.

Regent to the "Lord of the Age"

The Bábís of Persia saw Quddús as the representative of the Báb Himself during His long imprisonment. According to a Muslim source from that time,

---

1 Hooshmand Dehghan, *Ganj-i-Pinhán,* p. 209.

2 Willem Floor, *The Economic Role of the Ulama in Qajar Persia,* p. 54.

3 Nabíl-i-A'ẓam, *The Dawn-Breakers,* p. 32.

4 Abbas Amanat, *Resurrection and Renewal,* p. 248.

5 Persians say the name as *Mullá Ḥusayn-i-Bushrú'í.* These days, similar names are recorded in English texts as *Mullá Ḥusayn Bushrú'í.* Shoghi Effendi transliterated these names in the Dawn-Breakers based on how they are pronounced in Persian. Still, the second form is used in nearly all non-Bahá'í publications nowadays.

6 Ruhollah Mehrabkhani, *Mullá Ḥusayn: Disciple at Dawn,* p. 21.

7 John Walbridge, *Mulla `Abdu'l-Karim Qazvíni (Mirza Ahmad Katib),* 1997. Available at: https://bahai-library.com/walbridge_encyclopedia_abdul-karim_Qazvíni

8 Nabíl-i-A'ẓam, *The Dawn-Breakers,* p. 592

9 The Báb, *Persian Bayán,* 9:2.

10 *Selections from the Writings of E. G. Browne on the Bábí and Bahá'í Religions.,* p. 61

Quddús used to say: "I am the regent to the Lord of the Age [the Báb]."[1] An Orthodox Muslim source, Shaykhu'l-'Ajam, certainly biased, wrote that Quddús began

> ... seducing people who came frequently and gladly to see him [telling them]: "I am the man of God. I am the representative of the Lord of the Time [the Mahdí]. Whatever I say, harken unto me: These mullás of ours, whatever they say, is a lie. [But] what I say is the truth." And they replied: "Whatever you say, is the truth."[2]
>
> He [Quddús] said: "Garlic is forbidden by religion, do not eat it! Onion is prohibited; do not eat it! Water pipe is unlawful; do not smoke it!" One by one, those who cherished him refrained from eating garlic and onion and from smoking the water pipe. Whatever he said, they would take his words. One night he was taken as a guest to somewhere. That night the meal was chela pilaf.[3] He had eaten two or three mouthfuls of the pilaf [when] he became aware that there were raisins in it; he stopped eating. Then they brought him water for ablution. He rinsed his hands and lips. People said: "Why did he do so? Was the pilaf unclean that he rinsed his hands and lips?" Later on, on two or three occasions [a similar episode] took place and he did the same thing. Little by little, [those] who were not his intimates said: "He must be a Bábí; if he is not, [then] why does he do this?"[4]

---

1 Habib Borjian, *A Mázandaráni Account of the Babi Incident at Shaikh Ṭabarsí*, p. 390.

2 Shaykh ol-Ajam (1866, p. 205). Cited in Kurt Greussing, *The Babi Movement in Iran 1844–52*, p. 262.

3 White rice cooked in garlic, onion, raisins, etc.

4 Habib Borjian, *A Mázandaráni Account of the Babi Incident at Shaikh Ṭabarsí*, pp. 390–391.

The author Avarih, before apostatising from the Faith, wrote two volumes of history where he stated that garlic and onion were proscribed in the Bábí religion.[1,2]

The opposition of Mullá Qásim

Because he was speaking publicly about the Faith of the Báb, Quddús was forced to stop preaching and was isolated. He was later expelled from the neighbourhood of his father's house at the instigation of the local cleric, Mullá Qásim,[3] owing to growing hostility. A non-Bahá'í source relates that:

> The news came to the attention of Mullá Qásim, the Imám. "Curse be upon him .... One who is a Moslem does not do this. He must be exiled from this neighbourhood. If he stays here, he will commit many evil things and will lead the people astray." By Mullá Qásim's order he [Quddús] was expelled from Chihar Shambih Písh. He left and with him all his companions. A while later, he came back and stayed for about a month. He was driven out again. He went. A couple of months later he returned. He was refused to stay. [Finally] he lodged there in Píá-kúlá [پی کلاه].[4,5]

The same source states that when Mullá Ḥusayn arrived in Mázindarán in April of 1848, Quddús was still in Píá-kúlá a small agricultural village engaged mainly in rice farming which hosted a small shrine of a Muslim saint where people went for pilgrimage. The short ten-kilometre distance from Bárfurúsh would have allowed him to pay short visits, which would go unchecked, from his "exile"

---

1 This account was written by a Muslim source most likely misinformed about the new Faith. The Báb forbade smoking and using *asafoetida* (Persian انگژه, *anguzha*), a spice with a strong unpleasant smell and taste, because both "are of an odor contrary to purity" (*Persian Bayán* 9:7). Perhaps the statement cited is unreliable, exaggeration or a personal preference from Quddús. The Báb did not ban raisins, garlic and onion as the text suggests. There is a hadith (tradition) indicating that Muḥammad prohibited eating raw garlic and onions before coming to a mosque because of the bad breath. Another hadith forbids mixing raisins and dried dates. What the Báb recommended was the use of nice odours as part of His concept of refinement (*laṭáfat*): *"Whosoever is adorned with the virtues of God, glorified and exalted be He, must make use of perfumes, and inhale sweet-smelling substances such as clove or other creations of God, the Exalted, the Mighty"* (*Selections of the Writing of the Báb*, p. 79). Intoxicating liquors, and drugs were definitely prohibited in the *Persian Bayán* (9:8) and opium was allowed on medical reasons as it was the only pain relief available in those times.

2 It is possible that the alleged controversial prohibition of garlic and onion might have circulated among the Bábís. The author Avarih, before apostatising from the Faith, wrote two volumes of history (*al-Kawākeb al-dorrīya*, 1914) where, without providing any source, he stated that garlic and onion were proscribed. Thanks to Dr Khazeh Fananapazir for this information.

3 Habib Borjian, *A Mázandaráni Account of the Babi Incident at Shaikh Ṭabarsí*, p. 391.

4 Habib Borjian, *A Mázandaráni Account of the Babi Incident at Shaikh Ṭabarsí*, p. 391.

5 Píjá-kuláh (پیجا کلا) at 36.563889, 52.583056

away from there. Abbas Amanat wrote of this growing opposition to Quddús by the local clergy, with "persecutions, house arrest, and physical threats increased, culminating in banishment from his hometown".[1] In his words:

> No doubt other Mullás—including Mullá Qásim, the Imám Jum'ih of Aqrúd—were instrumental in manipulating the public, and particularly the lutls (brigands or ruffians), against Quddús. From the second day of his arrival in Bárfurús͟h, he remarks, he was the subject of allegations and mistreatment. He acted with "utmost modesty" and had no desire to benefit from "what they possess of worldly luxuries," but nevertheless he was the target of "shameless slanders". In spite of his appeals for opening a dialogue with the mujtahids, the growing concern over Quddús' popularity must have encouraged the gradual formation of a coalition against him—a coalition that most probably took advantage of urban rivalries and recruited from the lutls [ruffians] as well as the tulláb [religious students] of Bárfurús͟h's seven madrasas. Hence, even prior to 1264/1848, the seeds of the far broader conflict of Ṭabarsí had been sown. The chief actors—the nonconformist millenarian, the forces of established 'Ulamá supported by the state, the factional urban divisions, the conflicting economic interests—are all present.[2]

Quddús and the Sa'ídu'l-'Ulamá'

When Quddús returned to Bárfurús͟h he was warmly received by his family and by S͟harí'atmadár, his former mentor. However, the Sa'ídu'l-'Ulamá', did not like his presence in the city as the religious beliefs of the young man and S͟harí'atmadár were in opposition to his own. S͟harí'atmadár was a protector of the Bábís and some sources suggest that he might have secretly been a Bábí.[3]

Sa'ídu'l-'Ulamá' is referred to by Shoghi Effendi as the "the fanatical, the ferocious and shameless mujtahid of Bárfurús͟h".[4] Furthermore, his behaviour was characterised as immersed in "irreligion, immorality, and worldliness".[5] To this cleric, Quddús wrote before:

> And fear lest thou shouldst be held to account before the [Hidden] Imám (may God hasten his glad advent!) because thou art commissioned to oppose him. By thy truth, today is not as it was aforetime, and verily I have a great message of joy: were it permitted to me I would inform thee of it; but His will become manifest in its time.[6]

---

[1] Abbas Amanat, *Resurrection and Renewal*, p. 188.
[2] Abbas Amanat, *Resurrection and Renewal*, pp. 185–186.
[3] Moojan Momen, *The Bahá'í Communities of Iran*, vol. I, p. 304.
[4] Shoghi Effendi, *God Passes By*, p. 83.
[5] E. G. Browne, *Taríkh-i-Jadíd*, p. 92.
[6] E. G. Browne, *Materials for the Study of the Bábí Religion*, p. 210.

Sa'ídu'l-'Ulamá' was a mujtahid, an authorised expounder of Islamic law and the highest rank of Shí'ite divine.[1] As religious judges they had immense power over the citizens and presided over their own courts from their mosques. Moojan Momen wrote of one of his court members being drawn to Quddús:

> Mullá Mahdí, known as Áqá Dada<u>sh</u>, was a cleric who worked in the religious court of Sa'ídu'l-'Ulamá'. When Quddús came to Bárfurú<u>sh</u> and started to spread the religion of the Báb, Sa'ídu'l-'Ulamá' sent Mullá Mahdí, to investigate the matter. Mullá Mahdí, was captivated by Quddús's words and reported back to Sa'ídu'l-'Ulamá'. The latter was angry and dismissed him from his work. Owing to the extreme pressure exerted by Sa'ídu'l-'Ulamá', Mullá Mahdí, kept a low profile for some years and even migrated to Ṭihrán for a time. After Sa'ídu'l-'Ulamá's death in 1853, however, he was able to return to Bárfurú<u>sh</u> and became one of the leaders of the Bábí and later Bahá'í communities. He was skilled in medicine and alchemy.[2]

His rank as a mujtahid not only made Sa'ídu'l-'Ulamá' proud and arrogant, but it also made him jealous of the "little studied"[3] regarded Quddús who was rapidly gaining a growing local popularity for his sanctity and wisdom. Haughtiness was a common characteristic amongst the Persian divines. The Báb had previously delivered rebukes to well-known religious figures for their conceit and their failure to use their position of authority to guide their followers to the new Revelation. The Báb wrote that persecution of Him by the Islamic clergy was based on ignorance of their own religion:

> *As to those who have debarred themselves from the Revelation of God, they have indeed failed to understand the significance of a single letter of the Qur'án, nor have they obtained the slightest notion of the Faith of Islám, otherwise they would not have turned away from God ... thinking that they are doing righteous work for the sake of God.*[4]

There is also another story on the circumstances surrounding Quddús when he was actively teaching the Faith in Bárfurú<u>sh</u>. This involved a believer named Riḍá [Reza] <u>Kh</u>án and the Sa'ídu'l-'Ulamá'. Riḍá <u>Kh</u>án was the son of the Master of the Horse to Muḥammad <u>Sh</u>áh. As such, the family enjoyed many privileges and the respect of the people. Riḍá <u>Kh</u>án had previously met the Báb, Quddús and Mullá Ḥusayn. The following is an account of his activities in Bárfurú<u>sh</u>:

> When, for instance, Jináb-i-Quddús first began to preach the doctrine in Mázindarán, and the Sa'ídu'l-'Ulamá', being informed of this, made strenuous efforts to do him injury, Riḍá <u>Kh</u>án at once hastened to Mázindarán, and, whenever Jináb-i-Quddús went forth from his house, used, in spite of his high position and the respect to which he was

---

[1] The Báb in Todd Lawson, *The terms 'Remembrance' and 'Gate'*, p. 19.
[2] Moojan Momen, *The Bahá'í Communities of Iran*, vol. I, p. 306.
[3] Abbas Amanat, *Resurrection and Renewal*, p. 184.
[4] The Báb, *Selections*, p. 140.

accustomed, to walk on foot before him with his drawn sword over his shoulder; seeing which, the malignant feared to take any liberty .... For some while, Riḍá Khán remained after this fashion in Mázindarán, until he accompanied Jináb-i-Quddús to Mashhad.[1]

Exchanges between Quddús and the Sa'ídu'l-'Ulamá'

Quddús addressed these words to Sa'ídu'l-'Ulamá':

> For what worldly desires are you harassing this adherent to God's clan? Though I enjoy no high status, in the eye of my forefathers, may peace be upon them, I am no less than the dispersed people of Israel .... I do not know of any other refuge and retreat but to the Lord of the Time, may God hasten his Advent .... Neither have I claimed any cause, nor have I interfered in or disposed over anything. I have taken the path of Sayyid-i Sajjad ['Alí Ibn Ḥusayn, the Fourth Imám] peace be upon him, and it is going to be like this till God will reveal His command ....[2] Leave me alone and let me retire in the solitude of my abode and engage in what is the tradition of my forefathers.[3]

The following story highlights the relationships between Quddús, Sharí'atmadár and Sa'ídu'l-'Ulamá':

> When Quddús arrived at Bárfurúsh to settle, a prominent and wealthy cleric organised a feast inviting Sa'ídu'l-'Ulamá' who was the local Mujtahid [high level cleric] and Sharí'atmadár who was another prominent cleric.[4]
>
> His Holiness [Quddús] was invited to a meeting. The first person to arrive was Sa'ídu'l-'Ulamá' and he went straight to the seat of prominence, which is customarily located furthest from the door. Then the host asked him to explain the meaning of one of the verses of the *Qur'án* and Sa'ídu'l-'Ulamá' mentioned something which was not accepted by the host.
>
> Then Sharí'atmadár came in and sat down and the host repeated the same question to him but his commentary was not acceptable to the host.
>
> The host told them that when Quddús arrives, he will ask the same question of him so that everyone may benefit from his explanation. When Quddús arrived, the same question was asked of him, but Sa'ídu'l-'Ulamá' became very upset by this request from the host. He felt disrespected because his own response was not accepted, and the host wanted to repeat the same question to Quddús for everyone's benefit.

---

1 E. G. Browne, *Taríkh-i-Jadíd*, p. 99.

2 Great-grandson of the Prophet Muḥammad who was known for his patience and a spirit of conciliation.

3 Abbas Amanat, *Resurrection and Renewal*, pp. 185–186

4 Fazel Mazandarani, *Taríkh Ẓuhúr al-Ḥaqq*, vol. 3, pp. 355–368.

Sa'ídu'l-'Ulamá' was very disturbed and said, "Why are you unkind to me? Is it correct that after so many years of study, we ask this youth with little education and try to benefit from his knowledge?"

Quddús then entered the meeting. When the same question was asked of him, the sea of his words flowed over those present like waves of wisdom impressing everyone. Consequently, everyone was drawn into Quddús' sea of knowledge. Everyone was much impressed with Quddús except Sa'ídu'l-'Ulamá'.

The fire of Sa'ídu'l-'Ulamá's jealousy and animosity became higher and more severe. Before a meal, there is a tradition that the servant brings a jar of water for the guests to wash their hands prior to eating. The jar of water was brought to Quddús, but because of his respect for Sharí'atmadár, he did not wish to use the water first and instead offered it to Sharí'atmadár. Sharí'atmadár, in turn, did not accept the water and offered it politely to Sa'ídu'l-'Ulamá'. They wanted to make up for Sa'ídu'l-'Ulamá' who was upset and angry. However, rather than being grateful, Sa'ídu'l-'Ulamá' thought that they were trying to pick on him and became offended further. He shouted and asked for another jar of water from one of his servants, rejecting the host's offer.

After the meal, the host brought some silver coins and said, "Give them to Sa'ídu'l-'Ulamá' and say this is my contribution in honour of my father, and if you could please perform fasting and say obligatory prayers in the name of my father". However, Sa'ídu'l-'Ulamá' refused the coins and said, "I do not do such things", and told Sharí'atmadár, "you do it", in the presence of the guests. He said to give the coins back to Sharí'atmadár and told him, "Take the coins—you are the wise man and knowledgeable and free from all superstitions, you do it".

At this juncture, Sharí'atmadár began sharing some of the writings that Quddús had brought, and read them to Sa'ídu'l-'Ulamá':

"In His Name whom there is none other God but Him the Most Exalted, the Most Great. All praise be to God who hath verily created Muḥammad and His Descendants for the protection of His Religion in the realms of the seen and the unseen".

Thus Sharí'atmadár was reminding Sa'ídu'l-'Ulamá' that religion must be the source of protection for people rather than arguing or denying each other and creating disunity.[1]

Quddús predicts his martyrdom

There are several stories revealing how Quddús predicted the episode of Shaykh Ṭabarsí and his own martyrdom while he was still living in Bárfurúsh. According to Fazel Mazandarani:

---

1 Fazel Mazandarani, *Tarí*kh* Ẓuhúr al-Ḥaqq*, vol. 3, p. 322.

One day, after taking a public bath, Quddús was talking with some of the companions. He had a sharp pen-knife, paring his nails. He accidentally cut his fingers, and a drop of blood fell. Two of the friends, Áqá Rasúl Bihnamirí[1] and Mullá Riḍá Sháh upon observing this incident were upset. Quddús looked upon them and with a smile said: "If observing such a small injury makes you distraught and sad how you can bear to witness my body slaughtered and cut into pieces body and soaked in blood."[2]

So likewise, in the exhortation known as "the Eternal Witness", which he [Quddús] wrote to Jináb-i-Bábu'l-Báb [Mullá Ḥusayn] while on his way to Khurásán, and wherein, besides foreshadowing his martyrdom, he made known to him how he should die together with seventy righteous men. He wrote, "I shall bury my body with my own hands", by which expression he signified that none would bury him [but that one of themselves would succeed in accomplishing his interment]. Again in that same year, he had repeatedly said to his sister and his step-mother, "This year all manner of troubles will befall you because of the love ye bear me but be ye patient and thankful when affliction comes, and the predestined blow falls, and display resignation and fortitude."[3]

---

1 Áqá Rasúl was the chief of the village and also a wealthy and influential landowner. The village was one day away walking from Bárfurúsh. He had previously sent a messenger to Mashhad to interview Mullá Ḥusayn about the claims of the Báb. As a result of his conversion, a large number of people from his village converted. It has been said that up to one-hundred and twenty people from that locality joined later Shaykh Ṭabarsí (E. G. Browne, ed., *Taríkh-i-Jadíd*, p. 67, & Moojan Momen, *The Bahá'í Communities of Iran*, vol. 1, p. 312).

2 Fazel Mazandarani, *Taríkh Ẓuhúr al-Ḥaqq*, vol. 3, p. 333.

3 E. G. Browne, *Taríkh-i-Jadíd*, p. 90.

8
Two extraordinary friends reunited

Chapter content
Two prominent friends
Two Bábí leaders
Brilliant service records
The Hidden Treasure of God
Mullá Ḥusayn and Quddús reunited
Ascendency of Quddús
Leadership upon shoulders of Quddús
Mullá Ḥusayn and the Sa'ídu'l-'Ulamá'
Hands of the Cause of God

These are the beautiful words that Bahá'u'lláh revealed in honour of Mullá Ḥusayn and Quddús after their martyrdoms in February and May 1849, respectively:

> *Ye are the dawning-places of the Will of God and the daysprings of His Cause, the embodiments of His command and the sources of His might. Ye are the storehouses of His knowledge and the treasuries of His secrets, the repositories of His decree and the exponents of His behest. Ye are the pearls of the ocean of His generosity and the gems of the mines of His munificence, the suns of the firmament of His grace and the moons of the heaven of His bounty.*[1]

Other Letters of the Living were also given beautiful spiritual appellations, In referring to Ṭáhirih, the Báb once said "What am I to say regarding her whom the Tongue of Power and Glory [Bahá'u'lláh] has named Ṭáhirih (the Pure One)?".[2] The second Letter of the Living, Mullá 'Alíy-i-Basṭámí, who according to the Báb was "*the first to leave the House of God* (Shíráz) *and the first to suffer for His sake* ..."[3] was symbolically identified as the return to earth of 'Alí, the first Imám and son-in-law of Prophet Muḥammad.[4]

Two prominent friends

Among the eighteen Letters of the Living to accept the Báb between May and June 1844, Mullá Ḥusayn was the first and Quddús was the last. Both were among the most prominent believers and did not meet again for four years. After all those years of simply being theology students, they had now become true luminaires, if not spiritual giants in the field of service.

---

1 Bahá'u'lláh, *Tablet of Visitation for Mullá Ḥusayn and Quddús*. See Appendix part I.

2 Nabíl-i-A'ẓam, *The Dawn-Breakers*, p. 84.

3 Nabíl-i-A'ẓam, *The Dawn-Breakers*, p. 87.

4 Abbas Amanat, *Resurrection and Renewal*, p. 192; and The Báb, *Persian Bayán* 1:3.

Quddús and Mullá Ḥusayn had been very good friends for many years. They were both disciples of Siyyid Káẓim in Karbilá, prior to the Declaration of the Báb. Theirs was a deep and enduring friendship that weathered all the ups and downs of life. Both Letters of the Living studied at the same religious seminary in Mas͟hhad. Mullá Ḥusayn was about nine years older than Quddús.

All indications are that both were among the favourite students of Siyyid Káẓim. Quddús, although very young, about 18 years old at that time, had stood out, especially for his humility, purity and knowledge. Mullá Ḥusayn, distinguished himself for his courage, erudition, and his judgment and sensitivity for the Word of God and the sacred writings. Of course, in general, they shared all these qualities.

A reunion of these two spiritual giants occurred one day in April 1848 in Bárfurús͟h. Since the time they were last together in S͟híráz, and having both individually recognized the Báb, they each had experienced many significant events. As students of religion, they had undergone tests and episodes so extraordinary that very little of their original conditions remained. It could be said that they had been forged anew as a new race of heroes and saints.

If meeting an old friend is a pleasant experience—to dust off memories and talk with enthusiasm and curiosity about the passing of the years—it is not surprising how special was that meeting between Mullá Ḥusayn and Quddús. The former was a traveller *par excellence,* while Quddús, residing in Bárfurús͟h and surrounding areas, had been conducting extensive teaching among the local population.

They came from totally different backgrounds: whereas Quddús was the son of an illiterate and poor rice farmer having lost his mother while a child, Mullá Ḥusayn's parents were a wealthy cloth dyer and a talented poetess.[1] "The recognition of the station of Quddús," Adib Taherzadeh commented, "came to Mullá Ḥusayn in a mysterious way reminiscent of his memorable experience of his first meeting with the Báb some years earlier".[2]

Two Bábí leaders

There was a perception among some believers, because of the differences in their amazing individual capabilities and perhaps because Quddús' activities were circumscribed to his province, that Mullá Ḥusayn "was unrivalled in excellence and learning, while *Jináb-i-Quddús* appeared to possess no special merit or distinction, save that he had accompanied His Holiness the Supreme on the pilgrimage to Mecca."[3] As we shall see, this perception would change after the famous encounter described in this chapter.

---

1 In Ahang Rabbani, *The Genesis of the Bahá'í Faith in K͟hurásán*, Chapter 2, p. 2.

2 Adib Taherzadeh, *The Revelation of Bahá'u'lláh,* vol. 4, p. 210.

3 E. G. Browne, *Tarík͟h-i-Jadíd*, p. 43.

According to 'Abdu'l-Bahá, prior to their meeting in April at Bárfurúsh, Mullá Ḥusayn was considered *"the leader of all and the arbiter appealed to alike by the noble and the humble of this sect"* [the Bábís].[1] 'Abdu'l-Bahá, is reported to have said: *"In those days, His Holiness Quddús was not recognized as a man of high rank and authority. He was only accounted as a religious scholar ....*[2]

In the Bábí dispensation, the Báb, as the Primal Point, was at the highest level of authority. He wrote in the *Qayyúmu'l-Asmá*: *"I swear by the One true God, herein lieth the vicegerency of God."*[3] Below the Báb there is an unstructured hierarchy of living characters. The Báb honoured certain commendable disciples with the title of "Mirrors". Other prominent followers were called "Guides" and "Witnesses". Witnesses, or more precisely "Witnesses of the *Bayán*", were those who, until the advent of Bahá'u'lláh, were to testify to the validity and authenticity of the words of the Blessed Báb. Together, the *Letters of the Living, Mirrors, Guides*, and *Witnesses* formed a non-linear hierarchy in the Revelation of the Báb.[4] It was not a governance structure like in past religions but one for spiritual empowerment and nourishment.

The Báb seemed to have small regard for earthly ranks and stations:

> *... among the lowly servants whom no one would imagine being of any merit, how great the number who will be honoured with true faith and on whom the Fountainhead of generosity will bestow the robe of authority.*[5]

The Báb loved Quddús and Mullá Ḥusayn equally and once referred to them as *"My beloved ones, Quddús and Mullá Ḥusayn."*[6] However, the Báb wisely let Mullá Ḥusayn naturally recognise Quddús' primacy rather than dictating it at the first instance. With this arrangement, the Cause grew enormously in the years ahead. In all, humility was a quality highly praised by the Báb:

> *... know thou that neither being a man of learning nor being a follower is in itself a source of glory. If thou art a man of learning, thy knowledge becometh an honor, and if thou art a follower, thine adherence unto leadership becometh an honor, only when these conform to the good-pleasure of God.*[7]

Brilliant service records

The Báb spoke eloquently and lovingly of Quddús and Mullá Ḥusayn in His Writings because of the spiritual qualities shown by them in their services in the

---

1 'Abdu'l-Bahá, *A Traveller's Narrative,* p. 19.

2 Ali-Kuli Khan, *1906 Pilgrim Notes of Ali-Kuli Khan,* pp. 63–64. Available https://bahai-library.com/ali-khan_pilgrim-notes_1906

3 The Báb, *Selections,* p. 66.

4 See Shoghi Effendi, *God Passes By,* pp. 89–90.

5 The Báb, *Selections,* 83–84.

6 Nabíl-i-A'ẓam, *The Dawn-Breakers,* pp. 431–432.

7 The Báb, *Selections,* p. 124.

path of God. Mullá Ḥusayn was called the "Primal Mirror", the "Beloved of My Heart", and the "Gate of the Gate" *"whom 'the creatures, raised in the beginning and in the end' of the Bábí Dispensation, envy, and will continue to envy until the 'Day of Judgment'."*[1] Quddús, on the other hand, was praised as the "Last Name of God", a very exalted position.[2]

They both eventually offered their lives in the path of the Cause of God in the same year, during the episode of S͟hayk͟h Ṭabarsí, where Quddús affectionately called Mullá Ḥusayn "Sulṭán Manṣúr" [the Victorious King] and Mullá Ḥusayn affectionately called Quddús "Ḥabíb" [the beloved].[3]

Mullá Ḥusayn had been privileged to be in the blessed presence of his Beloved three times, including the Báb's Declaration in S͟híráz, and had performed dedicated service in risky and extensive teaching travels over several years. In turn, Quddús had the honour of being in the Báb's company for nine uninterrupted months on the occasion of the pilgrimage to Mecca. Quddús had visited many villages and cities, sowing the seeds of the Faith, and he was among the first to suffer persecution for the Cause of God in Persia.

It might have been a pleasant surprise for some that this youth, Quddús, had been chosen from among older and more experienced believers, or even from those of a higher socio-economic status. The issue of Quddús' age was raised in a disparaging way.[4] However, the same questions were raised regarding the youthfulness of the Báb, where His adversaries questioned, *"How can He speak of God while in truth His age is no more than twenty-five?"*[5]

Both Mullá Ḥusayn and Quddús had received important missions on behalf of the Báb. For his part, Quddús travelled to Kirmán in mid-1845 to convince Ḥájí Mírzá Karim K͟hán to stop pretending being Siyyid Káẓim's successor,[6] while Mullá Ḥusayn was the instrument through which Bahá'u'lláh, Mírzá Ḥusayn 'Alí, then publicly accepted the Faith of the Báb in September of 1844.[7] If Quddús was the "most esteemed disciple of Siyyid Káẓim",[8] Mullá Ḥusayn was "his leading representative".[9]

---

1 Shoghi Effendi, *God Passes By*, p. 50.
2 Shoghi Effendi, *God Passes By*, p. 49.
3 Sepehr Manuchehri, *Brief Analysis of the Features of Bábí Resistance*, n.p.
4 Nabíl-i-A'ẓam, *The Dawn-Breakers*, p. 297; & Fazel, Mazandarani, *Taríkh Ẓuhúr al-Ḥaqq*, vol. 3, p. 322..
5 The Báb, *Selections*, p. 47.
6 Nabíl-i-A'ẓam, *The Dawn-Breakers*, pp. 180-182
7 Nabíl-i-A'ẓam, *The Dawn-Breakers*, pp. 103-107.
8 Shoghi Effendi, *God Passes By*, p. 8.
9 Nabíl-i-A'ẓam, *The Dawn-Breakers*, p. 47.

The Hidden Treasure of God

Perhaps because Quddús' superb activities were to be confined to his own town and surrounding nearby areas, the Báb called him a "*Hidden Treasure*" [of God] (Ganj-i-Pinhán-i-Khudá).[1] A "hidden treasure" is a term used to designate a highly valuable trove whose location is either not revealed to everyone or, if found by luck, seeming to belong to no one. Hidden treasures are either left buried or been abandoned. Therefore, they are secrets, just as was the high position of Quddús. It was a treasure well-guarded by the green and dense forests of the Mázindarán region.

Some choose to keep any discoveries to themselves in order to covertly hide the treasures, just as they might conceal any treasure for fear of losing it. In the Parable of the Hidden Treasure, Jesus said: "The kingdom of heaven is like a treasure hidden in a field. When a man found it, he hid it again, and then in his joy went and sold all he had and bought that field" (*Matthew* 13:44). He reckoned immediately that the treasure was much more valuable than all his earthly possessions because for him it was not a sacrifice but a gain. To his wonder, God had placed the treasure as a free gift for him to find. In truth, it was a divine treasure that could only be seen and comprehended with spiritual eyes.

There are also those who, upon finding a treasure, decide to share their luck and happiness with others. Some might argue that a hidden treasure is not a true treasure until it has been discovered and appreciated by a community. In fact, any treasure is waiting to be discovered so that the glittering gems can dazzle people. The discoverer will display the gems and will not stop talking about his priceless discovery out of his happiness and delight. A mystical treasure is so spiritually valuable that it seems destined to be revealed for the delight of those who see with inner vision.

The initial reasons for the owner to keep the treasure secret are also important. The Báb, being "the proprietor" had restricted Quddús' to Mázindarán Province, unlike the other Letters of the Living, so that he could focus on teaching the Faith in that area and also to help him maintain a low profile to be protected from the martyrdoms that began to occur in Persia.[2] It appears that the Báb waited for an appropriate time for Quddús to have a national impact, a time when the multiplicative growth effect of the partnership of Quddús and Mullá Ḥusayn would trigger a major reaction throughout the country.

At their last meeting in the prison of Máh-Kú in March 1848, the Báb had commanded Mullá Ḥusayn to direct his steps to the province of Mázindarán where he would discover a precious, priceless treasure. He was given no other specific mission or hint other than to travel to Mázindarán where Quddús lived.

---

1 Nabíl-i-A'ẓam, *The Dawn-Breakers,* p. 262.

2 Peter Smith and Moojan Momen, *Bábí Martyrs.* In *Encyclopaedia Iranica.* Available https://iranicaonline.org/articles/martyrs-babi-babi

Mázindarán at the time was considered to be an Iranian "jungle" that was bordered by the vast Caspian Sea.

Mázindarán Province was the ultimate destination of Mullá Ḥusayn, where *"The nature of your task will ... be revealed to you, and strength and guidance will be bestowed upon you that you may be fitted to render your service to His Cause."*[1] During the 1,100 km journey, Mullá Ḥusayn was accompanied by his travel companion Qambar-'Alí. Mullá Ḥusayn must have been deeply reflecting on what the Báb intended. The chronicler Nabíl relates that Mullá Ḥusayn:

> ... faithful to the instructions he had received, stopped at every town and village that the Báb had directed him to visit, gathered the faithful, conveyed to them the love, the greetings, and the assurances of their beloved Master, quickened afresh their zeal, and exhorted them to remain steadfast in His way.[2]

The immanent reunion of Mullá Ḥusayn and Quddús would prove to be a very significant event in the history of the Bábí Faith. The Báb had inferred that the "Hidden Treasure" would be directing the main events of the Cause. This visit, though short—just two days—was unique. It was not only the informal meeting of two old friends but was also how one—Mullá Ḥusayn—recognised the elevated merits and the seniority of the other—Quddús. The account also reveals how Mullá Ḥusayn finally realised that he had found his "Hidden Treasure" promised by the Báb.

Mullá Ḥusayn and Quddús reunited

When Mullá Ḥusayn arrived in Bárfurú<u>sh</u>, he went straight to the house of Quddús in Píjá-Kulá,[3] who, with great affection, welcomed and attended him personally, wiping the dust from the trip and attending to the blistering wounds on his feet, the result of long days of travel. "Upon his arrival in that city," according to Nabíl, "Mullá Ḥusayn went directly to the home of Quddús and was affectionately received by him. Quddús himself waited upon his guest and did his utmost to provide whatever seemed necessary for his comfort."[4]

Some believers who had heard Mullá Ḥusayn had arrived came to meet and greet him. Quddús lavished praise on his guest and, with much respect, offered him the seat of honour. Quddús invited the believers from the village to his house for dinner. They all rejoiced at the presence of Mullá Ḥusayn as they had already heard of him, the First Letter of the Living. Although there is not much information about what transpired at the meal, we can imagine how joyful the meeting must have been and how the feelings of unity and service were renewed. After the guests had departed, Quddús asked Mullá Ḥusayn many questions about

---

1 Nabíl-i-A'ẓam, *The Dawn-Breakers*, p. 260.

2 Nabíl-i-A'ẓam, *The Dawn-Breakers*, p. 260.

3 A small village (36.563549, 52.583363) 8 km NW of Bárfurú<u>sh</u>.

4 Nabíl-i-A'ẓam, *The Dawn-Breakers*, p. 262.

the life of their Beloved Whom Mullá Ḥusayn had recently visited in the prison of Máh-Kú.

Mullá Ḥusayn responded by sharing many momentous insights from His words. For instance, His instructions about the service he would perform in the days ahead, especially at a "Feast of the Sacrifice" where he would be martyred. Mullá Ḥusayn also shared that the Báb did not promise that they would meet again, as He had done on previous occasions, from which Mullá Ḥusayn deduced that he himself would soon be sacrificed in His path. The Báb also forewarned him, saying, *"Arise and gird up the loin of endeavour, and let nothing detain you from achieving your destiny* [reference to Quddús's martyrdom]. *Having attained your destination, prepare yourself to receive Us, for We too shall ere long follow you"*.[1]

The Báb, Mullá Ḥusayn continued, shared with Quddús that in Mázindarán he would find a *"Hidden Treasure"* that *"will unveil to your eyes the character of the task you are destined to perform."*[2] When he finished narrating his impressions, Quddús asked whether he had brought any letter or epistle from the Báb. At Mullá Ḥusayn's negative response, Quddús handed him a manuscript and asked him to read it.[3]

Mullá Ḥusayn did so, and upon reading one of its pages, a sudden expression of great surprise and amazement appeared on his face. Nabíl wrote that Mullá Ḥusayn was able to appreciate "the transcendent sublimity of the writings of Quddús", realising "the true worth and merit of those special gifts with which both the person and the utterance of Quddús were endowed".[4]

Ascendency of Quddús

It was evident then that the manuscript's content was unique, particularly for a person like Mullá Ḥusayn, who was trained to analyse religious writings and to recognise anything that was inspired. "I can well realise that the Author of these words," Mullá Ḥusayn exclaimed, "has drawn His inspiration from that Fountainhead which stands immeasurably superior to the sources whence the learning of men is ordinarily derived. I hereby testify to my whole-hearted recognition of the sublimity of these words and to my unquestioned acceptance of the truth which they reveal."[5]

When Quddús did not respond, Mullá Ḥusayn realised his silence indicated that Quddús was the author of the manuscript. Suddenly, he stood and bowing his head, he solemnly declared:

---

1 Nabíl-i-A'ẓam, *The Dawn-Breakers,* p. 262.

2 Nabíl-i-A'ẓam, *The Dawn-Breakers,* p. 262.

3 Nabíl-i-A'ẓam stated that the writings shown were authored by Quddús (*The Dawn-Breakers,* p. 264).

4 Nabíl-i-A'ẓam, *The Dawn-Breakers,* pp. 264–5.

5 Nabíl-i-A'ẓam, *The Dawn-Breakers,* p. 263.

The Hidden Treasure of which the Báb has spoken of now lies unveiled before my eyes. Its light has dispelled the gloom of perplexity and doubt. Though my Master be now hidden amid the mountain fastnesses of Á<u>dh</u>irbayján, the sign of His splendour and the revelation of His might stand manifest before me. I have found in Mázindarán the reflection of His glory.[1]

'Abdu'l-Bahá has referred to Quddús' ascendancy and primacy over all Bábís that became evident at that meeting:

After a while certain manners and states issued from him such that all, acting with absolute confidence, considered obedience to him [Quddús] *as an impregnable stronghold, so that even Mullá Ḥusayn of Bushrúyih ... used to behave in his presence with great humility and with the self-abasement of a lowly servant.*[2]

According to 'Abdu'l-Bahá, Mullá Ḥusayn exclaimed, "I did not know before the station of Quddús. Tonight, I realize that I am less than the dust of his feet".[3] Recalling that episode, the Hand of the Cause of God Keith Ransom-Kehler wrote in 1932:

But in an unused portion of my being, like a treasure hidden in a field, lies something tremulous and unforgettable, something with a wistful fragrance and tenderness, something that lures and stills me, something strangely startling and tranquilizing—the recollection of how the Mullá Ḥusayn stood with folded arms upon the threshold, like a servant to the man [Quddús] who had been twice preferred before him[4] ... that no attention or respect might ever be lacking to that one whom he might so easily have regarded as a usurper of his position; of how, though numbers wished to acclaim him, he remained indifferent to their adulation; of how, in every instance, before and after the Declaration of his Lord, his eye never deviated from that Figure of Divine Perfection upon which his life was stayed.[5]

Leadership upon shoulders of Quddús

'Abdu'l-Bahá, is reported to have said:

During that night various conversations and explanations took place between the two. This acquainted Bábu'l-Báb [Mullá Ḥusayn] *with the lofty degree of knowledge possessed by the young scholar, as a consequence of which he made himself humble before him .... To be brief: the principal thing*

---

1 Nabíl-i-A'ẓam, *The Dawn-Breakers*, p. 263.

2 'Abdu'l-Bahá, *A Traveller's Narrative*, p. 19

3 'Abdu'l-Bahá in *Star of the West*, (3:10) 8 September 1912, p. 8.

4 The Báb had chosen Quddús to accompany Him on the pilgrimage to Mecca and later as His second in rank.

5 *Star of the West*, Volume 24, Issue 3, pp. 79–82.

in the Cause of God is humility, meekness and service to the Cause, and not leadership.[1]

From the moment of realising the station of Quddús, Mullá Ḥusayn, would place himself under Quddús' orders and, with tremendous confidence, would be strengthened with the thought that even when the blessed Báb was inaccessible in His confinement, Quddús could assume with justice and capacity the reins of the leadership of the community of the Bábís. From that moment, in addition to a frank and cordial friendship, a sentiment of reverence and respect was added towards Quddús who was now going to be their recognised leader.

Let us now see how this occurred.

The next morning the Bábís gathering again in the house of Quddús were surprised by the scene they were beholding. Whereas the day before, Mullá Ḥusayn was the object of all consideration, now the roles had changed, and Quddús was the centre of reverence and total respect. Mullá Ḥusayn was standing before the door's threshold, implying his complete humility towards Quddús. The believers came to understand the rank and position of Quddús who had patiently brought them into the Faith. They, too, had come to realise the "Hidden Treasure" announced by the Báb.

Mullá Ḥusayn and the Sa'ídu'l-'Ulamá'

On the second and last day together, Quddús entrusted to Mullá Ḥusayn an important mission. He should go to the city of Mashhad, the capital of the province of Khurásán, and build a house suitable for holding meetings of the believers. Quddús would join him afterwards.

Quddús also gave Mullá Ḥusayn the mission to go to the Sa'ídu'l-'Ulamá', the main clergyman of the local people, and clarify for him the verities of the Cause. That Muslim clergyman was perfidious and cruel, and had become a sworn enemy of the Cause of the Báb, directly opposing Quddús' activities.

Mullá Ḥusayn departed the following dawn and, in accordance with Quddús' instructions, went to the Sa'ídu'l-'Ulamá', and courageously defended his faith in front of a public assembly. Unable to respond to the words of Mullá Ḥusayn, the priest lashed out at him with insults.

Nabil relates that:

> Seeing that there was no hope of continuing a conversation, Mullá Ḥusayn came out of the meeting and asked one of the attendees who had been listening with interest to approach Quddús and report all he had seen and heard. "Say to him," Mullá Ḥusayn said, "Inasmuch as you did not specifically command me to seek your presence, I have determined to set

[1] Ali-Kuli Khan, *Pilgrim Notes of Ali-Kuli Khan, 1906*, pp. 63–64. Available https://bahai-library.com/ali-khan_pilgrim-notes_1906

out immediately for Khurásán. I proceed to carry out in their entirety those things which you have instructed me to perform".[1]

According to A. L. M. Nicolas, "After a full exchange of views [with Sa'ídu'l-'Ulamá'], the Bábu'l-Báb [Mullá Ḥusayn] continued his trip towards Khurásán, then, a few days after, our Bárfurúshí [Quddús], having been driven out of the city by Sa'ídu'l-'Ulamá',[2] would have gone to join his colleague in Khurásán."[3] That was most likely May 1848, the fourth anniversary of the Declaration of the Báb.

The future activities of Quddús and Mullá Ḥusayn in Mashhad, capital of Khurásán, represent a decisive move of the Bábí Faith to cast its influence from the west to the east of the country.

Hands of the Cause of God

The lives of Mullá Ḥusayn and Quddús, the first and the last of the Letters of the Living, run in parallel throughout the Dispensation of the Báb. It is noteworthy that in the *Arabic Bayán* the Báb exhorted His followers to prostrate themselves during obligatory prayers on a crystal box containing the dust of the first and the last Bábí believers.[4]

In a Tablet of Visitation[5] revealed by Bahá'u'lláh for Quddús and Mullá Ḥusayn, we read:

> *Ye are they who were awakened by the gentle winds of the dawn of Revelation and were enraptured by the voice of Him Who spoke on Sinai. Ye are they who inhaled the fragrance of the All-Merciful when it wafted from the realm of divine knowledge. By your guidance the thirsty hastened to the onrushing waters of everlasting life and the sinner to the vivifying river of forgiveness and mercy. Ye are the signs of God and His straight Path amongst His creation. Through you all faces turned to the Most Exalted Horizon and every poor one sought the Wellspring of wealth.*[6]

Bahá'u'lláh also referred to them as the "*hands of His Cause in His lands, and stars of His bounty amidst His servants ... they who were awakened by the gentle winds of the dawn of Revelation and were enraptured by the voice of Him Who spoke on Sinai*".[7]

In the Tablet of Visitation revealed in their honour (see Appendix part 1), Bahá'u'lláh addresses both of them in exalted terms and affirms that on account

---

1 Nabíl-i-A'ẓam, *The Dawn-Breakers*, p. 267.

2 4 April 1848, according to Hooshmand Dehghan, *Ganj-i-Pinhán*, p. 206.

3 A. L. M. Nicolas, *Seyyèd Ali-Mohammed dit le Bâb*, p. 289.

4 The Báb, *Arabic Bayán* 10:8. See A. L. M. Nicolas, *Le Beyan Arabe*.

5 Tablets of Visitation (Lawḥ-i-Ziyárih) are specific prayers revealed by the Báb, Bahá'u'lláh or 'Abdu'l-Bahá', to be read when visiting a resting-place of a person.

6 Bahá'u'lláh, Tablet of Visitation for Mullá Ḥusayn and Quddús. See Appendix part 1.

7 ibid.

of their suffering *"the Pen of the Most High hath wailed aloud"* and *"hath been prevented from moving in the realms of remembrance and praise"*, that *"the inmates of the loftiest Paradise have been sorely vexed"* and *"the Maids of heaven have swooned away in their crimson chambers".* Because of their affliction, *"the kindreds of the Verdant Isle* [Mázindarán] *were made to quake on the shore of the sea of glory, causing the sighs of the near ones to ascend and the tears of the sincerely devoted to rain down."*[1]

Moreover, through Quddús and Mullá Ḥusayn, Bahá'u'lláh asserts, *"the suns of knowledge dawned forth, the skies of religion were illumined, the rays of the lights of sciences shone radiantly among various peoples, and the spheres of arts were widened in the world".*[2] They were well aware of the Báb's exhortation to guide and teach others:

> *It is better to guide one soul than to possess all that is on earth, for as long as that guided soul is under the shadow of the Tree of Divine Unity, he and the one who hath guided him will both be recipients of God's tender mercy, whereas possession of earthly things will cease at the time of death.*[3]

The following benedictions of Bahá'u'lláh reflect how much He appreciated both Quddús and Mullá Ḥusayn:

> *Blessed is the poor one who hath set out towards the orient of your wealth, the thirsty one who hath hastened to the shores of the ocean of your favours, the lowly one who hath sought the court of your glory, the ignorant one who hath looked to the dawning-place of your knowledge, the distressed one who hath drawn nigh unto the tabernacle of your majesty and the pavilion of your grace, the ailing one who hath longed for the heavenly river of your healing, the weak one who hath turned to the kingdom of your might, and the friend who hath reached the soft-flowing stream of reunion with you and been honoured with your presence, which excelleth all that hath been fashioned in the universe or appeared in the realm of creation.*[4]

---

1 ibid.

2 ibid.

3 The Báb, *Selections*, p. 77.

4 Bahá'u'lláh, *Tablet of Visitation for Mullá Ḥusayn and Quddús.* See Appendix part 1.

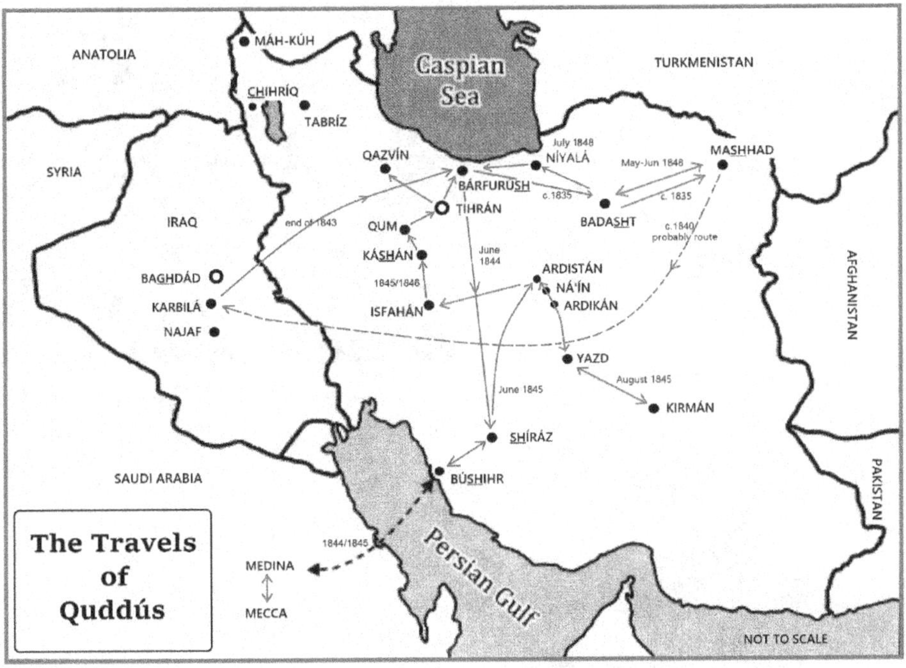

Figure 22: The travels of Quddús
(Courtesy of Pedro Donaires and M. W. Thomas)

Figure 23: Mírzá Karím Khán of Kirmán (Source: Bahá'í Media)

Figure 24: Áqáy-i Kalím, brother of Bahá'u'lláh (Source: Bahá'í Media)

Figure 25: House of Bahá'u'lláh in Ṭihrán (Source: Bahá'í Media)

Figure 26: Castle of Máh-Kú (Source: Bahá'í Media)

Figure 27: The ring of Quddús © Bahá'í World Centre

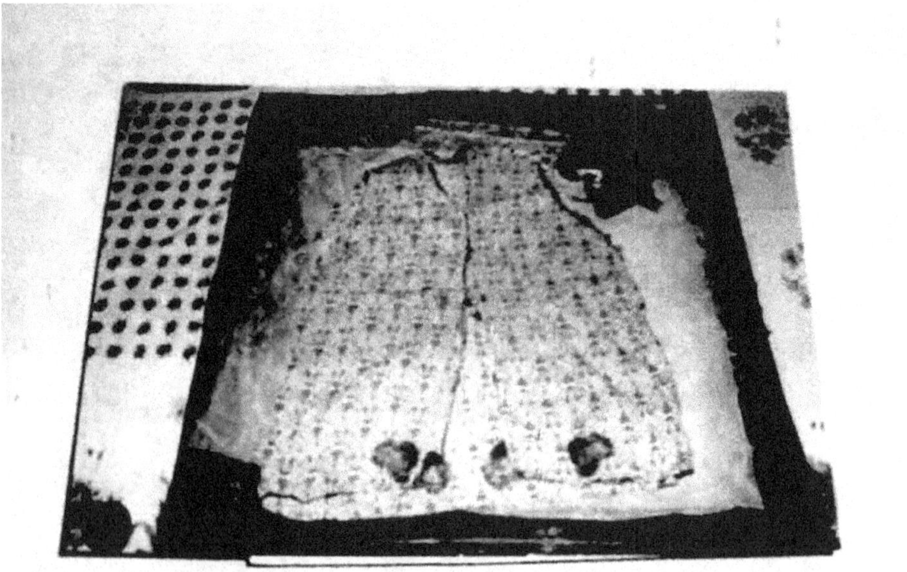

Figure 28: Quddús' shirt and shawl (courtesy of Hooshmand Dehghan)

Figure 29: House of Sa'ídu'l-'Ulamá' in Bárfurú<u>sh</u>

Figure 30: José Rey and Adam Mondschein as Quddús and Mullá Ḥusayn in the film "The Gate" (with permission)

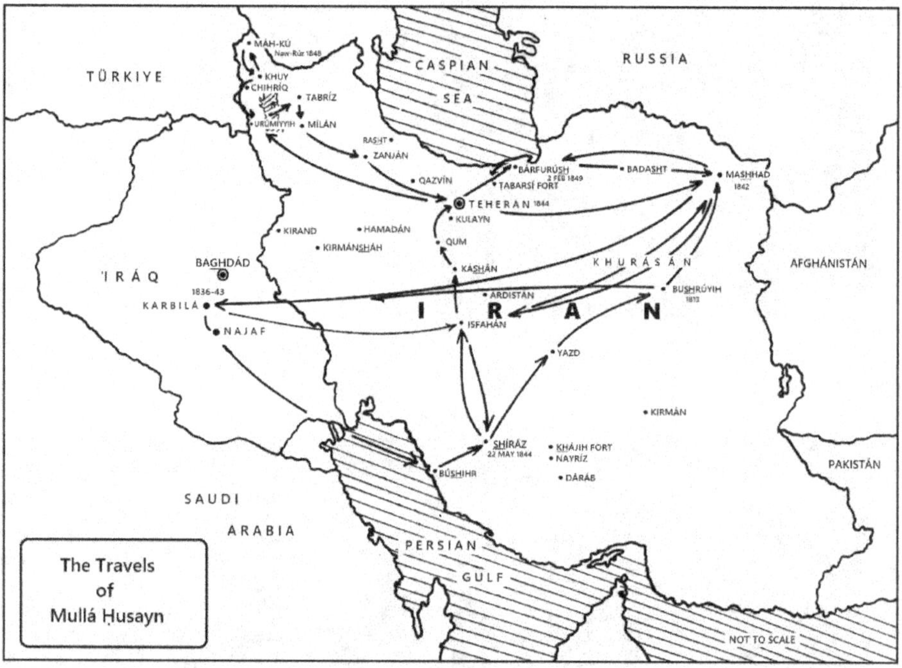

Figure 31: The travels of Mullá Ḥusayn (Courtesy of Pedro Donaires)

9
The House of Bábíyyih

Chapter content
About dates
Friends working together
Reactions of local authorities
Departure of Quddús
Mázindarán visit
Rendezvous with Bahá'u'lláh at Badas<u>h</u>t

Significant events were looming on the horizon of the Cause. The Báb from His prison in <u>Ch</u>ihríq Castle[1] instructed the Bábís to immediately head for the province of <u>Kh</u>urásán whose capital is Ma<u>sh</u>had: *"Hasten to the Land of <u>Kh</u>á* (<u>Kh</u>urásán)."[2] According to Nabíl, this call was made when Quddús was in Ma<u>sh</u>had around May-June of 1848 and was the reason why Ṭáhirih, who was in Karbilá teaching the Faith of the Báb, decided to return to Persia[3] [4] Other authors affirm that Ṭáhirih was asked to leave the country because of her teaching activities.[5] [6]

A multitude of seekers constantly poured from every direction into Ma<u>sh</u>had", Nabíl wrote, "eagerly sought the residence of Mullá Ḥusayn, and through him were ushered into the presence of Quddús".[7] That the believers needed to see Mullá Ḥusayn to attain Quddús's presence is an early indicator of the sense of ranks within the early Bábí community.

About dates

Nabíl wrote that Bahá'u'lláh first heard the Báb's call to go to Khurásán about the same time when Ṭáhirih has been put under house arrest in Qazvín[8] which

---

1 The ruins of the castle (38.080166, 44.589550) are on the end of a ridge with steep sides between the now largely dry Zúlá <u>Ch</u>áy River and a side stream. It is less than 1 km to the west of <u>Ch</u>ihríq-i-Ulya and 19 km southeast of the modern Turkish border.

2 The Báb in Nabíl-i-A'ẓam, *The Dawn-Breakers,* p. 269.

3 Nabíl-i-A'ẓam, *The Dawn-Breakers,* pp. 269-271.

4 According to Hussein Ahdieh and Hillary Chapman, Ṭáhirih left Baghdád on his way to Persia around March 1847 (*The Chosen Path,* p. 28). At that time Mullá Ḥusayn was in Ma<u>sh</u>had and Quddús in Bárfurú<u>sh</u>. She never reached Ma<u>sh</u>had but went directly to Qazvín, her hometown, arriving around July 1847 (Ahdieh and Chapman, *The Chosen Path*, p. 31), where he was eventually arrested (Siyamak Zabihi-Moghaddam, *Pírámún-i-kitáb-i-Ḥaḍrat-i-Báb,* pp. 136-137).

5 'Abdu'l-Bahá, *Memorials of the Faithful*, p. 105.

6 Martha Root, *Táhirih the Pure,* p. 37.

7 Nabíl-i-A'ẓam, *The Dawn-Breakers,* p. 288.

8 Nabíl-i-A'ẓam, *The Dawn-Breakers,* p. 278.

happened in October 1847.[1] By October 1847, the Báb was confined in Máh-Kú and Quddús was living in Bárfurú<u>sh</u>. According to Ruhollah Mehrabkhani,[2] about the same time Mullá Ḥusayn, at the Báb's request, had gone to <u>Kh</u>urásán residing first in Bu<u>sh</u>rúyih (his hometown) and then in Ma<u>sh</u>had.[3] Later, from <u>Kh</u>urásán, Mullá Ḥusayn undertook an 1,800-km pilgrimage on foot to Máh-Kú through Ṭihrán and Qazvín. In Ṭihrán, he secretly attained the presence of Bahá'u'lláh and in Qazvín met Ṭáhirih for the first time.[4] Nabíl wrote that Mullá Ḥusayn arrived in Máh-Kú in the eve of Naw-Rúz 1848,[5] stayed for nine days, thence he was instructed to go to Mázindarán. As discussed in the previous chapter, such a meeting took place around April 1848. From Mázindarán, Mullá Ḥusayn at Quddús' instructions, returned to Ma<u>sh</u>had to teach the Faith there. As seen in this chapter, the following month, around June 1848, that is, the following month, Mullá Ḥusayn was joined by Quddús in Ma<u>sh</u>had.

Hasan Fuadi Bushru'i wrote that, "According to The honored Mírzá Muhammad-'Alí Quddús who with a few other disciples came from Mázandarán to Ma<u>sh</u>had in accordance with a Tablet of the Báb and also a Tablet revealed in honor of Mírzá Aḥmad <u>Azgh</u>andí. Together with Mullá Ḥusayn and some other companions, he resided in the House of Bábíyyih and returned to Mázandarán prior to the departure of Mullá Ḥusayn."[6]

In general, it seems that there were two calls from the Báb encouraging the Bábís to go to <u>Kh</u>urásán: the first from Máh-Kú, around October 1847 when Mullá Ḥusayn was living in Ma<u>sh</u>had, and the second around May 1848, from <u>Ch</u>ihríq, when Mullá Ḥusayn and Quddús were residing in that city. It can also be hypothesised that instead of two discrete calls, there was only one continuous call between 1847 and 1848.

Friends working together

As previously noted, Quddús had asked Mullá Ḥusayn to build in the city of Ma<u>sh</u>had a centre where the Bábís could meet and teach their Faith:

> In the town of Ma<u>sh</u>had, you should build a house so designed as both to serve for our private residence and at the same time afford adequate facilities for the reception of our guests. Thither we shall shortly journey, and in that house we shall dwell. To it you shall invite every receptive soul

---

1. Moojan Momen, *A Chronology of some of the Persecutions of Bábís and Bahá'ís in Iran 1844-1978*, p. 380).
2. Ruhollah Mehrabkhani, *Mullá Ḥusayn*, pp. 133-135.
3. According to Hasan Fuadi Bushru'i, Mullá Ḥusayn returned to Bu<u>sh</u>rúyih at the beginning of 1846 CE (early 1262 AH) and then moved to Ma<u>sh</u>had around the end of the same year. See Ahang Rabbani, *The Genesis of the Bahá'í Faith in Khurásán*, pp. 13-16.
4. Ruhollah Mehrabkhani, *Mullá Ḥusayn*, pp. 136-137.
5. Nabíl-i-A'ẓam, *The Dawn-Breakers*, p. 255.
6. In Ahang Rabbani, *The Genesis of the Bahá'í Faith in Khurásán*, Chapter 2, p. 20

who we hope may be guided to the River of everlasting life. We shall prepare and admonish them to band themselves together and proclaim the Cause of God.[1]

Upon arriving in Mashhad, Mullá Ḥusayn acquired a piece of land on Bálá-Khíyábán Street close to the property of a local believer named Muḥammad-Báqir, who, as a builder, assisted in constructing an edifice named the House of Bábíyyih ("place of the Bábís").[2] Weeks later, Quddús travelled from Bárfurúsh to Mashhad, in the company of Riḍá Khán, to meet Mullá Ḥusayn and they resided in the House of Bábíyyih. Quddús knew Mashhad well as he had studied at a local religious seminary there for several years.[3]

The house would be used as their private home and to accommodate guests. Eventually, the house became a centre for the promulgation of the divine teachings, and it welcomed all interested seekers in the Cause of the Báb. It became the focal point that generated feverish Bábí activity in the area with believers coming from all over Persia following the Báb's call.

Due to the events taking place in the province of Khurásán, a pivotal period of transformation occurred around the middle of 1848. Something great, providential and historic was brewing, a time of expectation that a glorious drama was about unfold that would establish the unity of the Bábís and emphasise the independence of their Faith from Islam.

After the encounter between Quddús and Mullá Ḥusayn, as narrated in the previous chapter, the believers had realized that Quddús was the leader of the faithful while the Báb was confined in prison. A believer wrote:

> Early in the Cause, I had a deep devotion and a profound belief in the honoured Bábu'l-Báb [Mullá Ḥusayn], as he was the courier of divine knowledge, the first to believe [in the Báb], the first Letter of the Living and the gate to His Holiness the Báb [the Gate].
>
> After a few days, however, I noticed that in a gathering of the companions, it was His Holiness Quddús who was seated at the place of honor while all others stood reverently in his presence. That honored personage [Mullá Ḥusayn] was also standing in his presence with the utmost respect with hands folded over chest while waves of divine verses and wondrous utterances poured forth from the pearl-dispensing lips of Quddús.[4]

There were so many people in the Bábíyyih House that the available samovars were not enough to prepare tea. They had to boil water in a big copper pot to cook lunch and dinner for all of them.[5] Hushmand Dehghan commented,

---

1 Nabíl-i-A'ẓam, *The Dawn-Breakers,* pp. 265–266

2 The house was located on Kuchih Zardi in the Khiyaban Balla district.

3 Abbas Amanat, *Resurrection and Renewal,* p. 182

4 *The Narrative of Ḥájí Náṣir Qazvíní*, pp. 8–9.

5 Hushmand Dehghan, *Ganj-i-Pinhán*, p. 74.

"Although the Báb was imprisoned in Chihríq Castle and His faithful believers were deprived of seeing Him, the power of God woke up in Khurásán and kept the fire of faith burning in the hearts of the friends and believers".[1] The historian Nabíl described the impressive atmosphere:

> A steady stream of visitors whom the energy and zeal of Mullá Ḥusayn had prepared for the acceptance of the Faith, poured into the presence of Quddús, acknowledged the claim of the Cause, and willingly enlisted under its banner. The all-observing vigilance with which Mullá Ḥusayn laboured to diffuse the knowledge of the new Revelation, and the masterly manner in which Quddús edified its ever-increasing adherents, gave rise to a wave of enthusiasm which swept over the entire city of Mashhad, and the effects of which spread rapidly beyond the confines of Khurásán.[2]

These meetings in the Bábíyyih House in the early days of the Cause became a point of attraction for the Bábís and the broader community. An amazing flow of believers and supporters arrived from all parts of Persia. Within its walls, the thirst for service intensified and soon a heavenly host of brave spiritual soldiers would arise and seal with their very blood their faith in the Cause of the Báb. The love and enthusiasm that ignited in their breasts completely consumed their bodies so that in the days to come, they would become transformed, through faith and certitude, from people totally inexperienced in the use of weapons and fighting into incarnations of the most courageous heroes of antiquity.

A believer who visited that place described it in the following terms:

> Meanwhile, I had the bounty to visit the House of Bábíyyih, a humble but spacious abode with a large courtyard, where a staircase led to two upstairs room, designated as the temporary residence of Mullá Ḥusayn and Quddús. It had the usual characteristics of all the Mullá Ḥusayn's residences; simple furnishing to provide basic comfort for the occupant. The Bábu'l-Báb's [Mullá Ḥusayn] room had an annex for storing the bedding and belongings of the owner. In this windowless storage, we were shown a small opening in the earthen floor, where the Holy Writings of the Báb used to be hidden to protect them from frequent raids of Moslems. Ḥusayn used to take them out at night and study them in that storage room. Having access to all the Bahá'í books, and the relative freedom to read them in the privacy of my home, this blessed spot was the dearest and most touching place in that house.[3]

Reactions of local authorities

Hasan Fuadi Hasan Bushru'i wrote that "During this time the foes decided to rush to the House of Bábíyyih and slay all its occupants. Mullá Ḥusayn instructed twelve of his companions to charge the attackers with unsheathed swords, while

1 Hushmand Dehghan, *Ganj-i-Pinhán*, p. 75.

2 Nabíl-i-A'ẓam, *The Dawn-Breakers*, p. 267.

3 Shahla Behroozi Gillbanks, *Footprints in the Sand of Time*, pp. 60–61.

raising the cry of 'Yá Ṣáḥibu'z-Zamán!' meaning literally "O Thou the Lord of the Age", an invocation to the Báb. This they accomplished and compelled the enemy to withdraw as far as outskirts of the Bálá-Khíyábán district."[1]

The Bábíyyih House also greatly alarmed the local authorities because of its growing popularity and the number of visitors, and, more importantly, produced an intense jealousy in the local clergy who saw their prerogatives and influence undermined as the number of the faithful in the Bábíyyih House increased. Such distress within the civil authorities became evident when, in order to intimidate the population and diminish the zeal of the Bábís, they arrested Ḥasan, one of Mullá Ḥusayn's assistants. Without any judicial procedure, they decided to pierce his nose and pass a string through it with which to pull and parade him through the city streets. The news of this ignominy reached the ears of Mullá Ḥusayn while he was in the company of Quddús and without arousing the suspicions of his illustrious chief, Mullá Ḥusayn attempted at first to cool down the tempers of the Bábís who were seeking to avenge the fate of Ḥasan. Furthermore, Mullá Ḥusayn, urged them to observe moderation and be cautious, and that he would bring Ḥasan home.

Even so, without permission, a small group of them went to where Ḥasan was being held and liberated him at the call of "Yá Ṣáḥibu'z-Zamán!" Without considering the adverse effects of such a confrontational act, these Bábís disobeyed Mullá Ḥusayn, and in attempting to violently release Ḥasan, several soldiers were killed.

The incident caused great distress to Ḥamzih Mírzá (the prince) who was in charge of the military used for maintaining city order. The situation in Mashhad was still tense as it was emerging from a major civil insurgency, and the prince was ready to crush at any price whatever might upset the tranquillity of the population.

As soon as Mullá Ḥusayn learned of the killing of the guards and of the disobedience of the believers, he called them to his presence. Outraged by their behaviour, he harshly rebuked them for the consequences that could arise from having breached his instructions. Alluding to his own eventual martyrdom he told them: "You have refused to tolerate the trials to which Ḥasan has been subjected; how can you reconcile yourselves to the martyrdom of Ḥusayn?"[2] (Ḥasan and Ḥusayn are also the names of the two grandsons of Prophet Muḥammad).

Mullá Ḥusayn's retreat

The prince naturally feared that the situation could become critical and, therefore, in an attempt to reassure the city governor, he ordered the immediate arrest of Mullá Ḥusayn. He thought that bringing Mullá Ḥusayn to his camp would

---

1 In Ahang Rabbani, *The Genesis of the Bahá'í Faith in Khurásán,* Chapter 2, p. 24.

2 Nabíl-i-A'ẓam, *The Dawn-Breakers*, p. 289.

help to re-establish tranquillity, after which it would be safe to release Mullá Ḥusayn. The prince ordered one of his senior officers of the detachment to forcibly bring Mullá Ḥusayn to the camp.

To his surprise, the officer flatly refused to detain Mullá Ḥusayn and he even offered his own life to avoid such an action. He was very fond of Mullá Ḥusayn. The prince, trying to avoid disagreements with his officers, decided to personally write a letter politely inviting Mullá Ḥusayn to stay for some time in his military camp. In order to restore peace to the city, the prince pledged to provide security for Mullá Ḥusayn and to care for him for a few days. He also arranged that Mullá Ḥusayn use his personal accommodation. It was a diplomatically disguised, peremptory request.

Upon receiving the prince's communication, Mullá Ḥusayn quickly asked Quddús for advice, to which he recommended accepting the invitation and, therefore, he moved to the royal camp. While Mullá Ḥusayn was with the prince, a second clash occurred with the Bábís and a sector of the population:

> A young Bábí named Muḥammad-Ḥusayn became embroiled in an argument with a servant of Ḥájí Mírzá Ḥasan, a local religious leader, was arrested and, it seems, tortured by the chief constable of Mashhad... Mírzá Muḥammad-Báqir-i-Qá'iní, the owner of the Bábí house there, obtained permission from Mullá Muḥammad-'Alí Bárfurúshí [Quddús] to intervene, on condition that they should not strike until struck by the enemy-hardly a severe restriction since they could count on resistance once they began their rescue attempt. A party of seventy-two Bábís set off with swords bared after the youth and, in the course of effecting his rescue, engaged in several clashes with his captors.[1]

According to Nabíl, Quddús had informed Mullá Ḥusayn on the night of their conversation of his intention to leave the city for his native province. "No harm can befall you," Quddús comforted Mullá Ḥusayn. "As to me, I shall this very night set out in the company of Mírzá Muḥammad-'Alíy-i-Qazvíní, one of the Letters of the Living, for Mázindarán. Please God, you too, later on, at the head of a large company of the faithful and preceded by the 'Black Standards', will depart from Mashhad and join me. We shall meet at whatever place the Almighty will have decreed."[2]

"Mullá Ḥusayn joyously responded," Nabíl observed. "He threw himself at the feet of Quddús and assured him of his firm determination to discharge with fidelity the obligations which he had imposed upon him. Quddús lovingly took him in his arms and, kissing his eyes and his forehead, committed him to the Almighty's unfailing protection."[3]

---

1 Denis MacEoin, *The Messiah of Shíráz: Studies in Early and Middle Bábism*, p. 481.

2 Nabíl-i-A'ẓam, *The Dawn-Breakers*, p. 290.

3 Nabíl-i-A'ẓam, *The Dawn-Breakers*, pp. 290–291.

Mullá Ḥusayn, with complete confidence in the guidance and ability of Quddús, and with great emotion, bid him farewell. That evening after preparations were made, Mullá Ḥusayn departed on horseback for the military camp with complete serenity and dignity. Upon his arrival, the prince led him with great respect and reverence to the accommodations specially prepared for him. In that camp, located on the city's outskirts, Mullá Ḥusayn remained until July 1848.

Departure of Quddús

Before departing from the House of Bábíyyih, Quddús called together the leading believers and emphasised to them the need to fully obey Mullá Ḥusayn: "Tempestuous are the storms which lie ahead of us. The days of stress and violent commotion are fast approaching. Cleave to him, for in obedience to his command lies your salvation".[1] It has been conjectured that Quddús left Mas͟hhad because of the unrest that pervaded the city.[2]

As for the local believers in Mas͟hhad, their meetings and spirit of service continued to grow. As Nabíl recounted:

> The house of Bábíyyih was soon converted into a rallying centre for a multitude of devotees who were fired with an inflexible resolve to demonstrate, by every means in their power, the great inherent energies of their Faith.[3]

The following is an interesting anecdote of an event that occurred before the departure of Quddús:

> ... soldiers of Sám K͟hán of Armenia who were waiting outside of Quddús' house took him to Sám K͟hán. As soon as Sam K͟hán's eyes fell upon his radiant face he scolded his soldiers severely as to why they have brought him here and said to Quddús "you are free to go wherever you desire." So Quddús returned to the House of Bábíyyih and bid farewell to his companions and travelled towards Mázindarán in the company of Mírzá Muḥammad-'Alí Qazvíní and Karbilá'í Aṣg͟har Baná'í Qá'iní."[4]

Mázindarán visit

It is interesting that Nabil reports about this time that Bahá'u'lláh requested Quddús to go to His home in Ṭihrán to *"seek the presence, and revolve round the person of that Day-Star of Truth, to seek His advice, to reinforce His efforts, and to*

---

1 Nabíl-i-A'ẓam, *The Dawn-Breakers*, p. 291.

2 Negar Mottahedeh, *Resurrection, Return, Reform*, p. 395.

3 Nabíl-i-A'ẓam, *The Dawn-Breakers*, p. 267.

4 Mohammad 'Ali Malik Khosravi, *History of the Martyrs of the Cause*, vol 1, pp. 89–90. Cited by Hushmand Dehghan in *Ganj-i-Pinhán*, pp. 76–77.

prepare the way for His coming Revelation."[1] Apparently, this trip never took place but shows Bahá'u'lláh's leadership at that time.

The book *Ganj-i-Pinhán* relates the following anecdotes during the journey to Mázindarán:

> Quddús met some travellers at a mountain pass on the way to Mashhad, Mírzá Ḥaydar 'Alíy-i-Ardistání with six Bábís from Ardistán who were going to Mashhad, but they did not recognize him.[2] Quddús asked about their names and health, but they did not give a proper answer, and they wanted to pass. In the meantime, Quddús extended his hand and showed them his ring, which in secret code, the blessed name of the Báb had been engraved on it. It was incumbent upon each Bábí to have one of them in his hand for identification.[3] Then, suddenly, he touched the agate ring of Áqá Mírzá Ḥaydar-'Alí and gave instructions regarding it, as well as the prayer of the Temple (a prayer written in the form of a human figure or a five-pointed star, which male Bábís carried it around their neck). He instructed them to remove these pieces of jewellery from their fingers and around their necks and dissimulate in Mashhad.[4]
>
> He also met Mírzá Sulaymán-i-Núrí on the way. He told the story of the rescue of Ṭáhirih from Qazvín prison and her move to Khurásán, and also told him the news of Bahá'u'lláh's departure from Ṭihrán to Khurásán. After that, Mírzá Sulaymán and Mírzá Muḥammad-'Alíy-i-Qazvíní served Quddús until they reached Badasht.[5]

Badasht at that time was a small hamlet with a sparse population located on the route between Ṭihrán to Mashhad (Khurásán's capital) with a bifurcation to Bárfurúsh in Mázindarán Province. It is 500 km from Mashhad.

Rendezvous with Bahá'u'lláh at Badasht

Around that time, the Báb had revealed from His captivity, a Tablet requesting all His followers on Persian soil to immediately travel to the province of Khurásán, where Quddús and Mullá Ḥusayn had enkindled a great number of the population of Mashhad to accept the Cause of the Báb.

The Báb's summons spread quickly and soon reached Bábís dispersed throughout the country, even beyond the kingdom's borders. The believers felt His exhortation in their hearts and enthusiastically arose in support.

---

1 Bahá'u'lláh in Nabíl-i-A'ẓam, *The Dawn-Breakers,* pp. 268–269.

2 Fazel Mazandarani, *Taríkh Ẓuhúr al-Ḥaqq*, vol. 2, p. 216.

3 Mohammad 'Ali Malik Khosravi, *History of the Martyrs of the Cause*, vol 1, pp. 89–90. Cited by Hushmand Dehghan in *Ganj-i-Pinhán*, p. 77.

4 Fazel Mazandarani, *Taríkh Ẓuhúr al-Ḥaqq*, vol. 2, p. 216.

5 Hushmand Dehghan, *Ganj-i-Pinhán,* pp. 76–77.

Bahá'u'lláh had left Ṭihrán in compliance with the request of the Báb to travel to the province of Khurásán.[1] Badasht was at that time part of Khurásán Province. According to 'Abdu'l-Bahá, *"The Blessed Beauty made elaborate arrangements for Ṭáhirih's journey to* Badasht *and sent her off with an equipage and retinue. His own party left for that region some days afterward".*[2]

Quddús travelled from Mashhad towards his native province of Mázindarán and reached the village of Badasht at dawn. Hushmand Dehghan relates:

> When they approached Sháh-Rúd, Áqá Muḥammad-Hanásáb met Mírzá Sulaymán who was running behind them. Quddús was informed by him that Bahá'u'lláh and Ṭáhirih had gone from Sháh-Rúd to Badasht, and many Bábís from Iṣfahán, Qazvín and other parts of Iran were waiting to go to Khurásán with Bahá'u'lláh. In the meantime, Mírzá Sulaymán Khán turned to Áqá Muḥammad-Hanásáb and said: "Tell Mullá Aḥmad Abdál that a light shone on you this morning, but you did not notice it." But Áqá Muḥammad did not understand his meaning and asked him, "whether the horseman who was going to Sháh-Rúd was Mullá Ḥusayn." Mírzá Sulaymán replied "he is the master of Mullá Ḥusayn." Once Muḥammad Hanásáb, arrived in Badasht, he brought the matter of Quddús' moving to Sháh-Rúd to the attention of Bahá'u'lláh.[3]

Nabíl informs us that in Badasht Quddús found a large number of Bábís congregated there, but he continued towards the village of Sháh-Rúd, 8 km away. On his way, he was advised that many believers had arrived from different parts of Persia and were waiting in anticipation of accompanying Bahá'u'lláh on his projected trip. Individuals or small groups of travellers normally remain at a caravanserai until they can join the next caravan travelling in their direction. This enabled them to resume their journey in large groups due to the danger of highwaymen prevalent at that time. Camels or mules were normally part of the entourage as pack animals, and horses for the armed guards or just to pull carriages with children, women, elderly or the sick. The wait for the next caravan would take days or even weeks, adding time to the wearisome journeys.

In the meantime, Bahá'u'lláh and His entourage, travelling en route to Khurásán Province, learned of Quddús' whereabouts in Sháh-Rúd and changed His route to that nearby destination, where they met on the evening of the same day. That Bahá'u'lláh and Quddús met in Sháh-Rúd is because that town lies on the intersection of the road network joining Ṭihrán, Mashhad and Bárfurúsh. Sháh-Rúd "it was a place of assembly of caravans which combined their joint defences against possible Turkoman raids during the long four hundred kilometres of semi-desert to Mashhad".[4] (See map in Figure 36)

---

1 Khurásán Province was divided into three new provinces in 2004: North Khurásán, South Khurásán, and Raḍawí Khurásán.

2 'Abdul-Bahá, *Memorials of the Faithful*, p. 200

3 Hushmand Dehghan, *Ganj-i-Pinhán*, pp. 76–77.

4 David Ruhe, *Robe of Light*, p. 84.

Together they then travelled on to Badas_h_t, arriving the next sunrise. Bahá'u'lláh, Quddús and Ṭáhirih reached Badas_h_t one day in June in the hot Iranian summer of 1848.[1]

1 Iran is in the northern hemisphere.

Part III
The leader

10
The Bada<u>sh</u>t conference

Chapter content
Renewal of religion
Bada<u>sh</u>t village
Conference purpose
Old World Order abrogated
Laws of the *Bayán*
Conference organisation
A pre-arranged plan
"Him Whom God shall make manifest"
Ṭáhirih and "Him Whom God shall make manifest"
Quddús and Bahá'u'lláh
Ṭáhirih removes her veil
The role of the Báb in the conference
New Day celebrated
New Order proclaimed

During the summer of 1848 in Persia, the conference of Bada<u>sh</u>t took place, becoming one of the most historic developments of the Bábí Faith. It can be compared to the Council of Jerusalem held by the first Christians (*Acts* 15:1–23).

At the Council of Jerusalem, which occurred about twenty-five years after Jesus' crucifixion, early Christians gathered to make decisions about the applicability of the Jewish laws to the new converts. It is presumed that all of the apostles attended (including Matthias, who replaced Judas)—and we can glean from the text that Paul and Barnabas were also there. They were confused and needed to distinguish clearly between Judaism and Christianity. At that time, Christian identity was not well developed, and therefore, the believers were described as followers of "The Way"—a party within Judaism. One group advocated following the traditional Mosaic laws, while another believed no such need existed. The Council decided that the new converts were not required to follow most of the Mosaic laws, including male circumcision. Likewise, the participants at the Bada<u>sh</u>t conference wanted to establish the differences between Islám and the new Bábí Faith.

Renewal of religion

The Bábí conference took place amid jade green orchards in the small village of Bada<u>sh</u>t and was a dramatic turning point in the progress of the Faith of the Báb. The believers discarded Islamic laws at the conference and vowed to abide by the recently revealed new laws in the *Bayán*. This historic conference occurred in mid-June and early July 1848,[1] while the Báb being transferred from

---

[1] The conference occurred during the late Rajab and early <u>Sh</u>a'bán months of the

His prison in Chihríq Castle to Tabríz for His trial to be held in the last ten days of July 1848.[1] It was at this trial that the Báb announced publicly that He was the promised *Qá'im* ("He Who shall arise" or "He Who ariseth").

The Qá'im

Everyone in Persia anticipated the promised prophetic Qá'im in the nineteenth century. Therefore, the news that "the Qá'im has appeared" spread like wildfire throughout the country, which was carried on foot and horseback along roads and streets, via bazaars in cities and villages, and into people's homes and religious institutions. The Báb attracted thousands of adherents throughout the nation, and today the Bahá'í community is the largest non-Muslim religious minority of Iran. More importantly, the clerical system was based on the assumption that they ruled on behalf of the anticipated Qá'im. By equating Himself with the Qá'im, the Báb opposed their absolutist theocracy.

Written between July 1847 and April 1848, the *Persian Bayán* is considered, "the most weighty, the most illuminating and comprehensive of all His works."[2] In it, the Báb categorically declared Himself to be the Qá'im ("He Who will arise"), the Promised One of the Islamic Faith.[3] A few months after having been written, in July of 1848, at the religious court in Tabríz, the Báb openly proclaimed:

> *I am, I am, I am, the promised One! I am the One whose name you have for a thousand years invoked, at whose mention you have risen, whose advent you have longed to witness, and the hour of whose Revelation you have prayed God to hasten. Verily I say, it is incumbent upon the peoples of both the East and the West to obey My word and to pledge allegiance to My person.*[4]

Prior to Badasht, the Báb had proclaimed Himself to be the promised Qá'im and Mahdi, in the *Persian Bayán*[5] and to at least 'Alíd Sunní, the one-time Mufti of Baghdád,[6] before His proclamation in Tabríz.

The main Bábí leaders were aware of this claim before the conference. There is evidence that as early as 1846 the Bábís were openly teaching that the Báb was the Qá'im.[7] It is also known that the Bábís of Mashhad, as early as May 1848, were invoking the Báb as the Qá'im (the "Ṣáḥibu'z-Zamán", i.e., the "Lord of the Age"), following the visit of Mullá Ḥusayn who was returning from meeting the Báb in Máh-Kú.[8] Still, many Bábís held the belief that the Báb was only an intermediary

---

Islamic calendar.

1 David Merrick, *Martyrdom of the Báb.* Available www.paintdrawer.co.uk/david/folders/spirituality/bahai/bab/bab-martyrdom-outline.htm

2 Nabíl-i-A'ẓam, *The Dawn-Breakers*, pp. 248.

3 The Báb, *Persian Bayán* 1:15.

4 The Báb in Nabíl-i-A'ẓam, *The Dawn-Breakers,* p. 316.

5 The Báb, *Persian Bayán*, 1:15; 7:15.

6 Stephen Lambden, *From a Primal Point to an Archetypical Book,* p. 171.

7 In Ahang Rabbani, The Genesis of the Bahá'í Faith in Khurásán, Chapter 2, p. 15

8 Nabíl-i-A'ẓam, *The Dawn-Breakers*, pp. 248.

to the Qá'im who had been concealed since 941 CE and was to appear as a Messiah in the Latter Days. However, it is to Mullá Shaykh-'Aliy-i-Turshízí, known as 'Azím, that the Báb had given His categorical assertion of being the Qá'im just before His trial in Tabríz.[1] [2] The Tablet to the latter was copied and distributed among the Báb's adherents so establishing publicly His claim as the Qá'im.[3] [4]

The conference of Badasht was the vehicle to communicate this openly to all of the believers. However, for some, this powerful announcement was a test of faith.

In general, the summer of 1848 was a turning point in the destinies of the Bábí Revelation insofar as the aforementioned Tablet of the Declaration of the Báb, the Badasht summit, and the Báb's oral proclamation of His mission in Tabríz categorically and openly highlighted Him as being the promised Qá'im.

Bahá'u'lláh leading the conference

Shoghi Effendi wrote that Bahá'u'lláh Himself was behind the organisation of the conference:

> Bahá'u'lláh, maintaining through continual correspondence close contact with the Báb, and Himself the directing force behind the manifold activities of His struggling fellow-disciples, unobtrusively yet effectually presided over that conference, and guided and controlled its proceedings.[5]

According to Shoghi Effendi, Bahá'u'lláh chaired over the proceedings that were attended by 81 believers.[6] At the same time, Mullá Ḥusayn remained "by invitation" in the camp of Ḥamzih Mírzá in Mashhad and did not attend.

The mid-1848 summit held in Badasht, which had such a profound impact on the development of the Faith of the Báb, lasted twenty-two days. It was henceforth known as the Badasht conference in honour of the modest village that served as its stage. "At that time," Lowell Johnson wrote, "Bahá'u'lláh was not the leader of the Faith. Most of the Bábís looked to Quddús as their leader, because he was the closest to the Báb."[7] "After the Báb had been taken to the remote fortress of Máh-Kú, they rallied around His Holiness Quddús," wrote German historian Hermann Roemer.[8]

---

1 Fereydun Vahman, *The Báb: A Sun in a Night not Followed by Dawn*, p. 58.

2 The Báb, *Qismati az Alvah-i Khatt-i Nuqtih-'i Ula va Aqa Sayyid Husayn Katib* (Correspondence of the Báb and Sayyid Ḥusayn Katib), p. 23.

3 Denis MacEoin, *Sources for early Bábí Doctrine and History*, p. 96.

4 E. G. Browne, *Kitáb-i-Nuqtatu'l-Káf: Being the Earliest History of the Bábís*, p. 209. Also in *Iranian National Bahá'í Archives*, 58, p.172.

5 Shoghi Effendi, *God Passes By*, p. 35

6 Shoghi Effendi, *God Passes By*, p. 35

7 Lowell Johnson, *Quddús*, p. 13.

8 Hermann Roemer, *Die Bābī-Behā'ī, die jüngste mohammedanische sekte* p. 38.

Badas͟ht village

Today travellers can still see the village of Badas͟ht from afar. Its tall caravanserai stands on a perfectly horizontal plain flanked by distant hills. Like a gravitational point, Badas͟ht stands at the convergence of the ancient travelling routes to and from the provinces of Mázindarán, K͟hurásán and Ṭihrán, north, west, and eastbound of the country respectively, providing for trading caravans a place wherein to rest and replenish.

The little village of Badas͟ht[1] is 112 km southeast (180 km by road to Banda Gaz) of the Caspian Sea, with the main city of S͟háh-Rúd, the modern-day capital of Semnan Province, being only 8 km to the west (11 km by road). Shoghi Efendi referred to Badas͟ht as a "tiny hamlet".[2] It used to be a critical postal and communication centre on the old Silk Road to K͟hurásán towards the country's extreme west. At the 2006 census, its population was 466 people grouped in 143 families.

Like an oasis in the middle of arid lands, Badas͟ht refreshes the tired eyes of the exhausted traveller with the sights of fields of cotton, cereals, and a varied range of vegetables and fruits, including watermelons, cherries, apricots, apples, and gooseberries.

The Badas͟ht caravanserai dates back to the 17th century. It provided accommodation and hospitality to travellers on its six porches located on each side of the brick structure. Here travellers found a place to sleep, eat, exchange news and information about the country and recover from the inhospitable Iranian land routes. Given that travelling on land could be at most 20 km a day, travellers anticipated arriving at the next caravanserai by nightfall for safety because highwaymen swarmed the roads. Armed caravans were usually formed, leaving early in the morning after performing prayers and chants for protection. Whether on foot or in the saddle, travelling was always in the daytime and exposed to the elements of the climate—wind, heat and rain. The caravanserai later became an abandoned ruin that now forms part of the local airport. The ruined walls provide some protection from the wind for local youth to play volleyball. The village also has three ancient, semi-collapsed castles, serving as a reminder of past prosperity.

The warmest and driest month in Badas͟ht is July, with temperatures reaching 34 °C. Like most Iranian villages and towns, Badas͟ht had gardens (*bág͟h*)—spaces normally protected by informal mud walls with a beautiful arrangement of plants, trees, grass and flowers for the enjoyment and relaxation of citizens. These pleasant spaces were normally adjoined to houses or big mansions and connected to irrigated farming land.

A *bág͟h* is usually adorned with flowing water and pathways for the visitors. A citizen could rent some gardens for special occasions such as weddings or annual

---

1 Grid coordinates: 36.421515, 55.052773

2 Shoghi Effendi, *God Passes By*, pp 31–35.

calendar festivities like Naw-Rúz (New Year). More importantly, a *bágh* is associated with spiritual retirement and nourishment. Gardens are a common feature in Persian literature, often referred to as places of earthly paradise where altruistic sentiments can be found or cultivated. Interestingly, the English word *paradise* comes from the Old Persian *paridaidam* meaning "walled enclosure". According to Nattaj, a Persian garden is:

> considered a part of Iranian heritage, revealing Persian history, culture and lifestyle. Basically, when it comes to Iranian identity, a garden is reflected as a timely display of the Iranian historical identity .... The Persian garden is an ordered and organized space based on Iranian aesthetics, created by combination of natural elements such as water, plants and stones, and built elements such as belvedere [building with a view], wall, and so on.[1]

The history of the Bahá'í Faith shows a fascination with gardens. The Badasht conference occurred in the gardens of Badasht. Bahá'u'lláh revealed His Mission in the Najíbíya Garden,[2] located on the east bank of the Tigris River, opposite central Baghdád. The Blessed Beauty also visited several gardens in the 'Akká area, such as the Riḍván and Junaynih gardens. We know that Bahá'u'lláh had an immense love for gardens and nature. The beauty, both physical and material, of the extensive gardens surrounding the Shrines of the Báb and Bahá'u'lláh bear testimony to this tradition.

The conference of the Bábís in Badasht was held in a place with "pleasant surroundings", according to Shoghi Effendi and was hosted by Bahá'u'lláh Himself. According to 'Abdul-Bahá, *"there was a great open field. Through its centre a stream flowed, and to its right, left, and rear there were three gardens, the envy of Paradise. ... On the field amidst the three gardens, the believers pitched their tents."*[3] Bahá'u'lláh, Quddús and Ṭáhirih were each allocated one of the gardens. The garden of Badasht, according to Ṭáhirih was the fulfillment of the Quranic prophecy: *"Verily, amid gardens and rivers shall the pious dwell in the seat of truth, in the presence of the potent King"* (*Qur'án* 5:54–55).[4]

Conference purpose

At the time the conference was held, the Báb was imprisoned in the fortress of Chihríq. Some Bábís once offered to liberate the Báb while He was being conducted to Chihríq but the Báb responded, *"The mountains of Ádhirbayján too*

1 Vahid Nattaj, *The role of landscape elements,* pp. 6–7.

2 It was located on the east bank of the Tigris River (east of the former citadel and the modern bridge, Jisr Báb al-Mu'aẓẓim, 33.345294, 44.377532) just outside the upstream corner of the old city walls of Baghdád (now occupied by the Baghdád Medical City (Madína aṭ-Ṭibb, "City of Medicine").

3 'Abdu'l-Bahá, *Memorials of the Faithful,* p. 200.

4 Nabíl-i-A'ẓam, *The Dawn-Breakers,* p. 296.

have their claims."[1] The Báb was imprisoned in the Máh-Kú fortress from July 1847 to April 1848 and in the Chihríq fortress from May 1848 to June 1850. Both fortresses are in the province of Ádhirbayján.

Regarding the aims of the Badasht conference, the Guardian of the Faith stated:

> The primary purpose of that gathering was to implement the revelation of the *Bayán* by a sudden, a complete and dramatic break with the past—with its order, its ecclesiasticism, its traditions, and ceremonials. The subsidiary purpose of the conference was to consider the means of emancipating the Báb from His cruel confinement in Chihríq. The first was eminently successful; the second was destined from the outset to fail.[2]

"In those days," wrote 'Abdu'l-Bahá, *"the fact that the Báb was the Qá'im had not yet been proclaimed; it was the Blessed Beauty, with Quddús, Who arranged for the proclamation of a universal Advent and the abrogation and repudiation of the ancient laws."* 'Abdu'l-Bahá also remarked: *"The Blessed Beauty had previously said unto Quddús and Qurratu'l-'Ayn*[3] *that the Cause was to be fully proclaimed."*[4] *"Bahá'u'lláh made a solemn agreement with them,"* 'Abdu'l-Bahá stated, *"that the truth of the Cause would be proclaimed at Badasht, but no specific day was designated."*[5]

Prior to the conference at Badasht, the Báb had not openly made known His Mission to the people. Additionally, He had told those early believers not to inform others of His identity. In reality, all the Prophets of God temporarily hide Their position until the appropriate time to publicly proclaim, without any restriction, the greatness of Their Cause. According to the Báb:

> *His first Book enjoined the observance of the laws of the Qur'án, so that the people might not be seized with perturbation by reason of a new Book and a new Revelation and might regard His Faith as similar to their own, perchance they would not turn away from the Truth and ignore the thing for which they had been called into being.*[6]

At first, all Prophets of God hide their station. In the beginning, for instance, Christ "commanded his disciples not to tell anyone that He was the Christ" (*Matthew* 16:20). Similarly, Bahá'u'lláh, veiled His Divine Message from men's sight for over ten years until the open Declaration of His mission in Baghdád between 21 April and 2 May 1863.

---

1 Ḥasan Balyuzi, *The Báb*, p. 124.

2 Shoghi Effendi, *God Passes By*, p. 31.

3 Ṭáhirih's title means "Solace of the Eyes".

4 'Abdu'l-Bahá, *Light of the World*, p. 42

5 'Abdu'l-Bahá, *Ṭáhirih and the Conference of Badasht*.

6 The Báb, *Selections*, p. 119.

For this reason, the Bábís themselves took care not to reveal the name of the Báb while addressing prominent clerical and government authorities. Instead, they followed the explicit instructions of the Báb by only referring to Him by His titles.

The timing of the Bada<u>sh</u>t conference was significant in that it preceded the month when the Báb was placed on trial at a tribunal in Tabríz, where He publicly proclaimed that He was the Qá'im. "Shortly after the [tribunal] proceedings, it was decided to inflict corporal punishment upon the Báb ..."[1] When the Bábís learned that their Beloved leader had been brutally tortured with the feared bastinado, they became very distraught and began start making plans to forcefully rescue Him from His imprisonment in the fortress of <u>Ch</u>ihríq.

"The question of the Báb's precise claim and the nature of his mission was also raised," according to Negar Mottahedeh who has written about the concerns of many of the Bada<u>sh</u>t participants, "Who was the Báb? Was he the Qá'im—the Messiah whom they had been expecting for hundreds of years? Was his message a rejuvenation of the Islamic truth? Or did he intend to establish an independent claim?"[2] Hussein Ahdieh and Hillary Chapman suggest that "The Báb had revealed His Holy Book, the *Bayán* just the winter before so the Bábís did not know it well in those days you had to have a physical copy of a book to read it and things travelled much more slowly than today."[3]

Old World Order abrogated

The conference of Bada<u>sh</u>t was an opportunity to initiate a meeting of Bábís, who, according to a plan devised in advance by Bahá'u'lláh and Quddús, would openly proclaim the abrogation of the old order and the enactment of new laws revealed by the Báb in the *Bayán* for the New Day.

The number of Bábís had grown considerably since the initiation of the Bábí Faith four years before. However, many of the Bábís were unaware of the full extent of what the Manifestation of the Báb represented in all its dimensions. Although the Báb had not made a formal or public declaration of His exalted station as the expected Qá'im,[4] [5] He had indirectly alluded to this high prophetic station in His Writings. Some believed that the teachings of the Báb would comply strictly with the Islamic traditions they had been accustomed to without any changes.

---

[1] H. M. Balyuzi, *The Báb*, p. 145.
[2] Negar Mottahedeh, *Resurrection, Return, Reform*, p. 395.
[3] Hussein Ahdieh and Hillary Chapman, *The Chosen Path*, p.46.
[4] The word Qá'im ("He Who shall arise") comes from the expression Qá'im Ál Muḥammad ("He Who will rise from the family of Muḥammad"). The Qá'im was a Divine Messenger[4] and expected in Islám for over 1,000 years.
[5] The Báb is also the return of Elijah and John the Baptist (Malachi 4:5; Matthew 16:13-16) (Shoghi Effendi, *God Passes By*, p. 58 & William Sears, *Thief in the Night*, p. 92).

Some people believed the Qá'im must not be born from a mother[1] or that he was living in hiding in the mythical cities of Jábulqá and Jábursá. It was said that this Promised One will wear the garment of Joseph and carry the staff of Moses.[2] The general population expected the Qá'im would establish a kingdom of peace, justice and happiness; and all the supernatural signs associated with their interpretation of ancient prophecies would be literally fulfilled. Compare this expectation with the beliefs of ancient Jews who were waiting for their Messiah to come and destroy the mighty Roman army and to liberate them from their foreign yoke. They are still waiting for the mighty Messiah.

It was inconceivable for most Bábís, due to a lack of adequate information, and for most Muslims, due to their prejudices, to think that the Qá'im would annul many laws and ordinances of Islam and replace them with new laws. Whenever a new Messenger of God appears, the laws of the previous religious dispensation undergo a process of transformation that is rejected by the divines and the general populace, who label the new laws as heresies. Jesus Christ changed some of the laws of the Old Testament on divorce, the observance of Saturday *sabbath*, the *lex talionis* (an eye for an eye and a tooth for a tooth), and the ban on eating particular foods, etc. There has always been resistance from some converts to detach themselves from the laws of the previous religion dispensation. For instance, the laws of the Torah prohibit the eating of some foods, including pork (*Leviticus* 11:7); whereas Jesus declared all foods to be clean (Mark 7:15). A number of early Christian believers from a Judaic background still insisted on the Mosaic law prohibition of eating meat containing blood and meat of animals that were strangled (*Acts* 15).

After the Báb revealed the *Bayán*, His Book of Laws, prior to the conference of Badas͟ht, the majority of Bábís quickly realised the implications of the teachings they had embraced. Their enthusiasm and faith grew, and they were moved to disseminate the new teachings with zeal and perseverance. It is quite amazing, in spite of the lack of books and information available about the Báb's Writings, that the devoted early believers, even though only partially informed of the teachings, were unwavering in their faith.

The Báb broadly fulfilled the same roles as previous Messengers of God. He reformed or repealed the ordinances of Islam in His book, the *Bayán* ("Exposition"), revealed in the fortress of Máh-Kú. The *Bayán* established new laws and ordinances regarding personal behaviour, social observances and liturgies; and, in modifying or replacing past religious observances, there were significant differences in several cases.

However, it was very unusual in that the changes introduced by the Báb were not permanent—they would be valid for only a very short time—until the appearance of *Him Whom God shall make manifest*, namely, Bahá'u'lláh. Therefore, Báb's laws were of a transitory nature designed to annul the previous

---

1 Ahang Rabbani, *The Genesis of the Bahá'í Faith in Khurásán*, Chapter 2, p. 14.

2 Todd Lawson, *The Surát al-'Abd of the Qayyúm al-Asmá*, p. 116.

Islamic laws and to signal a break with the past, prior to the imminent appearance of Bahá'u'lláh. Regarding the looming advent of Bahá'u'lláh, the Báb stated:

> *I behold His appearance even as the sun in the midmost heaven, and the disappearance of all even as that of the stars of the night by day.*[1]
>
> *I Myself am but the first servant to believe in Him, and in His signs, and partake of the sweet savours of His words from the first-fruits of the Paradise of His knowledge. Yea, By His glory! He is the Truth. There is none other God but Him. All have arisen at His bidding.*[2]

In addition to the charges of heresy, the anti-Bábí propaganda stated that the believers "held their wives and possessions in common, allowed the drinking of wine and other immoralities forbidden in Islam, asserted that a woman could have nine husbands, and gave enchanted dates or tea to those visiting them which caused them to become Bábís."[3]

Laws of the Bayán

The *Bayán* ("Exposition"), the Mother Book of the Bábí Dispensation, was completed a short time before the conference of Badasht. The *Persian Bayán* can be characterized as the being the "epitome"[4] of His teachings and as "the most weighty, the most illuminating and comprehensive of all His works."[5] As previously indicated, in that holy book the Báb clearly declared Himself to be the *Qá'im* ("He Who will arise"), the Promised One of Islam.[6] The Islamic ecclesiastical system of Persia rested upon the foundation that they governed on behalf of the Qá'im. By identifying themselves with the Qá'im, the Báb was directly challenging their theocratic rule and assuming the leadership of the whole system.

The *Persian Bayán* was written by the Báb between 1847 and 1848 during His imprisonment in the Máh-Kú fortress. Of this sacred Book, Shoghi Effendi wrote:

> Peerless among the doctrinal works of the Founder of the Bábí Dispensation; consisting of nine Váḥids (Unities) of nineteen chapters each, except the last Váḥid comprising only ten chapters; not to be confounded with the smaller and less weighty *Arabic Bayán* revealed during the same period; fulfilling the Islamic prophecy that "a Youth from Baní-Háshim ... will reveal a new Book and promulgate a new Law"; wholly safeguarded from the interpolation and corruption which has been the fate of so many of the Báb's lesser works, this Book, of about eight thousand

1 Bahá'u'lláh, *Epistle to the Son of the Wolf*, p. 173

2 Bahá'u'lláh, *Epistle to the Son of the Wolf*, p. 141

3 Vernon Elvin Johnson, *A Historical Analysis*, p. 43. See E. G. Browne, *The Taríkh-i-Jadíd*, p. 25; and Appendix 2, p. 322.

4 Muḥammad Afnán, *The Báb's Bayán.*

5 Nabíl-i-A'ẓam, *The Dawn-Breakers*, pp. 248.

6 The Báb, *Persian Bayán* 1:15.

verses, occupying a pivotal position in Bábí literature, should be regarded primarily as a eulogy of the Promised One rather than a code of laws and ordinances designed to be a permanent guide to future generations.[1]

The Báb introduced in the *Bayán* a new corpus of laws and religious regulations in accordance with the exigencies of the New Day. What is more, the Bábí Religion introduced tremendous changes to the religious regulations of all three of the Abrahamic religions: Judaism, Christianity and Islám. The Báb declared in the *Qayyúmu'l-Asmá* that the time had come for a new Revelation with new rules, telling the priests and ministers of previous religious dispensations *to "Follow ye the Book which His Remembrance hath revealed in praise of God, the True One"*[2]

Many of the new prescriptions were at odds with Islamic regulations. The Báb abrogated and modified various Islamic laws (particularly those of Shí'a Islám) related to the individual and society. For instance, the Báb prohibited rituals and congregational prayers in general (except in the case of the congregational Prayer for the Dead), abolished the priesthood, removed former dietary injunctions, prohibited the use of pulpits and exhorted people to sit in chairs. The *Bayán* changed the penalties for adultery and murder. The Báb permitted the use of silk clothes, and of gold and silver dishes and cups, which were forbidden by religious regulations. He declared that animal hair, sable and bones do not nullify one's prayers. Moreover, the charging of reasonable interest on loans (as opposed to usury) was permitted as well as music. The Báb forbade making a public display of one's piety by means of the practices of reciting aloud the names of God, for example, and He prohibited the amputation of limbs for crimes. The Báb also abrogated the death penalty and abolished pilgrimages to "*tombs of prophets and patriarchs*"[3] so that people would not be veiled from the new Revelation due to their attachment to the past.

Shoghi Effendi wrote that the *Bayán* "at once abrogated the laws and ceremonials enjoined by the *Qur'án* regarding prayer, fasting, marriage, divorce and inheritance."[4] In the *Persian Bayán* 3:16, the Báb stated regarding the abolition of past religious observances:

> *It is not permissible to engage in religious acts save those ordained in the Writings of the Point of the Bayán, for in this Dispensation the writings of the Letters of the Living all proceed directly from the Sun of Truth Himself.*[5]

---

1 Shoghi Effendi, *God Passes By*, p. 25.

2 The Báb, *Selections*, p. 44.

3 The Báb, *The Persian Bayán* 4:12.

4 Shoghi Effendi, *God Passes By*, p. 25.

5 Nader Saiedi, *Modernity in the Writings of the Báb.* Last retrieved 30 September 2021 at https://user-hrqc9mo.cld.bz/Modernity-in-the-Writings-of-the-Báb/1 (page 4)

Thus, the Báb decreed a fundamental change in spiritual laws such as obligatory prayer and fasting. New personal status laws provided different guidelines,[1] among many other injunctions.[2]

Conference organisation

Altogether, 81 Bábís attended the conference of Badasht. Bahá'u'lláh was their host, and He rented a garden for Himself plus two other gardens. One was assigned to Ṭáhirih, whom the Bábís, based on a verse of the *Persian Bayán* (1:4) considered the return of Fáṭimih, the daughter of Muḥammad, the Islamic embodiment of charity and purity. The third garden was assigned to Quddús who was much revered by the followers of the Báb. "*One of those gardens was assigned to Quddús but this was kept a secret,*" noted 'Abdu'l-Bahá.[3]

'Abdu'l-Bahá said that "*Quddús remained concealed in one of the gardens ....*"[4] However, we do not know the exact reason for that—perhaps an element of surprise was required. While at the House of Bábíyyih, Mullá Ḥusayn explained to the believers the leadership role of Quddús. As someone said: "It was then that I understood that another mighty power and resplendent effulgence had appeared."[5] Some of the Bábís present went to Badasht and passed on this new guidance to other attendees, and from there the information was passed around the rest of the country. However, there were a few believers who initially challenged Quddús' leadership, as in the case of Ṭáhirih who said: "I deem him a pupil whom the Báb has sent me to edify and instruct. I regard him in no other light." Quddús reproached her for being "the author of heresy" and said that her supporters were "the victims of error"[6]

In reference to the Conference of Badasht, Shoghi Effendi has written:

> It was Bahá'u'lláh Who steadily, unerringly, yet unsuspectedly, steered the course of that memorable episode, and it was Bahá'u'lláh Who brought the meeting to its final and dramatic climax.[7]

Bahá'u'lláh "intervened" in the role of a "conciliator" to resolve the apparent differences." According to Nabíl, "This state of tension persisted for a few days until Bahá'u'lláh intervened and, in His masterly manner, effected a complete

---

1 The Báb. Marriage (*Persian Bayán* 6:7); dowry (*Persian Bayán* 8:16); divorce (*Persian* and *Arabic Bayán* 6:12); inheritance (*Persian Bayán* 6:7); obligatory prayer (*Persian Bayán* 7:19); fasting (*Persian* and *Arabic Bayán* 8:15); age of maturity (*Persian Bayán* 8:11); burial (*Persian* and *Arabic Bayán* 8:15); payment of tithes (*Persian Bayán* 8:17); pilgrimage (*Persian Bayán* 4:16); and location of the Qibla (*Arabic Bayán* 8:7), that is, the direction towards which one turns in prayer.

2 See Boris Handal, *The Dispensation of the Báb*, pp. 243–252.

3 'Abdu'l-Bahá, *Memorials of the Faithful*, p. 200.

4 'Abdu'l-Bahá, *Ṭáhirih and the Conference of Badasht.*

5 *The Narrative of Ḥájí Náṣir Qazvíní*, pp. 8–9.

6 Nabíl-i-A'ẓam, *The Dawn-Breakers*, p. 297.

7 Shoghi Effendi, *God Passes By*, p. 32

reconciliation between them. He healed the wounds which that sharp controversy had caused, and directed the efforts of both [i.e., Quddús and Ṭáhirih] along the path of constructive service."[1]

A pre-arranged plan

According to Shoghi Effendi "Quddús, regarded as the exponent of the conservative element within it, affected, in pursuance of a pre-conceived plan designed to mitigate the alarm and consternation which such a conference was sure to arouse, to oppose the seemingly extremist views advocated by the impetuous Táhirih."[2] As this abrupt change from one religious ordinance to another was too great a shock to be accepted so suddenly, it appears that Quddús and Ṭáhirih devised a plan by which the effect of the change would be somewhat softened. In front of the audience, they decided to pretend their disagreement and disapproval of each other before the audience. While Tahirih would insist on the independence of the Faith of the Báb and the absolute acceptance of the innovative precepts, Quddús would pretend to cling to the old ordinances and constantly oppose her.[3] In his edited translation of Nabil's Narrative, Shoghi Effendi added the following footnote:

> According to the "Kashfu'l-Ghitá," a decision had been previously arrived at between Quddús and Táhirih, in accordance with which the latter was to proclaim publicly the independent character of the Revelation of the Báb, and to emphasise the abrogation of the laws and ordinances of the previous Dispensation. Quddús, on the other hand, was expected to oppose her contention and strenuously to reject her views. This arrangement was made for the purpose of mitigating the effects of such a challenging and far-reaching proclamation, and of averting the dangers and perils which such a startling innovation was sure to produce. (P. 211.) Bahá'u'lláh appears to have taken a neutral attitude in this controversy, though actually He was the prime mover and the controlling and directing influence throughout the different stages of that memorable episode.[4]

Bahá'u'lláh was undoubtedly the Director of the gathering. At that time, Bahá'u'lláh was known by His given name of Mírzá Ḥusayn 'Alí, whereas Fáṭimih Baraqání, now referred to as Ṭáhirih, was known by her title of Qurratu'l-'Ayn ("Solace of the Eyes"), and Quddús as Mírzá Muḥammad-'Alí. According to Nabíl, it was Bahá'u'lláh at the conference who granted those designations. Later the Báb would reveal Tablets to these same participants and address them using new names He assigned to them. From that historical moment Mírzá Ḥusayn 'Alí became known as Bahá'u'lláh ("Glory of God"). Similarly, the names Quddús

1 Nabíl-i-A'ẓam, *The Dawn-Breakers*, p. 297.

2 Shoghi Effendi, *God Passes By*, p. 31.

3 Hussein Ahdieh and Hillary Chapman, *The Calling*, pp. 173-173

4 Nabí l-i-A'z am, *The Dawn-Breakers*, p. 294.

("The Holy") and Ṭáhirih ("The Pure") were to be universally used.[1] [2] Historian Mírzá Ḥusayn suggested that he "was named Quddús [literally, "holy", "sacred", "pure", "saint"], because he "recognized the Proof by its very nature (without any further sign).[3] Reverend Thomas Kelly Cheyne wrote:

> Of course, the new names were given with a full consciousness of the inwardness of names. There was a spirit behind each new name; the revival of a name by a divine representative meant the return of the spirit. Each Bábí who received the name of a prophet or an Imám knew that his life was raised to a higher plane, and that he was to restore that heavenly Being to the present age. These re-named Bábís needed no other recompense than that of being used in the Cause of God. They became capable of far higher things than before, and if within a short space of time the Báb, or his Deputy, was to conquer the whole world and bring it under the beneficent yoke of the Law of God, much miraculously heightened courage would be needed. I am therefore able to accept the Muslim authority's statement. The conferring of new names was not to add fuel to human vanity, but sacramentally to heighten spiritual vitality.[4]

Bahá'u'lláh, Quddús and Ṭáhirih were the three who guided the daily activities of the conference. Each day Bahá'u'lláh anonymously revealed a Tablet for the participants. *"Evenings,"* 'Abdu'l-Bahá has observed, *"Bahá'u'lláh, Quddús and Ṭáhirih would come together."*[5] It has been reported that Quddús wrote a treatise at the conference praising Bahá'u'lláh and paying homage to His elevated position.[6] Quddús and Ṭáhirih would both bow down in the presence of Bahá'u'lláh.

"Him Whom God shall make manifest"

The Báb referred to the prophetic figure of *"Him Whom God shall make manifest"* in the *Persian Bayán*. This was a designation given by the Báb to the Promised One to follow Him.

Prophecies from the Holy Books of previous religions warned of the Day when two Divine Messengers would appear. Prophet Muḥammad had said: *"Verily I say, after the Qá'im* [*"He Who shall arise"*] *the Qayyúm* [*"the Self-Subsisting"*] *will be made manifest."*[7] In the *Qur'án* we read:

---

1 Nabíl-i-A'ẓam, *The Dawn-Breakers*, p. 293.

2 Hasan Balyuzi stated that the Báb had previously named Quddús and Ṭáhirih (p. 163) were designed previously as such with those designations (Hasan Balyuzi, *The Báb*, p. 24 and 163).

3 Mírzá Ḥusayn Hamadání, *The New History (Taríkh-i-Jadíd)*, pp. 39-40.

4 Thomas Kelly Cheyne, *The Reconciliation of Races and Religions*, p. 82.

5 'Abdu'l-Bahá, *Memorials of the Faithful*, pp. 200–201.

6 Adib Taherzadeh, The *Covenant of Bahá'u'lláh,* p. 56.

7 Nabíl-i-A'ẓam, *The Dawn-Breakers*, p. 41.

And there was a blast on the trumpet, and all who are in the heavens and all who are in the earth expired, save those whom God permitted to live. Then was there sounded another blast, and, lo! arising, they gazed around them. And the earth shone with the light of her Lord, and the Book was set, and the Prophets were brought up, and the witnesses; and judgment was given between them with equity; and none was wronged.[1]

Zecharias referred to these two Messengers as the "Two Anointed" (4:14)[2] and by John the Evangelist in his *Apocalypse* as the two "woes" (Revelation 9:12), the "Two Witnesses", the "Two Olive Trees", and the "Two Candlesticks" (Revelation 11:3–5) that would appear in the *Last Days.*[3] Likewise, Zoroaster, anticipated the appearance of U<u>sh</u>idár-Máh and the <u>Sh</u>áh Bahram.[4]

These prophecies were fulfilled in 1863, nineteen years after the Declaration by the Báb of His mission in 1844, when Bahá'u'lláh, while in Ba<u>gh</u>dád, declared to be "*Him Whom God shall make manifest*".

In the third chapter of the *Persian Bayán*, the Báb affirmed:

If at the time of the appearance of Him Whom God will make manifest all the dwellers of the earth were to bear witness unto a thing whereunto He beareth witness differently, His testimony would be like unto the sun, while theirs would be even as a false image produced in a mirror which is not facing the sun. For had it been otherwise their testimony would have proved a faithful reflection of His testimony.

I swear by the most sacred Essence of God that but one line of the Words uttered by Him is more sublime than the words uttered by all that dwell on earth. Nay, I beg forgiveness for making this comparison. How could the reflections of the sun in the mirror compare with the wondrous rays of the sun in the visible heaven? The station of one is that of nothingness, while the station of the other, by the righteousness of God—hallowed and magnified be His Name—is that of the Reality of things ....[5]

By the time of the conference of Bada<u>sh</u>t, the theme of "Him Whom God shall make manifest" attracted intense interest and expectation within the Bábí community. This was because the Báb had written in the *Kitábu'l-Asmá'* ("Book of Divine Names")[6] that "He Whom God shall make manifest" is a normal human currently living among the believers:

---

1 *Qur'án* 39:60. Cited in Nabíl-i-A'ẓam, *The Dawn-Breakers*, p. 41.

2 William Sears, *Thief in the Night*, p. 93.

3 William Sears, *Thief in the Night*, p. 93.

4 William Sears, *Thief in the Night*, p. 92.

5 The Báb, *Selections*, p. 100.

6 The *Kitáb-i-Asmá'* ("The Book of Divine Names") was revealed in Máh-Kú and <u>Ch</u>ihríq between 1848–1849.

> *Say, He Whom God shall make manifest is but one of you; He will make Himself known unto you on the Day of Resurrection. Ye shall know God when the Manifestation of His Own Self is made known unto you, that perchance ye may not stray far from His Path.*[1]

Furthermore, in the *Kitáb-i-Panj-Sha'n* ("The Book of Five Modes or Grades"), one of His last books, the Báb definitely identified *Him Whom shall make manifest* with Bahá'u'lláh, *"Do ye know Bahá'u'lláh or not? For He is the glory of Him Whom shall make manifest."*[2] Historian Adib Taherzadeh wrote:

> It is important to note that although Bahá'u'lláh did not intimate His station to the Bábís, several souls among them recognized Him as "Him Whom God shall make manifest" during the Ministry of the Báb, long before Bahá'u'lláh's imprisonment in the Síyáh-Chál.[3] Mullá Ḥusayn, the one who first made contact with Him, was aware of His station. Likewise Quddús and Ṭáhirih had discovered that He, and no one else, was the Promised One of the *Bayán*. Indeed, when we study the events that took place at the Conference of Badasht, it becomes clear that these two outstanding disciples of the Báb had full knowledge of the station of Bahá'u'lláh. Some of those who took part in that conference were surprised to witness the expressions of utmost lowliness and humility by Quddús and Ṭáhirih towards Bahá'u'lláh. The reverence which they showed to Him at Badasht by far exceeded the homage they paid to the Báb.[4]

Ṭáhirih and "*Him Whom God shall make manifest*"

There is ample evidence to suggest that Ṭáhirih knew that Bahá'u'lláh was "Him Whom God shall make manifest".[5] In her poems, aware of Bahá'u'lláh's station, Ṭáhirih refers to Him as her Lord,[6] "Immaculate King", "unknowable King", "beneficent Moon", "King of Hearts".[7] In these verses, she portrays the sound of Bahá'u'lláh's footsteps outside her Badasht pavilion in these words:

> The sound of footsteps
> I hear from afar
> Suddenly enraptures

---

1 The Báb, *Selections*, p. 144.

2 The Báb in Adib Taherzadeh, *The Covenant of Bahá'u'lláh*, p. 44.

3 In 1853, Bahá'u'lláh was imprisoned in the Síyáh-Chál ("Black Hole"), a prison where He received the first intimations of His divine mission. The Síyáh-Chál was an underground dungeon infested with filth and vermin. It had previously been one of the water tanks of a public bath in the city.

4 Adib Taherzadeh, The *Covenant of Bahá'u'lláh*, p. 56.

5 Omid Ghaemmaghami, *The Hand of God is not Chained up*, p. 416.

6 Adib Taherzadeh, The *Covenant of Bahá'u'lláh*, p. 56.

7 Amrollah Hemmat and John Hatcher, *The Poetry of Ṭáhirih*, p. 86.

The essence of all that I am—
I recognise it.

Oh, it is the sound of
His footfall
It is His graceful gait
As He treads the pathway
Outside my pavilion![1]

The following stanzas reveal her clear understanding of Bahá'u'lláh's station:

O concourse of the realm on high,
Proclaim with joy the cry of reunion,
For the matchless beauty of the beloved's face'
Has appeared and is disclosed.

Since the veil has been lifted
From the face of Him whom we 'did not know',
Let your melodies be heard from every quarter:
'Light has subdued night's darkness!'[2]

Although at that time Bahá'u'lláh was *"still behind the veil of glory"*,[3] there is also evidence that Quddús had recognised the station of Bahá'u'lláh. The historian Stephen Lambden wrote:

> [Quddús] is said to have written tablets at Bada<u>sh</u>t and referred to a time when the Lord will cause a secret to be made manifest from the horizon of Bahá' in the land of 'or even nearer' [*aw ádná*, see *Qur'án* 53:9], shining resplendent from the "Point of Bahá'" ....[4]

Quddús and Bahá'u'lláh

Bahá'u'lláh stated in the *Lawḥ-i-Sarráj*[5] that Quddús announced the Revelation of Bahá'u'lláh at the conference of Bada<u>sh</u>t.[6] The *Lawḥ-i-Sarráj* was revealed in Adrianople circa 1867, about twenty years after the conference of Bada<u>sh</u>t. The repository was Mullá 'Alí-Muḥammad-i-Iṣfahání who was a saddler (*sarráj*) by trade. Dr Vargha Bolodo-Taefi explains:

> In the Tablet of Bahá'u'lláh addressed to Mullá 'Alí-Muḥammad-i-Iṣfahání, known as the *Lawḥ-i-Sarráj* (also referred to as the *Lawḥ-i-Siráj*), Bahá'u'lláh states that in Bada<u>sh</u>t, Quddús wrote and dispatched some letters, including some that foretold the advent of this most wondrous and

1 Amrollah Hemmat and John Hatcher, *The Poetry of Ṭáhirih*, p. 88.

2 Amrollah Hemmat and John Hatcher, *The Poetry of Ṭáhirih*, p. 85.

3 'Abdu'l-Bahá, *A Traveller's Narrative*, p. 4.

4 Stephen Lambden, *The Word Bahá*, p. 37.

5 Shoghi Effendi translated some passages of the *Lawḥ-i-Sarráj* in *Gleanings from the Writings of Bahá'u'lláh* (sections L and XCVII).

6 Nosratollah Mohammadhosseini, *Tahereh*, p. 338.

new Revelation (referring to the Revelation of Bahá'u'lláh). Bahá'u'lláh then quotes a few sentences from the writings of Quddús that prophesy the advent of Bahá'u'lláh's Revelation, states that these writings are still available, and affirms that they explicitly refer to this Cause (the Cause of Bahá'u'lláh).[1]

The following is an excerpt from the *Lawḥ-i-Sarráj* where Bahá'u'lláh quotes from the writings of Quddús:

> *And when the Lord revealed from the horizon of Bahá a Secret in the realm of "or even closer",[2] that resplendent Countenance appeared in a beauteous image from the point of Bá'.[3] And when the heavens of ecstasy were raised through the utterances of His Writ, in the form of written mystery, it shone resplendent above the horizon of our Cause unto the dwellers of the mystic realm.*[4]

Bahá'u'lláh explains that His modesty has prevented Him from uttering the words of Quddús, because He has never aimed to prove any station of Himself with words from the past. Bahá'u'lláh affirms in the *Lawḥ-i-Sarráj*, that His station is God's station, that He is nobody and that God's station is the midmost heaven of divine independence. Bahá'u'lláh adds that this truth is clear to everyone except the blind.

Ṭáhirih removes her veil

The Badasht conference witnessed the annulment of a number of Islamic precepts each day with the promulgation of new ones. In reality, the Persian population in the mid-nineteenth century was comparable in spiritual blindness to that of the Jewish faithful in the times of Jesus. Leading these ignorant people who were immersed in the most profound darkness of dogmas and traditions, often irrational, were their Muslim priests, zealous to the extreme in the Muslim compliance to strict religious rules, many man-made, and always ready to supress any subversiveness and to punish any transgressor.

There was an awareness that an abrupt change from one religious system to another was going to be met with opposition and rejection by some of the conference participants. Quddús and Ṭáhirih therefore devised a plan to mitigate, at least partially, the effect of this opposition and rejection.[5] They planned to give the participants the impression that they were in disagreement over the way to proceed and disapproved of each other's ideas. While Ṭáhirih was going to insist on the total independence of the Faith of the Báb from Islám and the absolute obedience to the innovative precepts of the Báb, Quddús would pretend to cling

---

1 Personal correspondence with Dr Vargha Bolodo-Taefi, 21 September 2023.

2 Alluding to the theme of the theophanic Presence of God in *Qur'án* 53:9.

3 Likely referring to Badasht.

4 Bahá'u'lláh, *Lawḥ-i-Sarráj*. Available www.bahai.org/r/666707945

5 Shoghi Effendi, *God Passes By*, pp. 31–35.

to the old Islamic ordinances and oppose Ṭáhirih's plans. People saw in Quddús a more moderate element within the Bábí community as opposed to "the seemingly extremist views advocated by the impetuous Ṭáhirih."[1]

Wearing a face veil was not a Qur'anic prescription. It was an interpretation of some religious sectors on sayings attributed to early religious Islamic figures. Such a practice was meant to represent chastity and purity in women. For most Muslim men of that epoch, it was impossible to accept that a woman would appear in public without the obligatory face veil. If such a situation were to occur, it was very likely that the woman would be insulted by the public and punished by religious authorities.

Nabíl reports that for the first believers "To behold her face unveiled was to them inconceivable. Even to gaze at her shadow was a thing which they deemed improper".[2] As Lowell Johnson commented:

> ... in those days, it was not proper for a woman to appear with the men. No man must ever look at the face of a woman, unless it were his wife. And certainly no man was supposed to look at Táhirih, because she was supposed to be the return of Fátimih, the daughter of the Prophet Muḥammad, a pure and holy woman.[3]

The Báb had ruled out the use of the veil. In the *Bayán*, He had written, "Those who have been brought up in this community [Bábís], men and women, are allowed to look [at each other] speak and sit together."[4] This was a very revolutionary statement in Muslim countries for that time, and in many Muslim countries even today.

An eyewitness recalled:

> Illness, one day, confined Bahá'u'lláh to His bed. Quddús, as soon as he heard of His indisposition, hastened to visit Him. He seated himself, when ushered into His presence, on the right hand of Bahá'u'lláh. The rest of the companions were gradually admitted to His presence, and grouped themselves around Him. No sooner had they assembled than Muḥammad-Ḥasan-i-Qazvíní, the messenger of Ṭáhirih, upon whom the name of Fata'l-Qazvíní had been newly conferred, suddenly came in and conveyed to Quddús a pressing invitation from Ṭáhirih to visit her in her own garden. "I have severed myself entirely from her", he boldly and decisively replied. "I refuse to meet her." The messenger retired immediately, and soon returned, reiterating the same message and appealing to him to heed her urgent call. "She insists on your visit," were his words. "If you persist in your refusal, she herself will come to you." Perceiving his unyielding

1 Shoghi Effendi, *God Passes By*, pp. 31–32.
2 Nabíl-i-A'ẓam, *The Dawn-Breakers*, p. 295.
3 Lowell Johnson, *Quddús*, p. 14.
4 Armin Eschraghi, *Undermining the Foundations of Orthodoxy*, p. 232. See The Báb, *The Persian Bayán* 8:09 and 8:10.

attitude, the messenger unsheathed his sword, laid it at the feet of Quddús, and said: "I refuse to go without you. Either choose to accompany me to the presence of Ṭáhirih or cut off my head with this sword." "I have already declared my intention not to visit Ṭáhirih," Quddús angrily retorted. "I am willing to comply with the alternative which you have chosen to put before me."

Muḥammad-Ḥasan, who had seated himself at the feet of Quddús, had stretched forth his neck to receive the fatal blow, when suddenly the figure of Ṭáhirih, adorned and unveiled, appeared before the eyes of the assembled companions. Consternation immediately seized the entire gathering. All stood aghast before this sudden and most unexpected apparition. To behold her face unveiled was to them inconceivable. Even to gaze at her shadow was a thing which they deemed improper ....[1]

Shoghi Effendi remarked on the same episode:

One day in His presence, when illness had confined Him to bed, Ṭáhirih, regarded as the fair and spotless emblem of chastity and the incarnation of the holy Fáṭimih, appeared suddenly, adorned yet unveiled, before the assembled companions, seated herself on the right hand of the affrighted and infuriated Quddús, and tearing through her fiery words the veils guarding the sanctity of the ordinances of Islam, sounded the clarion-call, and proclaimed the inauguration, of a new Dispensation.

Quddús, mute with rage, seemed to be only waiting for the moment when he could strike her down with the sword he happened to be then holding in his hand. [2]

Such an act also represented the fulfillment of an Islamic prophecy indicating that

The face of Fáṭimih, needs be revealed on the Day of Judgment and appear unveiled before the eyes of men. At that moment the voice of the Unseen shall be heard saying: "Turn your eyes away from that which ye have seen."[3]

Nabíl added:

Quietly, silently, and with the utmost dignity, Ṭáhirih stepped forward and, advancing towards Quddús, seated herself on his right-hand side. Her unruffled serenity sharply contrasted with the affrighted countenances of those who were gazing upon her face. Fear, anger, and bewilderment stirred the depths of their souls. That sudden revelation seemed to have stunned their faculties. 'Abdu'l-Kháliq-i-Iṣfahání was so gravely shaken that he cut his throat with his own hands. Covered with blood and

---

1 Nabíl-i-A'ẓam, *The Dawn-Breakers*, pp. 293-294.

2 Shoghi Effendi, *God Passes By*, p. 32.

3 Nabíl-i-A'ẓam, *The Dawn-Breakers*, p. 278

shrieking with excitement, he fled away from the face of Ṭáhirih. A few, following his example, abandoned their companions and forsook their Faith. A number were seen standing speechless before her, confounded with wonder. Quddús, meanwhile, had remained seated in his place, holding the unsheathed sword in his hand, his face betraying a feeling of inexpressible anger. It seemed as if he were waiting for the moment when he could strike his fatal blow at Ṭáhirih.

His threatening attitude failed, however, to move her. Her countenance displayed that same dignity and confidence which she had evinced at the first moment of her appearance before the assembled believers. A feeling of joy and triumph had now illumined her face. She rose from her seat and, undeterred by the tumult that she had raised in the hearts of her companions, began to address the remnant of that assembly. Without the least premeditation, and in language which bore a striking resemblance to that of the *Qur'án*, she delivered her appeal with matchless eloquence and profound fervour.[1]

The role of the Báb in the conference

"The Captain of the host was Himself an absentee," wrote Shoghi Effendi about the Báb, "a captive in the grip of His foes".[2] The Báb certainly had a role in planning the conference based on Shoghi Effendi's words:

> Bahá'u'lláh, maintaining through continual correspondence close contact with the Báb, and Himself the directing force behind the manifold activities of His struggling fellow-disciples, unobtrusively yet effectually presided over that conference, and guided and controlled its proceedings.[3]

The presence of personages such as Bahá'u'lláh, Quddús and Ṭáhirih also strengthen the above argument. Furthermore, it appears that, during the conference, the believers wrote to the Báb, Who was confined in the castle of Chihríq (1250 km away)[4] and also received a communication from Him. According to the book *Ganj-i-Pinhán*:

> ... for a few days, the conversation and debate between Quddús and Ṭáhirih continued until, at last, Bahá'u'lláh struck a balance stating that, "the parties should be quiet and calm and wait until the response to the questions regarding the needs and expectations of Qurratu'l-'Ayn [Ṭáhirih] which was brought to the attention of the Primal Point". When the Báb's

---

1 Nabíl-i-A'ẓam, *The Dawn-Breakers,* pp. 293–296.

2 Shoghi Effendi, *God Passes By*, p. 33.

3 Shoghi Effendi, *God Passes By*, p. 31.

4 George Nathaniel Curzon wrote that "The post which goes through from Mas͟hhad to Ṭihrán [900 km] without stopping, but with first claim upon the horses at each station, covers the distance in from five to six days" (*Persia and the Persian Question, Vol.* 1, p. 246). As such, covering the 2,500 km distance Badas͟ht-Chihríq-Badas͟ht might have taken 16-17 days. The Badas͟ht gathering took twenty-two days.

response reached Badasht after a few days, the companions realised that He explicitly endorsed Ṭáhirih's position and practice. He also subtly emphasised the repeal of earlier religious traditions. [1]

New Day celebrated

At Badas͟ht everything old was overturned and renewed. Ṭáhirih invited them all to celebrate the historic occasion with festivities. "This day is the day of festivity and universal rejoicing," she added, "the day on which the fetters of the past are burst asunder. Let those who have shared in this great achievement arise and embrace each other."[2]

"It was Bahá'u'lláh Who steadily, unerringly, yet unsuspectedly," wrote Shoghi Effendi, "steered the course of that memorable episode, and it was Bahá'u'lláh Who brought the meeting to its final and dramatic climax."[3]

Many were in a state of complete bewilderment. Then Bahá'u'lláh ordered the Surah of the Inevitable to be read, which is a chapter of the *Qur'án* that is read on exceptional occasions:

> *When the inevitable event occurs.*
> *then no one can deny it has come.*
> *It will debase ⌜some⌝ and elevate ⌜others⌝*
> *When the earth is shaken with a shock.*
> *And the mountains are crushed and crumbled.* (*Qur'án* 56:1–5)

'Abdu'l-Bahá explains, "*... thus was the new Dispensation announced and the great Resurrection made manifest. At the start, those who were present fled away, and some forsook their Faith, while some fell prey to suspicion and doubt, and a number, after wavering, returned to the presence of Bahá'u'lláh.*" Some of these distressed believers took their leave and moved to a derelict castle 10 km to the southwest.

New Order proclaimed

According to Shoghi Effendi, "The days immediately following so startling a departure from the time-honored traditions of Islám witnessed a veritable revolution in the outlook, habits, ceremonials and manner of worship of these hitherto zealous and devout upholders of the Muhammadan Law".[4]

This bold proclamation initiating the new laws moved the believers to detach themselves from the old standards and empowered them to look with fresh eyes at the horizon of the greatness of the Cause of God. Henceforth they would be firmer in the Faith they had adopted. The independent character of the Revelation of the Báb became clear to all, as also the depth of His teachings. With

---

1 Hooshmand Dehghan, *Ganj-i-Pinhán,* p. 82.
2 Nabíl-i-A'ẓam, *The Dawn-Breakers,* p. 296.
3 Shoghi Effendi, *God Passes By,* p. 32.
4 Shoghi Effendi, *God Passes By,* pp. 32–3.

joy and confidence, they were aroused to spread and share their experiences with their other co-religionists throughout Persia.

The believers carried the news of the Badasht conference to their own communities. It was the month of July 1848. Something marvellous had just happened. The Bábís were now prepared to vindicate the sacred character of their Faith, and even to sacrifice their own lives.

Many began their move towards the province of Mázindarán to re-enact, this time with the hope of success, their aborted experience in the city of Mashhad. Mázindarán Province represented a new teaching territory that had already been prepared by Quddús. In this same month, the Báb issued a directive for all believers to travel to that province and assist Quddús. Hence, the flow of believers was changed from Khurásán Province in the central east to the north of the country, initiating a series of events that would culminate with the episode of Shaykh Ṭabarsí.

11
August 1848 – Five stories

Chapter content
Ṭáhirih's journey to Núr
Quddús in Sárí
The Báb in the Chihríq Castle
Bahá'u'lláh in Bandar-i-Gaz
The long march to Bárfurúsh

On 19 August 1848 the New York Herald newspaper announced the discovery of large amounts of gold in California having accelerated a stampede of tens of thousands of people to the opposite coast of the United States by those searching for the precious metal.

Around the same time, a similar Gold Rush was taking place in Persia, albeit spiritual in nature. The Báb from His prison was summoning all believers to move to the northern province of Mázindarán to assist Quddús in his teaching efforts which had proven very successful.

Around August 1848, five episodes acting like communicating vessels took place accelerating what Danish sociologist Margit Warburg once called the "consummation", the apex and pinnacle of the Faith of the Báb. "The battles of Shaykh Ṭabarsí took place shortly after the Báb had announced that he was the Hidden Imám", wrote Professor Warburg, "and the millenarian expectations among the Bábís had grown to their heights."[1]

The following five stories, while not thematically exclusive and overlapping in time, are crucial for understanding the drama that unfolded over the next nine months and its tragic conclusion. Their locations vary, and each is distinctive having their own central protagonist: Bahá'u'lláh, the Báb, Ṭáhirih, Quddús or Mullá Ḥusayn.

After the Badasht conference, while travelling to his hometown, Quddús was abducted in Níyalá and subsequently confined in Sárí. During this 95-day confinement, the Báb remained imprisoned in the Castle of Chihríq, whereas Bahá'u'lláh visited Bandar-i-Gaz ("Gaz port") on His way to His ancestral home of Núr. Under the trust of a Bábí, Ṭáhirih was sent by Bahá'u'lláh to Núr for her safety. In turn, Mullá Ḥusayn was on his way to Bárfurúsh with 200 plus Bábís to meet Quddús. The details of these five stories are told below.

---

1 Margit Warburg, *Citizens of the World*, p. 135.

Ṭáhirih's journey to Núr

Níyalá is a beautiful and yet small Persian rural village in Mázandarán Province. It sits on a mountainous landscape, with mild and humid weather that blends perfectly with the lush green natural scenery, including waterfalls and forests. The population speaks Mázindaráni, a Persian dialect widely spoken in the province. Like any other Persian rural settlement, traditional agriculture and cattle herding are the population's main activity, with cereals and tea the primary harvests in the region. The Niká Rúd, a river flowing from the Alburz mountains to the Caspian Sea, provides the inhabitants of Níyalá with abundant water for human, plant and animal needs.

Níyalá is located village 110 km ESE of Badasht and 34 km south of the Caspian Sea. On horseback it would take ten days to travel from Badasht to Níyalá and about two days from Níyalá to the Caspian Sea coast.

After the Badasht conference, a number of incidents occurred in Níyalá. According to Nabíl:

> The remnant of the companions who had gathered in Badasht accordingly decided to depart for Mázindarán. Quddús and Ṭáhirih seated themselves in the same howdah[1] which had been prepared for their journey by Bahá'u'lláh. On their way, Ṭáhirih each day composed an ode which she instructed those who accompanied her to chant as they followed her howdah.[2]

Historian Dr David Ruhe adds:

> Quddús and Ṭáhirih chose to ride in the same howdah, now as true compatriots. And each day the poetess composed an ode which she taught to the company trudging behind them. Their exuberant shouts and chants echoed through the mountains and valleys as they proceeded, the words of the odes announcing the death of old ideas and the birth of the new day.[3]

Author Bradford Miller has underlined Quddús' support in assisting Ṭáhirih at the conference to come up with such a risky affirmation of women's rights: "Ṭáhirih, an enlightened woman, also introduced the revolutionary feminine in collaboration with a significant man, Quddús."[4]

Bahá'u'lláh, Quddús, and Ṭáhirih together with some other believers took the route to Mázindarán Province, passing through the village of Níyalá 200 km northwest of Badasht (See map in Figure 37). This happened around mid-July 1848,[5] in the middle of the month of Sha'bán 1264 AH (July 3-August 1, 1848 CE)

---

1 A seat or covered platform carried on the back of a mule, horse or camel to transport people in caravans.

2 Nabíl-i-A'ẓam, *The Dawn-Breakers,* p. 298.

3 David Ruhe, *Robe of Light,* p. 91.

4 Bradford Miller, *Seneca Falls First Woman's Rights Convention of 1848,* p. 1.

5 Nabíl-i-A'ẓam, *The Dawn-Breakers,* p. 301.

which was followed by the month of Ramaḍán. In Ramaḍán, the period of fasting takes place making travelling conditions more demanding in addition to the intense hot weather. According to Nabíl:

> Bahá'u'lláh's sojourn in Badasht lasted two and twenty days. In the course of their journey to Mázindarán [Bahá'u'lláh's ancestral home], a few of the followers of the Báb sought to abuse the liberty which the repudiation of the laws and sanctions of an outgrown Faith had conferred upon them. They viewed the unprecedented action of Ṭáhirih in discarding the veil as a signal to transgress the bounds of moderation and to gratify their selfish desires. The excesses in which a few indulged provoked the wrath of the Almighty and caused their immediate dispersion. In the village of Níyalá they were grievously tested and suffered severe injuries at the hands of their enemies. This scattering extinguished the mischief which a few of the irresponsible among the adherents of the Faith had sought to kindle, and preserved untarnished its honour and dignity. I have heard Bahá'u'lláh Himself describe that incident:
>
> *"We were all gathered in the village of Níyalá and were resting at the foot of a mountain, when, at the hour of dawn, we were suddenly awakened by the stones which the people of the neighbourhood were hurling upon us from the top of the mountain. The fierceness of their attack induced our companions to flee in terror and consternation. I clothed Quddús in my own garments and despatched him to a place of safety, where I intended to join him. When I arrived, I found that he had gone. None of our companions had remained in Níyalá except Ṭáhirih and a young man from Shíráz, Mírzá 'Abdu'lláh. The violence with which we were assailed had brought desolation into our camp. I found no one into whose custody I could deliver Ṭáhirih except that young man .... When the tumult had subsided, I approached a number of the inhabitants of the village and was able to convince them of the cruelty and shamefulness of their behaviour. I subsequently succeeded in restoring a part of our plundered property.*[1]

Bahá'u'lláh continued His indirect journey towards Núr, His ancestral home, via the port of Bandar-i-Gaz (See map in 33). According to author Janet Ruhe-Schoen, Baháu'lláh sent Ṭáhirih, with her female attendant, under the protection of another trusted person, to His home province of Núr, where he arranged shelter for her".[2] [3]

Meanwhile, Quddús continued to Bárfurúsh. Eventually, Quddús was seized and taken to the city of Sárí to be confined, while Ṭáhirih stayed concealed in Núr for about one year at Baháu'lláh's home.

---

1 Nabíl-i-A'ẓam, *The Dawn-Breakers,* pp. 298–299.

2 Janet Ruhe-Schoen, *Rejoice with My Gladness,* pp. 239-240.

3 Nabíl-i-A'ẓam, *The Dawn-Breakers,* p. 299.

Quddús in Sárí

Pietro della Valle, a seventeenth-century Italian traveller, wrote that the alternative name of the town of Sárí, Zadracarta (Pers. Zardshahr or "yellow town"), comes from its yellow appearance because of the large number of orange, lemon and other fruit trees surrounding the city.[1] The word *yellow* in Mázandaraní language is *sor*. Sárí is also known as Shahr-i-Tajin, the town on the Tajin River.

H. John Lewis wrote about Sárí, in 1854:

> Saru [sic] is still celebrated for its abundance of gardens, which emit a pleasing fragrance in the vernal and summer months. Oriental traditionary hyperbole declares, that the entrance to paradise derives sweetness from the air of Saru [sic], and the flowers of Eden their fragrance from its soil.[2]

Sárí, the capital of the province of Mázindarán, is 27 km from the Caspian Sea and by 1874 it had a population of about 15,000 people.[3] Its history goes to back to at least 658 BCE. The region mainly produces citrous fruit, cotton, sugar cane and rice. The city itself is renowned for its scenic surroundings and rich cultural history. Rich woodlands and forests hosting a wide range of plant and animal species surround Sárí.

According to Nabíl, Quddús had been arrested during the incident of Níyalá and subsequently taken to the town of Sárí, east of his native town of Bárfurúsh. Níyalá and Sárí are 100 km apart by road, but at the time it took at least two days to travel the distance.

In Sárí, Quddús was confined in the home of Mírzá Muḥammad-Taqí, a relative[4] and the chief Muslim cleric of Sárí. There are several versions as to how Quddús reached Bárfurúsh and Sárí. According to the historian Mohammad Ali Kazembeyki, "Quddús returned secretly to Bárfurúsh from which the Sa'ídu'l-'Ulamá' had expelled him to Sárí, where he remained confined in the house of Mírzá Muḥammad-Taqí"[5] and also according to Sa'ídu'l-Ulamá's command. Historian Abbas Amanat indicates that Quddús escaped in disguise to Bárfurúsh.[6] Moojan Momen, in turn, asserts that Quddús was arrested when he came back to Bárfurúsh and sent to Sárí.[7]

E.G. Browne adds that "His Holiness Quddús made his way secretly to Bárfurúsh, but his inveterate enemy the Sa'ídu'l-Ulamá, becoming aware of his

---

1 Edward Farr, *History of the Persians*, p. 67.

2 H. John Lewis, *The Merits of Protestantism,* Vol. 1, p. 260.

3 Moojan Momen, *The Bahá'í Communities of Iran,* vol. 1, p. 280.

4 Nabíl-i-A'ẓam, *The Dawn-Breakers,* p. 351.

5 Mohammad Ali Kazembeyki, *Society, Politics and Economics in Mazandaran,* p. 120.

6 Abbas Amanat, *Resurrection and Renewal,* p. 328

7 Moojan Momen, *The Bahá'í Communities of Iran,* vol. I, p. 280.

arrival, informed the governor of Sárí who [then] sent farrashes to arrest him and bring him thither."[1] In turn, Mangol Bayat, citing Bahá'í sources, indicates that Ṭáhirih "arrived together with Quddús in Bárfurúsh, where they were able to find help and shelter among Bábí converts."[2] After preaching at Sharí'atmadár's mosque in Bárfurúsh, Quddús secretly sent Ṭáhirih to the district of Núr where she would be under the protection of Bahá'u'lláh's household.

Hence, it is plausible that Quddús was somehow forced to move to Sárí due to disagreements with the Sa'ídu'l-'Ulamá', who had become his enemy in Bárfurúsh. A chronicler affirms this hypothesis: "His Holiness Quddús made his way secretly to Bárfurúsh, but his inveterate enemy the Sa'ídu'l-'Ulamá', becoming aware of his arrival, informed the governor of Sárí, who sent soldiers to arrest him and bring him thither."[3]

During his ninety-five days of confinement (from about mid-July to mid-October 1848) in the home of Mírzá Muḥammad-Taqí, Quddús had been trying to convince him of the fundamental truths of the Bábí Cause, though to no avail. Quddús was able to substantially support his statements and expand on the meaning of the teachings of the Báb by skilfully combining the seriousness of his arguments with a delicate humorous tone that left no room for heated conversations. According to Shoghi Effendi:

> While in Sárí, Quddús frequently attempted to convince Mírzá Muḥammad-Taqí of the truth of the Divine Message. He freely conversed with him on the most weighty and outstanding issues related to the Revelation of the Báb. His bold and challenging remarks were couched in such gentle, such persuasive and courteous language, and delivered with such geniality and humour, that those who heard him felt not in the least offended. They even misconstrued his allusions to the sacred Book as humorous observations intended to entertain his hearers.[4]

Quddús also used his confinement to begin writing a profound work known as the commentary on the Surah of Ikhlás. As he progressed with the writing, Quddús shared the content with his host, who, in turn, became more predisposed to show greater respect to the young author. Thanks to this admiration, the cleric was inclined to defend Quddús from the insults of a sector of the local population of Sárí.

Quddús' commentary, in the end, became so voluminous that it was three times larger than the *Qur'án* itself. Although Muḥammad-Taqí was related to Quddús, their relationship was based more on appreciation and admiration than on family links. Muḥammad-Taqí never admitted having arrested Quddús and felt that Quddús was his honoured guest. Quddús also had enough freedom to

---

1 E.G. Browne, *Taríkh-i-Jadíd or New History of Mírzá 'Alí Muḥammad the Báb,* p. 361.

2 Mangol Bayat, *Mysticism and Dissent,* p. 117.

3 Edward Granville Browne, *The Taríkh-i-Jadíd,* p. 360.

4 Nabíl-i-A'ẓam, *The Dawn-Breakers,* p. 351.

receive visits from believers. According to Nabíl, "Though confined, Quddús was treated with marked deference, and was allowed to receive most of the companions who had been present at the gathering of Badasht."[1]

While Quddús was still in confined in Sárí, Bahá'u'lláh passed through the town to obtain his release. The Blessed Beauty later recalled:

> *Whilst in Sárí, We were again exposed to the insults of the people. Though the notables of that town were, for the most part, Our friends and had on several occasions met Us in Ṭihrán, no sooner had the townspeople recognised Us, as We walked with Quddús in the streets, than they began to hurl their invectives at Us. The cry "Bábí! Bábí!" greeted Us wherever We went. We were unable to escape their bitter denunciations.*[2]

While confined in the house of his relative, Quddús was still receiving visitors. "To none," Nabíl wrote, "however, did he grant permission to stay in Sárí. Whoever visited him was urged, in the most pressing terms, to enlist under the Black Standard hoisted by Mullá Ḥusayn."[3]

Bábí chronicles relate that Mullá 'Abdu'l-Karím and another believer were detained before they reached Shaykh Ṭabarsí. "Hearing this," John Walbridge wrote, "Mullá Ḥusayn sent out a party under Mírzá Muḥammad-Báqir-i-Hirátí that brought them to the fort. A few days later Mullá Ḥusayn sent him to Sárí to attend Quddús who was detained there [Mullá 'Abdu'l-Karím was a scribe/copyist]. Quddús in turn sent him away with instruction to personally serve the Báb."[4]

Finally, Mohammad Ali Kazembeyki, a non-Bahá'í historian, shares information from the Muslim side on contacts between the tribal powers and Quddús during his three-month sojourn in Sárí:

> With the expulsion of Quddús [from Bárfurúsh] to Sárí, the crisis temporarily melted away but, at the same time, entered a new phase. The existing evidence indicates well how the local powers, under the leadership of 'Abbás-Qulí Khán Láríjání [a powerful tribal leader], taking advantage of the situation, endeavoured to improve their relations with both the government and the Bábís apparently, to gain better opportunities. While corresponding with Ṭihrán, the rebel Khán[5] held conversations with the Bábí side as well. According to Mírzá Jání, the son in law of 'Abbás-Qulí Khán was a Bábí. During the confinement of Quddús

---

1 Nabíl-i-A'ẓam, *The Dawn-Breakers,* p. 351.

2 Nabíl-i-A'ẓam, *The Dawn-Breakers,* p. 584.

3 Nabíl-i-A'ẓam, *The Dawn-Breakers,* p. 351.

4 John Walbridge, *Essays and Notes on Babi and Bahá'í History,* p. 32.

5 For many years 'Abbás-Qulí Khán-i-Láríjání had been challenging the central Persian government in attempting to gain greater tribal control.

at Sárí, 'Abbás-Qulí Khán paid him a visit and even confirmed his assertion.[1]

In this encounter between the regional leader 'Abbás-Qulí Khán-i-Láríjání (hereinafter 'Abbás-Qulí Khán) and Quddús, the latter spoke in eloquent terms citing the Words of God that, "Indeed, the most noble of you in the sight of God is the most righteous of you" (*Qur'án*, 49:13), claiming that nearness to him is through righteous deeds, and that social or financial standing made no difference in the way people should be treated. He also told the tribal authority that the kings of the world will become humbled before the Revelation of the Báb.[2]

The Báb in the Chihríq Castle

To explain the arrest of Quddús after the Conference of Badasht, it is important to understand that by that time persecution to the Bábís had become institutionalised as mentioned by Christian missionary Dr Austin Wright

The Chihríq Castle and the town of Urúmíyyih are 100 km apart. On His way to Tabríz for an interrogation in July 1848—that is, in the same month as the conference of Badasht—the Báb spent some days in Urúmíyyih.[3]

Dr Austin Wright (1811–1864) was residing in the city of Urúmíyyih close to the castle of Chihríq where the Báb had been imprisoned since April 1848.[4] Of that period Dr Wright wrote about how persecution of the Bábís had become an official policy of the Persian [5]government:

> [The Báb's] disciples became more and more numerous, and in some parts of the country they became involved in fierce quarrels with the so-called orthodox party. The affair became so serious that the Government gave orders that the founder of the sect should be brought to Tabriz and given the bastinado, and that his disciples should be arrested wherever they were found and punished with fines and beatings.[6]

In the meantime, the Báb remained captive in the fortress of Chihríq in the northwest of the country. The citadel of Chihríq is located 19 km southeast of the now Turkish (then Anatolia in the Ottoman Empire) border and about 0.8 km west of the village of Chihríq-i-Ulya (Upper Chihríq). There was an old Christian Armenian settlement (with a church) just below the citadel. The Armenian community left about 20 years before the arrival of the Báb. There was also a Christian church and cemetery to the south of the citadel. The pre-Islamic fortification was constructed on the end of a narrow, rocky ridge at an altitude of 2,000 m to defend Persia against potential foreign invaders, such as Ottoman

---

1 Mohammad Ali Kazembeyki, *Society, Politics and Economics in Mazandaran*, p. 120.

2 Fazel Mazandarani, *Taríkh Ẓuhúr al-Ḥaqq*, vol. 3, p. 413.

3 Nabíl-i-A'ẓam, *The Dawn-Breakers*, p. 301.

4 The linear distance between Chihríq and Urúmíyyih is 70 km.

5 Iran was known as Persia in the West until 21 March 1935.

6 Cited in Moojan Momen, *The Babi and Baha'i Religions 1844–1944*, p. 73.

Empire forces or Turkoman tribes. Andreh Marouti said that the fortress was over 80 m high in a 12,000 m² area and was protected by twelve main towers.[1]

Yaḥyá K͟hán was the castle warden whose home was inside the fortification. His sister was the wife of the sovereign. The Báb named C͟hihríq Castle the "Grievous Mountain" (Jabal-i-S͟hadíd) since He was subject to more severe confinement conditions there.[2]

The Báb had been transferred to C͟hihríq from the fortress of Máh-Kú at the insistence of the Russian government, which did not like the Báb to be too close to their borders for political reasons.[3] At that time, there was considerable disinformation regarding the Cause of the Báb, and His enemies claimed that the Bábís wanted to overthrow the sovereign. In addition, the Persian government was concerned about the number of Bábís reaching the presence of the Báb in Máh-Kú despite the severe isolation conditions imposed by Ṭihrán. The situation worsened again from their point-of-view after moving the Báb to C͟hihríq Castle as the number of Bábí pilgrims again gradually began to arrive in large numbers while His popularity grew among the locals. According to Nabíl:

> Despite the emphatic character of that injunction, and in the face of the unyielding opposition of the all-powerful Ḥájí Mírzá Áqásí [prime minister], Yaḥyá K͟hán found himself powerless to abide by those instructions. He, too, soon came to feel the fascination of his Prisoner; he, too, forgot, as soon as he came into contact with His spirit, the duty he was expected to perform. At the very outset, the love of the Báb penetrated his heart and claimed his entire being. The Kurds who lived in C͟hihríq, and whose fanaticism and hatred of the Shi'ahs exceeded the aversion which the inhabitants of Máh-Kú entertained for that people, were likewise subjected to the transforming influence of the Báb.

> Such was the love He had kindled in their hearts that every morning, ere they started for their daily work, they directed their steps towards His prison and, gazing from afar at the castle which contained His beloved self, invoked His name and besought His blessings. They would prostrate themselves on the ground and seek to refresh their souls with remembrance of Him. To one another they would freely relate the wonders of His power and glory, and would recount such dreams as bore witness to the creative power of His influence. To no one would Yaḥyá K͟hán refuse admittance to the castle. As C͟hihríq itself was unable to accommodate the increasing number of visitors who flocked to its gates, they were enabled to obtain the necessary lodgings in Iski-S͟hahr, the old C͟hihríq, which was situated at an hour's distance from the castle.

---

[1] Andreh Marouti, *Infrastructure for Trade Routes*, p. 252. The sketch indicates the castle was about 2,200 m² and the walled village about 5,900 m² = 8,100 m².
[2] C͟hihríq and S͟hadíd ("grievous") have the same abjad value of 318.
[3] Moojan Momen, *The Bábí and Bahá'í Religions, 1844–1944*, p. 9.

> Whatever provisions were required for the Báb were purchased in the old town and transported to His prison.[1]

M. Mochenin, a Russian traveller passed through Chihríq in June 1849 and described seeing the Báb at the castle:

> I saw the Bálá-Khanih [upper house] from the heights of which the Báb taught his doctrine. The multitude of hearers was so great that the court was not large enough to hold them all; most of them stayed in the streets and listened with religious rapture to the verses of the new Qur'án.[2]

The Báb spent more than two years (April 1848–June 1850) in Chihríq Castle. Several essential works were revealed in the fortress, such as the last two epistles to Muḥammad Sháh between April 1848–September 1848, before and after the trial in Tabríz (July 1848). In those epistles the Báb wrote to the monarch:

> *I swear by God, O Sháh! If thou showest enmity unto Him Who is His Remembrance, God will, on the Day of Resurrection, condemn thee, before the kings, unto hellfire, and thou shalt not, in very truth, find on that Day any helper except God, the Exalted.*[3]

> *Were ye to return, however, ye would be granted whatever ye desire of earthly possessions and of the ineffable delights of the life to come, and ye would inherit such glorious might and majesty as your minds can scarce conceive in this mortal life. But if ye fail to return then upon ye shall be your transgressions.*[4]

The Báb also wrote an epistle to Ḥájí Mírzá Áqásí (the prime minister) in condemnatory terms:

> *O minister of the King! be fearful of God, for there is no God except He who is the Truth, the Just. Withdraw your soul from the King. Verily, I am the one who has inherited the earth, and whatsoever is upon it by the leave of God the Wise.*[5]

In Chihríq Castle, the Báb also completed the voluminous 3,000-page *Kitáb-i-Asmá'* ("Book of Divine Names") where the new Badí' calendar, initially instituted in the *Persian Bayán*, was further elaborated.

From 19 March to 4 April 1850, the Báb revealed the *Lawḥ-i-Ḥurúfát* ("Tablet of the Letters") where He wrote, "*Had the Point of the Bayán no other testimony with which to establish His truth, this was sufficient—that He revealed a Tablet such as this, a Tablet such as no amount of learning could produce*".[6] The *Kitáb-i-Panj-*

1 Nabíl-i-A'ẓam, *The Dawn-Breakers*, pp. 304–305.

2 Moojan Momen, *The Bábí and Bahá'í Religions*, p. 75.

3 The Báb, *Selections*, pp. 41–21.

4 The Báb, *Selections*, p. 27.

5 The Báb in Abbas Amanat, *Resurrection and Renewal*, p. 204.

6 Nabíl-i-A'ẓam, *The Dawn-Breakers*, p. 304.

<u>Sha</u>'n ("The Book of Five Modes or Five Grades") was written during the same period. This book was one of the last works in which He categorically identifies "Him Whom God shall make manifest" with Bahá'u'lláh, *"Do ye know Bahá'u'lláh or not? For He is the glory of Him Whom God shall make manifest."*[1] It is in the Kitáb-i-Panj-<u>Sha</u>'n that the Báb refers to Quddús as the Last Name of God.[2] Communication between the Báb in <u>Ch</u>ihríq and Bahá'u'lláh in Ṭihrán was fluid.[3]

Bahá'u'lláh in Bandar-i-Gaz

Bandar-i-Gaz was an important commercial port on the Caspian Sea where Russian ships exchanged cloth, tea, sugar, metal and hardware for wool, silk and cotton.[4] There were also British trading personnel. Bandar-i-Gaz is 40 km north of Níyalá.

With magnificent vistas, the port itself sits in a region that is a rich ecological haven for migratory birds, plants, fish and mammals. The port is located on the southern edge of Gorgon Bay, a huge shallow wetland that is protected from sea swells. Today the Bay is threatened by siltation, growth of tourism and industrial development. The town is renowned for its stunning natural surroundings, including the forested hills standing to its south.

When Bahá'u'lláh reached Bandar-i-Gaz, Quddús was confined in Sárí and Mullá Ḥusayn was about two-thirds along on his long march from Ma<u>sh</u>had to Bárfurú<u>sh</u>. 'Abdu'l-Bahá said that when Bahá'u'lláh arrived, early September 1848, He became sick.[5]

By that time, the news of the Bada<u>sh</u>t conference had resonated in Ṭihrán. The <u>Sh</u>áh and the royal court learnt of the gathering and the role that Bahá'u'lláh had played there. Consequently, a royal arrest warrant was issued by the sickly king. Muḥammad <u>Sh</u>áh passed away on 4 September 1848. A few days before his passing, the despot issued a death sentence for Bahá'u'lláh. The <u>Sh</u>áh is alleged to say: "I have hitherto refused to countenance whatever has been said against him. My indulgence has been actuated by my recognition of the services rendered to my country by his father.[6] This time, however, I am determined to put him to death."[7]

However, Providence, extended her hands to protect the Blessed Beauty. According to Nabíl:

---

[1] The Báb in Adib Taherzadeh, *The Covenant of Bahá'u'lláh*, p. 44.
[2] See Nader Saiedi. *Gate of the Heart*, p. 36.
[3] David Ruhe, *Robe of Light*, p. 112.
[4] Xavier de Planhol, *Bandar-e Gaz*.
[5] Moojan Momen, *Two Episodes from the Life of Bahá'u'lláh in Iran*, p. 142.
[6] Mírzá Buzurg was the father of Bahá'u'lláh and a Persian aristocrat who served as a minister to the <u>Sh</u>áh. He passed away in Ṭihrán in 1839.
[7] Nabíl-i-A'ẓam, *The Dawn-Breakers*, p. 299.

He [the S̲h̲áh] accordingly commanded one of his officers in Ṭihrán to instruct his son, who was residing in Mázindarán, to arrest Bahá'u'lláh and to conduct Him to the capital. The son of this officer received the communication on the very day preceding the reception, which he had prepared to offer to Bahá'u'lláh, to whom he was devotedly attached. He was greatly distressed and did not divulge the news to anyone. Bahá'u'lláh perceived his sadness and advised him to put his trust in God.[1]

Given the threat of Bahá'u'lláh's imminent arrest, the officers of a Russian warship anchored in the bay at that time, as well as local notables, urged Bahá'u'lláh to board the vessel to escape. However, Bahá'u'lláh refused to accept their advice regardless of what they pledged. 'Abdu'l-Bahá stated that Bahá'u'lláh, responding to an invitation the following day, visited a village escorted by the adjutant of the Russian admiral.[2] Many prominent people in the district also attended.[3] Nabíl's account continues:

The next day, as He was being accompanied by His friend to his home, they encountered a horseman who was coming from the direction of Ṭihrán. "Muḥammad S̲h̲áh is dead!" that friend exclaimed in the Mázindarání dialect, as he hastened to rejoin Him after a brief conversation with the messenger. He drew out the imperial summons and showed it to Him. The document had lost its efficacy. That night was spent in the company of his guest in an atmosphere of undisturbed calm and gladness.[4]

After Bandar-i-Gaz, Bahá'u'lláh continued His journey on horseback westward along the coastal shore to Núr, His ancestral home. On his way, Bahá'u'lláh visited several small towns and villages where He was well-received with the honours due to a member of an aristocratic family that was well-known in the region.[5] *"Praise be to God that from the rays of the Sun of Truth all those regions became illumined in those days..."*,[6] once the Blessed Beauty wrote. He hoped to meet Quddús and Mullá Ḥusayn in the weeks ahead.

Bahá'u'lláh was desirous of meeting Quddús and Mullá Ḥusayn in the weeks ahead.

The long march to Bárfurús̲h̲

About the time Quddús was detained in Sárí, Mullá Ḥusayn was 600 km away in Mas̲h̲had, where he was an involuntary guest of Ḥamzih Mírzá. Mullá Ḥusayn had told the prince that he wished to go to the holy city of Karbilá for pilgrimage. Karbilá is where Iman Ḥusayn, Muḥammad's grandson, is buried. The prince

---

[1] Nabíl-i-A'ẓam, *The Dawn-Breakers*, pp. 299–300.
[2] Moojan Momen, *Two Episodes from the Life of Bahá'u'lláh in Iran*, p. 142.
[3] Hasan Balyuzi, *Bahá'u'lláh, King of Glory*, p. 50.
[4] Nabíl-i-A'ẓam, *The Dawn-Breakers*, pp. 299–300.
[5] Moojan Momen, *Two Episodes from the Life of Bahá'u'lláh in Iran*, p. 144.
[6] David Ruhe, *Robe of Light*, p. 93

volunteered to pay the expenses of the projected trip. During the following weeks, Quddús and Mullá Ḥusayn would be in touch through emissaries.

The prince's chief lieutenant also offered his resources to Mullá Ḥusayn, but the latter only accepted a horse and a sword, the two objects that would help him through the following epic months. Mullá Ḥusayn recommended that the prince devote the money he had offered for his expenses to the care of the needy and the poor.

In reality, the Bábís were expelled from Mashhad to alleviate the city's political problems. According to Mehrabkhani, "Mullá Ḥusayn's offer to make a pilgrimage to Karbilá was really a polite way of saying that he would leave the country".[1]

Over two hundred Bábís were willing to leave the city with Mullá Ḥusayn. Several hypotheses have been made regarding their destination. Some historians, such as Shaykh Káẓim-i-Samandar and Hidáyat Khán Riḍá Qulí, thought the group initially wanted to visit the Báb in Ádhirbayján,[2] perhaps to liberate Him.[3]

According to Nabíl, shortly after Mullá Ḥusayn was released from the prince's camp and returning to the Bábíyyih House, an envoy arrived with a message from the Báb sent from His prison in Chihríq Castle. The good news was that Mullá Ḥusayn had been given a new name, Siyyid 'Alí, the name of the Báb Himself, and one of His turbans as a gift. According to the wishes of the Báb, Mullá Ḥusayn should travel to Mázindarán Province, the Báb's "Green Island", to assist Quddús in Bárfurúsh.

In Islamic prophetology, there is a disputed story that the Green Island was an apocalyptic place where a major slaughter was going to occur before the Day of Resurrection, according to a prophecy attributed to Prophet Muḥammad. It was also supposedly the location where the hidden Qá'im lived and the spot where Christ would descend to help the former. For the Bábís, it was the place where Quddús resided, that is, Mázindarán Province.[4]

Since the Persian government had formally banned the Bábí Faith in the then Khurásán Province, it was an obvious choice that the next area for an intense teaching effort should be the adjacent Mázindarán Province. The Mázindarán region had previously been a centre of concentrated and successful teaching by Quddús at the request of the Báb. Mullá Ḥusayn was requested to promulgate the teachings and to unfurl the "Black Standard" along the journey, symbolising the fulfilment of a prophecy of Prophet Muḥammad that this would proclaim the advent of the Promised Qá'im.

---

1 Ruhollah Mehrabkhani, *Mullá Ḥusayn: Disciple at Dawn*, p. 173.

2 A. L. M. Nicolas, *Seyyèd Ali-Mohammed dit le Bâb*, p. 289.

3 Siyamak Zabihi-Moghaddam, *The Bábí-state conflict at Shaykh Ṭabarsí*, pp. 87–112.

4 Omid Ghaemmaghami, *To the Abode of the Hidden One*, p. 159.

Mullá Ḥusayn and a group of Bábís departed Mashhad on 21 July 1848. Many Bábís volunteered to accompany Mullá Ḥusayn on this journey. According to Nabíl:

> My pen can never adequately describe the devotion which Mullá Ḥusayn had kindled in the hearts of the people of Mashhad, nor can it seek to fathom the extent of his influence. His house, in those days, was continually besieged by crowds of eager people who begged to be allowed to accompany him on his contemplated journey.[1]

1 Nabíl-i-A'ẓam, *The Dawn-Breakers*, p. 324.

Figure 32: Muḥammad Sháh (r. 1834-1848)

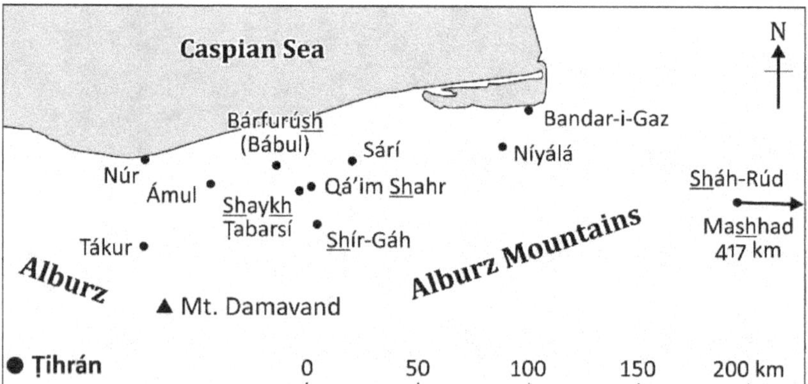

Figure 33: Northern Iran (Courtesy M. W. Thomas)

Figure 34: Bábíyyih house, Mashhad (Source: Bahá'í Media)

Figure 35: Bábíyyih house, Mashhad (Source: Bahá'í Media)

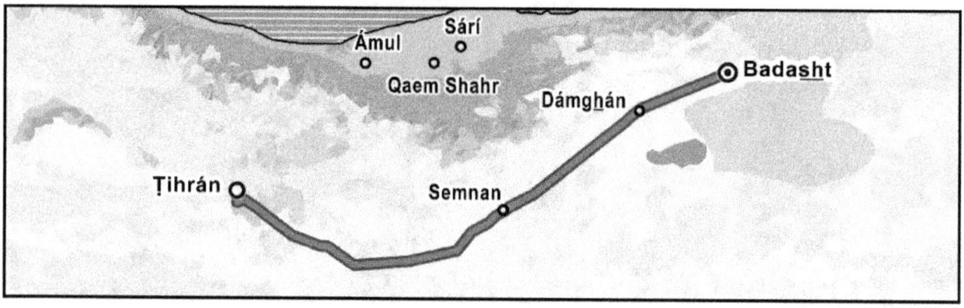

Figure 36: Route between Ṭihrán and Badasht
(Courtesy of Pedro Donaires)

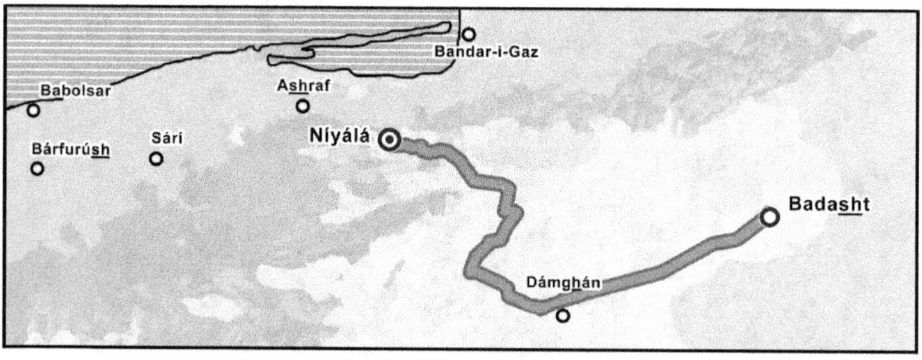

Figure 37: Route between Badasht and Níyalá
(Courtesy of Pedro Donaires)

Figure 38: Old view of Badas͟ht

Figure 39: Quddús wrongly attributed photograph – unknown source

Figure 40: C͟hihríq castle ridge (Source: Bahá'í Media)

12
The long march of Mullá Ḥusayn

Chapter content
Departure from Ma<u>sh</u>had Ní<u>sh</u>ápúr Sabzivár Message received when in Mazínán <u>Kh</u>án-i-<u>Kh</u>údí and Bíyár Jumand Mayámay Dih-Mullá Basṭám Mihmán-Dúst <u>Ch</u>a<u>sh</u>mah-'Alí Fúlád Maḥallih Message received in <u>Kh</u>úríyih <u>Ch</u>á<u>sh</u>m Message from the new governor Fírúzkúh Úrím <u>Sh</u>ír-Gáh Bárfurú<u>sh</u> (Babol) The sardár arrives

July 1848 was a momentous month for the Bábís of Persia. The conference of Badasht had concluded in mid-July. Shortly thereafter, the Báb was brought to trial in Tabríz, where He publicly declared Himself to be the Qá'im and as result was inflicted publicly with the bastinado.[1] Something eerie was in the atmosphere, building into a dramatic ending.

This chapter describes Mullá Ḥusayn's long journey from Ma<u>sh</u>had to Mázindarán Province showing evidence that on the road, at Mazínán and <u>Kh</u>awríyyih, he was in contact with Quddús through messengers.

Many of those places were just hamlets located along the road comprising of a few farms and families. This journey took the Bábí faithful to unfamiliar places, encountered diverse ethnic groups, and crossing hot, vast, hot deserts with only an occasional waterhole at which to rest. According to Ruhollah Mehrabkhani:

> Of course, many of these newly converted Bábís did not resemble the march of an orderly army. Most of the men were mullás or students of religion. Others were carpenters, masons, merchants, artisans, peasants, and so on. Each one who joined the company had to take care of his own

---

1 The punishment by bastinado was carried out with a long pole with a rope hanging from its ends. These ends were in the shape of knots where the victim's feet were placed and then adjusted. Two officers held each side of the stick, while a third strongly whipped the soles of the feet of the victim until they bled.

needs. Some had horses while others travelled on foot; each one carried his own clothing, bedding, and cooking utensils. They could not always find shelter in caravanserais, so at times they camped in fields or orchards, or rested under trees or in the shadow of a wall. They were open to thieves and robbers and had to guard their belongings carefully. [1]

Departure from Mashhad

At this same time, Mullá Ḥusayn had been politely asked to leave Mashhad by the local authorities. He told them that his new destination was Karbilá, Iraq. On 21 July 1848, at the head of 202 Bábís, Mullá Ḥusayn set out to the west on a route to Karbilá via the capital city of Ṭihrán. July is the hottest month in the Persian calendar.

Karbilá is a metaphor for pilgrimage, love and martyrdom. In the year 680 CE Ḥusayn, the beloved grandson of Prophet Muḥammad, was cruelly murdered there with his family. Since then, the city of Karbilá, 100 km east southeast of Baghdád—Iraq's capital—has become a prominent place of Shí'ih Islamic pilgrimage. By indicating Karbilá as their destination, Mullá Ḥusayn really meant that his next destination was going to be martyrdom. After all, the last time he saw the Báb, Mullá Ḥusayn was not given any re-assurance of another meeting.

Bábí history is not entirely clear on Mullá Ḥusayn's actual destination. There are some testimonies that his group's plan was to reach the presence of the Báb who was imprisoned in the castle of Chihríq, 1,500 km away. Some authors argued that the Bábís also wanted to liberate the Báb from His prison or, at least, reach there as a big crowd to demand that the government release the Báb.[2 3] That the Bábís wanted to visit the Báb was a distinct possibility as the Báb referred to Himself as the House of God[4]—a term used to refer to Mecca as a pilgrimage centre. Moreover, the Bábís had been lovingly encouraged to attain the presence of the Báb during their lifetime:

> *And hadst thou attained the presence of thy Lord in this land, and been of them that truly believe that the Face of God is beheld in the person of the Primal Point, it would have been far more advantageous than prostrating thyself in adoration from the beginning that hath no beginning until the present time ....*[5]

> *As soon as the Mover moveth make ye haste to attain unto Him, even though ye have to crawl over the snow.*[6]

---

1 Ruhollah Mehrabkhani, *Mullá Ḥusayn: Disciple at Dawn*, p. 182.

2 A. L. M. Nicolas, *Seyyèd Ali-Mohammed dit le Bâb*, p. 289.

3 Siyamak Zabihi-Moghaddam, *The Bábí-state conflict at Shaykh Ṭabarsí*, pp. 87–112.

4 Nader Saiedi, *Gate of the Heart*, p. 279.

5 The Báb, *Selections*, p. 36.

6 The Báb, *Selections*, p. 77.

However, just before leaving Mashhad Mullá Ḥusayn had received a message from the Báb requesting that he proceed to Mázindarán Province to assist Quddús. This message was most likely written at least one month earlier in order for it to reach Mashhad from Ádhirbáyján, since the messenger had to travel about 1,500 km through several mountainous areas. The historian Kazem Beg described the Iranian postal system at that time: "... a letter takes six to seven days to reach from one city to another, even when the distance does not exceed 200 km. Letters are not sent by post, but are entrusted to individuals who, on the way, stop for their own business, and deliver the letters they have taken care of, often a month after the due date."[1]

The question confronting historians is whether Mullá Ḥusayn's group was heading towards Mázindarán Province to see Quddús, or to Chihríq Castle to attain the presence of the Báb. Perhaps a combination of both goals was in mind, first go to Mázindarán Province and then proceed to Chihríq Castle. The advantage of taking this route was to bypass Ṭihrán, thereby allowing the large group of people to avoid public attention. However, the disadvantage was they would have to travel on a long and unfamiliar route through the dense, wet and humid climate typical of the northern region. There is also a possibility that the final destination and route was a working decision as they advanced westward along the road.

It is noteworthy that, in response to the prince-governor, Mullá Ḥusayn said that he left Mashhad "with the aim of spreading the truth, in whatever way might prove possible, whether by overcoming falsehood or by means of the sword or by suffering martyrdom."[2]

During the trip, they displayed proudly and enthusiastically the "Black Standard", citing Prophet Muḥammad's words: "Should your eyes behold the Black Standards proceeding from Khurásán, hasten ye towards them, even though ye should have to crawl over the snow."[3] Several Bábís and new converts joined the group along the way.

"Mírzá 'Alí-Riḍá [Reza] Mustashár al-Dawlih from Mashhad," wrote Sepehr Manuchehri regarding the financial support received for the long march, "was a well-known personality with numerous properties, shops and gardens. He financed the expenses of Mullá Ḥusayn and his party from Mashhad."[4]

---

1 Mirza Aleksandr Kazem-Beg, *Le Bab et les Bábís*, p. 481.

2 Siamak Zahibi-Moghaddam, *The Bábí-State Conflict at Shaykh Ṭabarsí*, p. 109.

3 Nabíl-i-A'ẓam, *The Dawn-Breakers*, p. 407.

4 Sepehr Manuchehri, *Brief Analysis of the Features of Bábí Resistance*, n.p.

The table that follows gives the geographical latitude and longitude co-ordinates of the places visited by Mullá Ḥusayn's during his long march. (See also Figures 41 and 42).

Mullá Ḥusayn—long march route

Town	Persian name	Latitude and longitude
Mashhad	مشهد	36.295990, 59.596677
Níshápúr	نیشابور	36.218930, 58.791107
Sabzivár	سبزوار	36.214164, 57.679404
Mazínán	مزینان	36.309642, 56.816666
Aḥmad Ábád	احمد آباد	35.766998, 56.602397
Zamán Ábád	زمان آباد	35.590591, 56.774878
Khán-i-Khudí	خانخودی	36.025232, 55.983626
Bíyár Jumand	بیارجمند	36.080556, 55.813056
Mayámay	میامی	36.410494, 55.653428
Armíyán (Urmíyán)	ارمیان	36.359722, 55.402778
Sháh-Rúd	شاهرود	36.418266, 54.968742
Basṭám	بسطام	36.484912, 54.999576
Dih-Mullá	ده مل	36.272722, 54.755498
Mihmán-Dúst	مهماندوست	36.218537, 54.555876
Dámghán	دامغان	36.165556, 54.341944
Ástánih	آستانه	36.271162, 54.096260
Chashmah-'Alí	چشمه‌علی	36.278608, 54.083590
Agarih	آگره	36.159520, 53.832541
Fúlád Maḥallih	فولاد محله	36.060963, 53.707101
Riḍá Ábád	رضا آباد	35.880193, 53.518999
Kharand	خرند	35.935449, 53.441426
Khúríyih-Bálá (upper)	خوریه بالا	35.907770, 53.364087
Khúríyih-Pá'ín (lower)	خوریه پائین	35.890498, 53.309956
Cháshm (Cháshm-Gáh)	چاشم	35.896950, 53.259297
Ásárán	اسران	35.857619, 53.290683
Fírúzkúh	فیروزکوه	35.759529, 52.775432
Úrím	آریم	35.946855, 52.975789
Dú-Áb	دوآب	36.017927, 53.046496
Pul-i-Sifíd	سفید پل	36.116207, 53.057324
Imám Zádih 'Abdu'l-Ḥaqq	امامزاده عبدالحق	36.172793 52.973558
Shír-Gáh	شیرگاه	36.299355, 52.887408
Bárfurúsh (Babol)	بابل	36.539797, 52.677346
Shaykh Ṭabarsí fort	شیخ طبرسی	36.436309, 52.805366

Note: Enter the latitude and longitude co-ordinates into your browser to view its location on a map.

Níshápúr

At the outset of the journey, when they passed through the town of Níshápúr (135 km away from Mashhad), 'Abá-Badí, the father of the immortal Badí,[1] joined the group. In a gesture of detachment, the father left behind a prosperous turquoise mine he owned. For two days, the Bábís stayed in Níshápúr, where they got provisions for the trip. According to a Hasan Fuadi Bushru'i:

> Once in Níshápúr, in accordance with the request of the martyred Ḥájí 'Abdu'l-Majid, [known as] the Aba-Badí, the companions tarried for two days. In addition to assembling the provisions for the believers' march, 'Abá-Badí joined their number. It was six farsangs to Sabzivár when a blessed Tablet of the Báb, addressed to Mullá Ḥusayn, Quddús and Mullá Ṣádiq Muqaddas (Ismu'lláhu'l-Aṣdaq), was received. Therein instructions were given for the three of them to change their turbans to green clothe – (at this time Quddús was in Mázandarán). Because of this, a large feast of celebration was organized and the villagers were served sweets and sherbet.[2]

Sabzivár

From Níshápúr the Bábís moved to Sabzivár (250 km from Mashhad) for two days, where several new enrolments occurred. Eventually, a community of 150 to 200 believers was established there due to the receptivity of the population.[3]

Message received when in Mazínán

It was in Mazínán that Mullá Ḥusayn received a letter from Quddús stating his destination was to be Bárfurúsh, Mázindarán Province. This letter has been known as Shahádatu'l-Azalíyyih ("Sermon or Epistle of the Eternal Witness"), although it has been lost to history. *Taríkh-i-Jadíd*[4] notes that Quddús wrote this letter on his way to Khurásán Province before reaching Bárfurúsh, which must be a reference to when he was going to Badasht. However, Fazel Mazandarani[5] indicates that Quddús wrote this letter before arriving in Bárfurúsh. According to Fazel Mazandarani:

> He [Mírzá Taqí Juviní Shahír] accompanied him [Mullá Ḥusayn], and then they left and reached a place that was around twenty miles away from Mazínán. A man by the name of Karbilá'í 'Alí Aṣghar, who had gone from Khurásán to Mázindarán in the service of Quddús, and was returning from there, visited the house where Mullá Ḥusayn was staying. He was carrying

---

1 Badí' (1852–1869) was a martyr of the Bahá'í Faith who delivered a Tablet from Bahá'u'lláh to the Sháh of Persia.

2 In Ahang Rabbani, *The Genesis of the Bahá'í Faith in Khurásán*, Chapter 2, p. 25.

3 Moojan Momen, *The Bahá'í Communities of Iran*, vol. I, p. 160.

4 E. G. Browne, *Taríkh-i-Jadíd*, p. 90.

5 Fazel Mazandarani, *Taríkh Ẓuhúr al-Ḥaqq*, vol. 3, p. 419.

a letter and a Tablet from Quddús for him (Mullá Ḥusayn), which is well-known as the "Tablet of the Eternal Witness".

This highly influential Tablet is full of hidden secrets foretelling the imminent martyrdom of Mullá Ḥusayn together with seventy souls from among his companions. Quddús praised him by calling Mullá Ḥusayn, Siyyid 'Alí, and summoned him to raise and assist the Cause. He also asked his companions and friends to follow his lead.

Then, that noble person [Mullá Ḥusayn] took a bath and put on new clothes, led the congregation of his companions, performing the obligatory prayers of midday and afternoon, and commanded them and emphasised to call him by the name of "Siyyid 'Alí", and to say that the destination of their journey is Karbilá. By Karbilá is meant love and sacrifice in the Green Island meaning Bárfurú<u>sh</u> (Babol) in Mázindarán, so that the secrets of "Return" on that Day of Resurrection will become evident, and the crusade for the triumph of the new Cause would appear, and that, they free Quddús from the oppression and malice of the 'Ulamá of Sárí and Bárfurú<u>sh</u>, and if possible, from there they should go to <u>Ch</u>ihríq because the road to Ṭihrán was not safe for them. Therefore, they had to go to Á<u>dh</u>irbáyján via Mázindarán and Gílán.[1]

The epistle's prediction of the martyrdom of Mullá Ḥusayn and 70 others of his companions, fulfils an Islamic religious tradition. In this epistle Quddús also asked Mullá Ḥusayn to join him in Mázindarán as soon as possible.[2] Quddús also predicted his own martyrdom.[3]

After reading this Tablet, Mullá Ḥusayn got ready to carry out the directive he had been given charged with, so as a result, he started off reaching Mayámay first.[4]

<u>Kh</u>án-i-<u>Kh</u>údí and Bíyár Jumand

The journey continued through the villages of <u>Kh</u>án-i-<u>Kh</u>údí and Bíyár Jumand (18 km apart) between Mazínán and Mayámay, where three mullás converted.[5] After stopping in these two small villages, they reached Mayámay, 120 km from Mazínán. Mayámay or Miyámay, was known as "the site of a well-fortified fortress".[6]

---

1 Fazel Mazandarani, *Taríkh Ẓuhúr al-Ḥaqq*, vol. 2, pp. 258–259.

2 A. L. M. Nicolas, *Seyyèd Ali-Mohammed dit le Bâb*, p. 290.

3 Ruhollah Mehrabkhani, *Mullá Ḥusayn: Disciple at Dawn*, p. 177.

4 A. L. M. Nicolas, *Seyyèd Ali-Mohammed dit le Bâb*, p. 290

5 Moojan Momen, *The Bahá'í Communities of Iran*, vol. I, p. 265.

6 Nabíl-i-A'ẓam, *The Dawn-Breakers*, p. 418.

Mayámay

From Mayámay, Mullá Ḥusayn sent a reply to Quddús' message that had been received in Mazínán. We do not know the content of the response.

The Bábís stayed at the old and beautiful caravanserai called located at the centre of the town. With a base area of 5,250 square metres, this structure is designed as a central courtyard with four brick porches. Nowadays it stands renovated as a UNESCO World Heritage site. There were ten of these inns in Mayámay which earned the designation as "the city of caravanserais". The city was located on the main Silk Road and was important not only for commerce, internally and linking the trade between East and West, but also for pilgrims going to the holy city of Mashhad. During those years roads were infested with robbers, and, therefore, caravanserais, which were built with defensive structures, protected travellers from thieves and provided accommodation and food for the travellers. With the advent of motor travel, the role of these building faded away.

Mullá Ḥusayn was allowed to lead the Friday congregational prayer at one of the local mosques. In that occasion, Mullá Ḥusayn delivered a powerful address about the "Black Standards", which resulted in the conversion of 31 local Muslims, the majority of them were *mullás*.[1] [2] Unfortunately, there was also opposition from the populace that resulted in a confrontation.

Another interesting incident happened in Mayámay:

> The leader of these [villagers] was a devout and saintly old man named Mullá Zaynu'l-'Abidín, a disciple of the late Shaykh Aḥmad Aḥsá'í. So great was his devotion and the ardour of his affection that he had said to his recently wedded son, a lad eighteen years of age, "Come with me, O my son, for this journey is to the Hereafter, and I imagine for thee a right goodly marriage." This white-bearded old man went also on foot everywhere.[3]

The next three towns were Armíyán (Urmíyán), Sháh-Rúd and Dih-Mullá. In Armíyán, they were attacked by "Áqá Siyyid Muḥammad, who, being surrounded by his friends, ordered them to withdraw, which they did, feeling that their numbers were not sufficient or rather, well-armed as they were, they not yet resolved to take that final step into all out violence."[4]

Sháh-Rúd was 500 km from Mashhad and is on the old border with the province of Mázindarán. They also stayed at the village of Badasht, 8 km from Sháh-Rúd. This was about one month after the famous conference.

---

1 Moojan Momen, *The Bahá'í Communities of Iran*, vol. I, p. 265.

2 According to Nabil, 33 people joined Mullá Ḥusayn's group. Eventually, 32 of them died as martyrs in Shaykh Ṭabarsí (*The Dawn-Breakers*, pp. 418-419).

3 E. G. Browne, *Taríkh-i-Jadíd*, p. 45.

4 Gobineau in Nash and O'Donoghue, *Comte de Gobineau and Orientalism, p.* 148.

Dih-Mullá

In Dih-Mullá, around mid-August 1848, Mullá Ḥusayn received a second message from the Báb. The content of the message is unknown. In this village, Luṭf 'Alí Mírzá S͟hírází, a descendant of the Afs͟háriyán royal dynasty (r. 1736–1796), joined the entourage:

> On the twelfth of Ramaḍán, AH 1264 (12 August 1848), when this worthless atom, after returning from waiting upon the Supreme Source [the Báb], set out for the *Land of K͟há* (K͟hurásán), I had the honour of kissing the dust at the feet of His Holiness the Báb [Mullá Ḥusayn][1] (upon whom be the Peace of God) at a station named Dih-i-Mullá, one of the dependencies of Dámg͟hán, and illuminated my dimmed eyes with the light of his comeliness, and had the honour of waiting on the Friends [Bábís].[2]

Luṭf 'Alí Mírzá was also a Súfí *darvish*.[3] Typically, *darvish*es wear white garments. Moojan Momen wrote that, "when Luṭf 'Alí Mírzá joined Mullá Ḥusayn Bus͟hrú'í's party dressed in the garb of a [Súfí] darvish, he was instructed by Mullá Ḥusayn to change his clothing."[4] The Persian word "dervish" means "needy" or "poor" and suggest living an ascetic and humble life.

Basṭám

Near Dih-Mullá was the village of Basṭám, which was visited by the Bábís. Basṭám was the home of Mullá 'Alí Basṭámí the second Letter of the Living and the first martyr of the Faith of the Báb in Istanbul in 1846.[5] Like Quddús and Mullá Ḥusayn, he was a student of Siyyid Káẓim in Karbilá. According to Momen, Mullá 'Alí Basṭámí was a native of Naṣírábád, a tiny village 13 km northeast of Basṭám.[6]

Mihmán-Dúst

The next stop was Mihmán-Dúst where they camped outside the settlement, followed by Ástánih where Mullá Ḥusayn sent two messengers to Quddús informing him about their journey. Ástánih was about 180 km from Bárfurús͟h. At Ástánih more Bábís joined the march, but due to the large number, and to avoid arousing any suspicions, the believers walked in smaller groups. From Ástánih, the group moved to C͟has͟hmah-'Alí, a further 2 km where they stayed a few days.[7]

---

1 Mullá Ḥusayn, the Bábu'l-Báb ("The Gate of the Gate").
2 Luṭf 'Alí Mírzá S͟hírází, *A Chronicle of the Babi Uprising*, pp. 71–72. See also E. G. Browne, *Materials for the Study of the Bábí Religion*, p. 238.
3 A Súfí is a practitioner of Súfís, a mystical and contemplative form of Islam. They aim at finding God and His love through meditation and personal inner search.
4 Moojan Momen, *The Social Basis of the Bábí Upheavals in Iran*, p. 304.
5 Moojan Momen, *Alí Basṭámí*, Mullá (d. 1846)".
6 Moojan Momen, *The Bahá'í Communities of Iran*, vol. 1, p. 262.
7 Ruhollah Mehrabkhani, *Mullá Ḥusayn*, p. 179.

Chashmah-'Alí

The village of Chashmah-'Alí sits near the city of Dámghán, where roads branch off to Mashhad, Iṣfahán, Ṭihrán and Sárí. The word Chashmah means *spring of water* since there is a huge natural water source in the village that now supplies a recreational resort.

It is in Chashmah-'Alí where another important decision was made after Mullá Ḥusayn had a premonition about the death of Muḥammad Sháh. Mullá Ḥusayn and the friends chose to make a short stop. "We stand at the parting of two ways .... We shall await His decree as to which direction should we take," Mullá Ḥusayn said to the travellers. While he was asking Providence for Divine assistance there was a sudden strong wind that ripped a tree branch from one of the trees near their camping place. This incident was interpreted by the Mullá Ḥusayn as a signal of the imminent loss of the power of the current sovereign, a prediction confirmed when the death of Muḥammad Sháh[1] was officially proclaimed in September 1848.

As Mullá Ḥusayn was departing the village on the third day, he resolutely pointed towards Mázindarán Province and said, "This is the way that leads to our Karbilá. Whoever is unprepared for the great trials that lie before us, let him now repair to his home and give up the journey,"[2]

The road from Chashmah-'Alí, to Agarih and Fúlád Maḥallih, traverses parallel to and north of the main Dámghán to Ṭihrán route, thus avoiding the main Ṭihrán route. This was advisable because of the worsening social conditions and the immanent dangers of travelling caused by the turmoil and the delays that accompanied a change of monarch.

"In Persia", wrote the Spanish Ambassador, "when the sovereign dies, everyone considers themselves authorized to do as they please because they are imbued with the idea that the rulers and authorities are all servants of the Shah. Therefore, once the master dies, they are stripped of their authority, and everyone participates equally".[3] The Orientalist E. G. Browne wrote in this regard:

> When a king dies in Persia, a period of anarchy and lawlessness ensues, to which European countries are fortunately strangers. The local authorities, uncertain of the continued tenure of their offices, hasten to the capital to make favour with the new government, or else employ the days of disorder for their own ends. The mechanism of the State is for the time being unhinged and thrown out of gear, laws are practically suspended, plunder and rapine are rife, and life and property are imperilled. Such was the state of things which Mullá Ḥusayn was called upon to confront. It demanded all his judgement and all his energies; for if on the one hand there was a hope that the new government might prove more favourably disposed

1 Muḥammad Sháh died on 4 September 1848.

2 Nabíl-i-A'ẓam, *The Dawn-Breakers,* p. 326.

3 Adolfo Rivadeneyra. *Viaje and Interior de Persia*, vol. 1, p. 240.

> towards the Báb than its predecessor had been, there was on the other hand great immediate danger to be apprehended from the unrestrained lawlessness of the ill-disposed, from which almost ever check had for the present been removed. Mullá Ḥusayn accordingly pushed on rapidly to the village of Badasht, situated near the borders of the province of Mázindarán, and there effected a junction with another band of his co-religionists under the leadership of Mullá Muḥammad-'Alí of Bárfurúsh [Quddús].[1]

Chashmah-'Alí is situated at an altitude of 1,100 meters. From there, an alternative road branches off traversing the reddish mountains of the Alburz range before descending into the drainage basin of the Caspian Sea leading to Bárfurúsh. This route is more rugged compared to the main road, though the difference in distance is minimal. The main advantage of this route was to avoid public scrutiny for at least a quarter of the journey from Mashhad to Bárfurúsh. For this reason they travelled to Fúlád Maḥallih instead of the conventional (and more comfortable) route on the main road (See Figures 41 and 42).

Fúlád Maḥallih

The next destination was through Ástánih to Fúlád Maḥallih, at an altitude of 1,860 m, where "people rushed to welcome them and did not refrain from hospitality towards them and providing grass for the horses ...."[2]

From Fúlád Maḥallih the 200-strong group of men had to walk through the mountains for 136 km, representing a theoretical twenty-eight hours of uninterrupted walking. The five horses[3] were probably used to transport the elderly, the sick and some provisions. They were travelling through a rugged area where the route twists and winds along the contours of the hills. Therefore, the travellers had to walk along an undulating road—the shortest distance between two places was rarely a straight line—making the journey more difficult for the already exhausted Bábís who had been on the road for 640 km, particularly walking under high temperatures that can reach up to 44 °C, in a desert-like climate where little water was available. Ruhollah Mehrabkhani describes the travelling conditions at that time:

> In those days it was common for travellers to journey day and night. When it was very hot, they would rest during the day and travel at night. The horses could follow the roads, even in the dark, and the riders would often sleep part of the way on the animals' backs. Not only those who were riding, but even those on foot would follow the caravan half asleep.[4]

On their way they passed through isolated villages to ultimately arrive in the lustrous province of Mázindarán, a region with a totally different vegetation,

---

1 E. G. Browne, *Bábísm,* p. 339.

2 Fazel Mazandarani, *Taríkh Ẓuhúr al-Ḥaqq,* vol. 2, p. 266.

3 Siamak Zahibi-Moghaddam, *The Bábí-State Conflict at Shaykh Ṭabarsí,* p. 97.

4 Ruhollah Mehrabkhani, *Mullá Ḥusayn,* p. 126.

climate and language. On arrival in Fúlád Maḥallih the companions found that they had already reached the area where the local people spoke the *Tabarí* language.[1]

Quddús' message received in Khúríyih

While travelling along the remote Khúríyih Road (the location of the present-day agricultural settlements of Khúríyih-Pá'ín (lower) and Khúríyih-Bálá (upper), a messenger arrived from Quddús encouraging them to continue their trip to Bárfurúsh. From Khúríyih they continued through the Sangsár area, 140 km distant from Bárfurúsh. At that time, Quddús had been confined in the town of Sárí for 95 days (see the previous chapter).

According to the historian Moojan Momen, the group moved across the pastures of Sangsár.[2] The reason to avoid the important towns of Sangsár and Shahmírzád was probably because these two populations were highly fanatical.

Cháshm

During the journey the companions learnt that the new Governor of Mázindarán was nearby. The prince governor, prince Khánlár Mirzá, a few days after arrival at his new post of Mázindarán (August 1848), went back to the capital as soon as he heard of the death of Muḥammad Sháh (in the first week of September 1848). He remained until December 1848 as the governor of the Mázindarán province then being replaced by prince Mihdí-Qulí Mírzá. The previous governor was Ardishír Mírzá. These three princes were stepbrothers to Muḥammad Sháh. Historian A.L.M. Nicolas wrote that "The death of Muḥammad Sháh worried [Khánlár Mirzá] much more for himself than the cries of the Mullás and he prepared to go to Ṭihrán to greet the new sovereign [his nephew] whose good graces he hoped to gain."[3] He did not come back to the province and was not engaged with its governance at all. The story of the prince's encounter with Mullá Ḥusayn is as follows:

> ... they reached Cháshm-gáh (or Chásht-gáh),[4] the first land of Mázindarán, where they learned that Ardishír Mírzá, the governor of Mázindarán had

---

1 A modern source provided the following travel sequence: Abbas Ábád-i-Sabzivár → Aḥmad Ábád va Zamán Ábád → Asgushu → Khankoli → Bíyár Jumand → Mayámay → Sháh-Rúd → Chashmah-'Alí → Agarih → Fúlád Maḥallih → Riẓá Ábád → Tang-i-Kharand → As Kharand-i-Darabi jade-i-gadimi Imám-Zádih Razi gareh → Khúríyih → Asárán → Dahaniyyih Dú-Áb → Farím Zahrá → Halalband → Shír-Gáh → Shaykh Ṭabarsí fort.

2 Moojan Momen, *The Bahá'í Communities of Iran*, vol. 1, p. 246.

3 A. L. M. Nicolas, *Seyyèd Ali-Mohammed dit le Bâb*, p. 296.

4 The names of many villages seem to have been changed and some settlements have disappeared over the last 170 years. Some errors and inaccuracies would have occurred when the chroniclers recalled events and placenames many years, even decades, later. Hence, Chásht-gáh is probably Cháshm in Semnan Province (in Mazandaran Province in the 1800s) at 35.896950, 53.259297. Less likely is the village

been deposed and Khánlar Mírzá had been appointed to rule that province. He had reached Savadkúh,[1] the first land of Mázindarán. Afterwards, they reached the village of Imámzádih,[2] soon after entering Mázindarán Province, when the nobleman [Mullá Ḥusayn] suddenly pulled his horse's reins and stopped, ordering his companions to stop. They all gathered around him and listened carefully to his words. He addressed them and said: "If anyone, in the middle of the road, asks you where you are heading for, answer that we are pilgrims to Karbilá, and since this route is safer and more appropriate, and the companions are poor and some on foot, we found the path more convenient." They [the Bábís] obeyed his orders wholeheartedly.[3]

Message from the new governor

The account continues:

> Two horsemen, sent by the Governor, arrived to this Imámzádih village and approached the companions inquiring about their condition, to which they answered according to the order of Mullá Ḥusayn. The two horsemen drove away and left, but it became clear to the companions that the new Governor of Mázindarán commissioned the riders to appraise the situation. When the companions left the place, they reached the main road to Mázindarán, settled in a place where two springs of pleasant and crystalline water flowed. From that place to the village known as Dih Surkh[4] (the village of Surkh) where Khánlar Mírzá (the prince) had paused,[5] there was a distance of a farsakh (about six km). When the prince heard the impressive news about the companions' strength, number and capacities, and was told about possible centres of rebellion and insurrection with the intention of attacking Mázindarán, he and his entourage would not sleep the whole night, out of fear and anxiety. They kept a watchful guard, and a group of armed men and women around them. He prepared his army and assigned some people to guard the passages and roads and prepared fortifications.
>
> To that place, two horsemen arrived, on his [prince's] behalf, to the group of companions to investigate Mullá Ḥusayn's affairs. He [Mullá Ḥusayn] replied according to the form mentioned earlier. He stated that a few

---

of Chásht Khúrán (35.699886, 53.617869), 40 km southeast of Cháshm.

1 Sawádkúd (Savádkúd) is the first county in Mazandaran on the Fírúzkúh to Babol road.

2 The location of Imámzádih is unknown.

3 Fazel Mázindarání, *Ẓuhúr al-Ḥaqq*, vol. 2, pp. 267–270.

4 Location is approximately that of Pá'ín Surkhábád (35.966649, 53.015793) on the main Ṭihrán-Babol road.

5 The new prince governor, Khánlár Mirzá, who a few days after arrival at his post (August 1848), went back to the capital when he learned of the death of Muḥammad Sháh (in the first week of September 1848).

> members of this congregation are travellers, and some are merchants, and they have goods suitable for the people of Mázindarán. They want to sell them and prepare them for the afoot pilgrims, and as we reached this place, we heard the news of the prince, the new governor, and we were planning to meet him [the prince] and ask for some riders and officials to protect pilgrims and travellers from the danger of robbers, and pass through the land of Mázindarán. As the riders heard this, they expressed their surprise and, concerning the calumnies reputed to these people, they expressed words of consternation and perplexity, and said that in order to correct the mistake and achieve their goal, the first thing is to send two of your wise men to the prince to clarify your content.
>
> He [Mullá Ḥusayn] sent Mullá Muqqadas Khurásání, Mírzá Muḥammad-Taqíy-i-Qá'íní, Áqá Siyyid Zaynu'l-'Ábidín Shírází, Mírzá Muḥammad-Taqí Juvíní and Siyyid 'Abdu'lláh-Kaní to the prince. He asked all the companions to hide their weapons and put on the turbans that they had disguised as hats during the journey. They became confused and as soon as the said messengers reached the governor and met and talked to him, answering his questions, the prince overcame his fear and concerns, gained confidence, and rode towards Mullá Ḥusayn and his companions. When the prince got near them and saw a group of scholars and disabled siyyids, he commanded them to spread a carpet in the shade of a tree and unhorsed, sat on the carpet, turned to the companions, and said, "You have to pay a fine for my sleepless nights, because I did not sleep last night for the fear of you." So, Mullá Ḥusayn told Mírzá Muḥammad-Taqíy-i-Qá'iní and Ḥájí 'Abdu'l Ḥámid Níshápúrí offer some money, turquoise fabrics, and handkerchiefs to the prince, and said that we are presenting these as a gift and congratulations for the government, and not as a fine. He was very pleased and sent a rider with the companions to safely reach Fírúzih Mountain. They set off, and as soon as they had travelled some distance, the rider stated that this road was public and safe from any dangers, and asked Mullá Ḥusayn's permission to return. Mullá Ḥusayn ordered he be given some reward, and he went back to the prince.[1]

The chronicler Mírzá Luṭf-'Alí informs us that the prince also said to the believers, "You are all Bábís and *mufsidúna fí'l-arḍ*" (literally, "the corrupt upon the land", from *Qur'án* 18:94), and killing you is obligatory, and the Sháh [Muḥammad Sháh] has ordered that wherever they find you, they kill you."[2] "Corruption has spread on land" is a term from *Qur'án* 30:41 (*al-fasád fí'l-barri*) which can be used as a serious accusation typified as a capital crime resulting in death.

---

1 Fazel Mázindarání, *Ẓuhúr al-Ḥaqq*, vol. 2, pp. 267–270.

2 Mírzá Luṭf 'Alí Shírází, *A Chronicle of the Bábí Uprising*, p. 14. Cited in Siyamak Zabihi-Moghaddam, *The Bábí-state conflict at Shaykh Ṭabarsí*, p. 105.

Fírúzkúh

The chronicles of the events, often written many years later, contain conflicting and obscure information regarding locations visited and their names. A possible route from Cháshm to Bárfurúsh would be west, a difficult mountain pass for two hundred people through steep hills, and then north to Dú-Áb on the main Ṭihrán-Bárfurúsh road. However, to travel through Fírúzkúh would mean backtracking a little, being more comfortable, and then go west to Fírúzkúh.

Finally, they arrived at Fírúzkúh, a village at the time, on the main Ṭihrán to Bárfurúsh road that is in the middle of the Alburz Mountains on a broad valley that cuts through most of the range. It is at the base of a massive mountain that towers 500 m above and to the southeast of the city.

They then made their way 35 km northeast along the main road and then turned off to the village of Úrím .

Mullá Ḥusayn would only travel a maximum of one or two farsakhs (12 km) after entering Mázindarán Province, stopping at caravanserais for a day or two before reaching the foothills of a mountain called Úrím and staying there for a few days.[1]

Úrím

Úrím[2] is 100 km from Bárfurúsh. When the group arrived, the locals protested about the Bábís occupying their pasture lands. The locals also complained that the Bábís were buying food at higher prices, and therefore, food was becoming scarce for the local population. It was the first-time people were became hostile to their presence, presaging the difficulties they would face in the following months. At this village, Mullá Ḥusayn again reminded the 232 Bábís about their eventual martyrdom if they decided to continue with him. He also advised that since they had entered Mázindarán Province, there would be no possibility of escape, and therefore, some might not endure the tests:

> Indeed, our supreme object in pressing forward to the goal of this our journey of woe is naught else than to bear witness to the truth and attain to the lofty rank of martyrdom. Whosoever feeleth himself able to bear steadfastly, contentedly, nay, rapturously, this heavy burden, let him remain; but if there be any who perceive in themselves, be it even in the least degree, signs of weakness, they are enjoined to depart, for it is not meet to lay on anyone more than he can bear. Let these, then (if such there be), bid a last farewell to their friends and comrades, and turn back even from this place.[3]

1 Fazel Mázindarání, *Ẓuhúr al-Ḥaqq*, vol. 2, pp. 267–270.

2 Also written as Oorim, Ourim or Owrim -pronounced as "oorim" like "door" in English)

3 E. G. Browne, *Taríkh-i-Jadíd*, p. 47.

According to Momen, "Here Mullá Ḥusayn succeeded in converting Mullá Mírzá Bábá Girún, a cleric who had studied under Mullá 'Alí in Iṣfahán and was considered one of the leading religious figures of the area."[1]

Thirty believers deserted the group after Mullá Ḥusayn's latest warning, with about 200 Bábís remaining for the last lap of the trip. In addition, Ḥájí Naṣír, one of the travelling Bábís, developed a severe illness. Luṭf-'Alí Mírzá Shírází, a fellow traveller, took care of him and nursed him back to health. He recovered his vigour and continued with the journey.[2]

It is in Úrím (a four-day walk from Bárfurúsh) where, according to Luṭf 'Alí Mírzá Shírází, the Bábís learned officially of the death of Muḥammad Sháh, therefore, they decided to leave the village as soon as possible.[3] Actually, the locals had asked them to leave and with the death of the sovereign, civil unrest and chaos were likely to break out, meaning that the roads would be repleat with robbers. This news made Mullá Ḥusayn happy because:

> Ever since he'd learned that the Báb had been tortured with the bastinado in Tabríz, Mullá Ḥusayn had dressed in mourning. Now he donned brighter garments and led his companions forward through "roads... like swamps" where the men, "unused to this kind of weather suffered terribly ..." [4]

It is known that when a Persian monarch dies, a period of lawlessness normally ensues. On the one hand, the Qájár dynasty did not have clear procedures for appointing the successor.[5] On the other hand, according to Gobineau, "during the interregnum there is neither legitimacy nor justification for any form of power".[6] Because of such a vacuum in the state, Gobineau remarked "... the death of the king and its consequences came as a wonderful help to Muḥammad-Ḥusayn Bushrú'í [Mullá Ḥusayn] and his troupe",[7] meaning they could proceed with more freedom.

It took about 45 days before the new Sháh was to be installed, so they decided to head directly for Bárfurúsh, which was a major town of 100,000 inhabitants, to reach a more stable region and to buy provisions.

Shír-Gáh

Before Shír-Gáh the companions stayed near the Imám Zádih 'Abdu'l Ḥaqq mosque, located in the village of Zíráb, 11 km beyond the village of Pul Safíd ("white bridge"), and 75 km from Fírúzkúh.[8]

---

1 Moojan Momen, *The Bahá'í Communities of Iran*, vol. I, p. 299.

2 *The Narrative of Ḥájí Naṣír-i-Qazvíní*, n.p.

3 He died on 5 September 1848.

4 Janet Ruhe-Schoen. *Rejoice with My Gladness*, p. 276.

5 Abbas Amanat, *Pivot of the Universe*, p. 32.

6 Gobineau in Nash and O'Donoghue, *Comte de Gobineau and Orientalism*, p. 154.

7 Gobineau in Nash and O'Donoghue, *Comte de Gobineau and Orientalism*, p. 154.

8 Luṭf 'Alí Mírzá Shírází, *A Chronicle of the Babi Uprising*, p. 22. The Imám Zádih 'Abdu'l

After passing through Shír-Gáh, Mullá Ḥusayn said to the believers, "The days of our rest have passed, and after this, the doors of hardships and calamities will be open to you, and various sufferings will come one after the other".[1]

Bárfurúsh (Babol)

Forty km after leaving Shír-Gáh the believers arrived at the doors of Bárfurúsh. Mullá Ḥusayn was familiar with the town due to his previous visit a few months earlier when he went to meet Quddús, and had openly defied the Sa'ídu'l-'Ulamá', the main cleric, at a public meeting.

The nearly 800 km trip from Mashhad to Bárfurúsh had taken 83 days on foot, sleeping in rustic caravanserais, tents or under the trees. They must have felt physically drained. Siyamak Zabihi-Moghaddam commented, "... several had fallen ill and one had died."[2]

It was 11 October 1848[3] [4] when they finally reached Bárfurúsh, their "Karbilá", the place of their eventual martyrdom. They were now in the Báb's "Green Island". They stayed in town for about nine tumultuous days.[5]

It is in Bárfurúsh where they were to receive their baptism of blood. About 5 km from Bárfurúsh, the companions learned that the Sa'ídu'l-'Ulamá' (the chief of the local clergy) had been instigating the populace to rise up in arms against the approaching Bábís in defence of the sacred interests of his sect. The word had spread that 500 Bábís were on their way to attack the city. It is likely that the news of the revolutionary Badasht Conference had spread to Bárfurúsh causing, in part, concerns of the clergy.

To those approaching him, Mullá Ḥusayn said:

> We are pilgrims and we have come a long way. The king has died and the roads are unsafe. This is the land of the believers; we shall be your guest for a few days, until the new king occupies his throne and the country is secure; then we shall go away.[6]

Mullá Ḥusayn reminded the local people of the exhortation of Prophet Muḥammad to strangers, "Honour thy guest though he be an infidel"[7] but the populace replied: "You are not pilgrims, and we shall not let you enter".[8]

Ḥaqq mosque (36.176665, 52.972883) is in the village of Zíráb.

1 Fazel Mazandarani, *Taríkh Ẓuhúr al-Ḥaqq*, vol. 2, p. 272.

2 Siyamak Zabihi-Moghaddam, *The Bábí-state conflict at Shaykh Ṭabarsí*, p. 96.

3 Ruhollah Mehrabkhani. *Mullá Ḥusayn: Disciple at Dawn*, p. 188.

4 According to Luṭf 'Alí Mírzá Shírází, the arrival date was 11 September 1848 (12 Shavval 1264). Problems using different contemporary calendars can be taken into account for those differences.

5 David Ruhe, *Robe of Light*, p. 101.

6 Ruhollah Mehrabkhani, *Some Notes on Fundamental Principles*, p. 34.

7 A. L. M. Nicolas, *Seyyèd Ali-Mohammed dit le Bâb*, p. 293.

8 Ruhollah Mehrabkhani, *Some Notes on Fundamental Principles*, p. 34.

A fanatical mob confronted the travellers, and a pitched battle broke out, initially resulting in the death of a highly valued Bábí. A seventy-year-old companion was shot dead and the patience and restraint, until then requested by Mullá Ḥusayn, had reached the limits of tolerance. Mullá Ḥusayn approached the tree behind which the author of the crime was hidden and in what constituted a supernatural blow, cut the tree in half, along with the man and his musket. Such a strength of power is difficult to explain considering that he was always a fragile man suffering from poor health and had a weak heart.[1]

Such an inexplicable feat greatly empowered the Bábís who soon inflicted such panic and havoc that the enemies had to run for their lives. Mullá Ḥusayn then went directly to the place where the Sa'ídu'l-'Ulamá' had taken refuge and, in a powerful voice and tone, rebuked him for his cowardly behaviour: "Have you forgotten that he who preaches a holy war must himself ride at the head of his followers?"[2] Soon the people started asking for peace, which was generously granted by Mullá Ḥusayn the same afternoon.

In subsequent weeks when Quddús was told about this account, he repeated the following verse from the *Qur'án*:

> *So it was not ye who slew them, but God who slew them; and those shafts were God's, not thine! He would make trial of the faithful by a gracious trial from Himself: verily, God heareth, knoweth. This befell, that God might also bring to naught the craft of the infidels.*[3]

The sincerity of their request was soon put to the test. On the same afternoon, the companions went to stay at a local caravanserai (inn). A local source wrote, "Everybody went there and saw that a great many Bábís were there, crammed in the caravanserai."[4] When the Bábí entourage was resting at the inn behind closed doors, the populace yelled furiously once again. The attack happened at the same time that Mullá Ḥusayn had requested someone to go to the inn's roof and chant the traditional call for congregational prayers. A young man resolutely determined to fulfil this desire, hastened to the roof but was shot dead by the besiegers. Two other young men who volunteered to conclude the unfinished task were likewise killed in the same way.

Witnessing this incident, Mullá Ḥusayn ordered a general assault against the attackers gathered around the inn. Such was the impetuousness of their charge from the inn with a loud cry of "Yá Ṣáḥibu'z-Zamán!" ("O Thou Lord of the Age"—a reference to the Báb)—that a few of the attackers, who were too stunned to move, were killed by the Bábís, the rest scattered in terror in all directions. The friends of God had clearly achieved a victory.

Ruhollah Mehrabkhani wrote:

---

1 In Ahang Rabbani, *The Genesis of the Bahá'í Faith in Khurásán*, Chapter 2, p. 4.

2 Ruhollah Mehrabkhani. *Mullá Ḥusayn: Disciple at Dawn*, p. 196.

3 Nabíl-i-A'ẓam, *The Dawn-Breakers*, p. 331. See *Qur'án* 8:17–18.

4 Habib Borjian, *A Mázandaráni Account of the Babi Incident at Shaikh Ṭabarsí*, p. 391.

> One of the Bábís was caught outside the inn and buried alive in a well. The well outside the caravanserai, which supplied the friends with water, was filled with earth. The enemies tried to set fire to one part of the caravanserai and wounded some of the Bábís who stopped them. During the night, the situation became unbearable. Mullá Ḥusayn called for his horse so that he could go out again to scatter his cowardly attackers. But the friends prevented him from doing this because of the darkness.[1]

The confusion and fear into which the city again sank into for several days induced a group of local notables and dignitaries to approach Mullá Ḥusayn and attempt to give him a satisfactory explanation of what had happened. Their explanation was that the infamy of the Sa'ídu'l-'Ulamá' was the real cause of the violent attack and this was in no way the real intention of the citizens.

Civil authority did not exist at that time in Bárfurúsh. During nearly four months the province did not have a governor in-situ. The prince governor, Khánlár Mírzá had left to the capital sometime in September of 1848 when he learned of the death of Muḥammad Sháh and his replacement prince-governor Mihdí-Qulí Mírzá arrived in the first half of January 1849. According to the French diplomat Count of Gobineau, prince-governor Khánlár Mírzá, had left for the capital seriously engaged in the governance of the province:

> Khánlár Mírzá had quite other things to worry about at that moment than the Mulláhs and their problems. He was waiting to see the effects of the ascension of the young king as Náṣiri'd-Dín Sháh to the throne. The latter, having been formally recognized by the legations at Tabríz, was about to set out for Ṭihrán, and Khánlár Mírzá, who did not know what would become of him under the new regime, lent only a fairly distracted ear to the supplications of the zealous Muslims.[2]

The sardár arrives

According to A.L.M. Nicolas, drawing from official government reports, Sa'ídu'l-'Ulamá' wrote directly to 'Abbás-Qulí Khán, the powerful tribal leader, asking him to intervene. 'Abbás-Qulí Khán was known as a sardár, that is, a commander. The latter sent 300 soldiers with an officer to put things back in order. According to Gobineau:

> The two parties confronted each other for several days; they paraded; the peaceful townspeople fled, stayed indoors, hid themselves; at the first sign of conflict the women uttered high-pitched cries and emptied the streets, only to return shortly afterwards and watch wide-eyed. In the mosques, the waiz [mullás] or preachers, hurled abuse at the Báb ...[3]

1 Ruhollah Mehrabkhani, *Mullá Ḥusayn*, p. 204.
2 Gobineau in Nash and O'Donoghue, *Comte de Gobineau and Orientalism*, p. 154-155.
3 Gobineau in Nash and O'Donoghue, *Comte de Gobineau and Orientalism*, p. 155.

While the hostilities were occurring around the caravanserai, 'Abbás-Qulí Khán finally turned up in Bárfurú<u>sh</u> to settle the matter.[1] In the absence of a governor, the negotiation was headed by him. In short, he was a warlord, then the ruler of a major tribe located in Láríján, about 100 kilometres southwest of Bárfurú<u>sh</u>, and half-way on the road to Ṭihrán. He was known as a sardár. A sardár is the Persian name for a commander and he was in charge of about 300 soldiers. They were his own soldiers that were recruited from among the local villagers, but it was not a regular government force. In Qájár Persia, regional powers historically have their own tribal forces. He has been described as a "local man with a very direct interest, who moreover, as chief of a tribe, more than any blood prince, which was one of the most undesirable trades in Persia, was far more assured of his rank and position under any regime." [2]

The sardár argued that although the city had not respected the principles of hospitality, public order had been disrupted, and he invited Mullá Ḥusayn to leave the city. In reality, he was not interested in theological discussion as he only understood the law of the sword being a purely military man. For him, the best approach was for the Bábís to move somewhere else and then the problem would be his.[3] According to the Count of Gobineau, Mullá Ḥusayn had written a letter to 'Abbás-Qulí Khán,

> ... in which it was stated that his Highness the Báb and his servants were essentially men of peace who wished only good and abhorred violence. That, in his infinite love for mankind, His Highness had ordered him and his collaborators to go and announce the truth in Mázindarán, and that it was for that cause he and his colleague, Ḥájí Muḥammad-'Alí [Quddús], had preached everywhere, as was well-known to all. But that if the inhabitants of Bárfurúsh really wished to remain attached to their old ideas, regardless of their flaws, it was not in his intentions to use force to convert them, and he asked only to be allowed to withdraw with his followers.[4]

When Mullá Ḥusayn reached Mázindarán Province, a wonderful alignment of four celestial stars occurred, because at the same time, Bahá'u'lláh was in Núr, Quddús in Sárí, Ṭáhirih (hidden in the Núr countryside), and these leaders of the Bábí Cause were all gravitating towards the same province, radiating singularly the light of the Báb who remained imprisoned in the castle of <u>Ch</u>ihríq.

---

1 A. L. M. Nicolas, *Seyyèd Ali-Mohammed dit le Bâb*, pp. 296-297.

2 Gobineau in Nash and O'Donoghue, *Comte de Gobineau and Orientalism*, p. 155.

3 A. L. M. Nicolas, *Seyyèd Ali-Mohammed dit le Bâb*, p. 297.

4 Gobineau in Nash and O'Donoghue, *Comte de Gobineau and Orientalism*, p. 155.

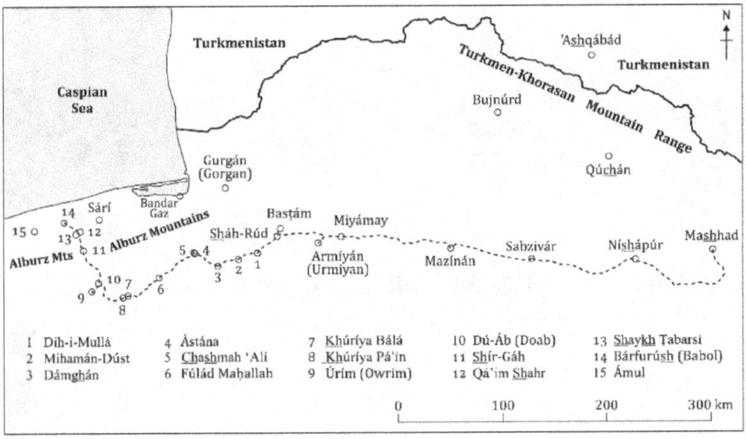

Figure 41: The long march (courtesy of M. W. Thomas)

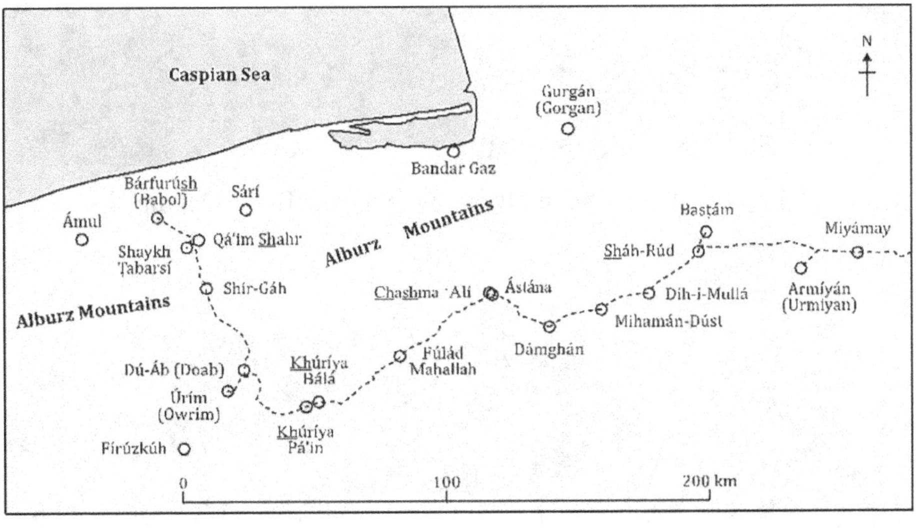

Figure 42: The long march – eastern end (courtesy of M. W. Thomas)

Figure 43: Village of Ní<u>sh</u>ápúr (Source: Bahá'í Media)

Figure 44: Village of Míyámay (Source: Bahá'í Media)

Figure 45: Village of <u>Sh</u>ír-Gáh (Source: Bahá'í Media)

Figure 46: Old view of the Caravanserai, Sabzih-Maydán, Bárfurúsh
(Source: Bahá'í Media)

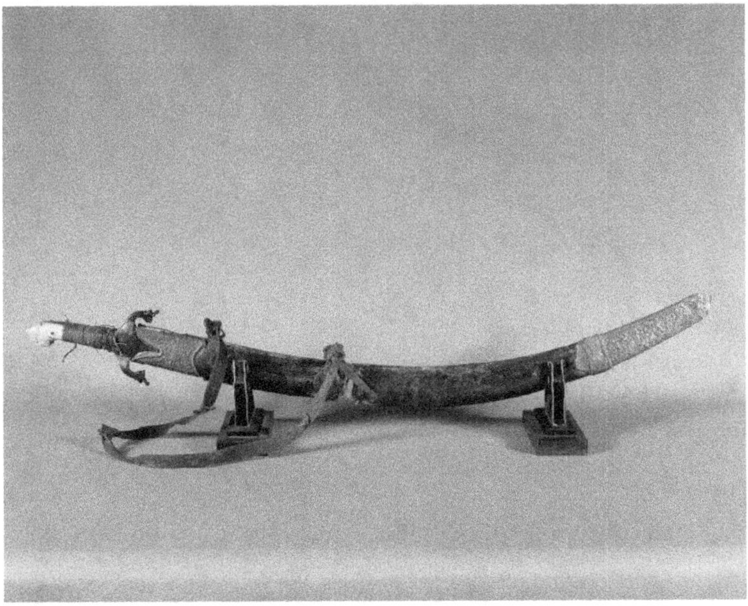

Figure 47: The sword of Mullá Ḥusayn © Bahá'í World Centre

Figure 48: Portrait of Násirí'd-Dín Sháh (r. 1848-1896)

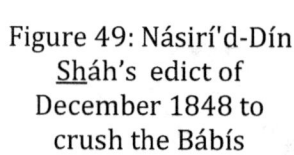

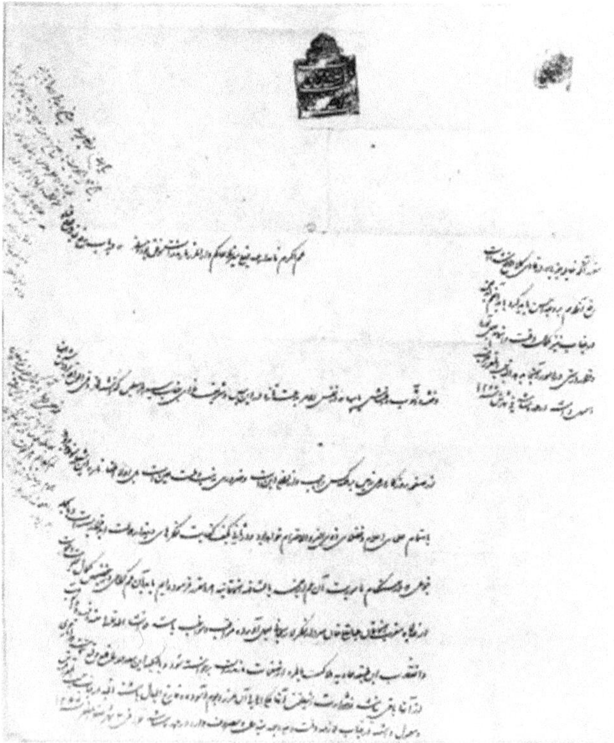

Figure 49: Násirí'd-Dín Sháh's edict of December 1848 to crush the Bábís

13
Settling into Shaykh Ṭabarsí

Chapter content
Leaving Bárfurúsh
The treason of Khusraw
Finding a refuge
Building the initial fort
Words of the Báb about the victory of His Faith

Leaving Bárfurúsh

The city officials promised to provide Mullá Ḥusayn maximum security for his protection if he left Mázindarán Province. Assurances were given that protected passage south to Shír-Gáh,[1] towards Fírúzkúh according to Luṭf 'Alí Mírzá Shírází,[2] including a guide, would be provided during the next part of their trip.

The mention of Shír-Gáh suggests that they were returning back down the same road, probably to travel in the direction of Chihríq in the province of Ádhirbayján where the Báb was imprisoned, 800 km away. Such a distant journey would mean passing through Ṭihrán.

Ámul was another way to get to Chihríq by the northwest of Bárfurúsh towards Gílán. At one point it seems that the Bárfurúsh city officials suggested Mullá Ḥusayn to leave through Ámul.[3] However, that route was not advisable according to Mohammad Ali Kazembeyki:

> [Mázandarán] was neither on the route to the holy places in 'Atabat ['Iráq], Mecca or Medina, nor on the road to Chihríq, south-west Ádhirbayján, where the Báb was imprisoned. Even if he was to proceed in those directions, the Bábís in Mázandarán should have been well aware that there was not a proper east-by-west road in the province on the one hand, in ordinary circumstances caravans, in order to go from Mázandarán to Gílán, had to cross the jurisdictions of several militant local powers of native, Turkish and Kurdish origins with a variety of faiths from Sunni to Shiite and Ahl-i Ḥaqq ....

The sardár promised to put at their disposal a detachment with the special task of watching over them and protecting them on the way. In order to give greater assurance of his commitment, he took a solemn oath on the pages of a copy of the *Qur'án* on which 'Abbás-Qulí Khán swore his veracity.

---

1 Nabíl-i-A'ẓam, *The Dawn-Breakers*, p. 340.

2 Thanks to Dr Siyamak Zabihi-Moghaddam for sharing this information.

3 Nabíl-i-A'ẓam, *The Dawn-Breakers*, pp. 339

Meanwhile, Quddús remained in confinement in the nearby city of Sárí 30 km east of Bárfurúsh. The route west to Ámul, in the opposite direction, was also 30 km distant. In other words, Bárfurúsh was between Sárí and Ámul. All these three cities were bordered to the north by the Caspian Sea and to the south by the dense, swamp ridden Mázindarán forest.

Why did the Bábís not proceed to Sárí to rescue Quddús from his confinement as initially planned? One hypothesis might be that the government did not give them that choice.

There is a letter written about the same time by Lieutenant-Colonel Francis Farrant, the British chargé d'affaires: "[Sárí] ... is the only town not in a disturbed state in all Mazandaran, and the roads are infested by robbers in every direction".[1] However, Sárí, the capital of the province, was where the hostile Governor resided, who, with his imperial forces, was hostile to the Bábís.

In general, accounts of the time show how disruptive and dangerous it was to travel, particularly for a large group that would intimidate many people, who would be harassed because of their beliefs. Far away from their native land, in an unhospitable jungle environment, with limited resources to sustain 200 travellers requiring accommodation and food, the Bábís had to make practical decisions. It is probably at this point that they had totally surrendered to the Will of God and their fate.

The question regarding where the Bábís were heading has not been answered by the chroniclers of these events.

The treason of Khusraw

The main head of the detachment assigned to protect the Bábís on their way out of the province was Khusraw, who was a notorious local ruffian. However, he would soon make clear his intention of not complying with the agreement.

It was evident that he had a close association with the Sa'ídu'l-'Ulamá' of Bárfurúsh. Taken through a misleading route, the Bábís fell into an ambush facing possible death. A hostile mob from the town pursued them seeking revenge for the death of their friends in Bárfurúsh[2] and to rob the Bábís.

During the march, upon reaching a certain point, Khusraw, the officer-in-charge, passed a message to Mullá Ḥusayn ordering him to surrender and relinquish his horse and sword. Mullá Ḥusayn flatly refused to answer and continued to observe his devotions in which he was engaged when, suddenly, the cry of "Yá Ṣáḥibu'z-Zamán!" was raised by the Bábís. This was the Bábí response to punish Khusraw and associates when they began to attack the companions.

---

1 Anonymous letter dated 12 September 1848, "Translation: Extract of a letter from a person sent to M. [Mazandaran] by Colonel F. [Farrant]", "Enclosed Farrant's No. 85 of 1848" in Public Record Office, FO 60/138, London.

2 E. G. Browne, *Tarí<u>kh</u>-i-Jadíd*, p. 53.

During this incident Khusraw himself was killed and the believers repelled the attack.

Sepehr Manuchehri relates that the companions' valuables might have attracted Khusraw's greed to attack the Bábís from the beginning:

> There were other Bábís from the outside who donated funds to assist Shaykh Ṭabarsí. Without this external support, it would have been impossible to resist against the onslaught of government attacks for nine months. Such assistance came in the form of hard cash, tea, sugar or animals. The degree of riches, goods and capital movement to the Bábís raised the envy of Khusraw Qádikaláí and his soldiers. The main cause of the preliminary clashes between the two sides could be attributed to this fact.[1]

Finding a refuge

Not knowing where to go in the middle of the dense and obscure forest after Khusraw's treason, they camped in the forest during the night. The next day, they continued walking, crossing difficult to traverse swamps and dense woodland.

"We are approaching our Karbilá, our ultimate destination,"[2] said Mullá Ḥusayn. "In this place will the blood of God's soldiers and saints will be shed, and many a pure spirit shall be quenched in dust and gore". A chronicler wrote that once Mullá Ḥusayn said these words "most of the companions knew that he intended to say,"[3]

Shortly, the companions reached an old Muslim shrine. Commonly known as the Shrine of Shaykh Ṭabarsí, this was the sanctuary of a revered Muslim saint and scholar named Shaykh Aḥmad Ṭabaristání-Mázindarání (1073–1153 CE).

Upon arriving on 12 October 1848[4] Mullá Ḥusayn uttered the words of the *Qur'án*: *"O my Lord, bless Thou my arrival at this place, for Thou alone canst vouchsafe such blessings"*.[5] There were about 300 men in the group, and they possessed about five horses and seven muskets. At one point, between November and December of 1848, there were 444 believers according to a headcount.[6] Gradually the number increased to about 500 men,[7] in that they were joined by believers from all over Persia and men from neighbouring villages who had converted to Bábísm.

---

1 Sepehr Manuchehri, *Brief Analysis of the Features of Bábí Resistance,* n.p.

2 Nabíl-i-A'ẓam, *The Dawn-Breakers,* pp. 343.

3 E. G. Browne, *Taríkh-i-Jadíd,* p. 55.

4 According to Luṭf 'Alí Mírzá Shírází, the arrival date at Shaykh Ṭabarsí was 20–21 September 1848 (22 Shavval 1264). Cited in: Siyamak Zabihi-Moghaddam, *The Bábí-state conflict at Shaykh Ṭabarsí,* p. 96.

5 Nabíl-i-A'ẓam, *The Dawn-Breakers,* pp. 343–4. *Qur'án* 23:29.

6 Luṭf 'Alí Mírzá Shírází, *A Chronicle of the Babi Uprising,* pp. 71–2.

7 Siyamak Zabihi-Moghaddam, *The Bábí-state conflict at Shaykh Ṭabarsí,* p. 96.

Immediately upon arrival the guardian of the sanctuary associated Mullá Ḥusayn with a dream that he had had the night before in which Imám 'Alí, the Prophet Muḥammad's chief disciple, had appeared to him surrounded by about 300 followers. The guardian fell at Mullá Ḥusayn's feet and asked to join him as his servant.

The Bábís had no choice but to take refuge in the shrine. They felt that could not make further progress through the jungle environment and the wild terrain where only narrow nature trails existed. The climate was rainy and humid, a climate unfamiliar to most of the group, and the local people spoke a different dialect. "For most of the Bábís at Ṭabarsí, Mázandarán was like a foreign country", wrote historian Ruhollah Mehrabkhani.[1]

The area was a difficult place for the troops to access as the shrine was surrounded by "swamps, marshes, quicksand, reed fields, bramble, high mountains with snow, heavy rain, and floods."[2] The dense forest camouflaged any attempt to gain a sense of direction and location. At the same time, the geographic features formed a gorgeous natural setting inhabited by wildlife such as brown bear, goats, red deer, roebucks, woodcocks, pheasants and wild ducks. The streams and rivers in the area were rich sources of fish. Some of these resources might have hunted for food by the Bábís. At the same time, according to 19th French diplomat Hyacinth Rabino who travelled throughout those lands at the beginning of the nineteenth century, "It is in these dense jungles and swamps which are the breeding places of all the illnesses and diseases, the hosts of flies, insects, and reptiles, and all other abominations that infest Mázandarán."[3] The climate of the region is has been described as volatile and capricious.

Mullá Ḥusayn warned the companions that the Shrine of Shaykh Ṭabarsí and the area around it would serve as a bright scene for their martyrdom and that they would soon be attacked. This meant the plan to visit the Báb had to be aborted.

Building the initial fort

The first requirement was to transform the old sanctuary into a secure fort for their protection. Muḥammad-Báqir, that same builder of the House of Bábíyyih in Mashhad, was asked to prepare a suitable plan. When Professor Browne visited the fort in 1888, he observed that "Shaykh Ṭabarsí is in a place of little natural strength".[4] The site is a short distance ESE of a small lake (now a 1.7 ha fishpond) and about the same distance west of the edge of the village of Afrá. Today there is also a 4.7 ha fishpond 100 m to the north. These are artificial lakes created last century and are not natural.

---

1 Ruhollah Mehrabkhani, *Mullá Ḥusayn*, p. 222.

2 Saghar Sadeghian, *Caspian Forests as Political Setting.*

3 Hyacinth Louis Rabino, *Mazandaran and Astarabad*, p. 4.

4 Edward Browne, *A Year Amongst the Persians*, pp. 616–19.

The initial fort, built with timber from the surrounding forest, had small towers and 1 m high walls. Its final form was in the shape of an octagon with several gates (see Figures 60 and 61). Believers from different cities were chosen to build one of the gates.

An eyewitness stated that "the companions, in groups of five or ten men, had built huts in the courtyard of the shrine. These were made of wood, and the roof was covered by hay to protect them from snow and rain. They served as their makeshifts dwellings".[1]

Later, the grounds were expanded and the walls strengthened. Each person was tasked with transporting twenty bricks to the fort from the neighbouring village. Mullá Ḥusayn also carried his twenty bricks and participated in the labour as well.[2]

From about 12 October 1848 until 10 May 1849, they defended themselves with all their energy from within their improvised fortress and in open battles outside it.

The nineteenth-century historian Kazem Beg described how the fortifications evolved with time:

> It consisted of an earthen rampart with two gates, one to the west, the other to the south-east; this rampart was flanked by twelve towers 18–20 feet [≈ 5.5–6 m] high and 600–720 feet [≈ 183–220 m] apart, to be easily defended by the neighbouring towers in case one of them should be attacked. The rampart (as well as the towers) was defended by earth embankments. with embrasures, buttressed by beams and encumbered with trees; it rose sloping to the level of the wall and ended in a ditch 10 feet wide and quite deep, filled with water supplied by the streams and small rivers in the vicinity. The tomb with its stone buildings and its enclosure was in the center and served as a citadel. It was also fortified by earth embankments in which there were secret underground passages; the inhabitants of the fortress, suitably armed, occupied the space comprised between the citadel and the ramparts and had built temporary lodgings there.[3]

A. L. M. Nicolas added:

> In these embankments, and from distance to distance, as well as in the ditch, deep wells were dug, the entrance to which was carefully concealed using branches covered with earth and the bottom of which was lined with bayonets planted pointing in the air.[4]

---

1 *The Narrative of Ḥájí Naṣír-i-Qazvíní,* n.p

2 Ruhollah Mehrabkhani, *Mullá Ḥusayn*, p. 315.

3 Mirza Aleksandr Kazem-Beg, "Le Bab et les Bábís", pp. 489–90.

4 A. L. M. Nicolas, *Seyyèd Ali-Mohammed dit le Bâb*, pp. 300–301.

Mírzá Ḥusayn Hamadání wrote how they were logistically organised and their spirit of collective sharing:

> During the day everyone was kept busy. When night came, they gathered around Mullá Ḥusayn, who spoke to them, words like the water of life—renewing their spirits and animating their bodies. But their calm was soon to be broken.[1]

Between September and November was harvest time, and therefore soon after their arrival the Bábís were able to buy their provisions locally at good prices, even if they paid more than the local people. Products included rice, barley, wheat, sugar, vegetables and other ingredients to cook for, at one point, about 500 people, roughly 1,000 kg of food every day, the size of a 10 m^3 container. A Muslim historian wrote that "the Bábís were good customers of village produce, while acting as evangelists of the Mahdí, his imminent victory over the oppressors, and coming justice".[2] That also helped to create a good relationship with the local villagers.

Words of the Báb about the victory of His Faith

About the purpose of His Faith the Báb declares:

> *Verily this is the true Faith of God, and sufficient witness are God and such as are endowed with the knowledge of the Book. This is indeed the eternal Truth which God, the Ancient of Days, hath revealed unto His omnipotent Word—He Who hath been raised up from the midst of the Burning Bush. This is the Mystery which hath been hidden from all that are in heaven and on earth, and in this wondrous Revelation it hath, in very truth, been set forth in the Mother Book by the hand of God, the Exalted ....*[3]

The Báb confidently affirms the eventual victory of the Cause of God in His Writings, a constant theme in His Writings, strengthening the faith of the believers in time of tribulations:

> *Say, God hath undisputed triumph over every victorious one. There is no one in heaven or earth or in whatever lieth between them who can frustrate the transcendent supremacy of His triumph.*[4]

> *In the Name of God, the Victor of the most victorious, proclaim: 'God will help all those who arise to serve Him! No one is able to deprive Him of His Majesty, His Dominion, His Sovereignty for in the heaven and the earth and in all the realms of God He is the Victorious and the Conqueror.'*[5]

It will not be long before the day of victory arrives:

---

1 Ruhollah Mehrabkhani, *Mullá Ḥusayn: Disciple at Dawn*, p. 223.
2 Mohammad Ali Kazembeyki, *Society, Politics and Economics in Mazandaran*, p. 121.
3 The Báb, *Selections*, p. 41.
4 The Báb, *Selections*, p. 164.
5 The Báb in *Star of the West* (10:1, 21) March 1919, p. 6.

> *Erelong God will bestow upon Thee rulership over all men, inasmuch as His rule transcendeth the whole of creation.*[1]
>
> *The Day is approaching when God will render the hosts of Truth victorious, and He will purge the whole earth in such wise that within the compass of His knowledge not a single soul shall remain unless he truly believeth in God, worshippeth none other God but Him, boweth down by day and by night in His adoration, and is reckoned among such as are well assured.*[2]

The Báb frequently prayed in the following or similar terms for the Cause of God's ultimate success:

> *O Lord! Assist those who have renounced all else but Thee, and grant them a mighty victory. Send down upon them, O Lord, the concourse of the angels in heaven and earth and all that is between, to aid Thy servants, to succour and strengthen them, to enable them to achieve success, to sustain them, to invest them with glory, to confer upon them honor and exaltation, to enrich them and to make them triumphant with a wondrous triumph.*
>
> *Thou art their Lord, the Lord of the heavens and the earth, the Lord of all the worlds. Strengthen this Faith, O Lord, through the power of these servants and cause them to prevail over all the peoples of the world; for they, of a truth, are Thy servants who have detached themselves from aught else but Thee, and Thou verily art the protector of true believers.*
>
> *Grant Thou, O Lord, that their hearts may, through allegiance to this, Thine inviolable Faith, grow stronger than anything else in the heavens and on earth and in whatsoever is between them; and strengthen, O Lord, their hands with the tokens of Thy wondrous power that they may manifest Thy power before the gaze of all mankind.*[3]

---

1 The Báb, *Selections*, p. 5.

2 The Báb, *Selections*, pp. 153–154.

3 The Báb, *Selections*, pp. 192–193.

Part IV
The hero

14
The eight Shaykh Ṭabarsí battles

Chapter content
First battle—the horsemen from Qáḍí-Kalá (October 1848)
Visit by Bahá'u'lláh and arrival of Quddús
A regional army is formed
Second battle—death of the commander (December 1848)
An imperial army is formed
Third battle—Quddús is injured (January 1849)
Fourth battle—death of Mullá Ḥusayn (February 1849)
Fifth battle—treason and triumph (March 1849)
Celebrating Naw-Rúz in the camp
Sixth battle— the enemy tower is captured (March 1849)
Seventh battle— new warfare technologies (April 1849)
Eighth battle—the last engagements (May 1849)

The military confrontations between the Persian state forces and the Bábís at the Shaykh Ṭabarsí fort during the period of October 1848 to May 1849 can be roughly divided into eight battles. According to the historian Zabihi-Moghaddam, "The episode lasted eight months and left an estimated fifteen hundred dead, almost a third of whom were Bábís"[1] representing "a turning point in the history of the Bábí movement."[2] It appears that the Báb predicted the upheaval in the year 1264 AH equivalent to December 1847 – November 1848 CE.[3]

About these battles, Shoghi Effendi wrote that they represent "a stirring episode, so glorious for the Faith, so blackening to the reputation of its enemies—an episode that must be regarded as a rare phenomenon in the history of modern times."[4] He referred to this episode of the history of the Faith as a "catastrophe"[5] a term which is defined by the Merriam-Webster Dictionary as "a momentous tragic event ranging from extreme misfortune to utter overthrow or ruin'.[6]

The non-Bahá'í sociologist, Margit Warburg, stated:

---

1 Siyamak Zabihi-Moghaddam, *The Bábí-state conflict at Shaykh Ṭabarsí*, p. 89.

2 Siyamak Zabihi-Moghaddam, *The Bábí-state conflict at Shaykh Ṭabarsí*, p. 89.

3 Abbas Amanat, *Resurrection and Renewal*, p. 279.

4 Shoghi Effendi, *God Passes By*, p. 42.

5 Nabíl-i-A'ẓam, *The Dawn-Breakers*, p. 653.

6 Merriam-Webster Dictionary. Available at: vhttps://www.merriam-webster.com/dictionary/catastrophe#:~:text=1,%3A%20utter%20failure%20%3A%20fiasco

> The battles of Shaykh Ṭabarsí took place shortly after the Báb had announced that he was the Hidden Imám, and the millenarian expectations among the Bábísm had grown to their heights.[1]

Her conclusion is that "the brief historical period from 1844 to 1853 ... saw the rise, culmination and collapse of Bábísm."[2]

The battles of Shaykh Ṭabarsí have been compared to the siege of the Masada fortress, in the Judaean Desert overlooking the Dead Sea, by the Roman army in 72–73 CE, where 960 Jewish zealots died—men, women and children.[3] Most of the army was made up of peasants who were compulsory recruits from various tribes without military training and somehow alien to the nature of the conflict. It also involved, tragically, members from the same family fighting from opposite sides.[4] The most affected were hundreds of women who were left alone in their rural villages with their children while the husbands were fighting in the frontlines, some of whom never came back.

During the siege of Shaykh Ṭabarsí there were three notable events: the visit of Bahá'u'lláh, the arrival of Quddús (both in October 1848), and the celebration of Naw-Rúz (New Year) in March 1849.

The Bábís were not the aggressors, but the continual danger and threats hovering over them would impel them to use any fair means to defend themselves and the Bábí Cause that they had come to worship so ardently. Their prime aim in establishing a defensive position at Shaykh Ṭabarsí was to seek refuge from their hostile enemies.

The believers fought off the Persian army forces in order to defend their lives, which is permitted under Islamic law in dangerous situations, including religious wars. The Báb never gave anyone permission to undertake holy wars, not even to the Bábís of Shaykh Ṭabarsí. Therefore, they were regularly reminded by Quddús and Mullá Ḥusayn to only defend themselves. "Never since our occupation of this fort," said Quddús once, "have we under any circumstances attempted to direct any offensive against our opponents. Not until they unchained their attack upon us did we arise to defend our lives."[5] Fighting, despite huge disadvantages in available weaponry, the Bábís valiantly distinguished themselves on the battlefield, even when "most of them were on foot, wearing felt hats with white scarves around their necks."[6] The government mistake was to underestimate the heroism of the Bábís.

---

1 Margit Warburg, *Citizens of the World*, p. 135.

2 Margit Warburg, *Citizens of the World*, p. 120.

3 Margit Warburg, *Citizens of the World*, p. 141.

4 A. L. M. Nicolas, *Seyyèd Ali-Mohammed dit le Bâb*, p. 321..

5 Nabíl-i-A'ẓam, *The Dawn-Breakers*, p. 396.

6 Mangol Bayat, *Mysticism and Dissent*, p. 120.

Historian Mangol Bayat's description is that: "The Bábís were determined to fight the government forces who were preventing them from establishing the rule of their religion throughout the nation."[1]

Professor Fereydun Vahdat clarified that the Báb:

> had neither called on the Bábís to launch these upheavals, nor had any doubts as to how disastrous they would end. From the earliest days of his ministry, he strove to erase from the minds of his new followers the conception of the bloodthirsty and vindictive Qá'im mentioned in Shí'ih hadiths, and replace it instead with an image of a peace-making prophet who had made it abundantly clear, orally and in writing, that he did not wish to see even the saddening of any soul.[2]

Moreover, during all those months, the Bábís seemed to be keener to be killed than to kill. The sardár 'Abbás-Qulí Khán once reported to the prince:

> One would imagine that in their eyes the keen sword and blood-spilling dagger were but means to the attainment of everlasting life, so eagerly did their necks and bosoms welcome them as they circled like salamanders round the fiery hail of bullets .... They used to expose their bodies to the bullets and cannon-balls not only fearlessly and courageously, but eagerly and joyously, seeming to regard the battle-field as a banquet, and to be bent on casting away their lives.[3]

It is important to note that the *Kitáb-i-Aqdas*, the Mother Book of the Bahá'í Dispensation, in which Bahá'u'lláh strictly forbids violence, struggle and strife,[4] was revealed much later, around 1873.

The following is a list of important places related to this chapter along with their geographical coordinates to be searched online.

---

1 Mangol Bayat, *Mysticism and Dissent*, p. 130.

2 Fereydun Vahman, "The Báb: A Sun in a Night not Followed by Dawn", p. 75.

3 E. G. Browne, *Taríkh-i-Jadíd*, pp. 108–109

4 See Bahá'u'lláh, *Kitáb-i-Aqdas*, p. 239.

Places associated with the Shaykh Ṭabarsí episode

Town	**Latitude and longitude**
Afrá	36.436642, 52.815196
Ámul	36.466423, 52.354574
Bárfurúsh (Babol)	36.538588, 52.676906
Dízábád (Dízvá)	36.423725, 52.806759
Qá'im Shahr (Also known as 'Aliyábád, Alí-Ábád or Sháhí)	36.463611, 52.858056
Qádí-Kalá	36.587500, 52.588056
Sabzih Maydán of Bárfurúsh	36.540257, 52.678379
Sárí	36.566292, 53.058604
Shír-Gáh, Shírgáh	36.299348, 52.887321
Vás-Kas	36.415021, 52.867400

Source: Michael Thomas, Glossary and transcription for Arabic & Persian terms (2024).

First battle—the horsemen from Qáḍí-Kalá (October 1848)

The very first night they arrived to Shaykh Ṭabarsí the Bábís were attacked by horsemen of the village of Qáḍí-Kalá to avenge the death of Khusraw who was from that locality.[1] Similar hostile attacks occurred after two weeks by the same Qáḍí-Kalá horsemen. Mírzá Ḥusayn Hamadání wrote:

> For about twenty days and nights [after the arrival at Shaykh Ṭabarsí] did they thus tranquilly await the fulfilment of divine destiny, but during all this time the continuous rain suffered none to leave his house. When the weather cleared, the comrades of Khusraw of Qáḍí-Kalá, banding themselves together, surrounded the Castle with a great host of horsemen and footmen, determined to shed the blood of its inmates. When news of this was brought to *Jenáb-i-Bábu'l-Báb* [Mullá Ḥusayn], most of his followers were without the fortress. But he said, "Let none of those who are without the castle stir from their places, and let those who are within go forth and sit down outside boldly and unflinchingly." And all obeyed his command."[2]

In the *Kitáb-i-Nuqtatu'l-Káf*, one of earliest Bábí chronicles, we read:

> After some time, once again, Khusrow's men assembled a large crowd, both mounted and on foot, and encircled the companions. [Mullá Ḥusayn] instructed everyone not to move, and to exit the fences, sit down and remain still. The narrator mentions that some of them approached us and began shooting. We were disturbed as they came so close that their rifle bullets passed near our ears.
>
> That honourable person [Mullá Ḥusayn] came to us and said, "You know we are from God, and you have come here to renounce your lives; so, why are you afraid to give up your lives? Be seated and submit yourselves. Whenever the Beloved desires your martyrdom, you too should desire it; and whenever He doesn't will it, you will not become martyrs. With such a belief, what are you afraid of?" Then he said, "Whoever believes in God, when the bullets come, if he moves his head to avoid them, has become an infidel and ungodly; his declaration and love have been false.
>
> The chronicler recounts that under the influence of those words from that esteemed individual, our fear dissipated, and the sound of the rifle bullets appeared quieter than that of a mosquito. We sat with utmost joy. Though those men fired many bullets, they did not dare to come close. Then, that esteemed person came out from the fort, threw a few grits in their direction, and said, "This is what Goliath did with Saul's army."

---

1 Nabíl-i-A'ẓam, *The Dawn-Breakers*, p. 345; & Mehrabkhani, *Mullá Ḥusayn*, p. 223.

2 E. G. Browne, *Taríkh-i-Jadíd*, pp. 55–56.

> With the blessing of his hand, that malevolent army was dispersed and no harm came to us. After that, the seeds of courage were planted in the fields of our hearts, and fear and apprehension were dissipated.[1]

Ḥájí Nasír Qazvíní, an eyewitness, wrote:

> For several days, they were anticipating such an attack, thinking that surely a mob [of the enemy] would assail them. The honored Báb [Mullá Ḥusayn], upon him rest God's peace, constantly assured everyone to rely upon God, saying, "Out of divine bounties and might, they will not be able to overcome us!"[2]

These hostilities were instigated by the Sa'ídu'l-'Ulamá' from Bárfurúsh and those seeking revenge for the death of Khusraw, who was a native of Qáḍí-Kalá, a village at least one day away from Shaykh Ṭabarsí.

The Bábís immediately responded to the attacks with a call of *Yá Ṣáḥibu'z-Zamán!* (*"O Thou Lord of the Age!"*) and then successfully repelled the aggressors. Based on their experience with Khusraw's dishonesty, the Bábís thought that the horsemen would soon return and therefore further punishment was necessary.

Not knowing the surroundings, the companions by mistake thought the adjacent village was Qáḍí-Kalá. A sortie was launched resulting in the demolition of the neighbouring houses and, accidentally, the death of the mother of the Naẓar Khán who was a tribal leader and head of sixteen villages. The head of the Bábí forces was profoundly regretful of this casualty and approached Naẓar Khán personally to explain the confusion. Such was the sincerity of his apologies that Naẓar Khán not only accepted them but also visited the fort the following day.

Naẓar Khán arrived when the congregational prayer was being performed, and he was very impressed by the religiosity and character of the defenders. Mullá Ḥusayn also profoundly apologised for the loss of Naẓar Khán's mother, explained the confusion, and their fear of a further attack that was largely based on the deceptive behaviour of Khusraw. Their intention was only to protect themselves from the enemy and no ill intention was harboured.

Naẓar Khán accepted Mullá Ḥusayn's words: "Afflict not your heart. Would that a hundred sons had been given me, all of whom I would have joyously placed at your feet and offered as a sacrifice to the Ṣáḥibu'z-Zamán" [the Báb].[3]

Their Karbilá

"We are approaching our Karbilá, our ultimate destination,"[4] Mullá Ḥusayn had said the night before their arrival in the middle of the jungle at the Shrine of Shaykh Ṭabarsí.

---

1 E. G. Browne, *Kitáb-i-Nuqtatu'l-Káf: Being the Earliest History of the Bábís,* pp.159-160.

2 *The Narrative of Ḥájí Naṣír-i-Qazvíní,* n.p.

3 Nabíl-i-A'ẓam, *The Dawn-Breakers,* p. 347.

4 Nabíl-i-A'ẓam, *The Dawn-Breakers,* p. 343.

For the believers, the reason for their great steadfastness and certitude was their acceptance and conviction that they had reached their Karbilá, their place of martyrdom. E. G. Browne reported that the Bábís compared their sojourn to the episode of Karbilá. [1]

As discussed in chapter 2, Imám Ḥusayn, the beloved grandson of Prophet Muḥammad, had been martyred with his family and companions at Karbilá in 680 CE. This town is 100 km southwest of Baghdád, now the capital of modern 'Iráq. In likening their spiritual experience as a spiritual recreation of the Battle of Karbilá, for the Bábís, Shaykh Ṭabarsí was their Karbilá, and Bárfurúsh represented the city of Kúfa, the intended destination of Imám Ḥusayn. Similarly, the lake around the royal garden in Bárfurúsh represented the Euphrates River that flowed to the east of Karbilá.[2] Ṭihrán (the Persian capital) was likened to Damascus, the government seat from whence was sent the order to kill Imám Ḥusayn.[3]

Being certain of their eventual and tragic death at their own "Karbilá", the Bábís fought with indomitable courage. They had no military training—they were religious scholars and ordinary citizens whose only desire was to uphold and demonstrate the legitimacy of the Cause of the Báb. They were equipped with only a few horses and riffles, and had little food or the means to communicate with others outside the fort, but they had oceans of faith and certitude.

With well organised regiments of the Persian army arrayed against them and the expectation of further inescapable bloody episodes hanging like a sword over their heads—like a series of nightmares with no end—the believers nonetheless persevered with courage and sacrifice. Their love for the Báb, still imprisoned, was limitless, and despite the danger surrounding them, they were never willing to surrender.

The friends of God dedicated their time to the chanting of prayers and praising their Creator in a seemingly endless wait for the ultimate end to their lives. The officers and soldiers of the Persian army marvelled at the spirit of the Bábís, and there were many times when they were reprimanded for the inability of the imperial forces to defeat the Bábís and capture the fort. They asked themselves what power was behind the Bábís that made them so powerful. They were astonished that the Bábís were able to resist such a formidable, and well-trained military force?

"Instead of the unconditional surrender which they expected," Nabíl wrote, "the call of the muadhdhin,[4] the chanting of the verses of the *Qur'án*, and the

---

1 E. G. Browne, *A Year among the Persians*, p. 615.
2 E. G. Browne, *A Year among the Persians*, p. 615.
3 Mírzá Ḥusayn Hamadání, *The New History*, p. 337.
4 The person who sounds the call to community prayers.

chorus of gladsome voices intoning hymns of thanksgiving and praise reached their ears without ceasing".[1]

Visit by Bahá'u'lláh and arrival of Quddús

There were two significant events that occurred after the Bábís had occupied the fort at Shaykh Ṭabarsí: Bahá'u'lláh's visit to the fort and the subsequent arrival of Quddús. Bahá'u'lláh might have arrived during the first week of October 1848, two weeks after the arrival of Mullá Ḥusayn, when the new settlement was recent and fresh.

Visit by Bahá'u'lláh

The news of Bahá'u'lláh's coming to Fort Ṭabarsí brought immense happiness to the heart of Mullá Ḥusayn and his companions. Mullá Ḥusayn ordered food for the occasion from the nearby village to hold a splendid banquet for the defenders.[2] Bahá'u'lláh's visit gave them strength and assisted them in remaining steadfast on the path of the Cause of God. He also gave instructions about improving the fortifications.

> "*The one thing this fort and company require,*" Bahá'u'lláh said during His visit, "*is the presence of Quddús. His association with this company would render it complete and perfect.*"[3]

Shortly after Bahá'u'lláh's visit, Mullá Ḥusayn gave preliminary instructions for the liberation of Quddús, and he sent a delegation of seven courageous horsemen to obtain his release from Muḥammad-Taqí, the cleric in whose house Quddús was confined.[4] Bahá'u'lláh had said to Mullá Ḥusayn: *"The fear of God and the dread of His punishment will prompt him* [Muḥammad-Taqí] *to surrender unhesitatingly his captive".*[5]

Bahá'u'lláh then left but said that He would come back and join them as another defender. However, His intention could not be fulfilled because, on His the next attempt to visit, sometime in late October or early November 1848, He was arrested by an armed detachment of men of the governor of Ámul, and then imprisoned and tortured. During Bahá'u'lláh's first visit the siege was not very rigorous, since senior officers were attending the coronation ceremony for the new monarch in Ṭihrán, but the controls had worsened by the time of His planned second visit. At that time, Bahá'u'lláh was about 12 km from the fortress when He was arrested with eleven other believers. He carried 4,000 tumans of silver plus other provisions to help the companions, but ultimately, He was detained and tortured.[6]

---

1 Nabíl-i-A'ẓam, *The Dawn-Breakers*, p. 392.
2 Hasan Balyuzi, *The King of Glory*, p. 51.
3 Nabíl-i-A'ẓam, *The Dawn-Breakers*, p. 350.
4 David Ruhe, *Robe of Light*, p. 104
5 Nabíl-i-A'ẓam, *The Dawn-Breakers*, p. 350.
6 A. L. M. Nicolas, *Seyyèd Ali-Mohammed dit le Bâb*, p. 307. See also David Ruhe, *Robe of*

The arrival of Quddús

The liberation of Quddús was relatively straightforward because Muḥammad-Taqí, gave his immediate assent for his release when the seven Bábís approached him. He said:

> I have regarded him only as an honoured guest in my house. It would be unbecoming of me to pretend to have dismissed or released him. He is at liberty to do as he desires. Should he wish it, I would be willing to accompany him.[1]

Mullá Ḥusayn prepared the Bábís in advance as to how to behave towards Quddús.

> As to myself, you must consider me as his lowly servant. You should bear him such loyalty that if he were to command you to take my life, you would unhesitatingly obey. If you waver or hesitate, you will have shown your disloyalty to your Faith. Not until he summons you to his presence must you in any wise venture to intrude upon him. You should forsake your desires and cling to his will and pleasure.
>
> You should refrain from kissing either his hands or his feet, for his blessed heart dislikes such evidences of reverent affection. Such should be your behaviour that I may feel proud of you before him. The glory and authority with which he has been invested must needs be duly recognised by even the most insignificant of his companions. Whoso departs from the spirit and letter of my admonitions, a grievous chastisement will surely overtake him.[2]

According to Nabíl, "Mullá Ḥusayn ... had enjoined them [his companions] to observe towards him [Quddús] a reverence such as they would feel prompted to show to the Báb Himself ...."[3] Mullá Ḥusayn also exhorted:

> O companions, I counsel you that whenever Quddús arrives here and if, hypothetically, I move against his opinion, you should turn your back to me and hold fast to his advice and directive.[4]

On the evening of 20 October 1848, Quddús arrived at Shaykh Ṭabarsí and was welcomed with candles and chants on a magical night. Interestingly, on that same night the new monarch entered Ṭihrán to be crowned as Náṣiri'd-Dín Sháh Qájár at the astrologically auspicious time of exactly seven hours and twenty minutes past sunset—i.e., in the early hours of 21 October 1848 (22 Dhu'l-Qa'da 1264).[5]

Light, p. 104.

1 Nabíl-i-A'ẓam, *The Dawn-Breakers*, p. 350.

2 Nabíl-i-A'ẓam, *The Dawn-Breakers*, p. 350.

3 Nabíl-i-A'ẓam, *The Dawn-Breakers*, p. 350.

4 Fazel Mazandarani, *Taríkh-i-Ẓuhúr al-Ḥaqq*, vol. 2, p. 296.

5 See Abbas Amanat, *Pivot of the Universe: Nasir Al-Din Shah Qajar and the Iranian Monarchy, 1831–1896*, p. 100

Quddús was not only the representative of the Báb because of his senior rank among the Bábís but also, he was a man characterised by *"radiant praise"*, supplication and devotion. In this regard the Báb wrote:

> *The loftiness of God, moreover, rest upon thy being and upon all who have been created through thy radiant praise, and upon thy spirit and all who have been created through thy supplication, and upon thy soul and all who have been created through thy belief in the Divine Unity, and upon thy self and all who have been created through the shining light of thy devotion.*[1]

Many of the believers had never previously met Quddús. He was accompanied by a number of additional local believers[2] estimated as large as ninety souls.[3] Nabíl narrates the details:

> The news of the impending arrival of Quddús bestirred the occupants of the fort of Ṭabarsí. As he drew near his destination, he sent forward a messenger to announce his approach. The joyful tidings gave them new courage and strength. Roused to a burst of enthusiasm which he could not repress, Mullá Ḥusayn started to his feet and, escorted by about a hundred of his companions, hastened to meet the expected visitor. He placed two candles in the hands of each, lighted them himself, and bade them proceed to meet Quddús.
>
> The darkness of the night was dispelled by the radiance which those joyous hearts shed as they marched forth to meet their beloved. In the midst of the forest of Mázindarán, their eyes instantly recognised the face which they had longed to behold. They pressed eagerly around his steed, and with every mark of devotion paid him their tribute of love and undying allegiance. Still holding the lighted candles in their hands, they followed him on foot towards their destination.
>
> Quddús, as he rode along in their midst, appeared as the day-star that shines amidst its satellites. As the company slowly wended its way towards the fort, there broke forth the hymn of glorification and praise intoned by the band of his enthusiastic admirers. "Glory be to Him, Quddús [Holy], our Lord and Lord of the Angels and the Spirit"[4] rang their jubilant voices around him. Mullá Ḥusayn raised the glad refrain, to which the entire company responded. The forest of Mázindarán re-echoed to the sound of their acclamations.[5]

While dismounting from his horse, Quddús revealed to the Bábís the greatness of the time in which they were living in. He alluded to a prophecy that signalled

---

1 The Báb, *Tablet of Visitation for Quddús.* See Appendix part 2.

2 'Abdu'l-Bahá, *A Traveller's Narrative*, p. 37.

3 Arthur Hampson, *The Growth and Spread of the Bahá'í Faith*, pp. 65-66.

4 See Footnote at the start of this subsection. In Arabic, *"sabbúḥun quddús rabbaná wa rabb al-malá'akat wa al-rúḥ"*. See: Abbas Amanat, *Resurrection and Renewal,* p. 187.

5 Nabíl-i-A'ẓam, *The Dawn-Breakers*, p. 352.

the advent of the Promised One and his heavenly hosts. When counting the total number of companions, they totalled 313, confirming with accuracy the prophecy of the Prophet Muḥammad regarding a heavenly host to appear in the times of the Promised One.[1]

Leaning his back on one of the sanctuary's walls, he exclaimed "The Baqíyyatu'lláh ("Remnant of God") will be best for you if ye are of those who believe".[2] With these words he was referring to Bahá'u'lláh who had recently visited the fortress and He had promised to return. "No sooner had he spoken them," a witness recalled, "that he made mention of Bahá'u'lláh and, turning to Mullá Ḥusayn, enquired about Him. He was informed that unless God decreed to the contrary, He had signified His intention to return to this place before the first day of Muḥarram."[3]

Effect of Quddús' arrival

The days that followed the arrival of Quddús witnessed the special spiritual ascendance of Quddús among the Bábís, whom they considered to be the representative of the Báb.

"The arrival of Quddús infused a new spirit into the companions," wrote Ruhollah Mehrabkhani. "The fort soon became a new teaching centre, similar to the one the believers had abandoned when they were forced to leave Mashhad. Quddús sent some of the Bábís to give the Message of the New Day to the people of the villages around the fort. Their missions were so successful that some of the chiefs of Mázindarán sought out the presence of Quddús. As they became acquainted with the believers, they realised how evil and false the accusations against them were. Some of the pure-hearted people of Mázindarán came to be believers in the Faith, and they joined the companions at the fort."[4]

According to the author of *Taríkh-i-Jadíd*: "After a little while Jináb-i-Quddús came forth from the Castle, picked up several small pebbles, and cast them towards the enemy, saying, 'This is what David did to the troops of Goliath'; whereupon, in the course of a few minutes, all were dispersed and incontinently fled."[5]

Day after day, these confrontations occurred after Quddús' arrival, and the Bábís always valiantly dispersed the royal troops trying to overrun the fort. At

---

1 See Biḥáru'l-Anwár 52, chapter 32, tradition 4. The Prophet Muḥammad while describing the features of the Promised Qá'im to one of His disciples affirmed, "God shall gather the same number of people as the companions of [the battle of] Badr (313) from different parts of the earth. The Imám has a tablet in which the details of his companions have been written down like their number, names, cities, natures, titles and even their family tree. These will be at the highest level of faith."

2 *Qur'án* 11:86.

3 Nabíl-i-A'ẓam, *The Dawn-Breakers*, p. 353. Return before 27 November 1848.

4 Ruhollah Mehrabkhani, *Mullá Ḥusayn*, pp. 234–5.

5 Mírzá Ḥusayn Hamadání, *The New History (Taríkh-i-Jadíd)*, p. 57.

Mullá Ḥusayn's call of "Mount your steeds, O heroes of God!",[1] the Bábís would astound the enemy by striking out from the fortifications on their horses. Despite their superior numbers, the royal troops learnt to fear the sound of the unique Bábí warrior calls of "Yá Ṣáḥibu'z-Zamán" and "Yá Quddús" and would abandon their artillery positions, and run for the hills in terror.[2]

Quddús' presence brought a new spirit to the Shaykh Ṭabarsí community who now numbered about 500 believers.[3] "The seats of His Holiness Quddús and of the honored Bábu'l-Báb, upon both be God's peace," wrote a survivor, "were in the midst of the mosque and Shrine of Shaykh Ṭabarsí. Group by group, the rest of the companions would gather for their meals in the courtyard."[4]

Quddús, who was then in his late 20s, impressed the Bábís as being a forceful and assertive leader endowed with superhuman powers. He was now much more than a theologian preaching a new Faith. He had become a strategist with consummate ideas that he had thought through a long time before. His worldview had evolved so far that he was able to mobilize others as witnesses that he had a message to proclaim to the world at all costs, even that of his own death.

To his roles as a missionary with mystical charisma, and the august role of a commander and main figurehead, Quddús now had added the responsibility for providing the defence and welfare of about 500 militarily untrained people, including some children, besieged in a constricted compound by a mighty imperial Persian army. This is the Quddús who, wearing the scars of torture, confinement and exile, was now fully exercising his status of being the First in Rank among the Bábís.

The conflict at Shaykh Ṭabarsí had attracted national attention, so Quddús was able to reach the top of his "spiritual mountain" to sound his clear clarion call. His leadership in the ensuing confrontations makes this very obvious. There is evidence that Quddús might have written to the Amír Kabír, the Grand Vizir or Prime Minister, calling for a meeting where the truth of the Faith of the Báb could be demonstrated.[5]

A regional army is formed

This section describes the building up of the regional armed forces to crush the Bábís. It shows the various political negotiations that took places between the central government, the regional leaders including representatives of foreign powers.

---

1 Nabíl-i-A'ẓam, *The Dawn-Breakers*, p. 341.

2 Sepehr Manuchehri, *Brief Analysis of the Features of Bábí Resistance*, n.p.

3 *The Narrative of Ḥájí Naṣír-i-Qazvíní*, n.p.

4 *The Narrative of Ḥájí Naṣír-i-Qazvíní*, n.p.

5 See E. G. Browne, *The Taríkh-i-Jadíd*, p. 169.

The new Sháh

The two Qáḍí-Kalá incidents forced the Bábís to remain on guard in case of another attack. However, November till before Christmas 1848 was, however, a period of relative tranquillity that was spent reinforcing their fortifications. While they were still able to move freely in the area, some teaching exchanges occurred with the local population and a number of them converted and joined the defenders.

"After the news of the goodly character of these distinguished men [the Bábís] had penetrated most hearts," wrote an eyewitness, "the townsfolk began to visit us as well. They would come in multitudes and ask various questions, and his honored person [Mullá Ḥusayn] would give answers suitable to each question."[1]

Although no further attacks are recorded by chroniclers during November, the Sa'ídu'l-'Ulamá' kept inciting the population and the authorities against the believers. The historian Mangol Bayat wrote:

> In fact, state officials in the capital were at first reluctant to carry on a full-scale war against the insurgents, both because they believed the revolt was religiously-oriented, and thus a matter of chief concern to the Ulamá rather than to the state, and because they feared it might turn into a political rebellion as well, should they react too strongly.[2]

One of the first acts of the new monarch was to appoint a Grand Vazir or Prime Minister in the person of Amír Taqí Khán, commonly known as Amír Kabír. This high-ranking government official was the one who prepared a war strategy to destroy the Bábís of Shaykh Ṭabarsí. High-level consultations were held in state circles to adopt his strategy to the point the Sháh, on 29 December 1848, wrote to the prince-governor, "It is decided that the mild disturbances which occurred in Qáḍí-Kalá must be quelled in the most efficient manner."[3]

New orders from Náṣiri'd-Dín Sháh Qájár

The conflict with the Bábís could not have come at a worst time for the new, 17-year-old Sháh and his new prime minister, Mírzá Taqí Khán, a ruthless man. The former Sháh had died on 5 September, but it took about 45 days for the crown prince to travel to Ṭihrán. A couple of months before, this same prince had presided over the interrogation of the Báb in Tabríz and ordered Him to be bastinadoed.

The interregnum between the old and the new monarch took two months. The widow of the late Sháh presided over a temporary government that consisted of four administrators. Finally, after much debate among the Qájár tribes and advice from foreign powers such as Russia and the United Kingdom, the young prince Náṣiri'd-Dín Mírzá, Governor of Ádhirbáyján, was permitted to ascend the

---

1 *The Narrative of Ḥájí Naṣír-i-Qazvíní*, n.p.

2 Mangol Bayat, *Mysticism and Dissent*, p. 119.

3 Ruhollah Mehrabkhani, *Mullá Ḥusayn*, p. 251.

throne.[1] In reality, as Mehran Kamrava points out, "the question of succession was never fully and adequately settled [in the Qájár dynasty], and the death of each shah was followed by intense internal squabbling among different pretenders to the throne."[2] The Qájár was a conglomerate of tribes which together decided on the successor to the throne.

Representatives of the province of Mázindarán attending the coronation ceremonies presented the monarch with alarming descriptions of the Bábís' insurrection, depicting it as a potential threat to his sovereignty and one of the first challenges to his kingdom.

'Abbás-Qulí Khán-i-Láríjání, Ḥájí Muṣṭafá Khán and other tribal commanders arrived in the capital on 27 November 1848 for talks about how to defeat the Bábís. Both kháns had in October negotiated a peace with Mullá Ḥusayn while in Bárfurúsh when the Bábís arrived at that town, meaning that they knew well about the Bábí teachings. These khans or tribal chiefs had been brought to the capital at the instigation of Colonel Farrant, the British chargé d'affaires, who talked to the Prime Minister about the need to put order on the Bábís upheaval. [3] [4] It has been even suggested that these tribal were having conversations with the Bábís before and after their arrival to Shaykh Ṭabarsí, playing a double game for their own political reasons.[5] They were perceived by the central government as not fully collaborating with the crown and showing ambiguous loyalty. This would explain why these traditionally rebellious regional powers did not attack the fort during the months of October and November. [6]

It has been said that the son-in-law of the main tribal leader, 'Abbás-Qulí Khán-i-Láríjání himself had paid once a visit to Quddús in Sárí, and that his son-in-law was a Bábí.[7] That these encounters between regional authorities and the Bábís happened, it is not surprising because of the implications for both civil governance and ecclesiastical dominance. Professor E.G. Browne refers to the power struggles between these kháns and the ecclesiastical power:

> 'Abbás-Qulí Khán is described as having been on bad terms with the Sa'ídu'l-'Ulamá', and disposed at first to look favourably on the Bábís and their doctrine; and even after ambition and self-interest, as well as unwillingness to adopt the principles of fraternity which prevailed with them, had caused him to abandon the idea of joining them, he was very

1 Mírzá Aleksandr Kazem-Beg, *Le Bab et les Bábís ou le Soulevement Politique et Religieux en Perse de 1845 à 1853*, p. 367.

2 Mehran Kamrava, *Qajar Autocracy*, p. 14.

3 Mohammad Ali Kazembeyki, *Society, Politics and Economics in Mazandaran*, pp. 123

4 Mohammad Ali Kazembeyki, *Society, Politics and Economics in Mazandaran*, pp. 123

5 Mohammad Ali Kazembeyki, *Society, Politics and Economics in Mazandaran*, pp. 122-123

6 Colonel Farrant to Lord Palmerston, 24 October, 1848, FO 60/138. Cited in Mohammad Ali Kazembeyki, *Society, Politics and Economics in Mazandaran*, pp. 269.

7 E.G. Browne (ed.), *Kitáb-i-Nuqtatu'l-Káf: Being the Earliest History of the Bábís*, p. 162.

unwilling to fight against them. His son-in-law, Sádát-Qulí Big, is described as being actually a believer. [1]

It is not surprising either that there were informal communications between the regional tribal powers and the Bábís, conversations which were seen as suspicious by the central government. In this regard, the British diplomat wrote on 10 October 1848 to his superior that his recommendation to the Sháh had been approved and that the Sháh had instructed him to bring the Mázindarán tribal chiefs to Ṭihrán in order to deal collaboratively with the matter. "I have despatched a messenger to the chiefs calling on them to come to the royal presence and I have obtained from His Majesty an autograph for 'Abbás Qulí Khán, and the Governor of Sárí on which the Sháh promises to them his total protection."[2] The Mázindarán tribal chiefs brought a letter of repentance to the Sháh for their rebelliousness when they arrived in Ṭihrán, and the Sháh forgave them but ordered them to destroy the Bábís.

The international politics of the conflict

At this point, we digress from our topic to discuss the political situation of the region. At the time of Quddús, the British and the Russian empires were pursuing areas of influence on Iranian territory. Whereas the former operated in the south of the country, the latter had expanded its commercial dominance in the north along the Caspian Sea due to its close proximity. The British, though, wanted to reach the north to gain access to its foreign products, mainly clothing and industrial textiles, while the Russians were pursuing exchange of agricultural and mineral resources. The British were also watchful of the Russians who were pushing towards the south to militarily take over India,[3] the gem on the British crown.

The antagonism of the two major world powers struggled to get concessions on infrastructure or taxes from the Sháh, who resorted to benefiting alternately, one over the other, to ensure Persia's own political stability and existence. Such dramas were affecting the Faith of the Báb. For instance, the Báb was transferred from Máh-Kú to Chihríq because the Russian government insisted that He was too close to its borders[4] having fears of the Báb's influence at a time when the Bábísm was being accused of heresy and social disruption. In turn, as relates to the British, as outlined in the previous paragraph, Colonel Farrant's statements against the Fort Shaykh Ṭabarsí would not have been seen as inciting violence against it, but rather as a way of asserting British influence on the Royal Court over the Russians. With regard to investigations into the matter of Shaykh Ṭabarsí, it appears that the Russian diplomats were not concerned nor involved

---

1 E. G. Browne, *The Taríkh-i-Jadíd*, pp. 361-362.

2 K. E. Abbott, *Report by Consul Abbott of his Journey to the Coast of the Caspian Sea, 1847-1848*. Colonel Farrant to Lord Palmerston, 24 October, 1848, FO 60/138.

3 Jennifer Siegel, *Endgame: Britain, Russia and the Final Struggle for Central Asia*, vol. 25.

4 Soli Shahvar et al, *The Bahá'ís of Iran*, vol. 1, p. 53.

but were upset when the Mázandaráni delegation did not pay a courtesy visit to them when they arrived in the capital for talks with the central government.[1]

Meetings between the khâns and the central government in the capital

On the day after their arrival, the Mázindarán tribal chiefs were ceremoniously received by the Sháh who promoted their militia forces to formal regular Persian state regiments.[2] Negotiations with the government resulted in the commanders being issued with privileges to recompense them for their loyalty to the crown. It was also decided to nominate Mihdí Qulí Mírzá,[3] an uncle of the Sháh, as governor of Mázindarán Province.[4] These tribal chiefs assured the monarch that, at this stage, it was not necessary to involve the imperial Persian army as they themselves were confident in their ability and military power to defeat the Bábís.

These khâns assured the monarch that, at this stage, it was not necessary to involve the imperial army as they themselves were confident in their ability and military power to defeat the Bábís. To the Sháh, 'Abbás-Qulí Khán addressed the following words dismissing the Bábís' capacity to fight:

> I myself come from Mázindarán. I have been able to estimate the forces at their disposal. The handful of untrained and frail-bodied students whom I have seen are utterly powerless to withstand the forces which your Majesty can command. The army which you contemplate despatching is in my view unnecessary. A small detachment of that army will be sufficient to wipe them out. They are utterly unworthy of the care and consideration of my sovereign. Should your Majesty be willing to signify your desire, in an imperial message addressed to my brother 'Abdu'lláh Khán-i-Turkamán, that he should be given the necessary authority to subjugate that band, I am convinced that he will, within the space of two days, quell their rebellion and shatter their hopes. [5]

Interestingly, the two days promised became nine months due to the Bábís' resilience and resistance. In any case, such meetings and decisions at the highest levels of government explains how quick and brutal the Sháh's determination was to destroy the Bábís at Shaykh Ṭabarsí. Consequently, the government gave full authority to the regional leaders to form a regional army consisting of their own new forces and people recruited from the villages. According to Kazembeyki, they also managed to get an excommunication warrant for the Bábís from a high-ranking Ṭihrán cleric.[6] Consultation about the four Mázindarán khâns took place

---

1 Mohammad Ali Kazembeyki, *Society, Politics and Economics in Mazandaran*, p. 123.

2 See Mohammad Ali Kazembeyki, *Society, Politics and Economics in Mazandaran*, p. 123.

3 Mírzá after a name designates the person is a prince.

4 See Mohammad Ali Kazembeyki, *Society, Politics and Economics in Mazandaran*, p. 123.

5 Nabíl-i-A'ẓam, *The Dawn-Breakers*, p. 369.

6 Mohammad Ali Kazembeyki, *Society, Politics and Economics in Mazandaran*, p. 123.

while they were there and they stayed in the capital at least until 5 January. The discussions involved a leading ulama, the financial controller of Mázindarán, and other notables.[1] Their long stay could be considered as a sign of the regional powers' endorsement towards the new young Sháh at a time when there were other rebellions in the country especially in the province of Khurásán, from where Quddús and Mullá Ḥusayn were before, and now coming to Bárfurúsh.[2]

The kháns' decisions were communicated by writing from Ṭihrán to their subordinates in Mázindarán. Their secondments should not wait but it was required to organise a regional power to attack the Bábís as soon as possible without waiting for their return or from a government army. 'Abdu'lláh Khán, son of the aforementioned Ḥájí Muṣṭafá Khán, were both heads of the powerful Hazár-Jaríb tribe. The government also wrote to Mírzá Áqá the Mustúfí (the government accountant and the Sa'ídu'l-'Ulamá' "to hasten the preparations and to warm up the zeal of the defenders of Islam."[3]

In turn, Sa'ídu'l-'Ulamá' continued to repeatedly write to the citizens warning them not to visit the fort or to sell them food. He also wrote to warn Náṣiri'd-Dín Sháh that Mullá Ḥusayn was organising an insurrection against him and that he wanted to usurp the crown. The cleric persisting message to the young monarch was to send troops to the area to crush the Bábís.[4]

How was the regional army formed?

Coming back from the capital, after been received by the Shah, the Mázindarán kháns had a meeting to take the offensive in regard to the Bábís in Bábís. Based on government chronicles, Gobineau wrote:

> The result of the deliberations was that Áqá 'Abdu'lláh Khán put together two hundred hand-picked men from his village of Hazár-i Jaríb; then a certain number of tufangchí [riflemen], recruited here and there, and a few noble horsemen of his tribe. With this company he took up position at Sárí, ready to initiate the campaign. For his part, the controller of the finances levied a troupe from amongst the Afghán living in Sárí and added a few men from the Turkish tribes under his administration. 'Alí-Ábád,[5] the village so rudely chastised by the Bábís and which aspired to revenge, furnished what it could, reinforced by some of the men of Qádí, who enrolled because they were from a neighbouring village. It was agreed that

1 Gobineau in Nash and O'Donoghue, *Comte de Gobineau and Orientalism*, p. 159.

2 Mohammad Ali Kazembeyki, *Society, Politics and Economics in Mazandaran*, p. 123.

3 A. L. M. Nicolas, *Seyyèd Ali-Mohammed dit le Bâb*, p. 303.

4 Abú-Ṭálib-i Shahmírzadí, Mír, *Untitled history*, p. 40.

5 "Qaem Shahr (Qaemshahr and Qá'em Shahr; formerly (pre-1979) known as Sháhí) is a city in and the capital of Qaem Shahr County, Mazandaran Province, Iran. Originally known as Aliyabad ('Aliyábád or 'Alí-Ábád). 155 km NE of Ṭihrán. It is 6 km NE of the Shrine of Shaykh Ṭabarsí" (Michael Thomas, *Glossary and transcription for Arabic & Persian terms*, Qaem Shahr entry).

Áqá 'Abdu'lláh Khán would assume command and march against the enemy forthwith.

From Áb-i Rúd he set out in fine spirits for the high valley of Lár, and having arrived at the village of the same name called a halt. He was hosted by Nizár Khán Giraylí. The night passed in the greatest tranquillity, although the proximity of the Bábís kept them on their guard. The next day they marched on, additionally reinforced by a troupe of men from the district of Kudar, and finally came into sight of the castle at Shaykh Ṭabarsí. The garrison had withdrawn inside; outside nothing stirred; the valley was completely silent. At once Áqá 'Abdu'lláh Khán set resolutely to work. He ordered a sort of trench to be dug and positioned some tufangjis [riflemen], there, who began to maintain fairly rapid constant fire against the wall. This continued all day without producing any result, the Bábís content to answer fire only sporadically, so that both parties went off to sleep with no clear notion of the events of the day.[1]

'Abdu'lláh Khán and his tribal army arrived in the Shaykh Ṭabarsí area on 19 December 1848. Immediately, they began putting the fort under siege and Bábís' communication with the external world ceased including purchase of food and access to water as this had to be carried from outside. Thereafter, at Shaykh Ṭabarsí , "Guards had been stationed at different places to ensure the isolation of the besieged".[2] The army surrounded the fort with barricades and shot anyone who escaped via the gate. 'Abdu'lláh Khán was very arrogant of his 12,000 men power but on a few days, he was going to meet death.

There is evidence that the Báb communicated with Quddús and other disciples from Chihríq through His courier Sayyáḥ ("Traveller')[3] and other believers.[4] Messages from the Báb might have continued until the beginning of the siege. Above all, the Báb had said four years before that communication between Him and Quddús happened *"in the world of the spirit"*.[5]

The siege

In order to win, the regional army decided to deploy siege tactics at Shaykh Ṭabarsí. Besieging the enemy is an ancient and effective combat technique because it disrupts communications with the outside world and prevents supplies from being delivered. Nobody can access or leave the site once it has been surrounded. Psychologically, it seeks to demoralise the defenders through propaganda, continuous minor strikes, and displays of military advantage and superiority to terrify the defenders. Furthermore, it permits the besieging forces to damage or destroy their opponent's defences by breaching defensive walls

1 Gobineau in Nash and O'Donoghue, *Comte de Gobineau and Orientalism,* pp. 158-159.

2 Nabíl-i-A'ẓam, *The Dawn-Breakers,* p. 369.

3 Hasan Balyuzi, *The Báb,* p. 149.

4 John Walbridge, *Essays and Notes on Babi and Bahá'í History,* p. 32.

5 Nabíl-i-A'ẓam, *The Dawn-Breakers,* p. 70.

with artillery, battering rams, or explosives placed in tunnels under them. Besiegers are also able to place siege towers near or against the walls where attackers can fire heavy weaponry like cannons and mortars. Siege warfare's ultimate goal is to capture the fortifications or to force the defenders to negotiate a surrender, usually after severely damaging their defences over an extended period.

The following dialogue between the prince-governor and his main commander, the Sardár, reflected these intentions:

> They spent there a few days [and] put heads together as what to do [next]. "The Bábís have killed many of our men.
>
> Dear prince, propose a plan!" [requested the Sardár].
>
> The prince said: "Be patient, dear Sardár! God favors the patient. Wait a while till their store of provisions is all consumed. [Then] they will surrender themselves. As a result, we will capture and kill them all."
>
> "That's not a bad idea," replied Sardár, "We shall wait."[1]

The regional army camped very close to the village of Afrá, less than 1 km east of the fort, and were armed with heavy artillery. They were so close that the defenders could hear their movements and see their campfires. The defenders had about six weeks in which they were able to obtain supplies from neighbouring villages. It seems that the companions were aware that a blockade was going to be imposed and they spent those first six weeks collecting and storing provisions.[2] A dossier from the Russian Legation in Ṭihrán reported that the believers have "stored food as well as everything else necessary for a siege of several months."[3]

Eventually, during November 1848, the regional army was able to impose a total blockade of the fort that stopped food, messages and other provisions from reaching the Bábís. Thereafter, "Guards had been stationed at different places to ensure the isolation of the besieged."[4]

When the Báb heard from His prison of the severity of the siege, He urged all friends throughout Persia to join the companions to aid Quddús and Mullá Ḥusayn.[5] The historian Hasan Balyuzi adds that the Báb, through His courier, sent Quddús, "the gift of a valuable pen-case and a silk turban."[6]

---

1 Habib Borjian, *A Mázandaráni Account of the Babi Incident,* pp. 392–393.

2 Moojan Momen, *The Bábí and Bahá'í Religions, 1844–1944,* p. 94.

3 World Order, A Bahá'í Magazine. *Excerpts from Dispatches Written During 1848-1852 by prince Dolgorukov, Russian Minister to Persia*, p. 20.

4 Nabíl-i-A'ẓam, *The Dawn-Breakers,* p. 369.

5 See Nabíl-i-A'ẓam, *The Dawn-Breakers,* p. 31.

6 Hasan Balyuzi, *The Báb,* p. 149.

Second battle—death of the commander (December 1848)

Mount your steeds, O heroes of God![1]

The second confrontation was with the newly-formed regional Persian army and started on 22 December 1848. It was initially an attack by the soldiers positioned around the fort, but it extended to those positioned in the village of Afrá where part of the army was located. The edge of Afrá village was only 100 m to the east, with its civic centre and mosque about 1 km to the east, and the Tálar River was over 2 km to the east.

By the time of the second confrontation, the regional army had recruited and trained about 12,000 men, mostly from local tribes. According to E. G. Browne "Hostilities commenced by an attack made by Áqá 'Abdu'lláh Surtej, with 200 Hazár-Jaríb *tufangchís*. His camp was surprised by the Bábís the day after his arrival."[2] The story of this confrontation is given below.

Sortie of 22 December 1848

A few among the Bábís became dispirited because of their deprivations and started having regrets about joining the defenders at Shaykh Ṭabarsí, but their plight was eased in one way or another by the ever-present Divine Providence. When there was a shortage of water, as predicted by Quddús, an unexpected heavy rain fell one night. It not only supplied large amounts of much needed water to the companions, who managed to store large quantities of it, but it also ruined the ammunition of the enemy. This downpour was followed the next night by snow, which was unusual for the region. Quddús said: "Praise be to God who has graciously answered our prayer and caused both rain and snow to fall upon our enemies; a fall that has brought desolation into their camp and refreshment into our fort."[3]

To protect themselves from the unusual snow, the army soldiers slept under covers and had neglected their sentinel duties.

The army had been making preparations for a concerted attack, but at dawn after the snow fell (22 December of 1848),[4] the companions took them by surprise during their slumber. "Mount your steeds, O heroes of God!"[5] was the Bábís' call

---

1 Cited by Shoghi Effendi, *God Passes By*, p. 40.

2 E. G. Browne, *Materials for the Study of the Bábí Religion*, p. 241. *Tufangchís* are matchlock armed men. Hazár-Jaríb is the name of a tribe.

3 Nabíl-i-A'ẓam, *The Dawn-Breakers*, p. 361.

4 Nabíl wrote that the date was 25 Muḥarram 1265 AH equivalent to 22 December 1849 CE (*The Dawn-Breakers*, p. 368). Mohammad Kazembeyki indicates late Muharram 1265 AH (*Society, Politics and Economics in Mazandaran*, p. 124). Siyamak Zabihi-Moghaddam, also cites 22 December 1848 CE (*The Bábí-state conflict at Shaykh Ṭabarsí*, p.98).

5 Nabíl-i-A'ẓam, *The Dawn-Breakers*, pp. 341 & 365.

to arms raised by Quddús and Mullá Ḥusayn. Quddús and Mullá Ḥusayn, with a group of Bábís came out of the fort to punish the army led by sardár ("commander") 'Abdu'lláh Khán. He was the brother of Ḥájí Muṣṭafá Khán who, the week before, was received with other tribal chiefs in the capital by the Sháh[1] who was still in the capital after meeting the Sháh.[2]

According to *Tarí<u>kh</u>-i-Jadíd*[3] the Bábí force consisted of 15 horsemen and five men on foot. They created such confusion among the tribal troops that they ran in desperation back to the village where the officers were quartered. A local historians wrote that the attack was motivated by 'Abbás-Qulí Khán who was still in the capital.[4]

In under an hour the small group of Bábís, led by the two Letters of the Living, managed, despite their inadequate weapons, to kill four hundred and thirty soldiers, [5] including the sardár, 'Abdu'lláh Khán and two of his senior officers. According to Dawn-Breakers "not one of the followers of the Báb lost his life in the course of that encounter. No one except a man named Qulí, who rode in advance of Quddús, was badly wounded."[6] Furthermore, the village of Afrá was burned down.[7]

According to Nabíl-i-A'ẓam:

> Quddús returned to the fort while Mullá Ḥusayn was still engaged in pursuing the work which had been so valiantly performed. The voice of Siyyid 'Abdu'l-'Aẓím-i-Khu'í was soon raised summoning him, on behalf of Quddús, to return immediately to the fort. "We have repulsed the assailants," Quddús remarked; "We need not carry further the punishment .... What we have already achieved is sufficient testimony to God's invincible power. We, a little band of His followers, have been able, through His sustaining grace, to overcome the organised and trained army of our enemies.[8]

According to the French historian A. L. M. Nicolas:

> The news of this victory and this terrible execution spread in Mázindarán with the rapidity of lightning. The whole province trembled with terror and the soldiers themselves felt their hearts sinking at the thought of having to defend themselves against such adversaries. Muḥammad Sulṭán,

---

1 See Mohammad Ali Kazembeyki, *Society, Politics and Economics in Mazandaran,* p. 124.

2 See Mohammad Ali Kazembeyki, *Society, Politics and Economics in Mazandaran,* p. 124.

3 See Mírzá Ḥusayn Hamadání, *The New History (Tarí<u>kh</u>-i-Jadíd),* p. 74.

4 See Mohammad Ali Kazembeyki, *Society, Politics and Economics in Mazandaran,* p. 124.

5 Luṭf 'Alí Mírzá's account has 175 soldiers killed and an unknown number drowned (*Untitled history*,, p. 76 & 81). Mír Abú-Ṭálib-i-Shahmírzadí's account has 400 or more (*Untitled history,* p. 10).

6 Nabíl-i-A'ẓam, *The Dawn-Breakers,* p. 362.

7 Gobineau in Nash and O'Donoghue, *Comte de Gobineau and Orientalism,* p.160.

8 Nabíl-i-A'ẓam, *The Dawn-Breakers,* pp. 362–363.

the Laríjání aide-de-camp thought only of fortifying Bárfurúsh in anticipation of an attack by the Bábís; in the same spirit, Mírzá Áqá the Mustúfí[1] did similar with the city of Sárí.[2]

Following the brief attack, many retreating soldiers drowned in the Tálar River and others were attacked again by the Bábís when they retreated to the village of Afrá.[3] Others continued to run as far as Sárí. By the end of the skirmish, the 12,000 strong army had vanished. "They also captured a huge amount of ammunition, provisions, and about a hundred horses," wrote author Siyamak Zabihi-Moghaddam. "This was of great importance to the Bábís, as their own equipment was completely inadequate. On their arrival at Shaykh Ṭabarsí, the Bábís had probably many swords and daggers, but only seven muskets, and perhaps five horses.[4]

The people of Bárfurúsh were so fearful of being attacked during the siege of Shaykh Ṭabarsí, that they cut slits in building walls (some still visible today) with raised bench steps on the inside, and placed gates across some streets.[5]

'Abdu'lláh Khán's body was taken to the capital. When news of the fantastic Bábí victory reached the Sháh's ears, he ordered the imperial army to be sent from the capital. He is reported to have said:

> We thought that our army would go without hesitation through fire and water, that, fearless, it would fight a lion or a whale, but we have sent it to fight a handful of weak and defenceless men and it has achieved nothing! Do the notables of Mázindarán think that we approve of this delay? Is it their policy to allow this conflagration to spread in order to magnify their importance in case they later put an end to it? Very well, let them know that I shall act as though Alláh had never created Mázindarán and I shall exterminate its inhabitants to the last man![6]

Bribing the soldiers

Mírzá Ḥusayn Hamadání reported that due to the strength of the Bábís, soldiers were bribed to assail them but, as a matter of course, were resisted with extraordinary courage:

> The first attempt of the enemy to storm the fortress was made on the covered way. As soon as they approached the Castle in force, fifteen [mounted] men [and five] on foot sallied forth and attacked them. Many of the soldiers were slain, and amongst them fell the Sardár 'Abdu'lláh Khán. Of the defenders only two were killed. The attacking force retired in

1 A government accountant.

2 A. L. M. Nicolas, *Seyyèd Ali-Mohammed dit le Bâb*, p. 304.

3 Ruhu'llah Mehrabkhani, *Mullá Ḥusayn*, p. 245.

4 Siyamak Zabihi-Moghaddam, *The Bábí-state conflict at Shaykh Ṭabarsí*, p. 97.

5 See Mohammad Kazembeyki, *Society, Politics and Economics in Mazandaran*, p. 122.

6 A. L. M. Nicolas, *Seyyèd Ali-Mohammed dit le Bâb*, p. 322.

> despair, while the garrison collected the bodies of their slain, and carried them into the Castle. The disastrous result of the attack on the covered way was openly admitted in the royalist camp, but nevertheless, seeing that the garrison did not repair the breach in the walls, they again prepared to make an attempt to carry the Castle by storm.
>
> It was arranged by the royalist leaders that there should be five standards, and that to him who should first succeed in planting one of them on the Castle wall should be awarded a sum of five hundred túmáns, to the second four hundred, and to each subsequent one a hundred túmáns less, by which arrangement the bearer of the last standard would receive one hundred túmáns. They then disposed the artillery, marshalled out seven thousand regulars, horse and foot, and boldly began the advance.
>
> When they were near the Castle, the first standard-bearer succeeded in planting his standard on the ramparts, but a bullet struck his foot and he fell. He bravely regained his feet, but a second shot struck him in the breast, and he fell down headlong with his standard. The defenders of the Castle, hungry and barefooted as they were, hurled themselves upon the enemy sword in hand, and displayed that day a courage and heroism which the world had never before seen, and which must appear to such as consider it little short of miraculous. So fiercely did they drive back that mighty host that many even of the bravest and boldest were unable to escape from their hands, while the rest, overcome with panic, could neither fight nor flee.[1]

The Bábís were aware of the increasing military threats they would meet in future confrontations, so with great effort they undertook significant steps to further fortify the fort. Over the next 19 days they dug a moat around the fort to make it much harder for the enemy to reach the fort.

An American Bahá'í visited the site in 1965 and described

> While Quddús and Mullá Ḥusayn had quarters in the fort itself, their Bábí soldiers dug themselves in outside, by the end of the siege being well protected, it is said, by a moat about 10 feet (about 3 m) deep and 10 feet wide outside the walls and several deep dugout chambers within. They even built themselves a sizeable pool for bathing about 50 yards north of the fort.[2]

For bathing, the defendants used to go to a public bath in the nearby village. According to Sepehr Manuchehri there were "extensive repairs made by the Bábís to a run down and disused bath inside the compound dedicated to Quddús who

1 Mírzá Ḥusayn Hamadání, *The New History (Taríkh-i-Jadíd)*, pp. 83-85.

2 Guy Murchie, *Visit to Fort Tabarsi*, pp. 8-10.

practiced and preached cleanliness, and bathed every day".[1] They also attempted to make the walls cannon-safe.[2]

The Bábís also dug a 50-foot (15 m) water well to alleviate the lack of water due to the siege.[3] By 1965 the well was still providing crystalline water for human consumption (see Figure 56). "Digging the well took some days, and during this time Mullá Ḥusayn would sit at the side of the well and converse with the workers," historian Mehrabkhani stated. "He deepened their knowledge of the Faith and advised them on all matters".[4] Guy Murchie also noted that "One of the large smooth-barked trees (perhaps a live oak) north of the fort still has a 'cannon ball hole' in its split trunk".[5]

---

1 Sepehr Manuchehri, *Brief Analysis of the Features of Bábí Resistance,* n.p.

2 Ruhu'llah Mehrabkhani, *Mullá Ḥusayn,* p. 247.

3 Guy Murchie. Visit to Fort Tabarsi, pp. 8-10.

4 Ruhu'llah Mehrabkhani, *Mullá Ḥusayn,* pp. 263-264.

5 Guy Murchie, Visit to Fort Tabarsi, p. 9.

Figure 50: Doorway to Shaykh Ṭabarsí shrine

Figure 51: Old view of entrance to Shaykh Ṭabarsí shrine
(Source: Bahá'í Media)

Figure 52: Old interior of Shaykh Ṭabarsí shrine

Figure 53: Old photo of Shaykh Ṭabarsí shrine (Source: Bahá'í Media)

Figure 54: Old photo of Shaykh Ṭabarsí shrine (Source: Bahá'í Media)

Figure 55: Old photo of Shaykh Ṭabarsí shrine (Public domain)

Figure 56: Well dug by the Bábís near Shaykh Ṭabarsí (Source: *Bahá'í News,* no. 411, 1965)

Figure 57: Modern interior of Shaykh Ṭabarsí shrine

Figure 58: Modern exterior of Shaykh Ṭabarsí shrine (Public domain)

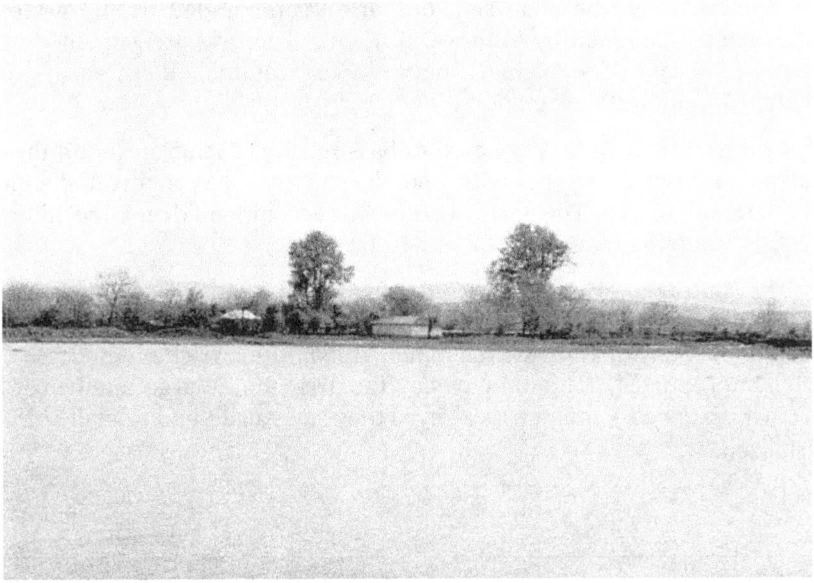

Figure 59: View of Shaykh Ṭabarsí from a distance, 1964

An imperial army is formed

Our dispute concerns religion.[1]

This section describes how a state army was created at the order of the monarch who commissioned a prince to lead the fight against the Bábís with full power.

The new prince-Governor

As previously mentioned, the new Sháh had appointed his uncle, Mihdí Qulí Mírzá, as governor of Mázandarán Province. News of the 22 December humiliating defeat must have reached the sovereign very quickly.

On 29 December 1848 Naṣiri'd-Dín Sháh wrote an edict appointing the prince Mihdí-Qulí Mírzá, his uncle, to march towards Mázindarán with a powerful army and achieved the total destruction of the Bábís who are called a "fresh heresy":

> It is true: Mihdí-Qulí Mírzá, you must exert yourself to the utmost in this affair. This is not a trifling amusement. The fate of our religion and Shi'i doctrine hangs in the balance. You must cleanse the realm of this filthy and reprobate sect, so that not a trace of them remains. Devote your utmost diligence to this [...][2]

Two armies were expected from the capital

From the capital, the Sháh sent one army commanded by the prince and another one commanded by 'Abbás-Qulí Khán. The first arrived sometime up until mid-January.[3] The distance between the capital and Bárfurúsh is 220 kilometres about one week on horse.

The prince Mihdí Qulí Mírzá and 'Abbás-Qulí Khán left Tehran on the 1st of Muharram. He left the capital with a small army that was augmented along the way to the conflict area. The new governor was accompanied by three other royal princes. He took the road to the Sawád-Kúh.

On the route, the prince instructed 'Abbás-Qulí Khán to go to Ámul through the Damáwand and Laríján direction, which was his jurisdiction, and then proceed to the Shaykh Ṭabarsí area. When 'Abbás-Qulí reached Ámul, the Conde of Gobineau reported, "The old city saw the arrival of a large number of black tents: Turkish tribes, Persian tribes, or, as they say, Kurds, and a small army soon materialized."[4]

---

1 Abbas Amanat, *Resurrection and Renewal,* p. 188

2 Ruhu'llah Mehrabkhani, *Mullá Ḥusayn,* p. 251.

3 Siyamak Zabihi-Moghaddam, *The Bábí-state conflict at Shaykh Ṭabarsí,* p. 97-98.

4 Gobineau in Nash and O'Donoghue, *Comte de Gobineau and Orientalism,* p. 161.

In turn, the prince continued on the Sawád-Kúh route, recruiting horsemen from Hazár-Jaríb and Kurdish and Turkish populations. These were taken straight to the village of Vás-Kas, which is 12 km away from Shaykh Ṭabarsí. Vás-Kas was situated among several villages on the other side of the Talar River, which did not have any bridges. The fort was a 30-minute walk. In Vás-Kas, the prince began to train the soldiers whose background was only peasantry with no experience in warfare at all.

Upon arrival, part of the army stayed at Vás-Kas while the remainder were deployed around the village of Afrá next to the fort harassing and preventing any supplies from reaching the Bábís.

The prince did not want to launch an attack until the army led by 'Abbás-Qulí Khán arrived. The prince and 'Abbás-Qulí Khán arrived within three or four days of each other around the middle of January. The Bábís were now facing two mighty armies.[1] Eventually the total forces numbered some 10,00 to 12,000 men.[2]

What the prince found in Shaykh Ṭabarsí

The prince's army arrived first. With the mandate of the 28 December 1848 royal edict, the prince left the capital with a small army by the end of that month. It consisted of 1,000 soldiers[3] plus heavy artillery, including some newer cannons mounted on field carriages. What the prince found in Shaykh Ṭabarsí was not of his complacency:

> For them [the prince's entourage] this new affair showed that the situation of the country was going from bad to worse. It was not just that a number of [army] men had succumbed in a badly led mission, but that everyone could see that the Bábís' authority in the province was growing, that a large number of still undeclared people were just waiting for them to take one step forward in order to join them, that their emissaries were so daring and supported by the atmosphere of fear that no one anywhere dared arrest them although they were well known, and finally, that if another conflict were necessary one could scarcely count on troops who had been beaten and mis- treated each time they had come to blows with the sectarians. Reasonable people concluded from all this that rather than wandering all over the mountain, laying themselves open to some new disaster that might ensue at any moment from their incurable carelessness and rare incapacity in all fields they would be better advised to reflect very carefully over what should be done and to strike only when they were almost sure of attaining their goal.[4]

---

1 Siyamak Zabihi-Moghaddam, *The Bábí-state conflict at Shaykh Ṭabarsí*, p. 97.

2 Siyamak Zabihi-Moghaddam *The Bábí-state conflict at Shaykh Ṭabarsí*, p. 98.

3 Ḥájí Nasír Qazvíní mentions 5,000 soldiers in his chronicle (See *The Narrative of Ḥájí Nasír Qazvíní*). Around mid-January 1849, the prince based his army in and around the village of Vás-Kas.

4 Gobineau in Nash and O'Donoghue, *Comte de Gobineau and Orientalism*, p. 170.

At the village of Afrá, next to the fort, the prince gave initial strategic instructions. Gobineau's narrative shows the ethnic diversity of the local conscripts:

> [The prince] began to build a siege wall around the fortress, and decided that this time they would set about the matter in such a way as to shut the Bábís in behind their walls, harass them continuously with sustained fire, and so that when they tried to leave the castle they would be pushed back from the high ramparts that were being built. The prince stationed guard posts at regular intervals along the siege wall; he put Ḥájí Khán Núrí and Mírzá 'Abdu'lláh Naváí in charge of provisions. As chief officers he chose 'Abbás-Qulí Khán-i-Laríjání, who since his lack of success was of more interest to him; then Naṣru'lláh Khán Bandábí, another tribal chief, and Muṣṭafá Khán, of Ashraf, to whom he gave command of the brave tufangchís [riflemen] of that town and of those from Suratí.
>
> Less distinguished lords commanded the men of Dúdánghih and Balá-Rasták, as well as a certain number of Turkish and Kurdish nomads, who felt misunderstood in the bands of the great leaders. These Turkish and Kurdish nomads were in particular given the task of keeping watch over the enemy. Their numerous bad experiences had begun to make them acknowledge that it might be a good idea to keep a better watch in the future. The Turks and the Kurds then, were ordered not to lose sight of enemy activity, day or night, and to keep a sharp look-out so as to avoid surprises.
>
> Having established these precautions, holes and trenches were dug for tufangchís [riflemen], who received orders to fire on any Bábís who might appear. Towers were built, as high as or higher than the different levels of the fortress, and by means of continuous falling fire it was made more difficult for the enemy to walk around on their walls or even to cross the interior courtyard. It was a considerable advantage. But after a few days the Bábí leaders, taking advantage of the long nights, raised their fortifications above the height of the offensive towers.[1]

Four days after arriving at the fort, the prince gave orders to build a solid fortification around Shaykh Ṭabarsí:

> Having the regiments occupied the points whose guard was entrusted to them, he [the prince] ordered accesses to be dug and towers built dominating the fortress so as to prevent the Bábís from leaving their homes, and from circulating within the interior of the fort. But Ḥájí Muḥammad-'Alí [Quddús] took advantage of the moonless nights to raise its walls and their own towers so that his companions could go about their activities and their duties peacefully.[2]

---

1 Gobineau in Nash and O'Donoghue, *Comte de Gobineau and Orientalism,* p. 170.

2 A. L. M. Nicolas, *Seyyèd Ali-Mohammed dit le Bâb*, p. 319.

> ... in a few days, the Bábí chiefs, taking advantage of the long nights, raised their fortifications so that their height exceeded that of the attacking towers of the enemy.[1]

A royal emissary is sent

When the prince Mihdí Qulí Mírzá arrived in the region, he conferred with the divines and local authorities to gather more information about the Bábís in Shaykh Ṭabarsí. Mihdí Qulí Mírzá at one point harboured the idea of peacefully solving the conflict but Quddús and Mullá Ḥusayn had doubts about him and, therefore, rejected the offer of a conference. There were reasons for that: a short time before this new Governor had been arresting anyone suspected of being a Bábí.

When Quddús was in confinement in Sárí, it appears that once he personally told 'Abbás-Qulí Khán-i-Láríjání , "we are the rightful sovereign, and the world is under our signet-ring, and all the kings in the East and the West will become humble before us."[2] For this reason the sardár had formed the opinion that for this "sovereignty" was meant "the sovereignty of the people of oppression, meaning that dominion must be obtained through oppression and cruelty, and the blow of the sword, and covetousness for worldly possession, and all sorts of deception".[3] At one point, the sardár understood that such was not Quddús' mission, rather, he realised the Bábís' creed was purely religious and within the spiritual domain. Nonetheless, with this alternative narrative, the sardár pursued a stronger military strategy to later request additional army support from the sovereign.[4] Obviously, there were mixed feelings about the matter on the side of 'Abbás-Qulí Khán-i-Láríjání.

Quddús and Mullá Ḥusayn at that point, were firmly set on neither leaving the fort nor the province as had been suggested by the Governor-prince and the Sardár. This could have been a strategy to get the Bábís to leave the fort in order to kill them. Mullá Ḥusayn defiantly replied to the prince, "I shall make manifest the cause of God by means of the sword." Fresh in mind was the treason of Khusraw and this new proposal sounded like another government stratagem that could not be trusted. According to one source, the prince also deceitfully intimated to the Bábís, to join forces with him to dethrone the sovereign.[5]

An emissary was sent to confer with the companions. A carpet was placed outside the fort gates where the emissary and Mullá Ḥusayn talked. To the

---

1 Joseph Arthur Gobineau, *Les Religions et les Philosophies dans l'Asie Centrale*, p. 181. Cited in Nabíl-i-A'ẓam, *The Dawn-Breakers*, p. 391.

2 E. G. Browne, E. G. (ed.), *Kitáb-i-Nuqtatu'l-Káf: Being the Earliest History of the Bábís*, p. 162.

3 E. G. Browne, E. G. (ed.), *Kitáb-i-Nuqtatu'l-Káf: Being the Earliest History of the Bábís*, p. 163.

4 Siyamak Zabihi-Moghaddam, *The Bábí-state conflict at Shaykh Ṭabarsí*, p. 111.

5 Siyamak Zabihi-Moghaddam, *The Bábí-state conflict at Shaykh Ṭabarsí*, p. 111.

emissary, Mullá Ḥusayn expressed in clear terms that the mission of the Bábís was spiritual in nature and that they had absolutely no hidden political agenda, as had been attributed to them by some detractors; neither did they have any intention to undermine the authority of the Sháh. Their mission was limited to religious matters aimed at establishing proofs and arguments ascertaining the truth of the divine Cause of the Báb. Mullá Ḥusayn stated:

> Let the prince [Mihdí Qulí Mírzá] direct the 'Ulamás of both Sárí and Bárfurúsh to betake themselves to this place, and ask us to demonstrate the validity of the Revelation proclaimed by the Báb. Let the prince himself judge our case and pronounce the verdict. Let him also decide as to how he should treat us if we fail to establish by the aid of verses and traditions, the truth of this Cause.[1]

Quddús summarised their position in this statement to Mihdí Qulí Mírzá: "Our dispute concerns religion. First the 'Ulamá [divines] must converse with us and understand our legitimacy and submit to it. Then the sultán [the Sháh] of Muslims should obey and support the truthful religion and the subjects also should acknowledge [it]."[2] Quddús argued that they were acting in self-defence against forced recantation of their Faith. The Governor-prince did not respond to the challenge but continued to prepare to attack the fort. He was stalling for time to train his military recruits and to obtain more reinforcements from the capital.

According to Amanat, in summary, Quddús wrote to the prince that the subject of disagreement between both parties was religion and therefore the divines must attend a meeting where the Bábís were given the opportunity to prove the validity of the Báb's religious claims. Subsequently, to their acceptance, the monarch should also embrace the new Faith and defend it. Quddús argued that they were acting in self-defence against forced recantations of their Faith.[3]

Mihdí Qulí Mírzá's emissary might have been Mírzá Qurbán-'Alí. Historian John Walbridge wrote:

> Mírzá Qurbán-'Alí became a Bábí in 1845 ... he was prevented by severe illness from going to join the Bábís at Shaykh Ṭabarsí. ... he reached the government camp and, not being known as a Bábí, was asked to serve as Mihdí-Qulí Mírzá's emissary to the Bábís. At the fort he told Quddús of the situation in the government camp and then returned to Mihdí-Qulí Mírzá with samples of the writings of the Báb.[4]

---

1 Nabíl-i-A'ẓam, *The Dawn-Breakers,* p. 365.

2 Abbas Amanat, *Resurrection and Renewal,* p. 188

3 Abbas Amanat, *Resurrection and Renewal,* p. 188

4 John Walbridge, *Essays and Notes on Babi and Baha'i History,* p. 41.

Third battle—Quddús is injured (January 1849)

> Though my body be afflicted, my soul is immersed in gladness.[1]

While the second confrontation had occurred in the early daylight hours of 22 December 1848 in and around the adjacent village of Afrá, the third confrontation was at night on the night of 24-25 January 1849[2] and took place in the main royal military camp around the village of Vás-Kas, 6 km ESE of the fort on the eastern side of the Tálar River.

The new sortie

According to Gobineau, the new combined army after their catastrophic December defeat "had largely regrouped in the mountain village of Vaskas [Vás-Kas], where the prince, very tired, had installed in the best house, dined, had gone to bed and was sleeping"[3]

On the night of 24-25 January 1849 the Bábís surprised the army and "some two hundred Bábís sortied from their fortifications and routed the government forces."[4] [5] Led by Quddús and Mullá Ḥusayn on horse, keeping at minimum the noise, walking on the snow in a cold winter, the Bábís attacked the enemy in Vás-Kas on the other side of the Tálár river. The Talar River did not have bridges. Covered by the obscurity of the night, they moved silently not to be noticed by the four villages in between and the military camp in Afrá next to the fort.

When they arrived at the royal camp, the Mázandarání speaking companions called to the military sentinels in their local language pretending to be soldiers in order to avoid being identified as Bábís. Soon after, at the call of *Ṣáḥibu'z-Zamán!—O Thou Lord of the Age!*, the Bábís began their assault on the camp, catching the army off guard. A chronicler described the incident:

> But when they came to the magazine [ammunition depot] they set fire to it, and then surrounded the prince's quarters. Then cries and shouts arose from the soldiers on all sides, and the fire of battle blazed high. The royalist troops, unable to withstand the attack, were utterly routed and took to flight, while the followers of Jináb-i-Quddús continued to fight with the utmost courage, and succeeded in releasing such of their companions as were confined in the camp.... [6]

---

1 Quddús in Nabíl-i-A'ẓam, *The Dawn-Breakers*, p. 368.

2 Nabíl wrote that the second battle took place on 21 December 1848 (*The Dawn-Breakers*, p. 368). However, this is not possible because the 'Abbás-Qulí Khán-i-Láríjání's army arrived around mid-January from the capital (See: Siyamak Zabihi-Moghaddam, *The Bábí-state conflict at Shaykh Ṭabarsí*, pp. 97-98).

3 Gobineau in Nash and O'Donoghue, *Comte de Gobineau and Orientalism*, p. 162.

4 Siyamak Zabihi-Moghaddam, *The Bábí-state conflict at Shaykh Ṭabarsí*, p. 97.

5 Mírzá Ḥusayn Hamadání refers to 300 men (*Taríkh-i-Jadíd*, p. 66).

6 Mírzá Ḥusayn Hamadání, *The New History (Taríkh-i-Jadíd)*, pp. 67-68.

The companions attacked the three regiments of infantry and another of cavalry, and burst into the enemy headquarters. In a tremendous clash they routed the enemy. The court chronicle of the time, *Nasikh al-tawarikh* ("The Superseder of Histories"),[1] describes how "royal troops were running away from the Bábís like a herd of sheep escaping from wolves."[2]

Mullá Ḥusayn, in the meantime, was looking for the prince who was at his well-protected two-storey house with two other princes. The news of the Bábís' attack woke up the sleepy sentinels of the prince's house but they continued to sleep when told that the new regiment from the capital had arrived. During the fight described below, the building was set on fire in order to break into it by a valiant young man who "climbed into a room from the back part of the house".[3] According to Nabíl:

> The prince, who was observing the movements of Mullá Ḥusayn, saw him approaching, from his fort, and ordered his men to open fire upon him. The bullets which they discharged were powerless to check his advance. He forced his way through the gate and rushed into the private apartments of the prince, who, with a sudden sense that his life was in danger, threw himself from a back window into the moat and escaped barefooted. His host, deprived of their leader and struck with panic, fled in disgraceful rout before that little band which, despite their own overwhelming numbers and the resources which the imperial treasury had placed at their disposal, they were unable to subdue.[4]

The resulting panic and disarray were increased by a false declaration that the governor Mihdí Qulí Mírzá had been killed. However, the prince had managed to escape barefoot through a window. Wandering alone through the night in the forest, he finally was found by a peasant who gave him refuge in his barn.[5]

When the Bábís entered the room abandoned by the prince, they found valuable art objects and jewels which they did not touch, with a very few exceptions. The Bábís also managed to liberate a Bábí prisoner

---

1 Mírzá Muḥammad-Taqí Lisan al-Mulk Sipihr, *Nasikh al-tawarikh* Qájáríyyah.

2 Mangol Bayat, *Mysticism and Dissent*, p. 93.

3 Ruhollah Mehrabkhani, *Mullá Ḥusayn*, p. 257.

4 Nabíl-i-A'ẓam, *The Dawn-Breakers*, p. 366.

5 "We left [prince] Mihdí-Qulí Mírzá running far from his burning house and wandering alone in snow and darkness through the countryside. At dawn he found himself in an unknown gorge, lost in some godforsaken spot but in reality less than half a league from the scene of the carnage. The wind carried the sound of musket fire to his ears. In this sad state, and not knowing what was to become of him, he was found by a Mázandarání on a fair mount who recognized him as he was passing by. The man dismounted, bade the prince take his place in the saddle and offered to serve as his guide. He took him to the house of some peasants, where he installed him in the stable; in Persia this is in no way considered an unworthy lodging "(Gobineau in Nash and O'Donoghue, *Comte de Gobineau and Orientalism*, p. 161.)

Quddús is injured

Later, but still very early in the same morning, both forces were engaged in a massive clash on the outskirts of Afrá village. Mullá Ḥusayn had regrouped his men on the outskirts of the village and was watching on horse the enemy's movements fearing a renewed attack. Suddenly, a number of soldiers ran unto him, being defended by the Bábís at the call of "*Yá Ṣáḥibu'z-Zamán!*". According to *Taríkh-i-Jadíd*:

> Now some thousand of the royalist soldiers had hidden themselves in the defile of a mountain hard by, and when these perceived that the Bábís were but few in number, and that, in addition to this, many of them were scattered abroad or laden with booty, they took courage, surrounded them, and opened fire. Jináb-i-Bábu'l-Báb attacked them with drawn sword, and was pressing them hard, when suddenly a bullet was fired which struck Jináb-i-Quddús in the mouth...[1]

The bullet that passed through his mouth, tongue and throat, causing profuse bleeding. The bullet entered below the right ear and exited through the lower lip—breaking seven teeth.[2]

Mullá Ḥusayn, who witnessed the injury, ran to help his beloved leader. In desperation, Mullá Ḥusayn began beating his head, but Quddús stopped him. According to Nabíl:

> Obeying his leader instantly, he [Mullá Ḥusayn] begged him to be allowed to receive his sword from his hand, which, as soon as it had been delivered, was unsheathed from its scabbard, and used to scatter the forces that had massed around him. Followed by a hundred and ten of his fellow-disciples, he faced the forces arrayed against him. Wielding in one hand the sword of his beloved leader and in the other that of his disgraced opponent [the prince], he fought a desperate battle against them, and within thirty minutes, during which he displayed marvellous heroism, he succeeded in putting the entire army to flight.
>
> The disgraceful retreat of the army of Mihdí-Qulí Mírzá enabled Mullá Ḥusayn and his companions to repair to the fort. With pain and regret, they conducted their wounded leader to the shelter of his stronghold. On his arrival, Quddús addressed a written appeal to his friends who were bewailing his injury, and by his words of cheer soothed their sorrow.
>
> "We should submit," he exhorted them, "to whatever is the will of God. We should stand firm and steadfast in the hour of trial. The stone of the infidel broke the teeth of the Prophet of God; mine have fallen as a result of the bullet of the enemy. Though my body be afflicted, my soul is immersed in

---

1 Mírzá Ḥusayn Hamadání, *The New History (Taríkh-i-Jadíd)*, pp. 67-68.

2 Hushmand Dehghan, *Ganj-i-Pinhán*, p. 96.

> gladness. My gratitude to God knows no bounds. If you love me, suffer not that this joy be obscured by the sight of your lamentations."[1]

Mullá Ḥusayn was infuriated though:

> Mullá Ḥusayn blamed the Bábís who had remained to collect booty for delaying the company's march back to the fort and causing injury to their beloved Quddús. The companions were sorrowful and realized that their material desires had resulted in a grievous loss from which they would never be relieved. They begged forgiveness of Quddús and Mullá Ḥusayn.[2]

Quddús' recovery took three months on a diet based on liquids, tea and soups. The Bábís managed to get a medicine to prepare an ointment.[3] Surprisingly, despite his diet and injuries, he never lost his stamina and the colour of his face did not change.

A triumph

The attack on the enemy headquarters was an important victory for the Bábís because they were able to acquire about 100 horses along with additional weapons and ammunition for their defence. The defeated royal army ignominiously retreated in absolute chaos. Three royal princes and 70 soldiers died. According to Gobineau:

> Everywhere people lost their heads: the unfortified towns felt themselves exposed to all manner of dangers, and, despite the harsh weather, caravans of peaceful but distressed inhabitants carried the women and children off into the wilds of Damavand to spare them the inevitable dangers that the sháhzádih's [prince] prudent conduct clearly suggested to all. When Asiatics lose their heads it is not by halves. However, that situation could not long go on, least of all for the prince. Being afraid was insufficient justification, he had above all not to irritate the terrible Amir Nizam [Grand Vazir], who would certainly be far from satisfied when he heard the news. Bringing the wrath of that minister down upon his head was perhaps even worse than having to deal with Mullá Ḥusayn Bushrú'í. In his perplexity the poor man, not knowing which way to turn, gave orders to recruit new forces and to form a new army. The populations of the towns showed scant enthusiasm for serving a leader whose worth and intrepidity they had so recently seen in action.[4]

The French historian A. L. M. Nicolas wrote:

> The rumor of the Bábís victory spread throughout the Province, increasing from mouth to mouth: the most appalling stories circulated, which spread everywhere the maddest terror; a sudden attack, a pillage, an assault was

---

1 Nabíl-i-A'ẓam, *The Dawn-Breakers,* p. 368.

2 Ruhu'llah Mehrabkhani, *Mullá Ḥusayn,* p. 259.

3 Hushmand Dehghan, *Ganj-i-Pinhán*, p. 97.

4 Gobineau in Nash and O'Donoghue, *Comte de Gobineau and Orientalism,* pp. 164-165.

> expected at every moment. The women and children fled into the mountains, where they were soon joined by their brothers or their husbands, abandoning the villages in their turn; desolation and fear reigned supreme.[1]

Needless to say, the royal court in Ṭihrán was very upset about this outcome. The Grand Vizir, wrote to Mihdí Qulí Mírzá:

> I have charged you, with the mission of subduing a handful of young and contemptible students. I have placed at your disposal the army of the Sháh, and yet you have allowed it to suffer such a disgraceful defeat. What would have befallen you, I wonder, had I entrusted you with the mission of defeating the combined forces of the Russian and Ottoman governments?[2]

A report from prince Dolgorukov, Russian Minister to Persia to his government, dated 15 March 849, revealed how contrary was the public and state opinion about the prince's performance in handling the Bábís:

> The governors of Mázindarán realized the danger which the presence of this crowd engendered for the peace of this province and twice tried to penetrate their retreat and destroy the crowd. The first campaign was undertaken by Muḥammad Qulí Khán [22 December 1848], the son of 'Abbás Khán, who ruled the province in his father's absence; the second, by the now Governor of Mázindarán, Mihdí-Qulí Mirzá [24-25 January 1849]. Both campaigns ended ingloriously for the Mázindaránís who were repulsed with great losses. In the army of Mihdí-Qulí Mírzá there are several cannons, but it seems that no one know how to use them.[3]

Food supplies

Feeding 500 people every day is a major logistic undertaking. With dwindling provisions due to the blockade, and depleted monetary resources, the Bábís were thankful for any comestibles and cattle obtained as spoils from the battle. Ḥájí Nasír Qazvíní, a survivor, remarked:

> Therefore, the command was issued that whatever belongings were left in the village could be seized as spoils. The companions hurried and appropriated many possessions and much food, including, rice, wheat, grains and clothing, as possible.[4]

That was the last time they had the opportunity to obtain fresh supplies necessary for their survival in that inhospitable forest region.

---

1 A. L. M. Nicolas, *Seyyèd Ali-Mohammed dit le Bâb*, p. 310.

2 Nabíl-i-A'ẓam, *The Dawn-Breakers*, p. 332.

3 World Order, *A Bahá'í Magazine. Excerpts from Dispatches Written During 1848-1852 by prince Dolgorukov, Russian Minister to Persia*, p. 19

4 *The Narrative of Ḥájí Naṣír-i-Qazvíní*, n.p.

Fourth battle— the death of Mullá Ḥusayn (February 1849)

Are you well pleased with me?[1]

Following their catastrophic defeat in the third battle, the Persian military officers were being publicly reproached by all government circles for their failure to defeat the Bábís. There was extreme disappointment that despite being provided with enormous and powerful military resources, such as the 10,000-man royal army commanded by Mihdí-Qulí Mírzá, the Bábís were still defiant.[2]

It was evident that a subsequent confrontation was in the making as new developments were occurring in the field. The second army from the capital led by the sardár 'Abbás-Qulí-i-Láríjání arrived four days after the third battle. A tension developed between him and the humiliated prince. This sardár (commander) was a bold character and a powerful leader of various tribes, among them nomad groups, which were enlisted to attack Shaykh Tabarsí:

> Turkish and Persian nomads spend their lives hunting, often, too, waging war, and above all talking about hunting and warfare", wrote Gobineau. "But what these nomads are in a consistent and uniform manner is great talkers, great razers of towns, great massacrers of heroes, great exterminators of multitudes; in short, naive, openly showing their feelings, very vivid in expressing that which exalts them, extremely amusing. 'Abbás-Qulí -i-Láríjání, most assuredly a man of good birth, was the very embodiment of the type.[3]

He himself rode at their head, and in a bold stroke went straight to attack the Bábís in their refuge instead of joining the royal army. Then he announced the prince that he had arrived at and was laying siege to the fort at Shaykh Ṭabarsí. An eyewitness stated:

> Therefore, they began to advance from their locations, and established a new camp for themselves near the shrine of Shaykh Tabarsí, at a distance of approximately five hundred steps. Until that time, the opposing army had not completely surrounded the shrine, because their number was no more than two or three thousand, and they were insufficient to completely encircle [the Fort]. Subsequently, they had stayed [only] on one side. One last time, they assembled and further summoned men from all regions of Mazandaran. Together with soldiers from Tehran, they gradually came together and thoroughly encircled us.[4]

Moreover, the sardár arrogantly announced that he had no need of help or assistance and that his own people sufficed..."[5] Gobineau mentioned that for the

---

1 Mullá Ḥusayn in Nabíl-i-A'ẓam, *The Dawn-Breakers,* p. 381.

2 Muḥammad Sháh died on 5 September 1848

3 Gobineau in Nash and O'Donoghue, *Comte de Gobineau and Orientalism,* p. 165.

4 *The Narrative of Ḥájí Naṣír-i-Qazvíní,* n.p.

5 Gobineau in Nash and O'Donoghue, *Comte de Gobineau and Orientalism,* p. 165.

next few days some negotiations took place between 'Abbás-Qulí -i-Láríjání and the Bábís to no avail, and so he promised to hang them.

The Russian Minister in Ṭihrán prince Dolgorukov reported that same month to his government:

> I have heard that 'Abbás-Qulí Khán-i-Láríjání has secretly sent a message to the Bábís that he would not prepare for a further attack but, since he is forced to obey the Shah's orders, he would only appear to be engaged in combat with them. But the Láríjání commander ['Abbás-Qulí Khán] did not remain faithful to his word and when the Bábís realized that he was preparing to do battle with them, they anticipated him and killed several hundred of his men.[1]

In the meantime, the water supply in the fort—the most indispensable element required for survival—became scarce and there was little to eat due to the siege, then the enemy became emboldened, and they began to apply all possible means to annihilate the Bábís expecting that they would soon surrender. Aware of the impending danger, the Bábís kept reinforcing the fortification to strengthen it.

Preparations of Mullá Ḥusayn for his martyrdom

On 2 February 1849 the Bábís conducted a surprise strike on the troops led by 'Abbás-Qulí-i-Láríjání. Quddús did not participate because he was injured from the third battle. An eyewitness described previous days to the battle where Mullá Ḥusayn lost his life:

> During those days Mullá Ḥusayn used to sleep in front of the tower guarded by comrades from Iṣfáhán, rather than retreating to his room. One day, when he gathered the companions around him, he said to them, "since the aim of the believers since they left Khurásán has been to give their lives in the way of God, they must always be ready for this". Then he said that godly men must never shrink from danger but must be prepared to face it and welcome sacrifice for the beloved. The true believer should not desire anything of this world that they do not desire for their beloved. His own desires shall die before death comes. In this way death shall not disturb him. Then he revealed that that very night he would again advance and all those who were prepared to sacrifice themselves would get ready to follow him...[2]

Sepehr Manuchehri wrote:

> Mullá Ḥusayn first requested the permission of Quddús to be martyred. Quddús initially refused and then reluctantly agreed ....

1 Moojan Momen, *The Bábí and Bahá'í Religions, 1844–1944*, p. 93.

2 Ruhu'llah Mehrabkhani, *Mullá Ḥusayn*, p. 265.

> Mullá Ḥusayn used to preach to all of the believers for three consecutive days [prior to his martyrdom] to respect and obey the instructions from Quddús. One day Mullá Ḥusayn addressed all believers and said whom amongst you is prepared to accompany me [to the battle]. Everyone responded positive and he replied "If all of you accompany me, my 'Habíb' [Beloved] will be left on his own. Only some of you must come with me".
>
> When Mullá Ḥusayn finally left the fortress, he observed that nearly all of the Bábís had also come out with him, leaving only a handful in the compound. He advised that his beloved is alone and requested that people return to the fortress to serve Quddús. Bábís again lamented at the sorrow of losing Mullá Ḥusayn, but he clearly ordered them to return and assist Quddús.[1]

The Bábís had begun digging a well inside the fort to extract groundwater. It was then that Mullá Ḥusayn confidently expressed to them that on that same night they would find enough water for him to take his last earthly bath before martyrdom. That night, purified from any stain, he would be transferred from the plane of limitations to God's presence. Mullá Ḥusayn then announced:

> Today we shall have all the water we require for our baths. Cleansed of all earthly defilements, we shall seek the court of the Almighty, and shall hasten to our eternal abode. Whoso is willing to partake of the cup of martyrdom, let him prepare himself and wait for the hour when he can seal with his life-blood his faith in his Cause. This night, ere the hour of dawn, let those who wish to join me be ready to issue forth from behind these walls and, scattering once again the dark forces which have beset our path, ascend untrammelled to the heights of glory.[2]

Author T. K. Cheyne suggested that the fourth battle was a punishment of the whole army in response to the wounding of Quddús.[3] It is in this context that Mullá Ḥusayn said to Quddús, "I can no longer bear to look upon the wound which mars your glorious visage. Suffer me, I pray you, to lay down my life this night that I may be delivered alike from my shame and my anxiety."[4] According to an eyewitness:

> After dark Mullá Ḥusayn came to see Quddús and indicated his desire to become martyred, and requested his permission. Quddús was not happy to lose his close companion and after vigorous persistence from Mullá Ḥusayn, he reluctantly agreed. They hugged one another for the last time. Many Bábís were standing near the doorway. Some were happy [to be

1 Sepehr Manuchehri, *Brief Analysis of the Features of Bábí Resistance,* n.p.

2 Nabíl-i-A'ẓam, *The Dawn-Breakers,* p. 379.

3 Thomas Kelly Cheyne, *The Reconciliation of Races and Religions,* p. 103.

4 Mírzá Ḥusayn Hamadání, *The New History (Taríkh-i-Jadíd),* p. 69.

> martyred], some were saddened by the impending separation, and others were completely overwhelmed by emotion.[1]

Feeling the nearness of his martyrdom, Mullá Ḥusayn made his ablutions, put on his best clothes and the turban given to him by the Báb.

The sortie of 2 February 1849

At midnight, when the army troops were sleeping, and after Mullá Ḥusayn had held an intimate conversation with Quddús, he, with a band of no less than 200 men, with superhuman strength, tore down the army's barricades that had been constructed around the fort. Around midnight, the call "O Thou, Lord of the Age!" was resonating loudly, causing panic and confusion among the soldiers. In the confusion, as in the previous confrontation, the royal troops were shooting at each other in the darkness.[2] A Muslim source reported:

> In the confusion following the Bábís' sortie, the Sardár's men [unintentionally] killed each other [in the dark]. As soon as the night turned to day, the Sardár's men realized that they had been killing one another all night long.[3]

Because of that, the number of fatalities increased to about 400 soldiers, including 45 high ranking officers, thirty "colonels" and 1,000 soldiers injured,[4] while the Bábís had only 40 casualties. Two of the commander's nephews were among those killed.[5] Up to that time, 70 Bábís had been martyred, fulfilling Quddús' prophecy in the "Sermon on the Eternal Witness" (see chapter 12, "The long march of Mullá Ḥusayn", section "Message received when in Mazínán").

Mullá Ḥusayn is wounded

During the battle, the leg of Mullá Ḥusayn's horse got entangled in a tent tie rope. While trying to get out of the situation, Mullá Ḥusayn was shot in the back by the sardár who had been hiding behind a tree, observing his movements and "disguised himself in change of raiment" disguise.[6] Another source informs that the sardár "he aimed his rifle and fired without knowing who the horseman was".[7]

Three of his companions hurried to where Mullá Ḥusayn lay unconscious and covered in blood and took him back to the fort to Quddús' presence. According to Professor E. G. Browne, Mullá Ḥusayn had already died on his horse as he entered the fort.[8]

---

1 Sepehr Manuchehri, *Brief Analysis of the Features of Bábí Resistance,* n.p.
2 Gobineau in Nash and O'Donoghue, Comte de Gobineau and Orientalism, p. 161.
3 Habib Borjian, *A Mázandaráni Account of the Babi Incident at Shaikh Ṭabarsí,* p. 393.
4 Sepehr Manuchehri, *Brief Analysis of the Features of Bábí Resistance,* n.p.
5 Moojan Momen, *The Bábí and Bahá'í Religions, 1844–1944,* p. 93.
6 Mírzá Ḥusayn Hamadání, *The New History (Tarí<u>kh</u>-i-Jadíd),* p. 70.
7 Ruhu'llah Mehrabkhani, *Mullá Ḥusayn,* p. 267.
8 E. G. Browne, *Tarí<u>kh</u>-i-Jadíd,* p. 363.

Although Mullá Ḥusayn no longer showed any signs of life, he miraculously woke up and sat at the side of Quddús when the latter uttered his name. An eyewitness remarked:

> "Leave me alone with him," were the words of Quddús as he bade Mírzá Muḥammad-Báqir close the door and refuse admittance to anyone desiring to see him. "There are certain confidential matters which I desire him alone to know."
>
> We were amazed a few moments later when we heard the voice of Mullá Ḥusayn replying to questions from Quddús. For two hours they continued to converse with each other.
>
> We were surprised to see Mírzá Muḥammad-Báqir so greatly agitated. "I was watching Quddús," he subsequently informed us, "through a fissure in the door. As soon as he called his name, I saw Mullá Ḥusayn arise and seat himself, in his customary manner, on bended knees beside him. With bowed head and downcast eyes, he listened to every word that fell from the lips of Quddús, and answered his questions."
>
> "You have hastened the hour of your departure," I was able to hear Quddús remark, "and have abandoned me to the mercy of my foes. Please God, I will ere long join you and taste the sweetness of heaven's ineffable delights."
>
> I was able to gather the following words uttered by Mullá Ḥusayn: "May my life be a ransom for you. Are you well pleased with me?"[1]

Death of Mullá Ḥusayn

Then the door was opened and the dismayed believers were able to see with great sorrow Mullá Ḥusayn lying dead on the bed. It was the night of 2 February 1849. Kissing Mullá Ḥusayn on his eyes and forehead, Quddús remarked:

> Well is it with you to have remained to your last hour faithful to the Covenant of God, I pray God to grant that no division ever be caused between you and me.[2]

Quddús dressed him in his own shirt and buried him with his own hands. The burial, in an atmosphere of blood, tension and pain, as well as the depth of Quddús' own pain was such that the Bábís present wished they themselves had been killed instead.

An eyewitness remembered, "The honored Quddús instructed that a burial shroud be prepared for the honored Báb and that he be buried in the corner of the shrine of Shaykh Ṭabarsí while still wearing his own garments."[3] Quddús instructed that the location of the grave should be kept confidential.

---

1 Nabíl-i-A'ẓam, *The Dawn-Breakers,* p. 381.

2 Nabíl-i-A'ẓam, *The Dawn-Breakers,* p. 381.

3 *The Narrative of Ḥájí Nasír Qazvíní.*

Mullá Ḥusayn was then 36 years old. One of the brightest lights in the firmament of the Dispensation of the Báb had been extinguished. Next to the shrine the bodies of the other 36 fallen companions were buried and Quddús remarked: "Let the loved ones of God take heed of the example of these martyrs of our Faith. Let them in life be and remain as united as these are now in death."[1]

On Mírzá Muḥammad-Ḥasan Khán, Mullá Ḥusayn's brother, who was about thirty-two years old when he died.[2] The *Taríkh-i-Jadíd* states "After the death of Jináb-i-Bábu'l-Báb, he [Quddús] bestowed on him [Mírzá Muḥammad-Ḥasan Khán][3] the sword and turban of that glorious martyr, and made him captain of the troops of the True King."[4] He was bestowed the rank of Letter of the Living and served the Cause of God tirelessly until he sacrificed his life in the aftermath of the Shaykh Ṭabarsí tragedy.[5]

Of Mullá Ḥusayn, the Count of Gobineau wrote: "What is sure is that Mullá Ḥusayn-i-Bushrú'í was the first in the Persian Empire to give Bábísm the status in the minds of the people which a religious or political party only acquires after having demonstrated warlike virility".[6]

In a Tablet written at the end of 1849, the Báb "extolled, in moving terms, the unswerving fidelity with which Mullá Ḥusayn, served Quddús throughout the siege of the fort of Ṭabarsí".[7] The Báb revealed in honour of him, "eulogies, prayers and visiting Tablets of a number equivalent to thrice the volume of the *Qur'án*".[8] The Báb had also affirmed that the dust of Mullá Ḥusayn's grave, in Shoghi Effendi's words, "was so potent as to cheer the sorrowful and heal the sick."[9]

The burial of the martyrs

Burying the fallen of the 2 of February battle was saddening. All bodies were placed in one grave:

> There were many of our companions who had received bullet wounds, and had fallen with no strength left in them [fourth battle, 2 February 1849]. After the companions who had not been injured returned, the foes saw and recognized them as not being of their own, and killed them.
>
> At any rate, after the return of the companions who carried with them the honored [Mullá Ḥusayn] —upon him rest God's peace—it was only a short

1 Nabíl-i-A'ẓam, *The Dawn-Breakers,* p. 382.

2 Ruhu'llah Mehrabkhani, *Mullá Ḥusayn,* p. 284.

3 The seventeen year old Mírzá Muḥammad-Ḥasan Khán was Mullá Ḥusayn's brother.

4 Mírzá Ḥusayn Hamadání, *The New History (Taríkh-i-Jadíd)*, p. 95.

5 Boris Handal, *El Concurso en Lo Alto,* pp. 71–72.

6 Gobineau in Nash and O'Donoghue, *Comte de Gobineau and Orientalism,* p. 168.

7 Nabíl-i-A'ẓam, *The Dawn-Breakers,* pp. 431–2.

8 Shoghi Effendi, *God Passes* By, p. 50.

9 Shoghi Effendi, *God Passes By*, p. 50.

moment before the sanctified spirit of that noble person winged its flight to the Sacred Realm.

Of the friends, about fifty had suffered martyrdom. The opponents took their own fallen men and withdrew a distance. The esteemed friends, upon seeing their departure, went to the battlefield and carried back with them the bodies and the remains of the martyrs, among them the honored Mullá 'Abdu'l-Jalíl and Áqá Mírzá Muḥammad-i-'Alí [a Letter of the Living], who were martyred in that battle.

That day witnessed a great cataclysm in the shrine of Shaykh Ṭabarsí. On one side was the honored Báb —upon him be God's peace—who died as a martyr. On the other side were about fifty of our dearly-cherished companions who in the battlefield had each hastened to the Abode of the Merciful, Almighty God. The sacred remains of some of the martyrs were left in the opposing camp, while the enemy had severed some of their heads and carried these away with them as gifts and prizes.

... [Quddús] then ordered that the martyrs who had fallen in the enemy's camp be collected one by one, and brought to the courtyard of Shaykh Ṭabarsí. He further commanded that on the side of the door that entered the mosque of Shaykh Ṭabarsí, situated on the eastern flank of the courtyard, a ditch be dug about five or six meters (in length and depth) and that collectively the sanctified remains of the martyrs be placed in that grave, in the same clothes that they had worn [in the battle]. They were placed next to each other and earth was poured over them, thereby hiding their remains.

After the burial of the martyrs, everyone was profoundly sad and despondent, wondering how his own end would come about. Some hearts wavered, since what their frail minds had imagined had not come to pass. The honored Báb, who was their champion, and in the field of battle had shown the greatest valour and peerless leadership, was now gone. Gone were also some of the friends who had fallen in the battle just concluded. In addition to this, food provisions were essentially depleted as well.[1]

That day Quddús asked the companions to visit the martyrs' graves every morning and evening and read the Holy Words. He also wrote a prayer of visitation for Mullá Ḥusayn which he kept a copy for himself and placed another one outside the shrine for the friends to recite for the martyrs.[2]

Aftermaths of the fourth battle

Mírzá Ḥusayn Hamadání wrote in *The New History (Taríkh-i-Jadíd)* about the losses on the part of the army:

---

1 *The Narrative of Ḥájí Nasír Qazvíní.*

2 Hushmand Dehghan, *Ganj-i-Pinhán*, p. 100.

> The royal troops had that night suffered a disgraceful defeat, and were scattered in flight. Many of the Bábís, too, had in the darkness and pouring rain missed the way to the Castle and become separated from their comrades, but, when the time for prayer came, these, guided by the sound of the *adhán* [call to prayers], found their way back thither. For it was customary with the garrison of the Castle to keep vigil during the last third of the night, to read and pray aloud with fervent devotion until day-break, and to offer up their petitions to the Just and Gracious Lord.[1]

When dawn broke, the royal commanders began counting their losses. In Gobineau's words:

> They began to cry out to advert and summon any of their comrades who might still be nearby and able to hear them; and in fact the sardár and the isolated pockets of men spread around the area immediately came to join them. They went over the battlefield and buried those of the dead who could be identified as Muslims. As for the Bábí corpses, their heads were cut off; this booty was placed aside as a trophy, and a few days later these remains were sent to Bárfurúsh and the other towns of Mázindarán in order to show that the Bábís were not invincible.[2]

Nicolas added: "'Abbás-Qulí Khán [the sardár] sent a messenger named 'Abdu'lláh Khán to the prince Mihdí Mírzá: he gave him a letter and some enemy heads ....[3] A Muslim source reported that

> Sardár [Abbás-Qulí Khán] sent men off to Sárí [the capital of the province] to Mihdí Qulí Mírzá, [with the message]:
>
> "Dear prince, take all the soldiers you have and come [to our aid] to slay these Bábís; if we do not repel them, they will kill all Mázandaránís."
>
> The prince gathered all the men he had and took them to Shaykh Ṭabarsí. Sardár, [on the other hand,] went to Láriján, recruited many men, and once again came to Shaykh Ṭabarsí.
>
> [There] he saw that the prince too had recruited many men and had come to Shaykh Ṭabarsí.[4]

---

1 Mírzá Ḥusayn Hamadání, *The New History (Taríkh-i-Jadíd)*, p. 71.

2 Gobineau in Nash and O'Donoghue, *Comte de Gobineau and Orientalism*, p. 167.

3 A. L. M. Nicolas, *Seyyèd Ali-Mohammed dit le Bâb*, p. 314.

4 Habib Borjian, *A Mázandaráni Account of the Babi Incident at Shaikh Ṭabarsí*, p. 393.

Fifth battle—treason and triumph (March 1849)

Yá Ṣáḥibu'z-Zamán!—O Thou Lord of the Age!

The fourth confrontation was seen as a major Bábí victory, one which seriously demoralised the troops, their senior military officers, and the Sa'ídu'l-'Ulamá' 20 km away in Bárfurú<u>sh</u>. The fifth confrontation occurred before Naw-Rúz (21 March) 1849.

Background to the fifth battle

At the time, the prince-governor was already being severely criticised by officials of the Government regarding his inability to quell the upheaval. Since the army was mostly made up of soldiers who had been recruited locally, appeals were made to the capital to send a military regiment that had received professional training and was outfitted with cannons.[1]

"On the following day, the government troops attacked the fort, apparently in order to collect the wounded and some of their dead and bury other bodies where they had fallen." Siyamak Zabihi-Moghaddam wrote, "When they retreated, the Bábís went out to the battlefield to fetch their own dead. They found that the Bábí corpses had been decapitated, burned, or both."[2] [3]

To allay public apprehensions, the army had the Bábís' heads paraded throughout the province's towns. Nicolas continued,

> Be that as it may, the Bábís, furious that the corpses of their people had been desecrated, dug up the Muslim soldiers, cut off their heads and stuck them on the top of long pikes planted in front of the Fort. They threw the mutilated bodies into the prey of wild beasts, and mercifully buried their own.[4]

Also, surprise attacks became the recognised successful strategy of the Bábís and therefore, "guards were posted, all possible order was established in the camp; briefly, everything was so arranged that this time the question, whether the Governor of Mázindarán could manage the Bábís with his own forces, had to be finally solved." [5]

Troops were deserting the army and the officers blamed the clergy, and they demanded that if this was truly a holy war then by example the clergy must stand at the battle front. Moreover, the population was afraid that the Bábís would leave the fort and conquer Bárfurú<u>sh</u>. A number of soldiers had deserted and hid in villages outside the city, while many others were wounded. "Sa'ídu'l-'Ulamá'

---

1 Moojan Momen, *The Bábí and Bahá'í Religions,* p. 94.

2 Siyamak Zabihi-Moghaddam, *The Bábí-state conflict at <u>Sh</u>ay<u>kh</u> Ṭabarsí*, p. 98.

3 A. L. M. Nicolas, *Seyyèd Ali-Mohammed dit le Bâb*, p. 314.

4 A. L. M. Nicolas, *Seyyèd Ali-Mohammed dit le Bâb*, p. 314.

5 World Order, A Bahá'í Magazine. *Excerpts from Dispatches Written During 1848-1852 by prince Dolgorukov, Russian Minister to Persia*, 15 March 1849, p. 15.

out of his fear", an early chronicle reads, "paid a group to protect his house, their habit was to spend a group every day, and he paid a lot of money in order to protect himself."[1]

The death of Mullá Ḥusayn was supposed to be kept secret; however, a traitor within the fort wrote to the sardár: "They [the Bábís] are worn with famine and are being grievously tested".[2] Such a small piece of information was great news for the army because the latter believed that food storage was plenty in the fort, or at least there was enough to sustain a long siege. He suddenly became bolder and more confident in his effort to destroy the fort but without letting anyone know the reason for his new-found courage.

It appears that Sa'ídu'l-'Ulamá' was not on good terms with the prince. The prince was still in the capital of the province reorganizing a new army when he received a communication from the sardár. The letter did not mention his defeat but was accompanied with heads of Bábís, a fact that emboldened the prince and gave him confidence to accelerate his march towards the fort. However, two officers let the prince know the reality of the sardár's tragedy.[3]

When the news of Mullá Ḥusayn's death broke later on to the community, Sa'ídu'l-'Ulamá' also become hopeful and who wrote to him:

> I congratulate you on your courage and discretion, but how much to be deplored it is that after you have been at such pains, lost so many of your kinsmen, and gained at length so signal a victory, you did not follow it up. You have made a great multitude food for the sword, and have returned, leaving only a few decrepit old men as survivors. Alas, that, after all your efforts and perseverance, the prince is now prepared to march against the castle and take captive these few poor wretches, so that after all he will get the credit of this signal victory, and will appropriate to himself all the money and property of the vanquished! You must make it your first and most important business to return to the castle ere he has set out, for the government of a province like Mázindarán is not a thing to be trifled with. Strive, then, to gain the entire credit of this victory, and let your exertions accomplish what your zeal has begun.[4]

In such a power struggle between the prince, Sa'ídu'l-'Ulamá' and 'Abbás-Qulí Khán, the former put pressure on the divines to fulfil his religious duties of holy war and join the army. "If indeed this be a religious war", the prince wrote to the clergy, "you, who are such zealous champions of the faith, and to whom men look for example, should take the lead, and make the first move, so that others may follow you."[5] As a result,

1 E.G. Browne, *Kitáb-i-Nuqtatu'l-Káf*, p. 174.

2 Nabíl-i-A'ẓam, *The Dawn-Breakers*, pp. 384-385.

3 A. L. M. Nicolas, *Seyyèd Ali-Mohammed dit le Bâb*, p. 327.

4 Mírzá Ḥusayn Hamadání, *The New History (Tarí<u>kh</u>-i-Jadíd)*, p. 72.

5 Mírzá Ḥusayn Hamadání, *The New History (Tarí<u>kh</u>-i-Jadíd)*, p. 73.

> A great company of tradesmen, common people, and roughs was assembled, and these, with the clergy and students, set out, ostensibly for the accomplishment of a religious duty, but really bent on plunder and rapine. Most of these went to Bárfurúsh and there joined the advance of prince Mihdí-Qulí Mírzá, who, on reaching a village distant one parasang from the Castle, sent a body of his men to reconnoitre and collect information about the movements of the Bábí garrison.[1]

The battle

Ten days before Naw-Rúz, the sardár, leading two regiments of infantry and cavalry positioned near the fort, gave orders to shoot at the Bábís guarding the fort towers. In response, Quddús ordered Muḥammad-Báqir—[2] who had built the House of Bábíyyih—to go out with 18 believers and harshly punish the sardár's efforts. They did so, at the cry of "Yá Ṣáḥibu'z-Zamán!" ("O Thou Lord of the Age") and with great courage and without any injury they returned to the fort. By then, Muḥammad-Báqir had taken Mullá Ḥusayn's role as the Bábí military commander. Nabíl wrote:

> The whole army fled in confusion before so terrific a charge. All but a few were able to escape. They reached Bárfurúsh utterly demoralised and laden with shame. 'Abbás-Qulí Khán was so shaken with fear that he fell from his horse. Leaving, in his distress, one of his boots hanging from the stirrup, he ran away, half shod and bewildered, in the direction which the army had taken. Filled with despair, he hastened to the prince and confessed the ignominious reverse he had sustained.
>
> Mírzá Muḥammad-Báqir, on his part, emerging together with his eighteen companions unscathed from that encounter, and holding in his hand the standard which an affrighted enemy had abandoned, repaired with exultation to the fort and submitted to his chief, who had inspired him with such courage, this evidence of his victory.[3]

The *Taríkh-i-Jadíd* presents a similar scenario describing the sardár's defeat:

---

1 Mírzá Ḥusayn Hamadání, *The New History (Taríkh-i-Jadíd)*, p. 73.

2 "Mullá Muḥammad-Báqir Qáiní (sometimes known as Harátí), a Shaykhí from Mashhad with some local influence, was an outstanding example of Bábí radicalism. It was perhaps due to past acquaintance with Mullá Ḥusayn that he was brought to the movement. As already indicated, he was the cofounder of the Bábíya (the House of Bábíyyih) and a devoted preacher of the Bábí cause from the pulpit. His financial support covered the expenses of the Bábíya... Qáiní's conversion was followed by that of many other relatives and followers, including his wife, his son, and his brother. According to one source, as a result of his open preaching "as many as four hundred followers gave their support to the cause." A large number of Bábís who prayed with Qá'iní in the Bábíya were to form the backbone of the forces that started the Mázandarán campaign in 1264/1848" (Abbas Amanat, *Resurrection and Renewal*, pp. 279-280).

3 Nabíl-i-A'ẓam, *The Dawn-Breakers*, pp. 387–388.

> But Jináb-i-Quddús was well aware of the circumstances just detailed, and said to his followers, "Go, and set up on posts the heads of such of our antagonists as were slain, arranging them in regular order round the ramparts of the Castle." So they did as he commanded. And when the royal troops, with the rabble who accompanied them, drew nigh to the Castle, and saw these heads, with mouths gaping horribly and blackened faces, set up on posts round the fortress, they were filled with indescribable terror. And even as they stood gazing thus, fifteen horsemen emerged from the Castle crying "Yá Ṣáḥibu'z-Zamán!" and scattered before them the cavalry of the enemy (though these were more than five hundred strong), slaying not a few.[1]

Interestingly, Mihdí Qulí Mírzá rejoiced at the sardár's failure in the previous fourth battle as prince saw an opportunity to be credited with achieving a victory and of impressing the Sháh. Hence the governor-prince ordered that even more and heavier artillery for his army to assault the fort. He had brought from the capital "four batteries of cannons and mortars, and two howitzers"[2] increasing his military firepower.

A secondary consequence, product of further recruitment, was that the enemy got enough soldiers to encircle completely the fort. Before they only could guard one side because their number was between 2,000 and 3,000. More troops were moved close to the fort getting their camps as closer as 500 steps.

Celebrating Naw-Rúz in the camp

Food was becoming a serious issue within the fort. However, despite the hardships, the lack of food and water, and being away from their families and the aggravating situation they were enduring, Quddús and all the friends of God, joyfully celebrated Naw-Rúz.

Naw-Rúz means literally *New Day* and constitutes the start of a New Year in the millennium-old Persian calendar. Naw-Rúz occurs at the vernal equinox when the day and night are of equal length. It usually occurs around 20 March. In the *Bayán*, the Báb set apart Naw-Rúz as the day for *Him Whom God shall make manifest.*[3] The Báb wrote that "*permission is given at that time* [Naw-Rúz] *to use all musical instruments and luxuries which at other times are not permitted.*"[4] From being a secular national holiday, the Báb changed it to a religious festival.

By Naw-Rúz, all their gunpowder had been used up. In Nabíl's words:

> Whilst their enemies were preparing for yet another and still fiercer attack upon their stronghold, the companions of Quddús, utterly indifferent to the gnawing distress that afflicted them, acclaimed with joy and gratitude the

---

1 Mírzá Ḥusayn Hamadání, *The New History (Taríkh-i-Jadíd)*, p. 73-74

2 Siyamak Zabihi-Moghaddam, *The Bábí-state conflict at Shaykh Ṭabarsí*, p. 98.

3 Moojan Momen, *Selections from the Writings of E. G. Browne*, p. 362.

4 Moojan Momen, *Selections from the Writings of E. G. Browne*, p. 383.

approach of Naw-Rúz. In the course of that festival, they gave free vent to their feelings of thanksgiving and praise in return for the manifold blessings which the Almighty had bestowed upon them.

Though oppressed with hunger, they indulged in songs and merriment, utterly disdaining the danger with which they were beset. The fort resounded with the ascriptions of glory and praise which, both in the daytime and in the night-season, ascended from the hearts of that joyous band. The verse, "Holy, holy, the Lord our God, the Lord of the angels and the spirit", issued unceasingly from their lips, heightened their enthusiasm, and reanimated their courage.[1]

Another chronicler wrote about their "New Year gift":

On the eve of the festival of the Naw-Rúz or Persian New Year's Day (19 March 1849 CE) it was represented to His Holiness Quddús by some of his followers that their gunpowder was all used up. He replied, "To-morrow I will give you a New Year's present of gunpowder." The Bábís supposed that he had promised them a victory over their enemies whereby they should obtain possession of the ammunition stored in the camp, and accordingly were filled with joy at the anticipated triumph; but his Holiness Quddús smiled to himself.

Next day they were subjected to an unusually heavy bombardment from the enemy, and showers of bombs and cannon-balls fell amongst them. In the midst of this His Holiness Quddús came out from his quarters and said, "My men, this is God's New Year's gift, which He hath sent down from the heaven of glory and trial for you much-suffering ones." Then he added, "Affliction is love's portion," and recited the following verses:

"We vouchsafe affliction to none till we have inscribed him amongst the saints.

This affliction is the jewel of our treasure-house: we do not bestow jewels on everyone."

Then he instructed them to pour water over the shells as soon as they touched the ground, and, having thus extinguished the fuses, to extract the powder with which they were filled. "This," added he, "will suffice you, for soon you will need no more powder." These words were understood by those most advanced in faith as signifying that their martyrdom was at hand; but the weaker brethren imagined that a speedy triumph was promised to them.[2]

---

1 Nabíl-i-A'ẓam, *The Dawn-Breakers*, p. 389.

2 Edward Granville Browne, *The Taríkh-i-Jadíd*, p. 367.

Sixth battle— the enemy tower is captured (March 1849)

In his frustrations about conquering the Bábís, the prince assembled a war council that consulted about how to storm the fort and bring it down once and for all. According to an eyewitness from the army side:

> We went to Qia Qéla where a war council was held. A few rare officers advised marching forward; the others affirmed that it would be better to camp where we were. Finally, we agreed that the troops were scared to death of the Bábí, that they had to be exercised and reassured before doing anything, and that a new victory would instantly make the Bábí masters of Mázindarán.[1]

Another Muslim source reported:

> They spent there a few days [and] put heads together as what to do [next]. "The Bábís have killed many of our men. Dear prince, propose a plan!" [requested the Sardár Abbás-Qulí Khán]. The prince said: "Be patient, dear Sardár! God favors the patient. Wait a while till their store of provisions is all consumed. [Then] they will surrender themselves. As a result, we will capture and kill them all." "That's not a bad idea," replied Sardár, "We shall wait."[2]

The entourage stayed four days in Qia Qéla from where they marched towards Shaykh Ṭabarsí. Getting to that vicinity the prince's entourage met with the sardár and for three days consulted on the next strategies which included further recruitment.

Artillery power

Quddús, through a written message, had already warned the Bábís of the growing tests that would surround them and of the imperative need to increase their resolve and to not waver in the face of the enemy's demonstrations of strength that they saw on a daily basis. As a matter of fact, the Mihdí Qulí Mírzá had placed his regiments closer to the fort and intensified the bombardment with recently arrived heavy artillery. Nabíl wrote:

> On the ninth day of the month of Bahá [the ninth day after Naw-Rúz—about the end of March 1849] the commanding officer gave orders to those in charge of his artillery to open fire in the direction of the besieged. While the bombardment was in progress, Quddús emerged from his room and walked to the centre of the fort. His face was wreathed in smiles, and his demeanour breathed forth the utmost tranquillity. As he was pacing the floor, a cannon-ball fell suddenly before him. "How utterly unaware," he calmly remarked, as he rolled it with his foot, "are these boastful aggressors of the power of God's avenging wrath! Have they forgotten that

---

1 A. L. M. Nicolas, *Seyyèd Ali-Mohammed dit le Bâb*, p. 317.

2 Habib Borjian, *A Mázandaráni Account of the Babi Incident at Shaikh Ṭabarsí*, p. 393.

> a creature as insignificant as the gnat was capable of extinguishing the life of the all-powerful Nimrod? Have they not heard that the roaring of the tempest was sufficient to destroy the people of 'Ád and Thamúd[1] and to annihilate their forces? Seek they to intimidate the heroes of God, in whose sight the pomp of royalty is but an empty shadow, with such contemptible evidences of their cruelty?"[2]

The tall tower

The prince had ordered the construction of a tall tower on the west side of the fort close to its walls, a job that he completed in an intensive three-day period. That job would normally have taken three months —which shows the army's desperation.[3] Men were working on the site day and night. The hurry was due to the potential Bábís interventions endangering the construction and their carpenters' safety. The enemy tower was surrounded by a had a moat ten meters deep and ten meters wide with a bridge made of two tree trunks.[4] [5]

From the tower, the army pointed his cannons and began firing towards the fort interior. "The shells would ascend high and land in the Fort's courtyard," an eye witnessed later stated, "and upon contact would go into the ground about a half meter, then explode and kill several men in its range".[6]

"The Sháh's artillery", wrote Guy Murchie, "used cannon balls about 5½ inches in diameter and hollow, the casing being about three quarters of an inch thick... The Muslim artillery was firing from a small hill perhaps 100 feet high and half a mile or so to the south."[7] According to *Taríkh-i-Jadíd*:

> They [soldiers], therefore, employed carpenters to construct scaling ladders and battering-rams, which they carried to the Castle and erected during the night. They also began to dig trenches, and thus gradually advanced. Many came from the surrounding district to help them; ammunition and artillery began to arrive daily from Ṭihrán; and the garrison of the Castle came forth but seldom, only firing occasional shots from the tops of their towers.[8]

---

1 Ṣáliḥ was a Prophet of God sent to the tribe of Thamúd, considered the successor of the Adites (7:74) who moved from 'Ád to Al-Ḥijr where they lived in rooms made inside cut rocks. They hamstrung a camel that Ṣáliḥ brought as a sign from God. It is said that they were destroyed by a noise from the sky. Some identify Ṣáliḥ with the Peleg of the *Bible* (Genesis 10:25). He admonished his people for 100 years according to tradition. Thamúd is identified with the Havila of the Old Testament, the country of the Edomites that was also ancient Petra.

2 Nabíl-i-A'ẓam, *The Dawn-Breakers*, p. 391.

3 A. L. M. Nicolas, *Seyyèd Ali-Mohammed dit le Bâb*, p. 320.

4 A. L. M. Nicolas, *Seyyèd Ali-Mohammed dit le Bâb*, pp. 324-325.

5 Gobineau in Nash and O'Donoghue, *Comte de Gobineau and Orientalism*, p. 172.

6 *The Narrative of Ḥájí Naṣír-i-Qazvíní*, n.p.

7 Guy Murchie, *Visit to Fort Tabarsi*, pp. 8-10.

8 Mírzá Ḥusayn Hamadání, *The New History (Taríkh-i-Jadíd)*, p. 74.

> ... all men, with no exception, had to participate in the construction, those who had worked all nights as well as those who had slept. Vain protests were offered that many of the men were fasting and needed at least some time to rest. He [the commander] insisted, he went into a rage, and the stubborn, bored soldiers dispersed in all directions and hid so as not to have to obey. [1]

A chronist reported that the soldiers working on the tower were not happy due to the working conditions and therefore ran away. "All that Ja'far Qulí Khán, of Balá-Rasták, and Mírzá 'Abdu'lláh [two army officers] could do", a chronicler wrote, " was to keep back thirty or so men with whom they marched off towards the site.[2]

God's lion-hearted warriors

One day, the 35 soldiers guarding the tower fell asleep due probably to exhaustion because of the construction and the bridge was not raised.[3] In accordance with Quddús' command, Muḥammad-Báqir burst from the fort with eighteen companions shouting louder than ever before, "Yá Ṣáḥibu'z-Zamán". Quddús had told them:

> Let him [the sardár] know that God's lion-hearted warriors, when pressed and driven by hunger, are able to manifest deeds of such heroism as not ordinary mortal can show. Let him know that the greater their hunger, the more devastating shall be the effect of their exasperation.[4]

Based on official records, Nicolas described the above incidents in more detail:

> ... with great difficulty that Ja'far Qulí Khán and Mírzá 'Abdu'lláh [the two officer] gathered 35 men whom they brought back to [work on] the tower. As soon as they arrived there, these men lay down and fell asleep. The Bábís observed from the top of their walls what was happening: they understood that an excellent opportunity presented itself to them: two hundred of them came out of their fortress and threw themselves screaming on the sleeping men. Mírzá 'Abdu'lláh, who was keeping watch, discharged his rifle and killed two of them, which instinctively made the attackers divert to the tower of Ja'far Qulí Khán, which they entered easily, killing everything in their path. Ja'far Qulí Khán killed two of them with his own hand while his soldiers also killed two others, but the Bábís threw themselves on him and attacked him with sabres. Having received several wounds, he threw himself into the tower ditch. The Bábí attacked and killed his nephew Tahmásp Qulí Khán, then leaving a few of them at the top of the tower who were firing in the direction of the royal army to

---

1 Gobineau in Nash and O'Donoghue, *Comte de Gobineau and Orientalism,* p. 173.

2 Gobineau in Nash and O'Donoghue, *Comte de Gobineau and Orientalism,* p. 173.

3 A. L. M. Nicolas, *Seyyèd Ali-Mohammed dit le Bâb*, pp. 324-325.

4 Nabíl-i-A'ẓam, *The Dawn-Breakers,* p. 394.

> prevent their approach, and swept the immediate surroundings. Finally, they sounded the retreat...[1]

The Bábís managed to capture the tower and the thirty-nine soldiers fell to their death including Ja'far Qulí Khán who died from his wounds later in the camp. The Bábís were able to obtain additional ammunition and horses for their defence. They also managed to destroy the enemy barricades but could not finish them off because of the approaching darkness. This was another victory for the Bábís.

Eating the horses

According to the historian Siyamak Zabihi-Moghaddam, by the beginning of April 1849 the nearly 500 Bábís had exhausted all of their rice and grain supplies and had already butchered and eaten their remaining horses.[2]

For about a month, the enemy offensive was relatively quiet, perhaps due to an explosion in the enemy's ammunition depot, which killed many officers and soldiers as well as destroying most of their ammunition. Meanwhile those in the fort companions were slowly starving. They had to gather what grass remained in the area and boil it for their daily sustenance. They were consuming everything that it was possible to eat: the meat of their horses, the leather saddles, the bark of the trees and the leather sheaths of their swords. A witness wrote:

> After the horse flesh was finished, our ration was limited to the horse skins. The skin of each horse was torn into pieces, divided among all, and then fried over the fire and consumed like kabab[3]—chewed and eaten.
>
> After the horse skins were finished, all that was left were the bones from the horses. These too were divided among everyone and each bone was fried over the fire, smashed and consumed with some warm water.[4] In such wise, the pangs of hunger were dealt with.
>
> No one was able to go out [of the fort] and even wild vegetation was unattainable. The situation had become most difficult.[5]

It was now the end of March 1849, five months after the Bábís arrived at Shaykh Ṭabarsí.

---

1 A. L. M. Nicolas, *Seyyèd Ali-Mohammed dit le Bâb*, p. 321..

2 Siyamak Zabihi-Moghaddam, *The Bábí-state conflict at Shaykh Ṭabarsí*, p.98.

3 A kind of roasted meat.

4 According to Sepehr Manuchehri, "For nineteen days their diet consisted of a warm plate of water in dawn and dusk" (*Brief Analysis of the Features of Bábí Resistance*, n.p.)

5 *The Narrative of Ḥájí Naṣír-i-Qazvíní*, n.p.

Seventh battle— new warfare technologies (April 1849)

Ye are come near to the spirit be ye therefore like unto the angels.[1]

Due to the rigorously observed blockade, the besieged lost all communication with the world, so much so that they were without food for another month, and were slowly —literally—starving.[2]

Days progressed under an interminable threat. "So every day, the final catastrophe drew nearer, and ever the royalist troops devised some fresh plan for capturing the Castle" wrote Mírzá Ḥusayn Hamadání.[3] With the arrival of Sulaymán-i-Afshár in April 1849, two warfare innovations were introduced at Shaykh Ṭabarsí: the use of mines technology and the deployment of flammable projectiles.

The army of Sulaymán-i-Afshár

The Sháh had grown impatient and ordered another army be sent under the command of Sulaymán-i-Afshár to help subdue the Bábís. Sulaymán-i-Afshár was known for his harshness and experienced military skills. He was "a man known for his severity and of great influence, not only over his own tribe, one of the most influential in Persia, but overall, warriors, who knew and respected him".[4] He had been appointed to appraise the situation and be in charge of the now three armies.[5] A communication from General Semino (1797-1852), a French working for the Persian Army, informs that:

> The Prime Minister sent Sulaymán-Khan-i-Afshár to that side to investigate the movements of Sardár 'Abbás-Qulí Khán-i-Láríjání, who was suspected of being a Bábí, because this person had not been able to defeat them with 6000 men and even 500 of his tufangchís [riflemen] were killed.[6]

Sulaymán-i-Afshár and his powerful army was dispatched by the monarch from the capital on 9 April 1849.[7] It takes about one week for an army to march between Ṭihrán and Bárfurúsh. Gobineau asserted that his royal mandate was such that he replaced the prince[8] implying also the sardár. Sulaymán Khán-i-

1 The Báb, *Tablet of Visitation for Quddús.* See Appendix part II.

2 Mirza Aleksandr Kazem-Beg, *Le Bab et les Bábís,* p. 509.

3 Mírzá Ḥusayn Hamadání, *The New History (Taríkh-i-Jadíd),* p. 83.

4 Gobineau in Nash and O'Donoghue, *Comte de Gobineau and Orientalism,* p. 172.

5 A. L. M. Nicolas, *Seyyèd Ali-Mohammed dit le Bâb*, p. 343.

6 Letter dated 16 June 1849 cited in Mansureh Ettehadieh (Nezam-Mafi) and Said Mir Muhammad Ṣádiq (eds), *General Semino dar khidmat-i Iran dar casr-i Qajar va jang-i Harat*, pp. 192-193.

7 Siyamak Zabihi-Moghaddam, *The Bábí-state Conflict at Shaykh Ṭabarsí*, p. 98.

8 Gobineau in Nash and O'Donoghue, *Comte de Gobineau and Orientalism,* p. 172.

Afshár[1] arrived with five infantry regiments, four powerful guns and calvary of six-thousand people.[2] [3]

As a result of these reinforcements, the imperial army recovered its confidence and increased the bombardment of the interior of the fort. The goal was to tear down a portion of the structure of the wall so that the troops might break in. Several regiments of artillery, infantry, and horsemen were assigned to this war strategy. It has been said that at this point the prince and the sardár came close to the fort but were met with a rain of bullets from the companions. On that occasion, the sardár received a minor shoulder wound. The incident shows how close was the fort from the army.

Mine warfare

Mines were then used to forcefully break into the compound with the troops. "Galleries were dug to the fort, and mines were placed under two of its towers", wrote Zabihi-Moghaddam, "and the fort was stormed from four directions".[4] For instance, it is reported that the army had "dug a mine under one of the towers, charged it with powder, fired it, and destroyed the tower; but during the following night the garrison, at the command of their illustrious chief [Quddús], rebuilt it, and completed it ere dawn."[5] For a visual outline of the towers please Figures 60 and 61.

A. L. M. Nicolas wrote based on official records about the effect of this warfare strategy:

> The mine dug to the west succeeded very well: fifty meters of wall fell under the explosion. The eastern mine, on the contrary, badly dug, produced no effect. The signal for the assault was given and the general attack began. The attack was livelier and more vigorous where the breach had opened. The Bábís were shot to their hearts' content.
>
> Mírzá Karím Khán [an army officer] raised his standard and, without worrying about bullets, came to the foot of the fortress. A Bábí placed took out his rifle through a loophole to shoot down the audacious assailant, but the latter seized the weapon by the barrel and by a vigorous weight snatched it from the hands of the enemy. He then climbed the tower, planted his flag there, and shouted to the soldiers to hasten to join him. Muḥammad Ṣáliḥ Khán, brother of Ja'far Qulí Khán, came running with the men from Balarestaq. Things were about to turn out very badly for the sectarians [Bábís] when, one knows not what vertigo taking hold of the prince, he sounded the retreat.[6]

---

1 Ruhu'llah Mehrabkhani, *Mullá Ḥusayn,* p. 271.

2 Mírzá Ḥusayn Hamadání, *The New History (Taríkh-i-Jadíd),* p. 150.

3 E. G. Browne, *The Taríkh-i-Jadíd,* p. 150.

4 Siyamak Zabihi-Moghaddam, *The Bábí-state conflict at Shaykh Ṭabarsí,* p. 98.

5 Mírzá Ḥusayn Hamadání, *The New History (Taríkh-i-Jadíd),* p. 88.

6 A. L. M. Nicolas, *Seyyèd Ali-Mohammed dit le Bâb,* p. 323.

The sound of the drums indicated that the attack has to be halted as no more support on ground was going to be provided. The prince's subordinates were not happy with this sudden retreat when victory was at their hand. Later, Sulaymán-i-Afshár reprimanded the prince for taking such a decision.

A Bahá'í version of the above reads as follows:

> A large number from the army suddenly attacked the fort, poured naphtha and gunpowder under the Khurásání tower and setting it on fire. The tower was immediately demolished and obliterated. They smashed and demolished the fortification allowing a large number of troops and the multitude to rush into the compound at the sound of trumpets and drums. Once they took possession of the tower, a flag was planted on top of the mound.
>
> When Hazrat[1] Quddús observed the situation in which the opposing forces had overrun the companions, he immediately took his sword which was always hanging on the wall of his dwelling and said that, "With ten companions, I shall drive the enemies out of the tower", and he charged towards them with the same leather shoes he was wearing, followed by a group of his companions.
>
> Muḥammad-Báqir also rushed to the other tower with drawn sword. All the companions, half following him and half following the Hazrat Quddús, risked their lives by rushing towards the enemies with the cry of "Yá Ṣáḥibu'z-Zamán!" ("O Thou Lord of the Age"). Bullets were pouring down on them from the opponents but they were not harmed. They surrounded the enemies, and engaged in fierce combat, shedding their blood until they turned to run away. Hazrat Quddús and his companions climbed the tower and removed, smashed and tore down the seven flags of the army that were hoisted on the top of it, and burnt them.
>
> In that battle, Reza Khán, the son of Muḥammad Khán Turkman, showed great courage and bravery. It is recounted that nine of the companions continuously loaded rifles and handed them to him to fire non-stop. Since he was a skilled marksman, his shooting was very precise killing about seventy soldiers.[2]

By that time, the Bábís had become skilled at repairing their fort in record times. "The original fortifications had been destroyed"; wrote the Count of Gobineau, "but the Bábís had replaced them with an energy that none could deny and worked day and night repairing and extending them." [3]

---

1 The term Hazrat means His Holiness or His Majesty.

2 Fazel Mazandarani, *Taríkh Ẓuhúr al-Ḥaqq*, vol. 2, p. 341-342.

3 Gobineau in Nash and O'Donoghue, *Comte de Gobineau and Orientalism*, p. 172.

Attacks with flammable projectiles

The second military strategy was the use of flammable projectiles through catapults,[1] an old warfare practice. The Count de Gobineau described the steps as follow:

> [Prince] Mihdí-Qulí Mirzá however, in order to neglect nothing, wanted to add something of modern invention to the ancient methods, and had two cannons and two mortars with the necessary munitions brought from Ṭihrán. At the same time, he enlisted the services of a man from Herat [Afghánistán] who possessed the secret of an explosive substance which upon being lit projected itself nearly half a mile and set everything on fire. A test was carried out, with satisfactory results.[2]

Further, Count de Gobineau shared the following outcome:

> This composition was thrown into the castle, setting aflame the rooms of reeds, straw or wood the Bábís had built inside, either in the courtyard or on the ramparts, and soon reducing them to ashes. While this destruction was taking place the bombs thrown by the mortars and the cannonballs were doing considerable damage to a construction hurriedly raised by people who were not architects, less yet engineers, and who had never dreamt that they could be attacked by artillery. In a short time, the defences of the castle were dismantled; there was nothing left but beams felled by the fire, debris of charred and smoking wood, piles of fallen stones.[3]

Bábís built subterranean tunnels

The *Tarík͟h-i-Jadíd* informs that "during the following night the garrison [after the mining of the towers], at the command of their illustrious chief [Quddús] rebuilt it, and completed it ere dawn."[4] However, the bombing continuously continued and flames and cannonballs kept reaching the inside of the fort.[5] The inside of the precinct was highly flammable: "rooms of reeds, straw or wood ... either in the courtyard or on the ramparts".[6] Kazem Beg also informs that the Bábís, in order to protect themselves from flames and cannon-balls, had to retire to their underground cellars.[7]

Nicolas added:

---

1 Siyyid Muḥammad-Ḥusayn, *Vaqa'i-i Mimiyyih*, p. 70.

2 Gobineau in Nash and O'Donoghue, *Comte de Gobineau and Orientalism*, p. 172.

3 Gobineau in Nash and O'Donoghue, *Comte de Gobineau and Orientalism*, p. 172.

4 Mírzá Ḥusayn Hamadání, *The New History (Tarík͟h-i-Jadíd)*, p. 83.

5 Mirza Aleksandr Kazem-Beg, *Le Bab et les Bábís*, p. 509.

6 Gobineau in Nash and O'Donoghue, *Comte de Gobineau and Orientalism*, p. 171.

7 Mirza Aleksandr Kazem-Beg, *Le Bab et les Bábís*, p. 509.

> The cannons and mortars rained death on the sectarian [Bábí] camp. Raining may be exaggerated to say but it is certain that the fire of the royal army bothered the defenders of Shaykh Ṭabarsí so much that Quddús went to settle in the embankments while his companions took shelter in the underground passages: and they made fun of the royal artillery.[1]

According to the *Taríkh-i-Jadíd*, "the ground of Mázindarán lies near the water and is saturated with moisture, added to which rain fell continually, increasing the damage, so that these poor sufferers dwelt amidst mud and water till their garments rotted away with damp ...."[2] Sepehr Manuchehri adds:

> Their insistence on defensive fighting techniques coupled with a decrease in their food supplies during the final weeks of the resistance, forced the Bábís to take some desperate actions ... Bábís immediately began to dig underground tunnels to take refuge. The natural water table in Mázindarán is fairly close to the ground, and hence tunnels were often flooded. To add to their misery, heavy rain also impeded their efforts. They found the tunnels unbearable and could not dwell in the compound because of the cannon fires. The ones inside the rooms had to endure constant firing and bombardments.[3]

Departures and desertions

Many factors were undermining the Bábís' brave resolve. The fort's structure had been severely damaged after eight months of fighting, and the defenders were exhausted, lacking not only food and water but also shoes, sanitary conditions, and other basic necessities for survival let alone sleep deprivation. For example, they were unable to gather tree branches from outside to repair their makeshift huts, which were leaking from the rain. As summer approached, temperatures in May sometimes soar to 40 degrees Celsius, making life increasingly miserable, compounded by high humidity and erratic downpours. For some, it was more than they could endure.

"Shortly afterwards [mining of the fort]", wrote Zabihi-Moghaddam, "thirty or more Bábís deserted the fort, but their leader [Áqá Rasúl] and perhaps a few others were killed and the rest captured by the troops and killed later."[4] On several occasions, Quddús would say, "We passed over the actions of Áqá Rasúl and God forgave him'".[5] Other companions managed to cross the enemies in the darkness and return home.[6]

---

1 A. L. M. Nicolas, *Seyyèd Ali-Mohammed dit le Bâb*, p. 320.

2 Mírzá Ḥusayn Hamadání, *The New History (Taríkh-i-Jadíd)*, pp. 81–2.

3 Sepehr Manuchehri, *Brief Analysis of the Features of Bábí Resistance*, n.p.

4 Siyamak Zabihi-Moghaddam, *The Bábí-state conflict at Shaykh Ṭabarsí*, p. 97.

5 Cited in Sepehr Manuchehri, *Taqiyyah (Dissimulation) in the Bábí and Bahá'í Religions*, p. 228.

6 A. L. M. Nicolas, *Seyyèd Ali-Mohammed dit le Bâb*, p. 324.

Gobineau reports that Rizá Khán, "one of the sons of Muḥammad Khán, the king's squire, who had followed Mullá Ḥusayn, and, up until then bravely shared the fortunes of the sect" ... "weakened by hunger, escaped during the night and went to beg mercy of the prince, who pardoned him. A few other Bábís were perhaps less guilty, but no less pardonable. They gathered up their weapons, crossed the sleeping royal army and, upon reaching the mountains split up and returned to their villages".[1]

On the last week of April 1849

Despite all the latest battle technologies, the army was not getting any significant advance and the resilient Bábís, even starving, were putting up a great resistance. Nabíl wrote that Quddús instructed Mírzá Muḥammad-Báqir and thirty-six defenders to repulse the attack:

> Never since our occupation of this fort, have we under any circumstances attempted to direct any offensive against our opponents. Not until they unchained their attack upon us did we arise to defend our lives. Had we cherished the ambition of waging holy war against them, had we harboured the least intention of achieving ascendancy through the power of our arms over the unbelievers, we should not, until this day, have remained besieged within these walls. The force of our arms would have by now, as was the case with the companions of Muhammad in days past, convulsed the nations of the earth and prepared them for the acceptance of our Message. Such is not the way, however, which we have chosen to tread. Ever since we repaired to this fort, our sole, our unalterable purpose has been the vindication, by our deeds and by our readiness to shed our blood in the path of our Faith, of the exalted character of our mission. The hour is fast approaching when we shall be able to consummate this task.[2]

On 26 April 1849 Muḥammad-Báqir skilfully managed to repel the aggression and put confusion among the royal ranks:

> Mírzá Muḥammad-Báqir once more leaped on horseback and, with the thirty-six companions whom he had selected, confronted and scattered the forces which had beset him. He carried with him, as he re-entered the gate, the banner which an alarmed enemy had abandoned as soon as the reverberating cry of "Yá Sáhibu'z-Zamán!" had been raised. Five of his companions suffered martyrdom in the course of that engagement, all of whom he bore to the fort and interred in one tomb close to the resting place of their fallen brethren.

Such was the declining course of events form the Persian government that prince Dolgorukov, the Russian Ambassador, reported to his government on 3 May 1849:

---

1 Gobineau in Nash and O'Donoghue, Comte de Gobineau and Orientalism, p. 173.

2 Nabíl-i-A'ẓam, *The Dawn-Breakers*, p. 396.

> In a political report I may not paint a less gloomy picture. According to the information received from Mázindarán, Sulaymán Khán Afshár, who was commissioned to subdue the Bábís by peaceful means, has failed in his attempts. Attacked by Sardár 'Abbás-Qulí Khán and Sulaymán Khán-i-Afshár, who wanted to take the fortifications by force, those fanatics, in spite of numerical inferiority to the attackers, repulsed them...[1]

Eighth battle—the last engagements (May 1849)

When informed of the fallen wall in the seventh battle, Quddús said,

> Do not rebuild it, for when we bade you repair the breach in the tower we had need of it for other six months, but now we need these things no longer. Let two marksmen sit there; so shall none be able to approach or enter in.[2]

Probably because of these instructions is that the army decided to capture fort using only the troops.

The last month

Eight months had passed since they arrived at that unhospitable forest, surrounded by blood-thirsty enemies, away from their families, excommunicated from the world and subsisting on scarce food and water, if nothing at all. All these tribulations were paying a heavy toll on their bodies although not in their spirit. "Because in the early days of hardship", said Abú-Tálib Shahmírzadí, eyewitness to these events, "we used to go outside the ditch in the dark nights to bring grass. When the enemies saw and understood, they used to shoot us from the top of the catapult [manjaníq] in the open until morning".[3] A chronicler affirmed that "their clothes were rotten from the moisture of water and mud".[4]

Psychologically warfare was also present. Their attacks were accompanied by the noise of trumpets and drums.[5] The same source stated that "every morning and evening, the sound of the army trumpet was raised. The companions thought that they would attack"[6] but it turned out the army were only trying to scare the companions. A survivor recalled that in the very last weeks of the siege "the companions were exhausted from the weakness of hunger, except for Quddús who was sitting on a chair with a bare sword in his blessed hand", defiant, in the middle of the courtyard.[7]

---

1 Moojan Momen, *The Babi and Baha'i Religions 1844–1944*, p. 92.

2 Mírzá Ḥusayn Hamadání, *The New History (Taríkh-i-Jadíd)*, p. 83.

3 Mír Abú-Tálib Shahmírzadí, *Untitled history*, p. 48,

4 E.G. Browne, *Kitáb-i-Nuqtatu'l-Káf*, p. 177.

5 Fazel Mazandarani, *Taríkh Ẓuhúr al-Ḥaqq*, vol. 2, p. 341-342.

6 Mír Abú-Tálib Shahmírzadí, *Untitled history*, p. 47,

7 Mír Abú-Tálib Shahmírzadí, *Untitled history*, p. 51

The last fighting engagements took place when the believers were starving due to the lack of food. There were frontal confrontations between both parties with lots of pushing and shoving. Based on the official historical record, the Count of Gobineau wrote:

> And struggling with that rage and exaltation that transformed them into more than ordinary soldiers, the two sides mingled together in one great ruck and fought more with pistol and dagger than with rifle and sabre. The men rolled around pêle-mêle in the moat, on the ruins of the wall, on the debris of the towers. Like a whirlwind of leaves, assailants and defenders fell indistinguishably in the vast courtyard of the fort, the living, the wounded, clinging to each other and pushing like the waves of a sea shaken by the swell. The main entrance had finally been breached. Sulaymán Khan's soldiers arrived from all sides and the Bábís could neither repel them, disband or make their escape. [1]

A Muslim source reports that a number of defendants were taken prisoners and locked up.[2]

Living without water

Conditions became more severe as the end of the siege was looming:

> The food of the companions, in the morning and in the evening, was limited to a warm cup of water. In the face of hardships and calamities, Quddús, every day after performing the evening prayer, used to spend one hour with preaching and exhortation, and encouraged the companions to be patient, resigned, surrendered, and be content with the calamities that befell them in the path of God.
>
> The companions were endowed with such power of faith and detachment, that they spent their time with joy and bliss. However, they were so frail and skinny that it was as if they could not breathe and move, and each one yearned for martyrdom. [3]

Days progressed under an interminable threat. 'Abdu'l-Bahá refers to the suffering of these servants of the Báb:

> Think, for example, how the enemy had completely hemmed in the Fort, and were endlessly pouring in cannon balls from their siege guns. The believers, among them Ismu'lláh, went eighteen days without food. They lived on the leather of their shoes. This too was soon consumed, and they had nothing left but water. They drank a mouthful every morning, and lay famished and exhausted in their Fort. When attacked, however, they would instantly spring to their feet, and manifest in the face of the enemy a magnificent courage and astonishing resistance, and drive the army back

---

1 Gobineau in Nash and O'Donoghue, *Comte de Gobineau and Orientalism,* p. 174.

2 Habib Borjian, *A Mázandaráni Account of the Babi Incident at Shaikh Ṭabarsí,* p. 393.

3 Fazel Mazandarani, *Taríkh Ẓuhúr al-Ḥaqq,* vol. 2, pp. 349-350.

> from their walls. The hunger lasted eighteen days. It was a terrible ordeal. To begin with, they were far from home, surrounded and cut off by the foe; again, they were starving; and then there were the army's sudden onslaughts and the bombshells raining down and bursting in the heart of the Fort. Under such circumstances to maintain an unwavering faith and patience is extremely difficult, and to endure such dire afflictions a rare phenomenon.[1]

Eventually, the Bábís were so famished that their bodies became barebones:

> So their bellies clave to their back-bones, as though to say, "Ye are come near to the spirit be ye therefore like unto the angels"; their bodies became like skeletons ... their cheeks grew pallid as amber, telling them that the signs of a faithful lover are a heart filled with woe, bitter sighs, and a sallow complexion.[2]

Before proceeding to narrate the end of the siege in chapter 16, the next chapter 15 dealing on the daily life of the companions in the fort of Shaykh Ṭabarsí has been compiled so that the reader can understand the severe conditions in which they lived for several months and the spiritual resilience that the Bábís demonstrated in the face of great adversity.

---

1 'Abdu'l-Bahá, *Memorials of the Faithful,* p. 7.

2 Mírzá Ḥusayn Hamadání, *The New History (Taríkh-i-Jadíd),* p. 82.

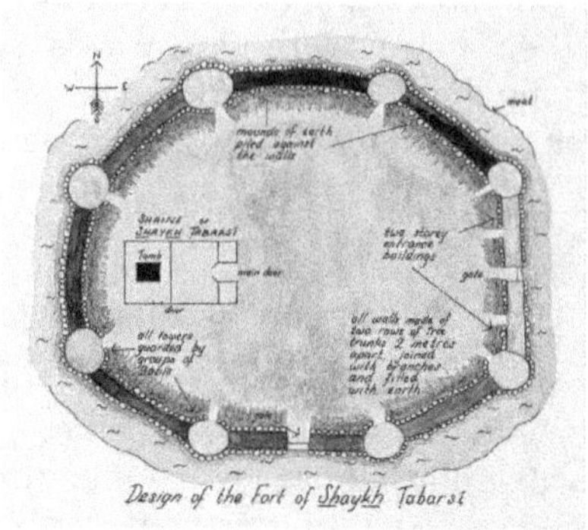

Figure 60: Shaykh Ṭabarsí plan (courtesy of Sue Podger)

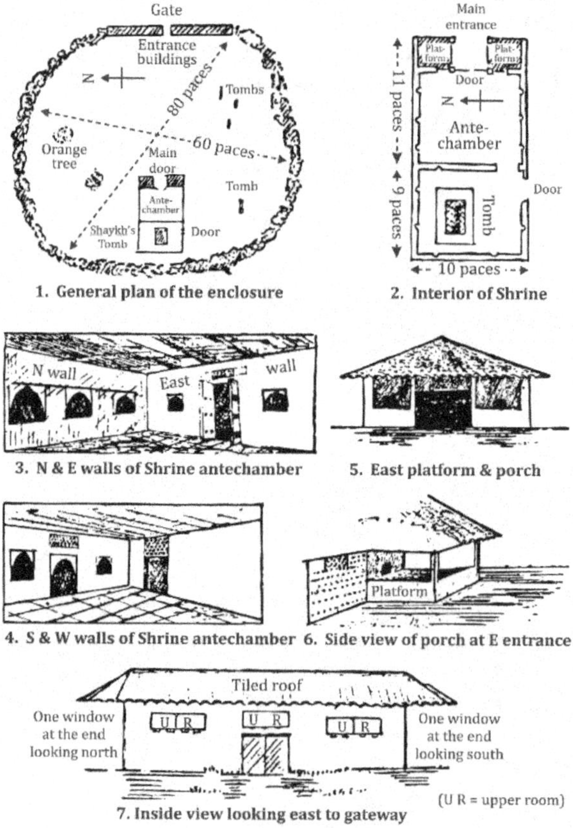

Figure 61: Layout of the Shrine of Shaykh Ṭabarsí by E.G. Browne

Figure 62: Sulaymán Khán-i-Afshár,
military commander at Shaykh Ṭabarsí
(Source: George Ronald Publisher)

Figure 63: Village of Afrá next to the Fort Shaykh Ṭabarsí

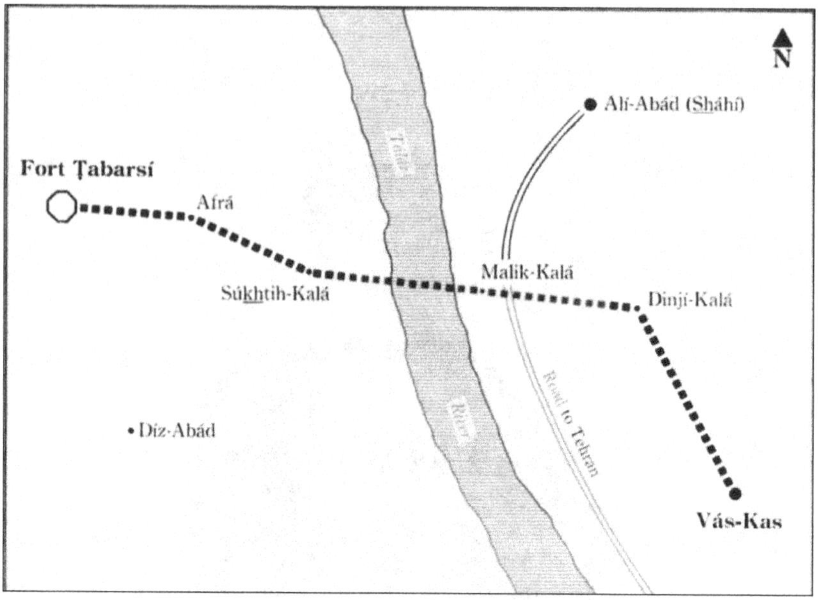

Figure 64: Route from the Vás-Kas military camp to Shaykh Ṭabarsí (Courtesy Kalimát Press)

Figure 65: Fictional image of Quddús (courtesy of Ivan Lloyd)

Figure 66: A cannon ball from the fort of Shaykh Ṭabarsí © Bahá'í World Centre

Figure 67: The defenders of Shaykh Ṭabarsí (courtesy of Ivan Lloyd)

Figure 68: The defenders of Shaykh Ṭabarsí (courtesy of Ivan Lloyd)

15
Living conditions in Shaykh Ṭabarsí

Chapter content
Shaykh Ṭabarsí as an early Bábí settlement
Arrivals at Shaykh Ṭabarsí
Teaching the Faith
Devotional environment
Community celebrations
Bábí heroism
Attacks on the fortifications
Hunger and starvation

This chapter will present illustrative vignettes associated with the daily life of the Bábís while defending themselves in Shaykh Ṭabarsí fort. These stories can be read in any order.

The sub-tropical northern Iranian sky, sometimes studded at night with innumerable stars sometimes shrouded by the temperamental weather of the day, stretched its vastness above the precarious fort. Providence cast its gaze upon the Bábís of Ṭabarsí, captives under an interminable siege with nowhere to go. Their only accompaniment was the dayspring and twilight warbling of thousands of birds stationed in the dense, foggy and luxurious forest. Resigned to their confines for months, they yet managed to develop a pattern of community life with its intense spiritual engagement so necessary to survive in such a hostile environment.

Coming from ordinary civilian lives, they were trapped and thrust into a dangerous, fluid, and unpredictable warfare situation.

There were frequent new arrivals, particularly before the beginning of the siege. Some believers could not endure the stoic conditions and left. Within the fort precincts, people of all ages were found including children and family members serving together. In a genuine communal life, regardless of their socio-economic background, they all shared their belongings and lives as if they had always lived under the same roof. "Quddús and Mullá Ḥusayn," Sepehr Manuchehri wrote, "went to great pains to stress that Bábís must share their possessions with one another and never lose sight of the ultimate purpose which was martyrdom in His cause."[1]

The source of such powerful motivation was Quddús, the Báb's mirror and His representative, who nurtured and inspired them through prayers, sermons and communal reading of the Báb's Writings and other devotional activities. If they shone brilliantly during the combat, like legendary warriors, it was because martyrdom was the full realisation of their earthly life. Defeat, surrender and

---

1 Sepehr Manuchehri, *Brief Analysis of the Features of Bábí Resistance*, n.p.

capture had no place in their adopted soldierly new life. With meagre food and harassed under intensive and continuous fire, the Bábís of Ṭabarsí gave their lives sacrificially for no other reason than to prove to government, clergy and the populace the messianic nature of the Cause of the Báb.

Such a display of immense inner power was even commented on by a military commander years later:

> ... they came forth to battle with such alacrity and joy, and engaged so eagerly and gladly in the strife, without displaying in their countenance any trace of fear or apprehension. One would imagine that in their eyes the keen sword and blood-spilling dagger were but means to the attainment of everlasting life, so eagerly did their necks and bosoms welcome them as they circled like salamanders round the fiery hail of bullets. And the astonishing thing was that all these men were scholars and men of learning, sedentary recluses of the college and the cloister, delicately nurtured and of weakly frame, inured indeed to austerities, but strangers to the roar of cannon, the rattle of musketry, and the field of battle. During the last three months of the siege, moreover, they were absolutely without bread and water, and were reduced to the extreme of weakness through lack of even such pittance of food as is sufficient to sustain life. Notwithstanding this, it seemed as if in time of battle a new spirit were breathed into their frames, insomuch that the imagination of man cannot conceive the vehemence of their courage and valour.[1]

Shaykh Ṭabarsí as an early Bábí settlement

In a way, Shaykh Ṭabarsí fit the mould of having become a self-contained settlement that ultimately reached about 500 people.[2] According to an eye-witness,

> Every manner of profession and worldly occupation could be found among the exalted companions. For instance, there were master-carpenters, builders, tailors, masseurs, engravers and cobblers, as well as many learned men of letters. In short, every profession was at hand.[3]

Luṭf 'Alí Mírzá Shírází was the registrar of Shaykh Ṭabarsí keeping a detailed account of who entered the fort, what type of work he did, who arrived and who left. They even had their own treasurer:

> Mírzá Khalíl Rashtí heard of the Bábí religion in his hometown of Rasht and came to Bárfurúsh where Quddús enrolled him as a Bábí. He accompanied Quddús on his journey to Mashhad and subsequently to Badasht. Because

---

1 Mírzá Ḥusayn Hamadání, *The New History (Taríkh-i-Jadíd)*, p. 108.

2 To visualize how 500-600 people can be accommodated standing, the area of a basketball playing area is 420 m², reaching 677 m² when run-off and sidelines are included.

3 *The Narrative of Ḥájí Nasír Qazvíní.*

> he was entrusted with the money for purchasing supplies for Quddús and his companions, he became known as Mullá Ámina (Ámina being from the root meaning trustworthy).[1]

Such a plentiful availability of human resources, added to a profound spiritual understanding, gave way to a rich and complex community life with a well-organised structure during the eight months in which the conflict took place.

Gradually, they experienced a communal metamorphosis. Here, a community was different in life skills and social backgrounds but united in devotion. The source of such a transformation may be found in their eight months of isolation from the external world, the extraordinary spiritual atmosphere and communion together, their sense of mission and the tests they had to go through to unanimously accept their destiny of martyrdom.

Although there is no historical evidence, it can be suggested that perhaps they wanted to create a proto-colony where there were going to communally live according to the teachings of the *Bayán* to create the foundations for a future Bábí society.

Arrivals at Shaykh Ṭabarsí

Before the noose of the siege tightened around the fort, there were always people coming and going at Shaykh Ṭabarsí. Since the Báb was summoning all Bábís throughout the country to join the defenders, their number increased to 540–600 people at one point according to a source.[2]

The visit of Bahá'u'lláh

One of the most notable visits was when Bahá'u'lláh arrived at the fort, which brought great joy to Mullá Ḥusayn. Quddús arrived at the fort a couple of weeks later. The historian Nabíl described the impact of the visit by Bahá'u'lláh:

> As soon as he [Mullá Ḥusayn] saw Him approaching with Naẓar Khán, he rushed forward, tenderly embraced Him, and conducted Him to the place of honour which he had reserved for His reception. We were too blind in those days to recognise the glory of Him whom our leader had introduced with such reverence and love into our midst. What Mullá Ḥusayn had perceived, our dull vision was as yet unable to recognise. With what solicitude he received Him in his arms! What feelings of rapturous delight filled his heart on seeing Him! He was so lost in admiration that he was utterly oblivious of us all. His soul was so wrapt in contemplation of that countenance that we who were awaiting his permission to be seated were kept standing a long time beside him. It was Bahá'u'lláh Himself who finally bade us be seated. We, too, were soon made to feel, however inadequately, the charm of His utterance, though none of us were even dimly aware of the infinite potency latent in His words.

---

1 Moojan Momen, *The Bahá'í Communities of Iran*, vol. I, p. 314.

2 See Moojan Momen, *The Social Basis of the Babi Upheavals in Iran*, p. 286.

Bahá'u'lláh, in the course of that visit, inspected the fort and expressed His satisfaction with the work that had been accomplished. In His conversation with Mullá Ḥusayn, He explained in detail such matters as were vital to the welfare and safety of his companions.[1]

The villagers of Bihnamír

People from the neighbouring villages also joined the companions:

> In Bihnamír[2] ... it was as a result of the conversion of a local landlord, Áqá Rasúl Bihnamirí, that a large number of persons was converted ... forty or more persons from the village who joined the Bábís at Shaykh Ṭabarsí did so under the leadership of the local landlord, Áqá Rasúl Bihnamírí.[3]

These men from Bihnamír

> ... accompanied Quddús to Ṭabarsí when he came to join the companions at the fort. As this group had prepared to leave their village, Qásim, a young boy, approached their leader, Áqá Rasúl, and asked to be allowed to go with them. Áqá Rasúl refused, saying that he was too young for such an undertaking. But Qásim would not give in. He hid himself near a bridge which he knew they would pass after midnight. When the villagers reached this place, he stood in their way and begged again not to be disappointed. So Áqá Rasúl accepted him.
>
> Sometime later, when the companions were severely tested, Áqá Rasúl could not bear the trials, and he abandoned his fellow believers. But the young Qásim was staunch to the end. During the last days of the siege, when the enemy cannons shelled the grounds of the fort, Qásim was struck in the stomach, his abdomen open. Holding his intestines in both hands, he ran towards Quddús, offered them to him, and fell dead.[4]

In Shaykh Ṭabarsí, the majority of these Bábís from Bihnamír were killed, but about five survived.[5]

The Bábís of Savád-kúh

> Their [the Bábís] numbers gradually increased from forty or fifty to between four and five hundred, and their recruits were chiefly men from the district of Savád-kúh. One of these latter was styled Amír-i-Tabardár, because his favourite weapon was the tabar, a poleaxe, from which the former name of the province Tabaristán was derived.[6]

---

1 Nabíl-i-A'ẓam, *The Dawn-Breakers,* pp. 347–9.

2 Bihnamír is located 20 km north-east of Babol.—Ed.

3 Moojan Momen, *The Social Basis of the Bábí Upheavals in Iran* (1848–53), pp. 177–9.

4 Ruhollah Mehrabkhani, *Mullá Ḥusayn: Disciple at Dawn,* p. 235.

5 See Moojan Momen, *The Bahá'í Communities of Iran,* vol. I, p. 312.

6 E. G. Browne, *Materials for the Study of the Bábí Religion,* p. 241.

Riḍá Khán enters the fort

Riḍá [Reza] Khán was a prominent Ṭihrán resident, a Turkman and a known Bábí who had been at the conference of Badasht and visited the Báb during His imprisonment. This is the exciting story as to how he joined Shaykh Ṭabarsí:

> Riḍá Khán's illness [at home] lasted for some while, and on his recovery the siege of the castle of Ṭabarsí had already waxed grievous. He at once determined to go to the assistance of the garrison. Being, however, a man of mark and well-known, he could not leave the capital without giving some plausible reason. He therefore pretended to repent his former course of action and begged that he might be sent to take part in the war in Mázindarán, and thus make amends for the past.
>
> The king granted his request, and he was appointed to accompany the force proceeding under prince Mihdí-Qulí Mírzá against the castle. During the march thither he was continually saying to the prince, "I will do this", and "I will do that", so that the prince came to entertain high hopes of him, and promised him a post commensurate with his services for till the day when battle was inevitable and peace no longer possible, he was ever foremost in the army and most active in ordering its affairs. But on the first day of battle he began to gallop his horse and practise other martial exercises, until, without having aroused suspicion, he suddenly gave it free rein and effected a junction with the Brethren of Purity. On arriving in their midst, he kissed the knee of Jináb-i-Quddús and prostrated himself before him in thankfulness.[1]
>
> After they had attacked three times and had been defeated, they [the enemy] retreated and, after a few days, wrote on a paper, attached it to a board, hung it on their trench border and shouted allowed calling us to read that paper. When the companions read the paper, they saw the bloody Mihdí-Qulí Mírzá [the prince] had written, "If you come out and leave the Fort, no one will hurt you, and there will be no revoke. Otherwise, we will keep surrounding you till you all starve to death."

People are allowed to leave

> In such circumstances of starvation [due to the strict siege], some companions left the fort begging for bread. They were Mírzá Ahmed Tarshízí, Mírzá Naṣru'lláh Hiraví and 'Alí Qazvíní.
>
> Áqá Rasúl Bihnámírí came to the presence of Quddús and said, "We cannot endure famine anymore; please remediate our plight." Quddús said, "Be well, be united, and in unity, with love and kindness towards each other, so that heavenly food be brought for you, and whatever you desire and wish may happen to you." Áqá Rasúl said, "I can go out, for I have a letter from the army commanders telling me to verify the situation in the Fort

---

1 Mírzá Ḥusayn Hamadání, *The New History (Taríkh-i-Jadíd)*, p. 100.

and what the companions think and say until they are back from Tihrán. They will not hurt me, for I will show the letter to the prince so they will see that they have sent me." Quddús said, "What you say is true. However, they will not let you reach the camp; they will shoot and kill you, and whoever you take along with you, they will chain you and keep you at their camp. And as they martyr all of us, they too will be martyred". Áqá Rasúl said, "The prince has spared us. What would be the problem if you release us to go out? Here we are perishing of hunger. So, we should go out. And when you overcome and defeat them, we will come back and join you.

As Quddús heard this, his blessed purple face turned into saffron, and said, "I do not hold back anyone, and I do not say you should stay. Whoever desires to be killed and hungry, may stay. He ordered Amán Yúsuf 'Alí Ardabílí to gather the companions and tell them, "Whoever desires to be killed, remain. Otherwise, you should leave. And I set you free from my pledge." Mullá Yúsuf 'Alí, by the order and command of Quddús, gathered the companions and released them from their allegiance. Therefore, Áqá Rasúl Bihnámírí and sixty of his followers who were from Mázindarán went to Quddús and kissed his hand before leaving.

Quddús said, Áqá Rasúl went out dreaming of bread at the camp, but he will taste neither bread nor water of the camp. He will be killed... As Áqá Rasúl Bihnámírí approached the vicinity of the enemy's camp, they suddenly fired at him, hitting his chest. He fell and died on the spot. Then they took his companions to the camp, chained and imprisoned them.[1]

The story of Áqá Siyyid Aḥmad

Of the number of those brave warriors of truth who were most eminent for their attainments was Áqá Siyyid Aḥmad of Semnan, a preacher of incomparable eloquence and rare powers of diction and delivery, well known throughout all Mázindarán for his godliness, simplicity of life, virtue, and piety. When he saw the faithful beleaguered in the Castle of Ṭabarsí, and ascertained them to be for the most part learned, wise, and virtuous beyond the generality of their` fellows, he was convinced by his natural acuteness of apprehension that they would not have embarked on so hazardous an enterprise or have thus imperilled their lives unless they had clearly recognized (in the new doctrine) something (worthy of their self-devotion). This was in the early days of the siege, before the garrison of the Castle were subjected to a rigorous blockade.

And the inhabitants of Sháh-Mírzá and Dasak-sar, two considerable villages situated near to the Tomb of Shaykh Ṭabarsí, moved by the same considerations as had influenced Áqá Siyyid Aḥmad, resolved to enquire into the matter, and waited upon him to unfold their views. "I also," replied he, "am filled with wonder at their behaviour, and am much disposed to

[1] Siyyid Muḥammad-Ḥusayn, *Vaqa'i-i Mimiyyih*, pp. 88-90.

examine their doctrine, and discover what object they have in view." To this the others replied, "We entertain no doubt concerning your piety and wisdom, and if you, having visited them, affirm the truth of their claims, we too will join ourselves to them and help them, so far as lies in our power, with men and supplies."

Now although at this time none dared so much as speak of the Bábís, much less go to their stronghold and converse with them, Áqá Siyyid Aḥmad actuated solely by his natural goodness and sincerity, manfully set out for the Castle to ascertain the truth of the matter. And it had been agreed that, so soon as he should have satisfied himself, he should return and inform the others of the state of the case, so that, if they held to their promise, they might all join the defenders of the Castle, and furnish them with supplies. So Áqá Siyyid Aḥmad, shutting his eyes to all worldly considerations, and impelled by zeal to discover the truth, set his feet within that vortex of affliction. And when he was come thither, and had met and conversed with Jináb-i-Quddús and others of the believers, the veil of doubt fell from his eyes, and he saw plainly that which he sought transcending the understandings of the wisest amongst mankind. So he believed with his whole heart, and thereafter turned not back from the path on which he had entered.

Then he sent word to the inhabitants of the two villages,

> "That which my heart hath long essayed to find
> Is found at length, concealed this veal behind."

So the villagers began to make preparations to go to the Castle, but just at that time the troops hemmed it in on all sides, closing every avenue of approach, so that they were unable to reach it. Surely men care naught for religious truth, and are held back by the bonds of passion and self- interest from taking thought of spiritual things, for of those, whether wise or simple, who set themselves to enquire into the matter not one but was convinced.[1]

Conversion of Mullá Yúsuf Ardibílí

Mullá Yúsuf Ardibílí a Shaykhí and an old, pious divine, had a room in the Madrisih Du-dar at the time when Mullá Ḥusayn would teach [the Faith] in that school. He and Mullá Ḥusayn debated for forty days until finally on the fortieth day the latter said to him, "The honored Akhúnd! When you leave this world and the Prophet of God inquires of you as to why you rejected the Call of His Descendent [i.e. the Báb] and instead of recognition showed stubbornness, how will you answer?" These words of Mullá Ḥusayn affected him in such wise that despite his advanced age and frail condition, and without any preparation for the journey and carrying only his walking stick, wearing solely his sandals and thin clothing, the late

1 Mírzá Ḥusayn Hamadání, *The New History (Tarí<u>kh</u>-i-Jadíd)*, pp. 105–6.

Mullá Yúsuf took the route for Ádharbayján the cold of that winter. With utmost difficulty, misery and hunger, and nearly at the door of death, he arrived at Máh-Kú where the Báb was confined. When he had finally reached the guards-station, he collapsed unconscious. Eventually, when he opened his eyes, he saw that his head was resting on the lap of a Siyyid who informed him. "I am here to deliver you to the Object of your desire." (This man was the amanuensis of the Báb, Áqá Siyyid Ḥusayn [Yazdí). They passed by the guards and arrived at the foot of a decayed fort, where on the top of an adjacent hill the Báb was imprisoned. Once there, the Siyyid said to him, "You are to wait here until I beseech permission for our admittance." However, when he returned, he reported, "The Báb has commanded, 'Since the Akhúnd has shown much stubbornness [in the path of God], he is to go forth to Shaykh Ṭabarsí and die a martyr's death so that We would be pleased with him.'" Instantly, he obeyed and took the road for Mázandarán, arriving on a night when the forest was set ablaze by the believers, and the sky was bright as a day and mortars constantly fell from every side. Under such conditions, Akhúnd Mullá Yúsuf entered the battle and fought in the frontline of defences, where a cannonball found him a ready target and thus he achieved the glory of martyrdom.[1]

An unusual visitor

An interesting anecdote happened on those days when an unexpected visitor showed up at the Fort:

> One day a woman came out with a black pitcher in her hand to sprinkle water on the dust. The Bábís seized her, and then discovered that she was really a man in disguise. They asked him what he was doing. He answered, "The clergy of the town have repeated spells over this water for forty days, and have given me twenty túmáns to sprinkle it, so that your people may be dispersed." Then they brought him before Quddús, to whom he said, "Six of the clergy have read prayers over this water for forty days and given it to me to bring and sprinkle here." Quddús said, "Their wickedness stands revealed, but no blame is attached to the messenger." Then he gave the man a present and dismissed him.[2]

The frightened divines

> The reverend divines, who with their pupils, had come to take part in the holy war, were scarce able to sleep at night for fear (though their quarters were in a place distant at about 10 km from the Castle).[3]
>
> Very little convinced of celestial assistance, believing their last day had arrived, they could not sleep and spent their nights lamenting. They cursed the prince and 'Abbás-Qulí Khán who had forced them to come into this

1 In Ahang Rabbani, *The Genesis of the Bahá'í Faith in Khurásán,* Chapter 2, pp. 21-22
2 Mírzá Ḥusayn Hamadání, *The New History,* p. 150.
3 Mírzá Ḥusayn Hamadání, *The New History,* p. 74.

mess, they anathematized Sa'ídu'l-'Ulamá' who had remained very quiet in Bárfurúsh even though he had sent them to the butchery.[1]

'Abbás-Qulí Khán and the prince, fearing that their [divines'] terror would spread to the soldiers, that their murmurs would find echo in the camp, hastened to send them away. They therefore left enchanted, at least deep down, but taking care to bless the army and to ask aloud the God of Islam to grant them victory.[2]

Teaching the Faith

The Bábís were actively engaged in teaching their Faith, particularly when Quddús arrived. It seems they wanted to replicate in Shaykh Ṭabarsí the success of the House of Bábíyyih. It has been related that Quddús asked the companions to visit the villages around and teach them the Cause of God. As a result, the inhabitants of the region realised that the Bábís were spiritual people.[3] As outlined earlier, Quddús was known well in the city of Bárfurúsh, 13 km away from Shaykh Ṭabarsí. He had participated in various debates with Sa'ídu'l-'Ulamá', the local cleric, on religious matters.

Quddús wrote a letter to the inhabitants of the city of Bárfurúsh which, in essence, reads:

> Whoever considers us believers and Muslims and does not come to our aid is an infidel. And whoever considers us unbelievers and non-Muslims and does not come to battle us is likewise an infidel.[4]

Gradually, Quddús' fame as a man of sanctity began to spread also in the villages around Shaykh Ṭabarsí. The villagers also understood that in the fort there were men of letters and sciences. Once a notable of the region of Núr forwarded several questions to Quddús through a messenger on matters related to the sciences of divination and astrology. Quddús passed this request to Mullá Sa'íd, a companion of the fort,

> Mullá Sa'íd though hurried by the presence of the messenger, and distracted by the turmoil of the siege, rapidly penned a most eloquent address, wherein, while replying to the questions asked, he introduced nearly a hundred well-authenticated traditions bearing on the truth of the new Manifestation of the promised Proof, besides several which foreshadowed the halting of those who had believed in the Lord about Ṭabarsí, and their martyrdom. The learned men of Núr were amazed beyond all measure at his erudition, and said, "Candour compels us to admit that such presentation of these matters is a great miracle, and that such erudition and eloquence are far beyond the Mullá Sa'íd whom we

---

1 A. L. M. Nicolas, *Seyyèd Ali-Mohammed dit le Bâb*, p. 317-318.

2 A. L. M. Nicolas, *Seyyèd Ali-Mohammed dit le Bâb*, p. 319

3 Ruhollah Mehrabkhani, *Mullá Ḥusayn: Disciple at Dawn*, p. 235.

4 *The Narrative of Ḥájí Naṣír-i-Qazvíní*, n.p.

> knew. Assuredly this talent hath been bestowed on him from on high, and he in turn hath made it manifest to us".[1]

Mullá Ḥusayn also heavily engaged in teaching the Cause of the Báb in Shaykh Ṭabarsí. The historian Nicolas describes the environment:

> Everything well developed, Mullá Ḥusayn Bushrú'í openly resumed his preaching, and announced, says the Muslim author, that the following year Mírzá 'Alí-Muḥammad [the Báb] would conquer the entire globe, organise it, make known the law of God and bring together into one all the religions. He thus attracted and converted a good number of Muslims.[2]

Devotional environment

It is Quddús' continuous deepening and collective devotional engagement that enabled the Bábís to endure the overwhelming military power of the enemy. The siege continued for such a long time and under such adverse conditions, both physically and psychologically, that it would humanly be impossible to withstand.

Prayers and devotions were essential components of the spiritual life of Shaykh Ṭabarsí. They had the Writings of the Báb.[3] About the spirit of those days, Nabíl wrote:

> Every morning and every afternoon during those days, Quddús would summon Mullá Ḥusayn and the most distinguished among his companions and ask them to chant the writings of the Báb. Seated in the Maydán, the open square adjoining the fort, and surrounded by his devoted friends, he would listen intently to the utterances of his Master and would occasionally be heard to comment upon them. Neither the threats of the enemy nor the fierceness of their successive onsets could induce him to abate the fervour, or to break the regularity, of his devotions. Despising all danger and oblivious of his own needs and wants, he continued, even under the most distressing circumstances, his daily communion with his Beloved, wrote his praises of Him, and roused to fresh exertions the defenders of the fort. Though exposed to the bullets that kept ceaselessly raining upon his besieged companions, he, undeterred by the ferocity of the attack, pursued his labours in a state of unruffled calm.[4]

These prayers sometimes lasted all night:

> The royal troops had that night suffered a disgraceful defeat, and were scattered in flight. Many of the Bábís, too, had in the darkness and pouring rain missed the way to the Castle and become separated from their comrades, but, when the time for prayer came, these, guided by the sound

---

1 Mírzá Ḥusayn Hamadání, *The New History (Taríkh-i-Jadíd)*, p. 79.

2 A. L. M. Nicolas, *Seyyèd Ali-Mohammed dit le Bâb*, pp. 301–2.

3 John Walbridge, *Essays and Notes on Bábí and Bahá'í History*, 2002.

4 Nabíl-i-A'ẓam, *The Dawn-Breakers*, pp. 355–6.

of the *adhán*,[1] found their way back thither. For it was customary with the garrison of the Castle to keep vigil during the last third of the night, to read and pray aloud with fervent devotion until day-break, and to offer up their petitions to the Just and Gracious Lord. Far otherwise was it in the royalist camp, where wine-bibbing, foul and licentious acts, dice-playing, and utter neglect of spiritual exercises universally prevailed.[2]

According to the historian Nabíl, they also read and chanted the *Qur'án*:

> He [Quddús] would sometimes ask his 'Iráqi companions to chant various passages of the *Qur'án,* to which he would listen with close attention, and would often be moved to unfold their meaning. In the course of one of their chantings, they came across the following verse: "With somewhat of fear and hunger, and loss of wealth and lives and fruits, will We surely prove you: but bear good tidings to the patient". "These words", Quddús would remark, "were originally revealed with reference to Job and the afflictions that befell him. In this day, however, they are applicable to us, who are destined to suffer those same afflictions. Such will be the measure of our calamity that none but he who has been endowed with constancy and patience will be able to survive them".[3]

These practices included reading the writings of Quddús:

> Despite these adverse circumstances, he unfailingly continued further to elucidate in his commentary the significance of the Ṣad of Ṣamad, and to exhort his friends to persevere till the very end in their heroic endeavours. At morn and at eventide, Mírzá Muḥammad-Báqir would chant, in the presence of the assembled believers, verses from that commentary, the reading of which would quicken their enthusiasm and brighten their hopes.[4]

The Qayyúmu'l-Asmá'

We do not know exactly which Writings of the Báb the Bábís read and chanted at Shaykh Ṭabarsí. It is very likely that they were familiar with the *Qayyúmu'l-Asmá*,[5] which was regarded by Bahá'u'lláh as *"the first, the greatest, and mightiest of all books"*.[6] It was revealed in Arabic and was considered to be the *Qur'án* of the Bábís.[7] The Báb instructed that the *Qayyúmu'l-Asmá* should be recited frequently:

---

1. Call to congregational prayers.
2. Mírzá Ḥusayn Hamadání, *The New History (Taríkh-i-Jadíd),* p. 71.
3. Nabíl-i-A'ẓam, *The Dawn-Breakers,* p. 356.
4. Nabíl-i-A'ẓam, *The Dawn-Breakers,* p. 390.
5. *Qayyúmu'l-Asmá* literally means "The Self-Subsisting Lord of All Names".
6. Bahá'u'lláh in Shoghi Effendi, *God Passes By,* p. 23.
7. See Bahá'u'lláh, *The Kitáb-i-Aqdas,* p. 213.

Recite ye as much as convenient from this Qur'án both at morn and at eventide, and chant the verses of this Book, by the leave of the eternal God, in the sweet accents of this Bird which warbleth its melody in the vault of heaven.[1]

The revelation of the *Qayyúmu'l-Asmá* began on the night of the Declaration of the Báb to Mullá Ḥusayn on 23 May 1844 as the Commentary on the Súrih of Joseph. The Báb stated that the *Qayyúmu'l-Asmá* "*had, in the first year of this Revelation, been widely distributed.*"[2] According to Him, "*This book is the Remembrance of God that, in truth, is revealed unto the Most Great Word for the entire world.*"[3] About the *Qayyúmu'l-Asmá*, the Báb also said that this Book is proof of His Revelation for East and West:

O peoples of the earth! By the righteousness of God, this Book hath, through the potency of the sovereign Truth, pervaded the earth and the heaven with the mighty Word of God concerning Him Who is the supreme Testimony, the Expected Qá'im, and verily God hath knowledge of all things. This divinely inspired Book hath firmly established His Proof for all those who are in the East and in the West, hence beware lest ye utter aught but the truth regarding God, for I swear by your Lord that this supreme Proof of Mine beareth witness unto all things ....[4]

Community celebrations

Community celebrations were also held among the companions to raise their spirituality. According to Mírzá Luṭf-'Alí:

On the day of the festival of Qurbán (sacrifice),[5] a few lambs were distributed among the believers. His Holiness Quddús used his sword to cut one of the lambs in two, and another was killed by Mullá Ḥusayn, which represented a certain saying (hadith) of the past regarding this occasion.[6]

The author of *Taríkh-i-Jadíd* comments on their spirit of unity and sharing:

After this several mounted men were sent to collect the baggage [that they left behind in the forest before arriving in the Shaykh Ṭabarsí for the first time] , and they gathered it together and brought it in. Then *Jináb-i-Bábu'l-Báb* [Mullá Ḥusayn], said, "If ye be united in spirit, it is contrary to the dictates of self-devotion and single-heartedness to make any distinction in these perishable possessions during the few brief days for which a respite

---

1 The Báb, *Selections*, pp. 55–56.

2 The Báb, *Selections*, p. 90.

3 The Báb in Nader Saiedi, *Gate of the Heart*, p. 141.

4 The Báb, *Selections*, pp. 59–60.

5 A religious festival in the Islamic calendar commemorating Abraham's willingness to sacrifice his son, Ishmael, in obedience to God's command.

6 Luṭf 'Alí Mírzá Shírází, *A Chronicle of the Babi Uprising*, pp. 71–2.

may be granted to you. Forsake, then, all such distinctions, and, for this short while, share what ye have in common."[1]

Quddús' words of encouragement:

> You are those same companions of whom Muḥammad, the Apostle of God, has thus spoken: "Oh, how I long to behold the countenance of my brethren; my brethren who will appear in the end of the world! Blessed are we, blessed are they; greater is their blessedness than ours". Beware lest you allow the encroachments of self and desire to impair so glorious a station. Fear not the threats of the wicked, neither be dismayed by the clamour of the ungodly.[2]

Bábí heroism

The beloved Guardian wrote about the detachment of the companions:

> We marvel at the spirit of renunciation that prompted those sore pressed sufferers to contemptuously ignore the possessions left behind by their fleeing enemy; that led them to discard their own belongings, and content themselves with their steeds and swords; that induced the father of Badí', one of that gallant company, to fling unhesitatingly by the roadside the satchel, full of turquoises which he had brought from his father's mine in Nishápúr; that led Mírzá Muḥammad-Taqíy-i-Juvayní to cast away a sum equivalent in value in silver and gold; and impelled those same companions to disdain, and refuse even to touch, the costly furnishings and the coffers of gold and silver which the demoralized and shame-laden prince Mihdí-Qulí Mírzá, the commander of the army of Mázindarán and a brother of Muḥammad Sháh, had left behind in his headlong flight from his camp.[3]

"Is there any who will help me?"

The sardár 'Abbás-Qulí Khán once related his admiration for the heroism of the Bábís of Shaykh Ṭabarsí and notably Mullá Ḥusayn challenging the army troops by asking, "Is there any who will help me?"[4] According to the *Taríkh-i-Jadíd:*

> I swear by the sacred plume of His Majesty the Centre of the Universe that one day Mullá Ḥusayn, having on his head a green turban, and over his shoulder a shroud, came forth from the Castle, stood forth in the open field, and [leaning on a lance which he held in his hand] said, "O people, why, without enquiry, and under the influence of passion and prejudiced

---

1 Mírzá Ḥusayn Hamadání, *The New History (Taríkh-i-Jadíd)*, p. 55.

2 Nabíl-i-A'ẓam, *The Dawn-Breakers*, p. 392.

3 Shoghi Effendi, *God Passes By*, p. 39.

4 This was the call for help from Imám Ḥusayn, Muḥammad's grandson, when he and his family were being massacred in Karbilá in 680 CE.

misrepresentation, do ye act so cruelly towards us, and strive without cause to shed innocent blood? Be ashamed before the Creator of the universe, and at least give us passage, that we may depart out of this land [to Europe, or Turkey, or India.]"

Seeing that the soldiers were moved, I opened fire, and ordered the troops to shout so as to drown his voice. Again I saw him lean on his lance and cry, 'Is there any who will help me?' three times so that all heard his cry. At that moment all the soldiers were silent, [and some began to weep], and many of the horsemen were visibly affected. Fearing that the army might be seduced from their allegiance, I again ordered them to fire [and shout].

Then I saw Mullá Ḥusayn unsheath his sword, raise his face towards heaven, and exclaim, "O God, I have completed the proof to this host, but it availeth not." Then he began to attack us on the right and on the left. I swear by God that on that day he wielded the sword in such wise as transcends the power of man. Only the horsemen of Mázindarán held their ground and refused to flee.[1]

Bombs inexplicably bursting in the air

On another day a bomb-shell fell on the wooden roof of the hut occupied by Jináb-i-Quddús. Mullá Muḥammad-Ṣádiq who was better known as Muqaddas-i-Khurásání, involuntarily sprang up, crying, "O my master, quit thy place!" But the other answered composedly, "If the Beloved of all worlds desires that we should fall by a bullet, then why should we flee, our object being gained? But if He desire it not, then shall we assuredly not be slain; wherefore then should we move?" Jináb-i-Muqaddas-i-Khurásání used to declare that forthwith the projectile rose up from the ground and burst in the air, and this notwithstanding the fact that bomb-shells commonly enter the ground where they fall, and then leap back and burst.[2]

Spirit of martyrdom is shown

They were ready to breast the steep ascent to martyrdom and bliss; they hovered like moths round the cannon-balls and bullets, which they hailed as a means of deliverance; they rushed towards immolation with an impetuosity which imagination can scarce conceive ....[3]

Much courage is needed

[Quddús said:] If the powers of the earth league themselves against you, they will be powerless, ere that hour strikes, to lessen by one jot or tittle the span of your life. Should you allow your hearts to be agitated for but one moment by the booming of these guns which, with increasing violence,

---

1 Mírzá Ḥusayn Hamadání, *The New History (Taríkh-i-Jadíd)*, pp. 106–9.

2 Mírzá Ḥusayn Hamadání, *The New History (Taríkh-i-Jadíd)*, p. 83.

3 Mírzá Ḥusayn Hamadání, *The New History (Taríkh-i-Jadíd)*, p. 82.

will continue to shower their shot upon this fort, you will have cast yourselves out of the stronghold of Divine protection.[1]

Divine protection

Mírzá Abú Ṭálib-i Shahmírzadí related that on arriving at the Fort, he went straight to the presence of Quddús who received them with much kindness and told them to take his place among the defenders and receive daily instructions from Mullá Ḥusayn. In seeing Mullá Ḥusayn, likewise, he uplifted them with his words of encouragement and then told that nothing happens in the Fort unless it is the will of Jináb-i Quddús at its appointed time.[2]

... when he returned from their last battle, his garment was full of bullet holes, but on opening his belt, bullets fell to the ground, none of them having harmed him in the least.[3]

The old man

Ḥájí Muḥammad-i-Karrádí, whose home was situated in one of the palm groves adjoining the old city of Baghdád, was a man of great courage who had fought and led a hundred men in the war against Ibráhím Páshá of Egypt. He had been a fervent disciple of Siyyid Káẓim and was the author of a long poem in which he expatiated upon the virtues and merits of the siyyid. He was seventy-five years old when he embraced the Faith of the Báb, whom he likewise eulogised in an eloquent and detailed poem. He distinguished himself by his heroic acts during the siege of the fort, and eventually became a victim of the bullets of the enemy.[4]

According to Sepehr Manuchehri, "Ḥájí Muḥammad-i-Karrádí, owned a number of gardens and properties. He was an expert in battle techniques and served in the Egyptian forces in his younger days. He joined Shaykh Ṭabarsí at the age of 80 but became paralysed whilst in the fortress".[5]

Attacks on the fortifications

Fort becomes a local attraction

The fortifications around the Shaykh Ṭabarsí Shrine were built with expertise and skill, and they became a great source of curiosity for the local people. People from the adjacent villages, and even from the Bárfurúsh, came to inspect the

---

1 Nabíl-i-A'ẓam, *The Dawn-Breakers,* p. 392.

2 Ahang Rabbani, *Miracles and history* (17 December 1995). Available www-personal.umich.edu/~jrcole/talisman/t95dec5b.htm

3 The Narrative of Ḥájí Naṣír-i-Qazvíní, n.p.

4 Nabíl-i-A'ẓam, *The Dawn-Breakers,* p. 426.

5 Sepehr Manuchehri, *Brief Analysis of the Features of Bábí Resistance at Sheikh Ṭabarsí,* n.p.

structure despite strict prohibitions issued by the Sa'ídu'l-'Ulamá'. According to Nabíl:

> The completion of the fort, and the provision of whatever was deemed essential for its defence, animated the enthusiasm of the companions of Mullá Ḥusayn and excited the curiosity of the people of the neighbourhood .... Quddús had no sooner ascertained the number of its occupants than he ordered that no visitor be allowed to enter it. The praises which those who had already inspected the fort had lavished upon it were transmitted from mouth to mouth until they reached the ears of the Sa'ídu'l-'Ulamá' and kindled within his breast the flame of unrelenting jealousy. In his detestation of those who had been responsible for its erection, he issued the strictest prohibition against anyone's approaching its precincts and urged all to boycott the companions of Mullá Ḥusayn.[1]

Sharing building tasks

> Of the detailed account of these transactions [there given] the following is an epitome of what is most material. When Jináb-i-Quddús had arrived at the Castle of Shaykh Ṭabarsí and interviewed those who already occupied it, he proceeded to determine the extent and limits of the fortress and ordered a wall to be built about it. He likewise commanded all such as were skilled in any craft to exercise that craft for God's glory in as perfect a manner as was possible, to the end that their brethren might be profited thereby. So, the mason busied himself with building, the tailor with tailoring, and the sword-maker with the manufacture of swords.
>
> The number of those amongst them who were craftsmen and artisans was but small; but what was intended by this command was that all should profit by the results of one another's gifts and talents. Wherefore in like manner such as were divines and men of learning busied themselves in searching out divine mysteries and expounding philosophic truths, whereby those who lacked learning and scholarship were enabled to partake in the advantages which these confer, and to advance towards perfection, learning to base their faith on grounds of reason, and not on mere imitation or blind devotion.[2]

There were "extensive repairs made by the Bábís to a run down and disused bath inside the compound dedicated to Quddús who practiced and preached cleanliness, and bathed every day."[3]

---

1 Nabíl-i-A'ẓam, *The Dawn-Breakers*, pp. 357–8.

2 Mírzá Ḥusayn Hamadání, *The New History (Taríkh-i-Jadíd)*, p. 57.

3 Sepehr Manuchehri, *Brief Analysis of the Features of Bábí Resistance*, n,p.

Hunger and starvation

Accommodation

According to the Narrative of Ḥájí Naṣír-i-Qazvíní:

> The esteemed companions were housed in the courtyard of the shrine of Shaykh Ṭabarsí. That is, before any hostilities had occurred, day and night all the companions had dug a trench around Shaykh Ṭabarsí, which had been a fort in previous times. The trench was three meters wide and three meters deep. The [excavated] earth was thrown behind the trenches and wooden, fortified fences built over it. Turrets were built in six locations and, on rotation, from the rank of companions a number of sharpshooters were selected to man them day and night. The rest of the companions, in groups of five or ten men, had built huts in the shrine's courtyard. These were made of wood and the roof was covered by hay to protect them from snow and rain. These makeshifts served as their dwellings. Food and provisions for each person was provided from what had been purchased and from the [war] spoils and stored in each hut.[1]

The single almond story

In the same Narrative we read:

> During the extreme days of the encirclement of the Fort in Mázindarán when the companions were suffering bitterly from the absence of food, one day I looked through my bag and travel sack and found a single almond. Even though I had been suffering from starvation for some time to the point that all strength had abandoned me, instantly I knew that I should take that almond to the illustrious Quddús. Therefore, I wrapped that single almond in a piece of silk and presented it before him.[2]

Some cow milk to share

Finally, there was just one last valuable resource in the fort, a cow whose milk was used to make a treat for Quddús. He divided that delectable feast with his companions, saving a few spoonfuls for himself. According to Nabíl:

> All that remained of the cattle they had brought with them to the fort was a cow which Ḥájí Násirí'd-i-Qazvíní had set aside, and the milk of which he made into a pudding every day for the table of Quddús. Unwilling to deny his hunger-stricken friends their share of the delicacy which his devoted companion prepared for him, Quddús would, after partaking of a few teaspoonfuls of that dish, invariably distribute the rest among them. "I have ceased to enjoy," he was often heard to remark, "since the departure of Mullá Ḥusayn, the meat and drink which they prepare for me. My heart

1 *The Narrative of Ḥájí Naṣír-i-Qazvíní,* n.p.

2 *The Narrative of Ḥájí Naṣír-i-Qazvíní,* n.p.

bleeds at the sight of my famished companions, worn and wasted around me."[1]

No place for gluttony

At the beginning when abundant food was available, Quddús counselled the Bábís about avoiding excessive eating.

> Thus Jináb-i-Quddús, coming forth one day from the room wherein he dwelt, saw lying a quantity of rice in the husk (choltook). Thereupon he said to his companions, "We came hither to shew forth God's truth, not to live gluttonously. If the aim in view were to maintain in luxury these perishable bodies, had you not in your own homes all manner of delicate foods? Why then did ye forsake these to come hither? But if ye came to die, then you need not fodder and provisions." To this his companions replied, "Whatever your orders may be, we are ready to obey them." Then said he, "Give the rice to the horses and sheep and cattle for them to eat it." For they had over two hundred horses, forty or fifty milch-cows, and three or four hundred sheep, most of which had been given to them by the people of Mázindarán, who, as many as believed, brought with them to the Castle of what they possessed. So the Bábís, eager to obey the commands of Jináb-i-Quddús, took no pains to husband their resources, so that in a little while their provisions were exhausted; while, inasmuch as the enemy had surrounded the Castle on all sides, they could not go forth to procure fresh supplies.[2]

Acquiring provisions

> Among the divines of Bárfurú<u>sh</u> was a good man, a friend of Quddús named Mullá Muḥammad-i-Ḥamzih. He was a pious Muslim who challenged everything that the Sa'ídu'l-'Ulamá' had done. When the people left the Bábís without food and water, he directed some of his men to take food and provisions to the caravanserai. Mullá Ḥusayn insisted that they accept full price for these supplies. Thus during the few days that they remained in Bárfurú<u>sh</u>, the believers were able to purchase what they needed to survive.[3]

Eating grass

> A sudden explosion in one of the ammunition stores of the enemy, which had caused the death of several artillery officers and a number of their fellow-combatants, forced them for one whole month to suspend their attacks upon the garrison. This lull enabled a number of the companions to emerge occasionally from their stronghold and gather such grass as they could find in the field as the only means wherewith to allay their hunger.

---

1 Nabíl-i-A'ẓam, *The Dawn-Breakers,* pp. 389–90.

2 Mírzá Ḥusayn Hamadání, *The New History (Taríkh-i-Jadíd),* p. 78.

3 Ruhollah Mehrabkhani, *Mullá Ḥusayn,* p. 204.

> The flesh of horses, even the leather of their saddles, had been consumed by these hard-pressed companions. They boiled the grass and devoured it with piteous avidity. As their strength declined, as they languished exhausted within the walls of their fort, Quddús multiplied his visits to them, and endeavoured by his words of cheer and of hope to lighten the load of their agony.[1]

Drinking only water

Áqá Muhammad-Mihdí Bá<u>gh</u><u>b</u>án-Bá<u>sh</u>í, was among those individuals who was alive until the end, and who, when the companions' food was reduced to horse meat and the skin and bones of the horses; this humble youth did not touch a morsel of food for seventeen days, and would only satisfy himself by drinking some warm water, until he finally drank the draught of martyrdom.[2]

When the food was finished

Ḥájí Nasír Qazvíní related that "After a while, the food ran out. There were some [provisions] in the kitchen of the dwelling occupied by the illustrious Quddús, who instructed that each day one or two *sír* [of ration] (the equivalent to 75 grams) be given to each person. It went like this until no trace of rice or wheat remained."[3] However, eventually they experienced total hunger and starvation and had to resort to horsemeat:

> When their stores were exhausted, and they began to suffer the hardships of privation, they represented to Jináb-i-Quddús that the horses[4] were perishing of hunger. So he ordered them to drive out from the Castle such as were lean, and to slay and eat such as were fat, seeing that this was now become lawful to them [*halál*]. One can readily imagine how grievous and how distasteful the eating of horse-flesh must have seemed to persons habituated to such luxuries as Russian sugar, Austrian tea, and fine aromatic rice. Yet they ate submissively and with contentment so much as was needful to sustain life, bowing patiently, yea, thankfully, before the Divine decree. Now there were in the Castle from olden time the remains of a bath, which the Bábís had endeavoured to repair. One day Jináb-i-Quddús, as he came forth from this bath, saw some of his companions roasting and eating horse-flesh. "Let me see," said he, "what this food, which the Beloved hath apportioned to us, is like." Then he took a little and sucked it in his mouth, and presently remarked that the meat was very pleasant to the taste, and sweet in savour. After this, horse-flesh seemed to the taste of all so sweet and so palatable that they were filled with

1 Nabíl-i-A'ẓam, *The Dawn-Breakers*, p. 395.

2 *The Narrative of Ḥájí Nasír Qazvíní*, n.p.

3 *The Narrative of Ḥájí Naṣír-i-Qazvíní*, n.p.

4 "They had two or three very fine horses." In Habib Borjian, *A Mázandaráni Account of the Babi Incident at Shaikh Ṭabarsí*, p. 393.

astonishment, saying, "It is as though our food savoured of paradise, for never have we tasted meat so delicious."[1]

"When the leaves were all consumed," another chronicler wrote, "they began eating dirt. Doing so for a couple of days, they realized that the mud harms them."[2] The Bábís therefore resorted to exhuming the dead horses. In Persian Shí'ih society, eating horses is both *ḥarám* ("forbidden") as well as *makrúh* ("abominable"), an injunction that was ignored when food disappeared and hunger pangs grew because of the blockade.

When meat from the dead horses was exhausted, they crushed the bones and ate that with water like a cream. One day when their needs became extreme, and after consultation, they decided to unearth Mullá Ḥusayn's horse that had died along with its master. They were saddened since the horse was so excellent that it had even "acquired human virtues".[3] Needless to say that the meat was spoiled. According to the Count de Gobineau:

> The horse of Mullá Ḥusayn had died of the wounds suffered during that fatal night which witnessed the death of its master. The Bábís had buried it out of regard for their holy leader and a little of the deep veneration which all felt for him hovered over the grave of the poor animal.
>
> They held council and, deploring the necessity for such a discussion, they debated the question whether extreme distress could justify them to disinter the sacred charger and eat the remains. With deep sorrow, they agreed that the deed was justifiable. They cooked the remains of the horse with the flour made from the bones of the dead, they ate this strange mixture and took up their guns once more![4]

The time came when not even dead horses were available:

> Eyewitnesses said that the Bábís often had to look for food in the holes of mice and rats.[5]
>
> Now when the horse-flesh came to an end they began to subsist on vegetables, until even the grass and the leaves of the trees within the fortress were all consumed, so that, as some have related, they ate even the leather off their saddles. Grass became harder to find than the Philosopher's Stone, and if they sought to gather it outside the Castle, they were at once exposed to the fire of the enemy.
>
> They therefore ceased to attempt to leave their fortress, and abstained from food, so that for nineteen days they took no sustenance (save that

---

1 Mírzá Ḥusayn Hamadání, *The New History (Taríkh-i-Jadíd)*, p. 80.

2 Habib Borjian, *A Mázandarání Account of the Babi Incident at Shaikh Ṭabarsí*, p. 393.

3 *The Narrative of Ḥájí Naṣír-i-Qazvíní*. n.p.

4 Joseph Arthur Gobineau, *Les Religions et les Philosophies dans l'Asie Centrale*, pp. 186–7. Cited in Nabíl-i-A'ẓam, *The Dawn-Breakers*, p. 395.

5 Bernard von Dorn, "Nachträge zu dem Verzeichniss ...", p. 381.

morning and evening they drank each a cup of warm water), drawing their strength from their converse with Jináb-i-Quddús.[1]

During a few days that elapsed after the last confrontations, the hostilities decreased and apparently, out of frustrations from the army's side on Wednesday, 9 May 1849, an invitation for negotiations was received from the prince.

1 Mírzá Ḥusayn Hamadání, *The New History (Taríkh-i-Jadíd)*, p. 81.

16
The massacre of 10 May 1849

Chapter content
Deceiving the Bábís: the final strategy
The Thursday massacre
Killing the survivors
Three poignant stories
Quddús' departure to Bárfurúsh

The alarming display of physical, mental, and spiritual resistance from the followers of the Báb—completely resigned to their fate—forced the prince to discard war strategies employed over the previous months. In *The New History (Taríkh-i-Jadíd),* we read:

> Even Sulaymán Khán-i-Afshár, a man wise in council and skilled in war, who had been sent from Ṭihrán to take the Castle at all hazards, gave up in despair, and retired to 'Alí-Ábád [Shír-Gáh] with the intention of returning [to the capital]. The Prince and 'Abbás-Qulí Khán also declared in the despatches which they forwarded to the King that in spite of the most strenuous efforts the troops could gain no advantage, and that it appeared certain that there was but little chance of their obtaining a victory.[1]

Deceiving the Bábís: the final strategy

Very concerned about the inexplicable incapacity of his troops, he consulted with his senior officers' plans for a new strategy. "We cannot carry the Castle by storm; every attempt to do so results only in defeat, disgrace, and useless loss of life," the officer said.[2] The military commanders therefore devised an infamous and wicked plan which took two days to be executed: Wednesday 9th and Thursday 10 of May 1849.

The prince and his war council sent a messenger to the fort with a message to Quddús proposing a negotiated peace. In reality, Sulaymán Khán-i-Afshár, fearful that his military tactics would fail again, suggested deceiving the Bábís with false promises to get them to leave the fort to secure their capture.

It could be possible that the Bábís were asked to apostasize as a condition for the talks.[3] However, this condition might be totally rejected by the Bábís as a matter of principle. On one hand, from the Bábís' point of view, martyrdom was

---

1 Mírzá Ḥusayn Hamadání, *The New History (Taríkh-i-Jadíd),* pp. 85-86

2 Mírzá Ḥusayn Hamadání, *The New History (Taríkh-i-Jadíd),* p. 85.

3 Gobineau in Nash and O'Donoghue, *Comte de Gobineau and Orientalism,* p. 174.

the ultimate goal whether through armed resistance or not. On the side of the government, a "no prisoners taken" policy was adopted. The prince himself might have discarded the option of absolution by having the Bábís renege on their faith because, according to historian A.L.M. Nicolas:

> ... it mattered very little to the Prince whether these people believed in God or the devil; then he knew very well that the Bábís would certainly not have consented to this apostasy [leaving the Faith of the Báb]; finally, and this is the most convincing reason, the Prince was already preparing the ambush into which he was going to make his unfortunate adversaries fall. From then on, he had no need to ask them for anything, risking an inadmissible demand to push the Bábís to a final act of despair that could have cost him many people.[1]

According to Gobineau, "After resolving a few difficulties, it was agreed that the Bábís surrender and with that being the sole condition that upon leaving their castle their lives would be guaranteed."[2] The details are provided below.

Wednesday 9 May morning – conversations with the prince

On Wednesday morning the prince asked Quddús to send two representatives to his camp to negotiate a process for resolving the stand-off. The prince presented to these two believers his desire to reach a friendly agreement to terminate the fighting and to avoid more bloodshed. The prince wrote in a copy of the *Qur'án* an oath in which he begged everyone to leave the fort assuring them that at all times they would be under the protection of his government, which had every intention of peacefully ending this fruitless confrontation, and that he wanted them to return home in peace. He said:

> I swear by this most holy Book, by the righteousness of God who has revealed it, and the Mission of Him who was inspired with its verses, that I cherish no other purpose than to promote peace and friendliness between us. Come forth from your stronghold and rest assured that no hand will be stretched forth against you. You yourself and your companions, I solemnly declare, are under the sheltering protection of the Almighty, of Muḥammad, His Prophet, and of Náṣiri'd-Dín Sháh, our sovereign. I pledge my honour that no man, either in this army or in this neighbourhood, will ever attempt to assail you. The malediction of God, the omnipotent Avenger, rest upon me if in my heart I cherish any other desire than that which I have stated.[3]

A clause in the prince's declaration included, "To whatsoever place ye desire to go, none shall let or hinder you in any way".[4] An eyewitness stated:

---

1 A. L. M. Nicolas, *Seyyèd Ali-Mohammed dit le Bâb,* p. 326.

2 Gobineau in Nash and O'Donoghue, Comte de Gobineau and Orientalism, p. 174.

3 Nabíl-i-A'ẓam, *The Dawn-Breakers,* pp. 399–400.

4 Mírzá Ḥusayn Hamadání, *The New History (Taríkh-i-Jadíd),* pp. 86-87.

> The prince wrote to us that you should come out and be assured that no one will harm you. We will send you to Sárí and Bárfurú<u>sh</u> and the divines of Sárí and Bárfurú<u>sh</u> will come and sit with you so that you can discuss to see who has the truth, and then we will give you money to return to your country and homeland.[1]

The two believers returned to inform Quddús of the solemn promise the prince had made. Quddús, reverently taking the copy of the *Qur'án* exclaimed, "*Oh our Lord! Decide between us and our people truthfully; because the one who can decide best is You.*" (*Qur'án* 7:88) "By our response to their invitation," Quddús addressed them, "we shall enable them to demonstrate the sincerity of their intentions"[2] and presaging the upcoming fateful events quoted a verse of Persian poetry, "My soul is a water bird, why would it complain about the deluge of misfortunes that surround it on all sides?"[3]

Although Quddús realised that betrayal lay hidden beneath the protocol and courteous words, as a gesture of goodwill he accepted the proposal and commissioned two highly regarded believers to carry his response to the prince. At the same time, he instructed the companions to leave the fort. According to a survivor, Quddús had warned that "they [the prince and his military officers] would deny sealing the *Qur'án* and attack us but we were not to engage in war. He said that all of us would become martyrs except for seven people who would survive to narrate the story of the <u>Sh</u>ay<u>kh</u> Ṭabarsí fortress and ensure that it was recorded in history. He advised that anyone who did not wish to be killed should leave. We replied that we had come to sacrifice our unworthy blood in the path of God."[4]

In taking the prince's proposal, Quddús observed trustworthiness. He was accepting the promise of free passage to the Bábís to their homes even thiugh this was doubtful. Swearing a false oath by the *Holy Qur'án* is not only a great sin but also perjury. Making false oaths is a great offence in Islam (*Qur'án* 5:89) resulting in a stern afterlife punishment as "*God will not speak to them, nor will He look upon them on the Day of Resurrection nor will He purify them, and they shall have a painful chastisement*" (*Qur'án* 3:77).

Fresh in their mind was <u>Kh</u>usraw's treason just before their arrival in <u>Sh</u>ay<u>kh</u> Ṭabarsí eight months before and the prince's deception on Áqá Rasúl after the death of Mullá Ḥusayn.

Interestingly, the figure of the bold 'Abbás-Qulí <u>Kh</u>án vanishes from the chronicles after the prince's swearing on the Qur'an. It is as if he disagreed with

---

1 Siyyid Muḥammad-Ḥusayn, *Vaqa'i-i Mimiyyih*, pp. 94-95.

2 Nabíl-i-A'ẓam, *The Dawn-Breakers,* p. 400.

3 A. L. M. Nicolas, *Seyyèd Ali-Mohammed dit le Bâb*, pp. 329. Cited in Nabíl-i-A'ẓam, *The Dawn-Breakers,* p. 320.

4 Shokrullah Ashqli Ardestani, *A Recollection*, p. 147.

such a strategy, either because of its moral falsity or because such a quick strategy undermined their own sense of tribal warrior, implying acceptance of defeat.

"According to a custom of the Persian court", Kazem-Beg wrote that the prince "sent as a sign of his benevolence a saddle horse to the leader of his new friends, with the assurance that special shelters were available.[1] Shortly afterwards, to appear to honor his promise, the prince sent his own favourite horse for Quddús, as well as a few more horses for them to ride. There was a tense atmosphere:

> Having agreed to this stipulation [the prince] Mihdí-Qulí Mírzá and the generals recalled their men and returned to camp. Their soldiers remained alert however to the manner in which the Bábís would fulfil their commitment.[2]

A.L.M. Nicolas recorded that, later,

> ... free of all anxiety, they [the military officer] went for a walk in the fortress: they agreed to admire the work that had been accomplished there and the science displayed in the defences: they applauded each other for not having had to force the enemies into their last entrenchment; they collected all the weapons that they encountered and all the booty that they found.[3]

Wednesday 9 May afternoon – leaving the fort

Quddús put on the green turban that the Báb had given him earlier, mounted the prince's horse and, in the company of a group of 220 believers, some on horseback and the rest walking on each side, set out for the tent that had been set up for Quddús near the local village of Dízvá (Dízábád) south of the military headquarters in Afrá, and 1,300 m from the fort.

An eyewitness left the following heart-wrenching account of the farewell to the fort:

> When the companions were leaving the fort, we all went to the tomb of Mullá Ḥusayn to say farewell to him. We all were weeping. And when at last we started to go, little Mírzá Muḥammad-Báqir [Mullá Ḥusayn's cousin][4] did not want to leave the tomb. He embraced it and wept bitterly.
>
> The companions tried to separate him, but he would not agree, and said that he would never leave that tomb. We told Quddús about it and, as he had already mounted his horse, he ordered us to mount him and take him with us. They put him on a horse, but after a short ride he fainted and fell

---

1 Kazem-Beg, Mírzá Aleksandr, *Le Bab et les Bábís ou le Soulevement Politique et June 1866*, vol. 7, p. 20.

2 Gobineau in Nash and O'Donoghue, *Comte de Gobineau and Orientalism*, p. 176.

3 A. L. M. Nicolas, *Seyyèd Ali-Mohammed dit le Bâb*, p. 327.

4 According to Ruhollah Mehrabkhani, Mírzá Muḥammad-Báqir was perhaps twenty-two years old (*Mullá Ḥusayn*, p. 284).

down. When he recovered his senses, we mounted him on a horse in the second line with Mullá Yúsif-i Ardibílí [a Letter of the Living], but he fell again, and died. Quddús, on seeing this, instructed us to carry his body as far as the bathhouse of Dízvá [Dízábád],[1] where it was washed and buried.[2]

Quddús' close entourage consisted of a selected group of believers prominent both in their civil life and in the Faith of the Báb. Depending on the source, they might have been seven or fourteen in number.[3] Soon, the entourage and the 220 companions arrived in the vicinity of the public bath of the village of Dízvá, 1,300 metres from the fort, and were accommodated in tents overlooking the army headquarters. On arrival, Quddús addressed to the 220 companions:

You should show forth exemplary renunciation, for such behaviour on your part will exalt our Cause and redound to its glory. Anything short of complete detachment will but serve to tarnish the purity of its name and to obscure its splendour. Pray the Almighty to grant that even to your last hour He may graciously assist you to contribute your share to the exaltation of His Faith.[4]

Wednesday 9 May evening – dinner

After sunset , both the entourage and the rest of companions were offered food. Nabíl wrote:

> The food that was offered them in separate trays, each of which was assigned to a group of thirty companions, was poor and scanty. "Nine of us," those who were with Quddús subsequently related, "were summoned by our leader to partake of the dinner which had been served in his tent. As he refused to taste it, we too, following his example, refrained from eating. The attendants who waited upon us were delighted to partake of the dishes which we had refused to touch, and devoured their contents with appreciation and avidity."
>
> A few of the companions who were dining outside the tent were heard remonstrating with the attendants, pleading that they were willing to buy from them, at however exorbitant a price, the bread which they needed. Quddús strongly disapproved of their conduct and rebuked them for the request they had made. But for the intercession of Mírzá Muḥammad-Báqir, he would have severely punished them for having so completely disregarded his earnest exhortations.[5]

---

1 The village of Dízábád 1,300 metres south of the fort (geographical co-ordinates (36.423725, 52.806759).

2 Mírzá Abú Ṭálib-i Shahmírzadí, cited in Ruhollah Mehrabkhani, *Mullá Ḥusayn,* pp. 284–5.

3 Mírzá Ḥusayn Hamadání, *The New History (Taríkh-i-Jadíd),* p. 86.

4 Nabíl-i-A'ẓam, *The Dawn-Breakers,* p. 401.

5 Nabíl-i-A'ẓam, *The Dawn-Breakers,* p. 401.

The recent developments about the fort defendants travelled fast and people to the central towns of Bárfurúsh and Sárí, located some hours aways from the military camp in Dízvá, and some people began to make arrangements to come in order "to share in the meritorious, act of inflicting the punishment of death to the companions of Quddús".[1] However, the prince had coldly calculated to terminate the whole episode by the next day.

Thursday 10 May 1849 morning

Early on Thursday morning, on 10 May 1849, Mírzá Muḥammad-Báqir, on behalf of Quddús' deputy was called to the presence of the prince and the military chief, Sulaymán Khán-i-Ja'far to receive details about the process of liberating the Bábís. With the consent of Quddús', this believer attended the meeting where these two officers reiterated the promise regarding free passage and safety. Upon returning to Quddús' tent one hour later, he informed that the prince would seek a royal pardon for all the companions. Furthermore, He reported:

> To-morrow [Friday] the prince intends to accompany you [Quddús] in the morning to the public bath, from whence he will proceed to your tent, after which he will provide the horses required to convey the entire company to Sang-Sar, from where they will disperse, some returning to their homes in 'Iráq, and others proceeding to Khurásán. At the request of Sulaymán Khán, who urged that the presence of such a large gathering at such a fortified centre as Sang-Sar would be fraught with risk, the prince decided that the party should disperse, instead, at Fírúz-Kúh

Mírzá Muḥammad-Báqir said to Quddús that he did not believe in the prince's intention, a remark that Quddús agreed to. Furthermore, presaging more clearly the enemy's ill intentions, Quddús sent instructions to the companions that they should abandon the camp that night.

In reality, the promise of the prince meeting Quddús face-to-face did not occur up until the following week and therefore the final liberation of the Bábís was never discussed. "The prince failed to redeem his promise", Nabíl wrote, "Instead of joining Quddús in his tent, he called him, with several of his companions, to his headquarters, and informed him, as soon as they reached the tent of the Farrásh-Báshí, 34 that he himself would summon him at noon to his presence".[2]

At one point in the day, Quddús and his entourage are reported to have been imprisoned at the army headquarters.[3] This stratagem of separating the Bábís from their leader allowed the military to take the Bábís that had accompanied Quddús to the tent as prisoners.

It has also been reported that the prince asked Quddús to instruct the believers to disarm because, according to a Bábí historian, "these were a menace

---

1 Nabíl-i-A'ẓam, *The Dawn-Breakers*, p. 407.

2 Nabíl-i-A'ẓam, *The Dawn-Breakers*, p. 403.

3 Siyyid Muḥammad-Ḥusayn, *Vaqa'i-i Mimiyyih*, pp. 114–117.

and a cause of fear to the troops".[1] Many companions were not happy about having to lay down their weapons. According to a chronicler:

> Quddús told them before leaving, "If a message comes from me bidding you lay down your arms, do just as you feel inclined: if you like, cast them away; if not, keep them." When, therefore, such a message came, some of the Bábís laid down their arms, while some retained them. Word of this was brought to the prince, who again urged His Holiness Quddús to command his followers to disarm. Another message was accordingly sent by Mullá Yúsuf 'Alí of Khúy, who, supposing that His Holiness Quddús really wished the Bábís to lay down their weapons, prevailed upon them with some difficulty to do so, whereupon ensued the massacre described ....[2]

Another chronicler wrote:

> ... [the prince] ordered Mullá Yúsif 'Alí [Ardibílí] to go and confiscate the armours and weapons of the companions and give them some money to return to their provinces. And that was pure ruse, for they took His Holiness and companions to a tower and imprisoned them. Mullá Yúsif 'Alí [Ardibílí] went to take the armours and weapons of the companions, and told them, "folks, I see the situation otherwise. You may give away the armours and weapons if you wish. And if you do not wish, don't give them." So, those deceitful pagans and shameless infidels [the officers] martyred Mullá Yúsuf 'Alí on the spot, took the armours and weapons of the companions, immediately fired with thousands of weapons on the companions of God, attacked those godly believers, and martyred them one and all.[3]

The Thursday massacre

Afterwards, the cunning prince and his officers ordered a human slaughter of great magnitude. "The prince, Mihdí-Qulí Mírzá", wrote Gobineau, "claimed that the honour of the religion, that the expressed laws of his faith and his loyalty towards his sovereign forced him to violate his word."[4] "The prince gave the order to massacre the rest," Nicolas wrote, "based on the Islamic law according to which any Muslim who denies his religion must be executed".[5]

On that day the companions, not including Quddús and his entourage, were invited to a breakfast-table like a banquet[6] in the public square of Dízvá next to the military and the fort. However, being disarmed, they were asked to line up in

---

1 Mírzá Ḥusayn Hamadání, *The New History (Taríkh-i-Jadíd)*, p. 86.

2 Mírzá Ḥusayn Hamadání, *The New History (Taríkh-i-Jadíd)*, p. 365.

3 Siyyid Muḥammad-Ḥusayn, *Vaqa'i-i Mimiyyih*, pp. 114–117.

4 Gobineau in Nash and O'Donoghue, *Comte de Gobineau and Orientalism*, p. 175.

5 A. L. M. Nicolas, *Seyyèd Ali-Mohammed dit le Bâb*, pp. 326–7.

6 Adolfo Rivadeneyra, *Viaje and Interior de Persia*, vol. 1, p. 242.

a row and were slain.[1] Nicolas wrote, "The exhausted Bábís were eating when suddenly they found themselves surrounded by Muslims [soldiers]."[2]

According to a survivor:

> We then started to eat, but they suddenly attacked us, killing everyone. They examined each corpse individually and severed their heads. For six days, we dared not move among the corpses. After six days, we raised our heads and realised there was nobody left. It was impossible to live amidst the smell of blood and decaying bodies.[3]

Those in charge of executing the orders were extremely cruel to those innocent victims remaining in the fort who, until the last moment of their lives implored the help of their Lord, who they had so fervently called upon. In their last words, they were heard saying, "Praise, praise, oh Lord our God, Lord of angels and of spirit."[4]

These firm believers won for themselves the crown and the glorious palm branches symbolic of martyrdom. As Shoghi Effendi annotated in *God Passes By*:

> ... a number of the betrayed companions of Quddús were assembled in the camp of the enemy, were stripped of their possessions, and sold as slaves, the rest being either killed by the spears and swords of the officers, or torn asunder, or bound to trees and riddled with bullets, or blown from the mouths of cannon and consigned to the flames, or else being disembowelled and having their heads impaled on spears and lances.[5]

A chronicler wrote, "And so much of their blood was collected in a hollow of the ground that the truth of a tradition which affirms that in that land shall be such bloodshed that a horse shall wade knee deep in gore was made manifest".[6] Others were laid on the ground and with their sabres they opened their bellies, finding to their surprise the grass they were eating. According to the Count de Gobineau:

> As to the other prisoners, they were made to lie down on the ground and the executioners cut open their stomachs. It was noticed that several of these unfortunates had raw grass in their intestines. This massacre completed, they found that there was still more to be done and they assassinated the fugitives who had already been pardoned.[7]

---

1 Mírzá Ḥusayn Hamadání, *The New History* (*Taríkh-i-Jadíd*), p. 90. See also A. L. M. Nicolas, *Seyyèd Ali-Mohammed dit le Bâb*, pp. 326–7.

2 A. L. M. Nicolas, *Seyyèd Ali-Mohammed dit le Bâb*, pp. 326–7.

3 Shokrullah Ashqli Ardestani, *A Recollection*, p. 147.

4 Nabíl-i-A'ẓam, *The Dawn-Breakers*, p. 404.

5 Shoghi Effendi, *God Passes By*, p. 41–2.

6 Mírzá Ḥusayn Hamadání, *The New History (Taríkh-i-Jadíd)*, p. 89.

7 Joseph Arthur Gobineau, *Les Religions et les Philosophies dans l'Asie Centrale*, p. 189. Cited in Nabíl-i-A'ẓam, *The Dawn-Breakers*, p. 404.

Non-Bahá'í sources reported that a few men escaped: "300 men were smeared with naphtha and burned alive or ... their stomachs were cut open."[1] The *Sacramento Daily Union* of 14 February 1874 compared the Sháh to Nero for setting fire to his victims at Shaykh Ṭabarsí.[2] An eyewitness later recalled, "One by one, they took them to the prince and martyred each of them in a different way. Some were stripped naked and cut to pieces with swords. Some of them were tied to trees, some of them were shot with cannons and mortars...",[3] the Count of Gobineau wrote, "the remaining captives were then lined up side by side and disembowelled one by one. It was observed that the entrails of several of those poor wretches were full of undigested grass"... "It was a full day. Many were killed and nothing was risked"[4]

Now the prince was free to satisfy his desire for revenge and blood on the one who caused and had challenged him at the royal court with humiliating public defeats. He removed Quddús and a few others with notable societal reputations or wealth and whom he planned to take to the capital.

He planned to submit Quddús to the authority of the Sháh and, to the others, to demand a substantial ransom as a price in exchange for their liberation. These captives were "men of recognised standing, such as the father of Badí,[5] Mullá Mírzá Muḥammad i-Furúghí, and Ḥájí Náṣir-i-Qazvíní,", Nabil wrote. [The prince] "charged his attendants to conduct [them] to Tihrán and obtain in return for their deliverance a ransom from each one of them in direct proportion to their capacity and wealth."[6]

Those few who survived, lived to tell the world the glorious story of Shaykh Ṭabarsí and how the companions achieved their Karbilá of martyrdom.

Firmness, not resignation, to the Faith of the Báb was their motto, serving as a testament to their honour and honesty. The words of their beloved rang like a melody in their ears:

> *Rest assured, the grace of the Almighty shall enable you to fortify the faint in heart and to make firm the step of the waverer. So great shall be your faith that should the enemy mutilate and tear your body to pieces, in the hope of lessening by one jot or tittle the ardour of your love, he would fail to attain his object. You will, no doubt, in the days to come, meet face to face Him who is the Lord of all the worlds, and will partake of the joy of His presence.*[7]

---

1 Bernard von Dorn, *Nachträge zu dem Verzeichniss*, p. 381.

2 The *Sacramento Daily Union*, 14 February 1874, p. 4, col. 4.

3 Mír Abú-Tálib Shahmírzadí, *Untitled history*, p. 55.

4 Gobineau in Nash and O'Donoghue, *Comte de Gobineau and Orientalism*, p. 175.

5 Badí' (1852–1869) was a martyr of the Bahá'í Faith who delivered a Tablet from Bahá'u'lláh to the Sháh of Persia.

6 Nabíl-i-A'ẓam, *The Dawn-Breakers*, p. 313.

7 The Báb in Nabíl-i-A'ẓam, *The Dawn-Breakers*, p. 404.

Killing the survivors

After the massacre, the soldiers walked among the fallen victims and, using their swords, killed those who were still breathing. Mírzá Ḥaydar-'Alí[1] was one of those fallen wounded. A soldier spotted him and went over to finish him off, but when he saw his wonderful face and his green scarf, he had a change of heart. Then he heard the victim reciting quietly a verse from the *Qur'án*. The soldier's eyes welled up with tears, and he left that abominable scene. The lifeless bodies of the brave and innocent martyrs remained in the square of Dízvá village. "Their bodies were left unburied," a chronicler wrote, "and were eaten by wild beasts or disintegrated by the elements."[2] Sa'ídu'l-'Ulamá' ordered that no one collect the corpses of those martyrs or bury them.[3]

When the military camp was removed and darkness of the night fell on the village, Mírzá Ḥaydar-'Alí rose up from the dead and, with much difficulty, dragged himself to the next village.

A Bedouin woman feeling pity for him, took him to her tent, and attended to his wounds. He rested and recuperated in the tent of that heaven-sent angel for a few days. Then he started his long and arduous homeward march. He had no provisions but plenty of pain from the effect of the bullets. He was afraid to enter any village, approach any person, or go to a suitable place to clean himself. So, he suffered greatly on his way back to Ardistán. Often, he wondered why and for what purpose he was still alive.

One night when he was sleeping in the wilderness, he had a dream in which he saw the Báb. The Báb told Mírzá Ḥaydar-'Alí that he was kept alive so that he could relate the events of the fort for posterity. From that night Mírzá Ḥaydar-'Alí was certain that he had an assignment and an obligation to fulfill. He therefore wrote down in detail all the events surrounding the struggle at the Shaykh Ṭabarsí fort for future generations. His written accounts of that defensive undertaking by a relatively small band of intrepid Bábís became one of the references used by Nabíl-i-A'ẓam, the immortal chronicler of *The Dawn-Breakers*.[4]

Three poignant stories

Murshid

The story of Murshid is equally heart-breaking:

---

1 The Mírzá Ḥaydar-'Alí referred to in this story is from Ardistán. He is not the same person as the *Angel of Carmel* who was from Iṣfahán.

2 Mírzá Ḥusayn Hamadání, *The New History (Taríkh-i-Jadíd)*, p. 365.

3 Siyyid Muḥammad-Ḥusayn, *Vaqa'i-i Mimiyyih*, p. 114.

4 Amir Badiei, *Dreams of Destiny*, pp. 42–3.

Now Sulaymán Khán [the military commander] was an old and intimate friend of Murshid's, and, as soon as his eyes fell upon him, he said, "How came you to be involved in this peril? Thank God that I was here, else you would certainly not have escaped." Murshid answered, "If you desire to do me a friendly service such that I may bear you eternal gratitude, do not intercede for me and thereby deprive me of the glory of martyrdom."

Sulaymán Khán, overcome with astonishment, strove by every means to dissuade him from this course, but he only replied, "I have tasted to the full the bitter and sweet of life, its hot and cold, its ups and downs. I have trodden every path, held converse with every class, associated with men of every sort and condition, and sought to fathom every creed, but nowhere have I beheld the Truth save in this supreme station, where I have seen with mine eyes and heard with mine ears things passing description. For a while I have walked with these in the path of love and with them have trod its stages, and I would not leave them now. Suffer me, then, to bear them company, and set me free from the trammels of this life.

'I know for sure that this my life is death;
My true life opens at my closing breath.'"

Thus so, he would not suffer himself to be moved by Sulaymán Khán's persuasions but continued looking towards the executioner and awaiting the death-blow; wherefore, seeing him so eager for the draught of martyrdom, they quenched his thirst with the bright sword. And Sulaymán Khán and the other officers were amazed beyond description at his steadfastness.[1]

The youth

Another source provided this tender story:

So in like manner there was another, a mere youth, whom the soldiers had hidden to save from death, [that advantage might accrue to them from his family.] But when his eyes fell on Jináb-i-Quddús, whom they were leading away in fetters and chains, he was overcome with uncontrollable emotion, and cried out, "Would that I were blind, that I might not see you thus!" Then he began to weep and cry out, saying, "Let me go to my master"; and though they bade him hold his peace and not make known his connection with the Bábís, he did but cry the more, "Do ye not see that I am one of them?" until at length the others perceived the true state of the case, and bore him away to death.[2]

---

1 E. G. Browne (ed.), *Taríkh-i-Jadíd or New History of Mírzá 'Alí Muḥammad The Báb*, pp. 105–6.

2 Mírzá Ḥusayn Hamadání, *The New History*, p. 102.

Mullá Muḥammad-i-Mu'allim-i-Núrí

After Quddús, Mullá Muḥammad-i-Mu'allim-i-Núrí was the person who suffered the most in his martyrdom following the fall of the fort:

> The prince had promised that he would release him [Mullá Muḥammad-i-Mu'allim-i-Núrí] on condition that he would execrate the name of Quddús, and had pledged his word that, should he be willing to recant, he would take him back with him to Ṭihrán and make him the tutor of his sons. "Never will I consent," he replied, "to vilify the beloved of God at the bidding of a man such as you. Were you to confer upon me the whole of the kingdom of Persia, I would not for one moment turn my face from my beloved leader. My body is at your mercy, my soul you are powerless to subdue. Torture me as you will, that I may be enabled to demonstrate to you the truth of the verse, `Then, wish for death, if ye be men of truth.' "The prince, infuriated by his answer, gave orders that his body be cut to pieces and that no effort be spared to inflict upon him a most humiliating punishment".[1]

With this massacre, an important Islamic tradition, as quoted by Bahá'u'lláh in the *Kitáb-i-Íqán*, was fulfilled:

> *Even as it hath been recorded in the "Káfi," in the tradition of Jábir, in the "Tablet of Fáṭimih," concerning the character of the Qá'im: "He shall manifest the perfection of Moses, the splendour of Jesus, and the patience of Job. His chosen ones shall be abased in His day. Their heads shall be offered as presents even as the heads of Turks and Daylamites. They shall be slain and burnt. Fear shall seize them; dismay and alarm shall strike terror into their hearts. The earth shall be dyed with their blood. Their womenfolk shall bewail and lament. These are indeed my friends!"*[2]

Friday 11 May 1849 – Departure to Bárfurú<u>sh</u>

On that day, Quddús and a group of prominent believers parted for Bárfurú<u>sh</u> in route to the capital, covering twenty kilometres through the forest. He had been away for eight months. According to Siyyid Muḥammad-Ḥusayn:

> [on] ... the next morning [the Friday, after the massacre] the detestable and base-born prince sent for some mules and mounted Quddús and the two companions upon a mule, with their hands tied up in their backs, and dispatched them to Bárfurú<u>sh</u>.[3]

1 Nabíl-i-A'ẓam, *The Dawn-Breakers*, pp. 425-426.

2 Bahá'u'lláh, *The Kitáb-i-Íqán*, p. 245.

3 Siyyid Muḥammad-Ḥusayn, *Vaqa'i-i Mimiyyih*, pp. 114–117.

Part V
The martyr

17
Martyrdom of Quddús

Chapter content
Entry into Bárfurú<u>sh</u>
The mob rejoices
Quddús' confinement
Demands for the right to kill Quddús
The trial
The role of the prince
The execution
After the martyrdom
Remains are recovered
Nuptials of fire
Other martyrdoms that same week
Martyrdom as a rendezvous
Further thoughts
Chronology of the life of Quddús

Quddús arrived in Bárfurú<u>sh</u> on Friday afternoon, 11 May 1849. There he was detained on the Baḥru'l-Arim (the Bárfurú<u>sh</u>'s inland lake) at the governor's residence,[1] for six days until he was martyred on Wednesday, 16 May 1849. Four years previously the Báb had told him to rejoice because he had been selected to become *"the standard-bearer of the host of affliction"*.[2]

'Abdu'l-Bahá said *"At length in the year 1265* [AH] *at the sentence of the chief of lawyers, the Sa'ídu'l-'Ulamá' the chief divine of Bárfurú<u>sh</u> he yielded his head and surrendered his life amidst extremest clamor and outcry."*[3]

Entry into Bárfurú<u>sh</u>

On the afternoon of that, Friday, prince Mihdí-Qulí Mírzá, *the prince of perjury*, stopped in Bárfurú<u>sh</u> on his way to Ṭihrán. Historians do not mention at this stage, the presence of Sulaymán <u>Kh</u>án Af<u>sh</u>ar and 'Abbás-Qulí <u>Kh</u>án, the two military commanders, who probably returned to their posts.

The prince was taking Quddús and a number of companions with tied hands as hostages to show them to the monarch in the capital. "Some of the Bábí chiefs were reserved to grace the prince's triumphal entry into Bárfurú<u>sh</u>," wrote E. G. Browne.[4] The prince was received by the Sa'ídu'l-'Ulamá' and the main clerics of the city with all honours.

---

[1] Hushmand Dehghan, *Ganj-i-Pinhán:*, p. 115.
[2] Nabíl-i-A'ẓam, *The Dawn-Breakers*, p. 142.
[3] 'Abdu'l-Bahá, *A Traveller's Narrative*, p. 19.
[4] Cited in E. G. Browne, *A Traveller's Narrative,* Note P, p. 307. Among them were:

Friday, the day after the massacre, is a day of worship where the community come together to pray. Ironically, it was the middle of spring and the air was filled with the scent of orange blossoms. It was the rice flowering season when the fields are covered in white blossoms and a time when Bárfurú<u>sh</u> weather is at its best.

At Quddús' hometown there had been a foul outcry for his blood, all instigated by the Sa'ídu'l-'Ulamá', the chief cleric, who was seeking his execution. As they entered the town, the holy hostages were received with loathing. According to Siyyid Muḥammad-Ḥusayn:

> When they reached the vicinity of the city, they were received by a huge crowd of populace who had come outside the city. A mob of thugs addressed Quddús and his companions with such impoliteness not worthy of mention and spat on the faces of that noble personage and his companions.[1]

Professor Edward Granville Browne observed that:

> Five or six of the chief Bábís only were reserved from the massacre to grace the prince's triumphal entry into Bárfurú<u>sh</u>; and, bearing with them these and the heads of the slain set on spears, the victorious army sets out with beating drums and blowing trumpets for the town.[2]

The clergy and the mob received them, acclaiming the prince for what he had achieved and asking him to hand over Quddús to them so they could kill him with their bare hands. The captives were not given any food.[3]

The mob rejoices

A local historian related that the populace "stayed awake all night long, constantly playing drums and trumpets."[4] According to *Taríkh-i-Jadíd*:

> They beat the drums to celebrate their victory, and displayed such pride in their prowess that one would have supposed that they had either retaken from Russia the territories once owned by Persia, or obtained some great victory over the English, which had replaced them in possession of India, or annexed Balú<u>ch</u>istán, Af<u>gh</u>ánistán, Bal<u>kh</u>, and Bu<u>kh</u>árá, or recovered their captives from the Turcomans, or won from the Turks Ba<u>gh</u>dád,

---

Quddús, Áqá Mírzá Muḥammad-Ḥasan (Mullá Ḥusayn's brother), Mullá Muḥammad-Ṣádiq of <u>Kh</u>urásán, Ḥájí Mírzá Muḥammad-Ḥasan of <u>Kh</u>urásán, <u>Sh</u>ay<u>kh</u> Ni'matu'lláh of Ámul, Ḥájí Náṣir-i-Qazvíní, Mullá Yúsuf of Ardabíl, and Áqá Siyyid 'Abdu'l-'Azím of <u>Kh</u>úy.

1 Siyyid Muḥammad-Ḥusayn, *Vaqa'i-i Mimiyyih*, pp. 114–117.

2 E. G. Browne, *Bábísm*, p. 348.

3 E. G. Browne, *Kitáb-i-Nuqtatu'l-Káf*, p. 197.

4 Habib Borjian, *A Mázandaráni Account of the Babi Incident at Shaikh Ṭabarsí*, p. 393.

> Karbilá, and Najaf, and brought back with them as prisoners of war many a proud Pásh<u>á</u> and great captain.[1]

Flags were waved, and bonfires were lit at night on the streets as the town celebrated the event. "On that day, the city of Bárfurúsh was filled with joy, Bárfurúsh was decorated with flowers and carpets," the French historian A. L. M. Nicolas wrote, "the cries of joy, the fireworks, the public spectacles made the entry into this city, of ten wretches who had been starving for three months, an event surpassing the conquests of Cyrus."[2] Siyyid Muḥammad-Ḥusayn stated "The mob played music in celebration, congratulating each other, till Quddús and his companions were placed in prison."[3] In turn, the author of *Taríkh-i-Jadíd* wrote: "When these few half-famished men, who for three months had suffered such pangs of hunger as can scarcely be conceived, were brought in (to Bárfurúsh), the people decorated the city and made great rejoicings."[4]

According to Nicolas:

> The victors, if they can be so called, wished to enjoy the intoxication of their triumph. They bound in chains Quddús, Mírzá Muḥammad-Ḥasan Khán, brother of the Bábu'l-Báb, Ákhúnd Mullá Muḥammad-Ṣádiq-i-Khurásáni, Mírzá Muḥammad-Ṣádiq-i-Khurásáni, Ḥájí Mírzá Ḥasan Khurásání, Shaykh Ni'matu'llah-i-Ámulí, Ḥájí Náṣir-i-Qazvíní, Mullá Yúsif-i-Ardábilí, Áqá Siyyid 'Abdu'l-'Aẓím-i-Khú'i and several others. These they placed at the center of the parade which started out at the sound of the trumpets, and, every time they went through an inhabited section, they struck them.[5]

A Muslim source reported what occurred during that tense period:

> The people came in groups to watch them. For two or three days, they were kept in Bárfurúsh for the men and women all to come and watch them. When everybody had watched, they were then taken around from quarter to quarter.[6]

It seems that during those six days, Quddús was at times paraded on a mule or barefoot.[7]

Quddús' confinement

Quddús was confined in the governor's house known as Bágh-i-Sháh (the "King's Garden") which was located on a man-made island on the outskirts of the

---

1 Mírzá Ḥusayn Hamadání, *The New History (Taríkh-i-Jadíd)*, pp. 87–8.

2 A. L. M. Nicolas, *Seyyèd Ali-Mohammed dit le Bâb*, p. 329.

3 Siyyid Muḥammad-Ḥusayn, *Vaqa'i-i Mimiyyih*, pp. 114–117.

4 Mírzá Ḥusayn Hamadání, *The New History (Taríkh-i-Jadíd)*, p. 88.

5 A. L. M. Nicolas, *Seyyèd Ali-Mohammed dit le Bâb*, pp. 329. Cited in Nabíl-i-A'ẓam, *The Dawn-Breakers*, p. 404.

6 Habib Borjian, *A Mázandaráni Account of the Babi Incident*, item No. 20.

7 Habib Borjian, *A Mázandaráni Account of the Babi Incident*, pp. 393–4.

town.[1] In those times, the concept of jail cells did not exist and people were detained in officers' houses, usually in the basements where each one administered their own justice in the absence of a proper judicial system. The delays during Quddús' trial was probably due to a need to wait for further instructions from the capital.[2]

In the second quarter of the last century, Reza Shah Pahlavi levelled the island and built a very beautiful palace in the middle of the Bágh-i-Sháh, which became known as the Shapur Mansion. Later, this palace became the Babol University of Medical Sciences. The Bágh-i-Sháh has now been subsumed into modern Babol. The local caravanserai, with the Sabzih Maydán (the "Green Square") in between, was located 1 km northeast of the Bágh-i-Sháh.[3]

According to Siyyid Muḥammad-Ḥusayn, with Quddús were also imprisoned Mullá Mírzá Muḥammad Mahvalátí and Mírzá Muḥammad-Ḥusayn-i-Mutavallí Qumí. With respect to the latter, a chronicler recorded:

> Mírzá Muḥammad-Ḥusayn-i-Mahvalátí Qumí,[4] who had left the fort before Quddús and his companions and had been captured by the despicable prince, was brought and imprisoned along with Quddús and companions. At that moment, Quddús stated that he was going to be martyred in three days.[5]

Sepehr Manuchehri added in regard to that person:

> Following the martyrdom of Mullá Ḥusayn and increasing hardships inside the fortress, a number of Bábís lad by Mírzá Muḥammad-Ḥusayn-i-Mutavallí-Qumí, decided to leave the fortress. Qumi became their spokesman and met with Quddús. Upon hearing his intentions Quddús replied 'Very well, leave whenever you can.' Mírzá Muḥammad-Ḥusayn-i-Mutavallí-Qumí surrendered to the government forces claiming: 'I had initially approached Bábís to investigate their cause. After spending some time with them I observed many words and no action. I did not see any truth in their claims and left.' A short time later he became disillusioned. Openly praising the Bábís and at other times questioning their resolve. When the prince learnt about his state of mind, he sent Qumí to the nearby city of Sárí fearing that he was a Bábí infiltrator.[6]

Mírzá Muḥammad-Ḥusayn-i-Mutavallí-Qumí must have been liberated in the next day or so because he is found spitting at Quddús at the place of execution.

---

1. Hushmand Dehghan, *Ganj-i-Pinhán*, p. 115.
2. Gobineau, Joseph Arthur, *Les Religions et les Philosophies dans l'Asie Central*, p. 234.
3. Vahid Nattaj, *The role of landscape elements*, pp. 5–20.
4. See Sepehr Manuchehri, *Taqiyyah*, p. 228; and Moojan Momen, *The Bahá'í Communities of Iran*, vol. 1, p. 412.
5. Siyyid Muḥammad-Ḥusayn, *Vaqa'i-i Mimiyyih*, pp. 114-117.
6. Sepehr Manuchehri, *Taqiyyah*, p. 228.

The second person in prison was Mullá Mírzá Muḥammad Mahvalátí[1] who remained incarcerated with Quddús and survived martyrdom because a ransom was paid to have him released. A chronicler stated:

> The honourable Mullá Mírzá Muḥammad Mahvalátí, who had undergone a radical transformation, requested Quddús and the companions to repent. Quddús then read a few passages from the sermon by Imám 'Alí to him, which awakened his consciousness. As a result, he recanted and asked Quddús for forgiveness, and that magnanimous individual pardoned him.[2]

Demands for the right to kill Quddús

The Sa'ídu'l-'Ulamá' demanded the prince deliver Quddús into his hands so that he could slay him. Other mullás also approached the Sa'ídu'l-'Ulamá', telling him: "... either Ḥájí Muḥammad-'Alí should stay [alive] or we should. If *he* stays, we will kill ourselves alive (sic) .... If *we* are to exist, we must kill him".[3] The Sa'ídu'l-'Ulamá' himself was inciting the population to assert to the prince their desire to kill Quddús. The mood on the streets was very volatile and dangerous, an atmosphere that the prince might have perceived as soon as he rode into Bárfurúsh.

Lowell Johnson writes that

> For three days the prince said nothing to anyone about what he intended to do with Quddús. He was afraid to do anything to him, himself. His plan was to take Quddús to Ṭihrán and hand him over to the Sháh, and let the Sháh decide what should be done. But the Sa'ídu'l-'Ulamá' had other plans. He had hated Mullá Ḥusayn, and now he hated Quddús. When he discovered the prince's plans, he argued and argued with him against the idea. When he found that the prince would not give in, he called everyone to the mosque. The Sa'ídu'l-'Ulamá' called upon the people of Bárfurúsh to help him prove to the prince that he must not take Quddús to the Sháh. He said to them, "I swear before God [that I] will take neither food nor sleep until I am able to end the life of this man Quddús with my own hands." When the prince learned that the people of Bárfurúsh were against him, he became afraid for his own life.[4]

The Sa'ídu'l-'Ulamá' warned the prince that he was opposed to his plan to take Quddús to the capital. "He is shrewd and eloquent", he said, "who knows what impression he will make on His Majesty's mind."[5]

There were two possible reasons why the prince hoped that Quddús would be taken to the capital.

---

1 A survivor of the fort brought to Bárfurúsh,

2 Siyyid Muḥammad-Ḥusayn, *Vaqa'i-i Mimiyyih*, pp. 114–117.

3 Habib Borjian, *A Mázandaráni Account of the Babi Incident,* item No. 30.

4 Lowell Johnson, *Quddús*, p. 31.

5 A. L. M. Nicolas, *Seyyèd Ali-Mohammed dit le Bâb*, p. 328.

Firstly, according to some sources,[1] after arriving at Bárfurúsh, Quddús asked the prince to send him to Ṭihrán to be placed on trial in front of the Sháh so that the monarch himself could decide his fate. "The prince was at first disposed to grant this request", wrote Reverend T.K. Cheyne, "thinking perhaps that to bring so notable a captive into the Royal Presence might serve to obliterate in some measure the record of those repeated failures to which his unparalleled incapacity had given rise".[2] For the prince, Quddús, being the representative of the Báb, represented an important war trophy to be offered to the monarch who in his Pyrrhic victory had lost over 1,000 soldiers, many more injured, the loss of huge military resources and that of three royal relatives, let alone the social instability resulting from the Shaykh Ṭabarsí confrontations.

Secondly, given the nation-wide political sensitivity of the Shaykh Ṭabarsí episode, it is reasonable to assume that the prince was waiting for instructions from the capital as to what to do with the prisoner. It might have been that the prince was buying time during those last eight days when Quddús was his captive. This is a possibility as the Count of Gobineau affirmed that the mullás, after the fall of the fort at Shaykh Ṭabarsí, insisted that the prince should kill Quddús and his companions in the same way as the recently massacred Bábís, without waiting for orders from the capital.[3] Persian relay riders could carry a message from Bárfurúsh to Ṭihrán within one day.[4]

At that time, there was a powerful insurrection in northeast Persia that had been raging for four years. It is therefore likely that the sovereign preferred to conclude once-for-all the Shaykh Ṭabarsí upheaval in Mázandarán Province so he could use all his military resources to deal with that insurrection.[5] He might have also thought that punishment in front of the local population would send a strong message to intimidate them. All of the above can explain the six-day Bárfurúsh delay for the prince to make a decision.

The trial

The trial of Quddús represented the first formal court case by the Persian state authority conducted against a follower of the Báb, one whose malign pattern of behaviour continues to be repeated up to the present.

A town in confusion and divided

At this point, the town was divided on what to do with Quddús. A Muslim source described what transpired in Bárfurúsh:

---

1 E. G. Browne, *Kitáb-i-Nuqtatu'l-Káf*, p. 197.

2 Thomas Kelly Cheyne, *The Reconciliation of Races and Religions*, p. 307.

3 Joseph Arthur Gobineau, *Les Religions et les Philosophies dans l'asie Centrale*, p. 231.

4 George Nathaniel Curzon, *Persia and the Persian Question*, Vol. 1, pp. 39–42.

5 Abbas Amanat, *Pivot of the Universe*, p. 114.

> When everybody had watched, they were then taken around from quarter to quarter. A few [of the captives] were claimed and ransom money was paid to gain [their release].
>
> Until it was Ḥájí Muḥammad-'Alí's [Quddús'] turn. Someone [in the crowd] said: "Kill him, [for] he is the one who has made all the trouble—that so much blood has been shed." [Another] one said: "Don't kill him; he is [a] fine young fellow, it is a pity to kill him." The prince said: "I have to take him alive to Ṭihrán to the king; he will decide what sort of person he is." "Take [him]!" said one; "Don't!" said another.[1]

Everyone found it difficult to decide on whether to kill Quddús. Within their own Islamic law, it was forbidden to kill a descendant of the Prophet Muḥammad. "Because of their descent," Willem Floor stated, "sayyids enjoyed general respect and immunity from normal state regulations."[2]

An assembly is called

As indicated earlier, the prince intended to take Quddús to the capital but the Sa'ídu'l-'Ulamá' warned the royal: "Beware that you meddle not in this matter, for he is a plausible fellow and hath a specious tongue; should he be suffered to appear before His Majesty the King, he will assuredly succeed in misleading him."[3] Quddús was the prince's opportunity to surrender him personally to the Sháh at the capital to receive royal honours and material rewards as per the Persian traditions. The prince was determined not to surrender Quddús. He showed no sign of yielding to the request of the Sa'ídu'l-'Ulamá', despite the priest's very insistent demands and the use of all possible means of persuasion. The prince, unwilling to expose Quddús—his valuable hostage—to that individual's savagery, gathered all the 'ulamá, the highest-ranking clergymen, to see how to appease the stormy crowd. A silk bundle containing a pen-case that the Báb had sent to Quddús and his writings, was now in the possession of the prince.

According to a chronicler:

> The prince ordered Quddús, Mírzá Muḥammad-Ḥusayn Qumí and Mírzá Muḥammad Mahvalátí be brought to a big meeting in which there were about 30 Uṣúlí and 10 Shaykhí scholars led by Mullá Muḥammad Ḥamzih [Sharí'atmadár].[4]

Nabíl described other details of the trial that occurred at the Sa'ídu'l-'Ulamá's residence with his religious court next to the Jum'ih [Friday] mosque:

> No sooner had the 'ulamás [high-ranking divines] assembled than the prince gave orders for Quddús to be brought into their presence. Since the

1 Habib Borjian, *A Mázandaráni Account of the Babi Incident*, pp. 393–4.

2 Willem Floor, *The Economic Role of the Ulama in Qajar Persia*, p. 58.

3 Mírzá Ḥusayn Hamadání, *The New History* (*Taríkh-i-Jadíd*), p. 88.

4 Siyyid Muḥammad-Ḥusayn, *Vaqa'i-i Mimiyyih*, pp. 114–117.

> day of his abandoning the fort, Quddús, who had been delivered into the custody of the Farrásh-Báshí [the prince's court chief], had not been summoned to his presence. As soon as he arrived, the prince arose and invited him to be seated by his side.[1]

Some rules for the trial were set by the prince: The prince told them [the clerics], "since you are Shaykhí and Uṣúlí[2] mullás, you should engage in conversation and debate with these individuals so that I can witness the evidence you present as well as the evidence they possess in support of their ideas and your supposed falsity. In this way we can determine the validity and falsehood of each argument."[3]

Turning to the Sa'ídu'l-'Ulamá', the prince urged that his conversations with him be dispassionately and conscientiously conducted. "Your discussions," he asserted, "must revolve around, and be based upon, the verses of the *Qur'án* and the traditions of Muḥammad, by which means alone you can demonstrate the truth or falsity of your contentions."[4]

It seems the prince was rather pleased to witness the conflict of opinions as a theatrical act. Deep inside, he was a very cruel man. He hated Quddús and had ordered the butchering of his younger brother Mírzá Ḥaydar, in Shaykh Ṭabarsí and destroy his fathers' home. The prince also knew that he had to hear the religious hierarchy because in the December 1848 royal edict he was instructed by the monarch "to extinguish this blazing flame will require the diligence of the most learned ulama and the most revered and respected scholars.[5] The divines' sights look like vultures impatient to put their hooks on their defenceless prey. It was probably only the presence of the prince that seemed to restrict their instincts.

Typical questions in these trials were about what flaws the defendant found in Islamic law and what perfection he said had been found in the Faith of the Báb. In other words, why he had abandoned his original religion. We know that Quddús was a consummate scholar in Islamic theology ready to respond the most complex questions. A chronicler wrote that at the first meeting:

> ... several writings and speeches by Quddús affirming the revelation of Qá'im were read aloud. These included interpretation of a hadith (a narrative record of the sayings or customs of Muḥammad and his companions) by Abí Abíd Makhzúní delivered with supreme eloquence along with compelling statements supporting the validity of this Revelation and refuting all other Islamic doctrines and sects.[6]

---

1 Hushmand Dehghan, *Ganj-i-Pinhán*, p. 124.

2 Sects of Islam.

3 Siyyid Muḥammad-Ḥusayn, *Vaqa'i-i Mimiyyih*, pp. 114–117.

4 Nabíl-i-A'ẓam, *The Dawn-Breakers*, pp. 409–10.

5 Ruhu'llah Mehrabkhani, *Mullá Ḥusayn*, p. 251.

6 Siyyid Muḥammad-Ḥusayn, *Vaqa'i-i Mimiyyih*, pp. 114–117.

It appears that the divines had previously agreed to sabotage the interchanges with indifference:

> As the prince was familiar with Shaykhí hadiths and principles, the frequent lack of comments on those works and on the writings of the Báb, made him address both groups of scholars asking, "Why do you remain silent and not engage in debate with these individuals?"[1]

Every evening, Quddús, Muḥammad-Ḥusayn Qumí and Mírzá Muḥammad Mahvalátí were returned to the prison and brought back to the assembly the following morning.

Jury bias

Apart from the fact that the jury was formed by clerics already prejudiced against the Cause of the Báb, there were other matters undermining their legitimacy. For Quddús, the jury did not have authority upon him since He was the supreme representative of the Manifestation of God. The Báb had already abolished the entire Islamic ecclesiastical system. The authority of the Shí'ih ecclesiastical system was based on the principle that they ruled in the name of the expected Qá'im. "Had the Báb in fact been acknowledged as the Hidden Imám," Hamid Algar wrote, "the function of the 'ulamá [Islamic clergy] would have ceased to exist. It may be conceded that they thus had a vested interest in the continued occultation of the Hidden Imám."[2] The Báb therefore challenged their absolutist theocracy by identifying Himself with the Qá'im and therefore head of the system.[3]

Above all, the purpose the trial "was not to enquire, but to find fault."[4] The jury was there for his blood and not for justice. According to Gobineau:

> They had been told in advance, doubtless as a precautionary measure, that even if they abandoned their religion and returned to Islam their apostasy would bring them no advantage and would not prevent them from being delivered into the hands of the executioner. They received that communication with cold disdain and died without a word.[5]

The court itself belonged to an obsolete and corrupt paradigm. About the contrast between the old and the new order, Jesus had said:

> And no one puts new wine into old wineskins; or else the new wine will burst the wineskins and be spilled, and the wineskins will be ruined. But new wine must be put into new wineskins, and both are preserved. And no one, having drunk old wine, immediately desires new; for he says, "The old is better". (Luke 5:37–39)

---

1 Siyyid Muḥammad-Ḥusayn, *Vaqa'i-i Mimiyyih*, pp. 114–117.

2 Hamid Algar, *Religion and state in Iran*, p. 148.

3 Armin Eschraghi, *Undermining the Foundations of Orthodoxy*, pp. 233-5.

4 E. G. Browne, *Taríkh-i-Jadíd*, p. 364.

5 Gobineau in Nash and O'Donoghue, *Comte de Gobineau and Orientalism*, p. 176.

Drunk on their old wine, there was no desire for the new Gospel. Furthermore, Quddús might have been aware by that time of the futility of the proceedings as the verdict was supposedly decided upon even before he was summoned. Sceptical of that judiciary circus, he listened to their diatribes and baseless accusations. How could he make these Pharisees understand, who ignored their ancestors' prophecies that God had changed them for other people according to the injunction of *Qur'án* (5:54). How could he explain to these religious dogmatists, indoctrinated in obscure, man-made traditions and superstitions, that the old order had been written off and that there was no place for their expired authority.

Nature of the interrogation

The proposed death sentence raised many issues. The basis for a death warrant was based on vague accusations of sedition and heresy.

On the charge of sedition, Quddús might have repeated what he wrote in response to the prince's letter when the latter arrived from the capital to Mázindarán Province—the gist of which was:

> Can gunners and soldiers distinguish right and wrong? This is the work of learned divines on whom devolves the duty of enquiring into the matter. If differences can be removed by reasonable discussion and argument, well and good ... we for our part have no quarrel with anyone, being strangers, who have suffered much in this wilderness, and are the objects of causeless persecution. Suffer us then to depart, that we may with all speed quit this land and pass to the holy shrines of Karbilá and Najaf. But if you encompass us on all sides and suffer us not to depart, and if ye be indeed bent on the slaughter of innocent folk, then we have no choice but to defend ourselves and to prove the sincerity of our belief by laying down our lives as martyrs to our cause. But do not thou, O noble prince, take part in bringing about this bloodshed.[1]

On the charges of heresy, these charges were considered to have gone against natural law. Nobody could have claimed complete knowledge of the truth of Islamic Revelation. From a realistic point of view, Islám was already divided into dozens of sects antagonistic to each other,[2] and therefore it was untenable for anyone to claim ownership of Truth. Furthermore, Muḥammad had predicted the disintegration of His religion into 73 sects.[3] Heresy was typified in their divines' man-made theology with the term *Bid'ah* meaning a "reprehensive innovation in matters of faith".[4] The term does not appear in the *Qur'án* but has been used

---

1 E. G. Browne, *Taríkh-i-Jadíd*, p. 363.

2 Carole Cusack and Muhammad Afzal Upal, *Introduction,* p. 2.

3 Carole Cusack and Muhammad Afzal Upal, *Introduction,* p. 2.

4 Hamid Algar. *Religion and State in Iran 1785-1906: The Role of the Ulama in the Qajar Period 1785-1906,* p. 123.

throughout history against political and religious adversaries.[1] Heresy was the charge in the fatvá that caused the martyrdom of the Báb the following year and His previous interrogation in July 1848, both in the city of Tabríz.[2]

On the other hand, It was a mistake in jurisprudence by Sa'ídu'l-'Ulamá' to typify Bábísm as heresy because, according to Muḥammad, heresy was not characterised in the Qur'án, "*For you is your religion, and for me is my religion*" (109:6). The Islamic civilization grew rapidly in other countries because of its pluralistic nature, tolerance and cosmopolitanism. Successful cultural exchanges with non-biblical religious communities occurred in Asia and Africa throughout the early centuries of Islamic growth, especially concerning Buddhism and Hinduism.[3]

Should it be the case that Quddús was accused of apostasy, he might have borne witness wholeheartedly to his belief in the truth of religion of Muḥammad. If tested about why he had disregarded the advice of Muslim doctors, as a skilled theologian, Quddús would have elaborated on his total reliance on the enduring principles of the *Qur'án*. His extensive knowledge of the prophecies about the Day of Resurrection to justify the advent of the Báb might have been brilliant. In the final analysis, according to Sharí'a law, following a religion outside of Islám does not make you a heretical outlaw. "*There is no compulsion in religion*" (*Qur'án*, 2:256), Muḥammad had categorically recited.

Quddús' lineage questioned

On the third and last day of the assembly, the matter was raised regarding Quddús being a descendant of the family of Prophet Muḥammad. The act of killing one of them was cursed. According to Nabíl:

> "For what reason," the Sa'ídu'l-'Ulamá' impertinently enquired, "have you, by choosing to place a green turban upon your head, arrogated to yourself a right which only he who is a true descendant of the Prophet can claim? Do you not know that whoso defies this sacred tradition is accursed of God?"[4]

Quddús replied:

> The lineage of Jesus, the son of Mary, traces back to the lineage where the Creator of the world bestowed the revered figure of Shem [in the *Bible*, a son of Noah and a traditional ancestor of the Semites] upon Prophet Adam. From the descendants of Jesus until the end, there has been no lineage except through His mother. Similarly, God established the lineage of the

1 Dina Yulianti, Otong Sulaeman, and Muhammad Ilyas. *Accusing Heresy is a Heresy. How Heresy Became an Instrument in Political Sectarianism*, p. 191.

2 Hamadání, Mírzá Ḥusayn, *The New History (Taríkh-i-Jadíd)*, p. 293.

3 Hasan Balyuzi, *Muḥammad and the Course of Islam*, p. 289.

4 Nabíl-i-A'ẓam, *The Dawn-Breakers*, pp. 409–10.

> Messenger [Prophet Muḥammad] only through Fáṭimah [Muḥammad's daughter], the truthful, peace be upon her, with no other lineage.[1]
>
> "Was Siyyid Murtaḍá," Quddús calmly asked, "whom all the recognised 'ulamás praise and esteem, a descendant of the Prophet through his father or his mother?"[2]

He added:

> According to the fatwas of the religious scholars, even Siyyid Murtaḍá Allámih al-Ḥudá himself was not in his lineage except through his mother. Furthermore, his fatwa, along with that of a group of previous scholars, states that those related to their mother and grandmother as descendants of the Prophet can take *khums* [which is a jurisprudential term meaning to pay one-fifth of the annual surplus income, or of mine and treasure, taking into account the required conditions in jurisprudence] and have a share of it.[3]

According to the chronicles:

> They all confirmed that nobody in this town would deny your mother's status as a siyyideh or Sayyida [feminine form of siyyid], her chastity, and nobility. Then Quddús asked "I testify before God, what is your opinion regarding my mother's reputation for possessing a good character among you?" When everyone silently nodded in confirmation, Mullá Muḥammad Hamzah [Sharí'atmadár] added, "There is no doubt about your mother being a siyyideh, her chastity, nobility, good character, knowledge and morality."[4]
>
> One of those present at that gathering instantly declared the mother alone to have been a siyyid. "Why, then, object to me," retorted Quddús, "since my mother was always recognised by the inhabitants of this town as a lineal descendant of the Imám Ḥasan? (Muḥammad's grandson) Was she not, because of her descent, honoured, nay venerated, by every one of you?"
>
> No one dared to contradict him. The Sa'ídu'l-'Ulamá' burst forth into a fit of indignation and despair. Angrily he flung his turban to the ground and arose to leave the meeting. "This man," he thundered, ere he departed, "has succeeded in proving to you that he is a descendant of the Imám Ḥasan. He will, ere long, justify his claim to be the mouthpiece of God and the revealer of His Will!"[5]

---

1 Siyyid Muḥammad-Ḥusayn, *Vaqa'i-i Mimiyyih*, pp. 114–117.
2 Nabíl-i-A'ẓam, *The Dawn-Breakers*, pp. 409–10.
3 Siyyid Muḥammad-Ḥusayn, *Vaqa'i-i Mimiyyih*, pp. 114–117.
4 Siyyid Muḥammad-Ḥusayn, *Vaqa'i-i Mimiyyih*, pp. 114–117.
5 Nabíl-i-A'ẓam, *The Dawn-Breakers*, pp. 409–10.

"It was completely confirmed that in the siyyid's (Quddús) status, decency, and lineage of his mother, there was no room for reflection or denial in this matter" wrote Siyyid Muḥammad-Ḥusayn. "Nobody spoke except Mullá Muḥammad Hamzah [Sharí'atmadár] who said that there is no rejection of her status, decency, goodness, knowledge and morals."[1]

As the prince insisted on engaging the scholars in debate, no one spoke. Consequently, the assembly ended, and the scholars dispersed.[2]

Death sentence

With no flanks open, with all questions answered appropriately, with a strong revindication of his convictions, Quddús emerged undefeatable, and it might be the case that some of the juries were reluctant to endorse a death warrant on the basis of religious infidelity. Even the charge of being against God fell off because all of his voluminous treatises testified the love for God. Given the influence of the Sa'ídu'l-'Ulamá', the sentence was probably passed on the nebulous and explainable charges of being an "*enemy of God*" (*Qur'án* 8:60) even when Quddús was going to die soon for God. Very likely, he was also accused of "*spreading corruption on earth*" (*Qur'án*, 18:94) ironically when the Báb had designated him as the "the Most Holy". These were typical accusations against innocent people in politically motivated trials.

"After three days, the totality of mullás, that is, the Bárfurúsh scholars (Shaykhis and Uṣúlís),"[3] wrote a chronicler, "rushed to the prince and told him that he had kept the main root [Quddús] and killed the branches. Why don't you kill him?"[4]

The role of the prince

That day, everybody was anxious to know what the prince would decide: either to take Quddús with him to the capital or to let the mullás kill him on the spot. Although a mujtahid [high level cleric] like the Sa'ídu'l-'Ulamá' had the religious prerogative to sign a death warrant, it was still necessary for the civil authority, represented by prince Míhdi Qulí Mírzá as the Governor of Mázindarán province and the monarch's representative, to endorse and authorize the sentence. Count de Gobineau stated that death sentences issued by Muslim clerics did not have full civil legal validity:

> But if the *Qur'án* condemns lapsed Muslims and heresiarchs to death [sic], this doctrine, it can be said, has not only fallen into disuse in Persia; it has never been accepted or practiced there by the political powers. In recent centuries as nowadays, we have seen the mullás insistently asking for its application and not obtaining it. Heresiarchs, heretics of all kinds have

1 Siyyid Muḥammad-Ḥusayn, *Vaqa'i-i Mimiyyih*, pp. 114–117.

2 Siyyid Muḥammad-Ḥusayn, *Vaqa'i-i Mimiyyih*, pp. 114–117.

3 Followers of the Shaykhi and Uṣúlí Islamic sects.

4 Siyyid Muḥammad-Ḥusayn, *Vaqa'i-i Mimiyyih*, pp. 114–117.

> always more or less openly set themselves as displayed themselves and have had nothing to fear from the secular arm.[1]

The Sa'ídu'l-'Ulamá's death sentence argued that Quddús was an apostate and an infidel. Interestingly, the *Qur'án* does not prescribe the death penalty for apostasy, hence the sentence was technically flawed.[2]

The prince surrenders Quddús

During the previous two days the Sa'ídu'l-'Ulamá' and his followers blackmailed the prince by politically threatening his governing of the province of Mázandarán. They were powerful and had great influence on people and the politics of the region. Besides that, the Sa'ídu'l-'Ulamá' had the monarch's backing.

The prince was addressed by all the divines, who advised him to either slay Quddús or expel him from Mázindarán Province.[3] Another account states that the Sa'ídu'l-'Ulamá' wrote a letter to the prince after learning that he had granted Quddús' request to be taken to the capital and placed on trial before the monarch:

> Be careful not to interfere in this matter, because he has a specious appearance and a deceptive language. If he is allowed to appear in the presence of His Highness, he will certainly mislead him. Send him to me and I will give you 1,000 tomans.[4]

Mírzá Ḥusayn Hamadání reported that he accepted 4,000 tumans as a gift to deliver Quddús.[5] According to a local source:[6]

> Sa'ídu'l-'Ulamá' wrote a letter, [stating]: "O prince! The moment you receive my letter, you will hand over Hájí Muḥammad-'Alí [Quddús] to [these] gentlemen [in order that] the clergy slay him." As soon as the prince saw the letter, he let them take the man. He was taken to 'Sa'ídu'l-'Ulamá', who said, "You have brought him again to me, what for? Get him killed!"

According to Siyyid Muḥammad-Ḥusayn, the prince pondered for two days and, on the morning of the third day, he avoided his official responsibilities and sent that revered personage [Quddús] to Sa'ídu'l-'Ulamá', and said, "do whatever you want to do with him."[7] Someone said that both in circle geometry and in politics, extremes come together—and this is what actually happened with

---

1 Joseph Arthur Gobineau, *Les Religions et les Philosophies dans l'Asie Centrale*, p. 262.

2 The Báb prohibited the issuing of the death penalty (*Arabic Bayán*, 11:16) particularly on a religious basis, when the ruling was used as a validation for killing non-Muslims by Islamic religious powers (*Persian Bayán*, 4:5).

3 Mohammad 'Ali Malik Khusraví, *Tarikh-e Shohada-ye Amr*, p. 404.

4 Hadi Letafati, *Biography and services of Saeed Ulama Mazandarani*, pp. 54–63.

5 Mírzá Ḥusayn Hamadání, *The New History* (*Taríkh-i-Jadíd*), p. 65.

6 Habib Borjian, *A Mázandaráni Account of the Babi Incident at Shaikh Ṭabarsí*, item No. 31.

7 See Siyyid Muḥammad-Ḥusayn, *Vaqa'i-i Mimiyyih*, pp. 114–117.

money finally settling the dispute. It might have been that by then he received instructions from the sovereign to kill Quddús.

Nabíl wrote:

> The prince was moved to make this declaration: "I wash my hands of all responsibility for any harm that may befall this man. You are free to do what you like with him. You will yourselves be answerable to God on the Day of Judgment." Immediately after he had spoken these words, he called for his horse and, accompanied by his attendants, departed for Sárí. [the provincial capital]. Intimidated by the imprecations of the 'ulamás and forgetful of his oath, he abjectly surrendered Quddús to the hands of an unrelenting foe, those ravening wolves who panted for the moment when they could pounce, with uncontrolled violence, upon their prey, and let loose on him the fiercest passions of revenge and hate.[1]

It was obvious that the prince

> ... was so afraid of the divines that he forgot that he had taken an oath, so he surrendered Quddús to the Sa'ídu'l-'Ulamá' and ordered his horse to be ready. He left with his servants towards Sárí and left Quddús under the claws of those blood-thirsty wolves.[2]

As soon as the Sa'ídu'l-'Ulamá' was told the prince had relinquished his official duty of care for Quddús, he went home and wrote a religious decree (fatwá) authorising the murder of Quddús.[3]

A double-faced personality

From the beginning, the prince seemed to act erratically while dealing with the Bárfurú<u>sh</u> divines who were his critics. At times, he is seen courteously dealing with Quddús' in front of the religious court.[4] He said that the assembly has been set up with the purpose of appraising the truth of the Faith of the Báb[5] and at times he reproaches the divines for not responding to Quddús arguments.[6] In those remarks he appears conciliatory and challenging the ecclesiastical hierarchy, an attitude that may have infuriated the mullás. Yet, on the other hand, he asked a survivor to insult the name of Quddús to be freed.[7]

The prince's double game was more a hypocritical manoeuvring recalling to what Bahá'u'lláh once said about another royal prince: "The faith which a

---

1 Nabíl-i-A'ẓam, *The Dawn-Breakers*, pp. 410.

2 Muḥammad-'Alí Malik <u>Kh</u>usraví, *Tari<u>kh</u>-i-<u>Sh</u>uhadáyi Amr*, p. 403.

3 Muḥammad-'Alí Malik <u>Kh</u>usraví, *Tari<u>kh</u>-i-<u>Sh</u>uhadáyi Amr*, p. 404.

4 Nabíl-i-A'ẓam, *The Dawn-Breakers*, p. 409.

5 Siyyid Muḥammad-Ḥusayn, *Vaqa'i-i Mimiyyih*, pp. 114-117.

6 Nabíl-i-A'ẓam, *The Dawn-Breakers*, p. 410.

7 Nabíl-i-A'ẓam, *The Dawn-Breakers*, pp. 425-426.

member of the Qájár dynasty professes cannot be depended upon".[1] He was the one directly responsible for the massacre of the survivors of the fort which totalled more than three hundred, an event that took place with the most chilling cruelty. This is not surprising given that Qájár governors often were "surpassing the Sháh in greed and in their harsh treatment of the local population... The primary responsibility of the provincial governors ... was to ensure that the royal treasury in Ṭihrán was sufficiently supplied."[2]

He knew that Quddús was an eloquent and knowledgeable speaker and that there were dissident voices among the divines themselves and within the population. The prince may have also wanted to assert his ultimate royal authority, already weakened by his costly victory. By preventing the final decision on Quddús' fate to happen smoothly and not in the hurried way the clerics planned to, he was passing a dominating message without totally contradicting them.

According to Mehran Kamrava, "the monarch could not wage battle against the Sharí'ah [religious law]" because his mandate was also religious and he "had a divine right to rule, conferred upon the king by God's grace" which "bestowed upon the person of the ruler a sense of religious sanctity"[3]. On the other hand, the Qájár ruling style was just personalized, arbitrary and autocratic.[4] In turn, the Shí'ih divines claimed that that they were given the rule in behalf of the Hidden Imám, a position that the Báb was now claiming for Him.[5] Power struggles between the two opposites, church and state, can explain the reason why the prince called for a public and open debate when he had no obligation for it as did the powerful governor of the province of Mázindarán, half-brother to the Shah and his representative to crush the Bábís of Ṭabarsí. It might even be hypothesized that the prince was playing this game to ultimately extract money from the Sa'ídu'l-'Ulamá' and his associates.

The maxim "Divide et impera" seems the more logical explanation to this paradox. Money, intrigues and corruption settled the dispute between the two parties.

The execution

Executions in Persia were normally held in public areas. There is no doubt that out of a population of about 20,000 people, a significant crowd formed in the open Sabzih-Maydán to witness the macabre spectacle that so many expected, this particularly included "the scum of its female inhabitants".[6] Nabíl-i-A'ẓam wrote:

---

1 Nabíl-i-A'ẓam, *The Dawn-Breakers,* p. 580.

2 Mehran Kamrava, *Qajar Autocracy,* p. 9

3 Mehran Kamrava, *Qajar Autocracy,* p. 8.

4 Mehran Kamrava, *Qajar Autocracy,* p. 9.

5 Armin Eschraghi, *From Bábí Movement to the Bahá'í Faith,* 381.

6 Shoghi Effendi, *God Passes By,* p. 42.

> No sooner had the prince freed them from the restraints which he had exercised than the 'ulamás and the people of Bárfurúsh, acting under orders from the Sa'ídu'l-'Ulamá', arose to perpetrate upon the body of their victim acts of such atrocious cruelty as no pen can describe.[1]

It is not known the exact timing of the execution. It is likely that it occurred during the day as the prince had surrendered Quddús in the morning of the third day. However, another source refers to the nighttime.[2] Based on this conflicting information it is supposed that the execution occurred late afternoon or early evening.

The parade around the city

Quddús suffered the greatest cruelties before his execution. He was again paraded barefoot through the Babol's alleys and marketplace. Shoghi Effendi related that the Sa'ídu'l-'Ulamá' "in his unquenchable hostility and aided by the mob whose passions he had sedulously inflamed, stripped his victim of his garments, loaded him with chains, in warm and humid weather, paraded him through the unpaved and muddy streets of Bárfurúsh"[3] around their moulded and compressed clay-tiled roof houses. The green silk turban that the Báb had given him was taken from him and muddied. This was done because the population would have had special pity for a descendant of Muḥammad. The clothes of that "most precious of all treasures in the world"[4] were torn to pieces by the crowd.

On that Wednesday, 16 May 1849,[5] that incomparable youthful figure of our Faith was being led to his ultimate sacrifice—a sacrifice which all past, present, and future generations of Bahá'ís will remember with unfailing appreciation and unshakable affection. Chained, barefoot, stripped of his clothes, and bleeding, he was led through the city's streets along with his other companions, accompanied by the beat of drums.

The *Taríkh-i-Jadíd* suggests that Mírzá Muḥammad-Ḥasan brother of Mullá Ḥusayn, was killed along with Quddús in the public square of Bárfurúsh.[6]

800 steps to Sabzih-Maydán

Hushmand Dehghan has reported that Quddús—this holy being—was dragged into the streets to trudge the 800 steps from the house of Sa'ídu'l-'Ulamá' to the Sabzih-Maydán, with his head wounded and his body bleeding.[7] Throughout that grim march the mob continued to beat him.

---

1 Nabíl-i-A'ẓam, *The Dawn-Breakers*, pp. 410–11.

2 E. G. Browne, *Kitáb-i-Nuqtatu'l-Káf*, pp. 199–200.

3 Shoghi Effendi, *God Passes By*, p. 42.

4 Siyyid Muḥammad-Ḥusayn, *Vaqa'i-i Mimiyyih*, pp. 114–117.

5 Twenty-third day of Jamádiyu'th-Thání in the year 1265 AH.

6 Mírzá Ḥusayn Hamadání, *The New History (Taríkh-i-Jadíd)*, p. 95.

7 See Hushmand Dehghan, *Ganj-i-Pinhán*, pp. 113–22.

At this stage, following months of inanition in the fort and the last six days in a prison, Quddús must have been totally exhausted. Further fatigued by being paraded barefoot 2 km around the market, Quddús, "that essence of the world's jewels",[1] needed the strength to complete the last steps on foot from the Jum'ih Mosque to the Sabzih-Maydán. That bushy open field was a 300 m walk from where Quddús was placed on trial. It was an eight hundred fatigued steps that represented an eternal march to the place of execution. The execution had already commenced with the first eight hundred steps to his death. Death had been prefaced by the wounds from the machetes and the hysterical screams of the women calling nauseatingly for his head along the way. That divine being, notwithstanding the moving body bleeding like a flagellated Jesus, had already celestially flown to the heavens of the expected martyrdom.

A martyrdom that would happily reunite him with his brother Ḥaydar, his mother whose memory was faint, and Mullá Ḥusayn—his spiritual brother—and the five hundred fallen companions, "my men" as he referred to them. Flash backs of his life must have come to his mind during those final and painful ten minutes. Ten minutes to recreate his short twenty-seven-year life but long enough to give him the strength needed to endure such a bath of blood in the green open field. Gone as a fading horizon was the greenery of his native Bárfurú<u>sh</u>, the sights of his school years in Sárí, Ma<u>sh</u>had and Karbilá, and the years spent with inspiring masters such as <u>Sh</u>arí'atmadár and Siyyid Káẓim. Both had instilled in him a love for the promised Qá'im. Having met the Qá'im in the person of the Báb, he was transformed into the new creation of being Quddús, the Holy, and became His personal companion to Mecca. The happy memory of sea and arid land on that occasion, and his association in the metropolis with Bahá'u'lláh probably made him sustain the remaining distance to the final place.

Many places must have come to mind during those last ten minutes: the deserts of Kirmán, the House of Bábíyyih, the plains of Bada<u>sh</u>t and the rudimentary <u>Sh</u>ay<u>kh</u> Ṭabarsí fort. Living in such a war sanctuary for eight months isolated from the world must have produced exultant sentiments of comradeship all of which were brusquely dissipated with the notorious royal treason provoking the brutal slaughter of his men. Their blood had profusely watered the forest of Mázandarán, being still fresh and red, and all had passed so quickly, like a hurricane of fury, in the past seven days. There would not be any more days to promote the Cause of the Báb, but he had successfully fulfilled all his missions—whereas now only the promise of martyrdom was needed to conclude his expected end of the journey.

Sadly, this was not indeed the expected end that his father Áqá Ṣáliḥ, his stepmother, and his surviving siblings Maryam and Muḥammad-Ṣádiq had wished for their beloved Quddús. He might have paid a final look at the crowd, looking for those sweet faces. Alas, all the present ugly and full of hatred faces looked drawn from a phantasmagorical scene belonging to Dante's inferno where

---

1 Siyyid Muḥammad-Ḥusayn, Vaqa'i-i Mimiyyih, pp. 114–117.

no saintly soul was recognisable. That day the city had debauched itself to its lowest end for a murder never to be forgotten.

Here, at the Sabzih-Maydán, Quddús comes with his head crowned with blood, his face bruised by blows and his ribs flagellated by sticks and whips. Would he be dismembered or beheaded? Would he die crushed or trampled under that wild horde acting in the name of God? Would they tie his limbs and shoot, or perhaps stab with swords? Nothing that the hysterical, ignorant and uncontrollable throng did was predictable. And nothing was more precious for him than seeing the martyr's palms and wreaths adorning the temples of his head. Looking at the infinite blue sky of Bárfurúsh, the only clean space left to him amid so much dross, knowing his abode was there waiting for him. They will want to destroy him but will not be possible since the Báb had promised him the immortality.

The Báb would write later about Quddús' tribulations, "*Thine affliction rose to such heights that the afflictions of no contingent being can be mentioned in connection to it.*"[1] He also affirmed: "*In all of God's creation, there is no drop of water so beloved in His sight than those which are shed in remembrance of thy suffering, or stream down in contemplation of thy trials*".[2]

At the Sabzih-Maydán

Historian Mohammad 'Ali Malik Khosravi wrote:

> Upon beholding Quddús, the Sa'ídu'l-'Ulamá' started to curse profanity and abusive obscenity at him ... With his own hands, he cut off the ears of that Blessed One, and then, ordered one of his servants who was holding a battle-axe to strike Quddús' on the mid-scalp of his head. Some have noted that 'Abidin the coolie was the person who, with the battle-axe, cut open his blessed mid-scalp. Next, Quddús was released into the hands of the mob and seminary religious students. Inhabitants of Bárfurúsh, according to the Sa'ídu'l-'Ulamá's instructions, attacked Quddús. The extent of hurt and injuries perpetrated upon that blessed soul were such that the pen is incapable of narrating and tongue is powerless to recount. O Lord, how could you ever empower the tongue to adequately make mention of his tribulations and martyrdom, all that injustice, or to commit in writing those grievous upheavals?[3]

Hushmand Dehghan added: "A low moral woman spat at Quddús' beautiful face, and everybody struck him with a blow, and Quddús had only a smile on his face."[4] Another historian wrote, "All the people heaped profanity and vulgarity upon that lord of the chosen ones while busy spitting upon his blessed face."[5]

---

1 The Báb, *Tablet of Visitation for Quddús*. See Appendix part II.

2 The Báb, *Tablet of Visitation for Quddús*. See Appendix part II.

3 Mohammad 'Ali Malik Khosravi, *Tarikh-e Shohada-ye Amr*, p. 404.

4 Hushmand Dehghan, *Ganj-i-Pinhán*, pp. 113–22.

5 Mohammad 'Ali Malik Khosravi, *Tarikh-e Shohada-ye Amr*, p. 404.

Mírzá Muḥammad-Ḥusayn-i-Mutavallí Qumí, who had betrayed him during the siege of the fort and was imprisoned a few days before him, remarked to Quddús, "You claimed that your voice was the voice of God. If you speak the truth, burst your bonds asunder and free yourself from the hands of your enemies", to which he replied: "May God requite you for your deed, inasmuch as you have helped to add to the measure of my afflictions".[1]

A mob had already gathered at the caravanserai. It is said that at the time of the martyrdom of Quddús, his blood was splattered on the wooden door of the building as a result of intense knife attacks at that place. Some years later, when the Bahá'ís approached the owner of the caravanserai to buy the door, he refused, saying, "how can you buy this door if this door is the cause of bounty to this place?"[2] The execution occurred less than 100 steps in front of the long tiled building that faced the extensive green space of the Sabzih-Maydán.

A Muslim source reported that:

> All the people of Bárfurúsh assembled. They led him to his death in Sabzih-Maydán. There was such a [thick] crowd that they could not kill him. So they killed him standing (i.e., on the spot).[3]

The final moments

At the prompting of the "diabolical"[4] Sa'ídu'l-'Ulamá', the mob became completely exasperated—spitting at him and brutally attacking him with their axes and knives. They were composed of religious students and the public who while passing hit and spat Quddús, and yet he kept smiling.[5] In the midst of intense and painful agony, he was heard to say:

> Forgive, O my God, the trespasses of this people. Deal with them in Thy mercy, for they know not what we already have discovered and cherish. I have striven to show them the path that leads to their salvation; behold how they have risen to overwhelm and kill me! Show them, O God, the way of Truth, and turn their ignorance into faith.[6]
>
> The time has come that I should be naked to leave my body and become alive.[7]

---

1 Nabíl-i-A'ẓam, *The Dawn-Breakers,* p. 413.

2 Hooshmand Dehghan, *Ganj-i-Pinhán*, p. 111.

3 Habib Borjian, *A Mázandaráni Account of the Babi Incident at Shaikh Ṭabarsí,* item No. 32.

4 Shoghi Effendi, *God Passes By*, p. 42.

5 Edward Granville Browne, *The Taríkh-i-Jadíd*, p. 197.

6 Nabíl-i-A'ẓam, *The Dawn-Breakers,* p. 411.

7 Hushmand Dehghan, *Ganj-i-Pinhán*, pp. 113–22.

Struck on his head

The *Taríkh-i-Jadíd* recounts, "With his own hands he [the Sa'ídu'l-'Ulamá'] first cut off both his ears, and then struck him on the crown of the head with an iron axe which he held in his hands, which blow caused his death. A similar version is given by A. L. M. Nicolas:

> The Sa'ídu'l-'Ulamá' was finally able to give free rein to his cowardice and his hatred: the illustrious captive was brought to him, and, after having ignominiously insulted him, he was seized by a horrible fit of fury—rushing towards Quddús he cut off both of his ears with a penknife and, with the intoxication of blood rushing to his brain, he grabbed a hatchet and struck on his enemy's skull until he fell.[1]

The last words of Quddús were: "Holy, holy, the Lord our God, the Lord of the angels and the spirit".[2]

After the martyrdom

Head of Quddús is severed

Next in that chain of modern barbaric acts, a spine-chilling event took place. "After that", the *Taríkh-i-Jadíd* remarked, at the command of the Sa'ídu'l-'Ulamá', "a student [of religion] severed his holy head from his [lifeless] body in the midst of the market-place",[3] and it was carried around the marketplace.[4] "People took warning," wrote a Muslim source on the eerie tension in the air.[5]

The body of Quddús is cut

'Abdu'l-Bahá said that Quddús "was torn to pieces".[6] "His body was chopped up," related French historian Nicolas.[7] Historian Hushmand Dehghan recorded, "Eventually the thugs and gangs whose core is evil, with knives and axes hit his body, and they tore his body to pieces."[8] In turn, the author of *History of the Martyrs of the Cause* wrote: "They attacked the body of Quddús and wounded him so much that the pen cannot relate it. 'O God! How a tongue can describe what happened on his martyrdom!'"[9]

The clerics then ordered that the body be cut into pieces. They made holes in the dead body of Quddús and mutilated him with their hands—they literally

---

1. A. L. M. Nicolas, *Seyyèd Ali-Mohammed dit le Bâb*, p. 329.
2. Hushmand Dehghan, *Ganj-i-Pinhán*, pp. 113–22.
3. Mírzá Ḥusayn Hamadání, *The New History*, p. 88.
4. Habib Borjian, *A Mázandaráni Account of the Babi Incident at Shaikh Ṭabarsí*, p. 394.
5. Habib Borjian, *A Mázandaráni Account of the Babi Incident at Shaikh Ṭabarsí*, p. 394.
6. 'Abdu'l-Bahá, *A Traveller's Narrative*, p. 19.
7. A. L. M. Nicolas, *Seyyèd Ali-Mohammed dit le Bâb*, p. 329.
8. Hushmand Dehghan, *Ganj-i-Pinhán*, pp. 113–22.
9. Malik Khusraví, *Muḥammad 'Alì, Tarikh-i-Shuhadáyi Amr*, p. 404.

hacked him into small pieces. Some people took body fragments as souvenirs, thus reaching down to the lowest ebb of human decency.[1]

Their ferocity had no limit. In the words of Nabíl, the historian:

> The absence of any restraint on the part of the government authorities, the ingenious barbarity which the torture-mongers of Bárfurúsh so ably displayed, the fierce fanaticism which glowed in the breasts of its shí'ah inhabitants, the moral support accorded to them by the dignitaries of Church and State in the capital—above all, the acts of heroism which their victim and his companions had accomplished and which had served to heighten their exasperation, all combined to nerve the hand of the assailants and to add to the diabolical ferocity which characterised his martyrdom.[2]

Body of Quddús is burnt

Another source related the heightened fear brought on by the Sa'ídu'l-'Ulamá', who had by that time returned the 800 steps to his residence. People were astonished that the decapitated body did not bleed. The Báb later said of such blood: *"I take thee and all created things as witnesses, that thy lifeblood is pure, holy, sanctified."*[3] The cleric's ruffians ran the 800 steps to his residence to secretly inform him of the strange phenomenon:

> And when they slew him, no blood came forth from his body. So they told this to the Sa'ídu'l-'Ulamá'. And he said: "He [Quddús] was afraid, and his blood left him".[4]

Consequently, the Sa'ídu'l-'Ulamá' ordered that the shattered limbs be set on fire, and people brought dried rice stalks which are highly flammable. Another source indicates that naphtha was used.[5] While they were collecting and bringing rice stalks from the surrounding area, the headless body of Quddús was left lying on the dirt. When they came back, the ruffians quickly lit a bonfire and put the remaining fragments on top of the flames. Again, another miracle occurred—the fire did not burn the body fragments. The normally quiet atmosphere of the Sabzi Maydán rapidly descended into chaos, the domain of the Devil.

The followers of the Sa'ídu'l-'Ulamá' again went secretly to his home to inform him that the fire was not burning the body fragments, and people were cursing the cleric, who became afraid.

---

1 Hushmand Dehghan, *Ganj-i-Pinhán*, pp. 113–22.
2 Nabíl-i-A'ẓam, *The Dawn-Breakers*, pp. 410–11.
3 The Báb, Tablet of Visitation for Quddús. See Appendix, part 2.
4 Mírzá Ḥusayn Hamadání, *The New History (Taríkh-i-Jadíd)*, p. 88.
5 Cited in E. G. Browne, *A Traveller's Narrative*, Note P, p. 308.

According to a historian, in desperation, "He [Sa'ídu'l-'Ulamá'] fearing lest men might know and condemn his action, bade them to scatter them in the fields."[1]

Mutilating and burning a body are strictly prohibited in Islam, let alone committing murder. It is condemned in the *Qur'án* 5:32: "*Whosever kills voluntarily, it is as if he has killed all men*".[2] The Sa'ídu'l-'Ulamá' blatantly infringed on six Islamic rulings within 24 hours, either by ignorance or purposefully: killing a descendant of the Prophet Muḥammad, bribing a government official, committing murder, mutilating a human body, burning a body, and later desecrating that body. His offenses must surely disqualify him from continuing to serve as the Islamic jurist he pretended to be.

Certainly, as the literature alluded to him, he was an Anti-Christ,[3] and the tyrant Nimrod[4]—the one who rose against God (Micah 5:6).

Scattering the remains

The significance of the occasion could not be underestimated for the hierarchy. The elite knew they were killing a man claiming to be the "regent of the Lord of the Age".[5] The holy prey, the most prominent of the Báb's believers throughout the country, was savagely slaughtered by the wolves of religion while the populace circled around chorusing their euphory and the government stood watching the ignominy. As A. L. M. Nicolas wrote, "Islam gave a shameful exhibition to the world".[6] This time was the Karbilá of Quddús being fully enacted after the martyrdom of Imám Ḥusayn 1,170 years ago, both descendants from Muḥammad's lineage. Approximately 367 Bábís[7] had succumbed in the Shaykh Ṭabarsí massacre including half of the Letters of the Living.

E. G. Browne wrote of a prophecy given by the Báb,

> that a day would come when in these spots [on the streets of Bárfurúsh], hallowed by the blood of his martyrs, representations of their sufferings and steadfastness should move the sympathetic lamentations and tears of the children of those who slew them, and obliterate the remembrance of the martyrs of Karbilá.[8]

---

1 Mírzá Ḥusayn Hamadání, *The New History* (*Taríkh-i-Jadíd*), p. 89.

2 al-Dawoody et al., Management of the dead under Islamic law, pp. 1–2.

3 See Abbas Amanat, *Resurrection and Renewal*, p. 187; & Mírzá Ḥusayn Hamadání, *The New History* (*Taríkh-i-Jadíd*), pp. 91–92.

4 Siyyid Muḥammad-Ḥusayn, *Vaqa'i-i Mimiyyih*, p. 17.

5 Reference to the Báb. According to the Shí'ih belief, the 12th Imám, a direct descendant of Muḥammad, disappeared in 874 CE and was expected to return on the Day of Judgement. The Báb fulfilled this prophecy as the Promised One of Islam or *Qá'im* ("He Who Will Raise").

6 Nabíl-i-A'ẓam, *The Dawn-Breakers*, p. 404.

7 Muḥammad-'Alí Malik Khusraví, cited in Denis McEoin, *A Note on the Numbers of Babi and Baha'i Martyrs in Iran*.

8 E. G. Browne, *A Year among the Persians*, p. 615.

After the completion of the above diabolic events, the blood covered mob were still not satisfied. There were hysterical cries for more brutality. They wanted to commit more cruelty, and nothing could restrain them from acting like scavenging hyenas. If the execution had been merciless, then so should the dishonouring of the burial of Quddús.

The outskirts of a city are traditionally dumping areas because of their distance from residences and businesses. As the disposal of Quddús' remains probably were not initially thought through, the savages turned what was left of their minds to the city swamps. A proper human entombment for an infidel was not sacramented in their religious books.

A Muslim source from around 1860 stated that the remains were thrown into a swampy area called 'Dezdak Chal' ("thief's cavern"), which one can imagine as a grassy marsh, overgrown with bullrushes and lotus flowers on the western side of Baḥru'l-Arim lake .[1] As previously mentioned, the place was chosen because it was located on the very outskirts of the city that did not directly face the town or the caravanserai—it was 1 km west of the Sabzih-Maydán.[2]

The horrific cortege carrying Quddús' limbs made it way through the old, long wooden bridge which connected the Sabzih-Maydán and the island on where the Governor's House stood. Then they dumped the corpse at the back of the land which was an everglade formation with lotus flowers and a duck-hunting place for the upper class of Bárfurú<u>sh</u>. Nicolas uses the expression "thrown into the city ditches".[3] One must wonder at the degree of hatred that provoked Islamic clerics to un-Islamically deny a person his place of rest? Additionally, perhaps, they feared turning the burial site of Quddús into a Bábí national sanctuary. Alternatively, they may have simply wished to hide their crime and leave no evidence.

Remains are recovered

There was a prophecy of Quddús made in the previous year, which was recorded in the *Epistle of the Eternal Witness,* stating "I shall bury my body with

---

1 The Mázandaráni term for Duzdk<u>ch</u>ál is دَزَكِ چال (Arabic) or دزدکچال (Persian). The toponyms Duzdik<u>ch</u>ál, Baḥru'l-Arim and Ba<u>gh</u>-i-<u>Sh</u>áh are synonyms across different times. The swamp where the body of Quddús was thrown used to be a duck hunting ground on the west of the lake (≈36.531718, 52.672004). It is now a residential area. According to an Iranian blogger: "'Dezdekchel' [Dezdakchal, Dezdkchal or Dezekchal] means a castle on top of a hill. The word 'dez' [diz] literally means 'fortress', and 'dezak' means 'fortress' and 'small fort' and 'chal' [<u>ch</u>ál] means 'pit' and it means that this area was located on a hill in the middle of water." (http://dezdekchal.rozblog.com)

2 Habib Borjian, *A Mázandaráni Account of the Babi Incident,* item no. 32.

3 "Son corps fut haché et les débris jetés dans les fossés de la ville". In A. L. M. Nicolas, *Seyyèd Ali-Mohammed dit le Bâb*, p. 329.

my own hands" meaning the absence of a proper burial. And this prophecy was now to be fulfilled by the believers.[1]

During that night, Sharí'atmadár (Quddús' mentor) secretly sent a few people to collect the charred remains to place them in a better and safer place, burying them nearby "after reading the midnight prayer".[2] The chosen place of internment was the School of Mírzá Zakí Khán[3] located near the Ḥaẓír Furúshán Square,[4] a religious seminary in the centre of the city, not far from the Sabzih Maydán. About this episode some years earlier Quddús had commented as recounted in *Taríkh-i-Jadíd:*

> One day, before ever these matters were talked of, I was in the company of that holy man. We were taking a walk in the country, and in the course of it chanced to pass by the gate of that same ruined college. He, speaking of the vicissitudes of the world, said by way of illustration, "This college, for instance, was once frequented and flourishing, and is now desolate and ruined. After a while some illustrious man will be buried here, men will come from afar to visit the place, and once again it will flourish".[5]

In reference to Sharí'atmadár and his attendants, Hooshmand Dehghan has stated that:

> ... at mid-night he buried the remains of Quddús at the school of Mírzá Zakí which was situated in the suburb of Panj Shambih Bazaar. The school of Mírzá Zakí is within a close proximity to Sabzih-Maydán where the martyrdom of Quddús took place. After becoming aware of this, Sa'ídu'l-'Ulamá' incited the evil doers to dig the grave of Quddús , take the body out and then completely destroy it. However, the same Shari'atmadar went to the governor of Bárfurúsh, angrily advised him that by carrying out such an act, the curse of God will come upon him (governor). He then took his own turban off and threw it to the ground while comparing the behaviour of Sa'ídu'l-'Ulamá' to the acts and behaviours of the enemies of God in the land of Karbilá , and as a last resort he threatened the governor that if he lets Sa'ídu'l-'Ulamá' does that, then he (Shari'atmadar) will be cursing the governor. This affected the governor and the seditious plan of Sa'ídu'l-'Ulamá' died away. [6]

---

1 See Ḥusayn Hamadání, *The New History,* p. 90.

2 Hooshmand Dehghan, *Ganj-i-Pinhán*, p. 113.

3 According to Hooshmand Dehghan, the school (36.548471, 52.682296) was founded by Mírzá Zakí 'Alíyábádí who was a contemporary of the first two Qájár kings, Áqá Muḥammad Khán (1794–1797) and Fatḥ-i-Sháh (1797–1834).

4 Nosratollah Mohammad-Hosseini, *Qoddus, Moḥammad-'Ali Bārforuši, n.p.*

5 Mírzá Ḥusayn Hamadání, *The New History (Taríkh-i-Jadíd),* pp. 89–90.

6 Hooshmand Dehghan, *Ganj-i-Pinhán*, pp. 113–22.

According to Professor E.G. Browne, a handwritten letter by Quddús was found in his pocket during his burial where he clearly states the date and manner of his death.[1]

It often happens that, almost immediately after disturbing or exciting events, legends start to arise and grow in the telling and retelling of the story until it becomes hard to distinguish between fact and fiction. In the case of the chronicles that were penned in the Persian tongue and then translated into English, we have to take into account the peculiarities of the culture and language that tends to speak in superlatives and metaphors. This also may give rise to contradictions. For example, according to the narrations presented earlier in this chapter, Quddús had been stripped of his clothing before his execution, and his body had been hacked to pieces. We must bear in mind that a man would never have been stripped naked in that society especially in the presence of women. He would have been stripped of his outer garment and head covering, which was considered a form of dishonour and figuratively left him naked according to the traditions and literary conventions of that time

That night, the people of Bárfurú<u>sh</u> probably did not sleep well. Macabre flashbacks of the brutality would have woken them in the middle of the night, haunting them with what their hands had wrought. Why had a man of God been killed? Where had he been finally placed to rest? The last words of the victim had been about God and salvation. Yet, what was worse, they had stained their hands with the blood descended from the Prophet Muḥammad. Where was the Islamic godliness prescribed by *Qur'án* 2:172 in its call for love and piety so often recited by the Sa'ídu'l-'Ulamá':

> *It is not piety, that you turn your faces*
> *to the East and to the West.*
> *True piety is this:*
> *to believe in God, and the Last Day,*
> *the angels, the Book, and the Prophets,*
> *to give of one's substance, however cherished,*
> *to kinsmen, and orphans,*
> *the needy, the traveller, beggars,*
> *and to ransom the slave,*
> *to perform the prayer [ṣalát], to pay the alms [zakát].*
> *And they who fulfil their covenant*
> *when they have engaged in a covenant,*
> *and endure with fortitude*
> *misfortune, hardship and peril,*
> *these are they who are true in their faith,*
> *these are the truly god-fearing.*[2]

---

1 E.G. Browne, *Taríkh-i-Jadíd* or *New History of Mírzá Alí Muḥammad the Báb,* p. 308.

2 Translation by A. J. Arberry.

With the passage of time, the believers began visiting this holy place about which the Báb said: "*... no thought of majesty and glory may subsist in any heart unless it cometh to thee first in meekness, and with the greatest humility falleth upon thy threshold.*"[1]

Nuptials of fire

"*Quddús sought companionship with the Beloved through glorious martyrdom,*" 'Abdul-Bahá has stated.[2] When, in the middle of the Sabzih-Maydán, the largest square in the city, with the whole of Bárfurúsh attending, the hour of martyrdom had arrived, he faced it with joy because it was his spiritual wedding day . "My soul is wedded to Thy mention!", Quddús once said, "Remembrance of Thee is the stay and solace of my life![3]

Near the place of execution and referring to the timeliness of his martyrdom, Quddús said: "Would that my mother were with me and could see with her own eyes the splendour of my nuptials!"[4] The following account related to Quddús has been recorded:

> Once, Quddús was walking with a group of his followers around the Sabzih-Maydán. Suddenly, Quddús turned around and looked at his people and said that the body of an important person [referring to himself], whom nobody knew at that moment, would be set on fire in this place. However, the fire, though kindled with rice husks, would not burn the body out of respect.[5]

Three different authors have narrated the following:

> While Quddús was in early youth, his stepmother and his sister were insisting that he get married. However, he did not pay attention to their request.[6]
>
> Quddús was then about twenty-five years of age, and she [his stepmother] often said to him, "I am afraid that I will go to my grave without having my happiness [of attending Quddús' wedding] made complete."[7]
>
> Once his stepmother said to him: "God willing, I will sew a wedding dress for you."[8]

In order to appease them, Quddús would say, "It is not befitting for my joyous and jubilant festivity to be so brief. It shall come to pass with great magnificence.

---

1 The Báb, Tablet of Visitation for Quddús. See Appendix part 2.

2 'Abdu'l-Bahá, *Writings and Utterances of 'Abdu'l-Bahá,* p. 664.

3 Nabíl-i-A'ẓam, *The Dawn-Breakers,* p. 354.

4 Nabíl-i-A'ẓam, *The Dawn-Breakers,* p. 413.

5 Fazel Mazandarani, *Taríkh Ẓuhúr al-Ḥaqq,* vol. 3, pp. 421–2.

6 Fazel Mazandarani, *Taríkh Ẓuhúr al-Ḥaqq,* vol. 3, pp. 421–2.

7 Lowell Johnson, *Quddús,* pp. 10–1.

8 Hushmand Dehghan, *Ganj-i-Pinhán,* p. 45.

It shall be carried out, in the Sabzih-Maydán, amongst the sounds of tambourine and trumpet, people's excitement and public exhilaration."[1]

That day, "refused to burn the holy remains," wrote Reverend Cheyne.[2] "Not even the blazing fire thus kindled would burn those holy remains," reaffirmed the chronicler Mírzá Ḥusayn Hamadání.[3] In turn, Hushmand Dehghan stated "the fire had shame and did not burn."[4]

Birth, marriage and death are perhaps the three most significant life stages, yet, for Quddús, marriage also symbolised martyrdom as portrayed in Persian poetry. In the verses of Bahá'í poets Na'ím and 'Abdí:

> These lovers who paced to the place of execution
> more eagerly than a groom hastening to the bridal chamber.[5]
>
> We are that very same captive bird they slaughter
> on the night of mourning or at the day of the wedding feast.[6]

Such was the wedding of Quddús, at night and in the open, with torches, excited crowds, music and fireworks.[7] Ṭáhirih, her Badasht companion, would follow same fate three years later also identifying her martyrdom with a wedding with the Beloved. She, Shoghi Effendi wrote, "aware that the hour of her death was at hand, she put on the attire of a bride, and unanointed herself with perfume..."[8] .

On that evening of the 16 May 1849, Quddús was about twenty-seven years of age. Dusk settled in Bárfurúsh at 8:40 pm.

Other martyrdoms that same week

Thursday, the day after the execution of Quddús, the sun was up at 5 am after a short and unsleeping night. It was the market day for the city and the day when the inhabitants from surrounding villages come to buy supplies or to sell their agricultural goods in the Panj-Shanbih-Bazár, but also to exchange regional and national information in the absence of newspapers. Having such a crowd in the city, no doubt, Quddús became the central topic of conversation.

The next day, Friday, was the last day of the Islamic week, the day for collective worship, when the clerics were going to symbolically tear their garments to hide their sins.

---

1 Fazel Mazandarani, *Taríkh Ẓuhúr al-Ḥaqq*, vol. 3, pp. 421–2.

2 Thomas Kelly Cheyne, *The Reconciliation of Races and Religions*, p. 308.

3 E. G. Browne, *Taríkh-i-Jadíd or New History*, p. 89.

4 Hushmand Dehghan, *Ganj-i-Pinhán*, pp. 113–22.

5 Hatcher and Hemmat, *Reunion with the Beloved: Poetry and Martyrdom*, p. 84.

6 Hatcher and Hemmat, *Reunion with the Beloved: Poetry and Martyrdom*, p. 147.

7 A. L. M. Nicolas, *Seyyèd Ali-Mohammed dit le Bâb*, pp. 327–8.

8 Shoghi Effendi, *God Passes By*, p. 75.

During that bloody week, four defenders suffered martyrdom in Bárfurú<u>sh</u>, and two were sent to Ámul. Other believers were sent to Sárí as a warning to the population. According to Nabíl, the head of Mírzá Muḥammad-Taqíy-i-Juvayní

> and that of his fellow-companion, Mírzá Muḥammad-Báqir, were impaled on spears and paraded through the streets of Bárfurú<u>sh</u>, amid the shouts and howling of an excited populace.[1]
>
> Mullá Riḍáy-i-<u>Sh</u>áh and a young man from Bahnimír were slain two days after the abandonment of the fort by Quddús, in the Panj-<u>Sh</u>anbih-Bazár of Bárfurú<u>sh</u>.[2]

In addition, the chroniclers named "Siyyid Ḥusayn-i-Kuláh-Dúz, a resident of Bárfurú<u>sh</u>, whose head was impaled on a lance and was paraded through its streets."[3]

The two defenders who were sent to Ámul to be killed as a lesson for the local population were: Mullá Ni'matu'lláh-i-Ámulí and Mírzá Muḥammad-Báqir-i-<u>Kh</u>urásáníy-i-Qá'iní. The latter was the builder of the House of Bábíyyih in Ma<u>sh</u>had and the fortifications at <u>Sh</u>ay<u>kh</u> Ṭabarsí. His son, Mírzá Muḥammad-Káẓim, survived the massacre and returned to Ma<u>sh</u>had.

Of their martyrdoms, the Count of Gobineau wrote:

> On his arrival at Ámul, Mullá Ni'matu'lláh was tortured with ruthless ferocity. Apparently, this scene threw Qá'iní [Muḥammad-Báqir-i-<u>Kh</u>urásáníy-i-Qá'iní] into a fit of rage. In any case, when the executioner approached, Qá'iní breaking his bonds, jumped upon him, snatched his sword and struck him with such violence that his head rolled about fifteen feet away. The crowd rushed upon him but, terrible in his strength, he mowed down all those who came within his reach and they had finally to shoot him with a rifle in order to subdue him. After his death, they found in his pocket a piece of roasted horse flesh proof of the misery that he had endured for his faith![4]

A few Bábís survived through the payment of monetary ransoms. 'Abdu'l-Bahá called them "the remnants of the sword".[5]

---

1 Nabíl-i-A'ẓam, *The Dawn-Breakers*, p. 417.

2 Nabíl-i-A'ẓam, *The Dawn-Breakers*, p. 425.

3 Nabíl-i-A'ẓam, *The Dawn-Breakers*, p. 425.

4 Comte de Gobineau, *Les Religions et les Philosophies dans l'Asie Central*e, pp. 329–330. Cited in Nabíl-i-A'ẓam, *The Dawn-Breakers*, p. 404.

5 The names of some were: Mullá Muḥammad-Ṣádiq-i-<u>Kh</u>urásání, Mullá Mírzá Muḥammad Mahvalátí-i-Du<u>gh</u>-Ábádí, Áqá Siyyid 'Abdu'l-'Aẓím-i-<u>Kh</u>ú'i, Ḥájí Náṣir-i-Qazvíní, Hájí 'Abdu'l-Majid-i-Ni<u>sh</u>abúrí and Mírzá Muḥammad-Ḥusayn-i-Qumí.

Martyrdom as a rendezvous

Martyrdom is an affirmation of faith. The word martyr means witness in both Greek (*mártyras*) and Arabic (*sháhíd*). Regarding the spiritual station of the martyrs of the Faith, the Báb stated:

> *Great is the blessedness of those whose blood Thou hast chosen wherewith to water the Tree of Thine affirmation and thus to exalt Thy holy and immutable Word.*[1]

He further said:

> *O My servants! Seek ye earnestly this highest reward, as I have indeed created for the Remembrance of God gardens which remain inscrutable to anyone save Myself, and naught therein hath been made lawful unto anyone except those whose lives have been sacrificed in His Path.*[2]

"*On the shores of the Great Beyond, however,*" the Báb had told Quddús when He had returned to His previous accommodation in Búshihr in June 1845 after the pilgrimage, "*in the realm of immortality, joy of eternal reunion awaits us*."[3] "I glory in that I was the first to suffer ignominiously for Thy sake in Shíráz," Quddús stated, "I long to be the first to suffer in Thy path a death that shall be worthy of Thy Cause."[4] On 16 May 1849 the last part of the Báb's divine promise was fulfilled.

Referring to his eventual martyrdom, Quddús was hoping to "taste the sweetness of heaven's ineffable delights."[5] He also said to the Bábís of Shaykh Ṭabarsí:

> Fear not; but if ye be indeed fighting for God, if ye be content with His good pleasure, ready to endure affliction and martyrdom, and freed from all worldly ties, then stand firm even where you are, and bow your heads in submission. If so be that God's will requireth your martyrdom, then great is your honour and happiness![6]

The zenith of the life-cycle of Quddús was fixed in his future—his destiny—rather than in his past. His life ended as he foretold earlier in Shaykh Ṭabarsí:

> Each one of you has his appointed hour and when that time is come, neither the assaults of your enemy nor the endeavours of your friends will be able either to retard or to advance that hour.[7]

---

1 The Báb, *Selections*, p. 190.
2 The Báb, *Selections*, p. 67.
3 Nabíl-i-A'ẓam, *The Dawn-Breakers*, pp. 142–3.
4 Nabíl-i-A'ẓam, *The Dawn-Breakers*, p. 354.
5 Nabíl-i-A'ẓam, *The Dawn-Breakers*, p. 381.
6 E. G. Browne, *Taríkh-i-Jadíd*, p. 56.
7 Quddús in Nabíl-i-A'ẓam, *The Dawn-Breakers*, p. 392.

The German historian Hermann Roemer wrote that Quddús preached to the Shaykh Ṭabarsí companions "about death as liberation from the earth and the prison of the body in order to ascend into the heights of the true being and to reach the presence of the Beloved."[1]

It should be noted that although martyrdom has an elevated station, the Bahá'í believers are nowadays discouraged from pursuing such a path as Bahá'u'lláh has clarified:

> *Today, the greatest of all deeds is service to the Cause. Souls that are well assured should, with utmost discretion, teach the Faith, so that the sweet fragrances of the Divine Garment will waft from all directions. This martyrdom is not confined to the destruction of life and the shedding of blood. A person enjoying the bounty of life may yet be recorded a martyr in the Book of the Sovereign Lord.*[2]

Further thoughts

Never has a citizen of such stature arisen from Bárfurúsh. Quddús is a native representing the Prophet of God and upholding his high rank among the faithful, directing a nascent national community from the central northern frontier of the country, a mind of vast scholarship and unparalleled sanctity. Bárfurúsh had gained so much not only from his appearance in that land but also with his bones being interned therein, conferring everlasting sacredness to the land. He was a resident who had received international tributes across the globe for his sense of justice and courage, a man who, despite the danger, stood up to the main ecclesiastical, military and political oppressors of his time, a soul who struggled for the spiritual awakening of his menfolk through extensive travels, one who deserves to be considered the most distinguished citizen ever to appear in his town.

On his martyrdom, the Báb wrote:

> *Thou hast ascended through the realm of existence unto a horizon wherein none hath preceded thee, and been seated upon the Throne of Might in the loftiest mansions of Paradise, a station that none, in the compass of God's knowledge, hath surpassed.*[3]

Sadly, "no one is a prophet in their own land" (*Luke* 4:24) and the universal adage "Nobody throws stones at a fruitless tree" is equally true. Too much ingratitude for a person who only wanted the betterment and development of their fellowmen. Such are the ebbs and flows of ignorance, blind imitation and jealousy of the human nature which still persist in that country. Peter, the prince of the Apostles, was crucified upside down at his request not to die like his Lord. Quddús, who held the same spiritual primacy, was likewise brutally murdered;

---

1 Quddús in Roemer, *Die Bābī-Behā'ī, die jüngste mohammedanische sekte*, p. 36.

2 Bahá'u'lláh, *Additional Tablets extracts from Tablets revealed by Bahá'u'lláh.*

3 The Báb, *Tablet of Visitation for Quddús.* See Appendix part 2.

his death marked the exact time, location, and mode of fulfillment as promised by the Báb. With the miraculous nature of his life, and the fruits it bore, we acknowledge the majesty and uniqueness of his divinely appointed station as the Last Name of God,[1] .

The fifth anniversary of the Báb's Declaration occurred within a week of the martyrdom of Quddús. The conclusion of the Bábí Revelation was fast approaching. The following year the Báb Himself would also be publicly executed.

Chronology of the life of Quddús

Quddús was born in Bárfurúsh	c. 1822 (1238 AH)
Went to a religious seminary in Sárí aged twelve	c. 1834
Went to study in Mashhad	Late 1830s
At 18 years old went to Karbilá and spent four years studying with Siyyid Káẓim	c. 1840–1843
Returned home after 13 years of study	1259/1843
Accepted the Báb when he was 22 years old	Beginning of July1844
Left Shíráz with the Báb on pilgrimage to Mecca and Medina	10 September 1844
Arrived in the port of Búshihr on-route to Mecca	19 September 1844
Left Búshihr on-route to Mecca	2 October 1844
Reached Mecca	12 December 1844
Completed pilgrimage rites in Mecca	24 December 1844
Left Mecca for Medina	7 January 1844
Arrived in Medina	16 January 1844
Left Medina	12 February 1844
Arrived in the port of Jidda to return to Iran	24 February 1844
Embarked on a ship	27 February 1844
Sailed for Iran	4 March 1844
Arrived at Búshihr	About May 1845
Expelled from Shíráz	June 1845
Travels to Yazd, Kirmán, Ardistán, Iṣfahán, Káshán and Ṭihrán where he meets Bahá'u'lláh	1845–1846
Returned and stayed in Bárfurúsh	Late 1846 for about two years
Mullá Ḥusayn visits Quddús	April 1848
Travelled to Mashhad	By May 1848
Conference of Badasht	Late June—early July 1848
Mullá Ḥusayn departs from Mashhad	21 July 1848
The Báb's trial in Tabríz	Early July 1828
Incident of Níyalá (110 km from Badasht)	Around mid-July 1848
Muḥammad Sháh died	5 September 1848
Quddús confined in Sárí	95 days
Mullá Ḥusayn arrived at Shaykh Ṭabarsí	21 September 1848
Bahá'u'lláh visited Shaykh Ṭabarsí	Early October 1848

1 Arabic إِسْمُ ٱللهِ ٱللآخِر transcribed as *Ismu'lláhi'l-Ákhir* (see *God Passes By*, p.49) or *Ismu'lláhu'l-Ákhar* (see *The Dawn-Breakers*, p. 414).

Martyrdom of Quddús

Quddús arrived to Shaykh Ṭabarsí	20 October 1848
Quddús wounded	Night of 22 December 1848
Mullá Ḥusayn died	2 February 1849
prince sent an emissary—fort evacuated	9 May 1849
About 220 Bábís disarmed and massacred	10 May1849
Quddús died in Bárfurúsh	Wednesday 16 May 1849

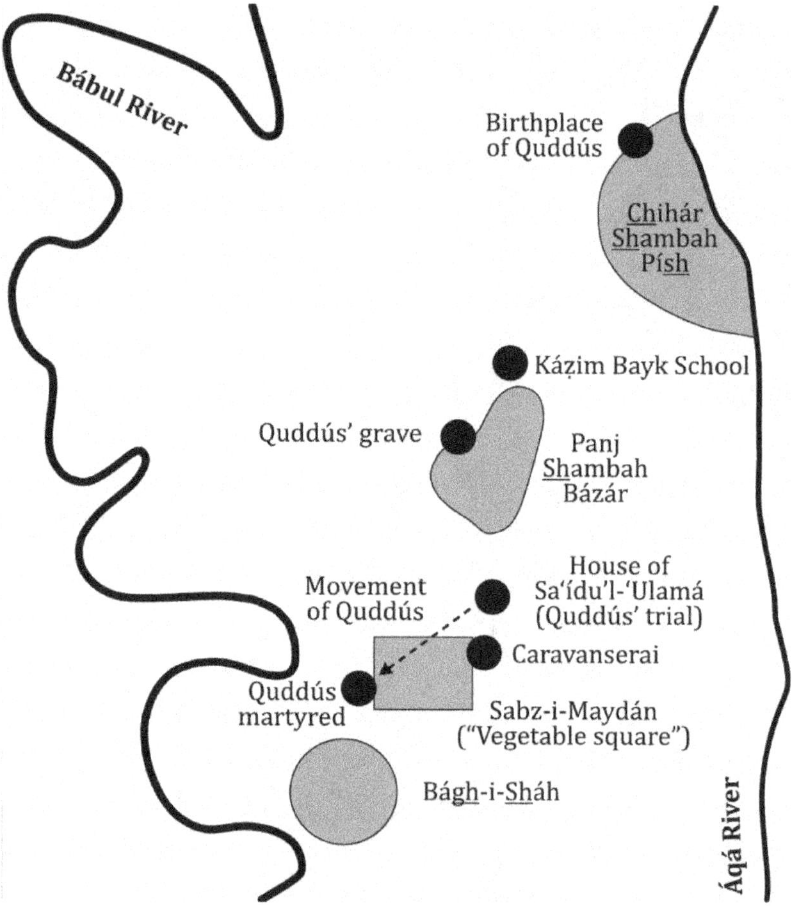

Figure 69: Old Bárfurúsh sketch
(Adapted from Ganj-i-Pinhán, p. 215)
(Courtesy of M. W. Thomas)

Figure 70: Portrait of Sa'ídu'l-'Ulamá'

Figure 71: Old view of the Jum'ih mosque of Bárfurú<u>sh</u> where Quddús was trialled

Figure 72: The Governor House where Quddús was arrested during his trial (public domain)

Figure 73: The bridge to the Governor House located in an island in the Bág͟h-i-S͟háh

Figure 74: Park (Sabzih Maydán) where Quddús was martyred (Source: Bahá'í Media)

Figure 75: Aerial view of the Sabzih Maydán (Source: Google Earth)

Figure 76: View of the old caravanserai gate where Quddús was beaten to bleed profusely

Figure 77: The lower border of the photo shows the possible span where Quddús was killed facing the caravanserai

Figure 78: Duzdekchál in the eastern side of Bahru'l-Arim lake where Quddús remains were scattered (photo around 1866)

Figure 79: The martyrdom of Quddús at the Sabzih Maydán
(Courtesy of Kamal Ma'ani)

18
The family of Quddús

Chapter content
Áqá Ṣáliḥ
The stepmother
Siblings

As described in the first chapter, Quddús' mother had died when he was an infant. His father later married a woman who cared for Quddús as if he were her own son. The name of Quddús' mother was never recorded. As indicated earlier, Quddús never married. The family was supported by the local cleric Sharí'atmadár who appeared to be inclined to the Cause of the Báb. Except for his father and stepmother, all Quddús' relatives came to believe in the Faith of the Báb. However, as his relatives, they all had to pay a high price as the stories quoted below reveal.

Áqá Ṣáliḥ

It seems that Quddús' father did not become a believer, and he passed away after Quddús' martyrdom.[1] He has been referred to as a "simple man".[2] According to Sepehr Manuchehri:

> Once during the battles, prince Mihdí-Qulí Mírzá arranged for the father, stepmother and sister of Quddús to come to the battle front. The prince asked the father, "What are the intentions of your son from causing such havoc?" He replied that "I am ignorant of the reasons behind his activities." The prince sent him near the fortress to talk to Quddús. It is reported that once he saw Quddús, he was shocked and temporarily lost his speech. After regaining his composure, he talked about their captivity and the prince's scheme. Quddús replied that captivity and suffering in the path of God are quite valuable.[3]

Áqá Muḥammad Ṣáliḥ's house was destroyed.[4] Quddús told his father to advise the prince regarding the spiritual nature of his endeavours and his refusal to give up. It has been said that the prince released Áqá Ṣáliḥ after a few days.[5]

"Later, all of the leading Bábís of Bárfurúsh," Moojan Momen wrote, "including Quddús' half-brother, became Bahá'ís, and the sons and family

---

1 Fazel Mazandarani, *Taríkh Ẓuhúr al-Ḥaqq*, vol. 3, pp. 421–2.

2 Fazel Mazandarani, *Taríkh Ẓuhúr al-Ḥaqq*, vol. 3, p. 423.

3 Sepehr Manuchehri, *Brief Analysis of the Features of Bábí Resistance*, n.p. See also Fazel Mazandarani, *Ẓuhúr al-Ḥaqq*, vol. 3, p. 423.

4 E. G. Browne, *Kitáb-i-Nuqtatu'l-Káf*, pp. 199–200.

5 Sepehr Manuchehri, *Brief Analysis of the Features of Bábí Resistance*, n.p.

> of Sharí'atmadár protected them against Uṣúlí [conservative] clerical opponents ...."[1]

The stepmother

Quddús' stepmother loved him like her own child but did not become a believer. She died many years after the martyrdom of Quddús. The author of *Ganj-i-Pinhán* relates that "Jináb-i-Doctor Atarian told the writer of this book that the old friends of the town of Qá'ím Shahr still remember that the honourable lady in the last year of her life, came to Chalih Samíní Qá'ím Shahr and associated with some of the Bahá'ís."[2]

As the time of his martyrdom approached, Quddús told his stepmother: "This year all manner of troubles will befall you because of the love ye bear me, but be ye patient and thankful when afflictions come and the predestined blow falls, and display resignation and fortitude."[3]

Siblings

Maryam

Maryam was Quddús' only sister.[4] The historian Fazel Mazandarani wrote:

> The other family member with utmost affection held was his sister. Quddús changed her name to Maryam. When he went to the Fort, Quddús sent her to the house of Ḥájí Mullá Muḥammad Sharí'atmadár [for her safety and security]. Quddús left all his books and works for safekeeping and Ḥájí [Mullá Muḥammad Sharí'atmadár] protected and safeguarded them.[5]
>
> However, Maryam after the martyrdom of her brother (Quddús) was melting like a candle. Ḥájí took her as his wife. She was very unsettled, with deep anxiety, and eventually she died.[6]

Mírzá Ḥaydar

Ḥaydar was Quddús' half-brother, the son of his stepmother. Quddús was very fond of him, and they called each other brothers.

> When Quddús went to Shaykh Ṭabarsí, like Maryam, he was sent to the house of Sharí'atmadár for protection. Sharí'atmadár was the custodian of Maryam. Ḥaydar was very impatient and did not want to stay at

---

1 Moojan Momen, *The Struggle for the Soul of Twelver Shi'ism in Qajar Iran*, p. 44

2 Hooshmand Dehghan, *Ganj-i-Pinhán,* pp. 119.

3 Mírzá Ḥusayn Hamadání, *The New History (Taríkh-i-Jadíd*), p. 90.

4 The chronicles are not very clear on whether Maryam was a full or half-sister to Quddús.

5 Fazel Mazandarani, *Taríkh Ẓuhúr al-Ḥaqq*, vol. 3, pp. 421–2.

6 Fazel Mazandarani, *Taríkh Ẓuhúr al-Ḥaqq*, vol. 3, pp. 421–2.

Sharí'atmadár's residence but finally Quddús told him he should. He was very fond of Quddús, crying for him, anticipating to receive some news about Quddús.

Eventually news was received via prince Mihdí-Qulí Mírzá, who was the governor of Mázindarán and the chief of the regiments at Fort Tabarsí, who had sent for Ḥaydar to come to the military camp under arrest. Riding his brother's horse [Quddús'], they took him to the prince Mihdí-Qulí Mírzá, who had issued a death warrant for Ḥaydar. When Ḥaydar arrived and was dismounting his horse, with one foot still in the stirrup, the executioners killed him and cut him into pieces.

Quddús' stepmother was very much affected when she was informed of Ḥaydar's death, and her heart was broken. She then travelled from Bárfurúsh (now Babol) to Fort Tabarsí to find her son and to bury him but was unsuccessful and returned to Bárfurúsh. In the middle of the night, the bloody mutilated body of her son was put on the same horse that he had been riding and was brought to her place in the city of Bárfurúsh—a short distance. However, the people of Bárfurúsh were not willing to allow the body of Ḥaydar to be buried in Bárfurúsh. As there was no choice, he was buried outside the city, in a place called Ázád Bin,[1] about half a farsang (3 km) away from the city.[2]

Áqá Muḥammad-Ṣádiq

Áqá Muḥammad-Ṣádiq was a half-brother of Quddús who managed to live a long life and recount to the friends the stories of Shaykh Ṭabarsí. According to Fazel Mazandarani:

> Another person in the family of Quddús was Áqá Muḥammad-Ṣádiq who was the [half] brother of Quddús, being the son of the second wife of Quddús' father. He was known as Dáí [dáí, "uncle"] Muḥammad-Ṣádiq and twice he entered the Ṭabarsí fort to help the Bábís who were besieged there. However, Quddús ordered him to return home. Years later he would relate to the other believers' stories of the Fort and the character of Quddús. His job was weaving quilts. At an old age and with pain, he endured much suffering from the hands of the people of Bárfurúsh because of his relationship to Quddús.[3]

One time, Áqá Muḥammad-Ṣádiq went to the mosque of Káẓim Bay. The prayer leader Imám was Muḥammad-Ḥasan Sharí'atmadár, the son of Shaykh Muḥammad-Ḥasan Sharí'atmadár the Great. There was a Mullá in the front row who recognised Muḥammad-Ṣádiq, and got angry and yelled "O Bábí, how come you come to the mosque and stand behind me", and he started to curse Áqá Muḥammad-Ṣádiq. Then the Mullá called Áqá Muḥammad-Ṣádiq a "najis"

---

1 In the local language: آزادبن (Azad ben).

2 Fazel Mazandarani, *Taríkh Ẓuhúr al-Ḥaqq*, vol. 3, pp. 421–2.

3 Hooshmand Dehghan, *Ganj-i-Pinhán*, p. 120.

("impure") and the Sharí'atmadár heard this and became angry and replied, "He is my uncle". The Mullá began to repeat his words that the man was a Bábí and Sharí'atmadár ordered his son Shaykh Muḥammad-Riḍá to slap the Mullá on the back of the head and kick him out of the mosque. Áqá Muḥammad-Ṣádiq stayed and said his prayers.[1]

> It is interesting to note that [Bahá'í historian] Jináb-i-Fazel Mázandaraní, when he was young, was learning from Muḥammad-Ṣádiq. Jináb-i-Muḥammad-Ḥusayní writes regarding this story, "This servant remembers that Jináb-i-Fazel-i- Mázandaraní told me that when he was a young boy, he was sent to Daí Muḥammad-Ṣádiq for learning. Muḥammad-Ṣádiq, despite my being a very young boy, he taught me the meaning of the Islamic hadith known as "I was a hidden mystery'."
>
> The wife of Muḥammad-Ṣádiq was Fáṭimih Khánum. They had nine children; all of whom passed away when they were very young. Fáṭimih Khánum was known as old Auntie. It is said that when she was lighting his charcoal to make it burn, with a Mázindaráni accent, she would say: "Te ruhe bezuse ..." ("Let your soul burn") meaning the Sa'ídu'l-'Ulamá'.
>
> Fáṭimih Khánum, during the last days of her life, lived in the home of one of the Bahá'ís of Babol, and died in the year 1319 AH (c. 1940).[2]

---

1 Fazel Mazandarani, cited in *Ganj-i-Pinhán,* pp. 113–22.

2 Hooshmand Dehghan, *Ganj-i-Pinhán,* p. 121.

Part VI
The saint

19
The station of Quddús

Chapter content
Testimonies from the Báb
Testimonies from Bahá'u'lláh
Testimonies from 'Abdu'l-Bahá
Testimonies from Shoghi Effendi
Universal House of Justice advice
The Last Name of God

The testimonies of the Báb, Bahá'u'lláh, 'Abdu'l-Bahá, Shoghi Effendi and the Universal House of Justice bear witness to the unfathomable position of Quddús in the Bábí community.

Testimonies from the Báb

As previously discussed, Quddús converted at the age of twenty-two years of age about late June 1844 in the city of Shíráz. On that occasion, the Báb stated, *"We have in the world of the spirit been communing with that youth. We know him already. We indeed awaited His coming."*[1]

The Báb also revealed a beautiful Tablet of Visitation at the martyrdom of Quddús (see Appendix part 2). In this Tablet of Visitation, according to Vahid Behmardi and William McCants, "Quddús is described with attributes of God found in the *Qur'án*".[2] An extract from this precious and sacred document reads:

> *From time immemorial and throughout eternity thou hast been immeasurably exalted with majesty, and wilt unto everlasting remain in the inaccessible retreats of holiness and beauty.*[3]

Furthermore, the Báb addressed Quddús as "beloved of my heart, my king of glory, and my irrevocable purpose, the sovereign Lord of my beginning and end!"[4]

The Last Name of God

In particular, in the *Kitáb-i Panj Sha'n* (Book of the Five Modes or Qualifications),[5] the Báb conferred upon Quddús the title of "The Last Name of

---

1 Nabíl-i-A'ẓam, *The Dawn-Breakers,* p. 70.

2 Vahid Behmardi and William McCants, *A Stylistic Analysis of the Báb's Writings,* p. 123.

3 The Báb, *Tablet of Visitation for Quddús.* See Appendix part 2.

4 The Báb, *Tablet of Visitation for Quddús.* See Appendix part II.

5 This book was written in April-May 1850.

God", transcribed as *Ismu'lláhi'l-Á<u>kh</u>ir*[1] or Ismu'lláhu'l-Á<u>kh</u>ar[2] (Arabic إِسْمُ آللهِ آللآخِر). The Arabic adjective *Á<u>kh</u>ir* can also be translated as last, utmost or the end.[3,4]

Amongst the names of God, are "the first" (Ismu'lláhi'l Ávval) which is defined as the "One before Whom there is nothing", and "the last" (Ismu'lláhi'l Á<u>kh</u>ir) is defined as the "One after Whom there is nothing". Furthermore, Quddús is the eighteenth and last "Letter of the Living", and a member of the first Unity (Váḥid) of the *Bayán*.[5]

The Last Sage

Previously, and equally significant, at the beginning of the *Arabic Bayán*, Quddús was referred to as *Ḥakím-i-Á<u>kh</u>ir* a term that can be translated as *The Last Sage.* The Báb wrote in a joyful way in the aforementioned paragraph that *Ḥakím-i-Á<u>kh</u>ir* has appeared.

At the beginning of the *Arabic Bayán*, the Báb refers to Quddús as the master of the seven consonant letters of his name *'Alí-Muḥammad* (the names are the reverse of the name of the Báb) which is composed of seven letters,[6] and in some of His Writings the Báb also refers to Himself in the same terms.

Similarly, as explained in chapter 8 the Báb referred to Quddús as the *Ganj-i-Pinhán* ("Hidden Treasure"). Around March 1848 when Mullá Ḥusayn was returning from a pilgrimage to the presence of the Báb in the Máh-Kú prison, he was told to go to the province of Mázindarán where a Hidden Treasure was going to be found.[7]

A companion to the Báb

There are several significant references to Quddús in the Writings of the Báb extolling his station. One of them appears in the *Persian Bayán* (4:18). Quddús was selected among all the disciples to accompany the Báb on His pilgrimage to Mecca and Medina, an episode which the passage below refers to:

---

1 Shoghi Effendi, *God Passes By*, p. 49.

2 Nabíl-i-A'ẓam, *The Dawn-Breakers*, p. 414.

3 Francis Joseph Steingass. *English-Arabic Dictionary,* p. 425.

4 Hans Wehr. *A Dictionary of Modern Written Arabic,* p. 10.

5 The first Váḥid (Unit) of the *Bayán* consists of the 18 Letters of the Living and the Báb ('Abdu'l-Bahá in *Light of the World*, p. 11—item 5). The Báb Himself is not a Letter of the Living, despite what is in a letter 30 November 1930 written on behalf of Shoghi Effendi (*The Unfolding Destiny*, p. 427). (See Muḥammad Afnán, "Number of the Letters of the Living")

6 "بلی ان اسم الله الاخر قد اشرق و لمع و ابرق و سطع طوبی لمن لا یری فیه الا الله". The written consonants of 'Alí-Muḥammad are: *' ('ayn), l, í m, ḥ, m* (double *m* is written as a single *m* with a mark indicating it is doubled), and *d.* The short vowels *u* and *a* are not written.

7 Nabíl-i-A'ẓam, *The Dawn-Breakers*, p. 262. Refer to chapter 8 for more information on this designation.

> The only person[1] who recognized Him and performed pilgrimage with Him is the one round whom revolve eight Váḥids[2] in whom God hath gloried before the Concourse on high by virtue of his absolute detachment and for his being wholly devoted to the Will of God.[3]

It is interesting to note in the above paragraph that the Báb affirmed that the only real pilgrim was Quddús implying that the only acceptable pilgrimage was achievable only through attaining the presence of Manifestation of God and recognizing Him.[4]

A mirror of the Báb

There are passages from the Writings of the Báb that refer to the immortality of Quddús. For instance, in a Tablet revealed to the 18th Letter of the Living (the Last, Quddús), the Báb affirms that Quddús is the reflection of Himself.[5] In addition, the Báb stated that the manifestation of Quddús was at the level of *takbir* meaning glorification. According to Nader Saiedi, "In the *Arabic Bayán*, the Báb speaks of Quddús as the realization of the Last—the return of the Islamic station of gatehood, or the station of magnification (takbir)".[6]

Similarly, Nader Saiedi wrote commenting on a passage of the *Arabic Bayán:*

> Quddús is thus a mirror of the First—the Báb—and indeed Quddús' own name, Muḥammad-'Alí, is the mirror image of the Báb's name, 'Alí-Muḥammad. Then the Báb calls Quddús the reality that is above eight unities [*Váhids*] of mirrors.[7]

---

1 This is a reference to Quddús (*God Passes* By, p. 49).

2 In the Abjad numerological system, eight units (wáḥid = 19) = 8 × 19 = 152. See Nader Saiedi, *The Gate of the Heart*, p. 285, for further elaboration. Váḥid also stands for a chapter of the *Bayán*. In Arabic wáḥid means "unity", "a unit", and usually symbolises unity (of God). Dr Saiedi suggests that the number 152 might represent the number of days that the pilgrimage lasted from 2 October 1848 to 15 May 1854 (excluding the about 90-day sojourn in Muscat on the way back).

3 The Báb, *Selections*, pp. 89–90.

4 Edward Granville Browne translated the paragraph as: "But he who recognised him and accompanied him on the Pilgrimage was he who truly performed the Pilgrimage" (In Moojan Momen, *Selections from the Writings of E. G. Browne on the Bábí and Bahá'í Religions*, p. 360).

5 Stephen Lambden, Muḥammad *'Ali Bārfurushi.* Available https://hurqalya.ucmerced.edu/node/4081

6 Nader Saiedi. *Gate of the Heart*, p. 285. The Báb in the *Arabic Bayán*, unity 1.

7 For an elaboration of the concept "eight unities", see Nader Saiedi, *Gate of the Heart*, p. 285.

'Abdu'l-Bahá also wrote that the Báb has said that *"Mirrors to the number of thirteen Váḥids abide beneath his* [Quddús'] *shadow."*[1] "Mirrors" were a designation used by the Báb for certain believers.[2]

The Bahá'í historian Abbas Amanat wrote that Quddús perfectly reflected the light of the Báb:

> In his appeal to the public, as in many other respects, Muḥammad-'Alí of Bárfurúsh [Quddús] was a redoubtable echo of 'Alí-Muḥammad of Shíráz [the Báb]. Though from a different social background and with bonds of loyalty to a community fundamentally different from Shíráz, he embodied many features apparent in the early Báb.

The position of the Letters of the Living

The Letters of the living were the first believers in the Báb. The eighteen Letters of the Living, together with the Báb Himself, comprise the Primal Unity of 19 unities. This Primal Unity gives rise to "all things" (*kullu shay'*, 361 = 19 × 19, or 19 unities in abjad gematria).[3] It is the perfect manifestation of the attributes of God as the First (the Báb, representing *Huva* ("He"), 11 unities in abjad gematria) and the Last (Quddús, representing 8 unities in abjad gematria) of the *Bayán*.[4] Each of these Letters were given their native province as the field of action of their apostolic work. In the *Persian Bayán*, the Letters of the Living are referred to as follows:

> All of these formed the name of the Living One, for these are the names that are the nearest to God; the others are guided by their clear and significant actions, for God began the creation of the *Bayán* through them, and it is to them that the creation of the *Bayán* will again return. [5]

Shoghi Effendi referred to them as:

---

1 'Abdu'l-Bahá, *Light of the World*, p. 11.

2 Certain distinguished disciples were given the title "Mirrors" by the Báb. The terms "Guides" and "Witnesses" were used to describe other worthy believers. Up until the advent of Bahá'u'lláh, Witnesses—or, more precisely, "Witnesses of the *Bayán*"—were people who attested to the truth and veracity of the blessed Báb's words. In the Bábí Revelation, a hierarchy was formed by the Mirrors, Guides, and Witnesses in addition to the Letters of the Living. (See Shoghi Effendi, *God Passes By*, pp. 89–90). In a way, according to the Báb, all believers are mirrors.

3 The abjad gematria or numerology is a writing system in which only consonants are represented or a term for the Arabic numeral system, where each consonant has an abjad numerical value. Abjad values of words are the sum of the digits for each consonant.

4 The *Bayán* ("Exposition") is the Mother Book of the Bábí Dispensation and was revealed by the Báb between 1847 and 1848. It is also considered the Book of Laws of the Báb.

5 Translation of A. L. M. Nicolas, *Le Béyan Persan*, vol. 1, pp. 24–25. Cited in *The Dawn-Breakers*, p. 94, fn. 1.

These "first Letters generated from the Primal Point," this "company of angels arrayed before God on the Day of His coming," these "Repositories of His Mystery," these "Springs that have welled out from the Source of His Revelation," these first companions who, in the words of the Persian *Bayán*, "enjoy nearest access to God," these "Luminaries that have, from everlasting, bowed down, and will everlastingly continue to bow down, before the Celestial Throne," and lastly these "elders" mentioned in the Book of Revelation[1] as "sitting before God on their seats," "clothed in white raiment" and wearing on their heads "crowns of gold" ....[2]

Tablets for Quddús by the Báb

It is not known how many Tablets the Báb wrote to Quddús. We do know that the Báb wrote Tablets to each of the Letters to the Living.[3] Facsimiles of these Tablets written in the Báb's exquisite handwriting are in the illustrated edition of *The Dawn-Breakers.*[4] Out of these eighteen Tablets, only those addressed to Ṭáhirih and Quddús are addressed by name.

The Tablet to the eighteenth Letter of the Living, Quddús, has still not been officially translated, but according to Stephen Lambden, Quddús "is intimately associated with the Báb to the degree that he shares or mirrors his subordinate Divinity."[5] In the aforementioned Tablet for Quddús, the Báb also refers to Himself the mouthpiece of the Divinity echoing the statement "Verily, I am God and there is none other God but Me",[6] echo in various sections of the *Persian Bayán* and other writings.

---

1 Revelation 4:4; 4:17; & 11:16.

2 Shoghi Effendi, *God Passes By*, pp. 7–8.

3 Letter of behalf of Shoghi Effendi to George Townshend dated 30 November 1930. In Shoghi Effendi, *The Unfolding Destiny of the British Bahá'í Community*, p. 425. In this letter the Guardian's secretary stated that "Shoghi Effendi has found in the papers of `Abdu'l-Bahá a complete set of the Bab's Tablets to the Eighteen Letters of the Living all written in His own handwriting and bearing His seal."

4 The *Narrative of Nabíl*, better known as *The Dawn-Breakers*, translated by Shoghi Effendi and published in 1932. Facsimile copies of the Báb's Tablets to the 19 Letters of the Living, the Báb and Bahá'u'lláh appear between pages xxii and xxiii.

5 Stephen Lambden, *Muḥammad 'Ali Bārfurushī*, n.p.

6 The Báb in Nader Saiedi, *Gate of the Heart*, p. 42. Also, in *The Báb, A. L. M. Nicolas' translation of "The Persian Bayán," v 1, p.128; The Dawn-Breakers, p.142.*

In that Tablet to Quddús published in the *Dawn-Breakers*,[1] [2] the Báb referred to him as the "Eighteenth Temple"[3] and affirms that Quddús is a "*manifestation of Myself*"[4] and that He has revealed unto him "*Mine own Essence*".[5]

Author Peter Terry adds that there is a Tablet addressed to Quddús stating "that the first descent of the spirit upon the innermost heart [*fu'ád*] of the Báb took place during the month of Rabí al-Awwal,[6] but without specifying the day of this descent."[7] According to Denis MacEoin, a letter to Quddús is listed in the Báb's *Kitábu'l-Fihrist* ("The Book Catalogue") revealed in June 1845[8] although its content is unknown. It is also reported that the book "Tá'rí<u>kh</u> al-Bábíyya wa miftáh báb al-abwáb" (published in Cairo in 1903) reproduces a letter from the Báb to Quddús with a Persian translation.[9] The Báb must have written numerous tablets to Quddús. It is possible that many of those tablets went lost along with his treatises written during the event of <u>Sh</u>ay<u>kh</u> Ṭabarsí. [10]

At Quddús' death, the Báb wrote eulogies and visitation prayers to his grave equivalent to a whole volume.[11] Appendix part II shows extracts from a beautiful *Tablet of Visitation* revealed by the Báb in honour of him: "A Tablet of Visitation for the martyrs, peace be upon them, who have offered themselves up as a sacrifice for the Last Name of God, Quddús, Quddús, Quddús."

'Alí-Muḥammad (the Báb) and 'Alí-Muḥammad (Quddús)

Interestingly, using abjad gematria the name of 'Alí-Muḥammad (the Báb) or 'Alí-Muḥammad (Quddús) are equivalent to the word Lord. Given that the name 'Alí ('a-70, l-30, í-10) stands for the number 110 and the name Muḥammad (m-40, ḥ-8, m-40, d-4) stands for the number 92, the abjad value for 'Alí-Muḥammad is 110 + 92 = 202. In turn, the number 202 is equivalent to the term *rabb* meaning Lord (r-200, b-2).[12]

Also, numerically speaking the statement *'Alí-Muḥammad, Bábu'lláh* ('Alí-Muḥammad is the Gate of God)" is equivalent to 273.[13] The number 273 was a kind

---

1 *The Dawn-Breakers: Nabíl's Narrative of the Early Days of the Bahá'í Revelation.* Wilmette, IL: Bahá'í Publishing Trust, 1970.

2 Lambden, Stephen. *Muḥammad 'Ali Bārfurushi, Quddūs*, n.p.

3 In Arabic, literally "haykal al<u>th</u>áman gabl 'a<u>sh</u>ar" (هيكل الثامن قبل عشر).

4 In Arabic, literally "Maẓhar nafsí" (مظهر نفسي).

5 In Arabic, literally "Gud tajalit lih benafsí" (قد تجلّيت له بنفسي).

6 5 April 1844.

7 Peter Terry, *A Prophet in Modern Times*, p. 104.

8 Denis MacEoin, *The Sources for Early Bábí Doctrine and History*, p. 50.

9 Denis MacEoin, *The Sources for Early Bábí Doctrine and History*, p. 97.

10 Nabíl-i-A'ẓam, *The Dawn-Breakers*, p. 132.

11 Fazel Mazandarani, *Taríkh Ẓuhúr al-Ḥaqq*, vol. 3, pp. 421–2.

12 Nader Saiedi, *Gate to the Heart*, p. 9.

13 The name *'Alí-Muḥammad* yields 202 and the term *Bábu'lláh* renders 71 (*b*-2, *á*-1, *b*-2, *l*-30, *l*-30, *á*-1, *h*-5).

of secret code to denote the station of the Báb which was concealed in the first years of His revelation. In the *Dalá'il-i-Sab'ih* ("Seven Proofs"), written in the Máh-Kú fortress between July 1847 and April 1848, He wrote, "... I did not wish My identity to be known by men, and gave instructions that My name should be concealed, because I was fully aware of the incapacity of this people ...."[1]

It is noteworthy that the Báb prescribed that all believers should wear a white agatha ring where the following statement is engraved "There is no God but God, Muḥammad is the Messenger of God, 'Alí is the Guardian of God" followed by the number 273.[2] [3] Such a prescription was revealed in the *Khaṣá'il-i-Sab'ih* ("The Seven Proofs or Qualifications") at the time when the Báb and Quddús were on pilgrimage to Mecca, a period where the Islamic laws had not been yet abrogated.[4] About three years later, the Báb instructed followers in the *Persian Bayán* to wear a red cornelian ring with specific verses on it.[5] This would let the wearer identify Him Whom God shall make manifest as He would eventually make His appearance. The inscription was "'Say that God is the Truth, and all else but God is His creation, and all are His worshippers."[6]

Testimonies from Bahá'u'lláh

Quddús

Bahá'u'lláh conferred upon Muḥammad-'Alí of Bárfurú<u>sh</u> the title of Quddús[7] at the Conference of Bada<u>sh</u>t, a designation that the Báb subsequently used in His Writings.

Bahá'u'lláh affirmed that His own Name (Quddús, "The Holy") was given to Muḥammad-'Alí of Bárfurú<u>sh</u> by the Concourse on High.[8] The term *Quddús* derives from *Qudsíyyih* ("sanctity, holiness or sacredness"). The state of *Qudsíyyih* is an exclusive attribute of God that is out of human reach.[9] In 19th-century Persia, it was not used as a personal name because of its religious connotations, unless preceded by the partial name—i.e., the first term of the *iḍáfah* or partial name ['Abdu (slave or servant) + 'l (the) = slave or servant of the ...], *Abdu'l* as in *'Abdu'l-Quddús ("servant of the Most Holy"*).

---

1 The Báb, *Selections*, p. 121.

2 Nader Saiedi, *Gate to the Heart,* p. 300.

3 Stephen Lambden. *The Bab- Risāla Khaṣā'il Sab`a ('The Treatise of the Seven Directives"),* n.p.

4 Denis MacEoin, *Sources for early Bábí Doctrine and History,* p. 62.

5 The Báb, *Persian Bayán* 6:10.

6 Moojan Momen, *Selections from the Writings of E. G. Browne on the Bábí and Bahá'í Religions,* p. 360.

7 Shoghi Effendi, *God Passes By*, p. 32.

8 Christopher Buck and Necati Alkan, *The Cradle of Christianity—and Islam.*

9 Nader Saiedi, *Logos and Civilization,* p. 101.

The Last Point

In the Tablet of All Food (*Lawḥ-i-Kullu'ṭ-Ṭa'ám*),[1] Bahá'u'lláh exalts Quddús with "the sublime appellation of *Nuqṭiy-i-Ukhrá* (the Last Point); whom He elevated, in another Tablet, to a rank second to none except that of the Herald of His Revelation"[2]

The term *Point* is normally used to denote a Manifestation of God. For instance, Muḥammad is the *Point of the Qur'án*, and the Báb is the *Point of the Bayán.* In explaining the symbology of the Point in the Bábí Dispensation, Bahá'u'lláh elaborates:

> *This Point*[3] *is the focal centre of the circle of Names and marketh the culmination of the manifestations of Letters in the world of creation. Through it have appeared indications of the impenetrable Mystery, the adorned Symbol, He Who standeth revealed in the Most Great Name—a Name which is recorded in the luminous Tablet and is inscribed in the holy, the blessed, the snow-white Scroll ....*[4]

In this regard, the Báb explains in the *Bayán* that He is like the sun and the other letters can be compared to mirrors set in front of the brilliant star. Further, the *Bayán* indicates that as *"words and letters are generated through the "Nuqṭih" (The Point, the Báb), similarly, through Him the realities of people will show forth and increase."*[5] The Báb called Himself *the Primal Point* (Nuqṭiy-i-úlá) and Bahá'u'lláh referred to Him with that designation. According to Adib Taherzadeh this designation, "closely identifies him [Quddús]with the Báb, the 'Primal Point', and alludes to the greatness his station."[6]

That Quddús has been named as a Point is a powerful assertion for which an official explanation does not exist. We can only conjecture that given that, firstly, the Báb and Quddús are the first and the last Letters that "together with the Báb, constitute the first Váḥid (unity) of the Dispensation of the *Bayán.*"[7] Secondly, because of the aforementioned principle the Last is a reflection of the First, then we can conclude that Quddús is a corresponding mirror of the Point (the Báb) and therefore both are comparable at the level of a spiritual image. The Báb also said referring to Quddús:

---

1 This Tablet in Arabic was revealed by Bahá'u'lláh prior to the Declaration of His mission in Baghdád, c. 1854–1856, in the first year of His arrival in Baghdád.

2 Shoghi Effendi, *God Passes By*, p. 49. Note that

3 The Báb.

4 Bahá'u'lláh, *Tablets of Bahá'u'lláh*, pp. 101–102.

5 The Báb, in LaFarge, "The Relation of the Báb to the Traditions of Islám", pp. 296–7.

6 Adib Taherzadeh, *The Revelation of Bahá'u'lláh*, Vol. 1, p. 60.

7 Shoghi Effendi, *God Passes By*, p. 8.

Thou art manifest through the manifestation of thy Lord, and art concealed through the concealment of thy Lord. Thou art the first, for there is no first save thee, and the last for there is no last save thee.[1]

Further, Adib Taherzadeh comments on the possibility that a believer can be given the rank of a Messenger of God: "The mind staggers at the thought that owing to the greatness of this Revelation some of its early disciples have been given the station of the Messengers of God."[2] The source of authority for such a command came from the Báb's own spiritual sovereignty: *"All the keys of heaven God hath chosen to place on My right hand, and all the keys of hell on My left ....*[3]

Given that God "doeth whatsoever He willeth and ordaineth whatsoever He pleaseth",[4] Bahá'u'lláh declares that with the same divine entitlement, *"... were He to take a handful of earth and declare it to be the One Whom ye have been following in the past, it would undoubtedly be just and true, even as His real Person ...."*[5] Likewise, Bahá'u'lláh affirmed: *"The station which he who hath truly recognized this Revelation will attain is the same as the one ordained for such prophets of the house of Israel as are not regarded as Manifestations 'endowed with constancy'."*[6]

It is noteworthy that the Báb Himself pronounced that Mullá Ḥusayn, the first believer, was the return of Prophet Muḥammad[7] meaning that he had been invested with *"... none other than the Cause of God"*.[8] This means that this is not a physical return but the return of spiritual attributes such as justice, kindness, service and worshipping God among others. These characteristics relate to the prophet's human personification instead of being associated with his inner divine essence.

In the *Persian Bayán*, the Báb highlights His human nature as distinct to His supernatural one: "The *Nuqta* ["The Point", the Báb] has two stations; one in which he speaks of God, and one in which he speaks of what is other than God: This last is the Station of Servitude wherein he worships God by night and by day".[9] It is perhaps to such a Station of Servitude that the return of Prophet Muḥammad is referring to.

The Báb stated that *He Whom God shall make manifest* (Bahá'u'lláh) also holds the divine prerogative to appoint any person a Prophet:

---

1 The Báb, *Tablet of Visitation for Quddús.* See Appendix part 2.

2 Adib Taherzadeh, The *Revelation of Bahá'u'lláh,* vol.4, p. 210.

3 The Báb, *Selections,* p. 12.

4 Bahá'u'lláh, *Gems of Divine Mysteries,* p. 61.

5 Bahá'u'lláh, *Tablets of Bahá'u'lláh,* p. 184.

6 Shoghi Effendi, *The World Order of Bahá'u'lláh,* p. 111.

7 Bahá'u'lláh, *Tablets of Bahá'u'lláh,* pp. 184.

8 Bahá'u'lláh, *Tablets of Bahá'u'lláh,* pp. 185.

9 Moojan Momen, Selections from the Writings of E. G. Browne on the Babi and Bahá'í Religions, p. 351.

Were He to make of every one on earth a Prophet, all would, in very truth, be accounted as Prophets in the sight of God.[1]

In the day of the revelation of Him Whom God will make manifest all that dwell on earth will be equal in His estimation. Whomsoever He ordaineth as a Prophet, he, verily, hath been a Prophet from the beginning that hath no beginning, and will thus remain until the end that hath no end, inasmuch as this is an act of God. And whosoever is made a Vicegerent by Him, shall be a Vicegerent in all the worlds, for this is an act of God.[2]

A mine of the Cause of God

Nader Saiedi gives an addition to Quddús' station:

> ... in the Tablet of All Food (*Lawḥ-i-Kullu'ṭ-Ṭa'ám*), Bahá'u'lláh ... identifies the Living Countenance [*Ṭal'at-i-Ḥayy*] as both Quddús and Him Whom God shall make manifest! Given the high station of Quddús, and his being the last of the primary "Unity" (Váḥid) of the Bábí dispensation, he is also the representative of the Báb in the Báb's lifetime.[3]

Similarly, in His *Book of the River* (Ṣaḥífiy-i-Shaṭṭíyyih) also revealed in Baghdád,[4] Bahá'u'lláh refers to Quddús as the Mine (or "source/treasure-house")[5] of the Cause of God and as His subsisting quintessence.[6] Treasures and mineral mines are similar because they kept gems of great value in their interiors and yet, nobody knows exactly their value.

Not a Manifestation of God

During the author's journey writing this book, he observed that due to the elevated station of Quddús and out of a love for him, some believers have developed confusing viewpoints regarding his position.[7] Concerning that, the Universal House of Justice has clarified that Quddús "despite these sublime stations [from the Bahá'í Writings,] he [Quddús] is not regarded as an

---

1 The Báb in Bahá'u'lláh, *Epistle to the Son of the Wolf*, p. 155.

2 The Báb in Bahá'u'lláh, *Epistle to the Son of the Wolf*, p. 155.

3 Nader Saiedi, *Concealment and Revelation in Bahá'u'lláh's Book of the River*, p. 48. In reference to Bahá'u'lláh, Nader Saiedi wrote: "The meaning of the title 'Living Countenance' becomes obvious from the Báb's and Bahá'u'lláh's writings: the Living Countenance refers to the return of the Báb (who is the Most Exalted Countenance), but after his own martyrdom, and in a living form", ibid, p.47.

4 Nader Saiedi, *Logos and Civilization*, pp. 29–34.

5 Bahá'u'lláh, *Tablet of All Food.* Provisional translation by Stephen Lambden, *Bahá'í Studies Bulletin*, 3(1), p. 53.

6 Peter Smith, *A Concise Encyclopedia of the Bahá'í Faith*, p. 285. See Juan Cole. *Bahá'u'lláh's Book of the Tigris.* Available www.h-net.org/~bahai/trans/shatt.htm

7 David Piff, *Bahá'í Lore*, p. 299.

independent Manifestation of God",[1] that "despite his uniquely high station, Quddús is not regarded as a Manifestation of God.[2]

According to the Báb, a Manifestation of God has a unique *"station that speaketh from God ... the station of His unknown and unknowable Essence, the Manifestation of His Divinity. Thus, all His revealed divine verses stream forth on behalf of God ... the Supreme Mirror of God, which hath never referred, nor will it ever refer, to aught but God."*[3] This supreme station is that of "*viceregency of God*" where the Manifestations of God[4] "*proclaim unto men the commandments of God which lie enshrined within the divine Spirit*"[5] and it cannot be shared with human beings as it is the spiritual privilege of the Messengers of God such as Krishna, Buddha, Abraham, Moses, Zoroaster, Jesus Christ, Muḥammad, the Báb and Bahá'u'lláh. *"All else beyond this supreme Sign present within Him is His creation,"* the Báb affirms categorically.

Further, the Central Figures of our Faith and the Guardian consistently described the Báb and Bahá'u'lláh as unparalleled by any other souls in their respective religions. 'Abdu'l-Bahá stated that the Bahá'í Faith is based on the following principle:

> *This is the foundation of the belief of the people of Bahá (may my life be offered up for them): "His Holiness, the Exalted One (the Báb), is the Manifestation of the Unity and Oneness of God and the Forerunner of the Ancient Beauty. His Holiness the Abhá Beauty (may my life be a sacrifice for His steadfast friends) is the Supreme Manifestation of God and the Dayspring of His Most Divine Essence. All others are servants unto Him and do His bidding."*[6]

Messengers charged with imposture

Finally, Bahá'u'lláh identifies Quddús as one of the three "*messengers charged with imposture*" mentioned in the *Qur'án* 36:13–14.[7] The other two personages are identified by Shoghi Effendi as the Báb[8] and Bahá'u'lláh.[9] The aforementioned *Qur'án* verse reads:

---

1. Letter to an individual 24 August 1975, written on behalf of the Universal House of Justice.
2. The Universal House of Justice, "Letters of Living, Dawn-Breakers, Quddús, Terraces".
3. The Báb, *Gate of the Heart* by Nader Saiedi, p. 46.
4. The Báb, *Selections,* p. 66.
5. The Báb, *Selections,* p. 64.
6. 'Abdu'l-Bahá, *The Will and Testament of 'Abdu'l-Bahá*, p. 19.
7. Shoghi Effendi, *God Passes By*, p. 49.
8. Shoghi Effendi, *God Passes By*, p. 58.
9. Shoghi Effendi, *God Passes By*, p. 96. See also Nader Saiedi, *Concealment and Revelation in Bahá'u'lláh's Book of the River*, p. 47.

> *Set forth to them the instance of the people of the city when the Sent Ones came to it. When we sent two unto them and they charged them both with imposture–therefore with a third we strengthened them:*
>
> *And they said, "Verily we are the Sent unto you of God."*
>
> *"They said, "Ye are only men like us: Nought hath the God of Mercy sent down. Ye do nothing but lie."*
>
> *They said, "Our Lord knoweth that we are surely sent unto you; to proclaim a clear message is our only duty."*[1]

Regarding this account, Bahá'u'lláh said that He Himself had sent both the Báb and Quddús.[2]

Tablet of the Confrontation

In the *Lawḥ-i-Mubáhilih* (Tablet of the Confrontation) in honour of the Hand of the Cause Mullá Muḥammad-Ṣádiq-i-Khurásání, Bahá'u'lláh praises the virtues and qualities of Quddús.[3] The *Lawḥ-i-Mubáhilih* was revealed in Adrianople in August-September 1867.[4] In the *Tablet of Mubáhilih*, Bahá'u'lláh refers to the protagonist as Muḥammad before 'Alí (that is, Muḥammad 'Alí, Quddús). The text is as follows:

> This is a Tablet which hath been expounded from the Preserved Tablet, that it may be a guide and mercy unto all who dwell in the heavens and on earth. And therein hath been mentioned a remnant of My kindred, he who hath endured in the path of his Lord that which caused the company of the well-favoured to tremble. Blessed art thou, O My Name, for the breezes of the fragrances of the garment of the mighty Joseph who hath been known as Muḥammad-'Alí, have wafted over thee. He, verily, is the one who hath been called by Our name, Quddús among the Concourse on High, and by Subbúḥ [the most Sanctified One] in the cities of eternity, and by all the names in the kingdom of names. Through him, My sovereignty and My power, My grandeur and My majesty were made manifest, if ye be of them that comprehend this truth. We sprinkled upon him from this Sea that which caused him to be severed from all other than Me, moving him from the west of stillness to the east of exhilaration, until he sacrificed his life in My Path. So was his inner being rejoiced, though the eyes of the favoured ones were made to weep. Blessed art thou that thou didst have the honour of meeting him, and of hearing his melodies, and of communing with his wronged and lonely soul. He standeth present before the Throne,

---

1 *Qur'án* 36:14–17 (Rodwell).

2 Christopher Buck and Necati Alkan, *The Cradle of Christianity—and Islam.*

3 Stephen Phelps, *The Writings of Bahá'u'lláh*, p. 60.

4 Bahá'u'lláh, *Lawḥ-i-Mubáhilih*, in Adib Taherzadeh, *The Revelation of Bahá'u'lláh*, vol. 2, p. 293.

and weepeth sore over that which hath been inflicted upon Me by the army of evil ones.[1 2]

It is in Adrianople that Mírzá Yaḥyá, Bahá'u'lláh's half-brother and the one who pretended to be the re-incarnation of Quddús,[3] openly unleashed his rebellion against Bahá'u'lláh after years of covert work sowing discord among the community of Bábís—now Bahá'ís. Mírzá Yaḥyá also claimed the station of prophethood and to be the successor of the Báb.[4] He was summoned to appear in a mosque and to raise his allegations in front of Bahá'u'lláh in public, but he failed to appear. As a result of his rebellion and claims, Bahá'u'lláh severed all ties and communication with this impostor and moved His residence to another location in Adrianople.

In referring to this episode, Bahá'u'lláh wrote in the *Lawḥ-i-Mubáhilih* to Mullá Muḥammad-Ṣádiq-i-Khurásání:

> *O Muḥammad! He Who is the Spirit hath, verily, issued from His habitation, and with Him have come forth the souls of God's chosen ones and the realities of His Messengers. Behold, then, the dwellers of the realms on high above Mine head, and all the testimonies of the Prophets in My grasp. Say: Were all the divines, all the wise men, all the kings and rulers on earth to gather together, I, in very truth, would confront them, and would proclaim the verses of God, the Sovereign, the Almighty, the All-Wise. I am He Who feareth no one, though all who are in heaven and all who are on earth rise up against me. ... This is Mine hand which God hath turned white for all the worlds to behold. This is My staff; were We to cast it down, it would, of a truth, swallow up all created things.*[5]

The name Quddús

The name Quddús means "absolutely holy", "the most sacred", "the most holy", "sanctified",[6] a title initially given to him by Bahá'u'lláh and subsequently used by the Báb. In a passage from the *Kitáb-i-Panj-Sha'n* ("Book of the Five Modes of Revelation"), the Báb says that "Quddús" (holy) is a name of God related to other

1 In 'Abdu'l-Hamid Ishraq-Khavari, *Má'iydih-i-Ásmání,* vol. 4, 277-281.

2 Provisional translation authorised by the Bahá'í World Centre.

3 Edward Granville Browne, *The Tarí<u>kh</u>-i-Jadíd,* p. 336.

4 Necati Alkan, *Dissent and heterodoxy in the late Ottoman Empire*, p. 84.

5 Shoghi Effendi, *God Passes By*, pp. 168–9.

6 Quddús (قدّوس) is the Arabicised Hebrew *Kadosh* (קָדוֹשׁ), being both Semitic languages. The proto-semitic root *q-d-s* (holy/sacred) root is found in several sections of the Old Testament (e.g, *Genesis* 2:1–3; *Genesis* 2:3–1; *Exodus* 19:5–6). For instance, *Leviticus* (19:1–2) reads: "I Yahve your God am Holy". In turn, there are many derivatives of the same root in the *Qur'án* (e.g., 59:23; 5:21; 20:12; 79:16; 2:87; 2:253; 5:110; 16:102; 2:30). For instance, *Qur'án* (62:1) states that God is "the Sovereign, the Holy, the All- Mighty, the All-Wise". In the Bahá'í Writings the derivatives are *muqqadas* (saint/holy), *aṣdaq*, or *aqdas* (sacred) from where the term *Kitáb-i-Aqdas* (the Most Holy/Sacred Book) comes from.

divine attributes such as "sanctified" (muqaddas) and "sacred" (al-aqdas).[1] According to The Merriam-Webster Dictionary, "Holy" means "exalted or worthy of complete devotion as one perfect in goodness and righteousness".[2]

Quddús (قدّوس) is the Arabicised Hebrew *Kadosh* (קָדוֹשׁ), being both Semitic languages. The proto-semitic root *q-d-s* (holy/sacred) root is found in several sections of the Old Testament (e.g., *Genesis* 2:1–3; *Genesis* 2:3–1; *Exodus* 19:5–6).

It is used to denote the attributes of God. For instance, *Leviticus* (19:1–2) reads: "I Yahve your God am Holy (קָדוֹשׁ)". In *Isaiah* (6:3) we read, "Holy (קָדוֹשׁ) , holy (קָדוֹשׁ), holy (קָדוֹשׁ) is the Lord Almighty; the whole earth is full of his glory".

"The name Quddús is somewhat difficult to account for", Reverend T.K. Cheyne remarked, "and yet it must be understood, because it involves a claim."[3] In a Tablet in honour of Quddús, the Báb calls him by his name three times:

Holy (Quddús), *Holy* (Quddús), *Holy* (Quddús)*! The Glory of God, besides whom there is no other God, rest upon thy heart and the heart of whomsoever is in thy heart, and upon thy spirit and the spirit of whomsoever is in thy spirit, and upon thy soul and whomsoever is in thy soul, and upon thy body and whomsoever is in thy body.*[4]

There are several derivatives of the word Quddús in the *Qur'án* (e.g., 59:23; 5:21; 20:12; 79:16; 2:87; 2:253; 5:110; 16:102; 2:30). For instance, in verse 62:1, Muḥammad mentions the term Quddús is used to describe God: "*Whatever is in the heavens and whatever is on the earth glorifies God, the King, the Holy* (ٱلْقُدُّوسِ), *the Almighty, the All-Wise*". Also, in the *Qur'án* (2:253), Muḥammad said, "*We assisted Him* [Jesus] *with the Holy Spirit* [bi-rúh al-Quddús]." In this regard, Nader Saiedi notes that, "Referring to the Qur'anic prophecy of the descent of the Spirit, the Báb identifies Himself with Jesus and the Holy Spirit".[5]

In Arabic the derivative is *Muqqadas* which is the most general form to describe anything that is regarded as holy or sacred, such as a shrine, a person or a religious text. Its superlative form is *Aqdas* (the holiest or the most sacred) from where the term *Kitáb-i-Aqdas* (the Most Holy/Sacred Book) comes from. The term *aqdas* is often used to describe God or a religious figure.

The term *rúḥ al-Quddús* is used in Persian mysticism to denote literally the Holy Spirit symbolized spiritually by the angel Gabriel.[6]." It is also interesting that

---

1 The Báb, *Kitáb-i-Panj-Sha'n*, pp. 223-224.

2 *Merriam-Webster.com Dictionary, Merriam-Webster*, "Holy". Available online at: www.merriam-webster.com/dictionary/holy. Accessed 28 Aug. 2023.

3 Thomas Kelly Cheyne, *The Reconciliation of Races and Religions*, p. 85.

4 The Báb, *Tablet of Visitation for Quddús*. See Appendix part II.

5 Nader Saiedi, *Gate of the Heart*, p. 31.

6 Suhrawardī. *The Philosophy of Illumination*, p. 151.

in the Qayyúmu'l-Asmá the Báb declares "Verily, I am Quddús ("Verily, I am the Holy One", "اني انا القدوس")[1]

The Báb changed the invocation "*In the Name of God, the Compassionate, the Merciful*" (Bismi'lláhi'r-Raḥmáni'r-Raḥím) which opens most of the chapters of the Qur'án, for another one where the sanctity of God is invoked, "*In the Name of God, the Most Exalted, the Most Holy*" (Bismi'lláhu'l-Amna'u'l-Aqdas). [2]As discussed earlier, *Aqdas* (Most Holy) is the superlative of the term *Quddús* (Holy).

In a Tablet in honour of Quddús, the Báb wrote of him:

> *Holy, Holy, Holy! The Glory of God, besides whom there is no other God, rest upon thy heart and the heart of whomsoever is in thy heart, and upon thy spirit and the spirit of whomsoever is in thy spirit, and upon thy soul and whomsoever is in thy soul, and upon thy body and whomsoever is in thy body.*[3]

In Christian liturgy, the aforementioned topos in Latin would be *Sanctus!, Sanctus! Sanctus!*[4]

Finally, it is noteworthy that Quddús is a popular first name in the Bahá'í community.

Testimonies from 'Abdu'l-Bahá

Three holy souls

On the same theme of the three messengers and the association mentioned above between Bahá'u'lláh, the Báb and Quddús, 'Abdu'l-Bahá interprets the identity of three birds seen in a dream of an inquirer. 'Abdu'l-Bahá wrote:

> *Verily, the three birds are the three holy souls. The one on the right is His Holiness the great Báb, the one on the left is His Honor the Quddús* [the Saint], *the glorious soul, and the great bird in the middle is the Greatest Name* [Bahá'u'lláh]. *The light shining from the Supreme Horizon is the Beauty of al-Abhá. These birds descended from an infinite height and the nearer they came to earth the more their majesty and glory became manifest. All nations were promised by a sure promise and were awaiting with anxiety and longing the coming of the Promised One. The two birds accompanying the great bird in the center signifies that the Báb and His Honor the Quddús were both under the wings of the Greatest Name. As those birds descended and their shadows extended vertically over the expectants, as the sun approacheth the zenith at noontide, at this time thou hast seen a majestic being in the form of man upon the back of the huge bird in the center. This person in the human form is the "divine station" mentioned in the Bible: "Let*

---

1 The Báb, *Qayyúmu'l-Asmá,* Sura 91, Al Rabí', "The Fourth", verse 7, p. 188.

2 The Báb, *Selections,* p. 111.

3 The Báb, *Tablet of Visitation for Quddús.* See Appendix part 2.

4 Claude Gilliot, *Is the Qur'an partly the fruit of a progressive and collective work?,* p. 92.

us make man in our image after our likeness." [Genesis 1:26] *And the divine lights were reflected from the reality of the Greatest Name. Although this station is far from the minds and understandings, yet its lights are apparent, its rays reflected and its brilliancy manifested throughout the universe.*[1]

Quddús is referred to in the Bible

Shoghi Effendi paraphrased the words of 'Abdu'l-Bahá when the latter wrote regarding the prophetic words in Chapter 11 of the *Book of Revelation* of John about Quddús that his

> ... appearance the Revelation of St. John the Divine anticipated as one of the two "Witnesses" into whom, ere the "second woe is past", the "spirit of life from God" must enter.[2]

On commenting on the above Apocalyptic chapter (Revelation 1:1–14), 'Abdu'l-Bahá confirmed that the Báb and Quddús were the "two witnesses", being the spiritual return of the Prophet Muḥammad and Imám 'Alí, respectively:[3]

> *And after three days and a half the Spirit of life from God entered into them, and they stood upon their feet; and great fear fell upon them which saw them." Three days and a half, as we explained earlier, is 1,260 years. These two Persons whose bodies were lying soulless—that is, the teachings and the religion that Muḥammad had established and that 'Alí had promoted, whose reality had vanished, and of which only an empty form had remained—were again endowed with spirit. That is, the spirituality of the religion of God that had become materiality, the virtues that had become vices, the love of God that had become hatred, the light that had become darkness, the divine qualities that had become satanic attributes, the justice that had become tyranny, the mercy that had become malice, the sincerity that had become hypocrisy, the guidance that had become error, the purity that had become carnality—all these divine teachings, heavenly virtues and perfections, and spiritual bounties—were, after three and a half days (which by the terminology of the Sacred Scriptures is 1,260 years) renewed by the advent of the Báb and by the allegiance of Quddús.*[4]

Moon of Guidance

For 'Abdu'l-Bahá, Quddús is considered as the *"Moon of Guidance"* and the Báb as the *"Sun of Reality"*.[5] This statement reaffirms the position of Quddús as the

---

1 'Abdu'l-Bahá Abbás, *Tablets of Abdul-Baha Abbas,* vol. 3, pp. 678–81.

2 Shoghi Effendi, *God Passes By*, p. 49.

3 'Alí (c. 600–661 CE), the cousin and son-in-law of the Prophet Muḥammad, was designated as His successor.

4 'Abdu'l-Bahá, *Some Answered Questions,* pp. 62–3.

5 Shoghi Effendi, *God Passes By*, p. 49. Also, in 'Abdu'l-Bahá, *Some Answered Questions,* p. 55.

Báb's most outstanding disciple. Bahá'u'lláh explains the divine metaphor of the sun and moon:

> *... that in every age and Dispensation, whenever the invisible Essence was revealed in the person of His Manifestation, certain souls, obscure and detached from all worldly entanglements, would seek illumination from the Sun of Prophethood and Moon of divine guidance, and would attain unto the divine Presence.*[1]

A promoter of the Faith of the God

'Abdu'l-Bahá said that the Báb and Quddús, *"these two great Personages—one the Founder and the other the promoter—arose and were as two candlesticks, for they illumined the whole world with the light of truth."*[2] For more than one year, between mid-1845 and almost all of 1846, Quddús had been travelling throughout Persia teaching the Cause of the Báb. A non-Bahá'í source referred to him as "the Bábí activist"[3] because of his prominence spreading the teachings of the Báb.

'Abdu'l-Bahá also affirmed of Quddús:

> *This personage set himself to exalt the word of the Báb with the utmost steadfastness .... In delivery and style he was "evident magic", and in firmness and constancy superior to all.*[4]

Testimonies from Shoghi Effendi

Quddús as the first in rank

Shoghi Effendi wrote, "The last, but in rank the first, of these Letters [of the Living] to be inscribed on the Preserved Tablet was the erudite, the twenty-two year old Quddús, a direct descendant of the Imám Ḥasan and the most esteemed disciple of Siyyid Káẓim ...."[5] In a letter written on his behalf, Shoghi Effendi stated that Quddús' "station was no doubt a very exalted one, and far above that of any of the Letters of the Living, including the first Letter, Mullá Ḥusayn."[6] Shoghi Effendi also referred to Quddús as "the essence of sanctity and purity""[7]

The Last Name of God

Much has been speculated about the infinite titles of the Divinity. According to a tradition, Prophet Muḥammad said, *"Verily, God has ninety-nine names, one*

---

1 Bahá'u'lláh, *The Kitáb-i-Íqán*, p. 221.

2 'Abdu'l-Bahá, *Some Answered Questions*, p. 63.

3 Mohammad Ali Kazembeyki, *Society, Politics and Economics*, p. 118.

4 'Abdu'l-Bahá, *A Traveller's Narrative*, p. 19.

5 Shoghi Effendi, *God Passes By*, p. 9.

6 Letter dated 11 November 1936, written on behalf of Shoghi Effendi to an individual believer. In The Universal House of Justice, "Letters of Living ...".

7 Shoghi Effendi, *Lawḥ-i-Garn-i-Áhibáy-i-Sharq*, p. 31,

hundred minus one, he who reckons them enters paradise",[1] and those names have been compiled by many scholars.[2] We know in the Bahá'í Faith that the Greatest Name of God (*Ism-i-A'ẓam*)[3] is Bahá' ("Glory").[4] The famous Islamic philosopher Muḥammad ibn Ḥusayn al-'Ámilí (known as Shaykh Bahá'í) (1547–1621) once wrote, "The Greatest Name is unknown to man, but in the list of all the Names of God it stands first."[5] He adopted the pen name Bahá'í after being inspired by the words of Imám Muḥammad al-Báqir (the fifth Imám) and Imám Ja'far aṣ-Ṣadíq (the sixth Imám).

The names of God are an important concept in the Bahá'í Faith since the Manifestations of God personify them:

> *It is therefore established that all names and attributes return unto these sublime and sanctified Luminaries. Indeed, all names are to be found in their names, and all attributes can be seen in their attributes. Viewed in this light, if thou wert to call them by all the names of God, this would be true, as all these names are one and the same as their own Being.*[6]

According to Islamic theological scholars, there are 99 Names of God—also known as Attributes of God—recorded in the Sunnah, most of which are to be found in the *Qur'án*, and some in the hadiths, although Muḥammad never specified them as a list. Many of the Names or Attributes of God are derived from the verbs referring to His "Doings" or are derivatives of the Arabic synonyms of those verbs. Hence, there are some variations over which names were to be included. Christian authors have also attempted to explore the names of God in their own traditions.[7]

We do not know what the specific names of God are. An indication can be obtained by reflecting on titles that Bahá'u'lláh and the Báb conferred upon some believers associated with a Name of God (Ismu'lláh). The Báb and Bahá'u'lláh conferred upon certain believers the title of *Ismu'lláh* ("The Name of God") and they were addressed by the believers as such by way of a courtesy. For instance, the Báb honoured Siyyid 'Abdu'r-Raḥím of Iṣfahán with the title *of Ismu'lláhi'r-Raḥím* ("The Name of God, the Merciful") which was later confirmed by Bahá'u'lláh.[8]

---

1 Yousef Casewit, *The Mystics of al-Andalus*, p. 139.

2 Boris Handal, *Muḥammad, Profeta de Dios*, pp. 115–6.

3 Bahá'í World Centre. *The Transliteration System Used in Bahá'í Literature.* Available at: https://www.bahai.org/library/transliteration/1#691938942

4 A. Q. Faizi, *Explanation of the Symbol of the Greatest Name*, p 10.

5 A. Q. Faizi, *Explanation of the Symbol of the Greatest Name*, p 7.

6 Bahá'u'lláh, *Gems of Divine Mysteries*, pp. 34–5.

7 See Ann Spangler, *The Names of God;* Máire Byrne, *The Names of God in Judaism, Christianity, and Islam;* & Stone et al, *Names of God.*

8 Moojan Momen, *The Bahá'í Communities of Iran*, vol. 2, p. 5. .

In turn, Bahá'u'lláh granted the title of *Ismu'lláhu'l-Mihdí* ("The Name of God, He Who is Guided") to Siyyid Mihdíy-i-Daháji; *Ismu'lláhi'l-Javád* ("The Name of God, the All-Bountiful") to Muḥammad-Javád-i-Qazvíní; *Ismu'lláhu'l-Jamál* ("The Name of God, the Beautiful") to Jamál-i-Burujirdí; *Ismu'lláhu'l-Aṣdaq* ("The Name of God, the True") to Mullá Ṣádiq-i-Khurásání; *Ismu'llahi'l-Muníb* ("The Name of God, the Mandator") to Jinab-i-Munír; and *Ismu'lláhu'l-Zayn* ("The Name of God, the Ornament") to Zaynu'l-Muqarrabín.[1] It was upon Quddús that the Báb granted the superior designation of Ismu'lláhu'l-Ákhar (the "The Last name of God").[2]

Also, several Bahá'í writers has referred to him in inspiring terms such as, "the one who had primacy in the company of His first eighteen disciples",[3] "the gentle, unwavering Quddús",[4] "the learned and confident Quddús, the most venerated of all the first disciples of the Báb",[5] "the flower of the Báb's disciples",[6] ""a redoubtable echo of 'Alí-Muḥammad of Shíráz [the Báb]",[7] "the greatest of all the believers",[8] "the last and greatest of the apostles"[9] "His most illumined follower"[10], "deeply versed in theology", [11] "His leading disciple",[12] "Though young in years, he showed that indomitable courage and faith which none among the disciples of his Master could exceed",[13]among other references.

From the above testimonies, it can be concluded Quddús was a human being endowed with a spiritual nature and powers distinctive from any other human being. He was created to live and serve as the regent of the Báb. With his belief in the Báb and His teachings, Quddús reached a great level of spiritual understanding and devotion.

---

1 Hasan Balyuzi, *Bahá'u'lláh King of Glory,* p. 33.

2 Nabíl-i-A'ẓam, *The Dawn-Breakers,* p. 414.

3 Hasan Balyuzi, *Edward Granville Browne and the Bahá'í Faith,* p. 42

4 Hasan Balyuzi, *Bahá'u'lláh, The King of Glory,* p.81.

5 Hasan Balyuzi, *Bahá'u'lláh,* p. 588.

6 Harriet Pettibone, *Quddús: The Companion of the Báb,* p. 139.

7 Abbas Amanat, *Resurrection and renewal,* p. 184.

8 George Townshend, *Nabíl's History of the Báb,* p. 431.

9 George Townshend, *Nabíl's History of the Báb,* p. 437.

10 Bertha Hyde Kirkpatrick, *Consultation and Sacrifice,* p. 77.

11 Hasan Balyuzi, *Bahá'u'lláh,* p. 588.

12 Moojan Momen, *The Bahá'í Communities of Iran,* vol. 2, p. 249

13 Nabíl-i-A'ẓam, *The Dawn-Breakers,* p. 72.

20
Reverence for Quddús

Chapter content
Love for Quddús A source of guidance Obeisance Spiritual authority Turning to Quddús. Circumabulating his chamber Spoke from behind a curtain Future predictions

"After the martyrdom of Quddús," wrote Nosrat Mohammad-Hosseini, "the Báb honored him with an exalted station that rivals that of the most venerated saints and holy persons of other religions".[1] Furthermore, the Báb testified:

> *Through thee* [Quddús]*, all beings extol God; through thee, all beings glorify His sanctity; through thee, all beings magnify His oneness; through thee, all beings celebrate His grandeur.*[2]

"Had it not been for My incarceration in this mountain fastness, I would have felt it My bounden duty to go in person to help My beloved Quddús,"[3] the Báb once stated. 'Abdu'l-Bahá commented that, *"... the Báb did full justice to speech in praising and glorifying him, accounting his uprising as an assistance from the Unseen.*[4]

Quddús' presence strongly radiated authority, majesty and ascendancy. Even when he was younger all of the believers respected him highly. His services, scholarship, his purity and station had drawn the admiration of the Bábís. Although his most significant title of being the "Last Name of God" was bestowed posthumously, it is clear from the chronicles that His supremacy as God's "Hidden Treasure" was always accepted prima facie. In particular, Mullá Ḥusayn was the first to surrender his spiritual entitlements and put himself lovingly at the service of Quddús, an example that all Bábís followed. This section bears testimonies of these dispositions.

---

1 Nosratollah Mohammad-Hosseini, *Qoddus, Moḥammad-'Ali Bārforuši, n.p.*

2 The Báb, *Tablet of Visitation for Quddús.* See Appendix part 2.

3 Hasan Balyuzi, *Bahá'u'lláh,* p. 67.

4 'Abdu'l-Bahá, *A Traveller's Narrative,* p. 19.

Love for Quddús

At Shaykh Ṭabarsí Mullá Ḥusayn commanded the Bábís to treat Quddús with the same respect they would have for the Báb Himself.[1] Mullá Ḥusayn whom Shoghi Effendi described as, the "lion-hearted Mullá Ḥusayn",[2] the "First Letter of the Living"; whom Bahá'u'lláh referred to as the recipient of "the effulgent glory of the Sun of divine Revelation" and averred that "[b]ut for him, God would not have been established upon the seat of His mercy, nor ascended the throne of eternal glory",[3] had in Quddús an object of his personal reverence:

> [Mullá Ḥusayn] ... pledged his undying loyalty to him who so powerfully mirrored forth the radiance of his own beloved Master. He felt it to be his first obligation to subordinate himself entirely to Quddús, to follow in his footsteps, to abide by his will, and to ensure by every means in his power his welfare and safety. Until the hour of his martyrdom, Mullá Ḥusayn remained faithful to his pledge.
>
> In the extreme deference which he henceforth showed to Quddús, he was solely actuated by a firm and unalterable conviction of the reality of those supernatural gifts which so clearly distinguished him from the rest of his fellow-disciples. No other consideration induced him to show such deference and humility in his behaviour towards one who seemed to be but his equal. Mullá Ḥusayn's keen insight swiftly apprehended the magnitude of the power that lay latent in him, and the nobility of his character impelled him to demonstrate befittingly his recognition of that truth.[4]

In the *Lawḥ-i-Kullu'ṭ-Ṭa'ám* ("Tablet of All Food"), revealed in Baghdád,[5] Bahá'u'lláh, five years older than Quddús, poignantly reflects on His afflictions and tenderly calls to memory Quddús, supplicating and hoping that he would be there to console and wipe away Bahá'u'lláh's tears of suffering. Bahá'u'lláh refers to him as the *"Countenance of My Love"* (Ṭal'at ḥubbí)[6] and wishes He could implore and entreat Quddús to let Him rest on the cushion of his sanctity as in the past times.[7]

---

1 Nabíl-i-A'ẓam, *The Dawn-Breakers,* p. 350.

2 Shoghi Effendi, *God Passes By,* p. 39.

3 Bahá'u'lláh, *The Kitáb-i-Íqán,* p. 223.

4 Nabíl-i-A'ẓam, *The Dawn-Breakers,* p. 265.

5 Shoghi Effendi, *God Passes By,* p. 118.

6 Bahá'u'lláh, *Tablet of All Food.* Provisional tr. by Stephen Lambden. *Bahá'í Studies Bulletin,* 3(1), pp. 4–67, 1984. Available https://bahai-library.com/bahaullah_lawh_kull_taam and https://hurqalya.ucmerced.edu/node/4221

7 *Ṭal'at ḥubbí* in Arabic طلعة حبّي. See Stephen Lambden, *Muḥammad 'Ali Bārfurushi, Quddūs.* Available https://hurqalya.ucmerced.edu/node/4081

Shoghi Effendi informs that around 1863 the believers in Baghdád commemorated together the memory of Quddús in "gatherings, lasting far into the night, in which they loudly celebrated, with prayers, poetry and song, the praises of the Báb, of Quddús and of Bahá'u'lláh ....[1] Moojan Momen adds: "One night they would chant the words of the Báb, the next those of Quddús, the foremost disciple of the Báb, and the next the writings of Bahá'u'lláh. Sometimes these recitals would go on until dawn."[2] 'Abdu'l-Bahá stated that Mullá Ḥusayn *"sacrificed his life in the path of Quddús."*[3] Hatcher and Amrollah told the story of Sa'íd-i-Jabbáví who at Shaykh Ṭabarsí showed amazing bravery:

> He was shot in the abdomen, and, though severely wounded, managed to walk until he reached the presence of Quddús. He joyously threw himself at his feet and expired.[4]

Such statements portray the devotion and respect Quddús attracted among the Bábís despite being younger than most of his fellow co-religionaries. Within their hearts, burned an unbreakable fervour for Quddús, a profound veneration for his sanctity, and an unwavering adherence to his utterances, that touched the depths of their souls. This reverence continued even after his death; and this despite the statement by Quddús that "I have no rank or station."[5]

Shoghi Effendi referred to him as the "venerated Quddús".[6] The Bábís referred to him as their "beloved leader",[7] "His Excellency the Most Holy",[8] "His Holiness Quddús" and as the "Countenance of the Friend".[9] The anecdotes in this chapter are intended to portray the nature and dimension of this love that people held for Quddús.

A source of guidance

The companions found in Quddús a fountain of knowledge and spiritual understanding:

> In my eagerness to unravel the subtleties of the traditions concerning the promised Qá'im, I several times approached Quddús and requested him to enlighten me regarding that subject. Though at first reluctant, he eventually acceded to my wish. The manner of his answer, his convincing and illuminating explanations, served to heighten the sense of awe and of veneration which his presence inspired. He dispelled whatever doubts

---

1 Shoghi Effendi, *God Passes By*, p. 135.

2 Moojan Momen, *A short biography of Bahá'u'lláh*, p. 82.

3 'Abdu'l-Bahá, *Star of the West*, III:10, 8 September 1912, p. 8.

4 John Hatcher and Hemmant Amrollah, *Reunion with the Beloved*, pp. 54–5.

5 Hooshmand Dehghan, *Ganj-i-Pinhán*, p. 209.

6 Shoghi Effendi, *God Passes By*, p. 90.

7 Nabíl-i-A'ẓam, *The Dawn-Breakers*, pp. 425.

8 Cited in E. G. Browne, *A Traveller's Narrative*, Note P, p. 307.

9 *The Narrative of Ḥájí Naṣír-i-Qazvíní*, n.p.

lingered in our minds, and such were the evidences of his perspicacity that we came to believe that to him had been given the power to read our profoundest thoughts and to calm the fiercest tumult in our hearts.[1]

Obeisance

Mullá Ḥusayn always encouraged the companions to obey Quddús as their spiritual leader. Siyyid Muḥammad-Ḥusayn wrote in this regard:

> His holiness the Qá'im of Khurásán [Mullá Ḥusayn], due to the injuries sustained to the blessed lips of his holiness the Qá'im of Gílán [Quddús], was beyond himself and had ceased to consume any food .... His holiness the Qá'im of Khurásán [Mullá Ḥusayn] gathered the companions and was giving them advice and consolation. He told them that acting in counter to his wishes and disobeying his command is not acceptable nor seemly. On the contrary, obedience to his eminence [Quddús] is obedience to God. He is the ark of salvation. If today you are working hard, tomorrow you will be in comfort and shall relax ...."[2]

Great reverence was shown to Quddús as the representative of the Báb and on account of his exalted station. It was written that:

> As his holiness [Quddús] would pace back and forth, all would collectively prostrate. Even his eminence the Báb [Mullá Ḥusayn] would prostrate towards him [Quddús]. He commanded that the companions not to sleep more than two to three hours at night and sleep with their weapons ready, and to spend the rest of the night in offering obligatory prayer, reading the verses of *Qur'án*, and the verses of His Holiness the Remembrance [the Báb]. They should not all sleep at the same time, but to sleep in turns. Since the inhabitants of Mázindarán are enemies, so those who have enemies should not sleep comfortably and without precaution.[3]

A hundred and seventy years ago, Persian culture obliged people to bow down before a person of higher rank. Presently, we only stand for an important person, but in those times, people prostrated themselves to rulers, high clergy, civil authorities or elders as a matter of respect. For instance, when Sayyáh returned from pilgrimage to Shaykh Ṭabarsí on behalf of the Báb, he visited the house of Bahá'u'lláh in Ṭihrán where the great Vaḥíd[4] was staying. Vaḥíd, "oblivious of the pomp and circumstance to which a man of his position had been accustomed, rushed forward and flung himself at the feet of the pilgrim [Sayyáh]. Holding his

---

1 Nabíl-i-A'ẓam, *The Dawn-Breakers,* p. 353.

2 Siyyid Muḥammad-Ḥusayn, *Vaqa'i-i Mimiyyih,* p. 54.

3 Luṭf 'Alí Mírzá Shírází, *A Chronicle of the Babi Uprising,* pp. 71–2.

4 The Guardian of the Faith pointed him out as "a man of immense erudition and the most preeminent figure to enlist under the banner of the new Faith" (Shoghi Effendi, God Passes By, p. 50) and "the most learned, the most influential, and the most accomplished among the followers of the Báb"(Nabíl-i-A'ẓam, The Dawnbreakers, p. 653).

legs, which had been covered with mud to the knees, in his arms, he [Vaḥíd] kissed them devoutly.[1]" It is noteworthy, that the Báb forbade the practice of kissing the hands of clergymen.[2] Likewise, in the *Kitáb-i-Aqdas,* revealed around 1872, Bahá'u'lláh "condemns such practices as prostrating oneself before another person and other forms of behaviour that abase one individual in relation to another"[3]

Spiritual authority

According to Nabíl:

> The knowledge and sagacity which Quddús displayed on those occasions, the confidence with which he spoke, and the resource and enterprise which he demonstrated in the instructions he gave to his companions, reinforced his authority and enhanced his prestige. These at first supposed that the profound reverence which Mullá Ḥusayn showed towards him was dictated by the exigencies of the situation rather than prompted by a spontaneous feeling of devotion to his person. His own writings and general behaviour gradually dispelled such doubts and served to establish him still more firmly in the esteem of his companions.[4]

Turning to Quddús

It is reported that on more than one occasion and as a sign of reverence, the companions would turn to Quddús as a Qiblih (Arabic Qibla) when they said their obligatory prayers:

> One day they decided to determine the total number of companions. It was four hundred and forty-four individuals. During the festivities of Qurbán [7 November 1848],[5] and Ghadír [15 November].[6] as per the specific instruction of his eminence the Báb[7] [Mullá Ḥusayn], all companions gathered for the mass prayer. Then, a sermon from his writings [Quddús] was read. A Tablet of Visitation was read by the honourable Mírzá Muḥammad-Báqir, the junior. His holiness Quddús commanded that the night prayer is obligatory, which needs to be observed. All the companions performed the *nafl* prayer [supererogatory prayer].
>
> In days to follow, a number of imáms (prayer leaders) were determined to

---

1 Nabíl-i-A'ẓam, *The Dawn-Breakers,* p. 432.

2 Armin Eschraghi, *From Bábí Movement to the Bahá'í Faith,* p. 381.

3 Bahá'í World Centre, *The Kitáb-i-Aqdas,* note #57, p. 193.

4 Nabíl-i-A'ẓam, *The Dawn-Breakers,* pp. 356–7.

5 A religious festival in the Islamic calendar commemorating Abraham's willingness to sacrifice his son in obedience to God's command.

6 A religious festival in the Islamic calendar commemorating Muḥammad's appointment of 'Alí as His successor.

7 Mullá Ḥusayn's designation was Bábu'l-Báb (The gate of the Gate). Not to be confused with His Holiness the Báb.

> lead the congregation in congregational prayer. The companions formed two lines of prayer behind them and to follow them in prayers. Ḥájí Mírzá Ḥasan, Jináb-i-Mullá Muḥammad-Ṣádiq, Mírzá Muḥammad Mahalátí and Mullá Zaynu'l-'Abidín Miyámaí were appointed imáms. While we were standing together in rows to offer prayers in congregation [facing the prayer leaders who in turn would be looking toward Mecca, the Islamic point of direction for prayers], Mírzá Amín instead turned towards his holiness [Quddús]. Mullá Jalíl also turned towards Quddús in prayer... [1]

The Qiblih (literally "direction", In Arabic) is that part to which people direct their prayers, which was in the Mecca for the Muslim (*Qur'án*, 2:144), Jerusalem for Jews (*Daniel* 6:10) and the East for Christians (*Ad orientem*). The Báb referred to Himself as the House of God—i.e. the new Qiblih[2] until the appearance of *Him Whom God shall make manifest*. That the Bábís in Shaykh Ṭabarsí decided to pray in the direction of Quddús was probably a reflection of their abandonment of the Mecca traditional practice, perceiving Quddús as the Báb's representative as their main spiritual leader, in those months, leading the congregational prayers. In Islam the imám (prayer leader) led the community devotions facing the Qiblih while the faithful observed their ritual prostrations behind him.

It appears that the Bábís had already disregarded the practice of turning to Mecca for their obligatory prayers as early as the beginning of 1846. A chronicler wrote that:

> On a number of occasions, Mullá Ḥusayn and the congregation of the believers came to the Maqṣúrih portico of the Masjid Gawhar-Shád [in Mashhad] and facing Shíráz would stand for the performance of the obligatory prayers, while others would follow his example.[3]

In general, Armin Eschraghi wrote that, in the *Kitáb al-Rúh* ("Book of the Spirit", sura 206) revealed during His pilgrimage to Mecca with Quddús, the Báb" declared all Friday prayers as unlawful if they were conducted by a leader not appointed by him."[4] Here in Shaykh Ṭabarsí, we found Quddús and Mullá Ḥusayn leading the congregational prayer with their authority as the First and the Last letter of the Living, the Báb's two "ablest lieutenants" as Shoghi Effendi called them.[5]

We can always speculate that Quddús and Mullá Ḥusayn considered themselves as congregational prayer leaders appointed by the Báb according to the provisions of the *Kitáb al-Rúh* ("Book of the Spirit", sura 206) discussed in the previous section.

---

1 Luṭf 'Alí Mírzá Shírází, *A Chronicle of the Bábí Uprising*, pp. 71–2.

2 Nader Saiedi, *Gate of the Heart*, p. 279.

3 In Ahang Rabbani, *The Genesis of the Bahá'í Faith in Khurásán*, Chapter 2, pp. 17-18.

4 Armin Eschraghi, *Undermining the Foundations of Orthodoxy*, p. 236.

5 Shoghi Effendi, in Nabíl-i-A'ẓam, *The Dawn-Breakers*, p. 653.

Circumabulating his chamber

The believers used to circumambulate[1] around the abode of Quddús:

> On the night of the festival of Qurbán, Mullá Ḥusayn circumambulated the house that was the residence of His Holiness Quddús. Other believers in obedience to the Bábu'l-Báb (Mullá Ḥusayn) also circumambulated the house of Quddús. This respect was repeated every night, and each night Mullá Ḥusayn circumambulated around the house of Quddús. Each time that Quddús appeared out of his residence or rode his horse, Mullá Ḥusayn circumambulated his Holiness [Quddús].[2]

On the matter of *Him Whom God shall make manifest,* Mullá Ḥusayn alerted the believers about the significance of the year "80" which refers to the year 1280 AH (1863–1864 CE) when Bahá'u'lláh declared His Mission in Baghdád. An eyewitness left this account:

> Many a night I saw Mullá Ḥusayn circle round the shrine within the precincts of which Quddús lay asleep. How often did I see him emerge in the mid-watches of the night from his chamber and quietly direct his steps to that spot and whisper the same verse with which we all had greeted the arrival of the beloved visitor! With what feelings of emotion I can still remember him as he advanced towards me, in the stillness of those dark and lonely hours which I devoted to meditation and prayer, whispering in my ears these words: "Banish from your mind, O Mullá Mírzá Muḥammad, these perplexing subtleties and, freed from their trammels, arise and seek with me to quaff the cup of martyrdom. Then will you be able to comprehend, as the year '80' dawns upon the world, the secret of the things which now lie hidden from you."[3]

Spoke from behind a curtain

Quddús sometimes would speak from behind a curtain. In the words of the historian Mangol Bayat:

> Sources generally agree that Quddús acquired saintly status, and assumed among the insurgents the position of supreme religious authority. He would rarely appear in public, and would grant audiences concealed behind a curtain. On the rare occasions when he would make a public appearance without cover, the Bábís would prostrate themselves at his feet. Even Bushrú'í (Mullá Ḥusayn) would bow to him, acknowledging him as his superior.[4]

---

1 Circumambulation is the act of moving around something sacred. It is a common practice in major religions of the world.

2 Luṭf 'Alí Mírzá Shírází, *A Chronicle of the Babi Uprising,* pp. 71–2.

3 Nabíl-i-A'ẓam, *The Dawn-Breakers,* p. 354.

4 Mangol Bayat, *Mysticism and Dissent,* p. 101.

Quddús is kept hidden from the believers:

> Mullá Ḥusayn only called him "Supreme Lord" (Ḥaḍrat-i-A'lá);[1] he bent his knees before him and hid him from view like a sacred being.[2]

According to an eyewitness:

> Each time his holiness [Quddús] decided to walk, his eminence the Báb [Mullá Ḥusayn] would order Mullá Ṣádiq Rashtí or Mírzá Báqir Kuchák to recite the sacred verses [given their beautiful voices]. Likewise, Quddús would usually ask one of these two to recite the sacred verses of His Holiness the Remembrance the Báb, or some other companions to do so. The companions would stand still to take heed. Blessed were those days.[3]

Future predictions

According to the book *Ganj-i-Pinhán*:

> A few hours before the arrival of Quddús at Shaykh Ṭabarsí fort, towards the afternoon, Ḥájj 'Alí Bárfurúshí [Quddús] entered and secretly announced his arrival to Mullá Ḥusayn.[4] Prior to his arrival, Quddús had dispatched certain utilities and gifts for the companions, including a letter for Mullá Ḥusayn.
>
> An inscription in the shape of number six had adorned the margin of this writing. The companions were amazed in seeing that number, but Mullá Ḥusayn interpreted it by saying that the siege of the castle will last for six months.[5]

The following is the story of a companion who miraculously survived the episode of Shaykh Ṭabarsí in October 1849, showing the capacity of Quddús to look into the future:

> ... when a wound had come to the mouth of His Holiness Quddús—upon whom rest the Glory of God, the Most Glorious, and may his remembrance be exalted above all others—then Ḥájí Naṣír presented him with a silk handkerchief to either wipe away [the blood] or to close the wound.
>
> When presenting this, uncontrollably, he made a sigh. His Holiness inquired, "For what reason do you sigh?" The Ḥájí was embarrassed and did not respond. His Holiness insisted, to which it was responded, "When

---

1 In the time of Bahá'u'lláh and 'Abdul-Bahá, *Ḥaḍrat-i-A'lá* ("Supreme Lord" or "His Holiness the Exalted One") was one of the titles believers used to address the Báb. It appears that during the Shaykh Ṭabarsí period, the companions used it to address Quddús.

2 Mirza Aleksandr Kazem-Beg, *Le Bab et les Bábís*, p. 509.

3 Luṭf 'Alí Mírzá Shírází, *A Chronicle of the Bábí Uprising, pp.* 71–2.

4 Luṭf 'Alí Mírzá Shírází, *A Chronicle of the Babi Uprising,* p. 53.

5 Fazel Mazandarani, *Taríkh Ẓuhúr al-Ḥaqq*, vol. 2, p. 297. See also Hushmand Dehghan, *Ganj-i-Pinhán*, p. 90.

> I was a merchant, among the items that I traded were such silk handkerchiefs. When I saw it again, without wanting to, I was reminded of that time and had that [sad] condition." The honoured Quddús responded, "You will once again trade in them."
>
> The esteemed Ḥájí Naṣír used to say, "I was most puzzled by this utterance since our fort was encircled by the enemy and we were engulfed in the most hopeless and grave situation."
>
> Nevertheless, truly because of the influence of Quddús' blessed utterance, for many years [he survived the Shaykh Ṭabarsí massacre] Ḥájí Naṣír worked as a merchant.[1]

There is the story of Mullá Mírzá Muḥammad who did not have a desire for martyrdom:

> As he [Mullá Mírzá Muḥammad] had no desire for martyrdom, Quddús assured him that he would leave Shaykh Ṭabarsí with his life spared.
>
> Now we see a man who had never had to wield a sword or a dagger, who would have been mightily astonished, a year before, if someone had put a sword in his hand and totally at a loss as to how to use the unfamiliar weapon, one who knew only the law, its intricacies and its applications, for whom fortifications and battlements and trenches were phantasmagorical removed from the world of reality, going out of Shaykh Ṭabarsí, sword in hand, to drive away the relentless enemy.
>
> He was wounded five times by bullets or sword; but as promised by Quddús he came through. Triumphantly he returned to Dúghábád to inform those ringleaders, who had sent him to Mázindarán in search of truth, that he had indeed found it ....[2]

As head of the Shaykh Ṭabarsí fort, Quddús led the defenders into the battlefield in person like the kings of Antiquity; he made strategical and tactical decisions about the front; delegated critical logistical matters such as negotiations, fortifications, food and weaponry, inspiring his men and gaining their loyalty and respect by example.

At all times, the believers were also reminded that they had been placed in an exceptional circumstance. Despite its severity and strangeness, they were to demonstrate a spiritual distinction between themselves and the enemy army, the hostile local clergy, the opposed civil authorities and the unfriendly population. Not surprisingly, Shoghi Effendi praised two converging dimensions in Quddús' personality, namely, his "serenity and sagacity".[3]

---

1 *The Narrative of Ḥájí Naṣír-i-Qazvíní*, n.p.

2 Hasan Balyuzi, *Eminent Bahá'ís in the Time of Bahá'u'lláh*, p. 157.

3 Shoghi Effendi, *God Passes By*, pp. 40–1.

21
The pen of Quddús

Chapter content
A prolific writer
Commentary on the letter Ṣad
The Sermon on the Eternal Witness

A prolific writer

Quddús was a prolific writer, although tragically most of his work has been lost. His literary production is estimated to be 30,000 verses—including prayers, learned discourses and homilies.[1] The Bible itself has 31,102 verses.

The attributes of Quddús were such that 'Abdu'l-Bahá referred to him as the "Moon of Guidance"[2] and Shoghi Effendi described him as the "erudite".[3] 'Some historians associate him with the position of *Mujtahid*, the highest rank in the Shí'ih hierarchy, a doctor of divinity, equivalent to the contemporary *áyatu'lláh*.[4] He has also been described as a man of "profound learning".[5]

The Báb has paid the following tribute to the creative dimension of being Quddús:

> *Verily, all that existeth hath been fashioned through thy light, and all that is hidden revealed by means of thy being.*[6]

The principal works of Quddús were: the Commentary on the Suríy-i-Tawḥíd (also known as Commentary on the Sura of al-ikhlás or Commentary on the Letter Ṣád); the Sermon on the Eternal Witness; and various letters to the Sa'ídu'l-'Ulamá'. These works will be discussed later in this chapter. There were also letters written to his mentor Sharí'atmadár. None of the surviving writings of Quddús are in his own hand.

In addition to the above works, in Shaykh Ṭabarsí Quddús composed homilies celebrating the Báb, Bahá'u'lláh and Ṭáhirih. In Nabíl's words:

---

1 Nosratollah Mohammad-Hosseini, *Qoddus, Moḥammad-'Ali Bārforuši,* n.p.

2 Shoghi Effendi, God Passes By, p. 49. Also in 'Abdu'l-Bahá, *Some Answered Questions,* p. 55.

3 Shoghi Effendi, *God Passes By*, p. 9.

4 Robert K. Arbuthnot, *The Bab and Babeeism,* Part 2, p. 595; A. L. M. Nicolas, *Seyyèd Ali-Mohammed dit le Bâb*, p. 289; & Bernard von Dorn, "Nachträge zu dem Verzeichniss ...", p. 378.

5 Jack McLean, *The Heroic in the Historical Writings of Shoghi Effendi and Nabíl*, n.p.

6 The Báb, *Tablet of Visitation for Quddús*. See Appendix part 2.

> Shortly after [his arrival at Shaykh Ṭabarsí], Quddús entrusted to Mullá Ḥusayn a number of homilies that he asked him to read aloud to his assembled companions. The first homily he read was entirely devoted to the Báb, the second concerned Bahá'u'lláh, and the third referred to Ṭáhirih. We ventured to express to Mullá Ḥusayn our doubts whether the references in the second homily were applicable to Bahá'u'lláh, who appeared clothed in the garb of nobility. The matter was reported to Quddús, who assured us that, God willing, its secret would be revealed to us in due time. Utterly unaware, in those days, of the character of the Mission of Bahá'u'lláh, we were unable to understand the meaning of those allusions, and idly conjectured as to what could be their probable significance.[1]

Two collections of manuscripts of the writings of Quddús are kept at the British Museum and the Cambridge University Library.[2] At the British Museum, the collection is entitled *Abharu'l-Quddúsiyyih,* which "includes ten pieces, eight in Arabic in the form of prayers (Munajat), and two others in the form of addresses".[3]

According to the Research Department of the Bahá'í World Centre, "... at present it is not possible to verify whether any of the manuscripts attributed to Quddús are indeed in his handwriting."[4] Similarly, the Bahá'í World Centre advised that Quddús' "writings do not appear to constitute 'part of our scripture'."[5]

We cannot understand the wisdom of why the writings of Quddús went missing and were lost. There is an indication in the chronicle of Siyyid Muḥammad-Ḥusayn that Quddús' writings were examined at his trial in Bárfurúsh.[6] Siyyid Muḥammad-Ḥusayn wrote that at one point of the proceedings, Quddús' writings were brought:

> These included interpretation of a hadíth (a narrative record of the sayings or customs of Muhammad and his companions) by Abí Abíd Makhzúní delivered with supreme eloquence along with compelling statements supporting the validity of this Revelation and refuting all other Islamic doctrines and sects. These materials were enclosed in a silk bundle,

---

1 Nabíl-i-A'ẓam, *The Dawn-Breakers,* p. 353.

2 Denis MacEoin, *The Sources for Early Bábí Doctrine and History*, p. 106.

3 Quoted in E. G. Browne, *Materials for the Study of the Bábí Religion,* p. 209. See Barfarushi Muḥammad 'Ali "Quddús": "al-Abhar al-Quddúsiyyah". Oriental and India Office Collections, British Library, London. Or. MS. Or. 5110. Foll. 36; "Al-Athar al-Qudsiyyah". Cambridge University Library. Browne Or. MS F. 43 (9). Foll. 20; "Az Farmayashat-i Hadrat-i Quddús". Oriental and India Office Collections, British Library. London. Or. 6256. Foll. 295–308.

4 Memorandum to the author dated 27 February 2023.

5 The Universal House of Justice. *Letters of Living, Dawn-Breakers, Quddús, Terraces.*

6 Siyyid Muḥammad-Ḥusayn. *Vaqa'i-i Mimiyyih,* pp. 114-117.

alongside a pen-case, originally sent by the Báb to Quddús, which was now in the possession of the prince. [1]

Perhaps Sharí'atmadár, Quddús' mentor and member of the panel, brought them to the meeting to prove his innocence. If so, it might have been the case that the government and ecclesiastical authorities promptly destroyed those texts. They were determined to eradicate the new movement not only by attacking its leaders and adherents but also their written records and sacred scriptures.

Quddús wrote mainly in Arabic and his writings "in both form and content" seem very similar to those of the Báb.[2] His mentor Sharí'atmadár once commented about the writings of Quddús:

> Out of the strength of his [Quddús'] intellect, his acumen, [Divine] confirmation (ta'yíd) and piety, there appeared in him the ability to compose and create ... many works of six or seven volumes each ... and similar to the [Divine] verses (áyát) and Quranic surahs, which would not have been out of place among the words of the *Qur'án*, and he composed or dictated orations, full of eloquence and in correct style, similar to the Ṣaḥífiy-Sajjádíyyih [of Imám Zaynu'l-'Ábidín].[3]

The Báb's writings are demanding to understand because of the intricacy of His written language in both Persian and Arabic, the terminology and context of the verses and the novel and complex grammatical constructions. "The style of the Báb's writings is new," Behmardi and McCants wrote, "and can't be compared with the standards of style of the people in the past."[4] On the same topic, historian Armin Eschraghi wrote:

> [The author Muḥammad] Afnán speaks of a 'spiritual revolution' (inqiláb-i-rúḥání) which was initiated by the Báb's Revelation and is clearly reflected in the grammatical peculiarities of his own writings as well as those of his disciples .... It seems that Quddús took the break with Arabic grammar to the extreme. In a manuscript of unknown origin but attributed to him we find incomprehensible and completely ungrammatical verb-forms such as y-q-sh-'-rr-t and y-k-f-h-rr-t, among others.[5]

It has been said that 'Abdu'l-Bahá had access to texts written by Quddús, remarking that his handwriting was illegible and difficult to read.[6] 'Abdu'l-Bahá used the verb "to reveal" (verses), i.e. he was "inspired", to describe how Quddús created his writings.[7]

---

1 Siyyid Muḥammad-Ḥusayn. *Vaqa'i-i Mimiyyih*, pp. 114-117.

2 Moojan Momen and Todd Lawson, *Ruḥ al-Quddús*, pp. 709–10.

3 Moojan Momen, *The Bahá'í Communities of Iran*, vol. 1, p. 304.

4 Behmardi & McCants, A *Stylistic Analysis of the Báb's Writings*, p. 114.

5 Armin Eschraghi, *Undermining the Foundations of Orthodoxy*, p. 242.

6 Nosratollah Mohammad-Hosseini, *Qoddus, Moḥammad-'Ali Bārforuši, n.p.*

7 Rabbani & Fananapazir, "'Abdu'l-Bahá's First Thousand-Verse Tablet", p. 120.

Commentary on the letter Ṣad

Another important missing work of Quddús was his Commentary on the Quranic *Súrat at-Tawḥíd* (*Qur'án* 112: "Sura of the Divine Unity"), also known as the *Súrat al-ikhlás* ("Sura of Sincerity") or Commentary on the Ṣád (letter "Ṣ") of the word Ṣamad, being the 112th and second shortest chapter of the *Qur'án*. This Quranic chapter consists of four famous verses that established monotheism as the central principle of Islam:

> *Say, He is God alone*
> *God, the Eternal [Ṣamad]!*
> *He begetteth not, and he is not begotten*
> *And there is none like unto Him.* (Rodwell translation)

The Commentary of Quddús focuses on the word Ṣamad ("Eternal") in the second verse and therefore, the work is better known as the interpretation by Quddús of the letter Ṣád (the letter "Ṣ") of the word Ṣamad. The text was about 20,000 verses, three times the volume of the Qur'án (6,348 verses),[1] although Nabíl, strangely, in another passage refers to 500,000 verses.[2]

According to Nabíl, the Commentary is a eulogy to Bahá'u'lláh.[3] "The slant and message of this work were solely on the oneness of God," wrote Sharí'atmadár.[4] It has been said that "that in a single night *Jináb-i-Kuddús* wrote a sublime commentary of some three thousand verses on the words "God the Eternal", and that in a brief space of time nearly thirty thousand verses of learned discourses, homilies, and supplications proceeded from him."[5] Some historians believe that the book might have been initiated while Quddús was living in Bárfurúsh.[6]

It also appears that Quddús started writing the book in the city of Sárí in the third quarter of 1848 when he was confined in the house of the cleric Mírzá Muḥammad-Taqí. According to Nabíl:

> In the days of his confinement in the town of Sárí, Quddús, whom Mírzá Muḥammad-Taqí had requested to write a commentary on the Súrih of Ikhlas ["Sincerity"], better known as the Súrih of Qul Huvá'lláhu'l-Aḥad ["Say, He is God alone"], composed, in his interpretation of the Ṣád of Ṣamad alone, a treatise which was thrice as voluminous as the *Qur'án* itself. That exhaustive and masterly exposition had profoundly impressed Mírzá Muḥammad-Taqí and had been responsible for the marked consideration which he showed towards Quddús, although in the end he joined the

---

1 Nabíl-i-A'ẓam, *The Dawn-Breakers*, p. 357.

2 Nabíl-i-A'ẓam, *The Dawn-Breakers*, p. 70.

3 Nabíl-i-A'ẓam, *The Dawn-Breakers*, p. 70

4 Sepehr Manuchehri, *Taqiyyah (Dissimulation) in the Bábí and Bahá'í Religions*, p. 236.

5 E. G. Browne, *Taríkh-i-Jadíd*, p. 44.

6 Denis MacEoin, *The Sources for Early Bábí Doctrine and History*, p. 105.

> Sa'idu'l-'Ulamá' in compassing the death of the heroic martyrs of Shaykh Ṭabarsí.[1]

Three times the volume of the *Qur'án*, it is equivalent to some 1,000 type pages except that it was written by hand with ink and quills.

Quddús kept working on that book when he was "besieged within the fort of Shaykh Ṭabarsí by the battalions and fire of a relentless enemy, engaged, both in the daytime and in the night-season, in the completion of his eulogy of Bahá'u'lláh—that immortal commentary on the Ṣád of Ṣamad ...."[2] Nabíl also stated:

> The rapidity and copiousness of his composition, the inestimable treasures which his writings revealed, filled his companions with wonder and justified his leadership in their eyes. They read eagerly the pages of that commentary which Mullá Ḥusayn brought to them each day and to which he paid his share of tribute.[3]

"We were so enraptured by the entrancing melody of those verses," said a Shaykh Ṭabarsí companion, "that were we to have continued for years in that state, no trace of weariness and fatigue could possibly have dimmed our enthusiasm or marred our gladness."[4] Certainly, Quddús inspired them with his writings and talks. Hushmand Dehghan adds:

> Despite all these sufferings and hardships [after the death of Mullá Ḥusayn on 2 February 2024], Jináb-i-Quddús continued to write his Commentary on the letter Ṣad. In addition, he also encouraged his companions to persevere and be steadfast. Mírzá Muḥammad-Báqir used to gather companions every morning and evening and recited to them a section of the Commentary on the letter Ṣad. Hearing those soul-enhancing words, the fire of courage was igniting again in the hearts of the companions and new hope was surging in them. Whenever there was a lack of food and provisions, like a dark specter to shake the will and determination of the companions, Jináb-i-Quddús would come and the companions would find strength and new life from meeting that luminous angel and hearing his celestial statements.[5]

There were not many writings of the Báb circulating at that time, and it is likely that the Bábís in Shaykh Ṭabarsí brought only a few copies into the fort. Hence, the treatises composed by Quddús and Mullá Ḥusayn inside the fort might have helped familiarise these isolated believers with the broader themes of the new Revelation.

---

1 Nabíl-i-A'ẓam, *The Dawn-Breakers*, p. 357.

2 Nabíl-i-A'ẓam, *The Dawn-Breakers,* p. 70.

3 Nabíl-i-A'ẓam, *The Dawn-Breakers,* p. 357

4 Nabíl-i-A'ẓam, *The Dawn-Breakers,* p. 390.

5 Hushmand Dehghan, *Ganj-i-Pinhán,* pp. 100-101.

According to Nabíl, before leaving the Shaykh Ṭabarsí fort, Quddús sent to his mentor Sharí'atmadár "a locked saddlebag containing the text of his own interpretation of the Ṣád of Ṣamad as well as all his other writings and papers that he had in his possession, the fate of which remains unknown until the present day."[1]

His mentor Sharí'atmadár wrote about this piece of Quddús' writings:

> The second Báb after Him was Jináb-i-Ḥájí Muḥammad 'Alí [Quddús] the son of a Mázindaráni farmer who lived at the same age and appeared slightly older than Him. He accompanied (the Báb) to Mecca ... and similar to (the Báb) had not studied conventional theory. After returning from Mecca, He wrote an incomplete commentary on the Surah of Oneness (Tawḥíd). I read approximately five to six thousand verses revealed by Him at a quick pace.[2]

'Abdu'l-Bahá has commented of the content of the treatise meaning that that at least some fragments had survived on His time.[3]

Sermon on the Eternal Witness

This important epistle of Quddús to Mullá Ḥusayn has been lost. In chapter 12, additional references were made to *Khuṭbiy-i-Sháhádat-i-Azalíya* ("Sermon on the Eternal Witness"). As stated earlier, Quddús reportedly authored this work before reaching Bárfurúsh,[4] however, another source indicated that Quddús wrote this work while travelling to Khurásán.[5]

We know from chroniclers that, in this epistle, Quddús predicted his martyrdom and the martyrdom of Mullá Ḥusayn with 70 of his companions—as occurred in the first half of 1849 in Shaykh Ṭabarsí. Before that episode Quddús had also recommended that Mullá Ḥusayn join him as quickly as possible in Mázindarán. In commenting on this historical epistle, the author of *Taríkh-i-Jadíd* wrote:

> Now inasmuch as Jináb-i-Quddús had, in the address known as the "Eternal Witness", made known the circumstances of his own and his companions' martyrdom in the plainest manner, and knowledge of this had reached most of the brethren whether far or near, who were firmly persuaded of the truth of his foreshadowings, these no sooner learned how he and his followers were hemmed in by so great a beleaguering force in the Castle of Shaykh Ṭabarsí that they knew for a surety in a little while the devoted band would to a man fall before the guns of the foe, and stain the earth with

1 Nabíl-i-A'ẓam, *The Dawn-Breakers,* p. 409.

2 Sepehr Manuchehri, *Taqiyyah (Dissimulation) in the Bábí and Bahá'í Religions,* p. 236.

3 'Abdu'l-Bahá, *Makātib-i Abd al-Bahā',* vol. 2 (Cairo, 1330/1912), p. 254; cf. p. 252. Cited in Denis MacEoin, *The Messiah of Shiraz,* p. 343.

4 Fazel Mazandarani, *Taríkh Ẓuhúr al-Ḥaqq*, vol. 3, p. 419.

5 E. G. Browne, *Taríkh-i-Jadíd*, p. 90.

> their life-blood. In spite of this knowledge, however, they eagerly set out from the most distant provinces to share the martyrdom of those already assembled in that fatal spot.
>
> I know not what these people had seen or apprehended that they thus readily cast aside all that men do most prize, and thus eagerly hastened to imperil their lives. Surely their conduct was such as to leave no room for doubt of their sincerity and devotion in any unprejudiced mind; and in truth what they did and suffered was little short of miraculous, being beyond mere human capacity. In them was exemplified the blessed verse, 'Desire death then if ye be sincere', while through their steadfastness the words, 'Those who strive in the way of God with their possessions and persons, these are highest in rank before God, and these are they who shall be happy', gained a new lustre ....[1]

Chapter 28 presents extracts from Quddús' writings in the form of prayers, letters to Sa'ídu'l-'Ulamá' and other passages.

---

1 E. G. Browne, *Taríkh-i-Jadíd*, p. 65.

Part VII
His legacy

22
In retrospect

Chapter content
Ministry of Quddús
Sorrow of the Báb
The fate of the enemies
The Persian religious leaders
Sharí'atmadár and the Bábís
The lasting impact of the siege
A tribute to the martyrs of Shaykh Ṭabarsí

This book has reviewed the major milestones and achievements in the life of Quddús, the mirror of the Báb. From his Islamic theological career to his conversion to the Bábí Faith, there was a path that Quddús traversed as a *seeker* and a *saint*. Later, Quddús emerged as a *promoter, leader, scholar* and *hero* of the Faith of the Báb, becoming its most outstanding disciple.

Ministry of Quddús

We can observe a chain of events in the life of Quddús that led to a massive spiritual transformation. He was a child orphaned by his mother and fathered by a modest rice farmer, receiving an elementary education from the local priest. During the twelve years before his conversion to the Cause of the Báb at the early age of twenty-two years, Quddús was engaged in the study of theological sciences in Persia and Iraq, becoming a consummate theologian. In five short years he traversed the distance from being a new convert to the highest-ranking disciple. In that process he became a religious leader and a warrior, and ultimately a martyr.

Quddús was chosen to undertake the pilgrimage to Mecca with the Báb and for one-year he was personally educated by Him to assume his future responsibilities as the Báb's representative.[1] "Praise be upon My Lord (the Báb)", he wrote, "Who with His divine Hands guided me from the beginning".[2]

Quddús travelled extensively, teaching the Faith of the Báb throughout Persia, approaching the rich, the poor, the clergy, the illiterate, the scholar and royalty with grace, maturity and skill. The Báb was in long-term captivity from the middle of His ministry, hence the leadership of Quddús proved to be vital in the ensuing years to rally the Bábí community of Persia in the midst of uncertainty, danger and a lack of internal networking.

---

1 Nader Saiedi, *Concealment and Revelation in Bahá'u'lláh's Book of the River*, p. 48.

2 Hushmand Dehghan, *Ganj-i-Pinhán*, p. 191.

In his native town Quddús managed to raise a strong Bábí community and alone withstood the opposition of the fierce Muslim ecclesiastics. Later he led the Bábís of Khurásán while using the historical House of Bábíyyih as his centre. Quddús also participated as a central protagonist in the famous conference of Badasht with Bahá'u'lláh and Ṭáhirih, subsequently endured confinement in Sárí, and finally succumbed to a brutal execution in the aftermath of the Shaykh Ṭabarsí siege. Moreover, the literary work of Quddús was prolific, being estimated to be in the tens of thousands of verses.[1] Since the Báb Himself was held in captivity for nearly two-thirds of His ministry, Quddús became the representative of the Báb to the believers throughout Persia.

Quddús stands as a unique beacon of guidance among the early Bábí community. He was familiar with the seminal works of the Báb, such as the *Qayyúmu'l-Asmá'* and the *Bayán*, among others, he maintained correspondence with the Báb from Mázindarán, he was the most prolific Bábí writer at that time, and he was commissioned by the Báb to teach the new Faith to accomplished Islamic theologians.

His position as a prominent disciple of the Báb has parallels with the roles of Isaac for Abraham, Joshua for Moses, Peter for Jesus, and 'Alí for Muḥammad. The Báb wrote about Quddús: "*Thou hast been exalted, and none is there above thee whose exaltation is like unto thine.*"[2]

Quddús, as the first in rank of the Bábís, held that level of leadership associated with the aforementioned religious figures. There are, however, two major differences with previous religions. Firstly, the Prophet of the Bábí Dispensation survived longer than His most important apostle. Secondly, the Báb explained that He did not leave a successor because of the imminence of the Revelation of *Him Whom God shall make manifest*:

> *Glorified art Thou, O My God! Bear Thou witness that, through this Book, I have covenanted with all created things concerning the Mission of Him Whom Thou shalt make manifest, ere the covenant concerning Mine own Mission had been established. Sufficient witness art Thou and they that have believed in Thy signs.*[3]

Bahá'u'lláh also confirmed the absence of successorship in the Dispensation of the Báb:

> *In My previous Dispensation* [the Báb], *the matter of successorship was totally obliterated from the Book of God. As all are aware, all that was revealed from the Pen of the All-Merciful was confined to the Letters and the Mirrors of the Bayán. Also, the number of Mirrors was not fixed.*[4]

---

1 Nosratollah Mohammad-Hosseini, *Qoddus, Moḥammad-'Ali Bārforuši, n.p.*

2 The Báb, Tablet of Visitation for Quddús. See Appendix part 2.

3 The Báb in Bahá'u'lláh, *Epistle to the Son of the Wolf*, p. 160.

4 Bahá'u'lláh, *Additional Tablets extracts from Tablets revealed by Bahá'u'lláh.*

The Báb's mission was centred on the coming of the next Messenger of God referred to as *Him Whom God shall make manifest*, that is, Bahá'u'lláh. The Báb made numerous allusions to this celebrated Figure, which attests to the care He took in preparing the world for that significant and very unusual spiritual phenomenon in the world—especially the need to rend the "spiritual veils" in order for the Bábís to accept the Cause of Bahá'u'lláh. The Báb wrote more about the characteristics and functions of the forthcoming Manifestation than any other previous Messenger of God had done.

In mid-1845, Quddús had met Bahá'u'lláh in the capital Ṭihrán[1] and there is evidence that Quddús was aware of Bahá'u'lláh's station as early as the time of the Badasht conference in mid-1848.[2] Upon arrival in Shaykh Ṭabarsí,[3] Quddús referred to Bahá'u'lláh as the *Baqíyatu'lláh* ("the Remnant of God"). The term itself is mentioned in *Qur'án* 11:86. In the Writings of the Báb, the "Remnant of God" is associated with "Him Whom God shall make manifest".[4] For instance, in the *Qayyúmu'l-Asmá*, revealed in 1844, the Báb affirmed:

> *O Thou Remnant of God! I have sacrificed myself wholly for Thee; I have accepted curses for Thy sake, and have yearned for naught but martyrdom in the path of Thy love. Sufficient witness unto me is God, the Exalted, the Protector, the Ancient of Days.*[5]

Likewise, in the *Persian Bayán* (3:3) the Báb stated, "*The Bayán and all that is therein revolved around Him Whom God shall make manifest ... The prolongation of the gaze of the Bayán is only towards the advent of the Remnant of God.*"[6]

As prophesied by the Báb, Bahá'u'lláh publicly announced His Mission in 1863, exactly nineteen years after the Báb's Declaration.[7]

Sorrow of the Báb

During the episode of the siege of the fort of Shaykh Ṭabarsí the Báb had, while confined 1,000 km away in the fortress of Chihríq, been greatly concerned regarding the fate of His loved ones. "Confined in His prison-castle of Chihríq," a chronicler wrote, "severed from the little band of His struggling disciples, He watched with keen anxiety the progress of their labours and prayed with unremitting zeal for their victory".[8] When the Báb heard about their ending, He fell prey to a great sadness that plunged Him into a long agony for the cruelty with

---

1 Nabíl-i-A'ẓam, *The Dawn-Breakers*, p. 183.
2 Stephen Lambden, *The Word Bahá*, p. 37.
3 *Qur'án* 11:86.
4 Nosratollah Mohammad-Hosseini, *The Commentary on the Sura of Joseph*, pp. 16–8.
5 The Báb, *Selections*, p. 59.
6 Nosratollah Mohammad-Hosseini, *The Commentary on the Sura of Joseph*, p. 17.
7 Nader Saiedi, *Gate of the Heart*, p. 356.
8 Nabíl-i-A'ẓam, *The Dawn-Breakers*, p. 430.

which the enemy had ended so many innocent and devoted lives. His mourning lasted five to six months.

In total, nine Letters of the Living[1] perished during the siege of the Shaykh Ṭabarsí fort. According to the Báb's amanuensis:

> The Báb was heart-broken at the receipt of this unexpected intelligence. He was crushed with grief, a grief that stilled His voice and silenced His pen. For nine days He refused to meet any of His friends. I myself, though His close and constant attendant, was refused admittance. Whatever meat or drink we offered Him, He was disinclined to touch. Tears rained continually from His eyes, and expressions of anguish dropped unceasingly from His lips. I could hear Him, from behind the curtain, give vent to His feelings of sadness as He communed, in the privacy of His cell, with His Beloved. I attempted to jot down the effusions of His sorrow as they poured forth from His wounded heart. Suspecting that I was attempting to preserve the lamentations He uttered, He bade me destroy whatever I had recorded. Nothing remains of the moans and cries with which that heavy-laden heart sought to relieve itself of the pangs that had seized it. For a period of five months He languished, immersed in an ocean of despondency and sorrow.[2]

After the martyrdom in Bárfurúsh, "The beloved Báb has written", Fazel Mazandarani stated, "the extent of a volume of statements for reading when visiting Quddús' grave." [3]

When the Báb learned about the deaths of Quddús and Mullá Ḥusayn, He became so despondent and downhearted that He stopped revealing texts for five months. The Báb later recommenced His work around November 1849.

According to Nabíl:

> He lavished His eulogies on his [Mullá Ḥusayn's] magnanimous conduct, recounted his exploits, and asserted his undoubted reunion in the world beyond with the leader [Quddús] whom he had so nobly served. He too, He wrote, would soon join those twin immortals, each of whom had, by his life and death, shed imperishable lustre on the Faith of God. For one whole week the Báb continued to write His praises of Quddús, of Mullá Ḥusayn, and of His other companions who had gained the crown of martyrdom at Ṭabarsí.

---

1 The Letters of the Living who died during the Shaykh Ṭabarsí episode were: Quddús, Mullá Ḥusayn, Mullá Muḥammad-Ḥasan (brother of Mullá Ḥusayn), Mullá Muḥammad-Báqir (cousin of Mullá Ḥusayn), Mullá Yúsif-i-Ardibílí, Mullá Jalíl-i-Urúmí, Mullá Aḥmad-i-Abdál-i-Marághi'í, Mullá Maḥmúd-i-Khu'í and Mírzá Muḥammad-'Alíy-i-Qazvíní (cousin and brother-in-law of Ṭáhirih).

2 Nabíl-i-A'ẓam, *The Dawn-Breakers*, p. 430.

3 Fazel Mazandarani, *Ẓuhúr al-Ḥaqq*, vol. 3, p. 22–423.

> No sooner had He completed His eulogies of those who had immortalised their names in the defence of the fort, than He summoned, on the day of 'Áshúrá, [26 November 1849], Mullá Ádí-Guzal, one of the believers of Marághih, who for the last two months had been acting as His attendant instead of Siyyid Ḥasan, the brother of Siyyid Ḥusayn-i-'Azíz. He affectionately received him, bestowed upon him the name Sayyáḥ ["traveller"], entrusted to his care the visiting Tablets He had revealed in memory of the martyrs of Ṭabarsí, and bade him perform, on His behalf, a pilgrimage to that spot.
>
> "Arise," He urged him, "and with complete detachment proceed, in the guise of a traveller, to Mázindarán, and there visit, on My behalf, the spot which enshrines the bodies of those immortals who, with their blood, have sealed their faith in My Cause. As you approach the precincts of that hallowed ground, put off your shoes and, bowing your head in reverence to their memory, invoke their names and prayerfully make the circuit of their shrine ... Strive to be back ere the day of Naw-Rúz, that you may celebrate with Me that festival, the only one I probably shall ever see again." [1]

"After Ṭabarsí," Abbas Amanat wrote, "he [the Báb] became increasingly tormented by the painful reality of frequent persecutions and bloodshed. He never learned of the execution of his uncle Sayyid 'Alí in early 1850, since, we are told, he had prohibited 'the mention of grief in his presence".[2]

According to Professor Edward Browne who visited Bárfurúsh in 1888, "I wondered whether the Báb's prophecy would ever be fulfilled, that a day would come when in these spots, hallowed by the blood of his martyrs, representations of their sufferings and steadfastness should move the sympathetic lamentations and tears of the children of those who slew them, and obliterate the remembrance of the martyrs of Karbilá."[3]

The fate of the enemies

An ancient proverb states *The mills of God grind slowly.* Those five most formidable opponents of the Faith of the Báb faced a sad end. In Shoghi Effendi's words:

> At present the state of affairs is in turmoil, tribulations are manifold, and the authorities have launched attacks from every direction. However, the invisible Hand of God is at work, and the wrathful Avenger is watching over the oppressed community of the righteous and the pious.[4]

---

1 Nabíl-i-A'ẓam, *The Dawn-Breakers*, pp. 431–2

2 Abbas Amanat, *Resurrection and Renewal*, p. 395.

3 E. G. Browne, *A Year among the Persians*, p. 615.

4 Bahá'í World Centre, *The Bahá'í World*, Vol. 18 (1979–1983), p. 36.

The life of Quddús (1820–1949) is a window into the decadent history of the corrupt Qájár dynasty founded by Muḥammad Khán (r. 1789-1797). Quddús was born during the reign of the second (Fatḥ-'Alí Sháh, r. 1797-1834), lived mostly during government of the third (Muḥammad Sháh, r. 1834-1848) and died at the beginning of the reign of the fourth (Naṣiri'd-Dín Sháh, r. 1848-1896).

Muḥammad Sháh Qájár

Muḥammad Sháh Qájár (1808–1848), the grandson of Fatḥ-'Alí Sháh Qájár, he was the one who ordered the exiles of the Báb to the mountains of Ádharbayján, and the issuing of an order for the execution of Bahá'u'lláh. Fortunately, the second order was terminated by the sudden death of this increasingly unwell sovereign at an early age. To him, the Báb wrote:

> *O King of Islám! Aid thou, with the truth, after having aided the Book, Him Who is Our Most Great Remembrance, for God hath, in very truth, destined for thee, and for such as circle round thee, on the Day of Judgment, a responsible position in His Path.*[1]

Náṣiri'd-Dín Sháh

Naṣiri'd-Dín Sháh Qájár (1831–1896), the son of Muḥammad Sháh, lost the Anglo-Persian wars (1856–1857), which resulted in humiliating conditions being imposed on Persia. Bahá'u'lláh had foretold that Náṣiri'd-Dín Sháh would be *"an object-lesson for the world"*,[2] and addressed him as the *"prince of Oppressors"*[3] for all the harm he had committed against the believers. Naṣiri'd-Dín Sháh Qájár was publicly assassinated on Friday 1 May 1896 on the eve of the fiftieth anniversary of his accession to the throne. Náṣiri'd-Dín Sháh had been responsible for the death of thousands of Bábís, including Quddús and Mullá Ḥusayn. Bahá'u'lláh addressed these recriminatory words to him:

> *Hast thou imagined thyself capable of extinguishing the fire which God hath kindled in the heart of creation? Nay, by Him Who is the Eternal Truth, couldst thou but know it. Rather, on account of what thy hands have wrought, it blazed higher and burned more fiercely. Erelong will it encompass the earth and all that dwell therein.*[4]

Ḥusayn Khán, the Governor of Shíráz

This governor ordered the torture of Quddús, Mullá Ṣádiq and Mullá 'Alí-Akbar in June of 1845 in Shíráz. According to Shoghi Effendi:

> Ḥusayn Khán, the governor of Shíráz, stigmatized as a "wine-bibber" and a "tyrant," the first who arose to ill-treat the Báb, who publicly rebuked Him and bade his attendant strike Him violently in the face, was compelled not

[1] The Báb, *Selections*, pp. 41–42.

[2] Shoghi Effendi, *The Promised Day Has Come*, p. 288.

[3] Shoghi Effendi, *God Passes By*, p. 197.

[4] Bahá'u'lláh, *The Summons of the Lord of Hosts*, p. 142.

> only to endure the dreadful calamity that so suddenly befell him, his family, his city and his province, but afterwards to witness the undoing of all his labors, and to lead in obscurity the remaining days of his life, till he tottered to his grave abandoned alike by his friends and his enemies.[1]

Dr Riaz Ghadimi added:

> The governor of Fárs Ḥusayn Khán Iravání, titled the Ájúdán Báshí or the Nizámu'd-Dawlih, imprisoned the Báb and ordered that He should be struck in the face. It was he, also, who ordered that Muqaddas receive a thousand lashes and that his beard and those of Quddús and Mullá 'Alí-Akbar Ardistání be burned and that they be haltered and paraded through the streets and bazaars. After four years as governor, he was suddenly dismissed from office and was pursued by the government. He finally found refuge at the embassies of foreign governments and in 1858 died in hiding in utter ignominy and misery. In Bahá'í Writings he is referred to as: the vicious Ḥusayn and the Tyrant of the Land of Shín (Shín refers to Shíráz).[2]

The Grand Vizir

The Grand Vizir, Mírzá Taqí Khán, was appointed by Náṣiri'd-Dín Sháh. The Grand Vizir was responsible for the Shaykh Ṭabarsí fort massacre and he was the "prime mover of the forces that precipitated the Báb's martyrdom".[3] He had been dismissed on 21 November 1852. "I [Mírzá Ḥáji Áqá Ján Káshání] heard that amongst the charges levelled by the Russian Tsar at the Prime Minister [Mírzá Taqí Khán, better known as Amír Kabír] which was instrumental in his removal from the office," wrote the author of the *Kitáb-i-Nuqṭat al-Káf*, "was the murder of this band of innocent people [Bábís]"[4] According to *A Traveler's Narrative,*

> And as His Majesty the King was in the prime of youthful years the minister fell into strange fancies and sounded the drum of absolutism in [the conduct of] affairs: on his own decisive resolution, without seeking permission from the Royal Presence or taking counsel with prudent statesmen, he issued orders to persecute the Bábís, imagining that by overweening force he could eradicate and suppress matters of this nature, and that harshness would bear good fruit; whereas [in fact] to interfere with matters of conscience is simply to give them greater currency and strength; the more you strive to extinguish the more will the flame be kindled, more especially in matters of faith and religion, which spread and acquire influence so soon as blood is shed, and strongly affect men's hearts.[5]

---

1 Shoghi Effendi, *God Passes By*, p. 83.

2 Riaz Ghadimi, *The Báb, The King of Messengers*, p. 30.

3 Nabíl-i-A'ẓam, *The Dawn-Breakers*, p. 526.

4 E. G. Browne. *Kitáb-i-Nuqtatu'l-Káf: Being the Earliest History of the Bábís*, pp. 233-234.

5 'Abdu'l-Bahá, *A Traveler's Narrative*, pp. 20-21.

Náṣiri'd-Dín Sháh issued an order that he [Mírzá Taqí Khán] was to be secretly murdered on 13th of January of the same year in the public bath of the city of Káshán. Dr Riaz Ghadimi wrote:

> As he relaxed in the pool, he was held in place by those agents in the presence of 'Alí Khán Ḥájib'ud'Dawlih (the court minister) while the veins in his right and left wrists were cut open. He was made to watch helplessly as blood poured out of him until he too was dispatched to his destined end. In the Writings he is referred to as the "Cruel Commander," "the Blood-Thirsty Amír," "the Blood-Thirsty Taqí," and "the Faithless Commander."[1]

Prince Mihdí-Qulí Mírzá

Prince Mihdí Qulí Mírzá, brother of the late Muḥammad Sháh and Náṣirid-Dín Sháh's uncle, who authorised the martyrdom of Quddús, was dismissed from his post for inefficiency in 1850 after two years as the governor of Mázindarán Province and died in 1854. Not portrait of him has remained and he has passed into history as the Pontius Pilate of Bárfurúsh.

Sulaymán Khán-i-Afshár

Sulaymán Khán-i-Afshár, the imperial general at Shaykh Ṭabarsí, who was also the head of the powerful Afshár tribe, was a rich man, a prosperous landowner, and an important influence at the imperial court. Sulaymán Khán-i-Afshár re-appeared in history in June 1850 bringing the Báb from the fort of Chihríq to Tabríz for His final martyrdom, at the request from the Prime Ministe.[2] He died in debt and indigence (d. 1309/1891). His family requested financial assistance from Bahá'u'lláh when He was in 'Akká. His son Riḍá-Qulí Khán escorted the Báb from Máh-Kú to Chihríq Castle and he became a Bábí and later a Bahá'í.[3]

'Abbás-Qulí Khán Láríjání

'Abbás-Qulí Khán Láríjání was the arrogant commander at Shaykh Ṭabarsí who fell into disgrace after being accused of embezzlement at a government post and had to take refuge at the United Kingdom of Great Britain and Ireland Legation in Ṭihrán.[4]

The Sa'ídu'l-'Ulamá'

Mullá Sa'íd was rewarded for his hostility to the Bábís by Náṣiri'd-Dín Sháh with the title of *Sa'ídu'l-'Ulamá'* ("Leader of the Learned").[5] The monarch saw the 1849 "victory" at Shaykh Ṭabarsí as a political opportunity to ally himself with the

---

1 Riaz Ghadimi, *The Báb, The King of Messengers*, p. 35.

2 Comte de Gobineau, Les Religions et les Philosophies dans l'Asie Centrale (p. 213), cited in Nabíl-i-A'ẓam, *The Dawn-Breakers*, p. 504.

3 Moojan Momen, *The Bahá'í Communities of Iran*, vol. I, pp. 421–3.

4 Abbas Amanat, *Pivot of the Universe*, p. 239.

5 Abbas Amanat, *Resurrection and Renewal*, p. 182.

religious hierarchy to further affirm his sovereignty in a province known for its rebelliousness to the crown.

S͟harí'atmadár, Quddús's mentor, died a few months before the 1865 visit of Náṣiri'd-Dín S͟háh to Bárfurús͟h. The Sa'ídu'l-'Ulamá' had died ten years before. The monarch called on S͟harí'atmadár's successor at his Káẓim Bayk madrasah in Bárfurús͟h.

In contrast, the power-hungry and corrupt Sa'ídu'l-'Ulamá' suffered a most grievous death. He died of cholera five years after the martyrdom of Quddús. His tomb was eventually set on fire and destroyed. A. L. M. Nicolas observed:

> The Bábís call attention to the fact that shortly afterwards a strange disease afflicted Sa'ídu'l-'Ulamá'. In spite of the furs which he wore, in spite of the fire which burned constantly in his room, he shivered with cold yet, at the same time, his fever was so high, that nothing could quench his intolerable thirst. He died, and his house, which was very beautiful, was abandoned and finally crumbled into ruins. Little by little, the practice grew of dumping refuse on the site where it had once so proudly stood. This so impressed the Mázindarán's that when they quarrel among themselves, the final insult frequently is, "May thy house meet the same fate as the house of Sa'ídu'l-'Ulamá'!"[1]

In turn, the *Taríkh-i-Jadíd* documents his fate:

> Moreover, after the martyrdom of Jináb-i-Quddús the Sa'ídu'l-'Ulamá' suffered a grievous punishment. For God deprived his body of the element of heat, so that in mid-summer, even while the sign of the Lion [summer] was dominant, two iron chafing-dishes filled with glowing fire were brought with him whenever he went to the mosque, and, although he always wore a sheep-skin cloak over his vest, and over the sheepskin a thick mantle, he would make haste to finish his prayers, and at once return to his home. And on his arrival there, they would put the chafing-dishes under a kursí[2] and cover him with many thick quilts, yet still his body would shiver and shake under the kursí by reason of the cold. So by reason of his lack of caloric and heat-producing power also one may describe him as bereft of virility and manhood.[3]

His tomb was burned several times and destroyed "under the pretext of widening the road"[4]

---

[1] A. L. M. Nicolas, *Seyyèd Ali-Mohammed dit le Bâb*, p. 330. Cited in Nabíl-i-A'ẓam, *The Dawn-Breakers*, p. 410.

[2] The *kursí* mentioned above has been described as "a low table under which a chafing-dish filled with burning charcoal is placed. The legs are put beneath it, and the remainder of the body, supported by pillows, is protected from the cold with rugs and quilts." (Browne in *The New History,* p. 91).

[3] E. G. Browne, *Taríkh-i-Jadíd*, pp. 91–2.

[4] RasaNews. (2 August 2011). *The opinion of authorities and scholars about the*

Abbas Amanat, in his book *Resurrection and Renewal*, wrote that "in the Days preceding Ṭabarsí, Quddús was recognised by the Bábís as the 'Spirit of the Messiah" who soon would descend in the 'Green Island' [Mázindarán] and destroy the forces of the Antichrist (Dajjál)."[1] In this regard the author of *Taríkh-i-Jadíd* stated:

> There is also a well-authenticated tradition to the effect that a bearded woman of Jewish extraction called Sa'ída shall compass the martyrdom of the Qá'im with an iron pestle in Fárán[2] of Ṭihrán. And since Jináb-i-Quddús had arisen to proclaim this teaching, he was in a sense Lord of the Dispensation, even as it runs in the tradition .... And the "iron pestle" was that same iron axe wherewith he smote the head of his illustrious victim, while as to his being a recent convert to Islám and of Jewish extraction there is no doubt, this fact being well-known to all the people of Mázindarán.[3]

To him, the author of the *Taríkh-i-Jadíd* dedicated these lines from the famous Persian poet Rumí:

> The doctor oft of wisdom hath no share,
> And is but wisdom's guardian, not its heir.
> 'Which beareth books,' saith God. A mere dead load
> Is knowledge which is not by Him bestowed.
> A sword in savage hands is not more dire
> A danger than the knowledge fools acquire!
> Rank, wealth, authority, and scripture lore
> In evil hands cause only strife and war.
> Whene'er the unjust judge controls the pen,
> Some Mansúr dies upon the gallows then.
> Whene'er fools wield authority, God's Word
> 'They slay the prophets' is a thing assured.[4]

His city eventually lost its 500 years old Safavid name of being Bárfurúsh (Barforushdeh- Market Town), and was autocratically changed to Babol (Bábul) in 1937 which relates to water supply.

The Persian religious leaders

The Báb severely condemns the Persian divines in His Writings:

personality of Allameh Saeed al-Ulama and Mulla Mohammad Ashrafi, n.p.

1 Abbas Amanat, *Resurrection and Renewal*, p. 187.

2 Arabicized form of the Mount Párán of the Old Testament *(Taríkh-i-Jadíd)*.

3 E. G. Browne, *Taríkh-i-Jadíd*, pp. 91–2.

4 E. G. Browne (ed.). *Taríkh-i-Jadíd or New History of Mírzá 'Alí Muḥammad The Báb*, pp. 92-93

> *O concourse of Shí'ihs! Fear ye God and Our Cause which concerneth Him Who is the Most Great Remembrance of God. For great is its fire, as decreed in the Mother Book.*[1]
>
> *O concourse of divines! Fear God from this day onwards in the views ye advance, for He Who is Our Remembrance in your midst, and Who cometh from Us, is, in very truth, the Judge and Witness. Turn away from that which ye lay hold of and which the Book of God, the True One, hath not sanctioned, for on the Day of Resurrection ye shall, upon the Bridge, be, in very truth, held answerable for the position ye occupied.*[2]
>
> *In all His Tablets, God hath verily ordained vain imaginings and conjecture to be a manifest sin ... God verily hath made it unlawful for you to pronounce, in clear defiance of truth, any injunction or to exercise any legal judgment while bereft of the absolute knowledge of this Book.*[3]

Further, the Báb wrote that the persecution unleashed by the Islamic clergy was based on their own spiritual ignorance:

> *As to those who have debarred themselves from the Revelation of God, they have indeed failed to understand the significance of a single letter of the Qur'án, nor have they obtained the slightest notion of the Faith of Islám, otherwise they would not have turned away from God ... thinking that they are doing righteous work for the sake of God.*[4]

Sharí'atmadár and the Bábís

In contrast, Sharí'atmadár, the clergyman who rescued the remains of Quddús, died between 1864–1865 CE (1281 AH) and passed into history with a good name. His full name was Mullá Muḥammad Ḥamzih Sharí'atmadár, and he was the mentor of Quddús during his childhood in Bárfurúsh. In his book *Asrár ash-Shaháda* ("The Secrets of the Martyrs"), written around 1856, he talks favourably about Quddús and his writings.[5] The author of *Taríkh-i-Jadíd* remarked:

> At all events it appears that after the martyrdom of Jináb-i-Quddús a pious divine Ḥájí Muḥammad-'Alíy-i-Ḥamzih [Sharí'atmadár] by name whose skill in exegesis and spiritual gifts was recognised by all, secretly sent several persons to bury the mutilated remains in the ruined college already mentioned. And he, far from approving the Sa'ídu'l-'Ulamá's conduct, used to curse and revile him, and never himself pronounced sentence of death against any Bábí, but, on the contrary used to obtain decent burial for those slain by the Sa'ídu'l-'Ulamá'.

---

1 The Báb, *Selections*, p. 55.

2 The Báb, *Selections*, p. 44.

3 The Báb in Nader Saiedi, *Gate of the Heart*, p. 137.

4 The Báb, *Selections*, p. 140.

5 Denis MacEoin, *Hierarchy Authority and Eschatology in Early Bábí Thought*, p. 146.

> And when men questioned him concerning the garrison of the castle, he would reply: 'I do not condemn them or speak evil of them.' For this reason, half of Bárfurúsh remained neutral, for at first he used to forbid men to traduce or molest the Bábís, though later when the trouble waxed great, he deemed it prudent to be silent and shut himself up in his house. Now his austerity of life, piety, learning, and virtue were as well known to the people of Mázindarán as were the irreligion, immorality and worldliness of the Sa'ídu'l-'Ulamá'.[1]

Hatcher and Amrollah told the story of how Sharí'atmadár assisted with the funeral of two Bábís:

> Mullá Ridáy-i-Sháh and a young man from Bahnimír were slain two days after the abandonment of the fort by Quddús, in the Panj-Shanbih-Bázár of Bárfurúsh. Hájí Mullá Muḥammad-i-Ḥamzih, surnamed the Sharí'at-Madár, succeeded in burying their bodies in the neighbourhood of the Masjid-i-Káẓim-Big, and in inducing their murderer to repent and ask for forgiveness.[2]

Some historians suggest that Sharí'atmadár was secretly a believer in the Báb.[3] Sepehr Manuchehri stated:

> He constantly assisted and protected the Bábís and in response to questions from the general public would say "I do not consider them bad and will not make negative comments about them", wrote ... Sharí'atmadár. "He set out to join the Bábís in Shaykh Ṭabarsí but was unable to get there due to the military embargo .... He performed final prayers for the funerals of the Bábí martyrs and sought forgiveness for their killers. Other Mullás became furious and called him a traitor and an infidel.[4]

According to *Ganj-i-Pinhán*, "After Sharí'atmadár, his son and grandson, who succeeded him, supported the Bahá'í friends. Another son, Shaykh 'Abdu'l Karím, and his son-in-law, Shaykh Muḥammad-Taqí, converted to the Bahá'í Faith during the time of 'Abdul-Bahá."[5]

The lasting impact of the siege

According to Shoghi Effendi, the episode of the siege of the Shaykh Ṭabarsí fort can be seen as one of the most powerful agencies to shape the Faith of the Báb, "generating the very seeds which, in a later age, were to blossom into world-wide

---

1. E. G. Browne, *Taríkh-i-Jadíd*, p. 92.
2. John Hatcher and Hemmant Amrollah, *Reunion with the Beloved*, p. 54.
3. Moojan Momen, *The Bahá'í Communities of Iran*, vol. I, p. 304.
4. Sepehr Manuchehri, *Taqiyyah (Dissimulation) in the Bábí and Bahá'í Religions*, p. 231.
5. Hooshmand Dehghan, *Ganj-i-Pinhán*, p. 30.

administrative institutions, and which must, in the fullness of time, yield their golden fruit in the shape of a world-redeeming, earth-encircling Order."[1]

For the Bábís, the upheaval represented an affirmation of their religious personality within the strict, highly-controlled, religious environment of Persia. The great epics of history, either real or legendary, have bequeathed an identity to nations and communities: the Persian *Sháhnámih*, the Greek *Iliad* and the *Odyssey*, the Indian *Ramáyana*, the Hebrew *Masada* gest, the Spanish *Cid Campeador*, the Chilean *Araucana*, and so forth. The siege of the Shaykh Ṭabarsí fort gave a sense of recognition to the nascent followers of the Báb, the Bábís. Their religious movement sent shockwaves throughout the Persian nation and abroad by proclaiming the emergence from obscurity of a global religion, with its own Prophet, Holy Book, shrines and martyrs.

It is interesting to note that the news of the siege at Shaykh Ṭabarsí quickly began to circulate around the world. In a dispatch dated 30 January 1849 the British Charge d'Affaires, Lt-Col. Farrant wrote to his government that the Bábís were followers of a prophet "who calls himself the door, or gate of the true Mahomedan religion and pretends to be the forerunner, and agent of the Imám Mihdí, who according to Mahomedan tradition, is to appear shortly before the termination of the world, and cause one religion to be established throughout the universe."[2] Similarly, prince Dimitri Dolgorukov (1797–1867), the Russian Minister (1845–1854) in Ṭihrán, in a dispatch dated 5 February 1849, reported that the Persian military commander "has stated that with the forces that he has under his command at present, he is not powerful enough to face the Bábís."[3] Likewise, Jose Ferrier, French agent in Persia, in a report dated 21 February 1850, noted the effects of the massacre: "This treacherous butchery, instead of halting the progress of Bábísm, only served to stimulate it further, and in a short time it had numerous adherents in every province."[4] Moreover, the *Journal de Constantinople*, a French periodical, published an article entitled *Nouvelles de Perse* that noted:

> There has been talk for some time of a religious sect which took up arms in Mázindarán to defend its dogmas and its leader who is currently in prison here. The Bábís, that is how they are called by the name of their chiefs, professing very advanced socialist ideas; they are as forceful as one can imagine, and they have already gone to extremes against the representatives of the authorities.[5]

1 Shoghi Effendi, *God Passes By*, p. 38.
2 Moojan Momen, *The Báb and Bábí Religions,* p. 92.
3 Moojan Momen, *The Báb and Bábí Religions,* p. 93.
4 Moojan Momen, *The Báb and Bábí Religions,* p. 95.
5 "Nouvelles de Perse", *Journal de Constantinople*, 24 March 1849. Available https://bahai-library.com/pdf/journal-de-constantinople/ocr-ed_pdfs/1849/journal_constantinople_1849-03-24_p1.pdf

The Count of Gobineau wrote, "All of Persia, we can say", "the whole country was shaking under the impression of the new doctrine and awaiting with extreme interest what the conclusions, that Mullá Ḥusayn Bushrú'í had been the first to draw from it, would produce".[1]

The clerical order and its absolute supremacy were openly challenged by the Faith of the Báb and, particularly, by the Shaykh Ṭabarsí upheaval. The clergy and government, once at odds with each other on the politics of the nation, joined forces in an unholy alliance to uproot the Bábí insurgency, effecting lasting change in the governance of the country. The incident of Shaykh Ṭabarsí also created an element of tension between the clergy and the government when the Bábís openly broke away from Islam. In this vortex of bloodshed, the Báb Himself was executed in the following year in order to exterminate His Faith. However, the faithful grew in number, devotion and courage, and other significant upheavals, even bloodier than Shaykh Ṭabarsí, occurred in Nayríz (27 May 1850–29 June 1850) and Zanján (5 May 1850–2 January 1851). As such, Shaykh Ṭabarsí represented the first of a number of systematic persecutions of the Faith of the Báb to be organised by the government.

On the wisdom behind the continual persecutions of His believers, the Báb wrote:

> *These decrees were ordained by Thee so that all created things might bear witness that they have been brought into being for the sake of naught else but Thee. Thou hast withheld from them the things that bring tranquillity to their hearts, that they might know of a certainty that whatever is associated with Thy holy Being is far superior to and exalted above aught else that would satisfy them; inasmuch as Thine indomitable power pervadeth all things, and nothing can ever frustrate it. Indeed Thou hast caused these momentous happenings to come to pass that those who are endued with perception may readily recognize that they were ordained by Thee to demonstrate the loftiness of Thy divine Unity and to affirm the exaltation of Thy sanctity.*[2]

---

1 Gobineau in Nash and O'Donoghue, *Comte de Gobineau and Orientalism,* p. 176.

2 The Báb, *Selections*, p. 189.

23
What happened next

Chapter content
Growth of the Bábí-Bahá'í Faith Abrogation of some Islamic practices Triumph of good over evil Ignorance versus truth Fruits of determination

Growth of the Bábí-Bahá'í Faith

The landscape of modern Bárfurúsh (now Babol) is radically different from that of the mid 1850s. It is now connected by an airport and modern highways to other major destinations in Iran, and the once-wild coastline has seen the building of many luxury resorts along the beautiful Caspian Sea. A booming tourist industry, vast oil reserves, flourishing real estate projects, along with the always thriving farming and fishing sectors, renders the province a leading economic region in the country. Yet, beneath the evident material progress, the embers of religious bigotry and fanaticism remain smouldering within their own ashes.

Persecution of the Bahá'ís of Iran has intensified since the establishment of the Islamic Republic of Iran in 1979. Wave after wave of brutal oppression has afflicted the Bahá'í community of Iran since its inception, a pattern that has become more insidious in the last forty-five years of the Islamic revolution.

The Báb said that the blood of the martyrs is the water that irrigates the tree of the Cause and makes it grow.[1] The idea that sacrifice is a pre-requisite for growth is not new. This is a spiritual principle governing the development of the great religious traditions throughout the annals of humanity, culminating in the greatest sacrifice—martyrdom. Likewise, Bahá'u'lláh wrote: *"The blood of the martyrs waters the sacred tree of the Cause of God. A tree, unless watered, does not grow and bear fruit".*[2] After Christianity, the Bahá'í Faith is regarded as the second most widely practised religion in the world.[3] It is practised by 2,100 ethnic and tribal minorities in 218 nations, and its literature has been translated into more than 700 languages and dialects.[4]

---

1. The Báb, *Selections*, p. 190.
2. Roger White, *Bahá'u'lláh and the Fourth Estate*, p. 977.
3. *Encyclopædia Britannica*, *Worldwide Adherents of All Religions by Six Continental Areas, Mid-2002*, n.p.
4. Douglas Martin, *The Bahá'í Faith in its Second Century*, pp. 61–66.

Abrogation of some Islamic practices

It has been reported that Quddús taught that Bábís were free of the old religious taxes and dues such as <u>kh</u>ums and zakát because the old order had been replaced.[1] This was in accordance with the Báb's abrogation of all previous religious obligations, including Islamic tithes and taxes, and the initiation of a new set of religious laws and obligations to constitute a complete break with Islam. These were subject to approval and modification by Bahá'u'lláh.[2] Seeking absolution from the clergy through any monetary means was also forbidden by the Báb.[3] Every <u>Sh</u>í'ih is required to give a fifth of their income as <u>kh</u>ums. Likewise, those believers are required to pay zakát (almsgiving to the poor).[4]

In the absence of the 12th (Hidden) Imám, the clergy self-authorised to collect and administer the <u>kh</u>ums. For instance, after passing away, the testator has control only over up to one-third of his estate while.[5] The deceased individual automatically forfeits the right to dispose of the other two-thirds of his property—they are administered by the clergy.[6]

Another obligation that is enjoined upon the Muslim believers is to participate in "holy war". For instance, some of the religious preachers and their students, who had been forced to fight against the Bábís at <u>Sh</u>ay<u>kh</u> Ṭabarsí, would "roundly abuse the prince and 'Abbás-Qulí <u>Kh</u>án and curse the Sa'ídu'l-'Ulamá'; for, they said, "these have, without sufficient reason, taken us away from our studies, our discussions, and the earning of our livelihood, besides bringing us into dire peril; since to fight with men like these, who have renounced the world, and carry their lives in their hands, is to incur great risk".[7] These religious preachers and their students argued:

> They [the clergy] regard knowledge but as a means of obtaining power and winning men's esteem; they barter religion for gold and silver; and they study the Law but to demand [money for] "restitution of wrongs", "Imám's money",[8] and thirds of the property left by persons dying, or to obtain

---

[1] M. S. Ivanov, cited in *Review of Ivanov's Bbidski Vostanii* by V. Minorsky, p. 880; & Peter Smith, *The Bábí and Bahá'í Religions*, p. 54.

[2] In the *Persian Bayán* 8:17, the Báb instituted a new form of religious contribution under the name of Ḥuqúqu'lláh ("Right of God"), the proceeds of which ultimately must be passed to *Him Whom God shall make Manifest* (Bahá'u'lláh). Levy taxes are enunciated in the *Arabic Bayán* 5:19.

[3] Eschraghi, Armin, *Undermining the Foundations of Orthodoxy*, p. 236.

[4] Amédée Querry, *Droit Musulman*, Vol 1, p. 162, pp. 175–82; & Moojan Momen, *An Introduction to Shi'i Islam*, p. 179.

[5] Amédée Querry, *Droit Musulman*, vol 1, pp. 394–397, & 610–38.

[6] Pavlovitch & Powers, *A Bequest May Not Exceed One-Third*, pp. 133–72.

[7] E. G. Browne, *Taríkh-i-Jadíd*, (pp. 74-6) quoted by Nabíl-i-A'ẓam, in *The Dawn-Breakers*, p. 74.

[8] For "Restitution of wrongs" and "Imám's money" is meant the practice of <u>Sh</u>í'ih believers of bequeathing a part of their estates to the clergy to be used for religious

> bribes in lawsuits and presents for pronouncing decisions contrary to what God hath revealed. Thus do they amass wealth without the trouble of engaging in commerce or agriculture.[1]

Síghih (concubinage) was another "legal" religious practice from which the 'ulamá' obtained a large income—it was banned by the Báb.[2] Síghih was based on a twisted interpretation of Islamic traditions where Shí'ih law sanctioned the public acceptance of prostitution or "husbands for a day". Shoghi Effendi refers to síghih as "hardly distinguishable from quasi-prostitution, and which made of the turbulent and fanatical Mashhad, the national center of pilgrimage, one of the most immoral cities in Asia."[3]

The English historian, Lord Curzon (1859–1925) particularly characterised Mashhad as the most immoral city on the Asian continent. He wrote:

> ... In recognition of the long journeys which they [the pilgrims] have made, of the hardships which they have sustained, and of the distances by which they are severed from family and home, they are permitted, with the connivance of the ecclesiastical law and its officers, to contract temporary marriages during their sojourn in the city. There is a large permanent population of wives suitable for the purpose. A mullá is found, under whose sanction a contract is drawn up and formally sealed by both parties, a fee is paid, and the union is legally accomplished. After the lapse of a fortnight or a month, or whatever be the specified period, the contract terminates; the temporary husband returns to his own *lares et penates* in some distant clime, and the lady, after an enforced celibacy of fourteen days' duration, resumes her career of persevering matrimony.[4]

Síghih is still practiced, widely and legally, in contemporary Iran. In addition to the "legal" Síghih houses in Mashhad, it is reported in various media that there were also 6,000 "unlicensed" ones in 2018.[5]

The misuse of religious endowments, or *waqf*, which were meant to fund charitable causes and meet community needs, was another instance of clerical embezzlement. Waqf money was diverted from their intended uses and used by them for their own benefit or to further their own goals.[6]

---

and philanthropic purposes, atoning for any wrongs the deceased may have committed against his fellow citizens while they were alive or when they cannot be located in life.

1 E. G. Browne, *Taríkh-i-Jadíd*, p. 77.

2 Moojan Momen, *The Social Basis of the Bábí Upheavals in Iran*, p. 303; & Muḥammad Afnán, *The Báb's Bayán*, pp. 7–16.

3 Shoghi Effendi, *The Promised Day Has Come*, pp. 93–4.

4 Lord Curzon, *Persia and the Persian Question.* Cited in Nabíl-i-A'ẓam, *The Dawn-Breakers*, p. xlvii.

5 Peter Smith, *The Babí and Baha'í Religions*, pp. 34–35.

6 Willem Floor, *The Economic Role of the Ulama in Qajar Persia*, p. 72.

In general, the Báb abolished in the *Bayán* the *status quo* of religious laws, and wrote to the Islamic theologians:

> *O Concourse of the Learned! Ye have been forbidden after [the revelation of] this Book to teach anything other than it. Acquaint the people with the prescriptions (ahkám) of the Book and turn away from the obsolete (báṭil) writings that are spread amongst you ....*[1]

For example, the Báb prohibited the religious custom of kissing the hands of clergymen.[2] Similarly, the Báb also abolished any ministerial interpretation of the Word of God, which had become an important ecclesiastical prerogative and a fundamental element of religious jurisprudence (*ijtihád*).[3] This practice was used by the senior clergy hierarchy to issue decrees (*fatwá*) for death sentences (*fatwá-yi qatl*) such as the decree issued by the Sa'ídu'l-'Ulamá' for the execution of Quddús. Most significantly, the Báb forbade the imposition of the death penalty,[4] especially on the basis of religion, when Islamic religious leaders[5] used the edict as justification for the execution of non-Muslims:

> *No one is to be slain for unbelief, for the slaying of a soul is outside the religion of God ... and if anyone commands it, he is not and has not been of the Bayán, and no sin can be greater for him than this.*[6]

Triumph of good over evil

On the occasion of the 200th anniversary of the Birth of the Báb, the President of India, Dr Ram Nath Kovind paid homage to the Teachings of the Báb in a public address in New Delhi:

> The Writings which He [the Báb] has left behind continue to guide and inspire us, as they express profound eternal truths and summon the world to an exalted standard of conduct. The contributions made by the Bahá'í community ... have helped build vibrant communities across India. This includes working for the education of both girls and boys, expanding the concept of worship to include work carried in a spirit of service, and seeking to bring about the spiritual, social, and material progress simultaneously. It is my hope that those gathered here today, along with every other Indian, strive to fulfill the vision of the Báb to arise to selfless

---

1 Armin Eschraghi, *Undermining the Foundations of Orthodoxy*, p. 237.

2 Armin Eschraghi, *From Bábí Movement to the Bahá'í Faith*, p. 381.

3 *Kayhan Life, How Temporary Marriage, or Sigheh, is Spreading in Iran.* 6 September 2018. Available https://kayhanlife.com/views/opinion-how-temporary-marriage-or-sigheh-is-spreading-in-iran/

4 The Báb, *Arabic Bayán* 11:16.

5 The Báb, *Persian Bayán* 4:5.

6 The Báb in "The Bayán". See *Journal of the Royal Asiatic Society*, Oct. 1889, art. 12, pp. 927–8; also cited in *The Dawn-Breakers*, p. 330.

> and steadfast service and to make the welfare of humanity their common and collective aim.[1]

In 2018, British historian Christopher De Bellaigue, commenting on the glory of the religion of the Báb, wrote in his book *The Islamic Enlightenment* that "The Bábí movement, which began in the 1840s, went on to become an important catalyst of social progressiveness in mid-nineteenth-century Iran, promoting interreligious peace, social equality between the sexes and revolutionary anti-monarchism."[2]

Modern scholars[3] endorse the contemporary academic view that the Teachings of the Báb, as promoted by Quddús, became an agency for moral, social, religious and intellectual transformation in nineteenth century Persia, in a religious and feudalist system that, with its rottenness, ignorance, and prejudice, had already ran out of steam and was doing more harm than good.[4]

Cemeteries have been bulldozed, shrines and holy places demolished, believers imprisoned or killed, businesses closed, and youths banned from higher education. Nevertheless, underneath all those realities lies a spirit ready to re-appear like the Greek Phoenix or the Persian Simurgh.

Ignorance versus truth

It was indeed the Islamic clergy's ignorance of their own religion that drove their persecution to the Bábís. According to the Báb:

> *As to those who have debarred themselves from the Revelation of God, they have indeed failed to understand the significance of a single letter of the Qur'án, nor have they obtained the slightest notion of the Faith of Islám, otherwise they would not have turned away from God ... thinking that they are doing righteous work for the sake of God.*[5]

The Báb warned the Shí'ih clerics not to mix their own religious theories with the original Scripture:

> *O concourse of divines! Fear God from this day onwards in the views ye advance, for He Who is Our Remembrance in your midst, and Who cometh from Us, is, in very truth, the Judge and Witness. Turn away from that which ye lay hold of and which the Book of God, the True One, hath not sanctioned,*

---

1 *Bahá'í World News Service*, 22 December 2019. Available at: https://www.youtube.com/watch?v=udFv71iIf-c

2 Christopher de Bellaigue, *The Islamic Enlightenment*, p. 96.

3 Nikie Keddie & Yann Richard, *Continuity and Change Under the Qajars.;* Tadd Graham Fernée, *Modernity and Nation-making;* Geoffrey Nash, *Aryan and Semite;* & Harsha Ram, "Literature as World Revolution".

4 Jürgen Osterhammel, *The Transformation of the World*; Richard Losch, *The Many Faces of Faith;* Jack Kalpakian, *Representing the Unpresentable.*

5 The Báb, *Selections*, p. 140.

for on the Day of Resurrection ye shall, upon the Bridge, be, in very truth, held answerable for the position ye occupied.[1]

In this regard, Quddús makes clear to Sa'ídu'l-'Ulamá' the importance of the independent investigation of truth and of giving proofs when discussing religious matters:

> It is imperative for every person to examine, before himself and his God, all matters to which he commits himself, and above all in matters of religion, with all fairness of mind and firmness of reason ... If anyone puts forth a claim and presents proofs from the precise verses of the Book of God and also from *akhbár*,[2] he then is rightful [in his claim] and his [claim] is justified amongst the wise and people of the faith. If on the other hand someone claims a position for which, may God forbid, he does not have a firm proof from the Book of God and from the reliable ḥadíth,[3] to the above-mentioned groups his [claim] is weak and void.[4]

The Báb has strongly condemned the religious leaders who opposed His Cause. To 'Abdu'ṣ-Ṣáḥib, a high-ranking Muslim divine, the Báb wrote the following statements equally applicable to Sa'ídu'l-'Ulamá':

> *Therefore unto thee shall be assigned the fire which was meant for those who turned away from God in that land, inasmuch as thou art their leader; would that thou might be of them who heed. Hadst thou faithfully obeyed the Decree of God, all the inhabitants of thy land would have followed thee, and would have themselves entered into the celestial Paradise, content with the good-pleasure of God forevermore.*[5]

> *Thou hast set thyself up as one of the learned in the Faith of Islám, that thou mightest save the believers, yet thou didst cause thy followers to descend into the fire, for when the verses of God were sent forth thou didst deprive thyself therefrom and yet reckoned thyself to be of the righteous ....*[6]

Fruits of determination

It is in human nature that we aspire to grow and develop morally and spiritually. However, the responsibilities, duties, and concerns for our day-to-day existence, unconsciously create conditions that attract us to this terrestrial plane. Life's journey is sometimes bumpy and rough. We suffer, endure pain and sickness, have setbacks, feel hunger and cold, harshness appears unpredictably,

---

1 The Bab, *Selections*, p. 44.

2 A<u>kh</u>*bár* are traditions and saying attributed to Muḥammad and the Imáms, the first twelve descendants of Prophet Muḥammad.

3 Prophetic tradition and narrative relating to the deeds and utterances of the Prophet and his Companions.

4 Abbas Amanat, *Resurrection and Renewal,* p. 185.

5 The Báb, *Selections*, p. 32.

6 The Báb, *Selections*, p. 32.

and randomness surrounds our existence for good and for bad. In order to survive, we dream, form hopes and aspirations, and draw upon metaphysical realities to calm our worries and obtain contentment.

Records of lives like Quddús' can provide us with guidance and appease our anxieties. Here is a young man, unassuming at first, born into a modest family, who studied the theological sciences of his times, and through perseverance, trust, and relentless effort to please his Beloved, he transformed himself into a hero and a saint, later sustaining the worst tests; and, yet, he died forgiving his enemies. He became "the possessor in a high degree of all manner of miraculous powers and divine illuminations.[1] So much was achieved in his short life that he instilled hope in many people from a broad range of backgrounds. Further, Quddús' life story shows that men and women are not always the product of their environments but the result of eagerness to improve and progress.

A number of characters in religious literature have shown that we can arise and triumph over this mundane reality with its vicissitudes, that life is more than the eventualities and the inclemencies from birth to death. Somehow, we relate to these personages, mortals as we are, as they show how the ladder from here to heaven can be happily attempted and, with drawbacks and successes, trials and errors, at times falling backwards, we finally begin to move forward. Sooner or later, slowly or quickly, we pick up our souls to be back on track towards achieving the world of the spirit.

Personages like Quddús inspire us to understand that discipline and perseverance in pursuing a goal are paramount and that effort can be more valuable than ability. Effort can improve through working incrementally harder and within a short time, while developing talents takes a long time. As a whole, we can improve more effectively as a result of working harder rather than only relying on self-ability.

Inspired by the divine magic of the Writings of the Báb and through his personal effort, Quddús soared up into the highest spheres of servitude and adoration. He showed us that the sky is the limit if you align to the Sun and to the brilliant stars. As 'Abdu'l-Bahá stated: *"Aim high, choose noble ends"*[2] *"To thank Him for this [being chosen], make ye a mighty effort, and choose for yourselves a* noble goal."[3] *"He who is associated with a great Cause becomes great"*.[4]

"Upon arrival at that city and meeting the Báb in the streets [of Shíráz]," wrote Mírzá Habíbu'lláh Afnán, a relative of the Báb, "without seeking proofs or signs, nor evidence or deductions, he [Quddús] instantly attained complete certitude.

---

1 Mírzá Ḥusayn Hamadání, *The New History (Taríkh-i-Jadíd)*, pp. 39-40.

2 'Abdu'l-Bahá, *The Secret of Divine Civilization,* pp. 104–5.

3 'Abdu'l-Bahá, *Selections from the Writings of 'Abdu'l-Bahá*, p. 35.

4 Words attributed to 'Abdu'l-Bahá'. Cited in Marzieh Gail, *Dawn Over Mount Hira*, p. 102.

From the moment of that meeting, he ranked among the foremost disciples, manifesting unsurpassed qualities, displaying all-embracing virtues.[1]

The Báb Himself makes clear that it is not about fortune or luck but about self-work: "*This doth not mean that he* [Quddús] *was made the object of a special favour, nay, his is a favour which God hath vouchsafed unto all men, yet they have suffered themselves to be veiled from it.*"[2] Quddús' last words bear witness of this truth: "I have striven to show them the path that leads to their salvation".[3]

---

1 Afnán, Mírzá Ḥabíbu'lláh. *The Genesis of the Bábí-Bahá'í Faiths in Shíráz and Fárs*, p. 43.

2 The Báb, *Selections*, p. 190.

3 Nabíl-i-A'ẓam, *The Dawn-Breakers*, p. 411.

24
Quddús as the mirror of the Báb

Chapter content
The Báb and Quddús
Religious hatred
A monument to infamy
Saints and heroes
<u>Sh</u>ay<u>kh</u> Ṭabarsí and the Bahá'í Identity
Message for the youth
Postscript

The Báb and Quddús

The Writings of the Báb indicate that the life of Quddús reflected the verses of the *Bayán*,[1] and that the Báb was the Primal or First Point[2] whereas Quddús was the Last Point.[3]

The Báb wrote that Quddús reflected Himself.[4] Shoghi Effendi also stated that Quddús "reflected more than any of the disciples of the Báb the light of His teaching."[5] Quddús "powerfully mirrored forth the radiance of his own beloved Master," said Nabíl the historian.[6] "He reflected the radiance of the beloved Báb," is another tribute to Quddús, "just as the still water reflects the face of the full moon."[7]

Although born from opposite socio-economic backgrounds, the Báb and Quddús had several things in common. For instance, they were both descendants of the Prophet Muḥammad. They were nearly of the same age[8] and bore the same compound name in reverse order: *'Alí-Muḥammad the Báb* and *Muḥammad-'Alí Quddús.*[9]

---

1 Nader Saiedi, *Gate of the Heart,* p. 285; & 'Abdu'l-Bahá, *Light of the World,* p. 11.

2 The Báb, *Selections,* p. 12.

3 Shoghi Effendi, *God Passes By,* p. 49.

4 Stephen Lambden, *Muḥammad 'Ali Bārfurushi, Quddūs.* Available https://hurqalya.ucmerced.edu/node/4081; & Nader Saiedi, *Gate of the Heart,* p. 285.

5 Letter dated 11 November 1936, written on behalf of Shoghi Effendi to an individual believer. In The Universal House of Justice, "Letters of Living ...".

6 Nabíl-i-A'ẓam, *The Dawn-Breakers,* p. 265.

7 Kamal Ma'ani, *Quddús: 1822–1849*, cover page.

8 Sepehr Manuchehri, *Taqiyyah (Dissimulation) in the Bábí and Bahá'í Religions,* p. 236.

9 The Báb's name was *Muḥammad-'Alí* whereas Quddús' name was 'Alí-Muḥammad.

Their virtues were acclaimed and recognised by the public[1] and both served the Cause of God in the prime of their youth. Their style and content of writing were similar.[2] Both are referred in the Writings of the Báb as "master of the seven letters".[3]

The Báb and Quddús attended sessions by the sage Siyyid Káẓim in Karbilá around the same time[4] and travelled together to perform the pilgrimage to Mecca—they remained together for a year. About the Báb, Siyyid Káẓim described Him to his disciples as "A highly esteemed and distinguished Personage".[5] In turn, of Quddús, Siyyid Káẓim said "... he has such a rank that I am not even worth[y of] serving him."[6]

The Báb and Quddús, while in Shíráz,[7] were among the first to suffer persecution in Persia—both were tortured.[8] They were struck on their faces and their Siyyid turbans were flung to the floor, a major insult during those times.[9] Their initial teaching effort was in their own birth towns but they were later forced to leave the towns.[10]

The Báb gave Quddús important missions to undertake on His behalf[11] and Quddús was seen as the Báb's deputy.[12] Further, Quddús wore the Báb's silk turban that he was given as a gift.[13] People noted in Quddús "the charm of his person"[14] and his "dignified and noble" appearance[15] whereas the Báb was described as "a Youth of radiant countenance".[16] Eyewitnesses have reported on their youthfulness.[17]

---

1 The Báb, *Selections,* p. 96; & Nabíl-i-A'ẓam, *The Dawn-Breakers,* p. 261.

2 Moojan Momen and Todd Lawson, "Ruḥ al-Quddús", pp. 709–10.

3 A. L. M. Nicolas, *Le Beyan Arabe,* p. 98. The seven letters written in Arabic for the name 'Alí-Muḥammad (على محمد) are: ' ('ayn), *l, í, m, ḥ, m* and *d.*

4 Hushmand Dehghan, *Ganj-i-Pinhán,* p. 42.

5 Nabíl-i-A'ẓam, *The Dawn-Breakers,* p. 26.

6 Ruhollah Mehrabkhani, *La Aurora del Día Prometido,* p. 63.

7 Moojan Momen, *The Bábí and Bahá'í Religions, 1844–1944,* p. 69

8 Nabíl-i-A'ẓam, *The Dawn-Breakers,* pp. 142–3; & 320.

9 A. L. M. Nicolas, *Seyyèd Ali-Mohammed dit le Bâb,* pp. 22–226; & Nabíl-i-A'ẓam, *The Dawn-Breakers,* p. 550 & 410.

10 Hooshmand Dehghan, *Ganj-i-Pinhán,* p. 206; & Shoghi Effendi, *God Passes By,* p. 13.

11 Ibrahim Ruhi, *Kitáb-i-Quddúsiyyíh,* p. 57. Cited in Hushmand Dehghan, *Ganj-i-Pinhán,* pp. 60–61.

12 Abbas Amanat, *Resurrection and Renewal,* p. 186; & Habib Borjian, *A Mázandaráni Account of the Babi Incident at Shaikh Ṭabarsí,* p. 390.

13 Hasan Balyuzi, *The Báb,* p. 149; & Nabíl-i-A'ẓam, *The Dawn-Breakers,* p. 400.

14 Nabíl-i-A'ẓam, *The Dawn-Breakers,* p. 183.

15 *Tarikh al-Quddosí,* by p. 57, cited in Hushmand Dehghan, *Ganj-i-Pinhán,* pp. 60–1.

16 Nabíl-i-A'ẓam, *The Dawn-Breakers,* p.526.

17 Nabíl-i-A'ẓam, *The Dawn-Breakers,* p. 145; & cited in Houri Faláhi-Skuce, *A Radiant Gem,* p. 172.

The chronicles reveal that the Báb performed numerous miracles.[1] Likewise, Quddús was involved in a few supranatural occurrences. According to historian Peter Smith, the Báb and Quddús performed "miracles—over 2,000 according to one Bábí cleric—but there were expressions of divine grace rather than magical practice as such."[2] Nonetheless, Quddús was reluctant that these occurrences or "miracles" should be divulged:

> So much was the case that Mullá Mírzá Muḥammad, one of the most eminent of those divines and highly-gifted men who hastened to accept the new Manifestation, one who had, moreover, himself witnessed the greater part of the occurrences connected with it, and who was amongst the remnant who escaped the sword at Shaykh Ṭabarsí, at the request of a certain learned and eminent enquirer set down in writing two thousand four hundred occurrences of a miraculous character which he had witnessed on the part of His Holiness, and, during the siege of the Castle of Shaykh Ṭabarsí, on the part of Jináb-i-Quddús and his companions and supporters.
>
> But when he had completed this, he became aware that His Holiness [Quddús] in no wise regarded these miracles, wonders, and supernatural occurrences as a proof of his mission, and did not desire them to be published; wherefore he effaced what he had recorded in that precious book, and refrained from publishing it.[3]

As with Islamic prophecies,[4] these indicated that the Qá'im would appear along with Jesus and that is possibly why Quddús, was regarded by a number of the Bábís as the return of Christ."[5] Both were alluded to together in the Bible and the *Qur'án*.[6]

Both were the subject of baseless accusations and calumnies. At His trial in Tabríz in July 1848, the Báb was accused of foolishness, slander, ignorance, presumptuousness, desecrating God's *Qur'án*, hypocrisy, heresy, and other absurd allegations.[7] Quddús was the victim of slander and calumny, and was referred to by his enemies as one who "deceives the people", an "unclean infidel",[8]

---

1 Boris Handal, *The Dispensation of the Báb*, pp. 53–4.

2 Peter Smith, *The Bábí and Bahá'í Religions*, p. 38.

3 E. G. Browne, *Tarí<u>kh</u>-i-Jadíd*, p. 42.

4 Abbas Amanat, *Resurrection and Renewal*, p. 11.

5 Moojan Momen, *Understanding Religion*, p. 558; & Abbas Amanat, *Resurrection and Renewal*, pp. 187.

6 Shoghi Effendi, *God Passes By*, p. 49; & 'Abdu'l-Bahá, *Some Answered Questions*, chapter 11, para. 30.

7 Denis MacEoin, *The Trial of the Báb*, pp. 272–317.

8 Habib Borjian, *A Mázandaráni Account of the Babi Incident at Shaikh Ṭabarsí*, p. 390.

a "hypocrite",[1] an "apostate"[2] and guilty of "aiming at the subversion of the Persian Government".[3]

The Báb was bastinadoed in Tabríz[4] while Quddús was flagellated in Shíráz.[5] They were accused of heresy and sentenced to death by leading divines.[6] Their martyrdoms closely followed,[7] as prophesied by the Báb, and a promise of immortal reunion was given at their last farewell.[8] Both were publicly martyred in public squares, in front of scores of people, after being paraded barefoot on the streets.[9]

Furthermore, around the time of their deaths, large numbers of believers were slaughtered: Quddús was killed six days after the holocaust of Shaykh Ṭabarsí whereas the Báb died ten days after the massacre of Nayríz when several hundred of believers were killed.[10] While Quddús at the time of his martyrdom was "the victim of the most refined and wanton barbarity at the hands of the enemy",[11] about the Báb's martyrdom, Bahá'u'lláh wrote, "They suspended Him in the air, and the hosts of misbelief flung at Him the bullets of malice and hatred, piercing the body of the One unto Whom the Holy Spirit is a humble servant..."[12]

The princes in charge of their custody washed their hands of their duty and surrendered their prisoners to the awaiting clergy.[13] At their executions, both the Báb and Quddús lamented the sad spiritual condition of their kinsmen.[14] Their dead bodies were thrown out on the city outskirts and later rescued by the believers.[15] Furthermore, immediate family members were martyred during their lives.[16] The Báb lost his paternal uncle whereas Quddús lost his step-

---

1 IslamHouse, *Una Breve Mirada sobre el Baabismo y el Baha'ismo.* Available https://islamhouse.com/fatwa/es/una-breve-mirada-al-baabismo-y-el-baha-ismo-2788716. Also Abdul Rahman Wakil, *Baha'i Faith*, p. 110.

2 Hushmand Dehghan, *Ganj-i-Pinhán*, pp. 60–1.

3 Maulana Muhammad Ali, *History and Doctrines of the Babi Movement*, p. 17.

4 E. G. Browne, *Materials for the Study of the Bábí Religion*, pp. 260–262.

5 Hasan Balyuzi, *Eminent Bahá'ís in the Time of Bahá'u'lláh*, p. 14.

6 Nabíl-i-A'ẓam, *The Dawn-Breakers,* pp. 508–10 & pp. 409–10.

7 The Báb's and Quddús' martyrdoms occurred on 9 July 1850 and 16 May 1849, respectively.

8 Nabíl-i-A'ẓam, *The Dawn-Breakers,* pp. 142–3.

9 E. G. Browne, *Bábísm,* p. 345; & Hushmand Dehghan, *Ganj-i-Pinhán,* pp. 113–22.

10 Nabíl-i-A'ẓam, *The Dawn-Breakers,* p. 499.

11 Nabíl-i-A'ẓam, *The Dawn-Breakers,* p. 415.

12 Bahá'u'lláh, *Days of Remembrance,* section 35.

13 E. G. Browne, *Taríkh-i-Jadíd*, p. 294; & Nabíl-i-A'ẓam, *The Dawn-Breakers,* pp. 409–10.

14 The Báb in Nabíl-i-A'ẓam, *The Dawn-Breakers,* p. 514; & Nabíl-i-A'ẓam, *The Dawn-Breakers,* p. 411.

15 Shoghi Effendi, *God Passes By,* p. 54; & Habib Borjian, *A Mázandaráni Account of the Babi Incident at Shaikh Ṭabarsí,* item No. 32.

16 Fazel Mazandarani, *Taríkh Ẓuhúr al-Ḥaqq*, vol. 3, pp. 421–2; & Ahang Rabbani, "The

brother on his father's side. Quddús died a week before the fifth anniversary of the Declaration of the Báb in Shíráz. A voluminous amount of the writings of the Báb disappeared His pilgrimage to Mecca,[1] and of Quddús during the Shaykh Ṭabarsí events, never to be recovered.[2]

A century-and-a-half later, the homes of the Báb and Quddús were demolished following the so-called Islamic revolution (January 1978–February 1979), acts that were condemned by the international community who echoed their names in many fora.[3] The House of the Báb is one of the Bahá'í Faith's most holy sites in Iran while the shrine of Quddús represents their most sacred sepulchre in Iran.

Bahá'u'lláh, in a fasting prayer, gives us a glimpse the mystery of the quasi-symmetrical relationship between the Báb and Quddús:

> *And all honor be upon him* [Quddús] *who was the last to come unto Him, whose arrival was like His arrival, and Thy manifestation in him* [Quddús] *like Thy manifestation in Him* [The Báb] *except that he was illumined with the lights of His face and prostrated himself before Him and testified to his servitude unto Him ....*[4]

There are many examples of reflection in nature. A reflection is the casting back of an image seen in a mirror or other shiny surface. Heat in the form of energy can be reflected by shiny objects. Sound waves are reflected back to a listener as an echo from a hard surface. A reflection can give the illusion of objects being equal when they are not. However, it is the best instructional metaphor, whether visual, sensory or aural, to explain similar qualities acquired from a more notable person, as in the case of the spiritual seal of the Báb being imprinted on Quddús, and how this reflected image can be appreciated by others.

This binary and reflective association between the Báb and Quddús is demonstrated by the meaning of the Báb being the "*First*" and Quddús the "*Last*",[5] of the Báb being the "*founder*" and Quddús the "*promoter*",[6] or the Báb being the "*sun*" and Quddús His "*moon*".[7] The latter was a metaphor from 'Abdu'l-Bahá,[8] perhaps because Quddús reflected many aspects of the Báb.[9]

Conversion of the Great-Uncle of the Báb", p. 28.

1 Nabíl-i-A'ẓam, *The Dawn-Breakers,* p. 132.

2 Nabíl-i-A'ẓam, *The Dawn-Breakers,* p. 132.

3 Office of the UN High Commissioner for Human Rights. *Mandates of the Special Rapporteur in the Field of Cultural rights; the Special Rapporteur on Freedom of Religion or Belief; and the Special Rapporteur on the Situation of Human Rights in the Islamic Republic of Iran.* Geneva, 2016.

4 Bahá'u'lláh in *The Importance of Obligatory Prayers and a Fasting.*

5 Nader Saiedi, *Gate of the Heart,* p. 285.

6 'Abdu'l-Bahá, *Some Answered Questions,* chapter 10, item 29.

7 'Abdu'l-Bahá, *Some Answered Questions,* p. 55.

8 'Abdu'l-Bahá, *Some Answered Questions,* p. 55.

9 Shoghi Effendi, *God Passes By,* p. 49; & 'Abdu'l-Bahá, *Some Answered Questions,* p. 63.

Furthermore, Bahá'u'lláh elevated Quddús as part of the divine triad of "*messengers charged with imposture*" *(Qur'án* 36:14)[1] along with Himself and the Báb; while 'Abdu'l-Bahá described him as one of the three holy birds descending "*from an infinite height*" with "*their majesty and glory*".[2] Quddús is also included in the reference to the "advent of the Báb, Quddús, and the Living Countenance [Bahá'u'lláh]",[3] all of which identifies Bahá'u'lláh, the Báb and Quddús as the stellar figures of the Bábí Dispensation.

Regardless of the difference in station between them, the above analogies, suggest that the Báb had Himself engraved onto the spirit of Quddús. Shoghi Effendi also referred to him as the "stainless mirror"4 of the Manifestation of the Báb.

These analogies should not be interpreted as a dimension of unicity (nor sameness) between the Báb and Quddús. In his book *The Dispensation of Bahá'u'lláh* Shoghi Effendi addresses the case of the relationship between Manifestation of God and the foremost believer in the context of the Bahá'í Faith. The Guardian explains, for instance, that articulating a possible "mystical unity" between Bahá'u'lláh and 'Abdu'l-Bahá—His Interpreter, Successor and Centre of His Covenant —is an "erroneous conception"[5] The only divine identities established are from a Manifestation of God to another Manifestation of God. Referring to His own essential identity with the Báb, Bahá'u'lláh wrote, "*He Who now voiceth the Word of God is none other except the Primal Point Who hath once again been manifest*".[6] Conversely, the Báb wrote of how He and Bahá'u'lláh both comprise a single reality:

> *Therefore let not your recognition become fruitless, inasmuch as the Bayán, notwithstanding the sublimity of its station, beareth fealty to Him Whom God will make manifest, and it is He Who beseemeth most to be acclaimed as the Seat of divine Reality, though indeed He is I and I am He.*[7]

Religious hatred

The religious atmosphere in Bárfurú<u>sh</u> was poisoned by the venom of the Sa'ídu'l-'Ulamá', a religious leader recognised by many as the most prominent cleric of the region. However, the Sa'ídu'l-'Ulamá', out of arrogance, could not tolerate a man like Quddús fifty years younger than himself can challenge his ideas.

1 Shoghi Effendi, *God Passes By*, p. 49.
2 'Abdu'l-Bahá, *Tablets of Abdul-Baha Abbas*, vol. 3, pp. 678–81.
3 Nader Saiedi, "Concealment and Revelation in Bahá'u'lláh's Book of the River", p. 48.
4 Shoghi Effendi, *Lawḥ-i-Garn-i-Áhibáy-i-Sharq*, p. 31,
5 Shoghi Effendi, *The World Order of Bahá'u'lláh*, p. 137.
6 Quoted in Shoghi Effendi, *The World Order of Bahá'u'lláh*, pp. 138-139.
7 The Báb, *Selections*, pp. 167–168.

The Sa'ídu'l-'Ulamá' was finally rewarded by the Sháh for his fight against the "infidels". The Sháh "valued [in the Bárfurúsh clerics] a trustworthy local ally against the troublesome local powers of Mázandarán," remarked Mohammad Ali Kazembeyki. As a result of the events at Shaykh Ṭabarsí, the Sháh "demonstrated much respect and attention to Sa'ídu'l-'Ulamá'. To indicate its commitment to Islam, the government increased the budget of the religious ceremonies of Muḥarram[1] in Mázandarán from 190 tumans in 1848 to 1,407 tumans in 1859 ...."[2] The arrangement did not last long because the Hand of God took the Sa'ídu'l-'Ulamá' to the other world about five years later.

It was easy for the Sa'ídu'l-'Ulamá' to mislead an ignorant population, who still thought that killing an unbeliever was a righteous religious deed, into becoming a bunch of intolerant and fanatical bigots whose merits included murder, acts of violence, and widespread looting. No wonder then that Bahá'u'lláh described religious leaders as a main cause of disunity in society. He wrote in the *Kitáb-i-Íqán:*

> *Leaders of religion, in every age, have hindered their people from attaining the shores of eternal salvation, inasmuch as they held the reins of authority in their mighty grasp. Some for the lust of leadership, others through want of knowledge and understanding, have been the cause of the deprivation of the people.*[3]

Just as religious love can unite people, so religious hatred leads to fake unity, ironically. It is astounding to note the number of conflicts and wars started in the name of God that are recorded by human history. 'Abdu'l-Bahá succinctly stated: "*If religion becomes a cause of dislike, hatred and division, it were better to be without it ....*"[4] Bahá'u'lláh stated in another warning: "*Should the lamp of religion be obscured, chaos and confusion will ensue, and the lights of fairness and justice, of tranquility and peace cease to shine.*"[5]

The attacks incited by the Sa'ídu'l-'Ulamá' on the fort at Shaykh Ṭabarsí were a clear demonstration of the importance of the above statements. It is interesting to note that the prohibition of force to convert people to Islam—an accusation frequently made by its detractors—occurs early in the *Qur'án*. In Islam, the principle of tolerance was categorically upheld in the Sura of the Disbelievers: "*To you your religion; to me my religion*".[6] On the use of force to convert Muḥammad said:

1 Muslim religious ceremonies to grieve over the death of Imám Ḥusayn.

2 Mohammad Ali Kazembeyki, *Society, Politics and Economics,* pp. 129–130.

3 Bahá'u'lláh, *The Kitáb-i-Íqán*, p. 15.

4 'Abdu'l-Bahá, *Paris Talks*, p.130.

5 Bahá'u'lláh, *Tablets of Bahá'u'lláh,* p. 125.

6 *Qur'án* 109:6 (Rodwell).

> *What! Will thou compel men to become believers? No soul can believe but by the permission of God* (10:99–100) .... *Surely, God loves not the aggressors*[1]

Conversely, discourse and reasoned communication were seen to be essential to calling people to the true Faith as the Báb reiterated:

> *Summon thou to the way of thy Lord with wisdom and with kindly warning: dispute with them in the kindest manner*[2]

Inclusion and acceptance were also advised in the *Qur'án* when interacting with individuals of different faiths:

> *Revile not those whom they call on beside God, lest they, in their ignorance, despitefully revile Him. Thus have we planned out their actions for every people; then shall they return to their Lord, and He will declare to them what those actions have been.* (6:108)[3]

The *Qur'án* also specifies tolerance is better than rigid fanaticism in the observance of laws, in contrast to current orthodoxies:

> *A kind speech and forgiveness is better than alms followed by injury*[4]

Muḥammad warned of the dangers of self-righteous theological disputes that lead to sectarian hostility and often violence as preached by the Sa'ídu'l-'Ulamá'.

> *And if God had pleased He had surely made you all one people; but He would test you by what He hath given to each. Be emulous, then, in good deeds. To God shall ye all return, and He will tell you concerning the subjects of your disputes*[5]

This clergy was used to a toxic way of speaking, which was very different from the verses of the *Qur'án.* For example, when addressing his congregation in Bárfurúsh, he stated:

> Awake, for our enemies stand at our very doors, ready to wipe out all that we cherish as pure and holy in Islam! ... It is the duty of all the inhabitants of Bárfurúsh, both young and old, both men and women, to arm themselves against these contemptible wreckers of Islam, and by every means in their power to resist their onset. To-morrow, at the hour of dawn, let all of you arise and march out to exterminate their forces.[6]

---

1 *Qur'án* 2:190 (Rodwell).

2 *Qur'án* 16:125 (Rodwell).

3 *Qur'án* 6:108 (Rodwell).

4 *Qur'án* 2:263 (Rodwell).

5 *Qur'án* 5:52–53 (Rodwell).

6 Nabíl-i-A'ẓam, *The Dawn-Breakers*, p. 328.

A monument to infamy

In a futile attempt to resuscitate the ignominious figure of the Sa'ídu'l-'Ulamá' of Bárfurúsh, forgotten by his own fellow townsmen for over a century, some prominent people in the city decided in 1980 to erect a statue for him in a different part of the city with its face turned away from the Sabzih-Maydán. The public backlash showed its mark in social media against such measures.[1]

Official news report continued this hate speech tradition:

> He [Sa'ídu'l-'Ulamá'] prevented the progress and expansion of Bahá'ísm in this city with his actions .... Sa'ídu'l-'Ulamá', along with the people and the ruler of Mázindarán, stood up against this group[2] and were able to execute two of the leaders of this misguided group in the current Sabzih-Maydán of Babol.[3]

Likewise, in recent decades some Muslims have preposterously celebrated the efforts of the Sa'ídu'l-'Ulamá' for uprooting the rebellion of the Bábís headed by Quddús. "Under the leadership of Sa'ídu'l-'Ulamá'," a non-Bahá'í author wrote, "the clerics of Bárfurúsh demonstrated well their ability to mobilize the masses."[4] "I have vowed," the Sa'ídu'l-'Ulamá' affirmed once, "to deny myself both food and sleep until such time as I am able to end the life of Ḥájí Muḥammad-'Alí [Quddús] with my own hands!"—as he did.[5]

Quddús had previously addressed these warning words to the Sa'ídu'l-'Ulamá':

> I counsel thee, O man, not to be deceived by the worldly pomp and splendour, and not to rely upon its possessions and riches. Verily, the Day of Resurrection shall come upon thee as the day of thy birth and thou shalt not have the power to do anything whatsoever. Verily, in that day, based on what thy hands hath wrought, thou shall be held accountable at the presence of the Lord.[6]

This infamous statue representing that "notorious and false-hearted tyrant"[7] looks away in shame from the sacred spot where he martyred Quddús with his own hands, now a beautiful and serene public park with "orange trees, palms and

---

1 Criticism of the new era of reconstruction of Babol Squares. (25 January 2013) https://www.facebook.com/mashahir.babol/photos/a.184081534991084/457966847602550/?locale=hr_HR

2 A reference to the Bábís.

3 *Rasa News Agency*, Wednesday 26 February 1980. Available https://rasanews.ir/fa/news/60509/

4 Mohammad Ali Kazembeyki, *Society, Politics and Economics in Mazandaran*, p. 139.

5 Nabíl-i-A'ẓam, *The Dawn-Breakers*, p. 409.

6 Hooshmand Dehghan, *Ganj-i-Pinhán*, pp. 214–5.

7 Nabíl-i-A'ẓam, *The Dawn-Breakers*, p. 265.

stately trees",[1] along with flowers and birds that together celebrate his life all day long. The humble sacred spot from the other side appears saying to the Sa'ídu'l-'Ulamá' that he had failed in his malice.

One would say that history has restored justice, setting in stone and reminding the world about his crimes and deceptiveness. Universal consciousness could not ask more from that pedestal of ignominy raising its voice demanding that the light of religious tolerance forever shine forth in Iran against barbarity and bestiality.

The Faith of the Shaykh Ṭabarsí companions nowadays encompasses more than 100,000 communities all over the world, each of them being the like of the old Bárfurúsh.[2] Indeed, as the Báb had promised, "... *God hath indeed pledged to establish Thy sovereignty throughout all countries and over the people that dwell therein.*"[3]

From Quddús' time, when 20,000 people including 6,000 families were resident, in 2016 the city was accommodating about 250,000 inhabitants in over 81,000 households.[4] After 170 years, the map of Bárfurúsh has undoubtedly evolved and reshaped. From being a conglomerate of small urban settlements and houses set apart from each other and spread throughout the green forest, it has now turned into an amorphous cartography with an ever-expanding forest of cement where green areas once appeared. The Bágh-i-Sháh (The Royal Garden), a little lake with a small island in the centre, where Quddús was imprisoned has long since dried up and the island paved in 1931 in order to create residential neighbourhoods.[5] [6]

The extended Sabzih-Maydán, the area where Quddús was executed, once an empty plain is now a conglomerate of parks including the Municipality park, the premises of the Babol University of Medical Sciences, the Department of Education and some hospital and sports complexes. It also includes the more specific "Sabzih-Maydán", the place where Quddús was executed, which is now a circular traffic roundabout garden 30 metres in diameter. That space used to be the entrance to the city for people coming inland and located on the main road to the capital.

At the old Palangh ("Panther") caravanserai, where three Bábís were shot, only two ruined sections of the original building now stand. Located in the Kásih Ghar (کاسه گر, "Potter") area of the Sabzih Maydán, the 6,000 square metre

---

1 Guy Murchie, *Journey through Northern Iran*, pp. 8-10.

2 Douglas Martin, "The Bahá'í Faith in its Second Century", pp. 61–66.

3 The Báb, *Selections*, p. 57.

4 The Statistical Center of Iran. *Census of the Islamic Republic of Iran, 1395 (2016).* Available at: https://web.archive.org/web/20211007110909/https://www.amar.org.ir/Portals/0/census/1395/results/abadi/CN95_HouseholdPopulationVillage_02.xlsx

5 Vahid Nattaj, *The role of landscape elements*, p. 13.

6 East Bahru'l-Arim West Bahru'l-Arim (Dezdak-Chal), Lady Park and Mollakola.

Palangh caravanserai today is used as a garage and a warehouse kept by a rusty and lonely metal gate. The remnants are now a registered historical monument.

The nucleus of the old city around the old Panj Shanbih bazaar and the mosques of Sa'ídu'l-'Ulamá and Sharí'atmadár, have also moved southwards due to construction developments during the last century. While the extended Sabzih-Maydán marked the far end of the city, it is now its geographical and cultural centre on the urban map, as if Divine Justice would like to honour on earth the most well-known of its citizens.

Unlike public statues of mortar and metal, the place of Quddús' execution is marked by numerous graceful trees, crafted by nature as a living monument to the world. Nourished by his sacred blood, the shrubs emerge from the bosom of the earth, reaching toward the sun and moon, while the stars keep eternal vigil. Standing tall in the park, these trees, with their semi-spherical green canopies, join countless other species, all inviting visitors to pray beneath their fresh shadows. As the breeze whispers from the Caspian Sea, their foliage seems to sing in a seraphic chorus, echoing Quddús' stanza: "Holy, holy [Quddús], the Lord our God, the Lord of the angels and the spirit!" Fragrant like the oranges, tangerines, mandarins, clementines, lemons, and limes—the emblematic fruits of Mázindarán—these trees blossom golden in spring, bear fiery fruit in fall, or dress in emerald throughout the year. The beautiful trees of the Sabzi Maydán, growing between heaven and earth, remind us that, despite the cruel treatment and fall of the Most Holy One in those hallowed surroundings, it is certain that Quddús is with the Well-Beloved. Stirred by the eternal soft breezes of the Sabzi-Maydán and warmed by the generous subtropical weather, these trees declare to the world that Quddús is not dead but alive, just as the Cause he championed lives on with devotion and renunciation.

Saints and heroes

There are many heroes in history. Interestingly, the proto Indo-European root of the term *hero* is to watch over, to be a protector, adding an element of mindfulness to the common soldierly connotation. Certainly, Quddús was a 'Hero' with a capital *H*. In addition to his bravery, Quddús protected the Bábí Faith with his work, writings and leadership. The actions of Quddús were driven by his strong desire to protect the lives of his companions.

Quddús reminded the besieged Bábís at Shaykh Ṭabarsí when they were facing a powerful military enemy that: "Our purpose is to protect ourselves that we may be able to continue our labours for the regeneration of men."[1] We all are born with the capacity to become a hero, either with a small or capital *H*, depending on the degree to which we decide to emulate the devotion, erudition and courage of souls like Quddús. Therefore, this broader definition encompasses devoted believers who never shed their blood, such as Bahíyyih

[1] Nabíl-i-A'ẓam, *The Dawn-Breakers*, pp. 362–3.

Khánum[1] to whom Shoghi Effendi referred as "the most outstanding heroine of the Bahá'í Faith".[2]

The Comte de Gobineau (1816–1882) wrote that Quddús was "... a great saint, a character who cannot be sufficiently venerated. His knowledge, the purity of his doctrine, the brilliance of his devotion, all that happened to him afterwards, recommend him in the most clear way to the veneration of believers."[3] He has also been referred to as "a close favorite of the Báb",[4] the "quiet, unassuming Bábí chief,"[5]" "the pietistic, self-effacing *'árif,*[6] and the mystic".[7]

Quddús felt himself to be created a new being, physically the same, but living on a spiritually different station. He once told his father that he was now a new being or at least someone whose inner self had drastically evolved over the last few years: "Your son lost his way one day when you sent him to collect fire-wood and now is in some other place."[8]

Can a saint wield a sword and become a hero, and can a valiant hero live a godly life? Such a paradox seems to find a satisfactory resolution when looking at the life of Quddús. He gallantly led his companions on the battlefield, defended the believers of his Faith in person at the frontline like the famous kings of antiquity; and, yet he preached like an apostle of the past. His pious qualities have been recognised as much as his bravery and courage.

Saints are like heroes in that they also are worthy of emulation. However, you can become a hero in a matter of minutes, but the path to sainthood takes longer. To become a saint is indeed the result of intense and continuous spiritual work on oneself rather than being the result of an incident.

Bahá'í biographies attempt to understand how people overcome their personal struggles in the service to their Faith, rather than to glorify them. Historian Graham Hassall clarifies this point:

> But the concept of the heroic conveyed in Bahá'í scriptures includes heroes and heroines whose arenas for victory are the 'inner life', or the life at home in the family—lives far less accessible to the biographical process. The 'hero', thus, need not be famous, and what is 'heroic' need not be 'public'."[9]

---

1 Bahíyyih Khánum (1846–1932) was the daughter of Bahá'u'lláh who was entitled the Greatest Holy Leaf. She is considered the greatest woman in the Bahá'í Faith.

2 Shoghi Effendi in Bahá'í World Centre, *Bahíyyih Khánum, the Greatest Holy Leaf,* p. 62.

3 Joseph Arthur Gobineau, *Les Religions et les Philosophies dans l'asie Centrale*, p. 166.

4 Denis MacEoin, *Early Shaykhī Reactions to the Báb and His Claims*, p. 17.

5 Jack McLean. *The Heroic in the Historical Writings of Shoghi Effendi and Nabíl,* n.p.

6 *Árif* means kind, knowledgeable, trustworthy.

7 Jack McLean, *The Heroic in the Historical Writings of Shoghi Effendi and Nabíl*, n.p.

8 E. G. Browne, *Kitáb-i-Nuqtatu'l-Káf,* pp. 199–200.

9 Graham Hassall, *The Modes and Intentions of Biography*, p. 85.

Saints in history have significantly influenced the development of their religion through the model of their life, teachings and detachment from material things. Shoghi Effendi said saints are people "who have achieved the highest degree of mastery over their egos."[1] They also exert a benevolent influence on their peers, empowering them to new heights of spirituality. That is how they finally passed into history; their lives are like fragrant flowers that, once gone, their perfume stays with us forever. Hence, the need to keep them in our memory. 'Abdu'l-Bahá commented on the nature of sainthood:

> Saints are men who have freed themselves from the world of matter and who have overcome sin. They live in the world but are not of it, their thoughts being continually in the world of the spirit. Their lives are spent in holiness, and their deeds show forth love, justice and godliness. They are illumined from on high; they are as bright and shining lamps in the dark places of the earth. These are the saints of God.[2]

Shoghi Effendi has explained that, in general, a new concept of heroism has emerged in the Bahá'í Writings:

> The champion builders of Bahá'u'lláh's rising World Order must scale nobler heights of heroism as humanity plunges into greater depths of despair, degradation, dissension and distress. Let them forge ahead into the future serenely confident that the hour of their mightiest exertions and the supreme opportunity for their greatest exploits must coincide with the apocalyptic upheaval marking the lowest ebb in mankind's fast-declining fortunes.[3]

Shaykh Ṭabarsí and Bahá'í Identity

The Shaykh Ṭabarsí episode has helped to shape the spiritual identity of the Bahá'ís having an influence that continues to show forth throughout the last two centuries.[4] Although the event happened within the parameters of the Bábí revelation, still its relevance and influence was carried out into the Bahá'í Dispensation in various facets. Firstly, nine Letters of the Living, participated and died, or ten if Ṭáhirih had not been prevented from doing so by Bahá'u'lláh who Himself visited the spot. Bahá'u'lláh, Quddús, Ṭáhirih and Mullá Ḥusayn constituted the cream of the Bábí community. Secondly, although these two independent religions had their own distinct aims, principles and regulations, yet the Universal House of Justice has noted they both form a Global Faith.[5] In a letter written on behalf of the Guardian this principle is elaborated:

---

1 Shoghi Effendi, *The Unfolding Destiny of the British Bahá'í Community*, p. 453.

2 'Abdu'l-Bahá, *Paris Talks*, pp. 60-61.

3 Shoghi Effendi, *Citadel of Faith*, p. 58

4 Warburg, Margit. *Citizens of the World*, p. 135.

5 Bahá'u'lláh, *The Kitáb-i-Aqdas*, p. 4.

> Shoghi Effendi feels that the unity of the Bahá'í Revelation as one complete whole embracing the Faith of the Báb should be emphasized ... The Faith of the Báb should not be divorced from that of Bahá'u'lláh. Though the teachings of the *Bayán* have been abrogated and superseded by the laws of the Aqdas, yet due to the fact that the Báb considered Himself as the Forerunner of Bahá'u'lláh, we would regard His Dispensation together with that of Bahá'u'lláh as forming one entity, the former being introductory to the advent of the latter.[1]

Thirdly, the spiritual courage of the Shaykh Ṭabarsí defendants was celebrated by the Báb,[2] Bahá'u'lláh[3] and 'Abdu'l-Bahá.[4] For instance, in *God Passes By*, Shoghi Effendi makes a review of Quddús', Mullá Ḥusayn's and their companions' prowesses in almost 2,000 words with magnificent terms such as:

> It [the Shaykh Ṭabarsí saga] demonstrated beyond the shadow of a doubt what the indomitable spirit of a band of three hundred and thirteen untrained, unequipped yet God-intoxicated students, mostly sedentary recluses of the college and cloister, could achieve when pitted in self-defense against a trained army, well equipped, supported by the masses of the people, blessed by the clergy, headed by a prince of the royal blood, backed by the resources of the state, acting with the enthusiastic approval of its sovereign, and animated by the unfailing counsels of a resolute and all-powerful minister.

Finally, Bahá'ís of the world, in their teaching plans, have also been drawing their inspiration on Quddús' and his companions as a source of emulation for their own service to the Cause of God [5] [6] [7] [8] [9] considering themselves as the "spiritual descendants of the Dawn-Breakers".[10]

---

1 Letter written on behalf of Shoghi Effendi included in Introduction to *The Kitáb-i-Aqdas*, p. 8.

2 Nabíl-i-A'ẓam, *The Dawn-Breakers*, p. 431.

3 *Zíyárat-Námiy-i-Bábu'l-Báb wa Quddús* revealed originally by Bahá'u'lláh in 'Akká. Mss: British Library Or15714.077. Included in list "Bahá'u'lláh's best known Works" prepared by Shoghi Effendi in *The Bahá'í World*, vol. 16, pages 574-575. The original Arabic version is available in *Bahá'í Reference Library from www.bahai.org/r/931357408* and the English version from www.bahai.org/r/262760797

4 'Abdu'l-Bahá. *Memorials of the Faithful*, p. 7.

5 "Leeward Islands", *Bahá'í News*, June 1990, p. 16.

6 J.A. McLean. *To Russian with Love: Journal of a Member of the Quddús Team*. 1990/2018.

7 Summary of the May 2011 collective teaching campaign. (May 2011). Available at: https://innermelbourne.wordpress.com/

8 Bahá'í News. *Americas.* April, 1998, p. 3.

9 Annette Reynolds, *Trudy and the Bahá'ís' Spiritual Path in South Carolina*, p. 50.

10 Rúḥíyyih Rabbání, *The Priceless Pearl*, p. 218.

Message for the youth

Shoghi Effendi said the station of Quddús was "a very exalted one".[1] The story of this young leader, saint, sage and hero was and still is one of the most dramatic and heart-rending dramas of the early history of the Bahá'í Faith.

Bahá'í youths can be proud to be heirs to the valuable spiritual legacy provided by the example of generations of young believers during the early years of the Bábí-Bahá'í Faith. Indeed, Bahá'í youth have always shown a special ability and potential to achieve great victories for their Faith. Shoghi Effendi singled them out for the "adventurous spirit which they possess, and the vigor, the alertness, and optimism".[2] They have always shone like stars in the firmament of service and detachment like Quddús, the "heroic youth".[3]

There are many examples provided by youths in the Bábí Faith: The Báb was twenty-four years old when He declared His mission. Quddús, His highest-ranking disciple, was twenty-two years when He embraced the Faith and died "in the full bloom of his youth".[4] Once he said, "I am but a youth, detached from all else but God's holy family".[5]

Mullá Ḥusayn, the first Letter of the Living, is another good example. Nabíl-i-A'ẓam, destined to be Bahá'u'lláh's poet laureate, chronicler and indefatigable disciple, embraced and served the Faith from the age of eighteen years, originally as a Bábí.[6] The list will go on *ad finitum*, naming, Anís, the young Zaynab, and many others including several Shaykh Ṭabarsí companions.

In the Revelation of Bahá'u'lláh, we can observe the sacrifice of Mírzá Mihdí,[7] the Purest Branch, at twenty-two years of age in the prison of 'Akká. Rúḥu'lláh, the child prodigy of the Bahá'í Faith, offered his life at the age of twelve, preferring to die in this world rather than recanting his beliefs. Badí' did the same sacrifice at seventeen and was later designated as one of the nineteen Apostles of Bahá'u'lláh by Shoghi Effendi.

'Abdu'l-Bahá—the Centre of the Covenant of God—rendered invaluable services to his Father during the successive banishments the family suffered, while still being very young. Young women have in Bahíyyih Khánum, the daughter of Bahá'u'lláh, the best example of self-sacrificing Bahá'í service. Shoghi Effendi, assumed the high office of the Guardian of the Bahá'í Faith at the age of twenty-four when he was a student at Oxford University in England.

1 Letter dated 11 November 1936, written on behalf of Shoghi Effendi to an individual believer. In The Universal House of Justice, "Letters of Living ...".

2 Shoghi Effendi, *The Advent of Divine Justice,* p. 69.

3 Nabíl-i-A'ẓam, *The Dawn-Breakers,* p. 410.

4 Shoghi Effendi, *God Passes By,* p. 49.

5 Hooshmand Dehghan, *Ganj-i-Pinhán,* p. 209.

6 Boris Handal, *A Trilogy of Consecration*, pp. 36–96.

7 Boris Handal, *Mírzá Mihdí,* pp. 139-154.

Bahá'u'lláh has referred to the invaluable divine confirmation manifesting itself in those young souls who arise to serve God and humanity:

> *Blessed is he who in the prime of his youth and the heyday of his life will arise to serve the Cause of the Lord of the beginning and of the end, and adorn his heart with His love. The manifestation of such a grace is greater than the creation of the heavens and of the earth. Blessed are the steadfast and well is it with those who are firm.*[1]

Postscript

Quddús was designated as the *Last Name of God*, the *Last Point* and the *Moon of Guidance* by the Báb, Bahá'u'lláh and 'Abdu'l-Bahá respectively.

Quddús was "the greatest man among the followers of the Báb".[2] It was like Abraham had been with Isaac, Moses and Aaron; Christ with Peter; Muḥammad and 'Alí; with the difference that in the case of the Bábí Faith, the Prophet (the Báb) survived the death of His most prominent disciple (Quddús). From St. Peter, Quddús shared his passion for service; from 'Alí, his youthfulness; the faithfulness with Aaron, and from Isaac, the attribute of obedience and submission to God.

The lives of the Báb and Quddús were both tragically cut short. The whole Bábí dispensation was destined to have a fleeting existence as regards the span of divine providence—only six years. Shoghi Effendi compared the Báb to a meteor that raises "above the horizon of Shíráz, traverse the sombre sky of Persia from south to north, decline with tragic swiftness, and perish in a blaze of glory."[3]

For the believers throughout Persia, Quddús became the representative of the Báb Himself during His captivity for nearly two-thirds of His Ministry. The Báb had been confined in the distant prisons of the kingdom (Máh-Kú and Chihríq Castle). In those circumstances, Quddús, like a moon, would assume the role of reflecting the light of the hidden Sun of Revelation on the persecuted community. For instance, a survivor of the Shaykh Ṭabarsí massacre stated:

> A glimpse of his face, the magic of his words, as he walked amongst us, would transmute our despondency into golden joy. We were reinforced with a strength of such intensity that, had the hosts of our enemies appeared suddenly before us, we felt ourselves capable of subjugating their forces.[4]

Of Quddús, Ṭáhirih penned down the following verses:

> He will manifest naught else save the mention of God:
> 'Indeed I am [Q]uddús, acting as befits this age.'[5]

---

1 Bahá'u'lláh, *Additional Tablets and Extracts*, p. 17.

2 Maulana Muhammad Ali, *History and Doctrines of the Babi Movement*, p. 11.

3 Shoghi Effendi, *God Passes By*, p. 3.

4 Nabíl-i-A'ẓam, *The Dawn-Breakers*, p. 390.

5 Amrollah Hemmat and John Hatcher, *The Poetry of Ṭáhirih*, p. 135.

> "He exemplified by his life and glorious martyrdom," Nabíl wrote of Quddús, "the truth of this tradition: 'Whoso seeketh Me, shall find Me. Whoso findeth Me shall be drawn towards Me. Whoso draweth nigh unto Me, shall love Me. Whoso loveth Me, shall I also love. Him who is beloved of Me, him shall I slay. He who is slain by Me, I myself shall be his ransom.'"[1]

Mírzá Ḥabíbu'lláh Afnán, a relative of the Báb, also highlighted his personal qualities: "Quddús was among the 'ulamá and learned divines famous for piety and godliness, and because of his inner spirituality and purity …."[2]

"People loved him very easily," wrote acclaimed writer Marzieh Gail about this brilliant youth orphaned at a young age by the death of his mother, "they could hardly turn their eyes away from him."[3] Quddús has also been described as a "charismatic clergyman" whose "piety and personal charm captured the admiration of every observer",[4] the prototype of the "scholar-hero-warrior"[5] and as a "man of singular excellence and noted for his piety and godliness."[6] The believers used to call him Ḥabíb ("beloved"),[7] perhaps because the Báb referred to him as such.[8] In fact, the Báb called Quddús the "*Beloved of My Heart, my king of glory, and my irrevocable purpose, the sovereign Lord of my beginning and end!*"[9]

His personality is full of colours. According to Shoghi Effendi, Quddús at Bada<u>sh</u>t "was regarded as the exponent of the conservative element".[10] We note in Quddús traces of a more-than-moderate religious disposition when in Ṭihrán, where he was observed performing scrupulously and devotedly the rituals of the Islamic obligatory prayer and ablutions.[11] He used to assert to the people of his town that "I am the representative of the Lord of the Time [the Mahdí]. Whatever I say, harken unto me".[12]

As part of his spiritual self-discipline, Quddús also followed strict religious dietary requirements set by the Báb when invited to a dinner,[13] and insisted that his companions follow a strict self-discipline in such matters. At <u>Sh</u>ay<u>kh</u> Ṭabarsí he admonishes the sieged Bábís, "not to live gluttonously" because "we came

---

1 Nabíl-i-A'ẓam, *The Dawn-Breakers*, p. 72.

2 Mírzá Ḥabíbu'lláh Afnán, *The Genesis of the Bábí-Bahá'í Faiths*, p. 43.

3 Marzieh Gail, *Dawn Over Mount Hira*, p. 82.

4 Nosratollah Mohammad-Hosseini, *Qoddus, Moḥammad-'Ali Bārforuši, n.p.*

5 Jack McLean, *A Celestial Burning*, p. 489.

6 E. G. Browne, *Taríkh-i-Jadíd*, p. 39.

7 Sepehr Manuchehri, *Brief Analysis of the Features of Bábí Resistance*, n.p.; & Peter Terry, *A Prophet of Modern Times*, p. 160.

8 Abbas Amanat, *Resurrection and Renewal*, p. 184.

9 The Báb, *Tablet of Visitation for Quddús*. See Appendix part 2.

10 Shoghi Effendi, *God Passes By*, p. 31.

11 Nabíl-i-A'ẓam, *The Dawn-Breakers*, p. 183.

12 Kurt Greussing, *The Babi Movement in Iran 1844–1852*, p. 262.

13 Borjian, *A Mázandaráni Account of the Babi Incident at Shaikh Ṭabarsí*, pp. 390–1.

hither to shew forth God's truth."[1] Instead, Quddús exhorted them to go to the battlefield with courage under the words "Wish for death if you are sincere"[2] and "Mount your steeds, O heroes of God!" In his prayers, he invokes, "O my God, my Lord, my Beloved, and my heart's desire"[3] and "Holy, holy, the Lord our God, the Lord of the angels and the spirit."

When projectiles were falling on his hut, a believer ran to Quddús asking to leave the place, however, giving us an example of observing divine trust, he said "If the Beloved of all worlds desires that we should fall by a bullet, then why should we flee, our object being gained? But if He desire it not, then shall we assuredly not be slain; wherefore then should we move?"[4]

People were impressed with "the God-given virtues which the spirit of this youth displayed"[5] including his vast scholarship and eloquence. At the same time, he was a man full of compassion. When seeing his companions starving, Quddús remarked, "My heart bleeds at the sight of my famished companions, worn and wasted around me"[6] and rejected special privileges. At one point he instructed one of four brothers at Shaykh Ṭabarsí to return home to help his mother.[7]

The Judaic, Islamic and Christian belief in angels has evolved to a higher level of mystical understanding in the Bábí-Bahá'í Faith. 'Abdu'l-Bahá explained:

> *The meaning of "angels" is the confirmations of God and His celestial powers. Likewise angels are blessed beings who have severed all ties with this nether world, have been released from the chains of self and the desires of the flesh, and anchored their hearts to the heavenly realms of the Lord. These are of the Kingdom, heavenly; these are of God, spiritual; these are revealers of God's abounding grace; these are dawning-points of His spiritual bestowals.*[8]

'Abdu'l-Bahá's description of angelic beings certainly fits the character and life of Quddús. He was truly the foremost Letter of the Living and the Hidden Treasure of God.

---

1 E. G. Browne, *Taríkh-i-Jadíd*, p. 78.
2 Hermann Roemer, *Die Bābī-Behā'ī, die jüngste mohammedanische sekte*, p. 36.
3 Hooshmand Dehghan, *Ganj-i-Pinhán*, pp. 175.
4 E. G. Browne, *Taríkh-i-Jadíd*, p. 83.
5 Nabíl-i-A'ẓam, *The Dawn-Breakers*, pp. 264–5.
6 Nabíl-i-A'ẓam, *The Dawn-Breakers*, pp. 389–90.
7 *The Narrative of Ḥájí Naṣír-i-Qazvíní*, n.p.; & Fazel Mazandarani, *Taríkh Ẓuhúr al-Ḥaqq*, vol. 3, p. 192.
8 'Abdu'l-Bahá, *Selections from the Writings of 'Abdu'l-Bahá*, p. 81.

Part VIII
Miscellanea

25
The Shrine of Quddús

Chapter content
History of the shrine
Confiscation and demolition
International pressure
Relics of Quddús
Recent persecutions in Babol
The fate of the fort
The shrines of the Letters of the Living

The seminary or madrasa of Mírzá Zakí in Bárfurús͟h, where Quddús was hastily buried at midnight, has became one of the significant historical Bahá'í holy places in Iran. As discussed earlier in chapter 17, Quddús had predicted this building as his place of burial. The school was open during the lifetime of Quddús. However, it was destroyed about ten years after his martyrdom. E. G. Browne described it in 1888 as an "old ruined madrasa"[1] but it seems that during Quddús' time the school was active.[2] [3]It was not a mosque.[4] It was subsequently converted into a school that was later acquired by the Bahá'ís around 1939 through a property transfer agreement.

Of the shrine of Quddús and the pilgrims who visit it, the Báb has revealed:

> *Methinks I see the angels of the Throne, the Seat, the heavens, the Most Exalted Paradise, and the Most Glorious Garden circling around thy dust, taking the tears that stream from the eyes of those that love thee to present them to the Lord thy God, that He may gaze upon one who hath achieved such a gracious favour, that His paradise may mourn for him, and that He may single him out for His bounties.* [5]

A visitor to the shrine of Quddús in Bárfurús͟h once wrote about the security of the place around the 1970s:

> A tombstone or marking was not permitted, in order to protect his remains and to prevent further desecration of his burial place. These precautionary measures limited the believers from visiting most of the Holy Spots in Iran

---

[1] Quoted in E. G. Browne, *A Traveller's Narrative*, Note P, p. 307. See https://bahai-library.com/books/tn/tn.p.html
[2] Hosseinzadeh Niaki Jafar, *Bábul, S͟hahr-i Zíbáiy Mázandarán (Babol, the Beautiful City of Mazandaran)*, 1ST volume, p. 168.
[3] Hooshmand Dehghan, *Ganj-i-Pinhán*, p.35.
[4] Hosseinzadeh Niaki Jafar. *Bábul, S͟hahr-i Zíbáiy Mázandarán (Babol, the Beautiful City of Mazandaran)*, 1ST volume, p. 168.
[5] The Báb, Tablet of Visitation for Quddús. See Appendix part 2.

> without special permission of the National Spiritual Assembly. As too much traffic would attract the enemies of the Faith and make their safekeeping at risk.[1]

In general, 'Abdul-Bahá has written about the importance of visiting sacred places:

> *Holy Places are undoubtedly centres of the outpouring of Divine grace, because on entering the illumined sites associated with martyrs and holy souls, and by observing reverence, both physical and spiritual, one's heart is moved with great tenderness.*[2]

History of the shrine

The building erected on the site of the old structure resembled a residence, but the gravesite of Quddús was retained. The so-called shrine of Quddús was owned by the Bahá'ís of Iran. According to the book *Ganj-i-Pinhán* by Hooshmand Dehghan:

> In the history of Mázindarán, about the resting place of Quddús, it is mentioned that, "the Bahá'ís believe that the place of his tomb is in the school of Mírzá Zakí". In the book Ẓuhúr-i-Ḥaqq, it is said that the resting place of Jináb-i-Quddús was bought by Bahá'ís in 1318 AH (c. 1939 CE) and came to the possession of the Bahá'í community after major renovations. However, according to other sources, in the year 1316 to 1317 [AH] the Madrisih-i-Mírzá Zakí came to the possession of the Faith. Ms Porandokht Ḥusaynzadeh has visited the resting place herself. In a fair and balanced book, she wrote,
>
> "The Madrisih-i-Mírzá Zakí that was refurbished in 1310 AH, by the Minister of Culture, and a government primary school was established. One or two years later, Dr Asadu'lláh Khán Sharif, who was a Bahá'í, bought that school from the Ministry of Culture and in the exchange, he gave the government today's current school, the School of the 7th Dai [month] which is on Pahlavi street and had a much higher value. This commercial deal caused a considerable uproar, and concerted efforts were exerted to nullify it, but with no success. The school of Mírzá Zakí at present has turned into a residence [hosting the shrine of Quddús]".[3]

The place was described at that time in the following words:

> The court of the house is quietly large with a lot of trees. The main entrance facing south opens to the Ibrahim alley way. In the west there is the Ḥaẓír-Fúrúshan (mat-weaver) alley. The yard used to have old chambers all around. During the construction of the school, the Ministry of Culture destroyed the house's old chambers. At the time there was no

1 Shahla Behroozi Gillbanks, *Footprints in the Sand of Time*, p. 40.

2 'Abdu'l-Bahá in *Synopsis and Codification of the Kitáb-i-Aqdas*, p. 61.

3 Hooshmand Dehghan, *Ganj-i-Pinhán*, pp. 113–22.

building to the east and south of the house. The west of the building looked like a storage area. The main part of the building, which is comprised of a few rooms and an atrium (a large open-air space surrounded by the building), is located in the north.[1]

A Bahá'í, in the year 2000, who visited the place for a second time, wrote:

> I, the writer (Púrándukht Ḥusaynzadih) went again to the house with the encouragement of Muḥammad-Riḍá Farzádniyá who was judge of the High Court and resident of Babol, and was confident of the location of the tomb of Quddús in that house. This time I was received with much more kindness because the owner had more confidence that I was not there to create problems but to write history.
>
> Therefore, she accommodated me further and took me to different parts of the house. She took me to the north of the house, where there was a basement where they kept poultry [hens and chickens], and there was no probability of the grave there. As I was saying good-bye to leave the house, the owner with a meaningful smile said: "If you are still interested to know where the grave is, it is located in the western part"; the same place that looked like a storage room. Then she led the way to that storage room, which was long and narrow where its length is a lot greater than its short width. The grave, she said, is in the north of that storage room but there was no sign of any headstone or writing. The floor of the storage is tiled with mosaic. In the four corners where the grave is supposed to be, they have placed traditional 'goleh-laleh' Persian lamps.[2]

Shoghi Effendi instructed the National Spiritual Assembly of the Bahá'ís of Iran to renovate the building. For instance, in a letter written dated 8 March 1946 on his behalf, the Guardian advised:

> About the blessed tomb of His holiness Quddús the Guardian instructed us to write that the protection of this holy place, during this time of revolution and tumult as well as to provide and to prepare all the necessary means for it is of the highest and holiest duties of the Assembly. However, the Assembly must act in such a manner not to arouse public attention, and not to intensify the animosities of the ignorant, the foes and their greed. Mr Varqá[3] is directed to offer a sum of 3,000 tumans to the Assembly to use for the repair and to provide the necessary items for that holy place.[4]

On 31 May 1955 the newspaper Khandaniha wrote:

---

1 Hooshmand Dehghan, *Ganj-i-Pinhán*, pp. 113–22.

2 Hooshmand Dehghan, *Ganj-i-Pinhán*, pp. 113–22.

3 Hand of the Cause of God and Trustee of the Ḥuqúqu'lláh, Valíyu'lláh Varqá (1884–1955).

4 Hooshmand Dehghan, *Ganj-i-Pinhán*, pp. 113–22.

In the city of Babol in Mázandarán, there is a mosque and a school in the area of the Hazír-Fúrúshan [mat sellers], where Bahá'ís believe that one of the leaders of the Bahá'í sect, Mullá Muḥammad-'Alí Quddús, was buried. Last week, several telegrams arrived from the people of Babol stating that, because the mosque and school building were still standing, its sale was inappropriate and basically illegal. They demanded that the mosque and the school be expropriated from the Bahá'í sect and again be used for congregational prayers and a residence for the religious students. Based on information received, actions have been taken and arrangements will soon be made for the school and the mosque to be taken from the Bahá'í sect and handed over to the Endowment Office.[1]

Confiscation and demolition

Unfortunately, the shrine of Quddús in Bárfurú<u>sh</u> was confiscated and demolished by the combined forces of the clergy and the Iranian government (January/February–April 2004).[2] Despite the pleadings and intervention of local Bahá'ís, the destruction was carried out with the full assistance from the authorities. The government also prevented local Bahá'ís from recovering the hallowed remains of Quddús.

Other Bahá'í properties had been previously demolished such as the House of the Báb in <u>Sh</u>íráz in 1981 where Quddús converted in 1844. The House of Bábíyyih in Ma<u>sh</u>had, where Quddús resided and taught, experienced the same fate the following year in 1982.[3] The Garden of Bada<u>sh</u>t where the famous 1848 conference was held led by Bahá'u'lláh, Ṭáhirih and Quddús was destroyed in April-May 1979.[4] The house of Quddús in Bárfurú<u>sh</u> was confiscated by armed men of the revolutionary committees in 1979.[5]

The book *Ganj-i-Pinhán* described the circumstances surrounding the confiscation of the Shrine:

> After the Islamic revolution in 1979, this holy place, like any of the Bahá'í holy places, was confiscated. Mrs Soraya Sabetian, custodian of the place, just before government agencies arrived there, around midnight removed

---

1 Khandaniha. *Falsafi against recruitment of Baha'is in government job.* 31 May 1955. Available at https://iranbahaipersecution.bic.org/index.php/archive/ khandaniha-newspaper-falsafi-against-recruitment-bahais-government-jobs

2 *Bahá'í World News Service.* 22 April 2004. *Bahá'í Holy Site Destroyed in Iran.* Available at: https://news.bahai.org/story/293/

3 *Letter of the Universal House of Justice to all National Spiritual Assemblies dated 9 March 1982.* Available www.bahai.org/library/authoritative-texts/the-universal-house-of-justice/messages/19820309_001/19820309_001.pdf?14edc826

4 *Bahá'í World News Service,* 22 April 2004. *Bahá'í Holy Site Destroyed in Iran.* Available https://news.bahai.org/story/293/

5 *The Bahá'í World,* vol. 17, p. 79. In her book *Dr Muhájir: Hand of the Cause of God, Knight of Bahá'u'lláh,* Írán Furútan wrote that in 1978, "Dr. Muhájir spent the night at the house of Quddús in prayer and meditation." (p. 249)

all precious belongings of the place such as carpets, silver candle holders, holy icons and images and took them to a safe place. However, she had no attachment to her own personal possessions and all her own belongings were confiscated. The writer of the book, saw with her own eyes in the last year of the life of Soraya Kh͟ánum, that her life belongings were a small carpet to sleep on, a framed tablet of visitation of Quddús as precious as her own eyes to her, and a small *kursí.*[1]

Upon the former site of the shrine, the government erected an Islamic learning centre dedicated to the Lord of the Age,[2] meaning the Báb, ironically, the purpose of Quddús' life devotion. The Bahá'í historian Hooshmand Dehghan wrote:

> After the confiscation of the tomb of Quddús, the title of deeds was nullified and the new ownership was given in the name of Valí 'Aṣr [Guardian of the Age] and it became a place of religious teachings and ordinances for women. This was changed on 25 May 2004. This place was completely destroyed and therefore one of the most holy and historical places of Iran was destroyed, and instead they built a school of religious sciences in the name of Mírzá Zakí. However, with the will of God the place of burial of Quddús was unharmed, and the remnants stayed on the basement safe, and still is a place of pilgrimage of the lovers of His holiness.[3]

During the demolition, the Bahá'ís were denied access to the location so they could not remove Quddús' remains. According to the International Bahá'í Community:

> Destruction of the gravesite [of Quddús] began in February [2004] but was temporarily halted after local Bahá'í demanded to see a legal permit for the demolition work. The Bahá'ís were referred to national authorities and for a time it appeared that the desecration had been halted. More recently [12 April 2004], it was discovered that the dismantling of the gravesite had continued surreptitiously over a period of days until the structure was entirely demolished.[4]

International pressure

Condemning such a desecration, Bani Dugal, the principal representative of the Bahá'í International Community to the United Nations, demanded on 22 April 2004: "It would be the least that the Government could do at this point to return to the Bahá'í community his sacred remains. We ask for the international

---

1 Hooshmand Dehghan, *Ganj-i-Pinhán*, pp. 113–22. A *kursí is* a type of low square table, traditionally used in winter in Iran, with a heater underneath it and blankets placed over the top.

2 Location at: https://balad.ir/p/مدرسه-علمیه-روحیه-babol_school-2d0bmmqZvkKobE#15/36.54738/52.68671

3 Hooshmand Dehghan, *Ganj-i-Pinhán*, pp. 113–22.

4 Bahá'í International Community. *Bahá'í Holy Site Destroyed in Iran.*

community's support in this goal."[1] "The Iran's Interior Ministry has not responded to requests for the remains," said Diane Ala'i, United Nations Bahá'í representative in Geneva.[2]

In response, world parliaments raised their voice protesting against the confiscation and demolition of the Shrine of Quddús. The United States House of Representatives expressed their distress for the fact that "the grave of Quddús, a revered saint and hero of the [Bahá'í] Faith was confiscated by the Islamic Committee."[3] Likewise, the US State Department's Annual Report on International Religious Freedom, 2004, observed:

> In February [2004] authorities initiated the destruction of the tomb of Quddús, a Bahá'í holy site. Local Bahá'ís attempted to prevent the destruction through legal channels, but the tomb was destroyed in the interim. The Bahá'ís were not allowed permission to enter the site and retrieve the remains of this revered Bahá'í figure.[4]

The Parliament of the United Kingdom of Great Britain and Northern Ireland passed the following resolution on 6 May 2004:

> That this House notes the final destruction by Iranian authorities on 20th April of the Shrine of Quddús, a Bahá'í holy site in the city of Babul; is deeply concerned by this act of desecration of a place of deep spiritual significance to the Bahá'ís of the world; observes that such an act is part of the ongoing persecution of the Bahá'í faith and its members in the state of Iran; and urges the Government to intercede with the Iranian authorities to effect the return of the body of Quddús to the local Bahá'í community so that the remains may be re-interred with proper respect immediately.[5]

Likewise, the Danish Secretary of State for Foreign and Commonwealth Affairs expressed his concern at the Parliament of Denmark for the Iranian religious government's levelling of "the shrine of Quddús at Babol, a sacred site of the Bahá'ís".[6] In addition, the Union European their expressed their concern at the destruction of the Bahá'í holy place in Babol and the government's opposition to the respectful reburial of the remains.[7]

Similarly, the 2004 UN report "Elimination of All Forms of Religious Intolerance" alerted that:

---

1 Bahá'í International Community. *Bahá'í Holy Site Destroyed in Iran.*

2 United Nations High Commissioner for Refugees. *Chronology of Events in Iran.*

3 United States House of Representatives. *Religious Persecution as a Violation of Human Rights.*

4 State Department (US). *Annual Report on International Religious Freedom*, p. 543.

5 UK Parliament. *Bahá'í Holy Sites.*

6 Denmark Secretary of State for Foreign and Commonwealth Affairs. *Third Report from the Foreign Affairs Committee Session 2003–2004 Iran.* May 2004.

7 European Union. EU *Annual Report on Human Rights.* 13 September 2004.

On 10 June 2004, the Special Rapporteur reported to the Government that the building over the grave of Quddús had reportedly been completely levelled. Despite attempts to protect this site, the demolition of the structure had continued gradually and quietly, in a manner designed not to attract attention. Subsequently, the Bahá'ís were allegedly prevented from retrieving the remains of Quddús.[1]

On 31 May 2016, the United Nations Special Rapporteur in the field of cultural rights; the Special Rapporteur on freedom of religion or belief and the Special Rapporteur on the situation of human rights in the Islamic Republic of Iran wrote to the Iranian Representative: "It is alleged that the destruction [of Quddús' grave] was carried out with the cooperation of government authorities."[2]

Like-minded organisations also publicly protested, supporting the preservation of the Shrine of Quddús through various media such as *the Network of Concerned Historians,*[3] *Iran Today,* Drama Circle, *Radio Liberty* (Czech Republic), the Hudson Institute, the Free Library, WallStreet Deutschland, Hindu Vivek Kendra, Harvard University[4] among many other regional, national and international newspapers:

The New York Times,[1] *Reuters,*[2] *Le Monde,*[3] *Janesville Gazette,*[4] *Valley Morning Star,*[5] *Placerville Mountain Democrat,*[6] *Annapolis Capital,*[7] *Cedar Rapids Gazette,*[8] *Tampa Bay Times,*[9] *The Record Searchlight,*[10] *Calgary Herald,*[11] *Fort Worth Star-Telegram,*[12] *Sunday Sun-Journal,*[13] *Journal and Courier,*[14] *The Baltimore Sun,*[15] *St. Louis Post-Dispatch,*[16] *News-Journal Ohio,*[17] *Iowa City Press-Citizen,*[18] *The Arizona Republic,*[19] *The Charlotte Observer,*[20] *The Courier-Journal,*[21] *Star Tribune,*[22] *Sunday Sun-Journal,*[23] *Richmond Times-Dispatch,*[24] *Austin American Statesman,*[25] *The Desert Sun,*[26] *The Columbian,*[27] *Santa Cruz Sentinel,*[28] *The Olympian,*[29] and *Benington Banner,*[30].[5]

---

1 United Nations General Assembly. *Elimination of All Forms of Religious Intolerance.*

2 Office of the UN High Commissioner for Human Rights. *Mandates of the Special Rapporteur in the field of cultural rights.*

3 Network of Concerned Historians, *Annual Report* 2005.

4 M. Kamrava, *Iran Today,* p. 62. Greenwood, Drama Circle, *Persecution to the Bahá'ís of Iran.* Radio Liberty, *Bahá'ís Launch Campaign against Alleged Iranian Abuses.* 13 November 2004. The Hudson Institute, *Religious Cleansing in Iran,* 22 July 2009. "In Iran, a renewed persecution aims at 'cultural cleansing'", 2004. WallStreet Deutschland, *Der Mythos vom toleranten Islam—Kulturelle Säuberung im Iran.* 17 September 2004. *Bahá'ís Decry Cultural Cleansing in Iran.* 12 September 2004. The Pluralist Project, *Bahá'ís Draw Attention to Destruction of Holy Sites in Iran.* 12 September 2004.

5 [1] 12 September 2004; [2] 23 April 2004; [3] 20 September 2004; [4] 30 October 2004; [5] 5 November 2004; [6] 5 November 2004; [7] 13 December 2004; [8] 16 November 2004; [9] 23 November 2004; [10] 29 May 2004; [11] 18 September 2004; [12] 17 October 2004; [13] 7 November 2004; [14] 9 November 2004; [15] 14 November 2004; [16] 19 December 2004; [17] 19 February 2005; [18] 11 November 2004; [19] 12

With the addition of international media coverage regarding Quddús between 1845–1846, as mentioned in chapter five, his impact at the world level was reported in nearly a dozen major countries (e.g., United States, Canada, France, Germany, Denmark, Czech Republic, United Kingdom, Australia, India, and New Zealand) and on three different continents. In addition, a related article appeared in the prestigious *Journal of War Crimes, Genocide, & Crimes against Humanity,* noting that "the gravesite of an early Apostle of the Faith, the resting place of Mullá Muḥammad-'Alí Bárfurúshí, known as Quddús, was destroyed in Babol."[1]

Furthermore, an extensive statement of the American Bahá'í community appeared on 12 September 2004 in the *New York Times* and in prominent newspapers in Australia, Canada, France, Germany, and the United Kingdom deploring the desecration of Quddús' grave.[2] In parallel, the news appeared in the various media in Spanish, German, Italian, Turkish, Russian, Persian, Arabic, French and Portuguese, etc.[3]

Relics of Quddús

All that remains of the physical possessions of Quddús are a colourful shirt, a shawl and a turquoise signet ring engraved with a Quranic verse. In one of his ring, like an epitaph, it reads, "If thou seest me, that I am less than thee in wealth and children",[4] [5]which is a reflection of his poverty and detachment. As Revered T. K. Cheyne has annotated, for Quddús this world was "a mere handful of dust".[6]

Whereas the shirt and shawl are in private Bahá'í hands, the ring is kept at the International Archives Building at the Bahá'í World Centre in Haifa, Israel. Today, thousands of Bahá'í pilgrims have the privilege of viewing this unique relic.

Hand of the Cause of God Zikru'lláh Khádim once told the story of the ring:

> Shoghi Effendi placed all the relics in this Archives. Amongst them, there is a ring from Quddús. Bahá'u'lláh says that the Primary Point is the Báb and the Final Point is Quddús. The ring of Quddús is mounted on a silver ring which, as far as its value is concerned, is not very precious, but it is wrapped in a paper in which the father of the beloved Shoghi Effendi had written on it when the Guardian was a small child. 'Abdu'l-Bahá called him

---

December 2004 [20] 5 December 2004; [21] 3 October 2004; [22] 18 October 2004; [23] 7 November 2004; [24] 27 November 2004; [25] 10 November 2004; [26] 21 January 2005; [27] 22 November 2004; [28] 14 November 2004; [29] 30 October 2004; [30] 11 December 2004.

1 Friedrich Affolter, *The Specter of Ideological Genocide*, p. 88.

2 Office of External Affairs of the NSA of the Bahá'ís of the United States. *Bahá'ís raise alarm over destruction of cultural heritage in Iran.* 13 September 2004.

3 *Bahá'ís Decry Cultural Cleansing in Iran.* 12 September 2004.

4 *Qur'án* 18:39.

5 Abbas Amanat, *Resurrection and Renewal,* p. 188.

6 Thomas Kelly Cheyne, *The Reconciliation of Races and Religions*, p. 114.

and said, "This is the ring of Quddús. It's very precious. You keep it and give to the apple of your eyes, Shoghi Effendi."[1]

Recent persecutions in Babol

The flames of religious bigotry are still alive 170 years after the passing of the Sa'ídu'l-'Ulamá'. Bahá'u'lláh issued an alert more than one hundred years ago that "*Religious fanaticism and hatred are a world-devouring fire, whose violence none can quench*".[2] For instance, over 100 Bahá'í-owned shops were closed by the authorities of the province of Mázindarán in 2016.[3] In the city of Quddús, Babol (formerly Bárfurú<u>sh</u>), students are expelled from their university studies solely because they are Bahá'ís.[4] This includes the Babol Noshirvani University of Technology, Babol University, Tabari University of Babol and the Technical University of Babol. These rules are based on the policy established in the 25 February 1991 secret memorandum of the Supreme Council of the Cultural Revolution prescribing that Bahá'ís "must be expelled from universities, either in the admission process or during the course of their studies, once it becomes known that they are Bahá'ís".[5] At one of these universities a student was advised in writing that her expulsion is due to the "impossibility of university education for Bahá'í citizens."[6] In another occasion, a Babol University wrote to a student:

> Your request for reconsideration of your case was received. As a review of your file indicates that you were dismissed from your course of study because of your membership in the wayward sect, it is necessary for you to provide proof of your recantation of your faith in the form of notices published in three highly circulated national newspapers (i.e., publication of the photocopy of your recantation), for our consideration. Failure to do

---

1 <u>Dh</u>ikru'lláh <u>Kh</u>ádim, *Address from the Hand of the Cause <u>Dh</u>ikru'lláh <u>Kh</u>ádim.* Available https://bahai.works/Transcript:Dhikrullah_Khadem/Address_from_the_Hand_of_the_Cause (original transcript has been edited for the sake of clarity).

2 Bahá'í World Centre, *One Common Faith,* p. ii.

3 HRANA News Agency (23 November 2016). Mazandaran authorities silent about the closure of 102 Bahá'í shops. Available https://iranbahaipersecution.bic.org/archive/hrana-mazandaran-authorities-silent-about-closure-102-bahai-shops

4 Bahá'í International Community. Archive of Bahá'í Persecution in Iran. Available https://iranbahaipersecution.bic.org/about

5 Archives of Bahá'í Persecution in Iran. Bahá'í International Community-Iran News Bulletin #18–2011. *Denial to access to higher education.* 30 May 2011. Available https://iranbahaipersecution.bic.org/archive/bahai-international-community-iran-news-bulletin-18-2011

6 HRANA. *Appeal Court of Administrative Justice confirms that Baha'is are not allowed to go to university"* 8 August 2019. Available https://iranbahaipersecution.bic.org/index.php/archive/hrana-appeal-court-administrative-justice-confirms-bahais-are-not-allowed-go-university

> so will result in [confirmation of the decision to expel you, as already recorded].[1]

Similarly, Babol women believers (e.g. Moshfegh Samandari (2009), Sheida Taeed (2016), Manijej Azamina (2021), and Shiva Khalil (2022)), have been arrested and imprisoned. In September 2013, another woman was arrested and charged for ten offences, including "holding memorial meetings and reciting the Bahá'í prayer for the dead at Bahá'í funerals held throughout the city and the province." Pejman Nikounejad and his wife Sharareh Kashaninejad had their house raided in 2011, they were attacked, and arrested. The couple was later released on bail.[2]

Furthermore, in the 1991 *Final Report to the Commission on Human Rights on the Situation in Iran* it is stated that Mr Bizhan Ahmadian "was shot in a street in Babol and that the authorities refused to return his body to the family. Subsequently, his parents and some other members of his family were allegedly arrested."[3] Another Babol born martyr in the line of Quddús was Asadollah Kamel-Moghaddam who died in a Tihran jail in 1984 and his death was suspiciously conveyed as an "accident".[4]

Quddús is certainly the most illustrious citizen in the history of Bárfurú<u>sh</u>. Through the silent "voice" of Quddús, the Cause of the Bahá'í Faith in international forums has been heard all over the world, even more than 170 years after of his execution. Through the echoes of history, Quddús is still championing the cause of Justice to eradicate oppression. In this regard, the words of Báb about him are most revealing:

> *The hosts of the Unseen will hasten forth to assist you, and will proclaim to all the world your heroism and glory.*[5]

The fate of the fort

The Shrine of Quddús and the one of Shaykh Ṭabarsí are twin Bahá'í sanctuaries 16 km away from each other. These buildings keep the remains of the

---

1 Archives of Bahá'í Persecution in Iran. Bahá'í International Community. *Need to recant your faith and publish three notices in newspapers, to continue your education.* 9 November 1988. Available https://iranbahaipersecution.bic.org/archive/need-recant-your-faith-and-publish-three-notices-newspapers-continue-your-education

2 Bahá'í International Community. Archive of Bahá'í Persecution in Iran. Available https://iranbahaipersecution.bic.org/about

3 United Nations Economic and Social Council. Final Report to the Commission on Human Rights on the situation in Iran, p. 19. 13 February 1991. Available https://iranbahaipersecution.bic.org/archive/final-report-commission-human-rights-situation-iran-1991

4 Gooya News. *Mass killings of the 80s and the Baha'is of Iran (25 November 2013).* Available https://iranbahaipersecution.bic.org/archive/gooya-news-mass-killings-80s-and-bahais-iran

5 Nabíl-i-A'ẓam, *The Dawn-Breakers,* pp. 142–3.

First [Mullá Ḥusayn], the Last [Quddús] and other seven Letters of the Living and soon after their deaths, the shrines became places of pilgrimage.

Sayyáḥ was a prominent believer who visited those two places on behalf of the Báb. On his return trip he passed through Ṭihrán and visited Bahá'u'lláh. It happened that that the great Vaḥíd[1] was also at His house. An eyewitness remarked.

It was the depth of winter when Sayyáḥ, returning from his pilgrimage, came to visit Bahá'u'lláh. Despite the cold and snow of a rigorous winter, he appeared attired in the garb of a dervish, poorly clad, barefooted, and dishevelled. His heart was set afire with the flame that pilgrimage had kindled.[2]

After the massacre the prince ordered that the fort should be raised to the ground. The Count of Gobineau wrote:

> All the Bábís, being dead, and being sure that henceforth they would at worst meet no more than their shades, the Muslims went to Shaykh Ṭabarsí castle and wandered around in the ruins. They were astonished at the extraordinary efforts it must have required of men without tools and above all without the necessary knowledge to build so many walls, hollow out so many tunnels, co-ordinate so many defences.[3]

Forty years later, Professor Edward Granville Browne of the University of Cambridge visited the fort of Shaykh Ṭabarsí and remarked as to the condition of the Bábí fortifications:

> ... of the elaborate fortifications, said by the Musulman historians to have been constructed by the Bábís, no trace remains. It consists at present of a flat, grassy enclosure surrounded by a hedge, and containing, besides the buildings of the shrine and another building at the gateway (opposite to which, but outside the enclosure, stands the house of the mutawalli, or custodian of the shrine), nothing but two or three orange-trees and a few rude graves covered with flat stones, the last resting-places, perhaps, or some of the Bábí defenders.[4]

It was subsequently visited in 1930 by Effie Baker, an Australian believer and photographer,[5] and by the Hand of the Cause of God Keith Ransom-Kehler in 1932. The latter wrote:

---

1 'Abdu'l-Bahá refers to Vaḥíd as "a remarkable man, a precious soul" (Nabíl-i-A'ẓam, *The Dawnbreakers,* p. 171) as the "great Siyyid Yaḥyá"' (Abdu'l-Bahá, *Memorials of the Faithful*, p. 125).

2 Nabíl-i-A'ẓam, *The Dawn-Breakers,* p. 432.

3 Gobineau in Nash and O'Donoghue, *Comte de Gobineau and Orientalism,* p. 175

4 Edward Browne. *A Year Amongst the Persians*, pp. 616–9.

5 Graham Hassall, *Ambassador at the Court: The Life and Photography of Effie Baker*, chapter 20.

> My heart nearly broke as in an abandonment of misery and repentance for all my negligence, unworthiness and arrogance, I fell prostrate upon this hallowed earth and besought God to teach me, at whatever cost, that sublime lesson of humility that had elevated this great devotee to a position of incalculable glory; to kindle within my breast, with the fuel of my very being, if necessary, this light of abandonment in His service that causes every personal wish to cast the shadow of death; to quicken in my soul that life eternal which alone can revitalize this earth into the promised Kingdom of God.[1]

Several distinctive Bahá'í villages began emerging around the fort. According to Shahla Behroozi Gillbanks:

> Some of the survivors of Fort Ṭabarsí decided to settle down in these [surrounding] villages and asked their families to join them. The result of this movement was a number of "all Bahá'í" villages in this region. We visited one of these in Mázindarán. It was in a lush forest. A single long bridge over a river was the only access to the village.
>
> The residents were proud that 'Abdu'l-Bahá, in one of his tablets called their village the "Lush Paradise." The emerald, green forest was a haven for foxes, deer, and birds. The abundance of wildflowers and murmuring rivers and streams truly created the picture of an earthly paradise.
>
> This village was a glimpse of what 'Abdu'l-Bahá described as the future Bahá'í villages in the years to come. The village was divided into a Bahá'í and a Muslim section. By entering the Bahá'í section, one immediately noticed the care shown for the cleanliness and beautification by its dwellers.[2]

Artifacts from the seven-month occupation appear still to be scattered in a zone rich for future archaeological work. An American visitor in 1965 recalled:

> As the nine of us sipped our tea, an old woman handed me a piece of iron cannon ball which she indicated had been dug up beside the fort. Although at first I thought she might have intended this as a gift, she soon intimated to one of the guides that she would like to be paid for it, and he handed her a few coins which she gratefully accepted. Since the siege lasted eleven months, probably there are enough cannon ball fragments about to keep the family in pocket money for many years.[3]

On the future of Shaykh Ṭabarsí, it is reported that Quddús made a prediction:

> Regarding the Ṭabarsí fort and its future, the following account from Quddús is recorded in the history of Mímíyyih [history of Mázindarán—

1 *Star of the West,* Volume 24, Issue 3, pp. 79–82.

2 Shahla Behroozi Gillbanks, *Footprints in the Sand of Time: Memories of a Maidservant,* pp. 36–7.

3 Guy Murchie, *Visit to Fort Tabarsi,* pp. 8-10.

S͟hayk͟h Ṭabarsí].¹ Jináb-i-Quddús said that the city of Bárfurús͟h would be destroyed, but the S͟hayk͟h Ṭabarsí fort would flourish. There is going to be a city built there, but the city of Bárfurús͟h will be destroyed. A great city will be established here (in S͟hayk͟h Ṭabarsí fort). Once the city is established, on the shrine of each of the martyrs' beautiful domes will be built, and great monuments will be built for each martyr and from every corner, people will rush for a pilgrimage to that place.²

Nowadays, the shrine of S͟hayk͟h Ṭabarsí sits within a renovated white modern structure, like a fair princess, with the green mantle of the dense forest and in front of and artificial lake acting as her mirror to reproduce its spiritual beauty. It is certainly an eternal monument to faith and courage, sheltering underneath the remains of hundreds of the beloved ones of God and reminding humanity that human goodness triumphs over evil and bigotry. An American Bahá'í visited the sanctuary 115 years later and recorded:

> We entered the recessed porch at the east end facing us, then, removing our shoes, went into the first of two inside rooms, each of which is about 20 feet square. This is of white plaster covered with faded banners on the west wall and indented with niches surmounted with pointed arches. Through a door we next entered the west room which contains the 700-year-old tomb of the famed Muslim saint, S͟hayk͟h Ṭabarsí, the presence of which is said to have caused this building to be chosen for their last stand by the three hundred-odd Bábís under attack by several regiments of the S͟háh's best troops, the site being thus assured immunity from desecration after their martyrdoms.

> Mullá Ḥusayn also is buried in this room, since Quddús, who survived him and who alone slept in this room during the siege, determined to keep his body safely hidden from the steadily approaching enemies. But the only visible object in the room is the dominating tomb of the shaykh, surrounded by a sort of cage of open woodwork about 12 feet long, 8 feet wide and 6½ feet high. The floor is of ancient turquoise tile and there are two niches in each of the plastered white walls. The ceiling is of wood, temporarily replacing the pyramid-shaped upper ramparts said to have been built by the c͟hádur for the siege and which the Bahá'ís hope some day to restore. Meantime the s͟hayk͟h's body holds the fort safe from destruction.³

In turn, the space that had housed the old Bárfurús͟h caravanserai is now a garage and a warehouse. It is situated in an area of 6,000 square metres at the back of a public school. Two rectangular brick houses stand as the only thing that remains.

---

1 *Vaqáyi' al-mímíyyih*—"Events of the letter Mím" (Mázindarán)". Published online at: https://www.h-net.org/~bahai/arabic/vol5/mimiyyih/mimiyyih.htm
2 Hooshmand Dehghan. *Ganj-i-Pinhán*, p. 113.
3 Guy Murchie. Visit to Fort Tabarsi, pp. 8-10.

The buildings are made of clay, and the exterior has brick decorations.[1] [2] [3] The Sabzih-Maydán, from being an unlimited green land, has turned into a critical four-exit roundabout thoroughfare. In the middle of that space, there is a leafy circular park with a small obelisk surrounded by a small pond where children used to catch goldfish.

During the Reza Sháh Pahlaví period, a much taller obelisk was erected as a sundial in a more extensive park than today's. However, during the Muḥammad Reza Sháh Pahlaví, the obelisk was removed, and instead where, four lions stood on each side. After the Islamic revolution, the appearance of the square changed dramatically where the lions disappear and only a small and ungraceful monolith remained standing. With its changing faces, along with the Shaykh Ṭabarsí fort, both monuments representing a collective memory that will never fade with the pass of time as one of the blackest periods in Iranian history.

The shrines of the Letters of the Living

The appropriation of the holy remains of Quddús and the illegal seizure of his shrine is a clear violation of the teachings of Islam about the sanctity of the dead. It also contravenes the explicit prohibition of destroying places of worship of other religions (*Qur'án* 42:20). Prophet Muḥammad even said, *"And do not insult those they invoke other than God, lest they insult God in enmity without knowledge. Thus We have made pleasing to every community their deeds. Then to their Lord is their return, and He will inform them about what they used to do"* (*Qur'án* 6:108).

In the *Persian Bayán* (4:13), the Báb commands that shrines should be built upon the graves of the Nineteen Letters of the first Unity (which includes the Báb Himself and the eighteen Letters of the Living) of the Bábí religion and pilgrimages should be undertaken to those places of reverence. We all know that the Shrine of the Báb stands sovereign on Mount Carmel in the Holy Land. Interestingly, the drum supporting the dome of the Shrine consists of eighteen beautiful stained-glass lancet windows honouring these first disciples of the Báb.

In the same chapter of the *Persian Bayán* (4:14) the Báb grants to the shrines of the Letters of the Living the capacity to provide safety and forgiveness to those looking for or intending to seek pardon or refuge. In verse 4:15 the asylum privilege is extended to people who live distantly and spiritually invoking this right. Furthermore, to add to the celestial magnificence of those shrines, the Báb prescribed (8:11) that all the graves of the Bábís were to contain the dust from the "first and last [Bábí] believers", a most likely reference to Mullá Ḥusayn and Quddús.[4]

---

1 Research in the history of Babol (11 December 2017). Available at: http://www.edugroup.blogfa.com/post/24

2 Panther caravanserai in the green area of Babol square.(15 April 1989). Available at: http://dabestanesabori.parsiblog.com/Author/صبوری/

3 Old neighborhoods of Babol city. (6 October 2012). Available at: http://www.joghrafiyapnu.blogfa.com

4 Many of the *Bayán* laws were inapplicable to be enacted in real life, mainly because of

Likewise, in the *Persian Bayán* (4:13), the Báb gives His benedictions to those who are prepared to construct these shrines because the angels of the heavens and earth descend on those sanctified spaces. He strongly affirmed that these shrines will be built since God commanded them. Moreover, God will reward those who would be prepared spend one mithqal[1] of gold on their construction with two thousand ones and all that could please them.[2]

In the light of all these tribulations and ordeals that have afflicted the believers in the Cradle of the Faith, the words of 'Abdu'l-Bahá gloriously resound to the future, *"Iran shall become a focal centre of divine splendours. Her darksome soil will become luminous and her land will shine resplendent."*

the short span of the Dispensation of the Báb and also because the new regulations were meant to abrogate past religious laws. As such they were to create an effect proclaiming a fresh Revelation rather than establishing a permanent legislative corpus. Shoghi Effendi explained in a letter written on his behalf that, "The Báb states that His laws are provisional and depend upon the acceptance of the future Manifestation. This is why in the *Book of Aqdas* Bahá'u'lláh sanctions some of the laws found in the *Bayán*, modifies others and sets aside many" Letter written on behalf of Shoghi Effendi included in Introduction to *The Kitáb-i-Aqdas*, p. 8).

1 A mithqál is about 3.64 g. Nineteen matháqíl (mithqals) of gold had a value of about $US4,000 in August 2021.

2 A. L. M. Nicolas, *Le Béyan Persan*, vol. 2, p. 144.

Figure 80: Old view of the Panj-Shambih bazar of Bárfurúsh scene of various martyrdoms (public domain)

Figure 81: Ḥaẓír-Fúrúshan (mat-weaver) alley near Quddús' grave

Figure 82: Mírzá Zakí Madrasih where Quddús was buried
(Source: Bahá'í Media)

Figure 83: Mírzá Zakí Madrasih where Quddús was buried
(Source: Bahá'í Media)

Figure 84: Shrine of Quddús in Bárfurú<u>sh</u> being demolished, 2004
(Source: Bahá'í Media)

Figure 85: Shrine of Quddús in Bárfurú<u>sh</u> being demolished, 2004
(Source: Bahá'í Media)

Figure 86: Shrine of Quddús in Bárfurúsh being demolished, 2004
(Source: *Ganj-i-Pinhán*)

Figure 87: Place where the shrine of Quddús was located (four-storey building)

26
Conceptions of the early Bábís

Chapter content
Transience of the Bábí Revelation
Internal confusion
Myths, legends and folklore about Quddús
Misconceptions about Quddús
First chronicles
The Shaykh Ṭabarsí fort defenders
Progressive claims and delegation of functions
The Qá'im
Quddús and Jesus Christ
Practising the new laws
Devotion over knowledge

This chapter covers the subject of some understandings and misunderstanding among the followers of the Báb. A number of potential factors should be considered, including the transience of the Bábí revelation, the background of the first chronicles, the relatively poor dissemination of Bábí literature, the strong reliance on oral transmission of knowledge and the followers' devotion to their leaders.[1]

Transience of the Bábí Revelation

A potential reason for the emergence of misunderstandings was the short Ministry of the Báb, the speed at which His Faith was disseminated, and the swiftness with which the major events occurred. Shoghi Effendi wrote in this regard:

> We behold, as we survey the episodes of this first act of a sublime drama, the figure of its Master Hero, the Báb, arise meteor-like above the horizon of Shíráz, traverse the sombre sky of Persia from south to north, decline with tragic swiftness, and perish in a blaze of glory. We see His satellites, a galaxy of God-intoxicated heroes, mount above that same horizon, irradiate that same incandescent light, burn themselves out with that self-same swiftness, and impart in their turn an added impetus to the steadily gathering momentum of God's nascent Faith.[2]

The Universal House of Justice wrote that the influence of the Báb: "... spread with extraordinary rapidity, reaching beyond the limits of Persia. Observers were astonished alike by the fast-swelling numbers of His followers and by their deeds

---

1 Hamid Algar, *Religion and state in Iran, 1785–1906*, p. 46.

2 Shoghi Effendi, *God Passes By*, p. 3.

of unsurpassed bravery and devotion."[1] The scope of such a rapid expansion was described by the Count of Gobineau as early as the 1860s:

> And so, here is a religion presented and promoted by a mere youth. In a very few years, that is to say from 1847 to 1852, this religion had disseminated throughout almost the whole of Persia, and counted within its fold numerous zealous adherents. In five years, a nation of from ten to twelve million people, occupying a territory which in bygone days had supported a population of fifty millions, a nation which does not possess those means of communication considered by us as so indispensable to the spread of ideas, I mean, of course, journals and pamphlets, and which did not have a postal service, nor even a single road fit for carriages in the entire extent of its empire; this nation, I say, had in five years been, in its entirety, penetrated by the doctrine of the Bábís, and the impression produced had been such that these most serious events, which I have recounted above, resulted therefrom. And it is not at all the ignorant part of the population that has been touched; it is eminent members of the clergy, the rich and learned classes, the women from the most important families; and lastly, after the Muslims, it is the philosophers, the Sufis in great numbers, and many Jews, who have been conquered by the new revelation ....[2]

Given such a short period of time, 'Abdu'l-Bahá explained how all prophecies and related events were fulfilled:

> *The Exalted One—may my life be offered up for Him—hath said that on the day of His Revelation all these events came to pass swifter than the twinkling of an eye, and that "fifty thousand years"*[3] *were traversed in a single hour.*[4]

Such a rapid and revolutionary passage of the Dispensation of the Báb was due to the imminence of *Him Whom God shall make manifest* "*Verily, the Rising of the Sun to its zenith is at hand and yet do ye not recognise that Day*",[5] the Báb had stated.

It is noteworthy that the Báb anticipated a period of confusion between His passing and the advent of *Him Whom God shall make manifest*:

> *The day will come when ye will earnestly desire to know that which would meet with the good-pleasure of God but, alas, ye shall find no path unto Him. Ye, even as camels that wander aimlessly, will not find a pasture wherein ye*

---

1 Message from the Universal House of Justice on the occasion of the Bicentenary of the Birth of the Báb, October 2019. Available https://www.bahai.org/library/authoritative-texts/the-universal-house-of-justice/messages/#20191001_001

2 Gobineau, *Religions et Philosophies* pp. 276–8 (tr. from French). In Moojan Momen, *The Bábí and Bahá'í Religions, 1844–1944*, pp. 70–1.

3 *Qur'án* 70:4.

4 'Abdu'l-Bahá, *Light of the World*, p. 152.

5 The Báb in Nader Saiedi, *Logos and Civilization*, p. 199.

may gather and unite upon a Cause in which ye can assuredly believe. At that time God shall cause the Sun of Truth to shine forth and the oceans of His bounty and grace to surge, while ye will have chosen droplets of water as the object of your desire, and will have deprived yourselves of the plenteous waters in His oceans.[1]

Internal confusion

The Research Department at the Bahá'í World Centre has advised that "in the period of turmoil and instability that prevailed in the Bábí community following the Martyrdom of the Báb, a number of people either announced themselves as the Promised One anticipated by the Báb or, in some instances, the community coalesced around one or more prominent believers."[2] For example, Adib Taherzadeh stated that in Qazvín the believers created "four sects, each bearing a name" and that "some followed Mírzá Yaḥyá, others identified their faith with Quddús or Ṭáhirih, and some considered themselves the followers of the *Bayán*, the Mother Book of the Bábí Revelation."[3]

Bahá'ís believe that all major religions in the past had a Lesser Covenant, whereby someone was appointed and authorised to lead the believers following the death of the Prophet. However, the Báb did not name a successor[4] or an authorised expositor of His teachings[5]—like the role fulfilled by 'Abdu'l-Bahá in the Bahá'í Faith.[6] Bahá'u'lláh has stated that in the Bábí Dispensation "*the matter of successorship was totally obliterated from the Book of God*."[7] This void was due to the imminence of *Him Whom God shall make manifest*. Who was going to be the principal expounder of the *Bayán*. The Báb ranked the Covenant of Bahá'u'lláh as higher than His own:

> *Glorified art Thou, O My God! Bear Thou witness that, through this Book, I have covenanted with all created things concerning the Mission of Him Whom Thou shalt make manifest* [Bahá'u'lláh], *ere the covenant concerning Mine own Mission had been established.*[8]

The Báb also stated in the *Persian Bayán* 3:16 that, after His passing, all Bábís, regardless of rank, would be sub servant to the authority of His Writings. He affirmed that *"from the setting of the Sun* [of the Báb] *until the rising of the Sun of Him Whom God shall make manifest, there will be no more binding Writings, and*

---

1 The Báb, *Selections*, p. 136.

2 The Universal House of Justice, letter 10 May 2023 to the author.

3 Adib Taherzadeh, *The Revelation of Bahá'u'lláh*, vol. 1, p. 68.

4 Bahá'u'lláh, *Additional Tablets extracts from Tablets revealed by Bahá'u'lláh.*

5 Shoghi Effendi, *God Passes By*, p. 28.

6 Bahá'u'lláh in His Will and Testament, called the *Kitáb-i-'Ahd* ("The Book of My Covenant"), designated 'Abdu'l-Bahá as the Head of the Faith, authorised Interpreter of His teachings and Centre of His Covenant.

7 Bahá'u'lláh, *Additional Tablets extracts from Tablets revealed by Bahá'u'lláh.*

8 The Báb in Bahá'u'lláh, *Epistle to the Son of the Wolf*, p. 160.

the Letters of the Living and all the believers in God will be under their shadow [the Writings] *of the Point of the Bayán."*[1]

In addition, the Báb declared that only *Him Whom God shall make manifest* [Bahá'u'lláh] would fully comprehend the Bayán, *"none shall encompass that which God hath revealed in the Bayán except Him Whom God shall make manifest, or the one who is taught such knowledge by Him, as well as the exalted Tree from which the Bayán hath emerged ...."*[2]

Myths, legends and folklore about Quddús

For information about the Bábí religion, the Bábís relied strongly on oral transmission of knowledge and devotion to their leaders.[3] On the one hand, at Shaykh Ṭabarsí there were key figures among the Báb's disciples. Within the fort there was Quddús, only second in rank to the Báb. There was also Mullá Ḥusayn who in the *Kitáb-i-Íqán,* Bahá'u'lláh has testified that "*But for him, God would not have been established upon the seat of His mercy, nor ascended the throne of eternal glory."*[4] Nine Letters of the Living were present, that is, half of the entire contingent, about whom the Báb has testified in the *Persian Bayán* as "*the lights which in the past have eternally prostrated themselves and will prostrate themselves eternally in the future, before the celestial throne*".[5] It is therefore reasonable to assume that the 500 companions grew stronger in their knowledge about the Faith of the Báb at their regular communal and devotional gatherings and through their close association.

On the other hand, it would appear that among some Bábís there was a degree of confusion about the stations of various people, such as that of Quddús' position, since, understandably, they were not very familiar with many of the Writings of the Báb.[6] Some of these misconceptions included ranking Quddús above the Báb, identifying the former with the return of Muḥammad, relating the Báb with the return of Imám 'Alí, identifying Quddús with Jesus Christ and implying that he was born from a virgin mother.[7]

The danger of divinising religious apostles has always existed. For instance, in Islam, a Shí'ih sect who called themselves 'Allíyu'lláhí (literally, "those who believe that 'Alí is God) considers Imám 'Alí as God.[8] Shoghi Effendi cautioned in *The Dispensation of Bahá'u'lláh* "those irrational and superstitious beliefs which

---

1 The Báb in Nader Saiedi, *Gate of the Heart,* p. 347.

2 The Báb in Nader Saiedi, *Gate of the Heart,* p. 65.

3 Hamid Algar. *Religion and state in Iran, 1785–1906: the Role of the Ulama in the Qajar Period,* p. 46.

4 Bahá'u'lláh, *The Kitáb-i-Íqán,* p. 223.

5 Emily McBride Périgord, *Translation of French Foot-Notes of The Dawn-Breakers,* pp. 14–5.

6 Adib Taherzadeh, *The Revelation of Bahá'u'lláh,* vol. 3, p. 332.

7 Kavian Milani, *NOQṬAT AL-KĀF,* n.p.

8 Hasan Balyuzi, *Muḥammad and the Course of Islam,* p. 224.

have insensibly crept in the first century of the Christian era, into the teachings of Jesus Christ, and by crystallizing into accepted dogmas have impaired the effectiveness and obscured the purpose of the Christian Faith."[1] In the early decades of the Bahá'í Faith, some Bahá'ís in the West struggled to understand the station of 'Abdu'l-Bahá. Some believers equivocally compared Him to the return of Jesus Christ or to a new Manifestation of God,[2] and others simply elevated Him so much that His position of servitude and self- effacement was hidden.[3] Due to the nature of history building based on oral sources, there was always the possibility in Bábí narratives that situations, memories or expressions were misinterpreted and distorted over time.

Misconceptions around Quddús

In brief, the Bábís lacked a coherent and well formulated notion about the stations of various people, such as that of Quddús, since they had limited knowledge of the Writings of the Báb.[4]

After the death of Quddús, some alienated Bábís themselves claimed the title and station of Quddús, one of them changing his name to *Quddús Effendi*.[5] [6] Even when Quddús was alive, some in the community held the belief that another believer held the same rank:

> Among the men who in Karbilá eagerly embraced, through the efforts of Ṭáhirih, the Cause of the Báb, was a certain Shaykh Ṣáliḥ, an Arab resident of that city who was the first to shed his blood in the path of the Faith, in Tihran. She [Ṭáhirih] was so profuse in her praise of Shaykh Ṣáliḥ that a few suspected him of being equal in rank to Quddús.[7]

There were also some believers who regarded Quddús as equal[8] or higher in rank to the Báb Himself.[9] As Nader Saiedi noted, "In the *Persian Bayán* the Báb explicitly and frequently stated that no one except the Báb and Him Whom God shall make manifest can reveal [divine] verses."[10] Furthermore, the Báb made

1 Shoghi Effendi, *The World Order of Bahá'u'lláh,* p. 138.

2 John Esslemont, *Bahá'u'lláh and the New Era*, pp. 68- 69.

3 Adib Taherzadeh, *The Covenant of Bahá'u'lláh*, p. 221.

4 Adib Taherzadeh, *The Revelation of Bahá'u'lláh*, vol. 3, p. 332.

5 Necati Alkan, *Bahá'u'lláh's Lawḥ-i-Istintáq*. See E. G. Browne, *The Taríkh-i-Jadíd*, p. 380; and Adib Taherzadeh, *The Revelation of Bahá'u'lláh*, Vol. 3, p. 225.

6 Effendi (Efendi, Afandí) is a "title of nobility meaning a lord, master or gentleman (after the name, when referring to non-Europeans wearing Western clothes and the tarboosh), In, Michael Thomas, *Glossary and transcription for Arabic & Persian terms,* Afandi entry.

7 Nabíl-i-A'ẓam, *The Dawn-Breakers,* p. 271.

8 Edward Granville Browne, *The Taríkh-i-Jadíd*, p. 336.

9 Mangol Bayat, *Mysticism and Dissent*, p. 115.

10 Nader Saiedi, *Concealment and Revelation*, p. 42. See *Persian Bayán* 6:8.

very clear that nobody was superior to Bahá'u'lláh in rank and gave the following warning:

> *And shouldst Thou behold, O my God, any branch, leaf, or fruit upon Me that hath failed to bow down before Him, on the day of His Revelation, cut it off, O My God, from that Tree, for it is not of Me, nor shall it return unto Me.*[1]

It is not always possible to track down the exact origin of many of the early Bábí perceptions, but they were certainly the product of the movement growing very quickly within a short period of time. Moreover, there was so little literature in circulation at a time of intense persecutions that it was inevitable that beliefs would have been borrowed from Islamic sources in response to the need for immediate answers to critical questions. Historian and Hand of the Cause Hasan Balyuzi asserts that some early Bábí historiography represents "a reflection of the anarchy of the darkest days of the Bábí Faith, and bears the indelible mark of that nihilism which did for a time overtake the community of the Báb."[2]

There was also a misconception among some believers that Quddús would have been designated as the Manifestation of God had the Báb not already declared Himself to be the next Manifestation of God.[3] The Research Department at the Bahá'í World Centre has written on behalf of the Universal House of Justice that "to date, it has not found any statement in the Bahá'í Writings to the effect that if the Báb had hesitated in announcing His mission, Quddús would have declared himself as a Messenger of God or been the chosen one for such a position."[4]

Certainly, there was an element of great devotion to Quddús that was sometimes exaggerated by the Bábís when they heard the exultant references made about him in the Writings of the Báb as discussed in detail in chapter 19 "The station of Quddús".

First chronicles

Chronicles about the Shaykh Ṭabarsí events were written several years, sometimes decades, after the death of Quddús. Those chronicles were written by eyewitnesses or gleaned from verbal accounts by survivors that were subsequently transcribed by the believers.

There are various untitled narratives from the survivors of the Shaykh Ṭabarsí conflict. Three years and three months after the conflict, Luṭf 'Alí Mírzá Shírází wrote his chronicle.[5] In addition, Mír Abú-Ṭálib-i Shahmírzadí[6] wrote his around

1 The Báb in Bahá'u'lláh, *Epistle to the Son of the Wolf,* p. 162.

2 Hasan Balyuzi, *Edward Granville Bowne and the Bahá'í Faith*, p. 73

3 David Piff, *Bahá'í Lore,* p. 299.

4 Letter of the Universal House of Justice 10 May 2023 to the author.

5 Luṭf 'Alí Mírzá Shírází, *Untitled history,* n.d. unpublished manuscript.

6 Abu-Talib-i-Shahmirzadi, Mir, Untitled history, n.d., unpublished manuscript.

1888 and Ḥájí Nasír-i Qazvíní,[1] wrote his story before he passed away in 1882–1883. Three of them died in prison. Mírzá Ḥaydar-'Alí Ardistání,[2] who wrote his own chronicle years later, died in 1905. His work was the basis of *Nabil's Narrative.*

In addition, there were Bábí secondary sources written using eyewitness accounts such as *Vaqa'i-i-Mimiyyih* ("Events of the letter Mím"—Mázindarán) by Siyyid Muḥammad-Ḥusayn Mahjúr-i-Zavári[3] around 1861–1862 based on oral reports from three survivors.[4] There is also an untitled account written by Áqá Siyyid Muḥammad Riẓá Shahmírzadí before his death in 1892-1893.[5] He derived his information from his brother Mír Abú-Ṭálib-i Shahmírzadí , a survivor and chronologist.[6] Nabíl had also access to this account.

It is also known an anonymous manuscript (although certain scholars attribute a large part of it to Mírzá Áqá Ján of Káshán) based on "the sayings of Jináb-i Ḥájí,[7] known as *Kitáb-i-Nuqṭat al-Káf*[8] ("The book of the Point of the letter Káf").[9] Other chronicles include *The New History (Taríkh-i-Jadíd)* by Ḥusayn Hamadání[10] a detailed narrative based on the *Kitáb-i-Nuqṭat al-Káf* but also from other unknown sources probably from oral accounts, and of course the classical *Narrative of Nabíl,*[11] which Shoghi Effendi said "will serve as a standard when future histories of the Faith will be written."[12] It is also worthy of note that Nabíl also relied on oral sources when he was writing his *Narrative in* 'Akká in 1887-1888.[13]

---

1 See https://bahai-library.com/rabbani_narrative_haji_Qazvíni

2 Thanks to Dr Amir Badiei for permitting the author to reproduce the story from his book *Dreams of Destiny in the Bábí and Bahá'í Faiths.*

3 Siyyid Muḥammad-Ḥusayn, *Vaqa'i-i Mimiyyih.* Available https://www.h-net.org/~bahai/arabic/vol5/mimiyyih/mimiyyih.htm

4 E.G. Browne, *Materials for the Study of the Bábí Religion,* p. 237.

5 Áqá Siyyid Muḥammad Rizá Shahmírzadí, *Unpublished manuscript,* nd. Available at: https://www.h-net.org/~bahai/arabic/vol5/aqariza/aqariza.htm

6 DenisMacEoin, *The Sources for Early Babi Doctrine and History,* pp. 162-163.

7 William McCants and Kavian Milani, *The History and Provenance of an Early Manuscript of the "Nuqtat al-Kaf"*, p. 448.

8 E. G. Browne, *Kitáb-i-Nuqtatu'l-Káf.*

9 According to Kavian Sadeghzade Milani, the manuscript is "the earliest general history of the Bábí religion spanning the years 1260/1844 to 1268/1851–52 with a theological preamble ... the text (p. 5) indicates that it [*Káf*] was derived from the Qur'anic injunction "kon fayakun" (["He merely says to it"] 'be', and it is"; Q. 19.35). (*Encylopaedia Iranica,* 2008, available www.iranicaonline.org/articles/noqtat-al-kaf)

10 Ḥusayn Hamadání, *The New History (Taríkh-i-Jadíd).*

11 Nabíl-i-A'ẓam, *The Dawn-Breakers.*

12 Shoghi Effendi letter dated 15 November 1932. Quoted in 'Alí Nakhjávání, *Shoghi Effendi,* p. 95.

13 Nabíl-i-A'ẓam, *The Dawn-Breakers,* p. xliii.

A brief account in Mázandarání language was written by a certain Shaykh al-'Ajam and written around 1860[1] [2] providing additional details about Shaykh Ṭabarsí and the martyrdom of Quddús. There were also two formal reports written for the government records: Násikh al-tawárrík ("The Superseder of Histories") and Rawzat al safá-yi Náṣirí ("Garden of Purity").[3] Since both authors were court historians for a despicable and corrupt administration, it was more crucial for them to adopt a strong anti-Bábí stance that would be accepted by their Qájár sponsors than it was for them to write objective and factual histories.[4]

A Traveler's Narrative written to Illustrate the Episode of the Báb is a valuable historical source written by 'Abdu'l-Bahá that provides context for understanding those times. In addition, four European scholars collected information about Shaykh Ṭabarsí (and the Bábí Faith in general) within Persia. Firstly, the Count of Gobineau (1816-1882), French diplomat to Ṭihrán, wrote his *Les Religions et les Philosophies dans l'Asie Centrale* [5]with the help of an "Israelite whom Gobineau had as [his] professor of Persian and who could only teach his student the little he knew of the sect"[6] and other oral sources presumably Bábí.[7] Gobineau also derived his sources from the government record *Násikh al-tawárrík.*[8]

In turn, A.L.M. Nicholas (1864-1939), another French diplomat who wrote *Siyyid 'Alí-Muhammad dit le Báb* [9] relied on narratives such as *Kitáb-i-Nuqṭat al-Káf*[10] and *The New History (Tarík͟h-i-Jadíd),*[11] oral narratives [12] and "collected documents widely, thanks to the indigenous secretary, Mírzá Ebrahim, of Ṭihrán, whom I discovered to be Bahá'í and who put me in touch with the believers." [13] [14] In turn, Adolfo Rivadeneyra (1841-1882), vice-consul and first Spanish diplomat to Persia, wrote three volumes of his *Viaje al Interior de Persia,* providing

---

1 von Dorn, Bernard, *Nachträge zu dem Verzeichniss der von der Kaiserlichen öffentlichen Bibliothek erworbenen Chanykov'schen Handschriften und den da mitgetheilten Nachrichten über die Baby und deren Koran,* p. 389.

2 Habib Borjian, *A Mazandarani Account of the Babi Incident at Shaikh Tabarsi,* pp. 386-394.

3 Siyamak Zabihi-Moghaddam, *The Bábí-state conflicts of 1848–1850,* p. 314.

4 Mina Yazdani, *Anti-Bahá'í Polemics and Historiography,* p. 89.

5 Joseph Arthur Gobineau, *Les Religions et les Philosophies dans l'Asie Centrale.* Bibliothèque Didier, 1866.

6 A.L.M. Nicolas, cited in Peter Terry, *A Prophet in Modern Times,* p. 11.

7 Geoffrey Nash, *Introduction,* p. 16.

8 Peter Terry, *A Prophet in Modern Times,* p. 92.

9 A.L.M. Nicolas. Siyyid 'Alí-Muhammad dit le Báb. Dujarric & Co, Paris. 1905.

10 E. G. Browne (ed.), *Kitáb-i-Nuqtatu'l-Káf: Being the Earliest History of the Bábís. Brill, 1910.*

11 Ḥusayn Hamadání, *The New History (Tarík͟h-i-Jadíd) of Mirza Ali-Muhammed the Bab (tr. E. G. Browne).* London: Cambridge University Press, 1893.

12 A.L.M. Nicolas, cited in Peter Terry, *A Prophet in Modern Times,* pp. 52-53.

13 A.L.M. Nicolas, cited in Peter Terry, *A Prophet in Modern Times,* p. 11.

14 Moojan Momen, *The Work of A.L.M. Nicolas (1864-1937),* n.p.

information about the Bábís of Iran some aspects of their history including Shaykh Ṭabarsí.[1] His sources seemed more oral and mostly based on Gobineau's book published ten years before Rivadeneyra' journey which took place in 1874. These European diplomas must have been very circumspect of their investigation as Rivadeneyra recorded:

> To give an idea of the fear that the Bábís still inspire today spread throughout Iran, it is enough to say that I, a European, would not dare to pronounce the name of that sect in a bazaar, fearing that it would immediately provoke a conflict.[2]

Their narratives were enriched by oral accounts from people working in their diplomatic legations. Based mostly on the two aforementioned documents, Professor E.G. Browne of the University of Cambridge wrote several historical essays about the Shaykh Ṭabarsí developments also partly using native oral accounts collected from Persian ground in his travels.[3]

The role of oral transmission of knowledge is fundamental in any religion. Jewish or Rabbinical oral transmission of Torah was a well-established discipline, so was it for the early reciters of the *Qur'án* who later had to commit their memories to paper to form that sacred Book. Many historical narratives about Shaykh Ṭabarsí went through the same formation. At times for some details those narrative differ but as a whole, they represent a valuable corpus of information about those years. A number of inconsistencies in dates among early Bábí chronicles has also been noted by Siyamak Zabihi-Moghaddam in his article *Pírámún-i-Kitáb-i-Ḥaḍrat-i-Báb.*[4]

In general, the sayings attributed to Quddús and other personages in the above narratives, unless referenced otherwise, should not be considered *ad verbatim* because these were not recorded on the spot. For instance, focusing on *The Dawn-Breakers*, John Walbridge asserts, "Nabíl followed the venerable historiographical tradition of having his characters say what they ought to have said under the circumstances."[5]

---

1 Adolfo Rivadeneyra, *Viaje and Interior de Persia*, vol. 1. Madrid: Imprenta y estereotipia de Aribau y ca, 1880.

2 Adolfo Rivadeneyra, *Viaje and Interior de Persia*, vol. 1, p.244.

3 E.G. Browne, *Materials for the Study of the Babi Religion*. Cambridge University Press, 1918.

4 Siyamak Zabihi-Moghaddam, "Pírámún-i-kitáb-i-Ḥaḍrat-i-Báb," review of *Ḥaḍrat-i-Báb [the Báb]*, by Nuṣratu'lláh Muḥammad-Ḥusayní (Dundas: Institute for Bahá'í Studies in Persian, 1995), pp. xiv + 1038, *Pazhúheshnámeh: A Persian Journal of Bahá'í Studies 2*, no. 2, pp. 130–59. Summer 1998.

5 John Walbridge, *Document and Narrative Sources for the History of the Battle of Zanjan*, n.d.

The Shaykh Ṭabarsí fort defenders

It is to be expected that the understanding of the Báb's revelation by the early Bábís was significantly influenced by their Islamic background. For instance, about one-third of the participants in Shaykh Ṭabarsí were religious scholars, ordinary citizens, merchants and lawmakers.[1] In *Tablets of the Divine Plan*, 'Abdu'l-Bahá quotes *Qur'án* 28:5: *"And We desire to show favor to those who were brought low in the land, and to make them spiritual leaders among men, and to make of them Our heirs."*[2]

There defenders were also merchants and farmers. About 270 believers were from small villages, while approximately 155 believers were from the neighbouring provinces of Mázindarán and Gílán.[3] One-hundred and twenty of them were exclusively from Mázindarán whose leader was Áqá Rasúl.[4] Therefore there was a significant presence of Bábís from a rural background, i.e., peasants. They were people of great faith for whom the coming of the Qá'im had been central to their lives since childhood.

In all religions, the poor and the destitute have had a special blessing. In Christian terms: "the abased will be exalted" (*Matthew* 23:12) and "the last will be first" (*Matthew* 20:16). Similarly, in the Tablets of the Divine Plan, 'Abdu'l-Bahá quotes this verse from the *Qur'án* (28:5) which warns, "But it was Our Will to favour those who were oppressed in the land, and to make them leaders, and to make them the inheritors"[5] [6] The Báb said something absolutely beautiful about them and the notion of spiritual wealth:

> *Glory be unto Thee, O Lord! Although Thou mayest cause a person to be destitute of all earthly possessions, and from the beginning of his life until his ascension unto Thee he may be reduced to poverty through the operation of Thy decree, yet wert Thou to have brought him forth from the Tree of Thy love, such a bounty would indeed be far better for him than all the things Thou hast created in heaven and earth and whatsoever lieth between them...*[7]

The "sifter of wheat" who accepted the Cause of the Báb in Iṣfahán is representative of the destitute person who embraced the Divine Teachings. In Shaykh Ṭabarsí, the "sifter of wheat" ultimately gave his life, and the *Persian Bayán* described him as a simple man of profound faith:

---

1 Moojan Momen, *The Social Basis of the Bábí Upheavals in Iran,* p. 284.

2 'Abdu'l-Bahá, *Tablets of the Divine Plan,* p. 34.

3 Moojan Momen, *The Social Basis of the Bábí Upheavals in Iran,* p. 288–9.

4 Mírzá Ḥusayn Hamadání, *The New History (Taríkh-i-Jadíd),* p. 67.

5 Matthew 20:16

6 'Abdu'l-Bahá, *Tablets of the Divine Plan,* p. 34.

7 The Báb, Selections, p. 189.

> *Iṣfahán, that outstanding city, is distinguished by the religious fervour of its shí'ah inhabitants, by the learning of its divines, and by the keen expectation, shared by high and low alike, of the imminent coming of the Ṣáḥibu'z-Zamán.*[1] *In every quarter of that city, religious institutions have been established. And yet, when the Messenger of God had been made manifest, they who claimed to be the repositories of learning and the expounders of the mysteries of the Faith of God rejected His Message. Of all the inhabitants of that seat of learning, only one person, a sifter of wheat, was found to recognise the Truth, and was invested with the robe of Divine virtue!*[2]

In the *Kitáb-Aqdas*, Bahá'u'lláh remarked about the "sifter of wheat":

> *Call ye to mind the shaykh whose name was Muḥammad-Ḥasan, who ranked among the most learned divines of his day. When the True One was made manifest, this shaykh, along with others of his calling, rejected Him, while a sifter of wheat and barley accepted Him and turned unto the Lord.*[3]

Highlighting again the value of a simple believer versus a prominent non-believer, according to Nader Saiedi, "the Báb explains that upon rejecting him, the king of Persia, Muḥammad Sháh (d. 1848), and his prime minister, Ḥájí Mírzá Áqásí (d. 1849), descended to the lowest abyss, while [Mubarak, servant of the Báb], who to outward appearance, was bereft of any power or earthly rank, ascended to the heaven of glory for 'having done good in the realm of faith'."[4]

Progressive claims and delegation of functions

It appears that at some stage during His life, the Báb delegated some of His titles to some of His followers. Such a delegation must not be understood neither as sharing of His divine station nor as a transfer of spiritual sovereignty. Rather such a mysterious process seems more a functional allocation of some ministerial roles associated the Báb's Revelation providing a degree of investiture and command to distinguished believers. For instance, among the many eschatological roles of the Qá'im were the spreading of a new religion and the establishment of justice.[5] Such a delegation might also emphasise the role of intermediary between the Báb with His believers when He was in custody due to persecution.[6]

1 *Ṣáḥibu'z-Zamán* ("Lord of the Age") is one of the prophetic titles of the Báb.

2 The Báb in Nabíl-i-A'ẓam, *The Dawn-Breakers*, p. 99.

3 Bahá'u'lláh, *The Kitáb-i-Aqdas*, para. 166.

4 Nader Saiedi, *The Ethiopian King*, p. 181.

5 Stephen Lambden, *The Messianic Roots of Babi-Baha'i Globalism*, p. 17.

6 Ruhollah Mehrabkhani, *Mullá Ḥusayn*, p. 129.

In the *Kitáb-i-Panj Sha'n* chapter related to the name of God, *Ajmal* ("The Most Beauteous"), the Báb affirms that He appeared in the station of the gates[1] over the first four years of His manifestation. Afterward, He removed that garment and emerged as the Promised One. The Báb continues to say that someone had to wear the (garment of) the title of Há'[2] (that is, the Báb).[3] The Báb then asks us to reflect how the new possessor of the title [Quddús] appeared to acquire it and then He utters the phrase, *"Quddús, Quddús, Quddús, Quddús"*.[4] Hence, Quddús was the one destined by Him to wear the Báb's previous station.[5]

In the same chapter the Báb reveals that only the Manifest is seen in the Hidden, and that only the Hidden is visible in the Manifest. In several of His Writings, the Báb ratifies this divine principle, that God is "the Manifest and the Hidden",[6] "the Manifest but the Hidden",[7] the "Seen and the Hidden".[8]

The Báb indicated that, in the beginning (al-Ávval) nothing is seen except the end (al-Ákhir), while in the end (al-Ákhir) nothing is seen except the beginning (al-Ávval).[9] It is then that the Báb says that the Last Name of God (Ismu'lláhu'l Ákhar, Quddús) certainly has shone forth, radiated and shed brilliance and gives His blessings to anyone who sees in Quddús nothing but God.[10] It has been said that in the same Book, the Báb "accorded him divine status"[11] and it is interesting to note that the Báb granted His own title of "Ḥaḍrat-i Aʿlá" (His Holiness the Exalted One) to Quddús in 1848.[12][13] Stephen Lambden adds that "towards the end

---

1 The "gates" (CE 874–941) were the four representatives of the twelfth (and final) successor of the Prophet Muḥammad (also called Imáms). The twelfth Imám was referred to as the "Lord of the Age". The Báb affirmed that He was the return of the Lord of the Age.

2 The Arabic letters *Há'* and *Wá'*, symbolizing the divinity (from "Huwá", Arabic pronoun for "He" referring to God).

3 Nader Saiedi, *Gate of the Heart*, p. 170.

4 The Báb, *Panj Sha'n*, p. 280.

5 The Báb, *Panj Sha'n* (*Five Modes*).

6 The Báb, *Selections*, p. 112.

7 Nader Saiedi, Gate of the Heart, p. 8.

8 The Báb, *Selections*, p. 159.

9 Stephen Lambden, *Muḥammad 'Ali Bārfurushi, Quddūs*, n.p.

10 The Báb, *Panj Sha'n (Five Modes)*. MS facsimile. Ṭihrán, 196X? [sic], p. 280.

11 Stephen Lambden, "A Tablet of Mírzá Ḥusayn 'Alí Bahá'u'lláh", p. 53.

12 Comment by the editor Dr Ahang Rabbani, in Mírzá Ḥabíbu'lláh Afnán, *The Genesis of the Bábí-Bahá'í Faiths*, p. 61.

13 The Báb also granted His own title to other followers: Mullá Muḥammad-'Alí Zanjání (1812 -1851) was given the designation of *Ḥujjat* (The Proof) and Mullá Shaykh 'Alíy-i-Turshízí was surnamed *Azím (Great, dignified, exalted).*

of the Báb's ministry leading Bábís saw the Báb and Quddús as the 'Alpha' and 'Omega' of the Dispensation of the *Bayán*".[1 2]

Similarly, Sharí'atmadár a local cleric referred to Quddús, in Amanat's words, as "the second báb, next to Sayyid 'Alí-Muḥammad-i-Shírází [the Báb]".[3] Sharí'atmadár, the teacher of Quddús in his early childhood became later his supporter, although a non-Bábí or perhaps himself one secretly.

Sharí'atmadár, a local cleric, referred to Quddús, in Amanat's words, as "the second báb, next to Sayyid 'Alí-Muḥammad-i-Shírází [the Báb]".[4] Sharí'atmadár was a supporter of Quddús, although he was not a Bábí or perhaps only in secret.

In the Shaykh Ṭabarsí chronicles, the companions used to call Mullá Ḥusayn "His Holiness the Báb".[5] Historian Ruhollah Mehrabkhani further asserts that:

> During those days (mid-1845], the Báb invested Mullá Ḥusayn with the new title of "Báb", which had been His own title until then. He Himself now used the title of "Sayyid-i-Dhikr".[6] Mullá Ḥusayn was made the intermediary between the believers and their Master. He was given authority to answer their queries, and the Bábís were instructed to direct their questions to him.[7]

About the evolution of the position of the Báb from being a *Gate* to become the *Qá'im*, the Promised One, and the *Primal Point,* Moojan Momen has commented:

> In 1848, when the Báb put forward his claim to be the Imám Mahdí, He began to apply to Himself such titles as "The Primal Point" (Nuqṭiy-i-Úlá). Some of the histories indicate that he then transferred the title of "Báb" to one or two of his leading disciples. With this transfer of title there appears to have also been a certain degree of function of authority ....[8]

That the Báb transferred His stations to distinguished believers and then assumed a higher one for Himself is accepted, then this is another unique feature of the Bábí Revelation that is enacted by the Báb in accordance to His "rank as one of the self-sufficient Manifestations of God", "invested with sovereign power and

---

1 Stephen Lambden, *A Tablet of Mírzá Ḥusayn 'Ali Bahá'u'lláh,* p. 7. See also *The Narrative of Ḥájí Náṣir Qazvíní*, n.p.

2 Stephen Lambden, *A Tablet of Mírzá Ḥusayn 'Ali Bahá'u'lláh of the Early* Iraq *Period: The "Tablet of All Food" (Lawḥ-i Kull Ṭa'ám)*, p. 7.

3 Abbas Amanat, *Resurrection and Renewal,* p. 186.

4 Abbas Amanat, *Resurrection and Renewal,* p. 186.

5 Mullá Ḥusayn was the Bábu'l-Báb ("The Gate of the Gate").

6 Sayyid-i-Dhikr" literally means "Siyyid of the Remembrance". It comes from the term *Dhikru'lláh* which can be translated as the "Remembrance or Utterance of God" in Arabic (Zikru'lláh in Persian). In Islamic theology the term *dhikr* is identified with the Creative Word of God or the Logos of the *Bible* (*John* 1:1-18) and the *Qur'án* (3:45) where the Logos is identified with Jesus (See: Nader Saiedi, *Gate of the Heart*, p. 96).

7 Ruhollah Mehrabkhani, *Mullá Ḥusayn*, p. 129.

8 Moojan Momen, *The Social Location of the Bábí Movement: A Preliminary Note*, p. 8.

authority" and exercising "all the rights and prerogatives of independent Prophethood".[1] As such, the Bábí Revelation as an independent religion did not totally transmute to the Bahá'í Revelation but conserved its uniqueness such as in Christianity and Islam. In this regard Shoghi Effendi wrote:

> The severe laws and injunctions revealed by the Báb can be properly appreciated and understood only when interpreted in the light of His own statements regarding the nature, purpose and character of His own Dispensation. [2]

The Qá'im

During the early days, Bábís taught their new Faith using mainly the claim that the "Qá'im has appeared".[3] Such a call thereupon spread like wildfire throughout the country, being carried on foot and on horseback along roads and streets, via bazaars in cities and villages, and into people's homes and religious institutions.

In those days people would be praying that the Qá'im would appear soon, "O Imám [the Qá'im], appear hastily, hastily, hastily, immediately in this hour and moment".[4] Iran Muhájir tells the story of a prominent person who "always kept dozens of horses saddled day and night, ready at the gate of his palace so that he would not lose even a moment in going to the Imám if he heard of his appearance, to assist him in his fight against the infidels".[5] In Iran, every Shí'ih believer appeals for the advent of the promised Qá'im by concluding their prayers with the formula: "'Ajal Alláhu farajahu" ("May God hasten his glad advent").[6]

It is important to note that there was a belief among some Bábís before the conflict at Shaykh Ṭabarsí that Quddús and Mullá Ḥusayn held not only the position of Letters of the Living but also the station of *báb* ("gate") to the Báb and afterwards they reached the station of *Qá'im* ("He Who shall arise"). Peter Smith and Moojan Momen have noted that Quddús and Mullá Ḥusayn "symbolically reenacted various of the prophecies relating to the coming of the Mahdí in the place of their imprisoned leader."[7]

Within Islamic theology there appear to be three different Qá'ims. The first was the Qá'im arising from the line of Muḥammad (Qá'im Ál-i-Muḥammad—"He Who will raise from the Household of Muḥammad"), that is, a Siyyid. The Báb was the Qá'im of the Household of Muḥammad.[8]

---

1 Shoghi Effendi, *The World Order of Bahá'u'lláh*, p. 123.
2 Shoghi Effendi, *Dawn of a New Day*, pp. 77–78.
3 Ḥaydar-'AlíUskú'í, *Monsieur Nicolas*, p. 102.
4 Írán Furútan, *Siyyid Muṣṭafá Rúmí*, p. 8.
5 Írán Furútan, *Siyyid Muṣṭafá Rúmí*, p. 24.
6 Ali Razi Naqavi, Bābism and Bahā'ism, p. 188.
7 Peter Smith and Moojan Momen, *The Bábí Movement*, p. 58.
8 William Collins, *Millennialism, the Millerites, and Historicism*, p. 18

The second one was referred to as the Qá'im from Khurásán (east of Persia), and the third one as the Qá'im of Gilán/Mázindarán (north of Persia), referring to Mullá Ḥusayn and Quddús, respectively. The reference to these two Qá'ims appear to come from an Islamic tradition:

> When the Qá'im will rise in Khurásán, he will proceed to Kufa and thence to Multan, passing through the jazira [island] of Banu Kawan; but the Qá'im among us will rise in [G]ílán among the people of Daylam [inland Gílán] and there will be for my son the Turkish flags.[1]

Qá'im of Khurásán

Mullá Ḥusayn was referred to as the *Qá'im of Khurásán* by the Bábís of Shaykh Ṭabarsí.[2] The title of Qá'im of Khurásán attributed to Mullá Ḥusayn might have come from a prophecy stated by the Prophet Muḥammad asserting that the Qá'im, the Viceregent of God, will appear from Khurásán to fight against the Anti-Christ unfurling the *Black Standards*.

In regard to Mullá Ḥusayn, we know that the Báb sent to Mullá Ḥusayn His Siyyid turban and conferred on him the new name of Siyyid 'Alí, effectively making him a member of the family of Muḥammad. As previously discussed, Mullá Ḥusayn left Mashhad with about 200 Bábís wearing the Báb's turban and displaying the Black Standards on his way to Mázindarán Province. "The raising of the Black Standard in Khurásán," wrote Moojan Momen, "appears to have been done by Mullá Ḥusayn in his new status as the Qá'im (the Qá'im being one of the titles of the Imám Mahdí and the prophecy relating to the raising of the Black Standards states that the Mahdí comes with the Black Standard)."[3]

Qá'im of Gílán

Some chroniclers spoke of Quddús as the *Qá'im of Gílán*.[4] [5] [6] Gílán is in the north of Iran, the region around which the episode of Shaykh Ṭabarsí occurred and where Quddús was born. Mullá Ḥusayn referred to Quddús as "the one whose advent you have awaited for one thousand two hundred and sixty years",[7] alluding to his position as Qá'im. Further, 'Abdu'l-Bahá in *Some Answered Questions* affirms that Quddús represents the renovation of religion after 1,260 years and the return of Imám 'Alí.[8] In turn, Nabíl affirms that Quddús' arrival at the Shrine of Shaykh Ṭabarsí fulfilled a Qá'im-related prophecy:

---

1 Cited in Stephen Lambden, *Antichrist-Dajjal*, p. 19.

2 Siyyid Muḥammad-Ḥusayn, *Vaqa'i-i Mimiyyih,* p. 54.

3 Moojan Momen, *The Social Location of the Bábí Movement*, p. 8.

4 Denis MacEoin, *The Bábí Concept of Holy War,* pp. 106–7 and p. 115.

5 Abbas Amanat, *Resurrection and Renewal,* p. 186

6 Moojan Momen, *The Social Location of the Bábí Movement: A Preliminary Note*, p. 8.

7 Siyyid Muḥammad-Ḥusayn, *Vaqa'i-i Mimiyyih,* p. 54. Cited in Denis MacEoin, *The Messiah of Shiraz*, p. 483.

8 'Abdu'l-Bahá, *Some Answered Questions,* chapter 11, para. 30 (p. 63).

> The first words that fell from the lips of Quddús after he had dismounted and leaned against the shrine were the following: "The Baqíyyatu'lláh ["The Remnant of God"] will be best for you if ye are of those who believe" [*Qur'án* 11:85]. By this utterance was fulfilled the prophecy of Muḥammad as recorded in the following tradition:
>
> "And when the Mihdí [the Qá'im] is made manifest, He shall lean His back against the Ka'bih [the Mecca Shrine] and shall address to the three hundred and thirteen followers who will have grouped around Him, these words: 'The Baqíyyatu'lláh [Bahá'u'lláh] will be best for you if ye are of those who believe.'"
>
> Quddús, on his arrival at the Shrine of Shaykh Ṭabarsí, charged Mullá Ḥusayn to ascertain the number of the assembled companions. One by one he counted them and passed them in through the gate of the fort: three hundred and twelve in all. He himself was entering the fort in order to acquaint Quddús with the result, when a youth, who had hastened all the way on foot from Bárfurúsh, suddenly rushed in and seizing the hem of his garment, pleaded to be enrolled among the companions and to be allowed to lay down his life, whenever required, in the path of the Beloved. His wish was readily granted. When Quddús was informed of the total number of the companions, he remarked: "Whatever the tongue of the Prophet of God has spoken concerning the promised One must needs be fulfilled, that thereby His testimony may be complete in the eyes of those divines who esteem themselves as the sole interpreters of the law and traditions of Islam. Through them will the people recognise the truth and acknowledge the fulfilment of these traditions."[1]

Finally, it also seems that the Bábís identified Quddús as "the Ḥasaní, the Nafs-i-Zakíya ("the pure soul") of the Shí'ite apocalyptic prophecies."[2] Nafs-i-Zakíya was a long-awaited prophetic saintly figure in Islam whose appearance would be one of the signs of the Promised One in the Latter Days.

Quddús and Jesus Christ

Some early Bábís saw in Quddús as the fulfilment of the Second Return of the Christ. It is interesting to note that the Qá'im, or Mahdí, was required to appear alongside Christ in Islamic prophecies. It seems that by the time of the Shaykh Ṭabarsí episode, the companions thought of the Báb as the Qá'im and Quddús as the second coming of Christ.[3] Consequently, it should not be surprising to come across these Christ-like stories among some early Bábís that the mother of Quddús was "three-months pregnant and a virgin" at the time of marrying her

---

1 Nabíl-i-A'ẓam, *The Dawn-Breakers*, pp. 352–4.

2 Abbas Amanat, *Resurrection and Renewal*, p. 186.

3 Abbas Amanat, *Resurrection and Renewal*, pp. 11–2.

husband.[1] Likewise, when Quddús died, according to a non-Bahá'í source, "The Bábís maintained that he would become alive again after three days."[2]

As mentioned earlier, Quddús was identified by some Bábís at Shaykh Ṭabarsí as the coming of "the Spirit of the Messiah" (rúḥ-i-masíḥá'í, "Christ-like spirit") in the second coming of Jesus, before the Day of Reckoning. In the same Muslim prophecies, it is foreseen that this Figure would descend on the "Green Island" (Mázindarán Province] and destroy the forces of the Dajjál (Arabic for "The Deceiver"). The Dajjál is the Islamic counterpart of the Biblical Anti-Christ[3] deriving his name from the *1 John* 2:18. The Bábís associated him with Sa'ídu'l-'Ulamá' because he opposed the Báb and Quddús.[4] [5]

There is nothing formal in the Writings of the Báb about the above associations which, like any other prophecy, can be taken as a metaphor rather than as a solid, concrete truth. It should be noted that neither is there is any official statement from the Báb or Bahá'u'lláh indicating that Quddús is the return of Jesus. Nevertheless, there are some interesting parallels between the lives of Jesus Christ and Quddús.

'Abdu'l-Bahá has likened the immolation of Quddús with the sacrifice of Jesus Christ.[6] *"And so that Sun of Reality* [The Báb] *and that Moon of Guidance [Quddús] both set, Christ-like, beneath the horizon of the supreme sacrifice and ascended to the realm of Heaven."*[7] Interestingly, in the *Qur'án* it is said that in the Latter days *"the sun and the moon shall be together"* (75:9).

Likewise, referring to the brutality of Quddús' martyrdom, Bahá'u'lláh assured His followers that not even Jesus had faced such cruelty in the hour of his greatest agony.[8] There is also a statement attributed to Quddús where he identifies himself with the spirit and truth of Christ.[9]

Ḥusayn Villar[10] has traced some comparisons between the circumstances before, during and after the death of Quddús and that of Christ:

---

1 "Sih mahih hamilih bud va dukhtar ham bud", cited by William McCants and Kavian Milan, *The History and Provenance of an Early Manuscript*, p. 441. See also E. G. Browne, *Kitáb-i-Nuqtatu'l-Káf*, p. 199.

2 Habib Borjian, *A Mázandarání Account*, p. 394.

3 1 John 2:18 & 22.

4 Abbas Amanat, Resurrection and Renewal, p. 187. See also E. G. Browne, *Taríkh-i-Jadíd*, pp. 91–2.

5 Mírzá Ḥusayn Hamadání, *The New History (Taríkh-i-Jadíd)*, pp. 91–2.

6 Shoghi Effendi, *God Passes By*, p. 49. Also 'Abdu'l-Bahá, *Some Answered Questions*, p. 55.

7 'Abdu'l-Bahá, *Some Answered Questions*, p. 55.

8 Shoghi Effendi, *God Passes By*, p. 49.

9 Sepehr Manuchehri, *Brief Analysis of the Features of Bábí Resistance*, n.p. See also Fazel Mazandarani, *Ẓuhúr al-Ḥaqq*, vol. 3, p. 423.

10 Husayn Villar, *Quddús*, 2008.

Quddús was trialed by the chief 'ulamá of the city.	Christ was questioned by the council of chief rabbis (Sanhedrin).
Sharí'atmadár, an 'ulamá who secretly practiced the Faith of the Báb, did not participate in the interrogation.	Joseph of Arimathea, a member of the Sanhedrin, did not participate in the questioning of Christ.
Sa'ídu'l-'Ulamá' threw his turban to the ground after a reply from Quddús.	Annas tore his clothes after one of Christ's responses.
Quddús was sold for 1,000 tuman	Christ by sold for thirty pieces of silver.
The prince responsible for what happened to Quddús, released himself from his responsibilities by literally washing his hands.	Pilate washed his hands of what would happen to Christ.
Quddús was execrated as he was led through the streets.	Christ was insulted and spat upon as he was led away to be crucified.
Quddús implored God to forgive the people who were torturing him.	Christ asked God to forgive his executioners.
Quddús was confronted to use his divine authority to rescue himself from his martyrdom.	Christ was challenged to use His divinity to save Himself from the cross examination.
Sharí'atmadár recovered the body of Quddús and buried him nearby.	The body of Christ was carried by Joseph of Arimathea to a tomb.

As previously mentioned, Quddús was not a Manifestation of God! However, the coincidences in Jesus' and Quddús' lives are inspiring.

Practising the new laws

It is also noticeable that, even when the Báb had previously abrogated the practice of congregational prayers, believers still attended mosques to offer individual prayers (*Persian Bayán* 9:9)[1] Either the Bábís were not aware of these new regulations or they decided to maintain the old practice to avoid misunderstandings and misgivings. Believers in Shaykh Ṭabarsí were celebrating Islamic festivals.[2]

Certainly, Quddús was a catalytic figure in bringing the believers from the old to the new order. It was not easy because believers were still accustomed to the Islamic rituals and practices. However, the element of devotion and faith was

1 Armin Eschraghi, *Undermining the Foundations of Orthodoxy,* p. 236.

2 Luṭf 'Alí Mírzá Shírází, *Untitled history,* p. 71

strong and with those resources in their hearts, along with Quddús' guidance and wisdom, the Bábís managed to make the big transition seamlessly.

It follows a process of patiently educating the believers in transitioning from one Revelation to another. Quddús and Mullá Ḥusayn must have been aware of this new prescription on congregational prayers. However, the Bábís needed a smooth transition between the old and the new order. It might also be that the conditions in Shaykh Ṭabarsí were not conducive to implementing the provisions of the *Bayán*. Therefore, there was an element of flexibility because of the rapid unfoldment of the Bábí laws. There is evidence of the gradual implementation of religious law in previous dispensations. For instance, Jesus said to the apostles "I was sent only to the lost sheep of Israel" [*Matthew* 15:22–24] but He also told them: "... go and make disciples of all nations." (*Matthew* 28:18–20).

It is interesting to note that the Báb in a Tablet to Mullá Muḥammad-'Alíy-i-Zanjání (entitled Ḥujjat—The Proof—d. 1851) indicated to him that congregational prayers were required.[1] "When the Báb wrote to him telling him to lead Friday prayers," John Walbridge wrote, "the Bábís went to the Friday mosque [to pray led by Ḥujjat]".[2] The incident showed not only the gradual unfoldment of the law but, also, the Bábís belief that "all existing institutions existed only at the sufferance of the Báb"[3] since He was the return of the Hidden Imám.

It is also known that during the times of the Báb, Bahá'u'lláh and 'Abdu'l-Bahá, the believers followed both the Muslim Ramaḍán fast and the Bahá'í fast.[4] [5] In contrast to Islamic fasting, the Bábí/Bahá'í fast occurs in the month of 'Alá' (Loftiness), the 19th month in the Bahá'í calendar, and is governed by other rules. The new regulations of the *Persian Bayán* on fasting prescribed that only believers between the ages of 11 and 42 were advised to fast, an age range that did not fit many Shaykh Ṭabarsí defendants. In general, religious laws have typically a transitional dimension as opposed to secular law where one stops automatically when the new one commences.[6] Such a process might have been exacerbated by the swiftness of the Bábí Revelation and the freshness of the new regulations.

---

1 'Abdu'l-Bahá, *A Traveller's Narrative,* p. 8.

2 John *Walbridge, The Bábí Uprising in Zanján, p. 44.*

3 John *Walbridge, The Bábí Uprising in Zanján, p. 45.*

4 Youness Khan Afroukhteh, *Memories of Nine Years in 'Akká*, p.295

5 John *Walbridge, The Bábí Uprising in Zanján, p. 44.*

6 According to Khalíl Shahídí: "I have heard that during the month of Ramadan, he [Shaykh Mahmúd] had spread a feast in 'Akká's bazaar and was offering food to every passer-by. When this news reached the blessed ears [of 'Abdu'l- Bahá], He quickly summoned him and strongly forbade him this conduct. He had asked, 'Is it not true that the laws have changed?" ['Abdu'l-Bahá] responded, 'Yes, but wisdom is required. Now is not the time.' 'Abdu'l-Bahá would remark, 'I can convert the entire population of 'Akká in three days, but the harm [of doing this] exceeds the benefit'" (Ahang Rabbani, *'Abdu'l-Bahá Reminiscences of Khalíl Shahídí*, p. 32)

Care had to be taken not to clash with the reigning society. Eating in public during Ramadan was and still is a major insult in a Muslim community.[1] Even in today's Iran such a transgression is punished with 74 lashes. Also, this author once saw government staff instructing shopkeepers in an Arabic country to close their shops because it was time for the Friday morning congregational prayers.[2]

As discussed earlier, although the Dispensation of the Báb was transient, it witnessed a drastic and rapid shift from the Islamic religious laws to establish a distinctive theological and liturgic identity as discussed in chapter 10. Not only did the *Bayán* introduce different or new laws, but some of these initial laws were later changed by the Báb. Also, the Báb did not formally identify Himself as the Qá'im until three years later in His Ministry. Around that time, a few months before the events at Shaykh Ṭabarsí, the Báb was placed on trial in Tabríz by a religious court where He publicly stated:

> *I am, I am, I am, the promised One! I am the One whose name you have for a thousand years invoked, at whose mention you have risen, whose advent you have longed to witness, and the hour of whose Revelation you have prayed God to hasten. Verily I say, it is incumbent upon the peoples of both the East and the West to obey My word and to pledge allegiance to My person.*[3]

Devotion over knowledge

While the first believers did not have a coherent understanding of the teachings of the Báb for various reasons as discussed above, we should note their strong sense of love, devotion and loyalty for the new Revelation.

Shoghi Effendi has highlighted that the confirmations bestowed upon a believer derive primarily from their active service and consecration to the Cause of God. His secretary wrote on his behalf:

> The early believers in both the East and the West, we must always remember, knew practically nothing compared to what the average Bahá'í knows about his Faith nowadays; yet they were the ones who shed their blood, the ones who arose and said: "I believe", requiring no proof, and often never having read a single word of the Teachings.[4]

Similarly, Shoghi Effendi remarked:

> How often—and the early history of the Faith in the land of its birth offers many a striking testimony—have the lowliest adherents of the Faith,

---

1 *Iran Human Righs.* Iran: 20 people lashed for eating or drinking during Ramadan fasting hours (12 June 2017). Available at: https://iranhr.net/en/articles/2909/

2 *Arab News, An ongoing debate: Shops closing for prayer in Saudi Arabia* (19 February 2024). Available at: https://www.arabnews.com/node/1615066/saudi-arabia

3 Nabíl-i-A'ẓam, *The Dawn-Breakers,* p. 316.

4 From a letter written on behalf of Shoghi Effendi to the National Spiritual Assembly of Central and East Africa, 8 August 1957, quoted by Rúḥíyyih Khánúm in *The Priceless Pearl,* p. 322.

> unschooled and utterly inexperienced, and with no standing whatever, and in some cases devoid of intelligence, been capable of winning victories for their Cause, before which the most brilliant achievements of the learned, the wise, and the experienced have paled.[1]

> Consider to what extent the Báb and those early leaders of the Faith suffered. It was not through a blind religious zeal but because they desired to bring about for the future generations that promised era that the Faith of the Báb promised to start—an era of peace, good-will and full realization of the spiritual significance of the life of man upon the earth. They suffered that we may be happy. They died that we may live in perfect bliss. What a sacred debt, therefore, we owe to them! How much we ought to labor to repay them for their sacrifices, and how willing and earnest we should be in consecrating our life in the path they trod![2]

One of the "veils" against the recognition of a Manifestation of God mentioned by the Báb is an arrogance of knowledge that may result in Him being rejected:

> *How often the most insignificant of men have acknowledged the truth, while the most learned have remained wrapt in veils. Thus in every Dispensation a number of souls enter the fire by reason of their following in the footsteps of others.*[3]

---

1 Shoghi Effendi, *The Advent of Divine Justice*, p. 46.

2 Letter dated 27 January 1933 written on behalf of Shoghi Effendi, in *Lights of Guidance*, no. 1928.

3 The Báb, *Selections*, pp. 90–91.

27
The role of women and families in Shaykh Ṭabarsí

Chapter content
Teachings of the Báb regarding women
Cultural restrictions and hardships
Women members of the family of Mullá Ḥusayn
Brides and grooms
Mothers and sons
Fathers and sons
The elderly

Tribute is paid here to the role of women, the unsung heroes of the Shaykh Ṭabarsí episode where about 500 men died.[1] The success and advancement of the Bábí Faith was not only the result of the resolve and determination by the men but also the sacrifices made by the women. Women stayed at home and raised their children, and very often the women were cared for by relatives who may not have been sympathetic to the new Faith. These courageous and abnegated women lent their full support to their husbands in the defence of the interests of the Cause of the Báb. They paid a high price for their support, as described in this section.

"How many homes were reduced to rubble;" 'Abdu'l-Bahá remarked, *"how many dwellings were broken into and pillaged; how many a noble building went to the ground; how many a palace was battered into a tomb."*[2] This chapter outlines some of their stories to show the reality of what happened at home while the men were away.

Teachings of the Báb regarding women

In the Revelation of the Báb, women held an equal status with men: *"God attributes both to Himself that haply neither men exalt themselves over women, nor women exalt themselves over men."*[3] The public removal of the Islamic face veil by women like Ṭáhirih, a Letter of the Living, undermined long-standing gender stereotypes deeply ingrained in a misogynistic society, and this resulted in a significant religious uproar.[4]

The Báb had written as early as the beginning of 1846 in the Ṣaḥífiy-i-'Adlíyyih ("Epistle of Justice") about Bábí women: *"Believing women are like the leaves of*

---

1 Siyamak Zabihi-Moghaddam, *The Bábí-State Conflict at Shaykh Ṭabarsí,* p. 89.

2 'Abdu'l-Bahá, *Selections from the Writings of 'Abdu'l-Bahá,* p. 73

3 The Báb in Saiedi, *Reconstruction of the Concept of the Human Being,* p. 4.

4 Nabíl-i-A'ẓam, *The Dawn-Breakers,* p. 293.

the heavenly camphor tree."[1] In the Persian Bayán 7:18 the Báb upholds a particularly high standard of justice in relation to behaviour of men towards women:

> *Therefore, in the Bayán there is no act of obedience that ensureth greater nearness to God than bringing joy to the hearts of the faithful, even as naught yieldeth more remoteness than causing them grief. This law is doubly binding in dealing with the possessors of circles (women),*[2] *whether in causing them joy or grief.*[3]

Cultural restrictions and hardships

Regrettably, chroniclers of those times did not provide much information about women due to cultural restrictions and their subservience to men. For instance, common regulations prohibited using women's names,[4] or a non-family male member asking about the welfare of a female member of a household. Homes did not even have windows that opened to the outer world.[5] Furthermore, historian Adib Taherzadeh has observed, "It was against the custom of the time for the female members of the family to entertain guests of the opposite sex."[6] Writing in the second decade of the twentieth century, 'Abdu'l-Bahá commented *"Until now, in Persia, the means for women's advancement were non-existent."*[7] However, He also notes, "*Some* [women] *there are in Persia who have become liberated through this cause, whose cleverness and eloquence the 'ulamá cannot refute.*"[8]

No women were present in the fort. Many of the defenders travelled on foot from Ma<u>sh</u>had to Bárfurú<u>sh</u>, traversing 770 km of rugged lands, suffering inclement weather, without any modern facilities. It was also unusual for women to travel on foot in nineteenth-century Persia. The oldest dweller in the castle was the seventy-year-old Ḥájí Muḥammad-i-Karrádí while the youngest was Áqá Siyyid Ḥusayn of about ten years of age.

In regard to Ṭáhirih, the great Bábí heroine who was martyred in August 1852 in Ṭihrán, the Hand of the Cause Martha Root wrote:

---

1 The Báb in Eschraghi, *Undermining the Foundations of Orthodoxy*, p. 232.

2 The Báb referred to men as the possessors of pentagrams and women as the possessor of the circle. In the *Persian Bayán* (5:10), the Báb states believers should wear around their necks inscriptions of the Holy Verses in the form of pentagrams (representing a temple) for men and in the shape of circles for women.

2 The Báb in Nader Saiedi, *Gate of the Heart*, p. 322.

3 The Báb in Nader Saiedi, *Gate of the Heart*, p. 322.

4 Navid Jamali, *The Lost Links*, n.p.

5 'Abdu'l-Bahá in *The Compilation of Compilations*, Vol. II, p. 368.

6 Adib Taherzadeh, *The Revelation of Bahá'u'lláh*, vol. 3, p. 177.

7 'Abdu'l-Bahá in *The Compilation of Compilations*, vol. II, p. 5.

8 'Abdu'l-Bahá in *The Compilation of Compilations*, Vol. II, p. 368.

> It is said that Ṭáhirih, when she heard of the Bábu'l-Báb's plight [to join the Shaykh Ṭabarsí defenders], determined to go in the disguise of a man into the fortress to help them. Bahá'u'lláh persuaded her not to do this. He said that first of all she could never succeed in entering, and moreover, war and strife are not desirable for anyone, above all for women; and besides this new Light had come to do away with war.[1]

A similar story is narrated by Janet Ruhe-Schoen:

> ... But if Ṭáhirih was able to see Quddús it would only have been fleetingly, before she went into hiding. Under the protection of different Bábís designated by Bahá'u'lláh, she moved from village to village, frequently changing her dwelling-place. After about a year she came to the farmhouse south of Ámul where she was able to remain for a time, frustrated at her inability to join Mullá Ḥusayn and his companions, who were by then under siege by the Sháh's army [at Shaykh Ṭabarsí]. Apparently, she "gave her signet ring to a woman to be eventually sent to Quddús ... The verse on the signet ring read, 'Lord of Ṭáhirih, remember her.'"[2]

The sacrifices made during the Shaykh Ṭabarsí upheaval involved entire families with children and their elderly parents and relatives. Mírzá Muḥammad-'Alí, the husband of Ṭáhirih's sister Marḍíyyih Khánum, was killed during the defence of Shaykh Ṭabarsí. Women were sometimes left on their own with little help from their extended families, placing them and their children in a precarious situation in a hostile town or village. These women were mothers, wives, daughters, sisters or brides. Likewise, it should be noted that when Mullá Ḥusayn was leaving Mashhad to join Quddús in Mázindarán Province, "Mothers brought their sons, and sisters their brothers, and tearfully implored him to accept them as their most cherished offerings on the Altar of Sacrifice."[3]

The loss of a beloved one at Shaykh Ṭabarsí was naturally a cause of deep distress in the martyr's family. 'Abdu'l-Bahá refers to their sufferings in a prayer for their families:

> *O Lord! These are the survivors of the martyrs, that company of blessed souls. They have sustained every tribulation and displayed patience in the face of grievous injustice. They have forsaken all comfort and prosperity, have willingly submitted to dire suffering and adversity in the path of Thy love, and are still held captive in the clutches of their enemies who continually torment them with sore torment, and oppress them because they walk steadfastly in Thy straight path. There is no one to help them, no one to befriend them. Apart from the ignoble and the wicked, there is no one to associate and consort with them.*[4]

---

1 Martha Root, *Ṭáhirih the Pure*, p. 88.

2 Janet Ruhe-Schoen, *Rejoice in My Gladness*, pp. 273-274.

3 Nabíl-i-A'ẓam, *The Dawn-Breakers*, p. 324.

4 'Abdu'l-Bahá in *Bahá'í Prayers*, p. 268.

Many of these families of the Bábís regarded the deaths of their loved ones as a blessing for their family. For instance, a chronicler reported "that the families of Bábí martyrs in these towns [Sangsár and Shahmírzád] celebrated the martyrdom of their loved ones, congratulated one another, dyed their beards and appeared very joyous."[1]

Finally, tributes also should be paid to the Maryam, the sister of Quddús and to his stepmother (name unknown). The latter saw her son Ḥaydar been literally dismembered in Shaykh Ṭabarsí at the order of the prince and her house totally destroyed. Full accounts of their sufferings are outlined in chapter eighteen.

While generally little is known about the women members of the families involved in the defence of the Shaykh Ṭabarsí fort, the gruelling circumstances of their lives are laid bare in the following examples.

Women members of the family of Mullá Ḥusayn

The Cause of God witnessed in the early years a formidable association and drive with these four outstanding women: Varaqatu'l-Firdaws (the sister of Mullá Ḥusayn), the mother of Mullá Ḥusayn, Ṭáhirih and Shams-i-Ḍuḥá. They all shared the attributes of detachment, sacrifice, courage, purity and consecration. The services of Mullá Ḥusayn's mother and sister, as well as the above-named lady known as Shams-i-Ḍuḥá, merit due attention.

The mother of Mullá Ḥusayn

The mother of Mullá Ḥusayn married a prosperous cloth dyer of Bushrúyih named Ḥájí Mullá 'Abdu'lláh. At the death of the patriarch, the family left for Karbilá to learn at the school of Siyyid Kaẓím. Her name has been lost, however, she became famous for being the mother of two Letters of the Living who died in Shaykh Ṭabarsí namely, Mullá Ḥusayn and Mírzá Muḥammad-Ḥasan.

The mother of Mullá Ḥusayn was a distinguished poetess greatly regarded for her high education.[2] She "was the daughter of the late Ḥájí 'Abdu'n-Nabí, a man of letter and an accomplished poet who possessed remarkable intellectual prowess and commanded universal esteem".[3] This lady became a staunch servant of the Cause of the Báb, and her life is a lesson in complete surrender while enduring opposition until the end of her life in Bushrúyih. She had three sons and two daughters: Mullá (Muḥammad), Ḥusayn, Muḥammad-Ḥasan, Bíbí Kuchák, Muḥammad-'Alí and Khadíjih.[4] The two sisters were younger than him. About the mother, it is written in the *Taríkh-i-Jadíd*:

> Although Jináb-i-Bábu'l-Báb had warned her of his approaching martyrdom and foretold to her all the impending calamities, she still continued to exhibit the same eager devotion and cheerful resignation,

1 Sepehr Manuchehri, *Brief Analysis of the Features of Bábí Resistance,* n.p.

2 Ruhollah Mehrabkhani, *Mullá Ḥusayn,* p. 2.

3 In Ahang Rabbani, *The Genesis of the Bahá'í Faith in Khurásán*, Chapter 2, p. 2.

4 Ruhollah Mehrabkhani, *Mullá Ḥusayn,* p. 2.

> rejoicing that God had accepted the sacrifice of her sons, and even praying that they might attain to this great dignity and not be deprived of so great blessedness. It is indeed wonderful to meditate on this virtuous and saintly family, the sons so conspicuous for their single-minded devotion and self-sacrifice, the mother and daughter so patient and resigned.[1]

Another distinguished member of the family was Mírzá Muhammad-Báqir, a Letter of the Living, who was the son of Mullá Ḥusayn's maternal uncle.[2] [3] Mullá Ḥusayn was accompanied in most of his travels by Mírzá Muhammad-Báqir and Mírzá Muḥammad-Ḥasan, cousin and brother, respectively, except for his pilgrimage to the Báb in Máh-Kú.

The sister of Mullá Ḥusayn (Bíbí-Kuchák)

Mullá Ḥusayn, his brother Muḥammad-Ḥasan, Mírzá Muḥammad-Báqir and sister Bíbí-Kuchák, along with their mother moved to Karbilá to attend the classes of Siyyid Káẓim[4] whereas Khadíjih, the other sister and the youngest child in the family, remained in Bushrúyih.[5] Khadíjih was four years younger than his brother Mullá Ḥusayn, who was eighteen when he travelled to that city.[6]

Bahá'u'lláh bestowed on Bíbí Kuchák the title of Varaqatu'l-Firdaws ("the Leaf of Paradise"), a name by which she was better known in the Bábí-Bahá'í community. Varaqatu'l-Firdaws married Shaykh Abú-Turáb-i-Qazvíní, hence, he was the brother-in-law of Mullá Ḥusayn

In turn, Khadíjih married Karbilá'í Muḥammad-'Alí[7] who also died at Shaykh Tabarsi.[8] They had two sons, Mírzá 'Abu'l-Ḥasan and Mírzá Muḥammad-Ḥusayn and, when Nabíl was writing his work (1887–1888) they were living in Bushrúyih and they were looking after their aunt Bíbí Kuchák.[9]

Years later, Shaykh Abú-Turáb-i-Qazvíní was arrested and incarcerated in the Síyáh Chál, the same prison where Bahá'u'lláh was imprisoned, and there he died. When Bíbí-Kuchák learned that her brother Mullá Ḥusayn had died, she settled in her hometown of Bushrúyih where she continued to serve the Bábí Faith, despite great difficulties, and later died in 'Ishqábád on 5 November 1902, five days after her arrival.[10]

---

1 E. G. Browne, *Taríkh-i-Jadíd,* pp. 93–5.

2 Siyamak Zabihi-Moghaddam, *Pírámún-i-kitáb-i-Ḥaḍrat-i-Báb,* p. 137.

3 Nabíl refers to Mírzá Muhammad-Báqir as the cousin of Mullá Ḥusayn (*The Dawn-Breakers,* p. 416).

4 Baharieh Rouhani Ma'ani, *Leaves of the Twin Divine Trees*, p. 93.

5 Siyamak Zabihi-Moghaddam, *Pírámún-i-kitáb-i-Ḥaḍrat-i-Báb,* p. 137.

6 Siyamak Zabihi-Moghaddam, *Pírámún-i-kitáb-i-Ḥaḍrat-i-Báb,* p. 137.

7 Hasan Fuadi Bushru'I, *Táríkh-i-Diyánat-i-Bahá'í dar Khurásán* ("The History of the Bahá'í Faith in Khorasan"), p. 347.

8 Ruhollah Mehrabkhani, *Mullá Ḥusayn*, p. 2.

9 Nabíl-i-A'ẓam, *The Dawn-Breakers,* p. 416.

10 Moojan Momen, *The Bahá'í Communities of Iran,* vol. I, pp. 219–23.

Through Bíbí-Kuchák, Ṭáhirih met another pious woman in Karbilá, Khurshíd Begum, who was better known by the title of Shams-i-Ḍuḥá ("Morning Sun") bestowed on her by Bahá'u'lláh. She did justice to her title since all recognized the quality of her character. Even Muslims called her the Bahá'í Lady of Light. She was the wife of an admired believer named Mírzá Hádíy-i-Nahrí. They had two children: a son, Siyyid 'Alí, who died in prison, and a daughter, Fáṭimih. Shams-i-Ḍuḥá also stood out as a distinguished female personality in the Cause of the Báb. Her life is described extensively by 'Abdu'l-Bahá in *Memorials of the Faithful.*[1] Her daughter Fáṭimih was the mother of Mírzá Muḥammad-Ḥasan (d. 1879), a rich merchant, who was designated as the *King of Martyrs* by Bahá'u'lláh.[2]

Brides and grooms

Newly-wed

Maḥmúd-i-Muqári'í was a noted cloth dealer. He was newly married and had attained the presence of the Báb in the castle of Chihríq. The Báb urged him to proceed to the Jazíriy-i-Khaḍrá[3] [Mázindarán] and to lend his assistance to Quddús. While in Ṭihrán, he received a letter from his brother announcing the birth of a son and entreating him to hasten to Isfahan to see him, and then to proceed to whichever place he felt inclined. "I am too much fired," he replied, "with the love of this Cause to be able to devote any attention to my son. I am impatient to join Quddús and to enlist under his banner."[4]

The bride

Twenty-two-year-old Mírzá Muḥammad-Ḥasan, on hearing in 1848 that a number of Bábís were on their way to Mázindarán, forwent his marriage on the eve of his wedding day and took the road with his fellow-believers to follow the standard raised by Mullá Ḥusayn. On the way to Shaykh Ṭabarsí he met martyrdom at the hands of the horsemen of Khusraw-i-Qádí-Kalá'í. Mullá Ṣádiq was the eldest of the brothers. He had sat at the feet of Ḥájí Siyyid Káẓim and had risen high in the circle of his disciples. But when his teacher had directed his steps to Iṣfahán he had accepted the great responsibility laid upon him.[5]

Mothers and sons

The four sons

Mír Abú-Ṭálib's father was among the Sádát [Siyyids, in Arabic] of Samnán and was entrusted with the guardianship of Imám-Zádih Qásim, northeast

---

1 'Abdu'l-Bahá, *Memorials of the Faithful*, pp. 175–190.

2 'Abdu'l-Bahá, *Memorials of the Faithful*, pp. 173–5.

3 Literally, the Green Island.

4 Nabíl-i-A'ẓam, *The Dawn-Breakers*, p. 422.

5 Hasan Balyuzi, *Eminent Bahá'ís in the Time of Bahá'u'lláh*, p. 10.

of Sangsár [now named Mahdí-Shahr] on the way to Shahmírzád. He was influential and respected in his native town, and while on a journey to Karbilá came upon some of the Báb's Writings, the perusal of which convinced him of the truth of the Báb's claim. Before his passing, he declared, "Whoever can assist this Cause must arise to its triumph."[1]

It must have been this advice that propelled his son, Mír Abú-Ṭálib, though not a Bábí at that time, to serve as a guide for three Bábís who were on their way to Shaykh Ṭabarsí. Upon encountering Mullá Ḥusayn and other companions at the Fort, he declared his allegiance to the new Faith. He then returned to his native town of Shahmírzád to inform the population of the events and the Qá'im's appearance. A number of people converted, and soon some of them joined Mír Abú-Ṭálib and his two brothers at Shaykh Ṭabarsí. The author [Ḥájí Naṣír-i-Qazvíní] indicates that inasmuch as his mother was old, she wrote a letter for Quddús stating that even though all believers were enjoined to hasten to the Fort to aid the defenders, she would keep the youngest of the four sons, Siyyid Muḥammad-Riḍá, for her needs.

Shortly after the arrival of these believers from Shahmírzád the battles with the Mázindarání forces commenced. The three brothers participated in the clashes and two of them were killed during those encounters. Mír Abú-Ṭálib states that miraculously he survived.

In the final days of the siege, Quddús summoned Mír Abú-Ṭálib and gave him a sealed envelope for his mother. When all the Bábís were arrested, Mír Abú-Ṭálib found his way home without the least objection from the opposing soldiers. He gave the letter to his mother in which Quddús had stated, "She had acted generously by giving up her three sons in God's path. But God was just and had taken two and allowed her to keep two", namely, Mír Abú-Ṭálib and Siyyid Muḥammad-Riḍá.[2]

According to Fazel Mazandarani: "The Báb subsequently advised her to keep the fourth son for her service and further pointed out that he is truly considered one of us [despite not participating in the battles]."[3] Similarly, according to Moojan Momen:

Quddús nonetheless considered him [Siyyid Muḥammad-Riḍá, the fourth son] "one who shared in the hardships endured by the people of the Fortress" (of Shaykh Ṭabarsí) ... much later on, 'Abdu'l-Bahá named Áqá Siyyid Muḥammad-Riḍá one of the *baqiyyat al-sayf* ("remnant of the sword", a title given to the survivors of the upheaval of Shaykh Ṭabarsí). When 'Abdu'l-Bahá was later asked by a certain Ghaḍanfar ["Lion"]—a

1 *The Narrative of Ḥájí Naṣír-i-Qazvíní,* n.p.

2 Ahang Rabbani in *The Narrative of Ḥájí Naṣír-i-Qazvíní,* n.p.

3 Fazel Mazandarani, *Taríkh Ẓuhúr al-Ḥaqq*, vol. 3, p. 192.

Bahá'í living in Mázindarán—why this appellation had been given to Muḥammad-Riḍá, he replied with a Tablet that begins as follows:

"O servant of the Holy Threshold! Thy letter hath been received. Although Áqá Siyyid Muḥammad-Riḍá, upon him be the Glory of the All-Glorious, was not physically present at the Fortress [of Shaykh Ṭabarsí], *yet he was there in spirit."*[1]

Helping mother (from previous story)

Of the two youngest sons of Áqá Mír Muḥammad-'Alí, Mír Abú Ṭálib-Shahmírzádí ... survived Shaykh Ṭabarsí, while Mír Muḥammad-Riḍá Shahmírzádí ... had been left behind to look after their mother. After the end of the Shaykh Ṭabarsí episode, a severe persecution erupted in Shahmírzád and after a time the family were forced to move in with their sister Ma'súmih in Sangsár. Even here they were relentlessly persecuted, at one stage being reduced to eating grass. Although still in their teens and early twenties, the two brothers took on extensive responsibilities looking after the dependents of those who had been killed at Shaykh Ṭabarsí. Their property had been looted and so they began as pedlars, eventually developing a pattern of travelling together through Mázindarán, in the winter months, taking with them salt, fruit and dried foods from Shahmírzád, and returning to the Sangsár in the summer with rice from Mázandarán. In all the years of their travelling, they faced many hardships and much persecution but they never hid their religion from anyone. Over the years, these two succeeded in converting many people in Mázandarán, in villages such as Ívil and Rawshánkúh and towns such as 'Alíyábád (Sháhí). The two brothers married the two daughters of a Bábí, Áminah of 'Arab-Khayl in Mázindarán, and also established a residence in that village.[2]

The two sons

Zaynab Bagum, her husband, her daughter, and her two sons were the earliest residents of Ardistán[3] to accept the message of the Báb. Soon after the declaration of the Báb, they all travelled to Iṣfahán,[4] where they had the honour of attaining the presence of Mullá Ḥusayn and joining the small band of the early believers.

In the year 1847, the Báb issued an injunction urging all the Bábís to gather under the black standard, in the name of Quddús,[5] which was being unfurled by Mullá Ḥusayn in Khurásán. Zaynab Bagum's two sons, Mírzá

1 Moojan Momen, *A Chronicle of the Bábí-Bahá'í Communities ...*, pp. 85–96.

2 Christopher Buck and Adib Masumian, *Bahá'u'lláh's Paradise of Justice*, p. 110.

3 A town about 260 miles south of Ṭihrán and 70 miles northeast of Isfahan.

4 Amir Badiei, *Dreams of Destiny*, pp. 42–43.

5 A Shí'ah Muslim tradition held that the army of the Qá'im would come from Khurásán, under a black banner, to conquer the world.

Ḥaydar-'Alí[1] and Mírzá Muḥammad, along with a few other Bábís from Ardistán, heeded this call and proceeded toward Khurásán. All took part in the struggle at the Fort of Ṭabarsí, and all died except Mírzá Ḥaydar-'Alí. He was also wounded by a few gunshots at the village of Dízvá [Díz-Ábád], where the government commander and his men treacherously murdered the Bábís who had left the fort after they were promised safety and freedom ....[2]

After a long and agonizing walk, Mírzá Ḥaydar-'Alí eventually reached his hometown. His mother, Zaynab Bagum, would not allow her son into the house. She told him that if he had run away from the fort, he did not deserve to live in that house. Neither did she want him to be counted as one of her sons any longer. Mírzá Ḥaydar-'Alí had to tell her about the death of his brother and his own dream. He told her that Almighty God had kept him alive so that he could inform the others about the events at Fort Ṭabarsí. After hearing his story and becoming certain that he was telling the truth, she opened the door and welcomed her son with open arms. After some two years of separation, they held each other and cried copiously for a long time.[3] The believers and the neighbours poured into that house and observed that remarkable reunion. Mírzá Ḥaydar-'Alí lived for many more years and had the bounty of seeing Bahá'u'lláh once in Baghdád and another time in 'Akká. He died during the ministry of 'Abdu'l-Bahá in the year 1905, when he was more than one hundred years old.[4]

Young Mírzá [Muḥammad] Káẓim

There were now two men at the fort by this name [Mírzá Muḥammad-Báqir]: one was Mullá Ḥusayn's nephew, and the other the one mentioned here. As they were of different statures, the friends called Mullá Ḥusayn's nephew "little Mírzá Muḥammad-Báqir" and the other "big Mírzá Muḥammad-Báqir".

---

1 Moojan Momen, *The Bahá'í Communities of Iran,* vol. 2, pp. 147–8.

2 Ḥájí Mírzá Ḥaydar-'Alí is reported to have said: "The seven of us went into the forest and survived by eating grass for seven months. Eventually, one of our friends found us, took us to his house and provided food. However, when we brought the spoon to our mouths, the smell made us vomit. They advised us to eat little by little in order to get used to it." (Shokrullah Ashqli Ardestani, *A Recollection*, p. 147)

3 Another version of this re-encounter between mother and son reads: "Ḥájí Mírzá Ḥaydar-'Alí used to say, "When I arrived in Ardistán, it was in the middle of the night. I went to the door of our house and knocked. My mother asked, 'Who is it?' I replied 'It's Ḥaydar 'Alí, open the door'. My mother responded, 'I will not open the door; you went to become a martyr in the path of God; why did you come back? I said, 'Mother, open the door, and I will undress for you to see my body. If I have to become a martyr, accept it. If not, then what you say is true.' When I undressed and she saw my wounded body, she said 'My son, I absolve you'" (Shokrullah Ashqli Ardestani, *A Recollection*, p. 147)

4 Amir Badiei, *Dreams of Destiny,* pp. 42–3.

The latter had been an important cleric whom thousands of people had imitated [emulated] as their mujtahid. When he accepted the Faith, four hundred of his followers embraced it as well. He was intelligent and erudite, a good organizer, very brave, and of noble spirit.

His wife was of the same spirit and followed him into the Faith. She stayed in Ma<u>sh</u>had, since no women were part of Mullá Ḥusayn's company. But her young son Mírzá [Muḥammad] Káẓim followed his father to Ṭabarsí. He was a handsome youth of fourteen who survived the upheaval. The enemy let him go at the end because of his age. It is said that when his mother saw him upon his return to Ma<u>sh</u>had, thinking that he had fled the battle, she expressed only dismay. But she was soon relieved to learn that he had been released by his captors.[1]

The child of Ṭabarsí (from previous story)

When Mullá Ḥusayn departed for Mázandarán, the late Mírzá Muḥammad-Báqir left in his company. At that time, his son, Mírzá Muḥammad-Kaẓím, was a mere child. However, Mírzá Muḥammad-Báqir did not wish his son to be deprived of the chalice of sufferings and, therefore, requested permission for the lad to accompany them in whatever capacity that was deemed appropriate. Mullá Ḥusayn consented to this request and appointed Mírzá Muḥammad-Kaẓím as the band's water-boy. This enabled Áqá Mírzá Muḥammad-Kaẓím to witness all the events of the fort [Ṭabarsí] from the beginning to the very end and afterwards he returned to Ma<u>sh</u>had.

Upon arrival, his mother expressed her great disappointment by saying, "Why were you not martyred like your father?"[2] To this, the young lad replied, "I did not try to save myself. But, alas, it so happened that I was not worthy of this august station." At that instant, the paternal uncle of the boy had entered the house and had offered expressions of condolences [for the loss of Mullá Muḥammad-Báqir], but ignoring his commiseration and tears, she instead had served sweetmeats [to celebrate this great bounty].

Mírzá Muḥammad-Kaẓím continued to maintain his residence in the House of Bábíyyih and devoted his time to transcribing the Sacred Writings. He passed away in the early days of 'Abdu'l-Baha's ministry and was buried in that same house.[3]

Bihnamír

After <u>Sh</u>ay<u>kh</u> Ṭabarsí, the situation became very difficult for the Bábís of Bihnamír. Four of the Bábí women, including Ṭávús <u>Kh</u>ánum, the daughter

---

1 Ruhollah Mehrabkhani, *Mullá Ḥusayn*, p. 214

2 The child survived the massacre probably because Islam prohibited the spilling of children's blood

3 In Ahang Rabbani, *The Genesis of the Bahá'í Faith in <u>Kh</u>urásán*, Chapter 3, pp. 32-33.

of Áqá Rasúl [the village chief], even spent some time hiding in the swamps around the village out of fear, during which time one of them died. With most of the Bábí men killed at Shaykh Ṭabarsí, it was the Bábí women who formed the backbone of the community initially. They remained strong in their faith and raised their children in the new religion. They included Ṭávús Khánum and Bíbí Khánum, the daughters of Áqá Rasúl; Gul-Dústí, the wife of Áqá Rasúl's brother (who was also killed at Shaykh Ṭabarsí), and her daughter Kháhar-Bájí; Jání Khánum, whose brother was killed at Shaykh Ṭabarsí; Zulaykhá, whose father was killed at Shaykh Ṭabarsí, and who married Áqá Muḥammad, Kulah-dúz Bárfurúshí; and others.[1]

Fathers and sons

Little Raḥmán

There is the story of a messenger from the royal army wanting to meet Mullá Mihdí who was a past acquaintance and now residing in the fort. In his mind he wanted to convince him to leave the fort and avoid being killed. By reminding Mullá Mihdí of his little boy Raḥmán he thought his heart would be induced to come out. Let us take a look at Mullá Mihdí's valiant response:

> Mullá Mihdí appeared above the wall of the fort, his countenance revealing an expression of stern resolve that baffled description. He looked as fierce as a lion, his sword was girded on over a long white shirt after the manner of the Arabs, and he had a white kerchief around his head. "What is it that you seek?" he impatiently enquired. "Say it quickly, for I fear that my master will summon me and find me absent." The determination that glowed in his eyes confused me. I was dumbfounded at his looks and manner. The thought suddenly flashed through my mind that I would awaken a dormant sentiment in his heart. I reminded him of his infant child, Raḥmán, whom he had left behind in the village, in his eagerness to enlist under the standard of Mullá Ḥusayn. In his great affection for the child, he had specially composed a poem which he chanted as he rocked his cradle and lulled him to sleep. "Your beloved Raḥmán," I said, "longs for the affection which you once lavished upon him. He is alone and forsaken, and yearns to see you." 'Tell him from me," was the father's instant reply, "that the love of the true Raḥmán ["Merciful"], a love that transcends all earthly affections, has so filled my heart that it has left no place for any other love besides His".

A ten-year-old child is killed in front of his father

> They seemed weary of life and of their bodies, and met the afflictions that continually beset them with the cry of "Is there more?" Whenever one of their comrades quaffed the draught of martyrdom before their eyes, instead of grieving they rejoiced.

---

1 Moojan Momen, *The Bahá'í Communities of Iran*, vol. I, p. 312.

Thus, for instance, on one occasion a bomb-shell fell on the roof of a hut, which caught fire. Shaykh Ṣáliḥ of Shíráz went to extinguish the fire. A bullet struck his head and shattered his skull. Even as they were raising his corpse a second bullet carried away the hand of Áqá Mírzá Muḥammad-'Alí, the son of Siyyid Aḥmad, who was the father of Áqá Siyyid Ḥusayn "the beloved". So, too, was Áqá Siyyid Ḥusayn "the beloved", a child ten years of age, slain before his father's eyes, and he fell rolling in mud and gore with limbs quivering like those of a half-killed bird. His father heaved a deep sigh and said, "May thy filial piety find acceptance!"[1]

Assisting Quddús

Mahmud-i-Muqari'í [was] a noted cloth dealer. He was newly married and had attained the presence of the Báb in the castle of Chihríq. The Báb urged him to proceed to the Jazíriy-i-Khaḍrá (literally, the "Verdant Island" meaning Mázindarán) and to lend his assistance to Quddús. While in Ṭihrán, he received a letter from his brother announcing the birth of a son and entreating him to hasten to Iṣfahán to see him, and then to proceed to whichever place he felt inclined. "I am too much fired," he replied, "with the love of this Cause to be able to devote any attention to my son. I am impatient to join Quddús and to enlist under his banner."[2]

The elderly

The old couple

In Sangsár, upon being informed of the Shaykh Ṭabarsí uprising, an old couple advised their son Ṣafar 'Alí to join the forces of the Qá'im. Later when the father heard that Ṣafar 'Alí was killed, he went to the local bath, dyed his beard [a traditional practice usually reserved for celebrations and weddings] and announced to the town "I have arranged a wedding for my son." Locals thought that he had turned insane after the tragedy and shunned him.[3]

Sangsár and Shahmírzád

The cruelty of the locals in Sangsár and Shahmírzád was particularly pointed ... and refused to sell them [to the families of the martyrs] any goods or services. Many children and elderly suffered from malnutrition due to the lack of milk and bread. A particular Bábí [Mírzá Aḥmad] escaped with his old mother from Sangsár to Shahmírzad where his sister was staying for some peace and quiet. The Muslim women in the town attacked the mother and sister in the streets, pulled their hair and accused them of betraying their religion for the benefit of infidels and foreigners.

---

1 Mírzá Ḥusayn Hamadání, *The New History (Taríkh-i-Jadíd)*, pp. 87–8.

2 Nabíl-i-A'ẓam, *The Dawn-Breakers*, p. 422.

3 Fazel Mazandarani, *Taríkh Ẓuhúr al-Ḥaqq*, vol. 3, p. 188. Cited in Sepehr Manuchehri, *Brief Analysis of the Features of Bábí Resistance*, n.p.

> This particular family suffered alone, and wept together from the persecutions. Mírzá Aḥmad was the guardian of his brothers' children as they had been martyred in Shaykh Ṭabarsí. He reports severe financial and emotional hardships. The locals had enforced a food embargo on the family to such an extent that they resorted to cooking and consuming weeds. Mírzá Aḥmad even attempted to sell the family properties and gardens in order to obtain food, but the locals refused to deal with him saying he is an infidel and a foreign agent. The family even suffered from close Muslim relatives. His uncle constantly tried to make life difficult for them. On one occasion he instigated a complaint to the local governor advising that they must be punished and killed. Mírzá Aḥmad reports that he maintained his dignity and respect for the rogue uncle at all times.[1]

Like the children, women are the past, present and the future of the Faith. The Bábí women were the spiritual ancestors of todays' generations who are achieving great victories making evident a statement from 'Abdu'l-Bahá:

> *Among the miracles which distinguish this sacred dispensation is this, that women have evinced a greater boldness than men when enlisted in the ranks of the Faith.*[2]

---

1 Sepehr Manuchehri, *Brief Analysis of the Features of Bábí Resistance,* n.p.

2 'Abdu'l-Bahá in *The Compilation of Compilations,* Vol. II, p. 406.

28
Prayers and letters by Quddús

Chapter content
Prayers revealed by Quddús
Letters to Sa'ídu'l-'Ulamá'
Other extracts from the writings of Quddús

The translations in this chapter of prayers and letters revealed by Quddús come from a set of his writings cited on pages 407-418 and 426-430 of *Tarikh-i Zuhúr al-Ḥaqq* ("History of the Manifestation of Truth")[1] by Fazel [Fáḍil] Mázandarání (1881–1957).[2] Much of the content requires having an Islamic theological background in order to understand it. Extracts from Quddús' writings in Persian and Arabic can be found online in *Ocean of Lights.*[3]

Fazel Mázandarání did not provide information on the original source although is known that he was also a native of Bárfurúsh and therefore had access to favoured information. For instance, he met survivors from the Shaykh Ṭabarsí massacre. As a child, he was a pupil of Muḥammad Ṣádiq, Quddús' half-brother.[4]

Prayers revealed by Quddús

The following prayer was written during the Shaykh Ṭabarsí period as a healing and protection prayer for the companions at the Fort.

> In the name of the Lord, the All-Subduing. Lauded and glorified art He who caused the healing to proceed for the love of His Testimony.[5] There is none other God but Him. He is the Ever-Forgiving, the All-Merciful.
>
> O my God, verily, Thou hath promised to respond to the prayer[6] of him who cometh to Thee in supplication. So, O Lord, cause healing to commence. Dispel that which has immersed him in sorrow, as Thou willeth, for the

---

1 Fazel Mazandarani, *Taríkh Ẓuhúr al-Ḥaqq ("History of the Manifestation of Truth")*, vols 2 & 3. n.p, Ṭihrán. 1944.

2 Moojan Momen, FĀŻEL MĀZANDARĀNĪ, MĪRZĀ ASAD-ALLĀH. *The Encyclopaedia Iranica,* Vol. IX, Fasc. 5, pp. 460-461. Available at: https://www.iranicaonline.org/articles/fazel-mazandarani

3 Ocean of Lights, Writings of Quddús. Available at: https://oceanoflights.org/table/Quddús-fa/

4 Hooshmand Dehghan. *Ganj-i-Pinhán,* pp. 121.

5 The Báb.

6 It is a reference to a verse from the *Qur'án* 2:186: "*When My servants ask you O Prophet about Me: I am truly near. I respond to one's prayer when they call upon Me*" and also *Qur'án* 40:60: "*Your Lord has proclaimed, 'Call upon Me, I will respond to you.'*"

sake of Thy innermost secret, manifest in the essence of the Há'.[1] Verily, Thou art amongst the people of the most sublime realm.

Disappoint not, him who has come unto thee, to attain the court of Thy presence.

Lauded and glorified art Thou, whose Benevolence is the innermost secret of Thy Essence. There is none other God but Him, and Thou art the Lord of all worlds.[2]

The following prayer was also written during the confines of the Shaykh Ṭabarsí period. In a section of this writing, Quddús appeals to Bahá'u'lláh about the tyranny of the adversaries, and has praised Him with numerous attributes.

O my God, my Lord, my Beloved, and my heart's desire.

Thy Glory beareth witness, there is no desire for me but Thee,
no station but in Thy presence,
no companion except Thee,
and no place of dwelling but Thine.

The one True God beareth me witness,
to Thy most Great Name,
to Thy Ancient Mystery,
to Thy most excellent names and most exalted attributes,
to Thy beauteous Countenances in the realms above,
to the warbling of Thy Phoenix in the countenance of the day-star of Praise, that Thou mayest dispel the sadness which Thou hast cause to descend upon Thy sincere lovers, amongst the chosen ones of Thy Love, Thy ardent trustees, and those who have no one in this world but them,
O Compassionate and Merciful One.[3]

In the name of God, there is none other God but Him, the Most Exalted, the Most Great.

All praise be to God who hath verily created Praise through the potency of His praise for His own praise. Through the means of His bounty, He hath verily, made it the manifestation of His countenance. There is none other God besides Him, He is the Most Exalted, the Ancient of Days.

All praise be to God who authorised the praise revealed through His inner mystery, and adorned His sentences with praise and attests to praise in the

1 A reference to the Báb. In abjad numerals, the value of the Báb (2+1+2) is equal to that of the letter H (Há' = 5)

2 Hooshmand Dehghan, *Ganj-i-Pinhán,* p. 172.

3 Hooshmand Dehghan, *Ganj-i-Pinhán,* pp. 175.

verses of His Remembrance. Haply, the blissful rapture of His beauty may not be concealed from the worlds, that perchance, none will question the Beauty of His praise as all are in ecstasy before Him.

All praise be to God who created Praise for praising Himself through the tokens of His Essence, and diffused it from the depths of His manifold Wisdom. He has illumined all the verses of grandeur, through the captivating influence of His Phoenix, by awakening the souls, to the extent of His heart's desire, that there is none other God except Him who is the Concealed Secret within the ancient Scroll.

O Lord, the King of all beings, and Master of the beauty of the Point,
O Thou who hast attracted all by the immortal verses,
O Warbler of the sweet scented heavenly leaves and by the Phoenix of the realms above,
O Concourse of the glorious ones [Bahá'íyát], by the scattering of the hidden blessings, reveal unto us the sign that Thou hast promised us in the past, and manifest the Cause Thou hast desired for the future.

Haste Thy victory and set open the gates by virtue of Thy grace. Gladden the hearts of Thy chosen Ones by gaining a glimpse of Thy countenance. Gather them together, out of Thy mercy, by bringing peace and security to their hearts. Dismantle the measures which prevent them from gathering at the threshold of Thy Remembrance.

Prepare the means, O Lord through Thy Bounty, a pathway for the manifestation of Thy Cause and the exaltation of Thy Command, and the perfection of Thy Handiwork, and quench the fire of those who have joined partners with God.

O Lord my God! Verily, I beseech Thee, by the appellation of
Há' in the Essence and
Bá' in the Name, and
Tá' in the Inner Secret, and

by the concealed Alif,
by the letters of the realms above,
by the numbers of the Words that encompasseth all creation,
by the Youth who is seated upon the throne of Glory in Thy presence,
by the People of Bahá in the ocean of Praise, and by He who in Thy voice, called "I truly am God" in the Burning Bush."[1][2]

---

1 It is probable that this paragraph in its entirety is in praise of Bahá'u'lláh. (translator's notes)

2 Hooshmand Dehghan, *Ganj-i-Pinhán,* p. 175.

Letters to Sa'ídu'l-'Ulamá'

In Bárfurú<u>sh</u>, Quddús wrote three letters to Sa'ídu'l-'Ulamá'.[1] Extracts from these letters are presented below.

According to the translator Babak Mohajerin:

> This letter is addressed by Quddús to Sa'ídu'l-'Ulamá', chief clergy of the city of Bárfurú<u>sh</u>, during the latter months of 1847. At this time, Quddús was twenty-five years old, and although he was a new arrival to the city of Bárfurú<u>sh</u>, his fame had preceded all of the other clerics of the town. This matter stirred the jealousy of some of the clergies and made him the target of indignation and harassment. In a sense, this letter is an appeal or complaint letter which Quddús is composing to Sa'ídu'l-'Ulamá'.[2]

These are Quddús' words to Sa'ídu'l-'Ulamá':

> After mentioning what is God's desire, that remembrance will be noted in this letter. At the presence of your sublime personage, an honourable figure, may God extend your life, may allow your hereafter worthier than this world, may God confer upon you attaining the stages of His good pleasure, may bestow His grace upon you, and may protect you from the worldly inclinations and desires which are contrary to His good pleasure.
>
> It is evident that people are not generally following their evil desire as much as not all of them desire God. As it is recorded in the Traditions, "If the truth is sifted from the falsehood, it will not be hidden from people of reason and if falsehood is cleared out of truth, no one will follow it. However, we seek refuge in God, that the fragments of truth and falsehood intertwine. In this case, Satan insnares his collaborators and those who divine grace has preceded upon them shall be saved." Thus is the word of the Commander of the Faithful, may my soul be a sacrifice for him.[3]
>
> Therefore, between him and his God, it is imperative for everyone to contemplate with utmost fairness and refined reason and intellect, in any matter he is engaged in, least of all in matters of religion. We take refuge in God and from His divine wrath, such that, we do not commit something which will lead one to regret, remorse, and contrition in the world to come.

---

1 According to Abbas Amanat, "All three letters by Quddús, one Arabic and two Persian ... must have been written sometime in late 1263 and early 1264/1847 and 1848, over the course of few months. Some idea of Sa'id al-'Ulama's criticism can be sensed from allusions in these letters." (*Resurrection and Renewal*, p. 184)

2 Correspondence to the author dated 22 September 2022.

3 The fiftieth sermon of Nahj al-Balá<u>gh</u>ah; "The Path of Eloquence", which is the best-known collection of sermons, letters, and sayings attributed to 'Alí ibn Abí Ṭálib, fourth Rashidun Caliph, first <u>Sh</u>í'a Imám and the cousin and son-in-law of the Islamic prophet, Muḥammad. (translator's notes, Babak Mohajerin)

The imperative necessity of certainty in the matters that a person wishes to act on, insofar as to delay the action until the certainty becomes evident like a sun in the mid-most sky. This will ensure that at the Day of Judgement, he will not cause himself and his followers to perish.

Therefore, it is the conviction of this band that, anyone who advances a claim which is based upon the confirmed verses of the Holy Book, as well as from the Traditions, he will be right with a strong case amongst the people of reason and religion. Anyone who, we seek refuge in God, claims something with no robust proof from the Holy Book and from the strong Traditions, will be regarded as refuted and weak.

The matters which have been brought to the attention of your eminence are no secret.

However, this detached person from all else but God's holy family is only mentioning them in passing.

From the moment this detached person from all else but God's holy family, may the peace of God be upon them all, entered this land up to now, under no circumstances I interfered in anyone's affairs, neither worldly nor hereafter.

Rather, I am staying at my own dwelling, busy with perusing the Holy Book, and holding fast to the Cord of God's holy family.

However, certain people, as your eminence know them better, for the mere reason that they have been residing in this land for some time and this detached person from all else but God's holy family has recently arrived in this city, continue to engage in unseemly conduct. Certainly, the matters have been repeatedly brought to your eminence's ears.

Notwithstanding your eminence's presence, it would be unlikely that the abject and meanest of people could commit wrongdoing.

Certainly, your eminence has made them understand that there are two possibilities. Either these actions are pertaining to the world and their worldly fears, in which case, your eminence himself has to intercede that to the extent of a needle's eye, no one has acquired anything from their worldly possessions. That haply their trepidation may turn to assurance.

If these actions are pertaining to the matters of religion, then, it is also strongly and categorically demonstrated. Repeatedly and in numerous occasions, they have spoken and through the blessing of the confirmation of the Lord of the Age, may God hasten His appearance, they have received compelling answers to the extent that they had nothing more to say, as the news of them, most certainly, have been brought to your eminence's attention.

There is no doubt, I take refuge in God, if there were any unanswered questions, your eminence is a scholar and as long as you are around, an unlettered person in the subject of jurisprudence, consisting of the Holy Book and Arabic Traditions, should he wish to act contrary, it would be regarded as a great insolence from him.

No one to the extent of a needle's eye can deviate from that which the Traditions and the Book are calling out.

God is the witness to the inner secrets of all and is aware that this detached person from all else but God's holy family, may the peace of God be upon them all, did not enter this land except for the sake of a few meek and lowly members of the household who had written repeatedly. Since they could not come to visit, they pleaded profusely for my arrival.

Therefore, this detached person from all else but God's holy family, may the peace of God be upon them all, decided to return and enter this land.

Otherwise, since I was twelve years of age, when I decided to take pilgrimage to that sacred land, may my soul and the soul of all the inhabitants of the kingdom of Cause and Creation be a sacrifice for the interred body therein,[1] up to now, which thirteen years has passed, I never had the intention to return.

Upon the return, as soon as I arrived in this land, I heard in the second day that which I heard from them.

Up to now, even though I acted towards them with humility, and self-effacement, never showed any greed or covetousness for what is amongst them from the material riches or their life hereafter.

They, themselves are present. They pleaded fervently and this person, detached person from all else but the God's holy family, did not accept. I became the target of calumny and slander.

I know not what their end purpose is. Are they excluded from death? What claimants are they in these matters?

Do they not consider this land the land of Islam? or do they envisage that the Lord of the Age, may God hasten His return, has suspended the religion and has not made it inflexible and weighty?

I do not imagine, should your eminence enquire them, can they stand in the position of lies and deception?

Make them swear to say, what was the driving force for these accusations? Why are you causing mischief? And why for the sake of some earthly matters, you are persecuting he who is holding fast to the Cord of God.

Although, I have no rank or station, but I am no less than the fish of Israelites[2] in the viewpoint of my holy ancestors, may the peace of God be

1 Reference to the shrine of Imám Ḥusayn in Karbilá.

2 Reference to a story mentioned in the *Qur'án* about a Jewish village that tried to

upon them. They have numbered me as one similar to themselves and have risen to torment me.

God beareth me witness, I have never been and will not be like one of them.

I know no haven or refuge but the Lord of the Age, may God hasten His return. I bear witness to that which the *Qur'án* and Traditions summon and direct.

From the exoteric and explicit verses to esoteric and inner mysteries, to ambiguous, allegorical and clearly decisive ones, from the general and specific verses or the absolute and conditional ones, to all that the Prophet Muḥammad, may God bless Him, has brought down, and all the utterances of the Holy Imáms, may God's peace be upon them.

I neither made any claims nor pronounced a religious edict on any matter. I did not interfere with any financial or material transactions.

I have followed the path of the fourth holy Imám, Siyyid Sajjád, may the peace of God be upon him, and I shall continue to do so till such time the divine decree commands otherwise.

For such is "God's method carried into effect of old"[1] and no change can ye find in God's method of dealing.

If their actions are not because of these two possibilities, and there is no reason behind it, then, leave me to myself as I am confined to the corner of my own dwelling, engaged in the tradition of my holy Ancestors.

The purpose behind sending this letter and the one preceding it was for your eminence, may God extend your healthy life, to be aware.

Blessings and peace be upon our Holy Imáms and their descendants, and those who follow them with detachment.

All glory be to God, the Lord of all worlds.[2]

Other extracts from the writings of Quddús

In the name of Him who is the Sublime, the Great, the Transcendent. All praise be to God who hath verily established the Throne on the air; covered the waters with the eternal mystery and sprinkled upon the fire the secret

---

circumvent the Sabath and to continue fishing as recorded in *Qur'án* 7:163—166. For the sin of working on the day of Sabath and fishing on that day, they were turned into monkeys. *Qur'án* 7:167: "*But when they stubbornly persisted in violation, We said to them, Be disgraced apes!*". It is probable that by invoking this Quranic reference and being a direct descendant of the holy figures of the Shí'ih Islam, Quddús is warning his antagonists of divine chastisement. (translator's notes, Babak Mohajerin)

1 The *Qur'án* 48:23: "*This is God's way, already long established in the past. And you will find no change in God's way.*" (translator's notes, Babak Mohajerin)

2 Hooshmand Dehghan, *Ganj-i-Pinhán*, p. 209.

of the irrevocable purpose that there is none other God except Him, He is Whom there is none other God but Him. He is the Ancient Tree. All praise be to God who hath verily commanded the mystery of manifestation to manifest upon the horizon of the Burning Bush with the concealed noble mystery. There is none other God except Him, the Exalted, the Ancient ....

In the name of the Lofty, the All-Glorious, the Almighty Lord. Verily, Thou knoweth O my God that I do not call upon Thy servants but to be humble and lowly at the door of Thy mercy and to summon them up to return unto Him, in all circumstances, before the manifestation of Thy countenance. Verily, O my God, Thou teacheth Thy Command, elucidateth Thy Mystery, and manifesteth Thy Cause. There is no doubt nor any uncertainty O my God, that it is not for anyone to [demand] a proof from Thee, but it is from you to [demand] a proof from the people. Thou hath chosen the highest of Thy servants and revealed upon him a proof from Thee, even if that be to the extent of a minuscule speck on a date stone ....

In the Name of the Lord, the All-Compelling, the Unconstrained, the All-Subduing. O Thou the warbling Nightingale in the incomparable mystic heaven of Glory. Were all to hearken unto the description of blissful rapture through the mystery of the Divine Essence that hath been inscribed, they would indeed be reckoned with the denizens of the everlasting realm by virtue of the secret imbued with the words "Verily, I am the Truth; there is none other God but Him" exaltedly enshrined in the secret of the verses. Say, hearken my call with the inmost versus from the crimson tree in the seas of Oneness, for the people of fidelity, in their entirety with the fire of light

In the name of the All-Compelling, the Unconstrained, the Almighty Lord. O Thou the warbling Nightingale in the incomparable mystic heaven of Glory. Hearken all the enthralling glorification of heavenly mystery in a single verse, that is the truth for the people of eternity, the contenders of the secret, that verily I am but the Truth, there is no other God but Him, Sublime in the mystery of the Verses. Say, hearken my call with the inmost verses from the Crimson Tree in the Seas of Oneness, for the people of fidelity, in their entirety with the fire of light ....

In the name of the All-Glorious, the Lofty, the Ancient Lord. All praise be to God who hath verily created the Oneness of all created beings from the sprinkling of the effulgence of the manifestation. And verily has illumined all created beings from the radiating light in the Burning Bush ...[1].

1 Tr. from E. G. Browne, *Catalogue and Description of 27 Bábí Manuscripts*, pp. 485–7.

29
Quddús in the arts

Content chapters
Film "The Gate"
Fictional images
Is there a photograph of Quddús?
Horrific death inflicted by a crazed mob
Poetry

Several forms of grassroots artistic endeavours, either individual, community or institutional, have emerged reflecting the love and admiration that Quddús has drawn from people's hearts despite the passage of time. Examples in electronic or printed media are found in film making, photography, painting, poetry, historical prose, drama and music. Believers have used these arts to express their love and admiration for the figure of Quddús in their hearts, either individually, community based or as corporations. *"All art is a gift of the Holy Spirit ...,"* said 'Abdu'l-Bahá.[1]

Although there are no physical descriptions or photographs of Quddús, various personal imaginary renderings have been depicted in electronic and printed media. This section describes some of the representations that have been used based on personal imaginations. It also provides a collection of images attributed to Quddús, which can consolidate some historical references in the narrative.

A description of Quddús' personality was given by Áqáy-i-Kalím, brother of Bahá'u'lláh, around 1846, referring to "his extreme affability, combined with a dignity of bearing, appealed to even the most careless observer"[2] and by others as a "dignified and noble person".[3] Quddús has been described as being of "youthful appearance and unconventional dress"[4] who preferred to dress in white Ṣúfí dresses.[5]

The present author surmises from the literature reviewed, that Quddús had a magnetic personality, a caring character and a strong leadership taking over his youthful natural aspect but endowed with a special spiritual power. By the time of his death, he was the conspicuous leader of a national religious community under persecution.

---

1 Lady Blomfield, *The Chosen Highway,* p. 167.

2 Nabíl-i-A'ẓam, *The Dawn-Breakers,* p. 183.

3 Ibrahim Ruhi, *Kitáb-i-Quddúsiyyíh,* p. 57. Cited in Hushmand Dehghan, *Ganj-i-Pinhán,* pp. 60–61.

4 Nabíl-i-A'ẓam, *The Dawn-Breakers,* p. 145.

5 Jack McLean, The Heroic in the Historical Writings of Shoghi Effendi and Nabíl, n.p.

Film "The Gate"

This film[1] was produced in the United States by Steve Sarowitz and directed by Bob Hercules in 2018 during the centenary of the Birth of the Báb. The power of the cinema magnificently represents the main historical events in the life of the Báb.[2] Actor José Rey played the role of Quddús (See Figure 30). Scenes in the movie include the one where Quddús was being barefoot paraded around the streets of Shíráz, his nose being pulled with a string by the torturers. The film is dubbed in Persian and distributed with English, Spanish, French, Persian, Polish, Japanese, Portuguese and German subtitles.

Fictional images

Figure 65 is a fictional image of Quddús as a warrior warlord, with swords and daggers as expected in military gear from that time, having an Islamic art backdrop. The illustration was drawn by Ivan Lloyd, a British artist specialising in Islamic art who has written and illustrated three books on Bahá'í history.

In the image, Quddús is wearing a white headdress, a purely fictional choice. Let us remember that the Báb had sent a fine green silk turban to Quddús as a gift at the beginning of the Shaykh Ṭabarsí siege.[3] However, he only used it for important occasions, such as when he would meet the prince at the end of the siege.

There might be another reason why Quddús is depicted wearing a white instead of a green turban. Nonetheless, he was a descendant of Prophet Muḥammad. Only descendants of Prophet Muhammad were entitled to that distinction, yet it was a matter of personal choice.

Figures 67 and 68 are beautiful illustrations representing the defenders of Shaykh Ṭabarsí drawn by Ivan Lloyd. Figure 67 shows both Bábís and soldiers fighting along the banks of the Ṭálár river. The dense forest of Mázindarán Province is seen on the right-hand side of the landscape, while the rustic Shaykh Ṭabarsí fort with its rudimentary walls is on the other side. Generously, the skies rest their sunrays upon the shrine, which, like a vivid character, seems to be watching the battle. Interestingly, the Bábís are mostly depicted wearing rudimentary clothes tied with waist belts and turbans of different colours. The troops in perfect blue uniforms were supported by artillery, while the Bábís relied more on their calvary. At the centre of the painting lie the dead bodies of Bábís and soldiers on both sides of the river as the army pushes towards the shrine. An officer with his gun points at a Bábí rider wearing a green turban who may represent Quddús or Mullá Ḥusayn.

---

1 Available at https://www.youtube.com/watch?v=GPKEkSXhtgw

2 *The Gate: Dawn of the Bahá'í Faith.* Available https://www.youtube.com/watch?v=GPKEkSXhtgw

3 Hasan Balyuzi, *The Báb*, p. 149.

Is there a photograph of Quddús?

There are no known photographs of Quddús. However, a non-Bahá'í Iranian writer published a book, *Babol, the Beautiful City of Mazandaran* (in Persian),[1] containing a photograph claimed to portray Quddús (Figure 39). If the picture is helpful, it is only to show a typical 19th century young Persian man. This image has also been circulated on internet social media and it could mislead Bahá'ís into thinking it was genuine. The historian Hushmand Dehghan categorically concluded after reliable research that the image is not genuine. Hushmand Dehghan has written:

> Is there any photograph of Quddús? The photography industry was invented in Europe in 1265 AH (1849 CE), exactly the same year Quddús was martyred. It became widespread in Iran a few years later. Therefore, the few photographs that were taken before this date and during the period of Muḥammad Sh́áh Qájár, should not be compared with today's prevalent photography industry. The use of the daguerreotype system was practised in the Muḥammad Sháh's period. Daguerreotype is the first successful method of recording permanent photos and commercial use of photography ... This method was invented by French inventor and photographer Louis Daguerre in 1837. In 1839, Nicholas I of Russia and Queen Victoria presented an exemplar of the daguerreotype machine to Muḥammad Sháh, and the first person commissioned to operate these machines in Iran was Jules Richard, a Frenchman. So, during the lifetime of Quddús, the photography industry, as it is known today, did not exist. Therefore, the picture displayed on page 551 of the book "Babol, the Beautiful City of Mázindarán", attributed to Quddús, cannot be of him and most likely belongs to someone else. During a phone call with the honourable author of this esteemed book, Mr Ja'far Niaki, in 2013, among other questions, I asked about the reason for ascribing the mentioned photo to Quddús. He said he did not remember why that photo had been chosen, and no compelling reason was given. Therefore, it can be stated that the mentioned photo is probably not an image of Quddús.[2]

In addition, the aforementioned portrait attributed to Quddús was probably drawn by hand rather than captured with a camera. The explanation is because daguerreotype cameras were first introduced to Iran in the early 1840s. However, the technology remained rare and in the hands of the royalty—the king had two cameras. During Quddús' life, it is very unlikely that cameras were available in Bárfurúsh. The so-called Quddús drawing has been enhanced in other publications giving the false impression of it being a photograph.[3]

---

1 Ja'far Niyákí, *Babol, the Beautiful City of Mazandaran*, vol. 1, p. 551.

2 Hushmand Dehghan, *Ganj-i-Pinhán*, p. 284.

3 Thanks to Dr Soroush Sedaghat for this commentary.

Horrific death inflicted by a crazed mob

There is an imaginary depiction of the martyrdom of Quddús at the Sabzih Maydán of Bárfurú<u>sh</u> (Figure 79). It is a portrayal of a crazed mob that horribly murdered Quddús on 16 May 1849. The image shows a massive crowd of people armed with sticks and machetes mercilessly attacking a figure on the ground. This drawing by Kamal Ma'ani was part of an 18-page fully illustrated story-telling book for children entitled "Quddús: 1822–1849". The booklet was published in Ireland in 2002.[1] The life of Quddús has also been portrayed in music,[2] [3][4][5][6][7][8][9]

---

1 Ma'ani, Kamal, *Quddús: 1822–1849*, p. 27.

2 *Quddús* – Bahá'í Rap. Available at: https://www.youtube.com/watch?v=sMj4nPAmUYQ

3 *Quddús* song by Jim Styan (with chords). Available at: https://www.youtube.com/watch?v=aS4E2hor55k

4 Luke Slott - Yá Quddús. Available at: https://www.youtube.com/watch?v=djhcNpI1Hsg&t=4s

5 Smith & Dragoman, 2004. *Quddús.* Available at: https://9starmedia.com/smith-and-dragoman-open-the-gates?zenid=vsthtacmd1nkqak1ccb7bp3nc6

6 *Fort Tabarsi* by Gordi Munro. Available at: http://bahaisongspoems.blogspot.com/2011/02/shaykh-tabarsi

7 Biblioteka Bahaicka. *Quddús.* Available at: https://www.youtube.com/watch?v=HQ8k2xZWcqM

8 Steve Carr Clark. *Fort Tabarsi.* Available at: https://www.youtube.com/watch?v=2tt8gsiUgco

9 Ahdi. *Tabarsi.* Available at: https://www.youtube.com/watch?v=pmNQbzT_avw

[1] drama, [2] [3] [4] [5] [6] historical prose,[7] [8] biography[9]story-telling[10] [11] [12] [13] and in poetry (see below).

Literature about him has also been produced in French,[14] Spanish, [15] Portuguese[16] and German[17] let alone the various aspects of his life portrayed in "Dawn-Breakers" [18] which has been published in several languages in at least Spanish, French, Portuguese, Dutch, Turkish, Hindi, Japanese and German.[19] There was even a Quddús football team, organized by the national youth committee of the Bahá'ís of Gambia![20]

---

1 Smith & Dragoman. *Fort Tabarsi.* Available at: https://www.youtube.com/watch?v=-PaAB8nGPgk&list=PLAR9iHdz7rAzRhi99d3iRclsIU-MbpVOr&index=11

2 Bahá'í International Community, 2017. Children rehearse a play on heroism. Available at: . https://bicentenary.bahai.org/the-bab/cards/children-rehearse-a-play-on-heroism/

3 Spiritual Bahá'í Videos, 2021. *Play on the Life of Quddús.* Available at: https://www.youtube.com/watch?v=ucQftWLoMhA

4 Barney, Laura Clifford. *God's heroes: a drama in five acts.* K. Paul, Trench, Trübner & Company, Limited, 1910.

5 Max Brand. *The Gate.* Scenic Oratorio for Soli, Chorus and Orchestra; Actors and Narrator. In Two Parts (19 Scenes). Associated Music Publishers, Incorporated,1944.

6 Spiritual Baha'i Videos. *Play on the Life of Quddús.* Available at https://www.youtube.com/watch?v=ucQftWLoMhA

7 Ruhi, Ibrahim, or Shaykh Ibrahim Kirmání. *Kitáb-i-Quddúsiyyíh* (Book of Quddús) also called *Tarikh al-Quddúsí.* Unpublished biography of Quddús. Kerman manuscript, Muharram 1339 A.H.

8 Lowell Johnson. *Quddús.* Johannesburg: The National Spiritual Assembly Bahá'ís of South and West Africa, 1982.

9 Stephen Lambden. *Quddús.* Available at: https://www.youtube.com/watch?v=p4fBI_a9BzU

10 Jacqueline Mehrabi. *Amazing Stories from the Dawn Breakers.* India Bahá'í Publication Trust India, 2009.

11 Ivan Lloyd. *Heroes of the Dawn Breakers: An Illustrated Bahá'í History.* Desert Rose Publishing, 2021.

12 Mine Rich in Gems. *The Story of Quddús.* Available at: https://www.youtube.com/@minerichingems

13 Darmain Segaran. *The Warrior & The Hidden Treasure.* https://www.youtube.com/watch?v=poL2aYR3zu4

14 Thomas, Die Bie Die (Illust). *Soulèvement de Mázindarán.* Maison d'Editons Fada'il, Niger.

15 Boris Handal. *El Concurso en Lo Alto.* PROPACEB, Lima. Peru, 1985. Available online at: https://bahai-library.com/handal_concurso_alto

16 Lowell Johnson. *Quddús (Coleção Letras da Vida).* Editora Bahá'í do Brasil

17 Zoe Meyer, Illustr. Katrin Hadji. *Das große Geheimnis.* Bahá'í Verlag, 2018.

18 Nabíl-i-A'ẓam. *The Dawn-Breakers: Nabíl's Narrative of the Early Days of the Bahá'í Revelation.* US Bahá'í Publishing Trust, 1932.

19 Nabíl-i-A'ẓam. *The Dawn-Breakers: Nabíl's Narrative of the Early Days of the Bahá'í Revelation.* US Bahá'í Publishing Trust, 1932.

20 Bahá'í International News Service. (23 January 2005) *Two Reasons for Festivities.*

Poetry

In poetry, Carl Fraver wrote the poem "For whom is the Tablet read?"[1] reflecting on the destruction of the resting place of Quddús and the Tablet of Visitation revealed by the Báb in his honour:

The grave of the Holy One is razed.
And raised in our hearts to a new knowing.
For whom is the tablet read?

These days know weeping, yet compassion.
Anticipating fresh victories,
we await their new faces fondly.

The tablet of visitation for Quddús ...
We say it for ourselves, and yet more
for those in the Cradle of the Faith.
May they ever see more gain
than the loss they feel today.

Watching our growing unity,
Quddús is radiantly happy,
urging us onward.

Allah'u'Abha!
Allah'u'Abha!
Allah'u'Abha!

The poem "Knowledge of graves"[2] was written by John Etheridge:

Quddús, the Forever Youth laughs:

So along came they
to tear down My grave
and Me up along with it.
I wish I had a hundred such plots
so they could desecrate them all.
I'd say, 'Look, there's the hundred and first!'
and off they'd scurry to dig that one up too.

And then He laughs again.

But I know whereof He speaks.
It is a place of mystery

Available at: https://news.bahai.org/story/346/slideshow/4/

1 Carl Fraver, *For whom is the Tablet read?*, 2004. Available https://fravel.net/2004/04/23/for-whom-is-the-tablet-read/

2 John Etheridge, *The Knowledge of Graves*, 2013. Available https://bookofpain.wordpress.com/2013/02/26/the-knowledge-of-graves/

yet a spot of clarity,
the conundrum at the crux of a knot.
There the worldly are lost, the dead live on,
and the living, while living are yet dead.
It whispers: *how do I empty the blood from my veins*
so that His flows there, instead?

A "Crimson Rain" by Roger White

And there shall be martyrs and saints
T. S. Eliot
Chorus No. 6 from The Rock

Fort of Ṭabarsí
Mázindarán
May 1849

His head now cushioned against my breast,
I see how lightly his closed lashes shadow the soft cheek;
even in death my friend is beautiful.
He has met his end with a startled, gentle courage,
his recumbent form assumes the chaste and artless grace
of a child or dancer. So must his mother have held him,
and so wept, but wept for his bright promise.
With what joy would I have led him to his wedding
in a season less sanguine. Never, now,
will I dandle his gurgling children on my knee.
Never again will we fatigue the aghast stars
with our chanting and our laughter,
or huddle, chilled and yawning, as the last candle fails,
talking of honour.
These slender hands-do they supplicate
for the accustomed book and pen?
My tears do not erase the bruises.

How young, how pale he is!
This pallor is not earned by dissipation.
What had this sheltered scholar need know
of soldiering or death?
It was no feat to kill him.
What resistance might this frail vessel offer
or rage this bosom store? That delicate
shattered cage held no aptitude for hate.

See how timidly his blood now stains my tunic.
Comrade-in-Faith, would that this thin, reluctant trickle
might brand your name upon my flesh for all to know.

His name? Ah world! you would not care,
nor does he need your tawdry accolades.
Lavish them upon your athletes,
your fawning princes, your debased divines.
God keeps his name! And I, his friend,
shall keep it while I draw breath, though
that may not be long—Ḥusayn felled,
Quddús injured, our number dwindling.
But in this moment this death, this name, are known,
and God's moments are eternal.

The siege resumes, and now I fight for two.
Weeping, I leave you, my gallant-in-God,
even my grief sacrificed to this awful hour.

Seminal your death, little brother—
all our deaths.
O Persia! Pitiless Persia! One day you shall,
you shall know what you have done.[1]

"The Heart of Quddús for the Báb"

How then by each day
does Thy orderly Pen fail
my Lord in my name,
but a name, between the
bold letters of Thy name.

And why do You not eat or sleep?
Then quick, swift, Lord; for
even as birds fly up unto
the skies and heavens and
looking down: and so I am.

My heart beats as wings of
a humming bird to see Thy
face, O Face above all!

Then pick up Thy pen and
move Thy sweet white
hand and speak for Quddús.

For witness how he flies.

To fly to Thee to catch
Thy tears, to wash Thy

1 Roger White, *Another Song*, pp. 79–80.

warm face, to swoon like
an eagle before Thee, O Lord.

Then order me to Thee,
for without Thy bidding
how can I approach thee,
or ever be near Thee:
Kind.

O kind clouds in the sky!
Soak up His tears!

How for that life again I
crave. To be torn as Thou
did witness and my flesh burned.

Yet I, Yet I! Quddús!
Quddús in his adoration
of Thy honey-sweet, warm face.

For I am but a Quddús
upon the dirt before Thee,
and thou art The Báb and
see how His calm hands
calm me when the heat of
the fire burns my body.

So see that bird, distant
and worshipping Thee
and over the people,
ever desiring Thee.

Then speak to me that Thy
heart is free of me. See me
my Lord, see me now for
just what God hath made me.

And God is over Glorious.

Say: All praise be to God
for the Báb! Who in His
kingship has made of a
single death
an infinitesimal number
of paradises and which
can reflect one another.

So great is His far ability!

And Quddús was the
Creator of earth and

heaven at that point,
had He so desired.[1]

[1] NewFormPoetry, 2013, *The Heart of Quddús for the Báb.* Available https://www.youtube.com/watch?v=9ROr-5_-Ryc

30
Social impact

Chapter content
The beginning of communal life
Allegations of communal sharing
Insurrectionist allegations
Holy war allegations
What happened at Shaykh Ṭabarsí?
Socialist allegations
A progressive social agenda
Echoes from the past
The rural factor
Popularity of the Bábís
The village of Ívil

Some scholars have erroneously represented Quddús as a revolutionary, socialist, peasant focused on social concerns. Some critics have suggested that Quddús had socialist ideas because "he belonged to a peasant family and was well acquainted with the grievances of his class".[1]

Likewise, the episode of the Shaykh Ṭabarsí fort has been misconstrued by some academics as a socialist insurgence[2] while other similar Bábí upheavals have been depicted as an uprising of "peasants, artisans, urban poor, and small trades-people" against the prevailing feudalism.[3] The purpose of this chapter is to clarify these unfair allegations.

The beginning of communal life

The Bábís at Shaykh Ṭabarsí shared their properties and their manual skills. The spiritual principle behind it can be better understood through an incident that occurred the day of arriving at the twelfth-century-old shrine for the first time. Khusraw, the government-designated escort to lead the Bábís peacefully out of the province, in fact, turned against them to rob them. In the middle of the forest, at night, the Bábís abandoned their belongings only to be recovered later on but as a collective property.

> He [Khusraw] said, "Deliver your horse and sword as well." Mullá Ḥusayn replied, "I cannot comply with such a request, as these were given to me by a great person, and it is impossible for me to surrender them to anyone." The evil man, [Khusraw] declared, "If you don't surrender them, I have the order to kill you all, and all your belongings would be considered lawful to

1 M. S. Ivanov, cited in Minorsky, *Review of Ivanov's Babidski Vostanii*, p. 880.

2 Mangol Bayat, *Mysticism and Dissent*, p. 119.

3 M. S. Ivanov, *Babi Uprisings*, p. 521. [See listing under V. Minorsky]

us", and he uttered some insults. One of the companions suggested to Mullá Ḥusayn, "If you allow me, I will hit his mouth," but he remained silent. The Bábís struck him with a stone, causing those malevolent ones to disperse. They regrouped in their nearby area and returned. Upon reaching the middle of the road, they prepared to loot and fight. As it was a forested area with a narrow road, Mullá Ḥusayn, said [to the Bábís], "Cast away your belongings and move along." They complied, and eventually, they reached the Shaykh Ṭabarsí fort. Mullá Ḥusayn gathered the companions and declared, "This is our abode".

Apparently, on their way to Bárfurúsh, when they arrived at this location, Mullá Ḥusayn had forewarned of potential bloodshed on this ground, hinting in a way that many companions understood that he was referring to himself and the group. Subsequently, he dispatched a number of mounted companions to collect the belongings to bring them back. The properties were gathered together in one place, and he stated that all possessions would be considered collectively. In Bárfurúsh, when he ordered the adhán, and the three individuals who made the call to prayer [in the caravanserai] were martyred, his intention was to emphasise that in proclaiming the Word of God, one should detach himself from earthly life, and your lives are one and the same. When he said to cast your possessions, Mullá Ḥusayn meant that they should not be attached to worldly possessions in the path of God.

Regarding gathering the belongings in one location, the words Mullá Ḥusayn signified that these possessions now belonged to God's property and to all of you. Everyone was free to use them fairly, aiming to prevent differences and disagreements. Mullá Ḥusayn appointed a supervisor and a cook to prepare the food. They took turns, sat together like brothers, and spent their time with utmost pleasure and happiness, and poverty and sadness disappeared from their midst.[1]

Allegations of communal sharing

The defenders of the makeshift Shaykh Ṭabarsí fort, sitting in the middle of nowhere in the jungle of Mázindarán Province, opted for a single communal kitchen, most likely out of necessity and a lack of resources. The arrangement logistically worked well for the believers while providing a sense of collective soul for their struggle. Unfortunately, such a communal approach has also been misconstrued as an overtly socialist concept. The Teachings of the Báb did not stipulate the collective sharing of food, but it was a wise strategy to provide food for over 500 men over a long period of time while coping with shortages. According to E. G. Browne,

> So they appointed a steward and a cook, and at breakfast and supper, they sat round like brethren, one plate containing a uniform portion being

1 E. G. Browne, *Kitáb-i-Nuqtatu'l-Káf: Being the Earliest History of the Bábís,* pp.159-160.

> placed before every two of them. Thus did they live happily together in contentment and gladness, free from all grief and care, as though resignation and contentment formed a part of their very nature.[1]

Sociologist Margit Warburg affirms that rather than being part of a political agenda, their collective living was related more to their "communal sharing of food and other possessions [in Shaykh Ṭabarsí, which] is a typical millenarian trait. The end is approaching, and the material world is losing its significance."[2]

Historian A.L.M. Nicolas recalls what happened when the Bábís arrived homeless, lost and hungry at the Shrine of Shaykh Ṭabarsí in October 1848, and also how their decisions were misrepresented by their adversaries:

> Then turning to his companions, he [Mullá Ḥusayn] said: "During these few days of life which remain to us, let us beware not to be divided and estranged by perishable riches. Let all this be held in common and let everyone share in its benefits." The Bábís agreed with joy and it is this marvellous spirit of self-sacrifice and this complete self-abnegation which made their enemies say that they advocated collective ownership in earthly goods and even women![3]

The above reference to women was, of course, insidiously fabricated as part of psychological warfare perpetrated by the clerical establishment, which continues to this date. A.L.M. Nicolas partly wrote from government records, hence the official malice. No women were present in Shaykh Ṭabarsí, and, further to these insidious allegations, they were even accused of cannibalism.[4]

Lord Curzon (1859–1925), a British politician, writer and Viceroy of India, dismissed the baseless socialist or communist allegations spread by the enemies of the Faith of the Báb and related their decisions to moral advances: "The only communism known to and recommended by him [the Báb] was that of the New Testament and the early Christian Church, viz., the sharing of goods in common by members of the faith, and the exercise of alms-giving, and an ample charity."[5] "Now the only sense in which the Bábís can be said to be communistic", Professor E.G. Browne observed, "is in the same sense as the early Christians might be so described; namely, in a readiness to share their possessions with one another, and a generous liberality in helping each other, such as is often witnessed in young and struggling faiths."[6] According to Peter Smith, "There is no evidence that this [communality of property] ever became part of formal Bábí practice and

---

1 E. G. Browne, *Taríkh-i-Jadíd*, p. 55.

2 Margit Warburg, *Citizens of the World*, p. 139.

3 A. L. M. Nicolas, *Siyyid 'Alí-Muhammad dit le Báb*, p. 299.

4 Ruhollah Mehrabkhani, *Mullá Ḥusayn*, p. 181

5 George Nathaniel Curzon, *Persia and the Persian Question*, pp. 496–7.

6 E.G. Browne, *The Bábís of Persia: Sketch of their History, and Personal Experiences amongst them*, p. 502.

doctrine."[1] As Farhad Kazemi commented regarding socialist or communist allegations, "this view of the social bases of Bábísm is impressionistic."[2] A similar conclusion can be drawn on the peasant dimension as Peter Smith and Moojan Momen suggest: "Iranian peasants were socially interlinked in a variety of ways, but as yet we have only been able to identify patronage relationships as an evident channel of Bábí diffusion."[3]

Conversely, there are no references in the Writings of the Báb to support allegations that the Báb suppressed the concept of private property.[4] For instance, the Báb explicitly forbids anyone from entering a house without the owner's permission and stipulates a monetary penalty for any offender (*Persian Bayán* 6:16).

It is equally unacceptable to reduce the glorious figure of Quddús "in whom God hath gloried before the Concourse on", "the Last Point"[5] and the "Moon of Guidance"[6] to that of a rural paladin because of his collective survival decisions or his agrarian provenance.

Insurrectionist allegations

A number of writers have posited the Faith of the Báb as an insurrectionist movement. For instance, Hamid Algar accused Bábísm of creating a "rebellion against the state."[7] and referred to the Shaykh Ṭabarsí episode as an "insurrection".[8]

In a report dated 19 February 1849, French diplomat M. de Bonnières wrote to the Minister of Foreign Affairs that the Bábís, a "sect of dissident Muslims... has just taken up arms and energetically defends its freedom of thought... which threatens to quickly become a political party."[9] In a more positive tone, British scholar Peter Avery argued that Bábísm "represented religious ferment preceding drastic social upheavals. This ferment ... contained a markedly millennial element in its aspirations."[10]

As with the accusations of political and earthly predisposition agendas, the teachings of the Báb are clear-cut on the apolitical character of His Faith. The Báb advised Muḥammad Sháh from His prison in Chihríq that "... *nor do I wish to*

---

1 Peter Smith, *The Bábí and Bahá'í Religions*, p. 46.
2 Farhad Kazemi, *Some Preliminary Observations*, p. 116.
3 Smith, Peter and Moojan Momen, *The Bábí movement*, p. 63.
4 Moojan Momen, *The Social Basis of the Bábí Upheavals in Iran*, p. 305.
5 Shoghi Effendi, *God Passes By*, p. 49.
6 Shoghi Effendi, God Passes By, p. 49; & Shoghi Effendi in 'Abdu'l-Bahá, *Some Answered Questions*, p. 55.
7 Hamid Algar, *Religion and State in Iran, 1785–1906*, p. 144.
8 Hamid Algar, *Religion and State in Iran, 1785–1906*, p. 140.
9 A. L. M. Nicolas, *Seyyèd Ali-Mohammed dit le Bâb*, p. 320.
10 Peter Avery, *Modern Iran*, p. 97.

occupy thy position. If thou followest Me not, then unto thee be the things thou dost possess, and unto Me the land of unfailing security.[1] As the Báb was not driven by the need to accumulate material possessions nor the achievement of earthly leadership, the Sháh need not worry that the Báb intended to usurp him of his kingship:

> *Methinks thou dost imagine that I wish to gain some paltry substance from this earthly life. Nay, by the righteousness of My Lord! In the estimation of them that have fixed their eyes upon the merciful Lord, the riches of the world and its trappings are worth as much as the eye of a dead body, nay even less.*[2]

The accusations of earthly leadership originated from correspondence from the Sa'ídu'l-'Ulamá' to the new young Sháh, suggesting that the Bábís wanted to establish their own kingdom:

> They [Bábís] have built themselves a fort, and in that massive stronghold, they have entrenched themselves, ready to direct a campaign against you. With unswerving obstinacy they have resolved to proclaim their independent sovereignty, a sovereignty that shall abase to the dust the imperial diadem of your illustrious ancestors.[3]

The Bábís categorically denied the above malicious charges. Mullá Ḥusayn clearly stated that the Bábís' mission was spiritual rather than political. Mullá Ḥusayn proposed a meeting to the prince that was never accepted. To the royal emissary, he said:

> Tell your master that we utterly disclaim any intention either of subverting the foundations of the monarchy or of usurping the authority of Náṣiri'd-Dín Sháh. Our Cause concerns the revelation of the promised Qá'im and is primarily associated with the interests of the ecclesiastical order of this country. We can set forth incontrovertible arguments and deduce infallible proofs in support of the truth of the Message we bear .... Let the prince direct the 'Ulamás of both Sárí and Bárfurúsh to betake themselves to this place, and ask us to demonstrate the validity of the Revelation proclaimed by the Báb. Let the *Qur'án* decide as to who speaks the truth. Let the prince himself judge our case and pronounce the verdict. Let him also decide as to how he should treat us if we fail to establish, by the aid of verses and traditions, the truth of this Cause.[4]

It seems that a similar response was received by the prince when a messenger arrived at the Shrine of Shaykh Ṭabarsí and asked Quddús about the nature of their mission: was it political or religious? Quddús wrote to him: "Our dispute concerns religion. First, the 'Ulamá must converse with us and, understand our

---

1 The Báb, *Selections*, p. 26.
2 The Báb, *Selections*, pp. 20–21.
3 Nabíl-i-A'ẓam, *The Dawn-Breakers*, pp. 358-359.
4 Nabíl-i-A'ẓam, *The Dawn-Breakers*, pp. 363-364.

legitimacy and submit to it. Then the sulṭán [the Sháh] of Muslims should obey and support the truthful religion, and the subjects also should acknowledge [it]."[1]

Quddús stated to him that they were totally loyal to the crown. He argued that they were only acting in self-defence in the face of forced recantations of their Faith. *Taríkh-i-Jadíd* remarked that Quddús wrote to the prince:

> We are exceedingly adverse to enmity and discord, much more to actual strife and warfare, especially with His Majesty the King. Only those who dream of lordship and dominion deliberately seek war with established authority, not such as these, who, foredoomed to destruction in this narrow enclosure, have nobly and devotedly cast from them such power, authority, and lordship as they formerly possessed, abandoning worldly success and supremacy to such as seek after these things ....[2]

Shoghi Effendi remarked on the "categorical repudiation, on the part of the Bábís, of any intention of interfering with the civil jurisdiction of the realm, or of undermining the legitimate authority of its sovereign."[3]

It is interesting to note Necati Alkan's view on how Persian government's fears and suspicions might have resulted from historical developments between organised religion and political matters in Persia, more than on concerns about the Bábi doctrine.

> The attention the Báb paid to religious and political authorities is an important point in his *Qayyúm al-Asmá'*. He asked them to turn toward him and to support his cause. The Báb assumed for himself "sovereignty" (*mulk*) and states that he would transfer it to the ruler who follows God's command through him. By claiming authority the Báb did not mean to claim the throne or political power and regarded the kings not as usurpers of power, on condition that they implement the laws of his new revelation. From the Iranian perspective this was threatening at any rate: the Safavids [Iranian dynasty r. 1501-1736] began as a Sufi order and turned into political rulers with their leader becoming the sháh. The Qájárs feared that the Ni'matulláhís, who called their leaders "sháhs" were going along the same path as the Safavids. And so when the Báb makes a claim to sovereignty, it would register as a threat in the minds of Iranian rulers.[4]

In regard to the allegation that Quddús' rural childhood had any influence on a potential "proletarian worldview", Moojan Momen has pointed out that "his [Quddús] theological training at Mashhad and Karbilá would have tended to make him identify with the 'ulamá class rather than the peasants and certainly whatever is extant of his writings confirms this view of him as one of the 'ulamá

1 Abbas Amanat, *Resurrection and Renewal,* p. 188.

2 Mírzá Ḥusayn Hamadání, *The New History (Taríkh-i-Jadíd),* pp. 59–60.

3 Shoghi Effendi, *God Passes By,* p. 43.

4 The Báb in Alkan Necati, *Dissent and Heterodoxy,* p. 52.

concerned with theological issues rather than a peasant revolutionary concerned with social ones"[1]

Holy war allegations

The spiritual and physical nature of jihád

In some of His early Writings, such as the *Qayyúmu'l-Asmá'*,[2] the Báb appears to allow some theoretical enactment of *jihád.* This Arabic root *jahada* stands literally for striving. It implies the use of strength and effort in order to accomplish a task within a praiseworthy context. Hence, jihád is a struggle that can be either physical or spiritual. The fundamental meaning of *jihád* is a struggle that may be physical, but more commonly, it is a struggle to achieve something cognitive or spiritual. It has a broader basis which can include scientific research or personal development. Because the root sometimes appears in the *Qur'án* along with the expression "in the path of God" (2:90), a military connotation has been added, usually for political aims or to justify religious violence.

In general, the Quranic jihád has an exclusive defensive parameter: *"Fight for the Cause of God against those who fight against you but do not transgress, for God does not love transgressors."* (*Qur'án* 2:190–191) Michael W. Thomas, has observed that:

> During and immediately after the time of Muḥammad, jihád was directed against pagans and idolaters—the polytheists—and was undertaken in defence of the realm of Islám. The meaning was later obscured and lost. There are two main forms: 1. *jihádí aṣghar* (the lesser warfare), war against infidels ...; 2. *jihádí akbar* (fem. *kubrá;* the greater warfare ...), war against one's own inclinations."[3]

Islám was born in a physically inhospitable environment and amongst a hostile population. The first Muslims were forced to physically defend themselves in order to survive. Otherwise, the evil idolaters of Mecca would have exterminated them. Initially, a few isolated individuals recognized Muḥammad as a Prophet of God. As time went by, Islám brought together families and tribes, consequently attracting the hostility of the enemies of the families and other tribes. Muḥammad, the first believers, and their families had to defend themselves against physical attacks from hostile neighbours and tribes.

Militancy of the Qá'im and the Messiah

The figure of the Qá'im ("He Who shall arise") is strongly associated in Islamic prophecies with the concept of jihád because the Qá'im had to fight the infidels to

---

1 Moojan Momen, *The Social Basis of the Bábí Upheavals in Iran,* p. 305.

2 The Báb, *Persian Bayán* 5:5.

3 Michael Thomas, *Glossary and transcription for Arabic & Persian terms,* jihád entry. See Frank Ayers, *Studying the Holy Qur'án,* vol. 4, pp. 64–5.

restore justice in the world.[1] Thus, jihád in the early Bábí revelation was a rhetorical theme that later was virtually annulled given the associated conditions placed around that concept by the Báb Himself in the Persian Bayán. At the time of the revelation of the *Qayyúmu'l-Asmá'*, the Báb had not proclaimed His station as the promised Qá'im. Such a proclamation occurred four years later in the *Persian Bayán*, where no specific section is dedicated to the topic, and the mention of religious war almost disappears. It is in the *Persian Bayán* where most of the previous precepts are reorganized and consolidated, as in the case of jihád or congregational prayers.[2] About the latter, the Báb initially validated and later abolished congregational prayers (*Persian Bayán* 9:9).[3] In addition, regulations about ring stones and the texts engraved on them were changed in the *Persian Bayán* from the original prescription, as discussed in chapter 9.

Muhammad Afnan and William Hatcher explain that "all of the laws contained in the *Qayyúmu'l-Asmá'*, including those relating to jihád, were regarded by the Báb himself as restatements (in virtually identical terms) of the corresponding Quranic laws"[4] and that "The *Bayán* contains no doctrine or law of jihád, and in fact contains only two explicit references to jihád (both incidental) in its entire corpus."[5] Further, the *Qayyúmu'l-Asmá'* was not a legislative book but a mystical interpretation of the story of Joseph. "In his *Dalá'il-i-Sab'ih*, written in 1847", Zabihi-Moghaddam wrote, "the Báb rejects the idea that the faraj (deliverance) of the Mahdí implies sovereignty, an army, and a kingdom".[6] The Báb wrote in the same book:

> *His first Book* [*Qayyúmu'l-Asmá'*] *enjoined the observance of the laws of the Qur'án, so that the people might not be seized with perturbation by reason of a new Book and a new Revelation and might regard His Faith as similar to their own, perchance they would not turn away from the Truth and ignore the thing for which they had been called into being.*[7]

It is possible that the clerics and the local population of Bárfurú<u>sh</u> related the Báb's claim to the violent Qáim portrayed in religious texts, and this association was wickedly used against the believers.[8] The idea of the Qá'im without a *jihád* in the Islamic world was unthinkable. which might partially explain their public reaction to the Bábí belief. On the one hand, it resembles the violence associated with the biblical prophecies of the promised Messiah (*Isaiah* 66:14–16). As such, *Isaiah* wrote that the Messiah would come with a sword, that "his chariots are like a whirlwind; he will bring down his anger with fury, and his rebuke with flames

---

1 Mehrabkhani, *Some Notes on Fundamental Principles*, pp. 22–43 (especially. 29–35).

2 Armin Eschraghi, *Undermining the Foundations of Orthodoxy*, p. 236.

3 Armin Eschraghi, *Undermining the Foundations of Orthodoxy*, p. 236.

4 Afnán and Hatcher, *Note on MacEoin's 'Bahá'í Fundamentalism*, p. 190.

5 Afnán and Hatcher, *Note on MacEoin's 'Bahá'í Fundamentalism*, p. 191.

6 Siyamak Zabihi-Moghaddam, *The Bábí-state Conflict at Shaykh Ṭabarsí*, p. 95.

7 The Báb, *Selections*, p. 119.

8 Siyamak Zabihi-Moghaddam, *The Bábí-state Conflict at Shaykh Ṭabarsí*, p. 95.

of fire" and he "will execute judgment on all people." But Jesus had no interest in the Jewish concept of a political Messiah—His Messianic kingdom was a spiritual one. At the Sanhedrin court, the high priest asked Jesus, "Are you the Messiah, the Son of the Blessed One?" Jesus responded, "*I am, and you will see the Son of Man sitting at the right hand of the Mighty One and coming on the clouds of heaven*" (Mark 14:61–62). There was another theological justification for such a prerogative: according to several Islamic traditions, it was illegitimate in the time of the Hidden Imám's concealment and only the promised Qá'im was entitled to call for jihád.[1]

Speaking to the Islamic world

Moreover, the *Qayyúmu'l-Asmá'* speaks in general and to a broader audience. This principle of accommodating the message to the audience's capacity was set up by the Prophet Muḥammad, "*Speak to people of that with which they are familiar; do you wish God and His Messenger to be called liars?*"[2]

According to Mírzá Abu'l-Faḍl, "This was because of the difficulty of explaining something to a person incapable of grasping it, and the equal difficulty of abandoning the effort lest this be attributed to impotence."[3] Hence, the teachings of the Manifestations of God refer to the previous ones in order to secure a chain of understanding between religious dispensations.

Importantly, it has been suggested[4] that later the Báb seemed to have recalled His early assertions on jihád invoking the Quranic concept (13:39) of *badá'* (literary, appearance or manifestation), that is, the "alteration of the Divine Will or the non-fulfilment of the Divine Will", an injunction "where God may alter the course of human history as is seen to be fit" on the basis of His essential sovereign.[5]

The spiritual jihád

In general, the use of the term jihád in the Báb's Writings appears to have a purely symbolic association with spiritual sovereignty and not with temporal sovereignty, and it has a rhetorical component related to the literal interpretation of Islamic prophecies that referred to the promised Qá'im as a conquering Messiah with might and power.[6]

According to the Báb, "*this law* [of jihád] *is confined to the sovereign Bábí kings and does not apply to everyone.*"[7] Even the decisions of future Bábí kings to take over new territories were subject to the Báb's approval, who never permitted

---

1 Denis MacEoin, *Early Shaykhī Reactions to the Báb and His Claims*, p. 34.

2 Mírzá Abu'l-Faḍl Gulpáygání, *Miracles and Metaphors*, p. 53.

3 Mírzá Abu'l-Faḍl Gulpáygání, *Miracles and Metaphors*, p. 56.

4 Stephen Lambden, From a Primal Point to an Archetypical Book, p. 206.

5 Michael W Thomas, *Glossary and transcription for Arabic & Persian terms*, pp. 36-36.

6 Nader Saiedi, *Gate of the Heart*, p. 87.

7 The Báb in Nader Saiedi, *Gate of the Heart*, p. 363.

anyone to use any type of violence.[1] According to Nader Saiedi, Bábí kings were supposed to appear at the time of *Him Whom God shall make Manifest*, that is, Bahá'u'lláh.[2] When the term jihád appears in the Báb's writings, it is only to condition the enactment to the appearance and sanction of Bahá'u'lláh.

It is noteworthy that Bahá'u'lláh categorically and unequivocally forbade religious warfare in 1863 when He announced: "... *in this Revelation the law of the sword* [jihád] *hath been annulled.*"[3] In the Tablet of Bis͟hárát, he also stated, "*the law of holy war hath been blotted out from the Book.*"[4]

Explicit Non-violence in the Bábí Faith

More importantly, the teachings of the Báb were categorically opposed to violence, and He placed impossible conditions for the enactment of any jihád in the form of religious violence. The Báb's stance on the use of force is characterized by a prohibition against engaging in religious controversies,[5] the statement that slaying a soul for unbelief is considered the greatest of all sins,[6] and the assertion that conversion is only possible through "evidence and proof, and testimony, and certitude."[7]

The Báb discouraged the use of force prohibited acquiring weapons unless essential[8] and prescribed fines for saddening another person. The *Persian Bayán* also asserts that the expansion of His Cause should be done without causing any sorrow[9] and that "not a single hair on anybody's head would be harmed."[10] Even kindness to animals is encouraged, nay demanded.[11] Furthermore, He stated the importance of holy deeds in converting new believers into His Faith:

> *The path to guidance is one of love and compassion, not of force and coercion. This hath been God's method in the past, and shall continue to be in the future! He causeth him whom He pleaseth to enter the shadow of His Mercy. Verily, He is the Supreme Protector, the All-Generous.*[12]

---

1 The Báb, *Persian Bayán* 6:16.

2 The Báb in Nader Saiedi, *Gate of the Heart*, p. 363.

3 Announced in the garden of Riḍván, Baghdád. Bahá'u'lláh in *Days of Remembrance*, para. 9.1.

4 Bahá'u'lláh, *Tablets of Bahá'u'lláh*, p. 21.

5 The Báb, *Selections*, p. 134.

6 The Báb, *The Bayán. cf. Journal of the Royal Asiatic Society*, Oct. 1889, art. 12, pp. 927–8; also cited in *The Dawn-Breakers*, p. 330.

7 The Báb in Nader Saiedi, *Gate of the Heart*, p. 368.

8 The Báb, *Persian Bayan*, 7:6

9 The Báb, *Persian Bayán* 4:5.

10 The Báb in Armin Eschraghi, *Promised One or Imaginary One?*, p. 119.

11 "Should at a stopping place, any hardship or pain be inflicted upon an animal, the latter would beseech God to torment its owner." The Báb in the *Persian Bayán* 6:16. (provisional translation by Nader Saiedi, *The Gate of the Heart*, p. 325)

12 The Báb, *Selections*, p. 77.

What happened at Shaykh Ṭabarsí?

In general, the actions of the defenders of the Shaykh Ṭabarsí fort were in self-defence. However, some authors have insidiously suggested that the Bábís at Shaykh Ṭabarsí purposely enacted an offensive jihád.[1] The use of force at Shaykh Ṭabarsí was not a call to implement a holy war but rather a self-preservation response to the threat of destruction. The Báb never called for anyone to wage war against the government.[2]

It is fair to say that the events occurring at Shaykh Ṭabarsí were totally unplanned. They were the outcome of a number of peculiar events coming unpredictably together at the same time. As the *first in rank*, Quddús had to do everything in his power to physically and morally protect the besieged believers in the Shaykh Ṭabarsí fort from an impending carnage of great magnitude. With no previous military training, he provided wise military guidance and spiritual wisdom in the face of impending chaos. A group of militarily untrained believers needed to take up arms in order to stave off constant attacks by a well-trained army that the clergy had incited the government to organize.

Responsible for the well-being of hundreds of believers of all ages, Quddús had to make difficult military decisions. For example, he had to order forays outside the protection of the fort to repel the imperial army despite possible heavy losses of life on both sides. During a very successful foray, Quddús ordered the defenders to retreat: "We have no intention whatever of causing unnecessary harm to anyone."[3] Followers of past religions have used force, whether they were Jews (Deuteronomy 20), Christians (*Matthew* 20:34) or Muslims (*Qur'án* 2:90).

Socialist allegations

The tremendous social and economic transformations introduced by the Báb upended the status quo and gave rise to the idea that His Faith was a socialist movement. Socialists of the 19th century, such as the British Robert Owen (1771–1858) and the French Henri de Saint-Simon (1760–1825), envisaged a society that was more equal, compassionate, and one that restrained the excesses of unchecked European capitalism.

The Industrial Revolution was booming in the West, encouraging people to migrate from rural to urban areas to work in factories. It was the time of steamships and locomotives. A by-product was the recrudescence of between-class tensions in Iran, originating from social contradictions between the current semi-feudal and the emerging capitalist modes of production. The quality, novelty, and lower cost of European-produced goods, especially textiles, greatly handicapped Indigenous artists and industries in Persia, which was still operating under a semi-feudal system. For example, the spinning and weaving of

---

1 Denis MacEoin, *The Babi Concept of Holy War,* p. 116

2 Peter Smith, *The Bábí and Bahá'í Religions*, pp. 21–22.

3 Nabíl-i-A'ẓam, *The Dawn-Breakers,* pp. 362–363.

textiles in Persia was still performed with manual labour, and the economy was basically agrarian. In addition, the bankrupted central government benefitted greatly from the customs duties levied on importing European textiles.

Throughout the 19th century, socialism was frequently linked to the goals of achieving social justice, reducing poverty, a fairer distribution of power and riches, and freeing the working class from repressive circumstances. Such ideals were supported by intellectuals, labour activists, and reformers, who shared the proletariat's desire to improve the workers' lives. Socialism was, therefore, associated with concepts of community, collaboration, and the conviction that the state should play a role in addressing social injustices.

Socialism at that time was not associated with the more radical and autocratic forms of the 20th century. Rather, it appealed to those who, in the midst of rapid societal change, sought a balance between individual and social initiative since it expressed a wide spectrum of contemporary ideas. Being a communist meant also to be an advocate of universal fraternity and love. It was not until the rise of authoritarian regimes in the 20th century, when socialism was called communism, that the term was associated with negative overtones such as economic inefficiency, repression, lack of individual freedoms and even insurgence and anti-monarchism.

Since the inception of the Bábí Faith, some observers from Europe and elsewhere have characterised some elements of the Faith to be socialist because of its avant-garde principles. Such observations were naturally affected by the observer's viewpoint and associated with a combination of positive and negative sentiments. For instance, according to an account in the *Revue of the Orient* in 1849, the Bábís "professed the most advanced socialist ideas".[1] Moreover, prince Dimitri Dolgorukov, the Russian Minister in Ṭihrán, in reporting to his government in February 1849, when the Shaykh Tabarsí conflict was raging, described the Bábí Faith as, "this sect, which is promoting communism through the force of arms"[2] He later added, "They plan to establish a new religion and are proponents of an equal division of property."[3] In turn, Joseph Ferrer, the French agent in Persia, reported to his government in June 1850 that "this religious sect is threatening to become a political party."[4] Lt. Col. Justin Shell, British Minister to Persia, wrote: "This is the simplest of religions. Its tenets are summed up in materialism, communism, and the absolute indifference of good and evil, and of all human actions."[5] Count de Gobineau referred to the Bábís as "these honest people who preach, like their brothers in Europe, the community of goods, etc.,

1 Moojan Momen, *The Bábí and Bahá'í Religions*, p. 11.
2 Moojan Momen, *The Bábí and Bahá'í Religions*, p. 9.
3 Cited in Moojan Momen, *The Bábí and Bahá'í Religions*, p. 10.
4 Cited in Mangol Bayat, *Mysticism and Dissent*, p. 119.
5 Cited in Moojan Momen, *The Bábí and Bahá'í Religions*, p. 6.

are extremely numerous."[1] These are the mixed messages that the Persian public opinion was receiving.

The Danish historian Margit Warburg, affirmed that the Bábí movement was portrayed as "a democratic popular movement supported by the peasants and small craftsmen".[2] Further, in his 1854 travel account throughout Persia, Christian missionary Henry A. Stern refers to the Báb as "the Persian socialist" without providing any justification.[3] Another historian thought of Him as "a 'dreamer' genuinely interested in religious and moral reforms."[4] Historian Nikki Kettie commented that throughout the country, "The Bábís continued to attract some converts and admiration, the latter based largely on the fact that they [Bábís] were the enemies of the disliked government and orthodox clergy."[5]

A progressive social agenda

"One fascinating aspect is that within only a few years," orientalist Armin Eschraghi wrote, "He [the Báb] revealed a whole new religion, with distinct teachings on creation, cosmology, epistemology, ethics, laws and ordinances as well as devotional practices".[6]

Although Bábísm did not enact a set of economic prescriptions, it is noteworthy that the Báb proclaimed to the Persian Grand Vizir that He is the *"Inheritor of the earth and all that is therein"*[7] while simultaneously telling Muḥammad S͟háh, *"I have no desire to seize thy property, even to the extent of a grain of mustard ...."*[8] Interestingly, the *Bayán* advises men and women to inscribe on their burial ring *"Unto God belongeth all that is in the heavens and on the earth and whatsoever is between them"*,[9] thus elevating the matter of personal property to a metaphysical dimension.

A number of Islamic academics still contend that it is immoral to charge interest on business dealings, misinterpreting the prohibition on taking usury in the *Qur'án* and forbidding reasonable interest charges. However, the Báb categorically ruled that buying and selling merchandise and charging interest are permitted as long as there is a set date for debt repayment and both parties are happy with the terms of interest.[10] The Báb Himself had been a successful

---

1 Letter to Mérimée, 20 Jan. 1856, in J. Gaulmier Mérimée, "Gobineau et les Bohémiens", *Revue d'Histoire Littéraire de la France*, vol. 66, no. 4, Oct-Dec. 1966, p. 685.

2 Margit Warburg, *Citizens of the World*, p. 149.

3 Henry A. Stern, *Dawnings of Light in the East*, pp. 260–262.

4 Mangol Bayat, *Mysticism and Dissent*, p. 94

5 Nikki Keddie, "Religion and Irreligion in Early Iranian Nationalism", p. 21.

6 In Boris Handal, *The Dispensation of the Báb*, p. xxiv.

7 The Báb in Shoghi Effendi, *God Passes By*, p. 7.

8 The Báb, *Selections*, p. 26.

9 The Báb in Bahá'u'lláh, *The Kitáb-i-Aqdas*, para, 19, pp. 64–65.

10 The Báb in the *Arabic Bayán* 5:18, and *Persian Bayán* 5:18.

businessman and, in His Writings, exhorted honesty and fairness in commercial transactions:

> *I who am your example have been a merchant by profession. It behoves you in all your transactions to follow in My way. You must neither defraud your neighbour nor allow him to defraud you. Such was the way of your Master. The shrewdest and ablest of men were unable to deceive Him, nor did He on His part choose to act ungenerously towards the meanest and most helpless of creatures.*[1]

According to the Báb, wealth is a gift from God and the rich are called trustees of God who should carefully consider the needs of those under stress, in debt or whose income has been cut off. With the same coin, He condemned mendicancy as practised in the Persian public markets and forbade giving handouts to those who beg.[2]

The Báb greatly emphasised education, saying, "*Educate then, O my God, the people of the Bayán in such wise that no product may be found amongst them but that the very utmost perfection of industry shall be manifest therein ....*"[3].

Likewise, the Báb encouraged His believers to pursue knowledge abroad because their knowledge should comprehend all the sciences and arts on the planet.[4] He praised Christian Europeans for using the telescope to investigate the universe.[5] The idea of emulating Christian practices was an anathema for the Muslim clergy, who considered them as infidel and unclean. However, the Báb encourages His followers to learn from Christians: "... *perfect then all your handiwork and industries, and seek to learn* [in that regard] *from the letters of the Gospel* [Christians]".[6]

On the Arts, He said:

> *Thus, just as today the letters of the Gospel [Christians] are distinguished amongst other communities in the art of ornament, the believers in the Bayán should likewise reflect in their handiwork naught but perfection within the limits of each endeavour, in such wise that a faithful believer in the Bayán in the East of the earth should be beloved in his station on account of his beauty and the beauty of all that he possesseth.*[7]

On handicrafts and industries, the Báb stated that:

> *Perfect ye then your own handiwork in all that ye produce with your hands working through the handiwork of God. Then would this indeed be a*

1 The Báb in Nabíl-i-A'ẓam, *The Dawn-Breakers*, p. 303.
2 The Báb in the *Arabic Bayán* 8:17.
3 The Báb in Nader Saiedi, *Gate of the Heart*, p. 316.
4 The Báb, *Arabic Bayán* 11:15.
5 The Báb, *Persian Bayán* 6:3.
6 The Báb in Nader Saiedi, *Gate of the Heart*, p. 319.
7 The Báb in Nader Saiedi, *Gate of the Heart*, pp. 317–318.

> *handiwork of God, the Help in Peril, the Self-Subsisting. Waste ye not that which God createth with your hands through your handiwork; rather, make manifest in them the perfection of industry or craft, be it a large and mass product or a small and retail one. For verily one who perfecteth his handiwork indeed attaineth certitude in the perfection of the handiwork of God within his own being.*[1]

About social equality:

> *Gaze ye then upon all even as ye behold the most exalted of the renowned amongst you. Verily, that which is shared by both the rulers and those who farm the lands is one thing: they all abide by the bidding of God. ...*[2]

About unity and fraternity, He remarked:

> *We have created you from one tree and have caused you to be as the leaves and fruit of the same tree, that haply ye may become a source of comfort to one another.*[3]

More importantly, the Báb appeared in a patriarchal and misogynistic society where women were kept hidden from public view. Fresh provisions in the *Persian Bayán*[4] such as discarding the veil, which was seen as groundbreaking.[5] Hence the action of Ṭáhirih[6] in publicly discarding the Islamic face veil (*niqáb*), undermined deep-seated gender-related beliefs and generated a great religious outcry.[7] The Báb never commented on Ṭáhirih's actions.[8] However, in contravention of conventional Islamic beliefs, the Báb commanded, according to Armin Eschraghi, that "*women should not be forced to hide their hair when saying their obligatory prayer.*"[9]

A growing number of scholars have attested that the Báb was an influential social, intellectual, religious, and moral reformer of nineteenth-century Persia. For instance, Christopher de Bellaigue wrote in his 2018 book *The Islamic Enlightenment* that "The Bábí movement, which began in the 1840s, went on to become an important catalyst of social progressiveness in mid-nineteenth-century Persia, promoting interreligious peace, social equality between the sexes and revolutionary anti-monarchism."[10] Several other Western scholars, including Richard Losch, Harsha Ram, Jack Kalpakjan, Tadd Fernée, Nikki Keddie,

---

1 The Báb in Nader Saiedi, *Gate of the Heart*, p. 316.
2 The Báb in Nader Saiedi, *Gate of the Heart*, pp. 80–81.
3 The Báb, *Selections*, p. 129.
4 The Báb, *Arabic Bayán* 8:9; & *Persian Bayán* 8:10.
5 The Báb in Armin Eschraghi, *Undermining the Foundations of Orthodoxy*, p. 232.
6 Janet Ruhe-Schoen, *Rejoice in My Gladness*.
7 Nabíl-i-A'ẓam, *The Dawn-Breakers*, p. 293.
8 Moojan Momen, *The Social Basis of the Bábí Upheavals in Iran*, p. 303.
9 Armin Eschraghi, *Undermining the Foundations of Orthodoxy*, p. 244.
10 Christopher de Bellaigue, *The Islamic Enlightenment*, p. 96.

Jürgen Osterhammel, and Geoffrey Nash[1] have expressed similar admiration for the Báb's vanguard ideas on social action and development. The Báb refers to His religion as *"a new Cause"*, *"the Wondrous Cause"*, and a *"new* [Prophetic] *creation"*.[2] *"These are the glorious days on the like of which the sun hath never risen in the past,"* the Báb wrote to Muḥammad Sháh.[3] He even brought a new calendar, thus creating a new framework to transform the social fabric of society in the future.

Echoes from the past

Many of the progressive teachings in the Writings of the Báb that benefitted community life and social development have been incorrectly interpreted as socialistic and hence advocating public ownership of production. These allegations are reminiscent of those made about the Ministry of Jesus. In considering Jesus' progressive teachings, former South African communist leader Joe Slovo remarked that "From my perspective, the Sermon on the Mount comes very close to a socialist manifesto."[4] After all, Jesus had clashed with the powerful Jerusalem merchants (*Matthew* 21:12–17) and had preached, "*It is easier for a camel to go through a needle's eye than for a rich man to enter into the kingdom of God*" (*Matthew* 19:23–26) and *"Blessed are you who are poor, for yours is the Kingdom of God"* (Luke 6:21-22). When the enemies of Jesus complained about His activities among poor people to Pontius Pilate, they made up false accusations against Him:

> We found this man subverting our nation, forbidding payment of taxes to Caesar, and proclaiming Himself to be Christ, a King ... He is stirring up the people, teaching all over Judea, starting from Galilee, as far as this place! (Luke 23:2, 5)

Similar behaviour by opponents of Muḥammad is evident in the history of Islám. The bitterness of Muḥammad was so great that He declared: *"No Prophet of God hath suffered such harm as I have suffered."*[5] God told Muḥammad there was no escaping His misfortune: "*But if their opposition is painful to you, look if you can for an opening in the earth or a ladder to heaven*" (*Qur'án* 6:35).

The *Qur'án* also records how people denounced Muḥammad: *"What manner of apostle is this? He eateth food, and walketh the streets. Unless an angel be sent down and take part in His warnings, we will not believe. (25:7) ... Work thou another miracle, and give us another sign! ... Make now a part of the heaven to fall*

---

1 Richard Losch, *The Many Faces of Faith*; Harsha Ram, "Literature as World Revolution"; Jack Kalpakian, "Representing the Unpresentable"; Tadd Graham Fernée, "Modernity and Nation-making"; Keddie & Yann, "Continuity and Change Under the Qajars"; Jürgen Osterhammel, *The Transformation of the World*, p. 896; & Geoffrey Nash, "Aryan and Semite".

2 Abbas Amanat, *The Persian Bayan and the Shaping of the Babi Renewal*, p. 337.

3 The Báb, *Selections*, p. 161.

4 Charles Villa-Vicencio, *Joe Slovo*, p. 268.

5 Bahá'u'lláh, *The Kitáb-i-Íqán*, p. 115.

down upon us" (26:187) ... If this be the very truth from before Thee, rain down stones upon us from heaven" (8:32) ... *Bring back our fathers [from their graves], if ye speak the truth!"* (45:24).

The rural factor

As mentioned in chapter 1, "Quddús was the son of a poor rice cultivator on the outskirts of Bárfurúsh."[1] Cast in this light, an author might be tempted to vicariously portray him as an outlawed rural hero, downtrodden by a semi-feudal society, who fights for justice and represents the aspirations of people with low incomes. Similarly, others might be impulsed to erroneously view him as an insurgent whose aim is to overthrow the government, one whose "destructive class" was represented by "mischief, sedition, riot, and revolution", quoting the sovereign's words.[2]

As mentioned previously, the mid-18th century Mázandarán economy and nationwide were changing due to the displacement of indigenous production by imported foreign goods. Another factor affecting the income of the poor rural workers was a change to the taxation system where taxes had to be paid solely in cash, often based on inflated agricultural produce values (as a result of falling prices), instead of the traditional half cash and half produce taxation.[3] Under these oppressive terms, the rural public opinion turned favourably to the fort occupants who paid in cash.

During this time of dire economic circumstances, a chronicler recorded that the Bábís of Shaykh Ṭabarsí "behaved very well towards the inhabitants of the villages in that area and in doing business, they paid more for products than other people."[4] As a result, the goodwill of the peasants towards the Bábís had an enduring impact. Indeed, there were around positive dispositions about the Shaykh Ṭabarsí settlers.

Interestingly, the Sa'ídu'l-'Ulamá' wrote to the Sháh, "The inhabitants of several villages near their headquarters have already flown to their standard and sworn allegiance to their cause".[5] Bahá'í and non-Bahá'í scholars have noted that most of the local converts who joined the defenders of the Shaykh Ṭabarsí fort were peasants from the surrounding villages.[6] For instance, forty or more people led by their landlord, Áqá Rasúl, of the village of Bihnamír, a seven-hour walk from the shrine, joined the defenders,[7] a figure that might ultimately have reached 120 locals according to E. G. Browne.[8] Moojan Momen has noted that

---

1 Abbas Amanat, *Resurrection and Renewal,* p. 179.

2 Ruhollah Mehrabkhani, *Mullá Ḥusayn*, p. 250.

3 Mohammad Ali Kazembeyki, *Society, Politics and Economics in Mazandaran,* p. 70.

4 E. G. Browne, *Kitáb-i-Nuqtatu'l-Káf,* p. 161.

5 Nabíl-i-A'ẓam, *The Dawn-Breakers,* p. 358.

6 Mohammad Ali Kazembeyki, *Society, Politics and Economics in Mazandaran,* p. 125

7 Moojan Momen, *The Social Basis of the Babi Upheavals in Iran,* p. 286.

8 E. G. Browne, *Taríkh-i-Jadíd,* p. 67.

"Some 36 per cent of the Bábí participants in the episode were from Mázindarán."[1]

The Báb also affirms, "*Through the poor and lowly of this land, by the blood which these shall have shed in His path, will the omnipotent Sovereign ensure the preservation and consolidate the foundation of His Cause.*"[2]

Popularity of the Bábís

Prince Dolgorukov reported that the Bábís at Shaykh Ṭabarsí were "being favoured by local inhabitants"[3] and that the locals expressed genuine sympathy towards them.[4] "They [the Bábís] received supplies from the locals who supported the rebels",[5] wrote historian Saghar Sadeghian. "A few out of sheer curiosity," Nabil wrote, "others in pursuit of material interest, and still others prompted by their devotion to the Cause which that building symbolised, sought to be admitted within its walls and marvelled at the rapidity with which it had been raised."[6] The story of a devoted shepherd is another excellent example of those sentiments:

> During those days, one of the shepherds who pastured his flock nearby heard of Mullá Ḥusayn and his companions and came to inquire about their religion. Mullá Ḥusayn talked to him about the Faith in some depth since the man had a good knowledge of religion and soon became a believer. His devotion grew so great that he offered all his flock—about four hundred sheep—to the companions, and he joined their ranks. His sheep were brought to graze near the fort, and their milk served as food for the friends.[7]

Unlike typical anti-heroes, legendary and popular folk heroes, such as William Tell, who challenged tyrannical political power or Robin Hood, who stole from the rich to benefit the poor, Quddús and Mullá Ḥusayn never resorted to unlawful means while interacting with their Mázindarán countrymen. "O brethren, do not disgrace your name by associating it with rapine," was Quddús' exhortation.[8] In particular, Mullá Ḥusayn became a popular folk figure whose name was praised later by Persian historians and poets.[9]

The fortifications around the fort were built with expertise and skill and became appealing for sightseeing in the area, increasing the popularity of the

---

1 Moojan Momen, *The Bahá'í Communities of Iran*, vol. I, p. 314.

2 The Báb in Nabíl-i-A'ẓam, *The Dawn-Breakers*, p. 213.

3 Moojan Momen, *The Bábí and Bahá'í Religions*, p. 94.

4 Cited in Mangol Bayat, *Mysticism and Dissent*, p. 119.

5 Saghar Sadeghian, Caspian Forests as Political Setting, n.p.

6 Nabíl-i-A'ẓam, *The Dawn-Breakers*, pp. 357-358.

7 Ruhollah Mehrabkhani, *Mullá Ḥusayn*, p. 225.

8 E. G. Browne, *Taríkh-i-Jadíd*, p. 67.

9 Nabíl-i-A'ẓam, *The Dawn-Breakers*, pp. 333.

Bábís. People from the adjacent villages and even from the Bárfurúsh itself became very curious about the structure and came to inspect it, despite strict prohibitions issued by the Sa'ídu'l-'Ulamá'. According to Nabíl:

> The completion of the fort, and the provision of whatever was deemed essential for its defence, animated the enthusiasm of the companions of Mullá Ḥusayn and excited the curiosity of the people of the neighbourhood ... Quddús had no sooner ascertained the number of its occupants than he ordered that no visitor be allowed to enter it. The praises which those who had already inspected the fort had lavished upon it were transmitted from mouth to mouth until they reached the ears of the Sa'ídu'l-'Ulamá' and kindled within his breast the flame of unrelenting jealousy. In his detestation of those who had been responsible for its erection, he issued the strictest prohibition against anyone's approaching its precincts and urged all to boycott the companions of Mullá Ḥusayn.[1]

After the massacre, the events at Shaykh Ṭabarsí soon became a myth among the population. When the imperial forces took over the fort, according to Gobineau, the "soldiers were in any case curious to see what remained of that formidable garrison, whose exploits had become legendary even before coming to an end."[2] "Decades later," wrote historian Siyamak Zabihih-Moghaddam, "its memory was still fresh in the minds of the people of Mázandarán."[3] Comte de Gobineau added, "The truth is that those Muslims were not at all far removed from considering Mullá Ḥusayn a prophet"[4] and "almost all the Muslims regarded the Bábís as something more than mere human beings, or at the very least as enchanted beings."[5] During one of the confrontations, in order to boost the troops' confidence

> A [soldier] man from Talish fired golden coins at those who seemed to him the most formidable of the champions. It is noteworthy that this superstition exists both in Persia and in Scotland, where the covenanters fired with silver bullets at those of their persecutors whom they believed enchanted.[6]

Author Shahla Behroozi Gillbanks has observed:

> Their [Quddús' and Mullá Ḥusayn's] courageous stand during the sustained siege of Fort Ṭabarsí and their heroic martyrdom and or captivity made a great impression on the surrounding villages. It eventually led to a number of them to embrace the Faith of the Báb.[7]

---

1 Nabíl-i-A'ẓam, *The Dawn-Breakers*, pp. 357–8.

2 Gobineau in Nash and O'Donoghue, *Comte de Gobineau and Orientalism,* pp 174–175.

3 Siyamak Zabihi-Moghaddam, *The Bábí-state Conflict at Shaykh Ṭabarsí*, p. 89.

4 Gobineau in Nash and O'Donoghue, *Comte de Gobineau and Orientalism,* p. 164

5 Gobineau in Nash and O'Donoghue, *Comte de Gobineau and Orientalism,* p. 174.

6 Gobineau in Nash and O'Donoghue, *Comte de Gobineau and Orientalism,* p. 175.

7 Shahla Behroozi Gillbanks, *Footprints in the Sand of Time*, pp. 36–7.

One of those villages was Ívil.

The village of Ívil

During the early days of the ministry of the Báb, with the conversion of Mullá Muḥammad 'Alí Bárfurúshí [Quddús], Mázindarán was illumined with the belief in the Faith of God. Sometime later, owing to the travels of Bahá'u'lláh in Núr and its environs, a group of those who were ready were attracted to the Faith. The events at Fort Ṭabarsí and the steadfastness and sacrifice of the followers of His Holiness Quddús spread the fame of the Faith in Mázindarán. Among the survivors of Ṭabarsí were two brothers, Áqá Siyyid Abú Ṭálib and Áqá Muḥammad Riẓá Shahmírzadí, who continuously travelled in Mazandaran and its surrounding villages to teach the Faith; this resulted in the spread and strengthening of the Faith in that region.

The belief in the Faith by Mullá 'Alí Ján Máhfurúzakí, the martyr, during the time of Bahá'u'lláh, had a strong influence on his friend Mullá Ḥusayn 'Alí Ayyúb Hizarjaribí. Mullá Ḥusayn-'Alí started to teach and was able to bring the light of the Faith to the hearts of half of the farmers of Ivel [Ívil]. In this way Ivel became famous in Chahardangeh and Hezarjarib.

Hezarjarib is one of the sectors of Mázindarán which is a mountainous area in its southern region spreading from east to west like a bow. It is situated at the borders of Savadkuh and Gorgan and is divided into two sections of four and two dangs [six shares of real estate]. The four dang section is divided into three parts: Chahardangeh Surtichi, Chahardangeh Mas'udu'l-Mulk and Chahardangeh Shahriyari. The village of Ivel is situated in Chahardangeh Surtichi, situated southeast of the city of Sari. The reason for calling this section Chahardangeh Surtichi is related to the participation of Áqá 'Abdu'lláh Surtichi in the early confrontations with the fighters of Tabarsi by the order of Náṣiri'd-Dín Sháh. He was killed in the fighting and as a reward for the shedding of his blood Náṣiri'd-Dín Sháh named this section for him ....

... In the year 1362 [1983], although Ivel was empty of Bahá'ís and apparently the enemies had succeeded in extinguishing the light of the Faith of God in that region, they did not realize that their actions had caused the spread of awareness of the Faith not only in that region but in far-off lands.[1]

1 Ali Ahmadi. History of the Bahá'í Faith in the Village of Ivel. In Archive of Bahá'í Persecutions. *January* 2023. https://iranbahaipersecution.bic.org/sites/default/files/PDF/English/020167E_0.pdf. Ívil (36.240230, 53.677921) is 12 km east of Kiyásar.

Afterword – My writing journey

Before the journey

The story of bravery and faith at the Shaykh Ṭabarsí fort drew me in as a new Bahá'í after I graduated from high school. It reminded me of epics such as the Persian Shahnameh and the Greek Iliad. Although the talk at a youth seminar was not long, the magic name of Quddús stuck in my memory, creating an intense desire to learn more about him. We were told that part of his story was available in the book *The Dawn-Breakers: Nabíl's Narrative of the Early Days of the Bahá'í Revelation*. A few weeks later, upon being paid my first salary, I went straight from my workplace to the local Bahá'í bookshop and I read it non-stop from cover-to-cover.

I have been thinking about Quddús for a long time. After my first pilgrimage to the Holy Land in 1984, I decided to dedicate myself fully to the task of collecting my biographical notes on the main characters in the history of the Bábí-Bahá'í Faith. My notes had previously served as study material for use at Bahá'í Institutes and Summer Schools. As a result, I wrote a chapter on the life of Quddús that was published as part of the book *The Concourse on High* in 1985.[1] Nearly forty years later, I felt there was a need in the English Bahá'í literature for a book focused solely on the figure of Quddús. I was amazed to find much more research material in English and Persian, both printed and electronic, which helped me to write a more extensive narrative. The original account has now been augmented with more information about Quddús' life and writings, and from extracts from especially translated Tablets of the Báb and Bahá'u'lláh that magnified his exalted station.

I have never had the opportunity of visiting Iran. However, there was a time when I stood and wet my feet on the opposite shore of Quddús' Caspian Sea gazing at the distant city of Bárfurúsh where he was born. From Bakú, the seaport capital of the Republic of Azerbaijan—once Persian territory—separated only by waters, I reflected on how far my research has mysteriously taken me. Iranian relatives of my wife and several friends who were also born in the land of Quddús, personally mesmerised me with tales and descriptions that vividly recreated in my mind those historical events in the Cradle of the Bahá'í Faith.

Many years ago, knowing of my interest in the episode of Shaykh Ṭabarsí, an Iranian Bahá'í friend returning from a trip to her country brought me an envelope containing dust from the fort itself, the place where Quddús and Mullá Ḥusayn fought their memorable battles as legendary warriors. I put that red dust in a transparent glass jar and kept it in my drawing room, an arm's length away from my desk, where I could always see and feel it. So precious is that soil that the Báb

---

1 Boris Handal, *El Concurso en Lo Alto*, PROPACEB.

referred to it as *"holy earth",*[1] once ordering a believer from His prison to go on pilgrimage and bring some of that soil to Him for His comfort for such an irreparable loss.[2]

The Orient always fascinated me, starting from the childhood stories of the "One Thousand and One Nights" and the rich Islamic heritage embedded in the Hispanic civilization. *"In the past, as in the present,"* 'Abdu'l-Bahá has said, *"the Spiritual Sun of Truth has always shone from the horizon of the East."*[3] From the paternal side, my Palestinian blood, a mixture of 13th century Crusaders and local Bethlehemites, made me feel closer to the Orient. My surname Ḥanḍal (حنضل, "Handal"), an Arabicised form of the Germanic Handal, became associated therefore with the standard Arabic word *ḥanẓal* and its meaning of a wild desert plant known as the "bitter apple", which was mentioned by Muḥammad in an oral tradition and by Bahá'u'lláh in the *Lawḥ-i-Sarráj* ("Tablet of the Saddler"). Having never been to Iran—Bahá'ís are at risk of being arrested—I have been fortunate enough to travel to three neighbouring countries and to a part of the old Persianate. The Spanish and Indigenous provenance from my mother's side taught me respect for the sacred and a concern for the poor, respectively.

During the journey

There are many characters in this story. Some arrive on the scene and perish at some stage, while others live on to take part in events not covered by the timeline of the book. As the storyteller, I become the invisible character travelling on dusty Persian roads, navigating the waters of the Persian, Arabian and Red Seas, visiting dozens of cities and villages, crossing the Alburz mountains, living in the Caspian jungles, fighting as another warrior, and travelling the interminable, arid landscapes on horse or on foot. There is undoubtedly a privilege in having had the opportunity to gather information from multiple sources to obtain a wide overview of the events, while simultaneously trying to understand the Divine Plan—the "God's Eye view"[4]—of the storyline rather than attributing events to the randomness of the world.

This imaginary, deeply personal immersion, in the journey and exploits of Quddús and his companions, made me feel as if part of the story—as the accompanying chronicler, speaking their language, eating their food, sleeping under the brilliant stars or in a remote caravanserai, or listening at night to their *dardi dil* ("pouring one's heart out"). It was sometimes difficult for this writer to remove himself from scenes so close to his inner eye. Some of the episodes were the work of such fanatical and genocidal cruelty that he wished he could traverse the curtain of time and play a part, however small, in the cause of the valiant but outnumbered Bábís.

---

1 Nabíl-i-A'ẓam, *The Dawn-Breakers,* p. 431.

2 Nabíl-i-A'ẓam, *The Dawn-Breakers,* p. 432.

3 'Abdu'l-Bahá, *Paris Talks,* p. 21.

4 Howard Sankey, Scientific realism and the God's eye point of view, p. 2.

Given my basic understanding of Fársí, many friends generously helped me to navigate through many of the Persian historical chronicles, published and unpublished. As a narrator of this beautiful story, I have been privileged to meet and correspond with descendants from the defenders of the legendary Shaykh Ṭabarsí fort. Although, as a Bahá'í, I have been unable to travel to that hallowed space, the magic of the internet in providing access to multimedia materials, allowed me to virtually travel and visit those places and to vividly recreate those spaces in my excited imagination.

As much as possible, Quddús' life has been described in the words of the original chroniclers so that we can hear their voices and emotions, as well as the accents of the time. The narrative has thus become a polyphonic account full of colours and nuances retaining the intimate touches of the actual events, even the brightness of the day and the gloom of the night.

Current Bahá'í narratives about Quddús are fragmentary. Strangely, unlike other heroes of the Bábí Faith, there is no comprehensive English biography of him. The process of writing about our protagonist resembled putting together a big puzzle of many pieces. In the Iranian culture the biographical genre literature has not developed as in the West. In fact, it was considered improper in traditional Persian culture to discuss one's personal life in depth. Hence, the need for an abundance of footnote references throughout the manuscript and a large bibliography at the end of the book to address this problem.

After the journey

The initial exploration of the life of Quddús through a linear research model eventually turned into a multi-dimensional study where his character was studied simultaneously in his overlapping roles as *seeker, promoter, leader, scholar, hero* and *saint* of the Bábí Faith. This turned the spotlight on the evolution of Quddús' personality from his peasant origins to that of the central protagonist at Shaykh Ṭabarsí who attracted national notoriety. Of Quddús' "*lifeblood*", the Báb said

> *By its mention the inmost beings of all created things were made manifest, the essence of every truth was sanctified, all wholly severed souls were set free and all things purified from the limitations of this world of allusion* .[1]

At the end of the journey, astounded by the narratives of the inspiring life of Quddús, I now dedicate these pages to his devotion, achievements and sacrifice. It is my hope that the accounts inspire all to acquire a personal connection with Quddús and the events surrounding his fleeting but impressive life.

Such a special personality harmoniously combined the modesty and simplicity of his peasant background, the disquisitions of the scholar, the patience of the saint, the bravery of the warrior, the lashing impetus of the youth, the lasting wisdom of the sage, the virtue of the consecrated, the passion for his new

---

[1] The Báb, *Tablet of Visitation for Quddús*. See Appendix part 2.

faith, the directness of the leader, the compassion of the pastor, the sacredness of his station, the humility of his life, his contemplative spirit and the friendliness of his gregarious soul—all attributes together in one name: Quddús.

Appendix

1. Tablet of Visitation for Mullá Ḥusayn and Quddús

Tablet of Visitation by Bahá'u'lláh for the first to arrive and the last to attain,[1] may the souls of all on earth be offered up for them both.

In the name of Him Who is the Compassionate, the All-Bountiful!

The peace that hath shone forth from the Dayspring of the Will of God, the Lord of all being, and the light that hath dawned above the horizon of His supreme mercy and His resplendent signs rest upon you, O ye who are the hands of His power in the kingdom of creation and the manifestations of His grandeur between earth and heaven!

Ye are they who were awakened by the gentle winds of the dawn of Revelation and were enraptured by the voice of Him Who spoke on Sinai. Ye are they who inhaled the fragrance of the All-Merciful when it wafted from the realm of divine knowledge. By your guidance the thirsty hastened to the onrushing waters of everlasting life and the sinner to the vivifying river of forgiveness and mercy. Ye are the signs of God and His straight Path amongst His creation. Through you all faces turned to the Most Exalted Horizon and every poor one sought the Wellspring of wealth.

At your suffering all things lamented, and every atom cried out between earth and heaven, and Adam forsook the Most Exalted Paradise and chose for Himself a place upon the dust. Ye are the dawning-places of power amidst the people and the daysprings of might amongst the righteous. Through you the springtime of inner meaning appeared in the world of utterance and the All-Merciful shed His effulgent splendour upon all created things.

Ye are the hands of His Cause in His lands, and the stars of His bountiful care amidst His servants. Through you the daystars of knowledge dawned forth, the heavens of all religions were illumined, the lights of the sciences shone brightly amongst the nations, and the sphere of the arts was expanded throughout the world. Ye are the dawning-places of God's Revelation upon the earth and the daysprings of His signs in the world of creation. By your arising did the people arise to serve the Cause and the river of mercy flow out amidst humankind.

Ye are the pearls of the Hidden Sea and the letters of the Treasured Book. Through your sublime word the Book of Names was expounded and the portals of blessings were opened wide before the inhabitants of earth and heaven. Through you the injunction "Be thou" was enforced, the Hidden Secret was divulged, and the choice Wine was unsealed.

---

1 Bahá'u'lláh states in another Tablet that the Báb used these descriptions in referring to Mullá Ḥusayn and Quddús.

Alas, alas! By reason of your sorrow, the inmates of the all-highest Paradise were overcome with grief and the denizens of the kingdom of names were moved to lament. At your suffering, trembling seized the inhabitants of the Verdant Isle on the shore of the Sea of Grandeur, causing the sighs of such as are wholly devoted to God to ascend and the tears of them that are nigh unto Him to rain down. Ye are the books of God and His scriptures, the epistles of God and His tablets. By virtue of your gladness the faces of all beings were wreathed in smiles, and by reason of your sorrow all things visible and invisible did wail aloud.

Ye are the arks of God sailing upon the ocean of His Will, and the people of God who have arisen to champion His Cause. Through you the Most Great Announcement was proclaimed and the limbs of all men were made to tremble. Through your call every sleeping one was awakened, every seated one rose up, and every reclining one rushed forth. Through that call the negligent were raised from slumber, the ignorant were enlightened, the agitated were assured, and the tongue of every stammerer was unloosed. Through your sweet remembrance all people hastened to the Most Exalted Horizon and the Crimson Ark sailed upon the sea of names.

Ye are the dawning-places of the Will of God and the daysprings of His Cause, the embodiments of His command and the sources of His might. Ye are the storehouses of His knowledge and the treasuries of His secrets, the repositories of His decree and the exponents of His behest. Ye are the pearls of the ocean of His generosity and the gems of the mines of His munificence, the suns of the firmament of His grace and the moons of the heaven of His bounty. Through you the banner "He, verily, is God" was hoisted upon the earth and every stranger came to recognize his ultimate goal and his true abode.

Through your allegiance did the pure in heart rush to the field of martyrdom and offer up that which they possessed in the path of God, the Lord of all names. Through you did they who enjoy near access to God attain unto the living waters of immortality, and the true believers unto that which hath flowed forth from the Luminous Spot in the All-Highest Paradise before the Divine Lote-Tree.

I testify that through you the breeze of the All-Merciful passed over all created things and the sweet savour of the All-Glorious wafted over all regions. Through you the Throne was established upon the land of Za'farán[1] *and the God of Mercy seated Himself thereupon. Through you the heaven of certitude shone resplendent and all things were moved to proclaim, "The Kingdom is God's, the Almighty, the Beneficent!" Through your names the*

---

1 Bahá'u'lláh states: *"The Holy Tree* [Sadrat] *is, in a sense, the Manifestation of the one true God, exalted be He. The Blessed Tree in the land of Za'farán* [Saffron] *referreth to the land which is flourishing, blessed, holy, and all-perfumed, where that Tree hath been planted."*

suns of inner meaning dawned above the horizons of utterance, and the streams of divine wisdom flowed in the gardens of true understanding. Ye are those inner meanings that can neither be apprehended through words nor expressed through speech.

Blessed is the poor one who hath set out towards the orient of your wealth, the thirsty one who hath hastened to the shores of the ocean of your favours, the lowly one who hath sought the court of your glory, the ignorant one who hath looked to the dawning-place of your knowledge, the distressed one who hath drawn nigh unto the tabernacle of your majesty and the pavilion of your grace, the ailing one who hath longed for the heavenly river of your healing, the weak one who hath turned to the kingdom of your might, and the friend who hath reached the soft-flowing stream of reunion with you and been honoured with your presence, which excelleth all that hath been fashioned in the universe or appeared in the realm of creation.

Great indeed is the blessedness of the wayward one who hath rushed to the dayspring of your guidance, the slumbering one who hath been awakened through your remembrance, the dead one who hath been stirred by the breezes of your utterance and adorned with the ornament of life beneath your shadow, the seated one who hath arisen in your service, the eloquent one who hath celebrated your praise and turned to the fountain of your generosity, and the rebellious one who through your intercession hath reached the ocean of forgiveness.

Through the sweet call you raised did all things draw nigh unto God, the Possessor of all names, and by your turning to the Most Exalted Horizon did all faces turn towards the dawning-place of the bounty of your Lord, the All-Glorious. Through you the treasures of all names were brought forth amongst the people. Through you the hearts of His ardent lovers were set ablaze in the world of creation.

The glory that hath dawned from the horizon of Mine utterance rest upon you and upon whomsoever hath turned towards you and fixed his gaze on the court of your glory. Through you the Dove of Eternity chanted and the birds of the Throne of glory warbled amongst the peoples, the seas surged and the winds blew, the lights were shed abroad and the skies were illumined. Through you the celestial Bird sounded its call, that which had been hidden was disclosed, the irrevocable decree was fulfilled, and the Hand of Mercy passed round the sealed wine. Through you the morn of certitude dawned forth, the lamp of vain imaginings was extinguished, and the gates of inspiration were flung open. Through you the secrets of the Book were divulged and the veils were rent asunder. Through you the emerald-green Nightingale warbled upon the Crimson Tree, testifying to that whereunto God Himself did testify ere the creation of earth and heaven.

Ye are the waves of this Sea through which every other sea hath surged and the mercy of God hath appeared in every land. I bear witness that ye are rivers branching out from the Most Great Ocean, luminous moons rising above the horizon of the world, and radiant lights shining upon its peoples. God hath made each of you a bough of this Ancient Root; an exponent of this glorious, this veiled and weighty Secret; a manifestation of His most noble Name; and a sign of His all-embracing grace. Well is it with him that hath been blessed by your breath during your lives and guided by your example after your deaths. Through you God's bounty was fulfilled, His mercy encompassed all things, His testimony was established, His heavenly sustenance was sent down, His Word was perfected, His breeze was wafted, and His proofs shone resplendent amidst all creation.

By your suffering, the kindreds of the cities of names were seized with agitation, the Pen of the Most High wailed aloud, the inmates of the loftiest Paradise were sorely vexed, the leaves of the Divine Lote-Tree withered, the Maids of heaven swooned away in their crimson chambers, the atoms of the universe cried out between earth and heaven, and the movement of the Pen of the Most Great Name was stilled in the realms of remembrance and praise.

Blessed is the one who hath been illumined with the light of your faces, hath drawn nigh unto the precincts of your court and circled round you, hath visited your resting-places and taken refuge with you, hath cleaved to the cord of your grace and held fast to the hem of your bounty, hath striven to the utmost in your path and suffered martyrdom for the sake of your love.

Through you the Supreme Horizon was illumined and all faces turned to God, the Lord of all Names. Through you were manifested His sovereignty and His might, His majesty and His grandeur. Ye are the lights of the Kingdom, the secrets of the Celestial Dominion, and the daysprings of the Cause of God in this nether world. Through you the sun of utterance shone forth, the ocean of understanding appeared, the heaven of certitude was upraised, and the throne of the All-Merciful was established in the realm of being.

Blessed are ye—the origin of your beings and their end, your outer temples and inner selves—and blessed is whosoever hath drawn nigh unto you and visited your graves, held fast to the cord of your favours, and clung firmly to the hem of the robe of your bestowals.

Lauded be Thy name, O Lord of Being and Possessor of all things visible and invisible! I beseech Thee by the showers of Thy mercy, through which Thy bounties and favours were manifested unto Thy servants, and by the mysteries of Thy knowledge and the pearls of the ocean of Thy wisdom, to forgive me, and my parents, and every servant who hath clung firmly to this exalted station and hastened to this sublime habitation.

I entreat Thee, O my Lord, by that Word wherewith Thou hast subdued the hearts of Thy chosen ones, to satisfy my needs and make me steadfast in Thy Cause, with my eyes fixed upon Thy horizon, wholly rid of all attachment to such as have disbelieved in Thee and in Thy signs.

O Lord! Thou seest Thy servant hastening to the ocean of Thy forgiveness, desiring only that which Thou hast ordained for them that love Thee. Thou art, in truth, that All-Powerful One Whom the pursuits of Thy servants can never frustrate nor the clamour of the people deter from Thy purpose. Thou doest, through the power of Thy might, what Thou willest, and ordainest as Thou pleasest. Thou, verily, art the All-Powerful, the All-Subduing, the Almighty.

Bahá'u'lláh[1]

---

1 *Zíyárat-Námiy-i-Bábu'l-Báb wa Quddús* revealed originally by Bahá'u'lláh in 'Akká. Mss: British Library Or15714.077. Included in list "Bahá'u'lláh's best known Works" prepared by Shoghi Effendi in *The Bahá'í World*, vol. 16, pages 574-575. The original Arabic version is available in *Bahá'í Reference Library from www.bahai.org/r/931357408* and the English version from www.bahai.org/r/262760797

2. Tablet of Visitation for Quddús

In the Name of God, the Most Exalted, the Most Holy.

Holy, Holy, Holy! The Glory of God, besides whom there is no other God, rest upon thy heart and the heart of whomsoever is in thy heart, and upon thy spirit and the spirit of whomsoever is in thy spirit, and upon thy soul and whomsoever is in thy soul, and upon thy body and whomsoever is in thy body. The loftiness of God, moreover, rest upon thy being and upon all who have been created through thy radiant praise, and upon thy spirit and all who have been created through thy supplication, and upon thy soul and all who have been created through thy belief in the Divine Unity, and upon thy self and all who have been created through the shining light of thy devotion. Thou hast been exalted, and none is there above thee whose exaltation is like unto thine. Thou hast drawn nigh, and none is there besides thee whose nearness is like unto thine. Each and every being doth lift up its voice in praise by means of thy praise. Each and every subtle reality hath voiced its thanksgiving out of the quintessence of thy thanksgiving. Each and every soul hath been united by the power of thy unity. Each and every living thing hath worshipped through the transcendence of thy worship. Through thee, all beings extol God; through thee, all beings glorify His sanctity; through thee, all beings magnify His oneness; through thee, all beings celebrate His grandeur. Verily, thy suffering waxed so grievous that the sufferings of all created things were as naught compared to it. Thine affliction rose to such heights that the afflictions of no contingent being can be mentioned in connection to it. I swear by the majesty of thy glory, there is no one in existence save God who hath not wept sore for thee; who doth not dwell beneath thy shadow, or praise God as thou didst praise Him; who hath not sanctified God in the manner thou didst sanctify Him; who is not a true believer in the Unity of God, just as thou hast believed; and who doth not magnify God even as thou didst magnify Him. From time immemorial and throughout eternity thou hast been immeasurably exalted with majesty, and wilt unto everlasting remain in the inaccessible retreats of holiness and beauty. Thou art manifest through the manifestation of thy Lord, and art concealed through the concealment of thy Lord. Thou art the first, for there is no first save thee, and the last for there is no last save thee. Thou hast ascended through the realm of existence unto a horizon wherein none hath preceded thee, and been seated upon the Throne of Might in the loftiest mansions of Paradise, a station that none, in the compass of God's knowledge, hath surpassed. I take thee and all created things as witnesses, that thy lifeblood is pure, holy, sanctified. By its mention, the inmost beings of all created things were made manifest, the essence of every truth was sanctified, all wholly severed souls were set free and all things purified from the limitations of this world of allusion. How, then, can I make mention of thee, O beloved of my heart, my king of glory, and my irrevocable purpose, the sovereign Lord of my beginning and end! Verily, all that existeth hath been fashioned through thy light, and all that is hidden revealed by means of thy being.

I take God and creation to witness that God hath sanctified thee from all likeness, and bestowed upon thee what hath never been conferred on any of His creatures: not the sovereignty of the earth and whatsoever is on it, but that of Paradise and those who dwell therein. Thus, no thought of majesty and glory may subsist in any heart unless it cometh to thee first in meekness, and with the greatest humility falleth upon thy threshold.

Methinks I see the angels of the Throne, the Seat, the heavens, the Most Exalted Paradise, and the Most Glorious Garden circling around thy dust, taking the tears that stream from the eyes of those that love thee to present them to the Lord thy God, that He may gaze upon one who hath achieved such a gracious favour, that His paradise may mourn for him, and that He may single him out for His bounties. In all of God's creation, there is no drop of water so beloved in His sight than those which are shed in remembrance of thy suffering, or stream down in contemplation of thy trials.[1]

[1] Provisional translation authorised by the Bahá'í World Centre. This Tablet of Visitation was originally published in Muḥammad-'Alí Malik Khusraví, *Tarikh-i-shuhadáyi Amr*, I. Ṭihrán, 130 B.E./1973-4, pp. 412-14.

3. A tribute to Mullá Ḥusayn

His full name was Mullá Muḥammad Ḥusayn-i-Bus͟hrú'í but was commonly known as Mullá Ḥusayn. According to the oriental form of that time to form the names: Mullá signifies he was a priest and scholar of theology and Muslim law; Ḥusayn is his birth name, and Bus͟hrú'í signifies he was a native of Bus͟hrúyih, a village in the province of K͟hurásán, at the eastern end of Iran. He was born around 1813.[1]

His father, Ḥájí Mullá 'Abdu'lláh, was a wealthy cloth dyer. Mullá Ḥusayn's mother was a devoted and gifted poetess. Two of their five children and a grandson would become outstanding defenders in the battles of the S͟hayk͟h Ṭabarsí fort that occurred in the first half of 1849 (see chapter fourteen).

For nine years, since he was eighteen years old, Mullá Ḥusayn sat at the feet of the wise Siyyid Káẓim in Karbilá in 'Iráq. He became one of the most esteemed and beloved of his students. Siyyid Káẓim had dedicated himself to teaching the minds and hearts of his disciples of the imminent advent of the divine Messenger that all the religions of the past had foretold.

Mullá Ḥusayn never married. We know that Siyyid Káẓim offered him his daughter's hand in marriage.[2] However, the proposition was respectfully declined as Mullá Ḥusayn had something else in mind for his future, as is seen in this book.

Mullá Ḥusayn is also known by his designation as the Bábu'l-Báb, the "Gate of the Gate" meaning the gate to access the Báb. Many believers just called him *Báb* because the Báb Himself had granted him His own title.[3]

Mullá Ḥusayn, the Bábu'l-Báb, holds a singular station in the Cause of the Báb because of his services and devotion, as discussed in chapter eight. Of him Bahá'u'lláh has said:

> *Among them was Mullá Ḥusayn, who became the recipient of the effulgent glory of the Sun of divine Revelation. But for him, God would not have been established upon the seat of His mercy, nor ascended the throne of eternal glory.*[4]

In the *Qayyúmu'l-Asmá*, the Báb also wrote of him "the beloved Siyyid, the exalted Ḥusayn"[5] although Mullá Ḥusayn was never a siyyid, meaning a descendant of Prophet Muḥammad.

---

1 In order to form a more comprehensive view of Mullá Ḥusayn's life, this section complements the reading of chapters 3, 8, 9, 12, 13 and the first six sections of chapter 14 dealing with his death

2 Ruhollah Mehrabkhani, *Mullá Ḥusayn*, p. 50.

3 Ruhollah Mehrabkhani, *Mullá Ḥusayn*, p. 129.

4 Bahá'u'lláh, *The Kitáb-i-Íqán*, p. 223.

5 Nader Saiedi, *Gate to the Heart*, p. 157.

His days were spent traversing the dusty roads and the ancient cities of the kingdom of Persia spreading tirelessly the new teachings of the Báb. Such was Mullá Ḥusayn's poverty that in his travels his main food during those days was a simple soup prepared with lettuce leaves called *bargh-i-káhú*. This type of food is mentioned in the *Persian Bayán* (2:9) as food for the poor.[1] The various travels of Mullá Ḥusayn can be observed on Figure 31.

All his travels led to his glorious spiritual victory at Shaykh Ṭabarsí, an old religious sanctuary precariously converted into a fort. Even before the Declaration of the Báb, Mullá Ḥusayn had succeeded in an important mission delegated by his mentor Siyyid Káẓim to argue favourably on the Shaykhi school to two leading Persian divines.[2]

The astounding events that occurred at the Shaykhi school during 1848–1849 spread like wildfire among all the people of his country and he became a source of inspiration for poets and writers.

Shoghi Effendi highlighted his role in Shaykh Ṭabarsí:

> The audacity of Mullá Ḥusayn who, at the command of the Báb, had attired his head with the green turban worn and sent to him by his Master, who had hoisted the Black Standard, the unfurling of which would, according to the Prophet Muḥammad, herald the advent of the vicegerent of God on earth, and who, mounted on his steed, was marching at the head of two hundred and two of his fellow-disciples to meet and lend his assistance to Quddús in the Jazíriy-i-Khaḍrá ("Verdant Isle")—his audacity was the signal for a clash the reverberations of which were to resound throughout the entire country.[3]

The life of this hero of God always revolved around fulfilling the pleasure of his Best-Beloved. At his passing on 2 February 1849, Mullá Ḥusayn's name was fully robed in glory with his becoming a celebrated personage in the annals of the world's religions. Endowed with unparalleled heroism, a shrewd judgement and consummate wisdom, he was able to enthuse and empower his co-religionaries into service to the Cause of the Báb.

Gifted with a virtuosity full of purity and a spiritual power worthy of admiration by all, Mullá Ḥusayn was admired even by those who declared themselves to be his adversaries. With a heart yearning to please his Lord, he set out to conquer the citadels of people's hearts and to enlist them for the promotion and defence of the Cause. So great and genuine was the devotion that radiated from him and so unassailable the power of his oratory that his dynamic presence in any place where he passed through ignited intense interest and he immediately became the focus of attraction. Even the most indifferent of the people were moved by the fervour of the sentiments he espoused. His fidelity was reflected in

---

1 Dr Nader Saiedi's personal communication to the author dated 20 March 2023.

2 Nabíl-i-A'ẓam, *The Dawn-Breakers*, pp. 20–4.

3 Shoghi Effendi, *God Passes By*, p. 38.

his actions, words, enthusiasm and oratory in promoting the Cause of the Báb, rapidly enlightening the spirits of any listener, spectator or audience. As the Báb had affirmed:

> *Let not the deeds of those who reject the Truth shut you out as by a veil. Such people have warrant over your bodies only, and God hath not reposed in them power over your spirits, your souls and your hearts.*[1]

There was even a slight yielding of resistance and opposition by the clerics to the preaching and mature knowledge he held, despite the Bábu'l-Báb publicly denouncing their vices and immoral practices. His overwhelming utterance, full of irrefutable proofs and arguments, easily defeated the few remaining opponents who still dared to challenge him. As seen in previous accounts, streams of seekers came looking for him, swearing allegiance to the Cause he professed. From whatever condition they came from, Mullá Ḥusayn's activities had prompted them to pursue with equal zeal and tenacity the dissemination of the seeds of Truth.

From Mullá Ḥusayn's point of view, every person, regardless of rank or social background, should have the opportunity to hear how he himself became enlightened with the teachings of the Báb. On his travels, he carried manuscripts and copies of the revelation of the Báb. With those sacred Writings, he addressed prominent ecclesiastical authorities and government officials throughout the country. Adolfo Rivadeneyra (1841–1882), a Spanish diplomat in Persia and an Orientalist, compared Mullá Ḥusayn to Saint Paul because of his intense missionary zeal.[2] When farewelled by the Báb in Shíráz, Mullá Ḥusayn was told:

> *Even as the cloud that rains its bounty upon the earth, traverse the land from end to end, and shower upon its people the blessings which the Almighty, in His mercy, has deigned to confer upon you.*[3]

When Mullá Ḥusayn entered a mosque, regardless of who was present, he would go up to the pulpit and begin to announce the Good News proclaimed from Shíráz. Without considering the danger and harassment he faced from an extremely cruel, fanatical and at the same time degraded Persian clergy, he continued to urge the population to approach and drink from the same Source of Life. He took advantage of the slightest opportunity to talk about the new Manifestation of God. His actions were like a fire that unexpectedly ignited at night when the city' is asleep, and ends up engulfing everything in the flames. As the Báb had written:

> *Regard not the all-sufficing power of God as an idle fancy. It is that genuine faith which thou cherishest for the Manifestation of God in every Dispensation. It is such faith which sufficeth above all the things that exist*

---

1 The Báb, *Selections,* pp. 161–2.

2 Adolfo Rivadeneyra, *Viaje and Interior de Persia*, vol. 1, p. 239.

3 The Báb in Nabíl-i-A'ẓam, *The Dawn-Breakers*, p. 85.

> *on the earth, whereas no created thing on earth besides faith would suffice thee.*[1]

Dr Farzam Arbab, a former member of the Universal House of Justice, once recalled:

> A Hand of the Cause once taught me how Mullá Ḥusayn, that immortal hero of our Faith, had written some stanzas of a poem on a wall in his house. The poet begins by saying: "True men have obtained their achievements only by great efforts" and then turning to himself, he asks: "What do you think, O feeble creature, who spends your time entirely in taking care of yourself?"[2]

Shoghi Effendi, the Guardian of the Bahá'í Faith, called him the "lion-hearted Mullá Ḥusayn".[3] He was worthy of such a designation because so he was undoubtedly daring in his interventions, impetuous and fierce in promoting the message he promoted, and irrepressible. With skill, courage, and dexterity, he proposed himself to win victories for the Cause of God. Like a majestic lion roaring in a thicket, the Bábu'l-Báb created confusion, chiefly among the faint-hearted, and an intense animosity among those who wished him ill, despite their awareness of Mullá Ḥusayn's superior merits. He showed every sign of being at the head of a host of angels. Fearless and unyielding, he scathingly lashed out at those tenets that had long been regarded as fundamental truths of religion, and declared them to be false.

His life principles were high and noble. He considered that presenting the teachings of the Báb was in itself a service to his nation and his fellow citizens. His determined character and achievements did not prevent him from revealing his soft and delicate nature, so that these two personality facets added together to form a leading personality. Mullá Ḥusayn also had a marked affinity for poetry and developed a keen literary judgement.

Mullá Ḥusayn' was an inseparable friend of Quddús. The following anecdote tell us about the affection between them while in the episode of Shaykh Ṭabarsí:

> A few days before Mullá Ḥusayn' death, His Holiness Quddús was walking with him in the enclosure of the Castle, resting his hand on his shoulder. In the enclosure were some lambs whose mothers had been carried off by the enemy, and these, deprived of milk, were bleating piteously. One of the Bábís, moved to pity by their evident distress, approached His Holiness Quddús and said, "These accursed men have wronged these poor beasts, and how great is the wrong done them!" Thereupon the eyes of His Holiness Quddús filled with tears, and he replied, "No, by God, it is not they who are wronged so much as we." Then he raised his hand and clapped Mullá Ḥusayn on the shoulder, adding, "By God, this is Ḥusayn the much-

---

1 The Báb, *Selections*, p. 193.

2 Farzam Arbab, *En camino hacia la gloria del servicio*, n.p.

3 Shoghi Effendi, *God Passes By*, p. 38.

> wronged, and no Antichrist." The narrator adds that he subsequently came across a tradition in the *Biháru'l-Anvár* to the effect that the Imám Ḥusayn will one day return to Karbilá in company with the Mahdí or Qá'im; that the army of the unbelievers will also return, and will declare the former to be Antichrist; that the Qá'im will deny this with an oath.; that the unbelievers will pay no heed to this, but will kill Imám Ḥusayn; that the Qá'im will demand his blood at their hands; and that forty days after his martyrdom all things will be plunged into confusion.[1]

When Mullá Ḥusayn was martyred on 2 February 1849, Quddús became extremely sorrowful. Hooshmand Dehghan, wrote:

> In this way [shooting of Mullá Ḥusayn], Jináb-i Quddús lost his best friend and supporter, and whenever the memory of Mullá Ḥusayn passed through his blessed mind, he became sad and sorrowful. So much so that when food was brought to him, he would say, "I have not enjoyed any food since the day Mullá Ḥusayn left me, because when I see that my friends are in the utmost state of hunger and are sitting around me with extreme weakness and frailty, my heart burns and my soul is set ablaze."[2]

After the burial, Quddús was the only person sleeping in that chamber as not wishing to separate in life and death from his friend.

In a Tablet written by the end of 1849, the Báb "extolled, in moving terms, the unswerving fidelity with which Mullá Ḥusayn, served Quddús throughout the siege of the fort of Ṭabarsí".[3] A Tablet revealed by Bahá'u'lláh for Mullá Ḥusayn's and Quddús is shown in the Appendix I with beautiful words of praise for these two distinguished believers such as:

> *Through your call*
> *every sleeping one was awakened,*
> *every seated one rose up*
> *every reclining one sped forth*
> *every negligent one was made heedful*
> *every ignorant one educated*
> *every agitated one assured,*
> *every stammering one eloquent.*
>
> *Through the guidance ye imparted,*
> *the thirsty hastened to the waters of life, and*
> *the rebel to the vivifying river of loftiness and pardon.*
>
> *Through your rising up*
> *did the people arise in turn to serve the Cause, and*

---

1 E.G. Browne, *Taríkh-i-Jadíd or New History of Mirzá 'Alí Muhammad the Báb,* p. 363

2 Hushmand Dehghan, *Ganj-i-Pinhán*, p. 100.

3 Nabíl-i-A'ẓam, *The Dawn-Breakers,* pp. 431–2.

the stream of clemency flow in the midst of mankind.

Through the Sublime Word ye promulgated,
the Book of Names was expounded, and
the gates of all good were opened to the inhabitants of earth and heaven.

Through your acceptance,
the purely devoted rushed to the field of martyrdom and offered up their substance in the path of God, the Possessor of all titles.

Through your names,
the suns of inner significance dawned from the firmaments of utterance, and the streams of revelation flowed in the gardens of understanding. Ye are those meanings that can neither be apprehended with words nor described through speech.

Through the supreme sweetness of your voice
Were all things drawn to God, the Possessor of every name... [1]

The Báb revealed in honour of Mullá Ḥusayn, "eulogies, prayers and visiting Tablets of a number equivalent to thrice the volume of the *Qur'án*".[2] The Báb had also stated that the dust of Mullá Ḥusayn's grave, in Shoghi Effendi's words, "was so potent as to cheer the sorrowful and heal the sick".[3]

When the Báb learned of the deaths of Quddús and Mullá Ḥusayn at Shaykh Ṭabarsí, He became so desponded and downhearted that He stopped revealing any Writings for five months. The Báb recommenced His work around November-December 1849 and commissioned Sayyáh to set out on pilgrimage on His behalf to visit the graves of the martyrs of Shaykh Ṭabarsí. "*Bring back to Me,*" the Báb requested, "*as a remembrance of your visit, a handful of that holy earth which covers the remains of My beloved ones, Quddús and Mullá Ḥusayn.*"[4]

Like Quddús, Mullá Ḥusayn lost his younger brother at Shaykh Ṭabarsí. When the Bábís were massacred, Mírzá Muḥammad-Ḥasan was placed in chains and later executed. Mírzá Jání noted:

> When I, Mírzá Jání, met Mírzá Muḥammad-Ḥasan, he was but seventeen years of age, yet I observed in him a dignity, gravity, composure, and virtue

1 *Zíyárat-Námiy-i-Bábu'l-Báb wa Quddús* revealed originally by Bahá'u'lláh in 'Akká. Mss: British Library Or15714.077. Included in list "Bahá'u'lláh's best known Works" prepared by Shoghi Effendi in *The Bahá'í World*, vol. 16, pages 574-575. The original Arabic version is available in *Bahá'í Reference Library from www.bahai.org/r/931357408* and the English version from www.bahai.org/r/262760797

2 Shoghi Effendi, *God Passes By*, p. 50.

3 Shoghi Effendi, *God Passes By*, p. 50.

4 Nabíl-i-A'ẓam, *The Dawn-Breakers*, pp. 431–2.

which amazed me. After the death of Jináb-i-Bábu'l-Báb, His Holiness Quddús bestowed on him the sword and turban of that glorious martyr, and made him captain of the troops of the True King. As to his martyrdom, there is a difference of opinion as to whether he was slain at the breakfast-table in the camp, or suffered martyrdom with Jináb-i-Quddús in the square of Bárfurúsh.[1]

1 *The Taríkh-i-Jadíd*, pp. 93–5, cited in Nabíl-i-A'ẓam, *The Dawn-Breakers*, p. 383.

Glossary and pronunciation guide

Glossary

Readers are advised that, as much as possible, the author has used the transcription standard adopted by Shoghi Effendi in 1923 for Bahá'í literature in the Persian and Arabic languages. However, authors often use their own styles or other systems currently in use. On some occasions, the author has taken the liberty of spelling some oriental terms differently from the original sources to adjust them to the Guardian's standard. For instance, the term Quddús is also transcribed as Qoddos, Quouddous, Quddús or Kuddus; or Tehrán as Ṭihrán. All Oriental terms have been adjusted to reflect the Bahá'í system while full referencing is provided to the original sources throughout the book.

Abjad	Alphabet. A writing system in which only consonants are represented or a term for the Arabic numeral system, where each consonant has an abjad numerical value. Abjad values of words are the sum of the digits for each consonant.
Ab	Ab (father) e.g., Abu'l-Qásim (father of Qásim)
'Abd	'Abd (slave or servant) e.g., 'Abdu'l-Bahá (Servant of the Glory)
AH	Anno Hejirae (Latin, "in the year of the Hijira", used in the West). H or Hijra for "after the Hijrah", the date (622 CE or AH). Muḥammad migration from Mecca to Medina marks the start of the Islamic calendar.
'Álim, pl. 'ulamá' (Pers. var. 'ulamá)[1]	Scholar, professional;—pl. learned ones; scholar (of Islamic law), scientist. Muslim scholars recognized as having specialist knowledge of Islamic sacred law and theology.
Áqá	Master, sire.
Azalí	A follower of Mírzá Yaḥyá (Ṣubḥ-i-Azal)
Báb	Door; gate; chapter, section, column. The Báb (*al-Báb*) is the title assumed by Siyyid Mírzá 'Alí-Muḥammad.
Bábí	A follower of the Faith of the Báb
Bahá'	Glory (often written as Bahá)
Bahá'í	A follower of the Faith of Bahá'u'lláh
BCE, CE	BCE ("before the common era") is a more general form of BC (before Christ). CE ("common or current era") is a more general form of AD (Latin, *Anno Domini*, "in the year of the Lord").
Caravanserai	An inn or accommodation for caravans.
Ḥadíth, pl. aḥádíth	Speech; discussion; narrative; Prophetic tradition, hadith. Narrative relating deeds and utterances of Prophet Muḥammad and his Companions.
Ḥaḍrat (Hazrat)	His Holiness
Ḥájí	A person who has completed the pilgrimage to Mecca.

[1] Variations are based on regional pronunciations.

Hand of the Cause	An appointed position for the propagation and protection of the Bahá'í Faith. Hands of the Cause were designated by Bahá'u'lláh, 'Abdu'l-Bahá and Shoghi Effendi.
Imám, pl. a'imma (English Imám)	A title of the first twelve linear successors of the Prophet Muḥammad. Title also used by religious leaders, especially in Iran. See Mullá entry below.
Jináb	Threshold; a place of refuge, hence, a title of respect, your honour, excellency.
Khán, fem. Khánum	Title of dignitary or a courtesy title, e.g., Muḥammad Khán, Maryam Khánum.
Lawḥ	Tablet, epistle, e.g. by the Báb, Bahá'u'lláh or 'Abdu'l-Bahá.
Mahdí	Literally "the rightly guided". The Promised One in Islam, a term used particularly within the Sunní tradition.
Mírzá	Preceding a name it refers to an educated person, e.g., Mírzá Muḥammad. A title of nobility (a son of a prince) when placed after a name, e.g., Muḥammad Mírzá.
Mujtahid	An original authority in Islamic law. Highest rank of Shi'ite divine. Now called an áyatu'lláh in contemporary Iran.
Mullá (Pers.)	School master, doctor, learned man, priest. The title has now degenerated into a derogatory term for a semi-literate, often bigoted village religious leader.
Qá'im	Literally "Rising". "He Who shall arise". Name given to the long-awaited Promised One of Islám. See Ṣáḥibu'z-Zamán.
Ṣáḥibu'z-Zamán	"The Lord of the Age". A title of the Qá'im or twelfth Imám, and the Báb. See Qá'im.
Sardár	A military commander; literally "headmaster"
Sayyid (var. Siyyid)	Master; gentleman; mister; sir; chieftain; title of Prophet Muḥammad's direct descendants.
Sharí'a	Sharia law or Islamic law that is based on the text of the *Qur'án*. Muslim traditions (hadiths) are often included. See ḥadíth.
Shaykh	A venerable gentleman; elder; chief; religious leader, e.g., Shaykh Yúsuf.
Shí'a (Pers. var. Shí'ih)	The second-largest branch of Islám—the dominant branch in Iran—follows the religious tradition of the twelve Imáms.
Shí'í (Pers. var. Shí'ih), pl. shí'yún	Adjective for member, follower. English: shiite, shi'ite.
Súra (Pers. var. súrih)	A row or series. Name given to a chapter of the *Qur'án*.

Titles can be combined in a single name such as in *Ḥájí Mírzá Siyyid Ḥusayn Bárfurúshí*, meaning a person who has made the pilgrimage to Mecca, coming from an educated background, a descendant of the Prophet Muḥammad, whose name is Ḥusayn, and being born in the city of *Bárfurúsh*.

Arabic and Persian pronunciation guide

Transliteration	Approximate pronunciation
a	a short *a* as in 'band', 'account', 'hat' or 'ran'
á	a long *a* as in 'ah', 'arm', 'wash' or 'father'
i	a simple 'e' sound as in 'met', 'ten' or 'egg'
í	the vowel sound 'ee' as in 'meet' or 'feet'
u	a 'o' sound as in 'put'
ú	a 'oo' sound as in 'boot', 'moon' or 'root'
y	'ye' as in "yoyo"
b	b
d	d
t ṭ	t
f	f
j	as in 'John' or 'yes'
l	l
m	m
n	n
p	p
r	r
v	v
Th, s or ṣ	s in 'see' or 'so'
ch	ch in 'church' or 'chat'
sh	sh in 'she', or 'sheep'
gh, g or q	g in 'get'
k	as 'cat'
h or ḥ	as in 'house'
kh	in 'Bach' or Scots 'loch'
ḍ, dh, z or zh	z
aw combination	as 'ow' sound in 'vowel'
’	silent 'uh'
‘	silent 'uh'

Adapted from

Leila Moshiri, *Colloquial Persian*. Routledge. 1988.
Marzieh Gail, *Bahá'í Glossary*. Bahá'í Publishing Trust, Wilmette, Ill. 1955.
M. W. Thomas (compiler), "Glossary and transcription for Arabic & Persian terms". Available https://bahai-library.com/glossary_arabic_persian_ transcription

Index of names

'Abbás-Qulí <u>Kh</u>án-i-Láríjání, 160, 161, 189, 190, 195, 207, 218, 220, 225, 234, 235, 236, 237, 239, 245, 254, 261, 267, 282, 283, 287, 296, 298, 311, 402, 410

'Abdu'l-Bahá, xvii, 4, 5, 15, 22, 44, 46, 47, 65, 66, 81, 106, 111, 113, 129, 137, 138, 143, 145, 148, 153, 164, 165, 214, 269, 311, 331, 337, 339, 357, 358, 360, 367, 371, 372, 373, 376, 378, 385, 387, 390, 401, 415, 417, 419, 421, 422, 423, 429, 430, 431, 432, 434, 438, 444, 457, 458, 463, 465, 470, 472, 474, 477, 478, 479, 482, 483, 485, 489, 498, 511, 529, 546, 547, 554, 556, 562, 568, 573

'Abdu'lláh <u>Kh</u>án-i-Turkamán, 220, 221, 222, 225, 226, 251

'Alí-Ábád, 221, 296

Afrá, xii, 198, 223, 224, 225, 226, 235, 236, 239, 241, 271, 299

Agarih, 175, 180, 182

Ámul, 195, 196, 212, 234, 312, 339, 479

Áqá Muḥammad Ṣádiq (Quddús' brother), 7, 352, 353

Áqá Ṣáliḥ (Quddús' father), 95, 328, 350

Áqá-rúd, 2

Áqáy-i-Kalím (Bahá'u'lláh's brother), 91, 498

Ardistán, 83, 128, 305, 342, 485

Asárán, 182

Ástánih, 175, 179, 181

Báb, The, 3, 7, xi, xv, xvi, xvii, xviii, xxi, 1, 6, 8, 12, 13, 16, 17, 18, 20, 21, 25, 26, 27, 28, 38, 39, 40, 41, 42, 43, 44, 45, 46, 48, 49, 50, 51, 52, 53, 54, 55, 56, 57, 58, 59, 60, 61, 62, 63, 64, 65, 66, 67, 69, 70, 71, 74, 81, 82, 83, 84, 85, 87, 88, 89, 91, 92, 94, 95, 96, 97, 98, 100, 103, 104, 105, 106, 107, 108, 109, 110, 111, 112, 113, 114, 123, 124, 128, 129, 133, 134, 135, 137, 138, 139, 140, 141, 142, 143, 144, 145, 146, 147, 149, 150, 152, 153, 154, 155, 157, 159, 160, 161, 162, 163, 164, 166, 172, 173, 174, 179, 181, 186, 187, 188, 189, 190, 195, 198, 200, 205, 206, 207, 210, 211, 213, 214, 216, 217, 219, 222, 223, 225, 238, 247, 249, 255, 275, 276, 277, 279, 284, 285, 286, 289, 296, 299, 304, 305, 311, 316, 317, 318, 319, 321, 323, 325, 326, 327, 329, 333, 337, 340, 341, 342, 350, 357, 358, 359, 360, 361, 362, 363, 364, 365, 366, 367, 368, 369, 370, 371, 372, 373, 374, 375, 376, 377, 378, 379, 380, 381, 383, 385, 386, 387, 390, 395, 396, 397, 398, 399, 400, 401, 402, 405, 406, 407, 408, 410, 411, 412, 413, 414, 415, 417, 418, 419, 420, 421, 422, 426, 430, 432, 433, 437, 440, 441, 444, 447, 456, 457, 458, 459, 460, 461, 463, 465, 466, 467, 468, 469, 470, 471, 472, 473, 474, 475, 476, 477, 478, 482, 483, 484, 491, 499, 503, 505, 506, 507, 509, 510, 511, 512, 514, 515, 516, 517, 518, 520, 521, 522, 523, 525, 528, 530, 532, 539, 540, 541, 542, 543, 544, 546, 547, 554, 556, 558, 559, 561, 563, 564, 565, 566, 568, 569, 571

Bábís, xi, xii, 28, 41, 76, 82, 96, 98, 106, 111, 112, 123, 125, 126, 128, 129, 134, 135, 137, 139, 140, 141, 143, 145, 154, 155, 160, 162, 166, 172, 173, 174, 176, 178, 179, 181, 184, 185, 186, 187, 188, 189, 190, 194, 195, 196, 197, 198, 199, 200, 205, 206, 207, 209, 210, 211, 212, 213, 214, 215, 216, 217, 218, 219, 220, 221, 222, 223, 224, 225, 226, 227, 228, 232, 234, 235, 236, 237, 238, 239, 240, 241, 242, 243, 244, 245, 246, 247, 248, 251, 252, 253,

254, 256, 257, 258, 259, 260, 261, 262, 263, 264, 265, 266, 267, 268, 269, 275, 276, 277, 278, 281, 282, 283, 284, 285, 287, 290, 292, 293, 294, 296, 298, 299, 301, 302, 303, 305, 306, 312, 314, 316, 326, 333, 339, 340, 350, 352, 369, 376, 377, 378, 382, 383, 395, 396, 397, 400, 401, 402, 403, 404, 406, 407, 408, 410, 413, 419, 425, 426, 427, 433, 447, 449, 456, 457, 458, 459, 460, 461, 463, 464, 465, 468, 469, 470, 471, 472, 473, 474, 480, 482, 484, 486, 499, 508, 509, 510, 511, 512, 513, 518, 519, 520, 524, 525, 526, 529, 542, 544, 555, 558, 562, 566, 568

Babol (Bárfurúsh), xi, 2, 3, 31, 93, 172, 175, 177, 183, 187, 208, 278, 314, 327, 352, 353, 409, 425, 426, 437, 439, 440, 442, 444, 445, 446, 450, 500, 559, 567, 568, 569

Badasht, xii, 92, 121, 128, 129, 130, 133, 135, 136, 137, 138, 139, 140, 141, 143, 146, 147, 148, 149, 152, 153, 154, 155, 156, 157, 160, 161, 164, 170, 171, 172, 176, 178, 181, 187, 276, 279, 328, 342, 363, 396, 397, 433, 440, 554

Baghdád, 24, 134, 137, 138, 146, 173, 211, 289, 312, 364, 366, 377, 378, 382, 485, 517, 571

Bahá'u'lláh, xi, xv, xvii, xviii, 1, 2, 6, 14, 19, 20, 21, 23, 24, 27, 40, 41, 42, 44, 60, 61, 63, 64, 81, 84, 85, 86, 90, 91, 92, 104, 105, 106, 107, 113, 114, 116, 117, 121, 127, 128, 129, 133, 135, 137, 138, 139, 140, 141, 143, 144, 145, 146, 147, 148, 149, 150, 152, 153, 155, 156, 157, 160, 164, 165, 176, 190, 206, 207, 212, 215, 277, 278, 285, 304, 307, 328, 341, 342, 357, 360, 361, 363, 364, 365, 366, 367, 368, 369, 371, 373, 374, 375, 376, 377, 378, 382, 383, 385, 386, 388, 389, 395, 396, 397, 400, 402, 409, 410, 421, 422, 423, 428, 429, 430, 431, 432, 440, 444, 445, 447, 458, 459, 460, 461, 466, 467, 468, 469, 471, 472, 474, 478, 482, 484, 485, 491, 492, 498, 517, 520, 523, 528, 529, 532, 533, 536, 539, 543, 546, 547, 554, 555, 556, 557, 558, 559, 560, 562, 563, 564, 565, 566, 568, 569, 570, 571, 573

Bandar-i-Gaz, 155, 157, 164, 165

Bárfurúsh (Babol), xi, xii, xiii, 1, 2, 3, 4, 5, 6, 7, 9, 10, 12, 13, 14, 23, 24, 25, 32, 36, 37, 42, 46, 92, 93, 94, 95, 96, 98, 99, 100, 101, 102, 103, 105, 106, 109, 119, 123, 128, 129, 155, 157, 158, 159, 160, 164, 166, 172, 175, 176, 177, 179, 181, 182, 185, 186, 187,189, 190, 193, 195, 196, 210, 211, 218, 221, 226, 234, 238, 251, 252, 254, 276, 283, 289, 292, 298, 307, 311, 312, 313, 315, 316, 323, 325, 327, 329, 330, 332, 333, 334, 335, 336, 337, 339, 341, 342, 343, 344, 345, 350, 352, 360, 363, 388, 390, 399, 402, 403, 405, 406, 409, 422, 423, 424, 425, 426, 437, 440, 445, 446, 449, 452, 454, 455, 471, 478, 490, 493, 500, 501, 509, 512, 515, 524, 526, 528, 545, 547

Basṭám, 172, 175, 179

Bayán, 6, 13, 45, 46, 50, 63, 89, 96, 98, 104, 106, 113, 133, 134, 138, 139, 140, 141, 142, 143, 145, 146, 147, 150, 163, 255, 277, 324, 358, 359, 360, 361, 363, 364, 365, 396, 397, 410, 411, 412, 417, 422, 430, 458, 459, 460, 465, 468, 473, 474, 475, 478, 511,514, 515, 517, 520, 521, 522, 540, 555

Bíyár Jumand, 172, 175, 177, 182

Búshihr, 24, 38, 48, 50, 52, 54, 55, 59, 61, 63, 64, 67, 70, 82, 91, 340, 342

Bushrúyih, 111, 539

Caspian Sea, 1, 3, 9, 109, 136, 156, 158, 164, 196, 219, 409, 528, 554

Cháshm (Cháshm-gáh or Chásht-gáh), 172, 175, 182, 183, 185

Chashmah-'Alí, 172, 175, 179, 180, 182

Chihríq, 121, 124, 134, 137, 138, 139,

146, 152, 155, 161, 162, 163, 164, 166, 173, 174, 177, 190, 195, 219, 222, 397, 402, 432, 482, 511
Dalá'il-i-Sab'ih, 38, 363, 515
Dámghán, 175, 179, 180
Dih Surkh, 183
Dih-Mullá, 172, 175, 178, 179
Dízvá (Dízábad), 299, 300
Dú-Áb, 175, 185
Fírúzkúh, 172, 183, 185, 186, 195
Ḥájí Naṣír Qazvíní, 483
Him Whom God shall manifest, 363
House of Bábíyyih, xi, xii, 121, 123, 124, 125, 127, 143, 166, 169, 198, 254, 283, 339, 396, 440
Imám Zádih 'Abdu'l Ḥaqq, 186, 187
Iṣfahán, 24, 62, 65, 90, 129, 180, 186, 305, 342, 465, 466, 482
Ívil, 484, 508, 527
Jesus Christ, 21, 22, 45, 48, 49, 108, 133, 140, 149, 307, 319, 321, 328, 367, 370, 396, 419, 456, 459, 460, 471, 472, 474, 516, 523, 561
Karbilá, xi, 4, 12, 14, 23, 24, 25, 26, 27, 28, 35, 36, 37, 38, 42, 61, 62, 65, 87, 105, 127, 165, 166, 173, 176, 177, 179, 180, 183, 187, 197, 210, 211, 287, 304, 313, 320, 328, 333, 335, 342, 399, 418, 460, 495, 513, 539, 543
Káshán, 90, 342, 402, 462
Khán-i-Khúdí, 172, 177
Kharand, 175, 182
Khaṣá'il-i Sab'ih, 63
Khurásán, 15, 17, 103, 112, 113, 121, 123, 124, 128, 129, 136, 154, 166, 174, 176, 179, 221, 245, 312, 379, 390, 396, 470, 484, 539, 558
Khúríyih, 172, 175, 182
Khusraw, 195, 196, 197, 209, 210, 237, 482, 508
Kirmán, xi, 81, 82, 83, 84, 86, 87, 88, 90, 107, 116, 328, 342
Kitáb-i-Aqdas, 207, 285, 369, 370, 380, 429, 430, 438, 466, 520, 557, 564
Kitáb-i-Íqán, 42
Letters of the Living, xv, 36, 41, 42, 43, 45, 48, 50, 63, 104, 105, 106, 113, 126, 142, 225, 249, 333, 358, 360, 361, 373, 398, 429, 447, 459, 469, 555
Luṭf 'Alí Mírzá, 179, 186, 187, 195, 197, 225, 276, 286, 379, 381, 382, 383, 461, 473, 564, 570
Máh-Kú, xi, 108, 110, 117, 135, 138, 140, 141, 146, 162, 358, 363, 402, 432
Maryam (Quddús' sister), 7, 36, 328, 351, 480, 547
Mashhad, xi, xii, 4, 12, 15, 16, 17, 18, 23, 24, 25, 33, 36, 101, 103, 105, 112, 113, 121, 122, 123, 124, 125, 126, 127, 128, 129, 135, 152, 154, 164, 165, 166, 167, 169, 172, 173, 174, 175, 176, 178, 180, 187, 198, 215, 254, 276, 328, 339, 342, 411, 440, 470, 478, 479, 486, 513
Mayámay, 172, 175, 177, 178, 182
Mazínán, 172, 175, 176, 177, 178, 247
Mázindarán, 1, 2, 7, 10, 13, 17, 38, 93, 98, 100, 108, 109, 110, 111, 114, 121, 126, 127, 128, 129, 136, 154, 155, 156, 157, 158, 165, 166, 172, 174, 176, 177, 178, 180, 181, 182, 183, 184, 185, 190, 195, 196, 214, 215, 218, 220, 221, 225, 226, 234, 243, 251, 252, 253, 257, 265, 267, 279, 280, 287, 288, 291, 292, 323, 324, 326, 352, 358, 379, 384, 390, 396, 399, 402, 404, 406, 407, 425, 438, 445, 448, 449, 462, 465, 470, 472, 479, 482, 484, 499, 500, 502, 504, 509, 525
Mecca, xi, 19, 23, 37, 38, 42, 48, 49, 50, 51, 52, 54, 55, 56, 57, 58, 69, 70, 74, 75, 94, 105, 107, 111, 173, 195, 328, 342, 358, 363, 381, 390, 395, 418, 421, 471, 514, 546, 547
Medina, 19, 48, 57, 195, 342, 358, 546
Mihdí-Qulí Mírzá (the Prince-Governor), 234, 244, 287, 352, 402
Mihmán-Dúst, 172, 175, 179
Mírzá Ḥaydar (Quddús' brother), 318, 328, 351

Mírzá Ḥaydar-'Alí Ardistání, 128
Mirzá Karím Khán Kirmání, xi, 81, 84, 85, 87, 88, 89, 90, 116, 262
Mírzá Taqí Khán (the Grand Vizir), 217, 401
Muḥammad (Prophet), 4, 7, 15, 19, 20, 23, 38, 40, 57, 101, 104, 145, 150, 166, 173, 174, 187, 198, 211, 215, 317, 321, 322, 333, 336, 365, 372, 373, 414, 417, 467, 470, 496, 499, 516, 539, 540, 546, 547
Muḥammad Sháh, xi, 17, 63, 68, 100, 163, 164, 165, 168, 180, 182, 183, 184, 186, 189, 244, 287, 342, 400, 402, 500, 511, 520, 523
Mullá 'Alí Akbar Ardistání, 66, 67, 400, 401
Mullá Ḥusayn, x, xi, xvii, xviii, 15, 17, 18, 19, 28, 36, 37, 38, 39, 40, 41, 43, 44, 62, 65, 90, 91, 92, 95, 96, 98, 100, 103, 104, 105, 106, 107, 108, 109, 110, 111, 112, 113, 114, 119, 120, 121, 122, 123, 124, 125, 126, 127, 128, 129, 135, 143, 155, 160, 164, 165, 166, 167, 172, 173, 174, 175, 176, 177, 178, 179, 180, 181, 182, 183, 184, 185, 186, 187, 188, 189, 190, 195, 196, 197, 198, 199, 200, 206, 209, 210, 212, 213, 214, 215, 216, 217, 218, 221, 223, 225, 227, 228, 237, 239, 240, 241, 242, 244, 245, 246, 247, 248, 249, 253, 254, 266, 275, 277, 278, 283, 284, 286, 287, 288, 289, 290, 291, 292, 294, 298, 299, 300, 312, 315, 328, 342, 343, 358, 365, 373, 376, 377, 378, 379, 380, 381, 382, 383, 386, 389, 390, 398, 400, 408, 429, 430, 431, 447, 449, 450, 459, 468, 469, 470, 471, 474, 477, 479, 480, 481, 482, 484, 485, 486, 487, 499, 508, 509, 510, 512, 524, 525, 526, 528, 532, 539, 540, 541, 542, 543, 544, 557, 565
Mullá Muḥammad-i-Mu'allim-i-Núrí, 307
Mullá Ṣádiq (Muqaddas), 63, 65, 66, 67, 68, 69, 81, 82, 84, 400, 482
Murshid, 305, 306
Najaf, 27, 58, 313, 320
Naṣiri'd-Dín Sháh, xii, 194, 234, 400
Níshápúr, 172, 175, 176
Níyalá, xii, 156, 157, 158, 164, 170
Núr, 1, 155, 157, 159, 165, 190, 283
Persian Bayán, 143, 450, 451
Pul-i-Sifíd, 175
Qá'im, 19, 20, 22, 25, 28, 44, 46, 49, 56, 62, 134, 135, 138, 139, 140, 141, 145, 166, 172, 207, 286, 318, 319, 333, 378, 379, 404, 419, 456, 465, 468, 469, 470, 471, 475, 483, 484, 488, 512, 514, 515, 516, 547
Qá'ím Shahr, 351
Qayyúmu'l-Asmá', 36, 40, 41, 42, 63, 66, 67, 69, 106, 142, 285, 286, 396, 397, 514, 515, 516, 539, 555
Qazvín, 28, 92, 128, 129, 458
Riẓá Ábád, 175, 182
Sa'ídu'l-'Ulamá', 5, 6, 37, 93, 95, 99, 100, 101, 102, 104, 112, 113, 158, 159, 187, 188, 189, 196, 210, 217, 218, 221, 252, 253, 283, 290, 292, 305, 311, 312, 315, 317, 318, 321, 322, 323, 324, 325, 326, 327, 329, 330, 331, 332, 333, 336, 353, 385, 391, 402, 403, 405, 406, 412, 414, 422, 423, 424, 425, 426, 445, 472, 473, 490, 493, 512, 524, 526
Sabzih-Maydán, xii, 93, 94, 193, 326, 327, 328, 329, 330, 334, 335, 337, 338, 425, 426, 427, 450
Sabzivár, 172, 175, 176, 182
Sangsár, 182, 566
Sardár, 190, 195, 207, 225, 237, 244, 247, 251, 253, 254, 255, 257, 259, 261, 262, 287
Sárí, 6, 12, 13, 15, 36, 92, 155, 157, 158, 159, 160, 165, 177, 180, 182, 190, 196, 218, 219, 221, 226, 237, 238, 298, 314, 325, 328, 339, 342, 388, 396, 512, 515
Shahmírzad, 488, 566
Sháh-Rúd, 129, 136, 175, 178, 182
Sharí'atmadár, xi, 5, 6, 9, 12, 24, 25, 32, 36, 37, 99, 101, 102, 159, 335, 350,

351, 352, 385, 387, 388, 390, 395, 403, 405, 406, 468, 473
Shaykh Aḥmad-i-Aḥsá'í, 12, 21, 22, 23, 24, 25, 37, 89, 178, 197
Shaykh Ṭabarsí fort, ix, xi, xii, xvi, xviii, 91, 92, 102, 103, 107, 154, 155, 160, 166, 173, 174, 175, 181, 182, 184, 187, 195, 197, 198, 205, 206, 209, 210, 211, 212, 213, 216, 217, 218, 219, 220, 222, 224, 226, 230, 231, 232, 233, 234, 235, 236, 237, 238, 239, 244, 248, 249, 250, 252, 255, 257, 260, 261, 262, 265, 269, 270, 271, 272, 273, 274, 275, 276, 277, 278, 279, 280, 283, 284, 285, 286, 287, 289, 290, 291, 298, 304, 305, 316, 318, 328, 333, 339, 340, 341, 342, 343, 351, 352, 362, 377, 378, 379, 381, 383, 384, 385, 386, 389, 390, 395, 396, 397, 398, 401, 402, 406, 407, 408, 410, 417, 419, 421, 423, 426, 427, 429, 430, 431, 432, 433, 434, 446, 447, 448, 449, 450, 456, 459, 461, 463, 464, 465, 468, 469, 470, 471, 472, 473, 474, 475, 477, 479, 480, 482, 483, 484, 486, 487, 488, 489, 490, 491, 499, 508, 509, 510, 511, 512, 515, 517, 518, 524, 525, 526, 528, 530, 539, 540, 542, 544, 573
Shí'ih, 19, 20, 21, 173, 207, 319, 326, 410, 413, 459, 469, 496, 547
Shíráz, xi, 17, 26, 37, 38, 42, 43, 48, 50, 55, 59, 62, 63, 64, 65, 66, 68, 69, 70, 73, 74, 75, 81, 82, 83, 84, 86, 91, 92, 104, 105, 107, 126, 157, 340, 342, 357, 360, 375, 400, 401, 415, 416, 418, 420, 432, 440, 456, 488, 499, 541, 554, 564
Shír-Gáh, 172, 182, 186, 187, 195
Shoghi Effendi, xv, xvii, 2, 5, 6, 24, 41, 51, 91, 92, 99, 106, 107, 135, 136, 137, 138, 139, 141, 142, 143, 148, 149, 150, 151, 152, 153, 159, 205, 224, 249, 285, 287, 303, 326, 327, 330, 357, 358, 360, 361, 363, 364, 365, 367, 369, 372, 373, 377, 378, 379, 381, 384, 385, 399, 400, 401, 406, 407, 411, 417, 418, 419, 420, 421, 422, 428, 429, 430, 431, 432, 433, 439, 444, 456, 458, 459, 460, 462, 469, 472, 475, 476, 498, 511, 513, 520, 536, 540, 542, 544, 546, 547, 557, 564, 567, 570
Shrine of Quddús, 421, 437, 438, 440
Siyyid Káẓim, xi, 12, 21, 22, 23, 24, 25, 26, 27, 28, 34, 36, 37, 38, 39, 65, 85, 87, 105, 107, 179, 289, 328, 342, 373, 418, 482, 539, 540
Siyyid Muḥammad Ḥusayn Mahjúr-i-Zavári, 264, 280, 298, 301, 302, 305, 307, 312, 313, 314, 315, 317, 318, 319, 322, 323, 324, 325, 327, 328, 333, 379, 386, 387, 462, 470, 570
Sulaymán Khán-i-Afshár, xii, 262, 267, 271, 296, 402
Sulṭán 'Abdu'l-Majíd, 58, 59
Sunní, 19, 20, 134, 547
Tabríz, 62, 134, 135, 161, 163, 186, 321, 402, 419, 420, 475
Ṭáhirih, 25, 42, 104, 121, 128, 129, 130, 133, 137, 138, 143, 144, 145, 147, 148, 149, 150, 151, 152, 153, 155, 156, 157, 159, 190, 338, 361, 385, 386, 396, 398, 429, 432, 440, 458, 460, 477, 478, 479, 522, 554, 561, 569
Universal House of Justice, The, xv, xvi, xvii, 41, 83, 357, 366, 367, 373, 386, 417, 429, 431, 440, 456, 457, 458, 461, 542, 556, 557, 559, 572
Úrím, 172, 175, 185, 186
Vás-Kas, xii, 235, 239, 272
Yazd, 24, 81, 83, 342

Bibliography

Abadis. *Mihdí-Qulí Mírzá Qájár.* Available at: https://abadis.ir/fatofa/مهدی قلی میرزا/

Abbott, K. E. *Narrative of a Journey from Tabriz along the Shores of the Caspian Sea to Ṭihrán in 1843/1844.* PRO (FO, 251 40), pp. 193–4.

________. "Extracts from a Memorandum on the Country of Azerbaijan", *Proceedings of the Royal Geographical Society of London*, 8(6), pp. 275–279, 1863–1864. Available from www.jstor.org/stable/1799149

________. Report by Consul Abbott of his Journey to the Coast of the Caspian Sea, 1847–1848. In A. Amanat (ed.), *Cities and Trade: Consul Abbott on the Economy and Society of Iran 1847-1866.* Ithaca Press, London. 1983.

'Abdu'l-Bahá. *A Traveller's Narrative.* Bahá'í Publishing Trust, Wilmette, Ill. 1980.

________. "Additional Tablets, Extracts and Talks". Bahá'í World Centre, Haifa. 2023. Available www.bahai.org/library/authoritative-texts/abdul-baha/additional-tablets-extracts-talks/

________. *Foundations of World Unity.* Bahá'í Publishing Trust, Wilmette, Illinois. 1979.

________. "Light of the World: 76 selected Tablets of 'Abdu'l-Bahá", 29 August 2021. www.bahai.org/library/authoritative-texts/abdul-baha/light-of-the-world/

________. *Memorials of the Faithful.* Bahá'í Publishing Trust, Wilmette, Ill. 1971.

________. *Light of the World: 76 Selected Tablets of 'Abdu'l-Bahá.* Bahá'í World Centre, Haifa. 2021.

________. *Paris Talks: Addresses Given by 'Abdu'l-Bahá in 1911.* Bahá'í Publishing Trust, London. 1972.

________. *The Secret of Divine Civilization.* Bahá'í Publishing Trust, Wilmette, Ill. 2007.

________. *Selections from the Writings of 'Abdu'l-Bahá.* Bahá'í World Centre. UK, 1978.

________. *Some Answered Questions.* 2nd edition. Bahá'í World Centre, Haifa. 2014. Last retrieved 30 September 2021 www.Bahái.org/library/authoritative-texts/abdul-Bahá/some-answered-questions/

________. *Tablets of Abdul-Baha Abbas.* Vol. III. Published by Bahá'í Publishing Society. Chicago, 1915. Available at https://bahai-library.com/writings/ abdulbaha/tab/

________. *Writings and Utterances of 'Abdu'l-Bahá.* Bahá'í Publishing Trust of India, 2000.

________. "Ṭáhirih and the Conference of Badasht". In *Twelve Table Talks given by 'Abdu'l-Bahá in 'Akká.* Available at : www.bahai.org/library/authoritative-texts/abdul-baha/twelve-table-talks-abdul-baha/3#608439669

________.. *Makātib-i Abd al-Bahā',* vol. 2 Cairo. 1330/1912.

________.. *Tablets of the Divine Plan.* Wilmette, US Bahá'í Publishing Trust. 1993.

________. *The Will and Testament of 'Abdu'l-Bahá.* Bahá'í Publishing Trust, Wilmette, Ill. 1990.

Abu'l-Faḍl-i-Gulpáygání, *Mírzá Abu'l-Faḍl: Letters and Essays 1886-1913.* Kalimát Press, 1985.

________.. *Mírzá Abu'l-Faḍl: Miracles and Metaphors.* Kalimát Press. 1981.

________. .*Kashfu'l-Ghitá.* Completed by Mahdi Gulpaygani. Ishqabad, n.d.

Adamson, Hugh C. *Historical Dictionary of the Bahá'í Faith.* Scarecrow Press. 2006.

Afnan, Abu'l-Qasim. *Black Pearls:* Servants in the Households of the Báb and Bahá'u'lláh. Kalimát Press, Los Angeles. 1988.

Afnán, Mírzá Ḥabíbu'lláh. *The Genesis of the Bábí-Bahá'í Faiths in Shíráz and Fárs.* Tr. Ahang Rabbani. Brill, 2008. Accessed 30 June 2022 at https://bahai-library.com/pdf/a/afnan_rabbani_genesis_faiths.pdf

Afnán, Muḥammad. "The Báb's Bayán: An Analytical Survey". *World Order*, 31:4, pp. 7–16. 2000.

________. "A General Introduction to the Qayyúmu'l-Asmá". In *A Most Noble Pattern* (eds Todd Lawson & Omid Ghaemmaghami), pp. 1–5. George Ronald, Oxford. 2012.

________. "Number of the Letters of the Living". *Lights of Irfán*, Vol. 5, p. 217. Accessed https://bahai-library.com/afnan_number_letters_living

Afnán, Muhammad and Hatcher, William S. Note on MacEoin's Bahá'í Fundamentalism. *Religion*, 16, 187-192. 1986.

Afnán, Muḥammad & Hatcher, William S. "Note on MacEoin's 'Bahá'í Fundamentalism'". In *Religion* (1986) 16, pp. 187–192. Available https://bahai-library.com/pdf/a/afnan_hatcher_note_maceoin.pdf

Affolter, Friedrich W. "The Specter of Ideological Genocide: The Bahá'ís of Iran". In *War Crimes Genocide & Crimes against Human*, 1 (75), 2005, p. 88.

Afroukhteh, Youness Khan. *Memories of Nine Years in 'Akká* (translated by Riaz Masrour). Oxford: George Ronald. 1952/2003.

Ahdieh, Hussein and Hillary Chapman. *The Chosen Path Tahirih of Persia and Her Search for God*. CreateSpace. 2020.

________. *The Calling: Tahirih of Persia and her American Contemporaries*. Ibex Publishers, Bethesda, Maryland. 2017.

Ahmadi, Ali. *History of the Bahá'í Faith in the Village of Ivel*. In Archive of Bahá'í Persecutions. *January* 2023. Available online from website: https://iranbahaipersecution.bic.org/sites/default/files/PDF/English/020167E_0.pdf

Al-Dawoody, Ahmed, Kristy A. Winter, and Oran Finegan. "International Committee of the Red Cross (ICRC): management of the dead under Islamic law". *Forensic Science International: Reports* 3, 2021, p. 100–196.

Algar, Hamid. *Religion and state in Iran, 1785–1906: the Role of the Ulama in the Qajar Period*. University of California Press. 1980.

Alkan, Necati. "Bahá'u'lláh's Lawḥ-i Istintáq (Tablet of the Interrogation) and the Murder of Three Azalís in Akká in 1872". Paper presented at the Irfan Colloquia. Centre for Bahá'í Studies, Acuto, Italy. July 5–8, 2016. Abstract available http://irfancolloquia.org/138/papers

________. *Dissent and Heterodoxy in the Late Ottoman Empire: Reformers, Bábís and Bahá'ís*. Gorgias Press. 2010.

Amanat, Abbás. *Pivot of the Universe: Nasir al-Din Shah Qajar and the Iranian Monarchy, 1831–1896*. University of California Press, Berkeley. 1997.

________. *Resurrection and Renewal: The Making of the Bábí Movement in Iran, 1844–1850*. Cornell University Press. 1989.

________. "The Shaping of the Babi Community: Merchants, Artisans, and Others". In *The Báb and the Bábí Community of Iran* (ed. Fereydun Vahman), pp. 101–150. OneWorld Academic. 2020.

Amanat, Mehrdad. Set in stone: Homeless corpses and desecrated graves in modern Iran. *International Journal of Middle East Studies* 44, no. 2, 257-283. 2012.

Áqá Siyyid Muḥammad Rizá Shahmírzadí. *Unpublished manuscript*, nd. Available at: https://www.h-net.org/~bahai/arabic/vol5/aqariza/aqariza.htm

Arbab, Farzam. "En camino hacia la gloria del servicio". Asamblea Espiritual Nacional de los Bahá'ís de Colombia.

Arbuthnot, Robert. "The Bab and the Babeeism", Part 1. In *Contemporary Review*, Vol. XI (May-August), pp. 581–601. Strahan & Co., London. 1869. Available https://bahai-library.com/arbuthnot_bab_babeeism_1

________. "The Bab and Babeeism, Part 2". In *Contemporary Review*, Vol. XII (September-December), pp. 245–266. Strahan & Co., London. 1969. Available https://bahai-library.com/arbuthnot_bab_babeeism_2

Ardestani, Shokrullah Ashqli. "A Recollection". In Áhang-i-Badí' (Persian), Masá'il no. 187. Mihr 1381 (1962). Available https://www.h-net.org/~bahai/docs/vol12/Ahangi_Badi.htm

Avery, Peter. *Modern Iran.* F.A. Praeger. 1965.

Ardestani, Shokrullah Ashqli. "A Recollection". In *Áhang-i-Badí'* (Persian), Mihr 1381 (1962), Masá'il no. 187. Available https://www.h-net.org/~bahai/docs/vol12/Ahangi_Badi.htm

Ayers, Frank. *Studying the Holy Qur'án.* Vol. 4. 2nd edn. Self-published with Amazon. 2022.

Báb, The. *Selections from the Writings of the Báb.* Bahá'í World Centre, Haifa. 1982.

________. *Panj Sha'n* (Five Modes). MS facsimile. Ṭihrán, 196X?[sic]. Published in digital facsimile. Lansing, Mi.: H-Bahai, 2000. Available www.h-net.org/~bahai/areprint/bab/M-R/panj/panjshan.htm

________. *Zíyárat-Námih-i-Mullá Muḥammad-'Alíy-i-Bárfurúshí* (Tablet of visitation for Quddús). A 2023 provisional translation authorised by the Bahá'í World Centre of three extracts from the "Tablet of visitation for Quddús" by the Báb. The Persian Tablet was published in Muḥammad-'Alí Malik Khusraví, *Tarikh-i-Shuhadáyi Amr,* I. Ṭihrán, BE 130/1973–1974, pp. 412–14.

________. *Qismati az Alvah-i Khatt-i Nuqtih-'i Ula va Aqa Sayyid Ḥusayn Katib* (Correspondence of the Báb and Sayyid Ḥusayn Katib). First published Tehran, n.d. Available at: https://www.h-net.org/~bahai/areprint/bab/M-R/qismati/qismati.htm

Badiei, Amir. *Dreams of Destiny in the Bábí and Bahá'í Faiths.* Bahá'í Publishing Trust, Wilmette, Ill. 2013.

Bahá'ís Decry Cultural Cleansing in Iran. Bahá'í World News Service. 12 September 2004. Available https://news.bahai.org/story/323/

Bahá'í International Community. *Bahá'í Holy Site Destroyed in Iran.* New York, 12 April 2004. Available www.bic.org/news/bahai-holy-site-destroyed-iran-0

________. *Bahá'í Holy Site Destroyed in Iran.* New York, 12 April 2004. Available www.bic.org/news/bahai-holy-site-destroyed-iran-0

Bahá'í News. Leeward Islands. June 1990, Bahai Year 147. Available at: https://bahai.works/Bahá'%C3%AD_News/Issue_710

Bahá'í World Centre. *The Bahá'í World.* Vol. 17 (1976–1979), 1981. Vol. 18 (1979–1983), 1986.

________. *Bahíyyih Khánum, the Greatest Holy Leaf: A Compilation from Bahá'í Sacred Texts and Writings of the Guardian of the Faith and Bahíyyih Khánum's Own Letters.* Haifa. 1982.

________. *The Compilation of Compilations*, vol. I. Bahá'í Publications Australia, Mona Vale. 1991.

________. *The Compilation of Compilations*, vol. II. Bahá'í Publications Australia, Mona Vale. 2000.

________. *The Importance of Obligatory Prayers and a Fasting. A Compilation.* Prepared by the Research Department of the Universal House of Justice. May 2020. Available www.bahai.org/library/authoritative-texts/compilations/importance-obligatory-prayer-fasting/4#725896087

________. *One Common Faith.* Bahá'í Publishing Trust, Wilmette, Ill. 2005.

Bahá'í Prayers: A Selection of Prayers Revealed by Bahá'u'lláh, the Báb, and 'Abdu'l-Bahá. Bahá'í Publishing Trust, Wilmette, Ill. 1991.

Bahá'í Publishing Committee. *The Bahá'í World, vol. 5 (1932-1934).* New York 1936.

Bahá'í World Centre. *The Transliteration System Used in Bahá'í Literature.* Available at: https://www.bahai.org/library/transliteration/1#691938942

Bahá'u'lláh. Additional Tablets extracts from Tablets revealed by Bahá'u'lláh. Available www.bahai.org/library/authoritative-texts/bahaullah/additional-tablets-extracts-from-tablets-revealed-bahaullah/additional-tablets-extracts-from-tablets-revealed-bahaullah.pdf?369f2267

________. *Days of Remembrance, Lawḥ-i-Ghulámu'l-Khuld (Tablet of the Immortal Youth).* Bahá'í World Centre. 2017.
Available at: https://www.bahai.org/library/authoritative-texts/bahaullah/days-remembrance/

________. *Epistle to the Son of the Wolf.* Bahá'í Publishing Trust, Wilmette, Ill. 1988.

________. *Gems of Divine Mysteries.* Bahá'í World Centre, Haifa. 2002.

________. *Gleanings from the Writings of Bahá'u'lláh.* Tr. Shoghi Effendi. Bahá'í Publishing Trust, London. 1978.

________. *The Hidden Words.* Tr. Shoghi Effendi. Bahá'í Publishing Trust, Wilmette, Ill. 1985.

________. *The Kitáb-i-Aqdas.* Bahá'í World Centre, Haifa. 1992.

________. *The Kitáb-i-Íqán.* US Bahá'í Publishing Trust, Wilmette, Ill. 1989.

________. Lawḥ-i-Sarráj. Bahá'í Reference Library. Available www.bahai.org/r/666707945

________. *A Synopsis and Codification of the Laws and Ordinances of the Kitáb-i-Aqdas.* Bahá'í World Centre, Haifa. 1992.

________. *The Call of the Divine Beloved.* Bahá'í World Centre. 2018. Available online at: https://www.bahai.org/library/authoritative-texts/bahaullah/call-divine-beloved/call-divine-beloved.xhtml?b496df9e

________. *The Seven Valleys and the Four Valleys.* US Bahá'í Publishing Trust. 1991

______. Tablet of All Food (Lawḥ-i Kullu'ṭ-Ṭa'ám). Tr. Stephen Lambden. *Bahá'í Studies Bulletin,* 3:1 (1984), pp. 4–67. Available https://bahai-library.com/bahaullah_lawh_kull_taam

________. *Tablets of Bahá'u'lláh Revealed After the Kitáb-i-Aqdas.* Bahá'í Publishing Trust, Wilmette, Ill. 1988.

________. *Gems of Divine Mysteries (Javáhiru'l-Asrár).* Bahá'í World Centre. 2002.

________. *Lawḥ-i-Mubáhilih.* Available on https://www.bahai.org/fa/library/authoritative-texts/bahaullah/additional-tablets-bahaullah/138668755/1#119537332

________. "*Lawḥ-i-Malláḥul-Quds (Tablet of the Holy Mariner) - Arabic*". Available from: https://oceanoflights.org/Baháullah-st-055-1-en/?lang=en&stems=arabian_youth&quotes=&paraId=para_33

________. *Zíyárat-Námiy-i-Bábu'l-Báb wa Quddús ("Tablet of Visitation for Mullá Ḥusayn and Quddús").* Revealed by Bahá'u'lláh in 'Akká. Mss. British Library Or15714.077. Available *www.bahai.org/r/931357408* (Arabic) and www.bahai.org/r/262760797 (English). See Appendix part 1 for the full English text.

Balyuzi, H. M. *The Báb: The Herald of the Day of Days.* George Ronald, Oxford. 1973.

________. *Bahá'u'lláh, the King of Glory.* George Ronald, Oxford. 1980.

________. *Edward Granville Browne and the Bahá'í Faith.* George Ronald, Oxford. 1970.

________. *The Summons of the Lord of Hosts.* Bahá'í World Centre, Haifa. 2002.

________. *Eminent Bahá'ís in the Time of Bahá'u'lláh.* George Ronald, Oxford, 1985.

________. Muḥammad and the Course of Islam. George Ronald, Oxford. 1976.

________. Bahá'u'lláh. In *The Bahá'í World, 1963-1968,* vol. 14, pp. 587-611. The Universal House of Justice, Haifa. 1974

Bayat, Mangol. *Mysticism and Dissent: Socioreligious Thought in Qajar Iran.* Syracuse University Press. 2000.

Behmardi, Vahid & McCants, William. "A Stylistic Analysis of the Báb's Writings". *Online Journal of Bahá'í Studies*, 114(1), pp. 114–136. 2007. Available https://bahai-library.com/pdf/b/behmardi_stylistic_ analysis.pdf

Bellaigue, Christopher de. *The Islamic Enlightenment: The Modern Struggle Between Faith and Reason*. Random House, UK. 2018.

Borjian, Habib. "A Mazandarani Account of the Babi Incident at Shaikh Tabarsi". In *Iranian Studies*, 39:3, pp. 381–400. 2006.

Browne, E. G. "Bábísm". In *Religious Systems of the World: A Contribution to the Study of Comparative Religion*. Swann Sonnenschein, London, pp. 333–353. 1890/1901. Available https://bahai-library.com/browne_Bábísm

________. "Catalogue and Description of 27 Bábí Manuscripts". *Journal of the Royal Asiatic Society of Great Britain and Ireland*, 1892, pp. 433–99. Available from: www.jstor.org/stable/25197107

________. The Bábís of Persia: Sketch of their History, and Personal Experiences amongst them. *The Journal of the Royal Asiatic Society of Great Britain and Ireland*, New Series, Vol. 21, No. 3, pp. 485–526. Cambridge University. (July 1889).

________. (ed.). *Nuqtatu'l-Káf: Being the Earliest History of the Bábís.* Brill. 1910. Persian text https://archive.org/details/in.gov.ignca.20700

________. (ed.). *Taríkh-i-Jadíd or New History of Mírzá 'Alí Muḥammad the Báb.* *Cambridge University Press.* 1893. English text https://archive.org/details/tarikhijadid

________. *Materials for the Study of the Babi Religion.* Cambridge University Press. 1918. Available at: https://ia800200.us.archive.org/3/items/materialsforstud00browuoft/materialsforstud00browuoft.pdf

Browne, E.G. (translator). *Traveller's Narrative Written to Illustrate the Episode of The Báb (English Translation and Notes), Vol.* 2. Cambridge University Press. 1891. Available online at: https://archive.org/details/in.ernet.dli.2015.530114/page/n5/mode/2up

Browne, E. G. "The Bábís of Persia. Vol. II: Their Literature and Doctrines". *The Journal of the Royal Asiatic Society of Great Britain and Ireland, New Series,* Vol. 21, No. 4, pp. 881–1009. Cambridge University. (October 1889). Last retrieved: 30 June 2022: https://www.jstor.org/stable/25208956

________. *Selections from the Writings of E. G. Browne on the Bábí and Bahá'í Religions.* George Ronald, Oxford. 1987.

________. *A Year Amongst the Persians: Impressions as to the Life, Character, & Thought of the People of Persia.* Cambridge University Press. 1927.

Buck, Christopher and Alkan, Necati. *The Cradle of Christianity—and Islam.* Bahá'í Teachings (6 August 2016). Available https://bahaiteachings.org/cradle-christianity-islam/

Buck, Christopher & Masumian, Adib (trs.). "Bahá'u'lláh's Paradise of Justice: Commentary and Translation". *Bahá'í Studies Review*, 20:1, pp. 97–134. 2014

Bushru'i, Hasan Fuadi. *Táríkh-i-Diyánat-i-Bahá'í dar Khurásán* ("The History of the Bahá'í Faith in Khorasan"). Eds. Minou D. Foadi and Fereydun Vahman. 1931/2022. Available https://bahai-library.com/bushrui_diyanat_bahai_ khorasan,

________. *Manāẓer-e tāriḵi-e nahżat-e amr-e Bahā'i dar Ḵorāsān.* Minou Dokht Fo'ādi and Faridun Vahman (editors), as Tāriḵ-e diānat-e Bahā'i dar Ḵorāsān. Darmstadt, 2007, 2nd rev ed, Satraap, London. 2022.

________. *Táríkh-i-Diyánat-i-Bahá'í dar Khurásán* ("The History of the Bahá'í Faith in Khorasan") - chapter 2 translated by Ahang Rabbani. Available online at: https://www.fazel.org/bahai/wp-content/uploads/2023/05/khur2.doc

________. *Táríkh-i-Diyánat-i-Bahá'í dar Khurásán* ("The History of the Bahá'í Faith in Khorasan") - chapter 3 translated by Ahang Rabbani. Available online at: https://www.fazel.org/bahai/wp-content/uploads/2023/05/khur3.doc

Byrne, Máire. *The Names of God in Judaism, Christianity, and Islam: A Basis for Interfaith Dialogue.* A&C Black. 2011.

Casewit, Yousef. *The Mystics of al-Andalus.* Cambridge University Press. 2017.

Cheyne, Thomas Kelly. *The Reconciliation of Races and Religions.* Adam and Charles Black, London. 1914.

Cole, Juan. "Bahá'u'lláh's Book of the Tigris (Ṣaḥífiy-i-Shaṭṭíyyih)". *Translations of Shaykhi, Babi and Bahá'í Texts,* No. 1 (April, 1997). Available www.h-net.org/~bahai/trans/shatt.htm

________. "Millennialism in Modern Iranian History". In *Imagining the End: Visions of Apocalypse from the Ancient Middle East to Modern America.* Eds. Abbas Amanat and Magnus Bernhardsson. pp. 282–311. I.B. Tauris, London. 2002. Available https://bahai-library.com/cole_millennialism_modern_iran

Collins, William P. "Millennialism, the Millerites, and Historicism". *World Order,* 30:1, pp. 18–21. 1998.

The Compilation of Compilations, vol. 2. Prepared by the Universal House of Justice 1963–1990. Bahá'í Publications Australia. 1991.

Curzon, George Nathaniel. *Persia and the Persian Question*, Vol. 1. Longmans, Green, London. 1892.

Cusack, Carole & Upal, Muhammad Afzal. "Introduction: Islamic Sects and Movements". In *Handbook of Islamic Sects and Movements.* Brill. 2021.

Dawoody, Ahmed al-; Winter, Kristy A. & Finegan, Oran. "Management of the dead under Islamic law". International Committee of the Red Cross (ICRC). 2021. Available https://www.sciencedirect.com/science/article/pii/S266591072100027X

Dūstḵāh, Jalīl & Yaġmā'ī, Eqbāl. The Traditional Elementary School (maktab). *The Encyclopaedia Iranica,* Vol. VIII, Fasc. 2, pp. 180-182. 2011. Available online at: https://www.iranicaonline.org/articles/education-iii

Dabashi, Hamid. *Shi'ism: A Religion of Protest.* Cambridge, Mass: Belknap Press. 2011.

Dehghan, Hooshmand. *Ganj-i-Pinhán: Sargozasht va Asare Hazrate Ghodoos.* Adel. 2016.

Denmark Secretary of State for Foreign and Commonwealth Affairs. Third Report from the Foreign Affairs Committee Session 2003–2004 Iran. 2004. Available www.bits.de/public/documents/iran/Iran-HoC-FA04-govtresp.pdf

Drama Circle. *Persecution to the Bahá'ís of Iran.* Available www.dramacircle.org/martyrdom-and-the-bahai-faith

Egea, Amín. *The Apostle of Peace,* vol. 1. George Ronald, Oxford. 2017.

Ekahi, Y. *Ax-haye tarikhi babol* ("Historical photos of Babol"). Resanesh, Ṭihrán. 2006.

Encyclopædia Britannica. *Worldwide Adherents of All Religions by Six Continental Areas, Mid-2002.* 2002. Available at: https://web.archive.org/web/20070313203604/http://www.britannica.com/eb/table?tocId=9394911

Eschraghi, Armin. "Undermining the Foundations of Orthodoxy: Some Notes on the Báb's Sharia Law (Sacred Law)". In *A Most Noble Pattern,* pp. 223–247 (eds Todd Lawson and Omid Ghaemmaghami). George Ronald, Oxford. 2012.

________. "From Bábí Movement to the Bahá'í Faith". In *The Báb and the Bábí Community of Iran,* pp. 377–406 (ed. Fereydun Vahman). OneWorld Academic. 2020.

________. "Promised One (maw'ūd) or Imaginary One (mawhūm)? Some Notes on Twelver Shī'ī Mahdī Doctrine and its Discussion in Writings of Bahā' Allāh". In *Unity in Diversity,* pp. 111–135 (ed. Orkhan Mir-Kasimov), Brill. 2014.

Esslemont, John. *Bahá'u'lláh and the New Era.* Wilmette: Bahá'í Publishing Trust. 1980.

Ettehadieh, Mansureh (Nezam-Mafi) and Mir Muhammad Ṣádiq, Said (eds). *General Semino dar khidmat-i Iran dar casr-i Qajar va jang-i Harat.* Tehran: Nashr-i Tarikh-i Iran. 1997. Available from: https://alfehrest.com/product/ژنرال-سمینو-در-خدمت-ایران-عصر-قاجار-و-جن/

European Union. *Annual Report on Human Rights.* 13 September 2004. Brussels.

Faizí, Abu'l-Qásim. *Explanation of the Symbol of the Greatest Name.* Bahá'í Publishing Trust. New Delhi, 197?. Also *In Conqueror of Hearts.* New Delhi, India: Bahá'í Publishing Trust. 1968.

Faláhi-Skuce, Houri. *A Radiant Gem: A Biography of Jináb-i-Fáḍil-i-Shírází.* Trafford, Bloomington, Indiana. 2004.

Fananapazir, Khazeh. "Bahá'u'lláh as fulfilment of the theophanic promise in the Sermons of Imám 'Alí ibn Abí Ṭálib". Tr. of al Ṭutunjiyya, Iftikhár and Ma'rifat bin-Nuràniyyat. *Bahá'í Studies Review,* 19, no. 1, pp. 191–213. 2013.

Farr, Edward. *History of the Persians.* Robert Carter & Bros., New York. 1850.

Fatheazam, Shahbaz. In Memoriam: Hushmand Fatheazam (1924-2013). *Lights of Irfan,* 15, pp. 404-411. Wilmette: Haj Mehdi Armand Colloquium. 2014. Available at: https://irfancolloquia.org/pdf/lights15_memoriam-fatheazam.pdf

Faizi, Naysan & Zohre. *Penned by A. Q. Faizi.* George Ronald, Oxford. 2021.

Fernée, Tadd Graham. "Modernity and Nation-making in India, Turkey and Iran". *International Journal of Asian Studies,* 9(1), 2012, pp. 71–97.

Floor, Willem. "The Economic Role of the Ulama in Qajar Persia". In *The Most Learned of the Shi'a: The Institution of the Marja' Taqlid* (ed. Linda Walbridge), pp. 53–81. Oxford University Press. 2001.

Fox, Carolyn Sparey. *Seeking a State of Heaven.* George Ronald, Oxford, 2018.Fraser, James Baillee. *A Winter's Journey (Tâtar,) from Constantinople to Tehran: with travels through various parts of Persia, &c.* 2 Vols. Richard Bentley, London. 1838. https://archive.org/details/awintersjourney01frasgoog (Vol. 1) & https://archive.org/details/awintersjourney02frasgoog (Vol. 1).

________. *A Narrative of a Journey into Khorasan in the Years 1821 and 1822, including some Account of the Countries to the North-East of Persia.* London, Paternoster-Row, 1825. Available at: https://archive.org/details/narrativeofjourn00frasuoft

Freeman, *Dorothy. From Copper to Gold: The Life of Dorothy Baker.* Oxford, George Ronald. 1984.

Furútan, Írán. *Dr. Muhájir: Hand of the Cause of God, Knight of Bahá'u'lláh.* Bahá'í Publishing Trust, London. 1992.

________. *Siyyid Muṣṭafá Rúmí, Hand of the Cause of God, Apostle of Bahá'u'lláh.* Bahá'í Publishing Trust, Wilmette, Ill. 2020.

Gail, Marzieh. *Bahá'í Glossary.* Bahá'í Publishing Trust, Wilmette, Ill. 1955.

________. *Dawn over Mount Hira and Other Essays.* George Ronald, Oxford. 1976.

Gaulmier, J. (ed.), Mérimée, Gobineau et les Bohémiens. *Revue d'Histoire Littéraire de la France,* vol. 66, no. 4, pp. 675-692. Oct-Dec, 1966

Ghadimi, Riaz. *The Báb, King of Messengers.* Juxta Publishing Limited, Hong Kong. 2009.

Ghaemmaghami, Omid. "A Youth of Medium Height: The Báb's Encounter with the Hidden Iman in Tafsír Súrat al-Kawthar". In *A Most Noble Pattern* (eds Todd Lawson & Omid Ghaemmaghami), pp. 175–195. George Ronald, Oxford. 2012.

________. "The Hand of God is not Chained up". In *The Báb and the Bábí Community of Iran* (ed. Fereydun Vahman), pp. 406–421. OneWorld Academic. 2020.

________. "To the Abode of the Hidden One: The Green Isle in Shīʿī, Early Shaykhī, and Bābī-Bahāʾī Sacred Topography". In *Unity of Diversity: Mysticism, Messianism and the Construction of Religious Authority in Islam.* (Ed. Orkhan Mir-Kasimov), pp. 137–173. Brill. 2013.

Gillbanks, Shahla Behroozi. *Footprints in the Sand of Time: Memories of a Maidservant.* The Afnan Library Trust, Sandy, Bedfordshire. 2019. Available https://afnanlibrary.org/footprints-in-the-sands-of-time/

Gobineau, Joseph Arthur de. *Les Religions et les Philosophies dans l'Asie Centrale.* Bibliothèque Didier, Paris. 1866.

Gödel, Rudolf. *Ueber den pontischen Handelsweg und die Verhältnisse des europäisch-persischen Verkehres* ("About the Pontic trade route and the conditions of European-Persian traffic"). Carl Gerold und Sohn, Vienna. 1849.

Gooya News. *Mass killings of the 80s and the Baha'is of Iran (25 November 2013).* Available https://iranbahaipersecution.bic.org/archive/gooya-news-mass-killings-80s-and-bahais-iran

Greussing, Kurt. "The Babi Movement in Iran 1844–1852: from Merchant Protest to Peasant Revolution". In *Religion and Rural Revolt, papers presented to the Fourth Interdisciplinary Workshop on Peasant Studies*, (eds Janos M. Bak and Gerhard Benecke), pp. 256–269. University of British Columbia, 1982. Manchester University Press, 1984.

Grolin, Daniel J. *Jesus and Early Christianity in the Gospels.* George Ronald, Oxford. 2002.

Gilliot, Claude. "Is the Qur'an partly the fruit of a progressive and collective work?" In *The Qur'an in Its Historical Context* (ed. G. Reynolds), pp. 88–108. Routledge. 2017.

Gulpáygání, Mírzá Abu'l-Faḍl. *Miracles and Metaphors.* Kalimát Press, Los Angeles. 1981,

Hamadání, Mírzá Ḥusayn. *The New History (Taríkh-i-Jadíd) of Mírzá 'Alí Muḥammad the Báb.* Ed. & tr. Edward G. Browne. Philo Press, Amsterdam. 1975. The *New History* is also available online at: https://bahai-library.com/hamadani_browne_tarikh_jadid

Hampson, Arthur. *The Growth and Spread of the Bahá'í Faith.* A dissertation submitted to the Graduate Division of the University of Hawaii in partial fulfillment of the requirements for the degree of Doctor of Philosophy in Geography. May 1980. Available at: https://scholarspace.manoa.hawaii.edu/server/api/core/bitstreams/4049ad72-2b6d-4137-a372-92ed3c87a325/content

Handal, Boris. *A Trilogy of Consecration: The Courier, the Historian and the Missionary.* IngramSpark, 2020.

________. *El Concurso en Lo Alto.* PROPACEB, Lima, Peru. 1985. Available https://bahai-library.com/handal_concurso_alto

________. *Mírzá Mihdí: The Purest Branch.* George Ronald, Oxford. 2017.

________. *The Dispensation of the Báb.* IngramSpark, 2023. Available https://bahai-library.com/handal_dispensation_bab.

________. *Muḥammad, Profeta de Dios.* Editorial Bahá'í del Peru. 2020.

Harper, Barron. *Lights of Fortitude.* George Ronald, Oxford. 2007.

The Pluralist Project, Harvard University. *Bahá'ís Draw Attention to Destruction of Holy Sites in Iran.* 12 September 2004. Available https://pluralism.org/religious-tradition/bahá%C3%AD?page=41

Hatcher, John S. & Amrollah, Hemmat. *Reunion with the Beloved: Poetry and Martyrdom.* Juxta Publishing, Hong Kong, 2004.

Hassall, Graham. *Ambassador at the Court: The Life and Photography of Effie Baker.* Available https://bahai-library.com/hassall_ambassador_court_baker&chapter=all

________. "The Modes and Intentions of Biography". *Bahá'í Studies Review*, 14, pp. 71–86. 2008.

Hemmat, Amrollah & Hatcher, John. *The Poetry of Ṭáhirih.* George Ronald, Oxford. 2002.

Hornby, Helen. *Lights of Guidance.* Bahá'í Publishing Trust, India. 1988.

Holley, Horace H. (ed.). *Bahá'í Scriptures: Selections from the Utterances of Bahá'u'lláh and 'Abdu'l-Bahá* (2nd ed). Bahá'í Publishing Committee, New York. 1923. Available https://bahai-library.com/holley bahai scriptures

Ibn Shu'ba al-Harrani. *Tuhaf al-'Uqul* ("The Masterpiece of the Mind"). Ansariyan Publications, Qum. 2000. Available at: https://www.al-islam.org/tuhaf-al-uqul-ibn-shuba-al-harrani

Imám'Alí. *Muslims Traditions of Human Rights.* N.d. Available at: https://ensani.ir/file/download/article/20120514173859-9017-320.pdf

Ishraq-Khavari,'Abdu'l-Hamid (ed.). Má'iydih-i-Ásmání, vol. 4, 277-81. Iran. 129 BE. Persian text available online at: https://www.bahai.org/fa/library/authoritative-texts/bahaullah/additional-tablets-bahaullah/138668755/1#119537332

Jamali, Navid. The Lost Links: An Introduction to the Matrilineal Genealogy of the Qajar Dynasty. Available from: https://www.academia.edu/37455230/The Lost Links An Introduction to the Matrilineal Genealogy of the Qajar Dynasty.

Hudson Institute, The. *Religious Cleansing in Iran,* 22 July 2009. www.hudson.org/ human-rights/religious-cleansing-in-iran

Ḥusayn, Sayyid Muḥammad. *Vaqa'i-i Mimiyyih.* Persian MS (authored c. 1849). University of Michigan British Manuscript Project 749(4), #1. East Lansing, Mi.: H-Bahai, 2001. Available www.h-net.org/~bahai/arabic/vol5/mimiyyih/ mimiyyih.htm & https://www.h-net.org/~bahai/arabic/vol5/mimiyyih/Tarikhi-i-Mimiyyih.pdf

"In Iran, a renewed persecution aims at 'cultural cleansing'". One Country, July 2004. Bahá'í International Community. Available www.thefreelibrary.com/ In+Iran%2C+a+renewed+persecution+aims+at+%22cultural+cleansing%22%3A+ in+its...-a0126851067

Jamali, Navid. *The Lost Links: An Introduction to the Matrilineal Genealogy of the Qajar Dynasty,* n.p.

Johnson, Lowell. *Quddús.* The National Spiritual Assembly Bahá'ís of South and West Africa, Johannesburg. 1982.

Johnson, Vernon Elvin. *A Historical Analysis of Critical Transformations in the Evolution of the Bahá'í World Faith,* 1974. Unpublished doctoral dissertation, Baylor University, Waco, Texas. Available https://studylib.net/doc/6874924/johnson_ transformations_evolution_bahai & https://bahai-library.com/johnson_transformations_evolution_bahai

Kalpakian, Jack. "Representing the Unpresentable: Historical Images of National Reform—From the Qajars to the Islamic Republic of Iran". In *Digest of Middle East Studies,* vol. 17, no. 2, pp. 162–166. Fall 2008.

________. *Iran today: an encyclopedia of life in the Islamic Republic,* p. 62. Greenwood. 2008. Available at: https://epdf.tips/iran-today-an-encyclopedia-of-life-in-the-islamic-republic-2-volume-set.html

Kamrava, Mehran. Qajar Autocracy. In: *A Dynastic History of Iran: From the Qajars to the Pahlavis.* Cambridge University Press; 5-34. 2022. doi:10.1017/9781009224628.003

Kamrava, M. *Iran today: an encyclopedia of life in the Islamic Republic,* 2008, p. 62. Greenwood. Available https://epdf.tips/iran-today-an-encyclopedia-of-life-in-the-islamic-republic-2-volume-set.html

Kazem-Beg, Mírzá Aleksandr. "Le Bab et les Bábís ou le Soulevement Politique et Religieux en Perse de 1845 *à* 1853". *Journal Asiatique.* June 1866, vol. 7, pp. 457–522.

Kazembeyki, Mohammad Ali. *Society, Politics and Economics in Mazandaran, Iran 1848–1914.* Routledge. 2013.

Kazemi, Farhad. "Some Preliminary Observations on the Early Development of Bábísm". *Muslim World,* LXIII, 1973, pp. 119–131 (Hartford, Conn.).

Keddie, Nikki R. & Yann, Richard. "Continuity and Change under the Qajars: 1796–1890". In *Modern Iran: Roots and Results of Revolution,* pp. 37–57. Yale University Press, 2006. Available www.jstor.org/stable/j.ctt5vkwwc.9.

________. Religion and Irreligion in early Iranian Nationalism. *Comparative Studies in Society and History,* 4, 274-75. 1962.

Kirkpatrick, Bertha Hyde. Consultation and Sacrifice. *Star of the West,* vol. 23, no. 1, p. 77. April 1932. Available online from https://file.bahai.media/6/64/SW_Volume23.pdf

Khan, Ali-Kuli. *Pilgrim Notes of Ali-Kuli Khan 1906.* Available https://bahai-library.com/ali-khan_pilgrim-notes_1906

Khusraví, Muḥammad-'Alí Malik. *Tarikh-i-Shuhadáyi Amr,* I ("History of the Martyrs of the Cause") pp. 412–14. Ṭihrán. BE 130/1973–1974. Available www.h-net.org/~bahai/areprint/authors/malikkhusravi/shuhadi/Shuhadi_1.pdf

LaFarge, Wanden Mathews. "The Relation of the Báb to the Traditions of Islám". In *The Bahá'í World: A Biennial International Record,* Vol. III, 1928–1930, comp. Bahá'í Publishing Committee, New York. 1930. Available https://bahai-library.com/pdf/l/lafarge_relation_bab_traditions.pdf

Lambden, Stephen. "Antichrist-Dajjal: Some Notes on the Christian and Islamic Antichrist Traditions and their Bahá'í Interpretation", part I. *Bahá'í Studies Bulletin* 1:2. September 1982.

________. "From a Primal Point to an Archetypical Book: Literary Trajectories through Selected Writings of the Bab (1819–1850)". In *The Báb and the Bábí Community of Iran,* pp. 151–234 (ed. Fereydun Vahman). OneWorld Academic. 2020.

________. *The Bab- Risāla Khaṣā'il Sab`a ('The Treatise of the Seven Directives").* 2016. Available online at: https://hurqalya.ucmerced.edu/node/411

________. "The Khutba al-Jidda (The Literary Sermon at Jeddah) of the Báb". In *A Most Noble Pattern* (eds Todd Lawson & Omid Ghaemmaghami), pp. 146–159. George Ronald, Oxford. 2012.

________.Muḥammad 'Ali Bārfurushi, Quddūs. Available online from the following website: https://hurqalya.ucmerced.edu/node/4081

________. "A Tablet of Mírzá Ḥusayn 'Alí Bahá'u'lláh of the Early Iraq Period: The 'Tablet of All Food' (*Lawḥ-i Kull al-Ta'ám*)". *Bahá'í Studies Bulletin* Vol. 3, no. 1 (June 1984), pp. 4–67. Available https://hurqalya.ucmerced.edu/sites/hurqalya.ucmerced.edu/files/page/documents/bsb_kullu_taam.pdf

________. "The Word Bahá: Quintessence of the Greatest Name". *Bahá'í Studies Review,* 3:1, 1993, pp. 13–45. Available https://bahai-library.com/pdf/l/lambden_word_baha.pdf

________. "The Surát al-'Abd of the Qayyúm al-Asmá". In *A Most Noble Pattern* (eds Todd Lawson & Omid Ghaemmaghami), pp. 116–1455. George Ronald, Oxford. 2012.

________. "The Messianic Roots of Babi-Baha'i Globalism." In *Baha'i and globalisation* (eds. Annika Hvithamar, Margit Warburg, Morten Warmind), pp. 17-34. Brill. 2005.

Lawson, Todd. "The terms 'Remembrance' (dhikr) and 'Gate' (báb) in the Báb's Commentary on the Sura of Joseph". In *Studies in Honour of the Late Hasan M. Balyuzi* (ed. Moojan Momen), pp. 1–64. Kalimát Press, Los Angeles. 1988.

________. Typological Figuration and the Meaning of "Spiritual": The Qur'anic Story of Joseph. *Journal of the American Oriental Society,* 132(2):221-244. 2012. DOI:10.7817/jameroriesoci.132.2.0221

________. "Interpretation as Revelation: The Qur'án Commentary of the Báb, Sayyid 'Alí-Muḥammad Shírází (1819–1850)". In *The Báb and the Bábí Community of Iran* (ed. Fereydun Vahman), pp. 235–274. OneWorld Academic. 2020.

Letafati, Hadi. "Biography and services of Saeed Ulama Mazandarani". In *Lessons from the School of Islam*, pp. 54–63. 2008. Available www.noormags.ir/view/fa/articlepage/322838/زندگینامه-و-خدمات-سعید-العلماء-مازندرانی

Lewis, H. John. *The Merits of Protestantism Demonstrated by the Character of Man*, Vol. 1. Astor House Bookstore, New York. 1854.

Losch, R. R. *The Many Faces of Faith: A Guide to World Religions and Christian Traditions*. Wm. B. Eerdmans Publishing. 2002.

Luṭf 'Alí Mírzá S͟hírází. *Untitled history, unpublished manuscript n.d.* University of Michigan British Manuscript Project 749(4), #3. Available www.h-net.org/~bahai/arabic/vol5/lutfali/lutfali.htm

Ma'ani, Baharieh Rouhani & Ewing, Sovaida Ma'ani. *Laws of the Kitáb-i-Aqdas—The Laws of Bahá'u'lláh Placed in Their Historical Context*. George Ronald, Oxford. 2004.

Ma'ani, Baharieh Rouhani. *Leaves of the Twin Divine Trees*. George Ronald, Oxford. 2008.

MacEoin, Denis. "A Note on the Numbers of Babi and Baha'i Martyrs in Iran". *Bahá'í Studies Bulletin*, 2/2, 1983, pp. 84–88.

———. *The Sources for Early Bábí Doctrine and History: A Survey*. Brill, Leiden and New York, 1992.

———. "Hierarchy Authority and Eschatology in Early Bábí Thought". In *Iran: Studies in Bábí and Bahá'í History* (ed. Peter Smith) vol. 3, pp. 95–14. Kalimát Press, Los Angeles. 1986.

———. *The Messiah of S͟hírāz: Studies in Early and Middle Bábísm*. Vol. 3. Brill. 2009.

———. "The Bábí concept of holy war". In *Religion*, 12, pp. 93–129, 1982.

———. *Rituals in Bábísm and Baha'ísm*. British Academy Press. 1994.

———. "The Trial of the Báb: S͟hí'ite Orthodoxy Confronts its Mirror Image". In *Studies in Honour of Clifford Edmund Bosworth, Vol. II*, (ed. Carole Hillenbrand), pp. 272–317. Brill. 2000.

———. "Early S͟hayk͟hī reactions to the Báb and his claims" In M. Momen (ed.), *Studies in Bábí and Bahá'í History* (pp. 1-47), Los Angeles, Kalimát. 1983.

———. "Muḥammad 'Alī Bārfurūs͟hī". In P. Bearman, Th. Bianquis, C.E. Bosworth, E. van Donzel, W.P. Heinrichs (eds), *Encyclopaedia of Islam*, second edition. 2002. Available online at: http://dx.doi.org/10.1163/1573-3912_islam_SIM_5382

Mahdavi, Shireen. Childhood in Qajar Iran. *Iranian Studies*, 47(2), pp. 305-326, March 2014.

Malik Khosravi, Mohammad 'Ali. *Tarikh-e Shohada-ye Amr (History of the Martyrs of the Cause)*, vol 1. Tehran, 130 Badi'/1972. Available online at: https://www.h-net.org/~bahai/areprint/authors/malikkhusravi/shuhadi/Shuhadi_1.pdf

McCants, William and Milani, Kavian. "The History and Provenance of an Early Manuscript of the 'Nuqtat al-Kaf' dated 1268 (1851–52)". *Iranian Studies* 37, no. 3, pp. 431–49. 2004.

McLean, Jack A. *A Celestial Burning: A Selective Study of the Writings of Shoghi Effendi*. Bahá'í Publishing Trust of India, 2012.

———. "The Heroic in the Historical Writings of Shoghi Effendi and Nabíl". Paper presented at Irfan Colloquia Session #72, November 2006. Available https://bahai-library.com/mclean_heroic_writings_shoghi-effendi

———. *To Russian with Love: Journal of a Member of the Quddús Team*. 1990/2018. Available online at: https://bahai-library.com/pdf/m/mclean_russia_journal.pdf

Ma'ani, Baharieh Rouhani. *Leaves of the Twin Divine Trees*. George Ronald, Oxford. 2008.

Ma'ani, Kamal. *Quddús: 1822–1849*. 2002. Irish Bahá'í Bookshop.

Manuchehri, Sepehr. "Brief Analysis of the Features of Bábí Resistance at Sheikh Tabarsi". Paper presented at the *Bahá'í Studies Conference in Sydney, Australia*, October 1998. Available https://bahai-library.com/manuchehri_analysis_Babi_resistance

_____. "Taqiyyah (Dissimulation) in the Bábí and Bahá'í Religions". *Australian Bahá'í Studies*, 2, 2000, pp. 219–251. Available https://bahai-library.com/manuchehri_taqiyyih_Babi_bahai

Markham, C. R. *A General Sketch of the History of Persia*. Longmans Green, London. 1974.

Marianoff, Dimitri & Gail, Marzieh. Thralls of Yearning Love. *World Order*, Series 2, Volume 6, Issue 4, pp. 7-42. Summer, 1972. Available at: https://bahai.works/World_Order/Series2/Volume_6/Issue_4/Text

Marouti, Andreh. "Infrastructure for Trade Routes in Western Azerbaijan, Iran: Caravanserais, Bridges, and Fortresses". In *Architectural Heritage in the Western Azerbaijan Province of Iran*, pp. 229-258. Eds Maurizio Boriani, Mariacristina Giambruno. Springer, Cham, Switzerland. 2021.

Martin, Douglas. "The Bahá'í Faith in its Second Century". In *The Bahá'í Faith and Islam* (ed. Heshmat Moayyad), proceedings of a symposium, McGill University, 23–25 March 1984, pp. 57–72.

Martin, Vanessa. *The Qajar Pact: Bargaining, Protest and the State in Nineteenth-Century Persia*. I. B. Tauris, London. 2005.

Mazandarani, Fazel. *Tarík͟h Ẓuhúr al-Ḥaqq* ("History of the Manifestation of Truth"), vols 2, 3 and 8. Ṭihrán. 1944. Available https://sites.google.com/site/adelsh09/TZHVol2TypedversionbyAdel.pdf & https://sites.google.com/site/adelsh09/Pagesfrom TZHvol3Pp.1-20pdf.pdf

_____. "The Life of Bahá'u'lláh". *Star of the West*, 14:10, p. 291. January 1924.

Mehrabkhani, Ruhollah. *Mullá Ḥusayn: Disciple at Dawn*. Kalimát Press, Los Angeles. 1987.

_____. "Some Notes on Fundamental Principles: Western Scholarship and the Religion of the Báb". *Bahá'í Studies Bulletin*, 2:4 (March 1984), pp. 22–43. Available https://hurqalya.ucmerced.edu/sites/hurqalya.ucmerced.edu/files/page/documents/rm-notes.pdf

_____. *La Aurora del Día Prometido* ("The Dawn of the Promised Day"). Terrassa: Editorial Bahá'í de España. 1974.

Merrick, David. *Martyrdom of the Báb: An Outline for Researchers*. 2017. https://www.paintdrawer.co.uk/david/folders/spirituality/bahai/bab/bab-martyrdom-outline.htm

Milani, Kavian. NOQṬAT AL-KĀF. *The Encyclopædia Iranica*. July 28, 2008. Available at: https://www.iranicaonline.org/articles/noqtat-al-kaf

Miller, Bradford. "Seneca Falls First Woman's Rights Convention of 1848: The Sacred Rites of the Nation". *The Journal of Bahá'í Studies* 8:3, pp. 39–52. 1998.

Minorsky, V. "Review of Ivanov's Babidski Vostanii". *Bulletin of the School of Oriental and African Studies*, 11:4, pp. 875–883, University of London, 1946. [Ivanov, M. S. Бабидские восстания в Иране (1848–1852 (Babidskiye vosstaniya v Irane (1848–1852)), "The Babi Uprisings in Iran (1848—1852)", Moscow, 1939.]

Mírzá Ḥusayn Hamadání. *The New History (Tarík͟h-i-Jadíd) of Mírzá 'Alí Muḥammad the Báb* (tr. E. G. Browne). Cambridge University Press, London. 1893. Available https://bahai-library.com/hamadani_browne_Taríkh_Jadíd

Mírzá Muḥammad-Taqí [Lisan al-Mulk Sipihr]. *Nāsikh al-tavārīkh, tārīkh-i salāṭīn-i Qajārīyeh*. Tehran, 1315 (1897) or Ed. Jamshid Kiyanfar. Tehran, 1998–1999.

Mohammad-Hosseini, Nosratollah. "Qoddus, Moḥammad-'Ali Bārforuši". *Encyclopædia Iranica*, 2009. Available https://iranicaonline.org/articles/qoddus-mohammad-ali-barforusi

_____. "The Commentary on the Sura of Joseph". In *A Most Noble Pattern* (Eds Todd Lawson & Omid Ghaemmaghami). George Ronald, Oxford. 2012.

_____. *Hadrat-i-Tahirih*. Fundacion Nehal, Madrid. 2018.

Momen, Moojan. "'Alí Bastámí, Mullá (d. 1846)". *Bahá'í Encyclopedia Project.* National Spiritual Assembly of the Bahá'ís of the United States, Evanston, Ill. Available www.bahai-encyclopedia-project.org/index.php?view=article&catid=37%3Abiography&id=68%3Aali-bastami-Mullá &option=com_content&Itemid=74

________. *The Bábí and Bahá'í Religions, 1844–1944: Some Contemporary Western Accounts.* George Ronald, Oxford. 1981.

________. *The Bahá'í Communities of Iran.* Vol. 1. George Ronald, Oxford. 2015.

________. *The Bahá'í Communities of Iran.* Vol. 2. George Ronald, Oxford. 2021.

________. "A Chronicle of the Bábí-Bahá'í Communities in Sangsár and Shahmírzad". *Bahá'í Studies Review,* 14, pp. 85–96. 2007.

________. *An Introduction to Shi'i Islam: The History and Doctrines of Twelver Shi'ism.* George Ronald, Oxford. 1985. Yale University Press. 2017.

________. "Persecution and Development: The History of the Bahá'í Community of Māhfurūzak in Mazandaran, Iran". *Bahá'í Studies Review,* 18:1, pp. 45–54, 2012. Available http://dx.doi.org/10.1386/ bsr.18.45/1.

________. *Selections from the Writings of E. G. Browne on the Bábí and Bahá'í Religions.* George Ronald, Oxford. 1987.

________. *A short biography of Bahá'u'lláh.* OneWorld. 2014.

________. "The social basis of the Babi Upheavals in Iran (1848–53): A preliminary analysis". *International Journal of Middle East Studies* 15 (1983), 157–183. Available in https://bahai-library.com/pdf/m/momen_upheavals_iran_1848-1953.pdf

________. "The Social Basis of the Bábí Upheavals in Iran". In *The Báb and the Bábí Community of Iran* (Ed. Fereydun Vahman), pp. 275–311. OneWorld Academic. 2020.

________. "The Social Location of the Bábí Movement: *A Preliminary Note*". *Bahá'í Studies Bulletin,* 3:3, pp. 8–26; September 1985. Available https://hurqalya.ucmerced.edu/sites/hurqalya.ucmerced.edu/files/page/documents/mm-socia_location.pdf

________. "The Star Tablet of the Báb". British Library, 2019. Available https://blogs.bl.uk/asian-and-african/2019/10/the-star-tablet-of-the-bab.html#_edn3

________. "The Struggle for the Soul of Twelver Shi'ism in Qajar Iran". *Die Welt des Islams,* 60:1, pp. 31–55, 2020. Available https://doi.org/10.1163/15700607-00600A01

________. "Two Episodes from the Life of Bahá'u'lláh in Iran". *Lights of Irfán* (Ed. Iraj Ayman), vol. 20, pp. 139–60. Available https://bahai-library.com/lights_irfan_20

________. *Understanding religion: A thematic approach.* Simon and Schuster, 2019.

________. The family and early life of Tahirih Qurrat al-'Ayn. *Bahá'í Studies Review,* 11, 35–52. 2003. Available at: https://bahai-library.com/pdf/m/momen_family_life_tahirih.pdf

________. "The Work of A.L.M. Nicolas (1864-1937)". In *The Bábí and Bahá'í Religions: Some Contemporary Western Accounts,* pp. 36-40. Oxford: George Ronald. 1981. Available online at: https://bahai-library.com/momen_work_alm_nicolas

________. FĀŻEL MĀZANDARĀNĪ, MĪRZĀ ASAD-ALLĀH. *The Encyclopaedia Iranica,* Vol. IX, Fasc. 5, pp. 460-461.

________. *The Star Tablet of the Báb.* British Library, 2019. Last retrieved 30 June 2022 at: https://blogs.bl.uk/asian-and-african/2019/10/the-star-tablet-of-the-bab.html#_edn3

________. "A Chronology of some of the Persecutions of the Bábís and Bahá'ís in Iran 1844-1978". In *The Bahá'í World (1979-1983),* vol. 18. Bahá'í World Centre. 1986. Available at: http://dl.bahai.org/bahai-world/the-bahai-world-vol18-1979-1983.pdf

Momen, Moojan & Lawson, Todd. "Ruḥ al-Quddús". In *Holy People of the World: A Cross-cultural Encyclopedia* (Ed. Jestice, Phyllis G.), Vol. 3. ABC-CLIO, 2004, pp. 709–710.

Moshiri, Leila. *Colloquial Persian.* Routledge. 1988.

Muḥammad-'Alí Malik Khusraví. *Tarikh-i-shuhadáyi Amr,* I. Ṭihrán. 130 B.E./1973-4,

Muhammad Mu'ín al-Saltanih. *Tarikh-i Amr.* 1921-1922. Digitally republished, East Lansing, Mi.: H-Bahai. 2000. Available at: https://www.h-net.org/~bahai/arabic/vol4/muin/muin.htm

Mottahedeh, Negar. "Resurrection, Return, Reform: Ta'ziyeh as Model for Early Babi Historiography". *Iranian Studies,* 32:3, pp. 387–399, 1999.

Muhammad Ali, Maulana. *History and Doctrines of the Babi Movement.* Ahmadiyya Anjuman Isha'at Islam Lahore Inc. 1998.

Munírih Khanum. *Memoirs and Letters* (tr. Sammireh Anwar Smith). Kalimát Press, Los Angeles. 1986.

Munro, Sarah. *Forget-Me-Not, Iran.* Intellect Books. 2013.

Murchie, Guy. "Visit to Fort Tabarsi'. *Bahá'í News,* no. 411, pp. 8-10. June 1965. Published by the National Spiritual Assembly of the Bahá'ís of the United States. Available online from: https://file.bahai.media/8/86/Baha%27i_News_411.pdf

Nabíl-i-A'ẓam. *The Dawn-Breakers: Nabíl's Narrative of the Early Days of the Bahá'í Revelation.* Bahá'í Publishing Trust, Wilmette, Ill. 1970.

Naqavi, Ali Razi. "Bábísm and Bahá'ísm. A Study of Their History and Doctrines". *Islamic Studies* 14, no. 3, 185–217, 1975. http://www.jstor.org/stable/20846959.

Nash, Geoffrey. "Aryan and Semite in Ernest Renan's and Matthew Arnold's Quest for the Religion of Modernity". *Religion & Literature,* 46:1 (spring 2014), pp. 25–50 (26 pages). The University of Notre Dame.

Nash, Geoffrey (tr.); & O'Donoghue, Daniel (ed.). *Comte de Gobineau and Orientalism: Selected Eastern Writings.* Routledge. 2009.

________. Introduction. In *Comte de Gobineau and Orientalism: Selected Eastern Writings. In* Geoffrey Nash and Daniel O'Donoghue (eds), pp, 1-20. Routledge. 2008.

Nakhjávání, 'Alí. *Shoghi Effendi: The Range and Power of His Pen.* Casa Editrice Bahá'í. 2006.

The Narrative of Ḥájí Naṣír Qazvíní. Tr. Ahang Rabbani. *Witnesses to Bábí and Bahá'í History,* vol. 8, 2007. https://bahai-library.com/rabbani_narrative_haji_Qazvíní

Naqavi, Sayyid Ali Razi. "Bābism and Bahā'ism: A Study of Their History and Doctrines". *Islamic Studies,* 14:3 (Autumn 1975), pp. 185–217.

Nattaj, Vahid Haidar. "The Role of Landscape Elements (Water and Geographic Context) in the Configuration of Bahrol-eram Garden" [Baḥru'l-Árám]. *Bagh-E Nazar,* 14:54, 2017, pp. 5–20. Available www.bagh-sj.com/article_53474.html?lang=en

Network of Concerned Historians. *Annual Report* 2005. Available www.concernedhistorians.org/ar/05.pdf

Niaki Ja'far, Hosseinzadeh. *Bábul, Shahr-i Zíbáiy Mázandarán (Babol the Beautiful City of Mazandaran),* 1st volume. Ramrang Publication. 2020.

Nouraei, Morteza and Andreeva, Elena. "Russian Migrants and Their Settlements in Iran in the Early 20th Century: A New Stage of Colonization". *Journal of Historical Researches*, Vol. 1, Issue 4, pp. 21-36. 2010.

Nicolas, A. L. M. *Le Béyan Persan.* 4 vols. Librairie Paul Geuthner, Paris. 1914.

________. *Le Beyan Arabe. Le Livre Sacre du Babysme.* Ernest Leroux, Paris. 1905.

________. *Seyyèd Ali-Mohammed dit le Bâb.* Dujarric & Co, Paris. 1905. Available https://bahai-library.com/nicolas_seyyed_ali_mohammed

Niyákí [Niaki], Ja'far & Ḥusaynzáda, Púrándakht. *Bábul, Shahr-i-Zíbáy-i-Mázandarán: Awḍá' Táríkhí* ["Babol, Shahre Zibaye Mazandaran: Auda' Tarikhi"] (Persian; "Babol, the Beautiful City of Mazandaran: Historical accounts"), vol. 1. Ramrang Publication. 1959.

Ocean of Lights. *Writings of Quddús.* Available at: https://oceanoflights.org/Quddús-02-fa/

Office of External Affairs of the National Spiritual Assembly of the Bahá'ís of the United States. *Bahá'ís raise alarm over destruction of cultural heritage in Iran.* 13 September 2004. Available http://dl.bahai.org/bwns/assets/documentlibrary/323_01.pdf

Office of the UN High Commissioner for Human Rights. *Mandates of the Special Rapporteur in the Field of Cultural Rights; the Special Rapporteur on Freedom of Religion or Belief; and the Special Rapporteur on the Situation of Human Rights in the Islamic Republic of Iran.* Geneva. 2016.

Osterhammel, Jürgen. *The Transformation of the World. A Global History of the Nineteenth Century.* Princeton University Press. 2014.

Pavlovitch, Pavel & Powers, David S. "A Bequest May Not Exceed One-Third: An Isnād-cum-Matn Analysis and Beyond". In *Islamic Cultures, Islamic Contexts*, pp. 133–172. Brill. 2014.

Périgord, Emily McBride. *Translation of French Footnotes of the Dawn-Breakers.* Bahá'í Publishing Trust, Wilmette, Ill. 1939.

Pettybone, Harriet. *Quddús, the Companion of the Báb.* In *World Order, The Bahá'í Magazine*, vol. xiv, No. 4. 1984.

Phelps, Steven. A Partial Inventory of the Works of the Central Figures of the Bahá'í Faith. 2 vols. June 2023. Available https://afnanlibrary.org/a-partial-inventory/

________. "The Writings of Bahá'u'lláh". In *The World of the Bahá'í Faith* (ed. Robert Stockman), pp. 51–71. Routledge, London. 2022.

de Planhol, Xavier. *Bandar-e Gaz.* Encyclopædia Iranica, 1988. Available https://iranicaonline.org/articles/bandar-e-gaz-a-port-on-the-southern-shore-of-the-astarabad-q

Poursoleiman, Z. & Khakpur, M. "An Investigation on Elements Creating Sense of Place in Historical Site of Babol". In *International Journal of Architecture and Urban Development*, 2:3, pp. 13–22. 2012.

Querry, Amédée (tr.). *Droit Musulman: Recueil de lois Concernant les Musulmans Schyites.* Vol 1. Imprimerie Nationale, France. 1871.

Rafati, Vahid. The Development of Shaykhí Thought in Shí'í Islam. Unpublished Ph.D. thesis, University of California, 1979. Available https://bahai-library.com/rafati_development_shaykhi_thought

Rabbani, Ahang. "The Conversion of the Great-Uncle of the Báb". *World Order*, 20:3, 1999, pp. 19–38.

Rabbani, Ahang. "The Bábís of Nayriz: History and documents." In *Witnesses to Bábí and Bahá'í History.* 2006. Available online at: https://bahai-library.com/pdf/r/rabbani_Bábís_nayriz.pdf

________. " 'Abdu'l-Bahá Reminiscences of Khalíl Shahídí". *In Witnesses to Bábí and Bahá'í History*, vol. 9. 2008. Available from: https://bahai-library.com/pdf/r/rabbani_reminiscences_khalil_shahidi.pdf

Rabbani, Ahang. *The Genesis of the Bahá'í Faith in Khurásán.* Unpublished. Available from: https://view.officeapps.live.com/op/view.aspx?src=https%3A%2F%2Fwww.fazel.org%2Fbahai%2Fwp-content%2Fuploads%2F2023%2F05%2Fkhur2.doc&wdOrigin=BROWSELINK

Rabbání, Rúḥíyyih. *The Priceless Pearl.* London: Bahá'í Publishing Trust. 1969.

Rabbani, Ahang & Fananapazir, Khazeh. "'Abdu'l-Bahá's First Thousand-Verse Tablet: History and Provisional Translation". *Bahá'í Studies Review,* Vol. 16, pp. 107–133, 2010. Available https://bahai-library.com/pdf/r/rabbani_fananapazir_thousand-verse_tablet.pdf

Rabino, Hyacinth Louis. *Mazandaran and Astarabad.* Luzac & Co., London. 1928.

Radio Liberty. *Bahá'ís Launch Campaign against Alleged Iranian Abuses.* 13 November 2004. Available www.rferl.org/a/1143241.html

Ram, Harsha. "Literature as World Revolution: Velimir Khlebnikov's Zangezi and the Utopian Geopoetics of the Russian Avant-garde". In Glaser, Amelia M. & Lee, Steven S. (eds). *Comintern Aesthetics*, pp. 31–80. University of Toronto Press. 2020.

Rází, Isfandíyár. *Táríkh-i va Jshahrughráfa-i Shahristán-i-Babol (History and Geography of Babol City).* Babol. Mobat, 1378 SH (1999-2000 C.E).

RasaNews (2 August 2011). *The opinion of authorities and scholars about the personality of Allameh Saeed al-Ulama and Mullá Mohammad Ashrafi.* Available at: https://hawzah.net/fa/News/View/88095/دیدگاه-مراجع-و-علما-درباره-شخصیت-علامه-سعیدالعلما-و-ملامحمد-اشرفی

Rezghi, Negin. Fort Tabarsi and The Courage of the Brave Bábís. *Elixir Journal,* Special Bicentenary Issue, #9. Autumn 2019. Available at: https://www.elixir-journal.org/issue9/castleattabarsi.php

Rivadeneyra, Adolfo. *Viaje and Interior de Persia*, vol. 1. Imprenta y estereotipia de Aribau y ca, Madrid. 1880.

Reynolds, Annette. *Trudy and the Bahá'ís' Spiritual Path in South Carolina,* Xlibris US. 2015.

Rivadeneyra, Adolfo. *Viaje and Interior de Persia*, vol. 1. Madrid: Imprenta y estereotipia de Aribau y ca. 1880.

Riza Quli Khan Hidayat. *Rawzat al safá-yi Náṣirí,* 10. Qum. 1960-6.

Rodwell, J. M. *The Koran.* Phoenix, London. 1994.

Roemer, Hermann. *Die Bābī-Behā'ī, die jüngste mohammedanische sekte.* Verlag der Deutschen orientmission, Potsdam. 1912.

Root, Martha L. *Ṭáhirih the Pure, Iran's Greatest Woman.* Los Angeles, Kalimat Press. 1981 (First published 1938).

Root, Martha. *Ṭáhirih the Pure.* Kalimát Press, Los Angeles. 1981.

Ruhe, David S. *Robe of light: the Persian Years of the Supreme Prophet Bahá'u'lláh; 1817–1853.* George Ronald, Oxford. 1994.

Ruhe-Schoen, Janet. *Rejoice in My Gladness: The Life of Ṭáhirih.* Bahá'í Publishing Trust, London. 2011.

Ruhi, Ibrahim (or Kirmání, Shaykh Ibrahim). *Kitáb-i-Quddúsiyyíh* (Book of Quddús) also called *Taríkh al-Quddsí.* Unpublished biography of Quddús. Kerman manuscript, Muḥarram AH 1339.

Rúḥíyyih Khánúm. *The Priceless Pearl.* Bahá'í Publishing Trust, London. 1969.

Sacramento Daily Union, The. 14 February 1874. Available https://cdnc.ucr.edu/cgi-bin/cdnc?a=d&d=SDU18740214.2.34&e=-------en--20--1--txt-txIN--------

Sadeghian, Saghar. Caspian Forests as Political Setting: A Socio-Environmental Study of the Babi Resistance at the Fort of Shaykh Tabarsi. n.p.

Sadeghzade Milani, Kavian. *Nuqtat al-Káf.* Encylopaedia Iranica, 2008. Available www.iranicaonline.org/articles/noqtat-al-kaf

Saiedi, Nader. "Concealment and Revelation in Bahá'u'lláh's Book of the River". In *The Journal of Bahá'í Studies,* 9:3, pp. 25–56. 1999. Available https://bahai-library.com/pdf/s/saiedi_book_river.pdf

________. "The Ethiopian King". Tr. Omid Ghaemmaghami. *Bahá'í Studies Review* 17:1, September 2012, pp. 181–6.

________. *Gate of the Heart: Understanding the Writings of the Báb.* Association for Bahá'í Studies and Wilfrid Laurier University Press, Canada. 2008.

________. *Logos and Civilization.* University Press of Maryland. 2000.

________. "Concealment and Revelation in Bahá'u'lláh's Book of the River". In *The Journal of Bahá'í Studies,* 9:3, pp. 25–56. 1999.

________. *Reconstruction of the Concept of the Human Being in the Writings of the* Báb. 2019. Available at https://user-hrqc9mo.cld.bz/Human-Being-in-the-Writings-of-the-Báb

________. Sulṭān-i h. abashī, Payám-i Bahá'í, 366, 2010, 10-13; trans. and annotated Omid Ghaemmaghami. "The Ethiopian King". *Bahá'í Studies Review,* 17, pp. 181-186. 2011. http://dx.doi.org/10.1386/bsr.17.181/1

Sankey, Howard. "Scientific realism and the God's eye point view". In *Epistemologia,* 27, pp. 211–226, 2004.

Savi, Julio & Mardani, Faezeh. "Prayers and rituals in the Bahá'í Faith: Introduction to A Tablet to Jináb-i-Mullá 'Alí-Akbar fí Ardi'l-Álif." *Lights of Irfan*, Vol. 9, pp. 321–350. Irfan Colloquia, Wilmette, Ill. 2008. Available https://bahai-library.com/savi_mardani_prayers_rituals

Siyyid Muḥammad-Ḥusayn. *Vaqa'i-i Mimiyyih.* Persian MS (authored c. 1849). University of Michigan British Manuscript Project 749(4), #1. East Lansing, Mi.: H-Bahai, 2001. Available at: www.h-net.org/~bahai/arabic/vol5/mimiyyih/mimiyyih.htm

Seyf, Ahmad. "Iran and the Great Plague, 1830–1831". *Studia Islamica,* 69 (1989), pp. 151–165.

Sears, William. *Thief in the Night.* George Ronald, Oxford. 1961.

Shahmírzadí, Mír Abú-Ṭálib. *Untitled history*, n.d., uncatalogued photocopy of autographed manuscript.

Shahvar, Soli; Gilbar, Gad; & Morozov, Boris (eds). *The Baha'is of Iran, Transcaspia and the Caucasus,* vol. 1. I.B. Taurus.

Siegel, Jennifer. *Endgame: Britain, Russia and the Final Struggle for Central Asia*, Vol. 25. IB Tauris. 2002.

Shírází, Luṭf 'Alí Mírzá. Tarikh-i Vaqa'i'-i-Mazandaran (A Chronicle of the Babi Uprising at Fort Shaykh Tabarsi in Mazandaran). Unpublished. Available https://www.h-net.org/~bahai/arabic/vol5/lutfali/lutfali.htm

Shoghi Effendi. *The Advent of Divine Justice.* Bahá'í Publishing Trust, Wilmette, Ill. 1990.

________. *Citadel of Faith: Messages to America 1947–1957.* Bahá'í Publishing Trust, Wilmette, Ill. 1980.

________. *God Passes By.* Bahá'í Publishing Trust, Wilmette, Ill. 1979.

________. *The Unfolding Destiny of the British Bahá'í Community.* Bahá'í Publishing Trust, London. 1981.

________. *The World Order of Bahá'u'lláh.* Bahá'í Publishing Trust, Wilmette, Ill. 1974.

________. *Lawḥ-i-Garn-i-Áhibáy-i-Sharq*, Tehran. Naw-Rúz, 101 B.E.

Siyyid Muhammad Tabíb Manshádí. "The Martyrs of Manshád". In *World Order*, translated by Ahang Rabbani and Naghmeh Astani, vol. 28, no. 1, pp. 21-36. Fall 1996.

Smith, Peter. *A Concise Encyclopedia of the Bahá'í Faith.* Oneworld, Oxford. 2000.

________. *The Bábí and Bahá' Religions: from Messianic Shi'ism to a World Religion.* Cambridge University Press. 1987.

Smith, Peter & Momen, Moojan. "The Babi Movement: A Resource Mobilization Perspective". In *Iran: Studies in Bábí and Bahá'í History*, vol. 3, pp. 33–93. Ed. Peter Smith. Kalimát Press, Los Angeles. 1986. Available online at: www.academia.edu/661036/The_Babi_Movement_A_Resource_Mobilization_Perspective

________. *Martyrs, Bábí.* In Encyclopaedia Iranica. Columbia University, New York, 2005. Available https://iranicaonline.org/articles/ martyrs-babi-babi

Spangler, Ann. *The Names of God: 52 Bible Studies for Individuals and Groups.* HarperChristian Resources. 2018.

Steingass, Francis Joseph. *English-Arabic Dictionary.* London: W.H. Allen & Co. 1882.

Star of the West. The Bahá'í Magazine, 8 vol. reprint. George Ronald, Oxford. 1978.

State Department (US). *Annual Report on International Religious Freedom, 2004*. Government Printing Office. 2005.

Stern, Henry A. *Dawnings of Light in the East; with Biblical, Historical, and Statistical Notices of Persons and Places Visited During a Mission to the Jews in Persia, Coordistan, and Mesopotamia*. C. H. Purday. 1854.

Stone, Nathan, Horton, T. C., Hurlburt, Charles E. & Pritchard, Ray. *Names of God/Names of Christ/Names of the Holy Spirit Set*. Moody Publishers. 2010.

Stokes, Jim. "Story of Joseph in Five Religious Traditions". In *World Order*, 28:3, pp. 35-46. Spring 1997.

Suhrawardī, Shihāb al-Dīn. *The Philosophy of Illumination* (*Hikmat al-Ishrāq*), (Eds & trs J. Walbridge and H. Ziai). Brigham Young University Press, Salt Lake City, Utah. 1999.

Sulaymānī, 'Azīzu'llāh. *Maṣābīḥ-i Hidāyat*. Bahá'í Publishing Trust, Tehran. BE 130/1974, 8:67. www.h-net.org/~bahai/areprint/authors/sulayman/masabih8/Masabih_Hidayat_v8_34_82.pdf. Provisional translation cited in Buck, Christopher and Masumian, Adib. "Bahá'u'lláh's Paradise of Justice: Commentary and Translation". *Bahá'í Studies Review*, Vol. 20 (2014, published 2018).

Tavakoli-Targhi, Mohamad. "Anti-Baha'ism and Islamism in Iran". In *The Baha'is of Iran: socio-historical studies* (Dominic Parviz Brookshaw and Seena B. Fazel, eds), pp. 200–231. Routledge, 2012.

Terry, Peter. *A Prophet in Modern Times*. Lulu Publications. 2008. Available https://bahai-library.com/pdf/t/terry_nicolas_prophet_modern.pdf

Taherzadeh, Adib. *The Revelation of Bahá'u'lláh: Baghdád 1853–1863*. Vol. 1. George Ronald, Oxford. 1974.

________. *The Revelation of Bahá'u'lláh: Adrianople 1863–1868*. Vol. 2. George Ronald, Oxford. 1977.

________. *The Revelation of Bahá'u'lláh: 'Akká, The Early Years: 1868–1877*. Vol. 3. Oxford: George Ronald, 1987.

________. *The Revelation of Bahá'u'lláh: Mazra'ih and Bahjí: 1877–1892*. Vol. 4. Oxford: George Ronald, 1987.

________. *The Covenant of Bahá'u'lláh*. George Ronald, Oxford. 1992.

Thomas, M. W. *Glossary and transcription for Arabic & Persian terms*. Compiler. Available https://bahai-library.com/glossary_arabic_persian_transcription

Thompson, Juliet & Marzieh Gail. *Diary of Juliet Thompson*. Los Angeles, Kalimát Press, 1983.

Townshend, George. Nabíl's History of the Báb. In *World Order*, Volume 5 No. 11. February 1940. Available online at: https://file.bahai.media/1/14/World_Order_Vol5_Issue11.pdf

Tsadik, Daniel. *Between Foreigners and Shi'is: Nineteenth-Century Iran and its Jewish Minority*. Stanford University Press. 2020.

UK Parliament. *Bahá'í Holy Sites*—EDM (Early Day Motion) 1145: tabled on 06 May 2004. Available https://edm.parliament.uk/early-day-motion/25322/bahai-holy-sites

United Nations General Assembly. *Elimination of All Forms of Religious Intolerance*. Report of the Special Rapporteur of the Commission on Human Rights on freedom of religion or belief, Asma Jahangir. UN, 16 September 2004. Available www.refworld.org/pdfid/4267be774.pdf

United Nations High Commissioner for Refugees. *Chronology of Events in Iran, April 2004*. UNHCR Ankara, July 2004. Available www.refworld.org/pdfid/4133432c4.pdf

United States House of Representatives. *Religious Persecution as a Violation of Human Rights. Hearing and Markup before the Committee on Foreign Affairs and its Sun Committee on Human Rights and International Organizations*. Washington, p. 168. 1983.

Universal House of Justice, The. "Letters of Living, Dawn-Breakers, Quddús, Terraces". Letter written on behalf of the Universal House of Justice to an individual believer dated August 1975. Available https://bahai-library.com/uhj_letters_Quddús_dawnbreakers

US State Department. *Annual Report on International Religious Freedom, 2004*, p. 543.

Uskú'í, Ḥájí Mírzá Ḥaydar 'Alí. *Monsieur Nicolas - the French: Extracts from Táríkh-i-'Amríy-i-Ádharbayján* ("History of the Bahá'í Faith in Azerbaijan"). Tr. Sepehr Manuchehri. 1950? pp. 96–110. Available https://bahai-library.com/manuchehri_tarikh_azarbeyijan_nicolas

Vahman, Fereydun (ed.). "The Báb: A Sun in a Night not Followed by Dawn". In *The Báb and the Bábí Community of Iran*, pp. 1–78. OneWorld Academic. 2020.

Villavicencio, Charles. "Joe Slovo, a Believing Unbeliever". In *The Spirit of Freedom: South Africa leaders on Religion and Politics*. University of California Press, pp. 260-273. 1996.

Villa-Vicencio, Charles. "Joe Slovo: A Believing Unbeliever". In "The Spirit of Freedom: South African Leaders on Religion and Politics". pp. 261–75. University of California Press. 1996. Available at:
https://publishing.cdlib.org/ucpressebooks/view?docId=ft4p3006kc&chunk.id=d0e5784&toc.id=d0e3131&brand=ucpress

Villar, Huseyn. *Quddús* (in Spanish). 2008. Available https://bahai-library.com/villar_Quddús_biography

von Dorn, Bernard. "Nachträge zu dem Verzeichniss der von der Kaiserlichen öffentlichen Bibliothek erworbenen Chanykov'schen Handschriften und den da mitgetheilten Nachrichten über die Baby und deren Koran". In *Mélanges asiatiques*. Tome V. Livraison 4. de l'Imprimerie de l'Academie Impériale des Sciences, St. Pétersbourg, pp. 377—419, 1866. Available www.orientalstudies.ru/rus/images/pdf/journals/Melanges_Asiatiques_05_1866_24_dorn.pdf

White, Roger. *Another Song, Another Season: Poems and Portrayals*. George Ronald, Oxford. 1979.

Walbridge, John. "Essays and Notes on Bábí and Bahá'í History". In *Occasional Papers in Shaykhi, Babi and Bahá'í Studies*, 6:1. East Lansing, Michigan. 2002. Available https://bahai-library.com/walbridge_babi_bahai_history

________. "Mullá 'Abdu'l-Karim Qazvíni (Mirza Ahmad Katib)". *Research Notes in Shaykhi, Babi and Baha'i Studies*, Vol. 1, no. 9, October 1997. Available online at: www.h-net.org/~bahai/notes/Qazvíni9.htm

________. *The Bábí Uprising in Zanján. Occasional Papers in Shaykhi, Babi and Baha'i Studies*, Vol. 6, No. 1, pp. 34-63. March, 2002.

Walker, Andy. "The Role of Genesis 37:1-11 in the Joseph Novella". *Leaven*, Vol. 24:(4), issue 3. 2016.
Available at: https://digitalcommons.pepperdine.edu/leaven/vol24/iss4/3

WallStreet Deutschland. *Der Mythos vom toleranten Islam—Kulturelle Säuberung im Iran*. 17 September 2004. Available www.wallstreet-online.de/diskussion/500-beitraege/854490-1-500/der-mythos-vom-toleranten-islam

Warburg, Margit. *Citizens of the World: A History and Sociology of the Baha'is from a Globalisation Perspective*. Vol. 106. Brill, 2018.

Watson, Robert Grant. *A History of Persia from the Beginning of the Nineteenth century to the Year 1858, with a Review of the Principal Events that led to the Establishment of the Kajar Dynasty*. London: Smith, Elder and Co. 1866.

Wehr, Hans. *A Dictionary of Modern Written Arabic*. Germany: Otto Harrassowitz Verlag, 1979.

Wei, S.Lc. (2022). Typological Figuration of Mystical Elements in Jesuit Figurists' Re-interpretation of Chinese Classics. In: Qi, L., Tobias, S. (eds) *Encountering China's Past. New Frontiers in Translation Studies*. Springer, Singapore. https://doi.org/10.1007/978-981-19-0648-0_9

White, Roger. "Bahá'u'lláh and the Fourth Estate". In *The Bahá'í World* (1979-1983), 1986. Available https://bahai-library.com/pdf/w/white_bw18_bahaullah_press.pdf.

________. *Another Song, Another Season: Poems and Portrayals*. George Ronald, 1979.

World Order, A Bahá'í Magazine. *Excerpts from Dispatches Written During 1848-1852 by prince Dolgorukov, Russian Minister to Persia*. Vol. 1, No. 1. Fall 1966. Available online: https://bahai.works/index.php?title=File%3AWorld_Order2_Vol1_Issue1.pdf&page=1

Yarshater, Ehsan. "Iranian National History". In *The National History of Iran* (ed. Ehsan Yarshater), Vol. 3, pp. 359–480. Cambridge University Press. 1983.

Yazdani, Mina. *The Writings and Utterances of 'Abdu'l-Bahá*. In *The World of the Bahá'í Faith* (ed. Robert Stockman), pp. 8–104. London, England: Routledge, 2022.

Yazdani, Mina. Anti-Bahā'ī Polemics and Historiography. *Bahá'í Studies Review*, 17(1), 87-100, 2012.

Yule, Henry. *The Travels of Marco Polo*. Cambridge University Press. 2010.

Yulianti, Dina, Sulaeman, Otong, and Ilyas. "Muhammad. Accusing Heresy is a Heresy. How Heresy Became an Instrument in Political Sectarianism". *Religió Jurnal Studi Agama-agama*, 10, no. 2, 189-208. 2020.

Zabihi-Moghaddam, Siyamak. "The Bábí-state Conflict at Shaykh Ṭabarsí". *Iranian Studies* 35, no. 1–3, pp. 87–112. 2002.

________. *The Bábí-state conflicts of 1848–1850*. In "The Báb and the Bábí Community of Iran" (Fereydun Vahman, editor). OneWorld Academic, 2020, pp. 313–376.

________. "Pírámún-i-Kitáb-i-Ḥaḍrat-i-Báb," review of *Ḥaḍrat-i-Báb [the Báb]*, by Nuṣratu'lláh Muḥammad-Ḥusayní (Dundas: Institute for Bahá'í Studies in Persian, 1995), pp. xiv + 1038, *Pazhúheshnámeh: A Persian Journal of Bahá'í Studies* 2, no. 2, pp. 130–59. Summer 1998.

Za'im al-Dawlah Tabrizi, Muhammad Mahdi Khan. *Miftah bab al-abwab ya tarikh-i bab va baha'i*. Farahani, 1967.

www.ingramcontent.com/pod-product-compliance
Lightning Source LLC
Chambersburg PA
CBHW071951290426
44109CB00018B/1982
9780645896329